THE
POPULAR
ENCYCLOPEDIA
OF BIBLE
PROPHECY

TIM LaHAYE
ED HINDSON
General Editors

WAYNE A. BRINDLE
Managing Editor

HARVEST HOUSE™ PUBLISHERS

EUGENE, OREGON

Cover by Dugan Design Group, Bloomington, Minnesota

The Bible version used by the contributor of each article in this encyclopedia is cited after the first Bible quote in the article.

THE POPULAR ENCYCLOPEDIA OF BIBLE PROPHECY
Copyright © 2004 by Tim LaHaye and Ed Hindson
Published by Harvest House Publishers
Eugene, Oregon 97402
www.harvesthousepublishers.com

Library of Congress Cataloging-in-Publication Data

The popular encyclopedia of Bible prophecy / Tim LaHaye and Ed Hindson, general editors; Wayne Brindle, managing editor.
p. cm.
Includes bibliographical references
ISBN 978-0-7369-1352-2 (hardcover)
1. Bible—Prophecies—End of the world—Encyclopedias. I. LaHaye, Tim F. II. Hindson, Edward E. III. Brindle, Wayne.
BS649.E63P67   2004
220.1'5'03—dc22   2004012971

Printed in the United States of America

09   10   11   12   / DP-CF /   13   12   11   10   9

ACKNOWLEDGMENTS

Our sincere appreciation to Kelly McBride,
who typed most of the original manuscript
and assisted in managing the electronic files.

Some material has been excerpted by permission from the following sources:

Gromacki, Robert. *The Holy Spirit.* Dallas: Word, 1999.

House, Wayne. "Progressive Dispensationalism." Paper presented to the Pre-Trib Research Center.

Jeremiah, David. *What the Bible Says About Angels.* Sisters, OR: Multnomah Publishers, 1996.

LaHaye, Tim, ed. *Tim LaHaye Prophecy Study Bible.* Chattanooga: AMG Publishers, 2000.

Mayhue, Richard. "The Prophet's Watchword: Day of the Lord." *Grace Theological Journal 6,* no. 2, 1985.

———. "Why a Pretribulational Rapture?" *The Master's Seminary Journal 13,* no. 2, Fall 2002.

Ryrie, Charles, Tom Davis, and Joe Jordan, eds. *Countdown to Armageddon.* Eugene, OR: Harvest House Publishers, 1999.

Stitzinger, James. "The Rapture in Twenty Centuries of Biblical Interpretation." *The Master's Seminary Journal 13,* no. 2, Fall 2002.

The following articles were excerpted substantially from the *Tim LaHaye Prophecy Study Bible,* NKJV Edition (Chattanooga, TN: AMG Publishers, 2001): "God's Covenants with Man" by Richard Mayhue (p. 20), "The Office of the Prophet" by Ed Hindson (p. 320), "The Resurrections" by Gary Frazier (p. 1361), and "The False Prophet" by Ed Hindson (p. 1516). Used with permission.

The following articles include statements excerpted from the *Tim LaHaye Prophecy Study Bible,* NKJV Edition (Chattanooga, TN: AMG Publishers, 2001): "Gog and Magog" by Mark Hitchcock (p. 972), "The Antichrist" by Ed Hindson (p. 1415), "The Book of Revelation" by Robert Thomas (pp. 1492-93), "Preterism and the Dating of Revelation" by Thomas Ice (p. 1611). Used with permission.

The chart "The Campaign of Armageddon" was excerpted from the *Tim LaHaye Prophecy Study Bible,* NKJV Edition (Chattanooga, TN: AMG Publishers, 2001, p. 1102). This chart is based on the work of Arnold Fruchtenbaum, and is used with permission.

Material from the article titled "Heaven" is used by permission of Crossway Books, a division of Good News Publishers, Wheaton, IL 60187, www.crosswaybooks.org.

The article titled "Imminence" by Wayne A. Brindle is based on an article on the topic that formerly appeared in the journal *Bibliotheca Sacra* (April-June 2001, pp. 138-151), and is used with permission.

TOPICS

CHART INDEX

GENERAL EDITORS

Tim LaHaye, Litt.D, D.Min.
President, Tim LaHaye Ministries and Cofounder,
Pre-Trib Research Center, El Cajon, CA

Ed Hindson, M.A., Th.M., Th.D, D.Min., Ph.D.
Assistant Chancellor and Dean of the School of Biblical Studies and the Tim LaHaye School of Prophecy,
Liberty University, Lynchburg, VA

MANAGING EDITOR

Wayne A. Brindle, Th.M., Th.D.
Chairman and Professor of Biblical Studies, Liberty
University, Lynchburg, VA

CONTRIBUTORS

Mark L. Bailey, Th.M., Ph.D.
President and Professor of Bible Exposition,
Dallas Theological Seminary, Dallas, TX

Paul Benware, Th.M., Th.D.
Professor of Bible and Theology, Philadelphia Biblical
University, Langhorne, PA

James Borland, M.Div., Th.M., Th.D.
Professor of Biblical Studies and Theology,
Liberty University, Lynchburg, VA

Mal Couch, Th.M., Th.D., Ph.D.
President, Tyndale Theological Seminary,
Fort Worth, TX

Robert Dean Jr., Th.M., Ph.D.
Senior Pastor, Preston City Bible Church,
Preston City, CT

Timothy J. Demy, Th.D., Ph.D.
Military Chaplain, Bible Teacher, Newport, RI

Paul R. Fink, Th.M., Th.D.
Professor of Biblical Studies, Liberty University,
Lynchburg, VA

Gary Frazier, M.A., D.D.
President, Discovery Ministries, Arlington, TX

James Freerksen, Th.M., Th.D.
Professor of Biblical Studies, Liberty Baptist Theological Seminary, Lynchburg, VA

Arnold Fruchtenbaum, Th.M., Ph.D.
Founder and Director, Ariel Ministries, Tustin, CA

Steven C. Ger, Th.M.
Founder and Director, Sojourner Ministries,
Garland, TX

Robert Gromacki, Th.M., Th.D.
Distinguished Professor of Biblical Studies,
Cedarville University, Cedarville, OH

Gary R. Habermas, M.A., Ph.D.
Distinguished Professor of Apologetics and
Philosophy, Liberty University, Lynchburg, VA

Mark Hitchcock, Th.M., J.D., Ph.D.
Pastor, Faith Bible Church, Enid, OK

David Hocking, Th.M., Ph.D.
President, Hope for Today Ministries, Santa Ana, CA

Wayne House, Th.M., J.D., Ph.D.
Professor, Oregon Theological Seminary, Salem, OR

Thomas Ice, Th.M., Ph.D.
Executive Director, Pre-Trib Research Center,
Arlington, TX

David Jeremiah, Th.M., D.D.
Senior Pastor, Shadow Mountain Community
Church, El Cajon, CA

Gordon Johnston, Th.M., Th.D.
Associate Professor of Old Testament Studies,
Dallas Theological Seminary, Dallas, TX

Joe Jordan, D.D.
Director of Word of Life Fellowship,
Schroon Lake, NY

Tony Kessinger, M.A.R., Ph.D.
President, Truth Seekers International, Melbourne, FL

John F. MacArthur, Th.M., D.D.
President and Professor of Pastoral Ministries,
The Master's College and Seminary, Sun Valley, CA

W.H. Marty, M.Div., S.T.M., Th.D.
Professor of Bible, Moody Bible Institute, Chicago, IL

Richard L. Mayhue, Th.M., Th.D.
Professor of Theology and Pastoral Ministry,
The Master's Seminary, Sun Valley, CA

Elwood McQuaid
Former Executive Director, The Friends of Israel
Gospel Ministry, Bellmawr, NJ

Daniel Mitchell, Th.M., Th.D.
Associate Dean and Professor of Theology, Liberty
Baptist Theological Seminary, Lynchburg, VA

J. Dwight Pentecost, Th.M., Th.D.
Distinguished Professor Emeritus, Dallas Theological
Seminary, Dallas, TX

Randall Price, Th.M., Ph.D.
President, World of the Bible Ministries,
San Marcos, TX

Renald E. Showers, Th.M., Th.D.
Professor, Institute of Biblical Studies, The Friends of
Israel Gospel Ministry, Bellmawr, NJ

Gary P. Stewart, Th.M., D.Min.
Military Chaplain, Marine Corps Base, Quantico, VA

James Stitzinger, Th.M.
Associate Professor of Historical Theology,
The Master's Seminary, Sun Valley, CA

Robert L. Thomas, Th.M., Th.D.
Professor of New Testament, The Master's Seminary,
Sun Valley, CA

Stanley D. Toussaint, Th.M., Th.D.
Senior Professor Emeritus of Bible Exposition,
Dallas Theological Seminary, Dallas, TX

Elmer Towns, Th.M., D.Min.
Dean of the School of Religion, Liberty University,
Lynchburg, VA

John F. Walvoord, Th.M., Th.D.
Late Chancellor and former President, Dallas Theological Seminary, Dallas, TX

John C. Whitcomb, Th.M., Th.D.
President, Whitcomb Ministries, Orange Park, FL

Harold L. Willmington, D.Min.
Dean, Liberty Bible Institute, Lynchburg, VA

Andy Woods, Th.M., J.D.
Doctoral Student, Dallas Theological Seminary,
Dallas, TX

Gary Yates, Th.M., Ph.D.
Professor of Old Testament, Liberty Baptist Theological Seminary, Lynchburg, VA

NEVER BEFORE HAS fascination with Bible prophecy been more acute than it is today. Part of that interest is due to the uncertainty of our times. Our world has become more and more marked by political instability and contentious strife, particularly in the Middle East. All over the globe, societies are characterized by this threat, along with our society's declining morals, rampant crime, and governmental turmoil. People living in these turbulent times want answers, and many are turning to the Bible to get them. Despite easy access to modern technologies and conveniences, including computers that can process billions of bits of information in the blink of an eye, many people still believe that the Bible, a book written thousands of years ago, holds the answers to life and the life hereafter.

Unfortunately, most seekers get little help in the area of prophetic study. Unless they take it upon themselves to make prophecy a special study, they are not fully equipped to answer many of the questions they may have on this vitally important subject. And important it must be, for 28 percent of the Bible was prophetic when it was written! Evidently God considered it important to include prophetic passages in nearly every book in the Bible, and He used, almost exclusively, prophets to record the Scriptures. As the apostle Peter said, "Holy men of God [the prophets] spoke as they were moved by the Holy Spirit" (2 Peter 1:21 NKJV). The accuracy of their inspired writing, particularly the prophetic portions, proves without question that the Bible is of divine origin.

Nothing motivates Christians like the study of prophecy. It puts an evangelistic fire in the heart of the church, it gives believers a vision for world missions, and it injects a desire to live a holy life in an age of unholiness. That is why the LaHaye Prophecy Library was launched in conjunction with Harvest House Publishers several years ago. This *Popular Encyclopedia of Bible Prophecy* is a key book in the series and may in fact be one of the most comprehensive. With the help of Dr. Wayne Brindle, we have compiled a team of prophecy experts who have written on the most important subjects of prophetic study. They may differ slightly on minor points of discussion, but they are all in agreement with the major issues of biblical eschatology, particularly in terms of holding to the pretribulational, premillennial view of the end times. The topics covered in this encyclopedia have been arranged alphabetically for ease of study, and the articles have been written to appeal to both those who are new to prophecy and those who are experienced students of the subject. We hope this volume will inspire you to search the Scriptures and become, as the apostle Paul admonished, "Approved to God...rightly dividing the word of truth" (2 Timothy 2:15).

Our sincere prayer is that these articles will inform your mind, bless your heart, and stir your soul with the blessed hope of Jesus' coming. As our Lord Himself instructed us, we are continually watching for His imminent return to call us home to be with Him. In the meantime, we are challenged and admonished to keep watching, be ready, and continue serving Him until He comes (Matthew 24:42-46).

Tim LaHaye
Ed Hindson

ABOMINATION OF DESOLATION

THE PHRASES *abomination of desolation, desolating abomination,* and *abomination that makes desolate* refer to violations of the ritual purity of the Jewish Temple in Jerusalem. They translate the Hebrew term *shiqqutz(im) m'shomem* and the Greek term *bdelugma tes eremoseos,* and they appear in prophecies about the desecration and defilement of the Temple in both A.D. 70 and at the end of the age.

OLD TESTAMENT TERMS

In the Old Testament, the phrase occurs only in Daniel (9:27; 11:31; 12:11). It conveys the feeling of horror that God's people feel when they witness criminal and barbaric acts of idolatry. These acts rendered the Temple ritually unfit for the worship and service of God.

Daniel laments the foreign domination of Jerusalem and desolation of the Temple: "How long will the vision about the regular sacrifice apply, while the transgression causes horror, so as to allow both the holy place and the host to be trampled?" (Daniel 8:13 NASB). In Daniel 12:11 we read of a foreign invader abolishing the regular sacrifice and substituting "an abomination of desolation." The word "abomination" shows how appalled Daniel is at the forcible intrusion of idolatry into a place of sanctity in order to cause defilement.

NEW TESTAMENT TERMS

In the New Testament, the phrase appears only in the Olivet Discourse (Matthew 24:15; Mark 13:14), where Jesus has Daniel's prophecy in mind. The term *eremos* ("desolation") does appear in Luke 21:20, but it does not refer to the technical phrase and describes the condition of Jerusalem in general, not the Temple in particular. Jesus uses the same word in Matthew 23:38, and even though He is referring to the Second Temple, He is predicting its destruction (rather than its desecration) and God's judgment upon it. This is quite distinct from the desecration caused by the abomination of desolation, which results in divine

judgment not upon the Temple but upon the one who desecrates it (see Daniel 9:27). Daniel's and Jesus' use of the phrase clearly influenced other prophetic scriptures (2 Thessalonians 2:3-4; Revelation 11:1-2).

The New Testament uses *bdelugma* (the Greek word translated "abomination") four times (Luke 16:15; Revelation 7:4-5; 21:27). The Septuagint (the Greek translation of the Old Testament) uses it 17 times. It comes from a root term that means "to make foul" and "to stink." Thus it refers to something that makes one feel nauseous, and by implication, something morally abhorrent and detestable. As with the Hebrew meaning in the Old Testament, the New Testament Greek term points particularly to idols or idolatrous practices. The Greek word *eremoseos* (translated "desolation") means "to lay waste, make desolate, bring to ruin" (see Matthew 12:25; Luke 11:17; Revelation 17:16; 18:17,19). The Septuagint uses it to describe the desolation of the Land as a result of desecration and exile.

THEOLOGICAL MEANING

In both Hebrew and Greek, the phrase *the abomination of desolation* is an unusual grammatical construction. The best explanation for this is the literary and theological linkage of *abomination* and *desolation* in the prophetic writings of Jeremiah and Ezekiel. These texts treat extensively the desecration and defilement of the Temple, and they frequently mention the abominations and desolations of pagan profanation of the Sanctuary (Jeremiah 4:1,27; 7:10; 44:22; Ezekiel 5:11,14-15; 7:20) as well as the foreign invaders who will further desecrate and destroy the Temple (Jeremiah 4:6-8; Ezekiel 6:11; 7:20-23). Jeremiah 44:22 in particular states that Israel's abominations have caused the desolation of the Land and made it "an object of horror" (compare Ezekiel 5:11,15; 7:20-24; 36:19-21).

This brief survey shows that the Israelites considered acts of ritual impurity and especially of foreign invasion of the Temple as ultimate violations of sanctity and as a sign of judgment. The Jews were extremely careful to prevent such acts and even built a protective fence around the Second Temple. It included a warning inscription promising death to any non-Israelite who passed beyond it into the court of the Israelites. The New Testament (Acts 21:27-28) records the violent opposition of a Jewish crowd who believed Paul had taken a Gentile proselyte (Trophimus) into the Temple to offer sacrifice. They accused Paul of "defiling the holy place" (the Temple). With this background, we can understand why the future act of desecration by the abomination of desolation is the climax of Daniel's seventieth week and signals the intensification of God's wrath in the second half of the Tribulation (Matthew 24:15-21; Mark 13:14-19).

HISTORICAL BACKGROUND

During the construction of the Second Temple, a host of actual and would-be desecrators of the Temple invaded Jerusalem. However, Daniel appears to be predicting the invasion of the Syrian–Greek ruler Antiochus IV Epiphanes (175–164 B.C.), who erected an idol in the Temple near the Brazen Altar. In Daniel 11:31 we read, "Forces from him will arise, desecrate the sanctuary fortress [Temple compound], and do away with the regular sacrifice. And they will set up the abomination of desolation." This occurred in 167 B.C. In response, the Jewish priests revolted and rededicated the Temple (an event commemorated as the Feast of the Dedication in John 10:22-23), leading to a Jewish military overthrow of Antiochus' forces.

Some critical scholars have dismissed an eschatological interpretation of the abomination of desolation in Daniel, assuming all references must refer to Antiochus' desecration and claiming Daniel was written *after* this event. However, Jesus understood that the historical application of the phrase to Antiochus' desecration was a pattern of the ultimate eschatological event—the abomination of the Antichrist. Citing Daniel's prophecy (some 200 years after Antiochus' desecration) and referring to the still-future abomination of desolation (Matthew 24:15; Mark 13:14),

Jesus affirmed both His and Daniel's awareness of the eschatological application of the phrase.

PROPHETIC IMPLICATIONS

Jesus saw His message as a continuation of the biblical prophets and evaluated His generation in the light of them. He frequently cited Jeremiah and Zechariah and applied these prophecies to the soon-coming judgment of Jerusalem in A.D. 70 as well as the more distant final judgment. For example, at the "cleansing of the Temple," Jesus quoted both Jeremiah 7 (which referred the threat of ritual defilement to the Temple following Jeremiah's Temple sermon) and texts in Isaiah and Zechariah (which referred to the Temple's future state). Jesus' Olivet Discourse also sets the Temple in an eschatological context. When the disciples heard Jesus' prediction of the Second Temple's destruction (Matthew 24:1-2; Mark 13:1-2; Luke 21:5-6), they apparently connected it to the messianic advent at the end of the age and asked for a *sign* (Matthew 24:3; Mark 13:4; Luke 21:7; see also 1 Corinthians 1:22). The "sign" He gave them was that of Daniel's abomination of desolation (Matthew 24:15; Mark 13:14). This, then, was the sign that the Jewish nation was nearing the time of messianic deliverance and restoration, for the desecration of the Temple would begin the persecution of the Jewish people (that is, the "great Tribulation," Matthew 24:16-22; Mark 13:14b-20). Only the Messiah Himself will be able to bring them redemption from their enemies (Matthew 24:30-31; Mark 13:26-27; Luke 21:28).

Luke's account does not include the abomination of desolation in the Temple because this is an eschatological event, and he has selectively focused on the immediate concern of the disciples (note the phrase "about to take place" in Luke 21:7) concerning *when* the predicted destruction of the Temple (and Jerusalem) would occur. For this reason he also omits the end-time persecution of the Tribulation (Greek, *thlipsis*), which is connected with this event, substituting the term "great distress"

(Greek, *anagke*), which better describes the local invasion and trampling of the city (Luke 21:23-24), fulfilled in the Roman conquest of Jerusalem in A.D. 70.

Matthew and Mark place the abomination of desolation in the time when "the end will come" (Matthew 24:14). It separates the period of "tribulations" or "birth pangs" (Matthew 24:6-12; Mark 13:7-9) from the "great tribulation" period (Matthew 24:21; Mark 13:19). Luke does this in Luke 21:24 by separating the event of Jerusalem's desolation (A.D. 70) and the times of the Gentiles (present age) from the time when "the times of the Gentiles are fulfilled."

The abomination of desolation marks the midpoint of Daniel's seventieth week, dividing the Tribulation into two divisions of lesser and greater intensity (Daniel 9:27). This corresponds to the "42 months" of Revelation 11:1-2 and the 1290 days of Daniel 12:11.

Preterists interpret the abomination of desolation (as they do most prophetic events) as having its ultimate fulfillment in the destruction of the Temple in A.D. 70. However, the events of the First Revolt that culminated with the destruction of A.D. 70 do not match the details in the "abomination of desolation" texts. None of the incursions by Roman officials during this time could be regarded as abominations that caused desolation because they did not affect the sacrificial system. Foreigners in the Temple may desecrate the Temple without defiling it. That is why the Jews could rebuild the Temple after its desecration and destruction by the Babylonians without the need of a purification ceremony (Ezra 3:2-13). Further, the entrance of the Roman general Titus (who destroyed the Temple) occurred only *after* the Sanctuary was already in flames and had been largely ruined and *after* the Jewish sacrifices had ceased. This is important to note since the abomination of desolation of which Daniel speaks, and to which Jesus refers, speaks only of the cessation of sacrifice in the Temple, not of the Temple's destruction.

ESCHATOLOGICAL FOCUS

Any interpretation except the eschatological leaves us with unresolved details that we must either interpret in a nonliteral, nonhistorical manner, or dismiss altogether. The eschatological view also explains the meaning of types that await their anti-type for ultimate fulfillment. Moreover, Daniel's seventieth week, and especially its signal event of the abomination of desolation, influenced the literary structure of the Olivet Discourse and the judgment section of the book of Revelation (chapters 6–19). Jesus' interpretation of the order of the events of the seventieth week in the context of prophetic history appears to confirm an eschatological interpretation for Daniel 9:27. Matthew 24:7-14 predicts that persecution, suffering, and wars will continue to the end of the age, climaxing in a time of unparalleled distress (verses 21-22). This corresponds to "the time of Jacob's distress" (Daniel 12:1; Jeremiah 30:7). Only *after* these events does Jesus make reference to Daniel 9:27 (verse 15) concerning the signal event of this time of Tribulation. If the seventy sevens (KJV, "weeks") were to run sequentially, without interruption, then why does Jesus place this intervening period *before* the fulfillment of the events of the seventieth week? The text of Matthew in particular shows that Jesus was answering His disciples' questions concerning His second coming and the end of the age (Matthew 24:3). Jesus here explains that His coming is necessary for divine intervention and national repentance (verses 27-31; Zechariah 12:9-10) and will occur "after the tribulation of those days" (Matthew 24:29). According to Matthew, the events described in this period prior to the messianic advent could *not* have been fulfilled in A.D. 70 with the destruction of Jerusalem because these events usher in and terminate with the coming of Messiah.

Although the phrase *abomination of desolation* does not appear in Paul's description of the end-time desecration of the Temple in 2 Thessalonians 2:4, he obviously has this event in view. For example, the Septuagint sometimes uses both *bdelugma* ("abomination") and *anomia* ("lawlessness") to refer to idolatrous practices. Thus in 2 Thessalonians 2:3-4, Paul describes the figure who magnifies himself above every idol as "the man of lawlessness." In fact, Paul's explanation of this event serves as a commentary on both Daniel's "abomination of desolation" texts (particularly Daniel 9:27) and Jesus' statement of it as a "sign" in the Olivet Discourse. Moreover, Paul uses the event to answer the same time-related question of the end time that Jesus' disciples asked. This further affirms the eschatological interpretation of the abomination of desolation.

Paul wrote to the Thessalonian church to admonish Christians who had abandoned the normal affairs of life. They believed the imminent coming of Christ that Paul had previously espoused (1 Thessalonians 4:13-18) was already set in motion (2 Thessalonians 2:2). Paul explained that before the "appearance" of the Messiah, the Antichrist must first appear (verses 3-9). The signal event that will manifest the Antichrist, whom this text refers to as "the man of lawlessness," "the son of destruction" (verse 3b), and "that lawless one" (verse 8), is his usurpation of God's place in the Temple (verse 4; see also Exodus 25:8). This act will reveal not only the Antichrist but also "the lie" (the deification of the Antichrist, Revelation 13:4-6,15) that will mark his followers (Revelation 13:16-18) and confirm them in the eschatological judgment that will occur at the coming of the Lord (2 Thessalonians 2:8-12).

ABOMINATION OF THE ANTICHRIST

Paul introduces the desecration of the Temple in 2 Thessalonians 2:4 by saying that the man of lawlessness "exalts himself." He elevates himself "over every so-called god or object of worship." While this might indicate a superlative blasphemy of God such as in Revelation 13:6, the immediate setting is the future (rebuilt) Jerusalem Temple, and so the "objects of worship" are sacred vessels (see 2 Chronicles 5:5-7; Hebrews 9:2-5) and the "desolation" occurs within the innermost sacred part of the Temple (the Holy of Holies), where God's presence was previously mani-

fested (Exodus 25:22; 30:6; see also Ezekiel 43:1-7).

The abomination, however, is the Antichrist's act of enthroning himself in the place of deity to "display himself" (Greek, *apodeiknunta*) as God (literally, "that he *is* God"). This blasphemous act fulfills Daniel's prediction that the Antichrist "will exalt and magnify himself above every god and will speak monstrous things against the God of gods" (Daniel 11:36). With the satanic background of Revelation 12:9,12-17; 13:4-10, the abomination has allusions to Isaiah 14:13-14 and Ezekiel 28:2-9, where the usurping figures "raise [their] throne above the stars of God," "make [themselves] like the Most High," and declare, "I am god; I sit in the seat of the gods."

Despite the precedent of the literal interpretation of the Olivet Discourse, which clearly refers to the desecration of the historic Jewish Temple in Jerusalem, some interpret 2 Thessalonians 2:4 in a nonliteral manner, taking "the temple of God" metaphorically as a reference to the church. They view the act of desecration by the "man of lawlessness" as apostasy in the church. However, writing to a first-century audience at a time when the Second Temple was still standing, Paul's reference to "the temple of God" could only mean one place—the Jewish Temple in Jerusalem.

We also have other reasons for rejecting the symbolic interpretation and applying the prophecy to a literal Temple (and therefore a literal abomination of desolation): (1) In the few places where Paul used the Greek word *naos* ("temple") to mean something other than the actual Holy Place at Jerusalem (1 Corinthians 3:16; 6:19; 2 Corinthians 6:16; Ephesians 2:21), he always explained his special meaning so that his readers would understand his metaphorical usage. (2) The word "temple" in 2 Thessalonians 2:4 has the definite article ("*the* temple") in contrast to Paul's metaphorical usage, where "temple" is usually anarthrous ("*a* temple"). (3) "In the temple of God" modifies the verb "takes his seat" (Greek, *kathisai*), a verb suggesting a definite locality, not an institution (such as the church). If Paul were referring to apostasy in the church, he would better have expressed this with a verb for "enthronement" or "usurpation" rather than a verb that referred to the literal act of "taking a seat."

The ante-Nicene church fathers affirmed the literal understanding of this passage. For example, Irenaeus (A.D. 185) wrote: "But when this Antichrist shall have devastated all things in this world, he will reign for three years and six months, and sit in the Temple at Jerusalem; and then the Lord will come from heaven in the clouds, in the glory of the Father, sending this man and those who follow him into the lake of fire; but bringing in for the righteous the times of the kingdom." Irenaeus' literal interpretation of the Temple's desecration is both eschatological and premillennial. By contrast, the symbolic or "spiritual" use of "temple" for the church does not appear in developed form until the third century A.D. with Origen, who was influenced by the allegorical interpretations of the Hellenistic idealist school of Philo.

Consequently, the eschatological interpretation of the abomination of desolation has both textual support and the witness of early church apologists. It warns us of the future day of deception and desolation at the midpoint of the Tribulation, which will call for divine judgment climaxing in the return of the Lord.

—RANDALL PRICE

BIBLIOGRAPHY

Dodd, C.H. "The Fall of Jerusalem and the Abomination of Desolation." *Journal of Roman Studies* 37 (1947), pp. 51-63.

Ford, Desmond. *The Abomination of Desolation in Biblical Eschatology.* Washington, DC: University Press of America, 1979.

Price, Randall. *The Desecration and Restoration of the Temple in the Old Testament, Jewish Apocalyptic Literature, and the New Testament.* Ann Arbor, MI: UMI, 1993.

Wenham, David. "Abomination of Desolation." In *Anchor Bible Dictionary.* New York: Doubleday, 1992.

Zmijewski, J. "Bdelugma." In *Exegetical Dictionary of the New Testament.* Edited by Horst Balz and Gerhard Schneider. Grand Rapids: Eerdmans Publishing Company, 1978.

ABRAHAMIC COVENANT

THE FOUNTAINHEAD of Bible prophecy begins with the Abrahamic covenant (Genesis 12:1-3,7; 13:14-17; 15:1-21; 17:1-21; 22:15-18). This agreement is the "mother of all redemptive covenants," and God's blessings springing forth from it extend to all mankind throughout the ages.

AN UNCONDITIONAL COVENANT

The Abrahamic covenant is an unconditional agreement or pact in which God reveals His sovereign election of Abraham and his descendants and declares His decrees for them. Arnold Fruchtenbaum (p. 570) explains, "An unconditional covenant can be defined as a sovereign act of God whereby God unconditionally obligates Himself to bring to pass definite promises, blessings, and conditions for the covenanted people. It is a unilateral covenant. This type of covenant is characterized by the formula 'I will' which declares God's determination to do exactly as He promised."

The covenant or treaty formats commonly used in the second millennium B.C. highlight the unconditional nature of the Abrahamic covenant. The Bible contains three kinds of covenants: (1) the royal grant treaty, (2) the suzerain–vassal treaty, and (3) the parity treaty.

The royal grant treaty is an unconditional, promissory covenant based on a king's desire to reward a loyal servant. Examples include the Abrahamic covenant (Genesis 12:1-3; 15), the Davidic covenant (2 Samuel 7:8-17), and the Land of Israel covenant (Deuteronomy 30:1-10).

God confirmed and sealed the Abrahamic covenant in Genesis 15 through a unique procedure whereby He put Abram into a deep sleep and bound Himself to keep the covenant regardless of Abraham's response. Since God is the only one who swore to keep the covenant, it is clearly an unconditional covenant, based solely on God. Thus, we can be absolutely confident that He will keep it and bring to pass in history every stipulation of the agreement.

Comparing the Abrahamic covenant with parallel expressions in the ancient Near East shows that it is a royal grant treaty. Genesis 26:5 (NASB) says, "Abraham obeyed me and kept My charge, My commandments, My statutes and My laws." The term "law" is from the Hebrew *torah,* which basically means "to direct, teach, or instruct." The first verb of Genesis 26:5 is "obeyed," referring to Abraham's obedience to sacrifice Isaac (Genesis 22:1-2). This is similar to terminology found at Amarna in covenant contexts. The second verb is "kept," paralleling an Assyrian grant in which Ashurbanipal rewarded his servant Bulta with a grant because he "kept the charge of my kingship." Both of these verbs indicate a personal relationship rather than a legal code of ethics. Thus, obedience to *torah* flows from a covenant relationship with God.

Abraham's obedience was not based on legalistic compulsion but rather expressed his faithfulness to God. "A close examination of the context reveals no covenant stipulations which could be viewed as pure legislative or ethical codes. What the context does reveal is that God has praised His servant Abraham because he has been faithful to do whatever the Lord instructed him to do. He did it not out of compulsion to legislation, but in a faith response to the instruction of God" (Dean, p. 13).

Royal grant treaties or covenants were unconditional. This point is important for Bible prophecy because they emphasize that God is obligated to fulfill His promise specifically to the original parties of the covenant. For example, we believe that God must fulfill the promises He made to national Israel through unconditional covenants such as the Abrahamic, Davidic, and Land covenants. If this is true, then they must be fulfilled literally, and many aspects of their fulfillment are yet future.

Eugene Merrill (p. 26) observes: "As most scholars now recognize, the covenant and its circumstances were in the form of a royal (land) grant, a legal arrangement well attested in the ancient New East....The Abrahamic Covenant...must be viewed as an unconditional grant made by Yahweh to His servant Abram, a grant that was to serve a specific and irrevocable function."

THE COVENANTAL STIPULATIONS

The Abrahamic covenant (Genesis 12:1-3) includes three major provisions: (1) *land* to Abram and Israel, (2) a *seed,* and (3) a worldwide *blessing.* A more complete breakdown of the covenant contains 14 provisions gleaned from the five major passages containing the treaty and its reconfirmations. Fruchtenbaum (p. 570) lists them as follows:

1. A great nation was to come out of Abraham, namely, the nation of Israel (12:2; 13:16; 15:5; 17:1-2,7; 22:17).

2. He was promised a land specifically, the Land of Canaan (12:1,7; 13:14-15, 17; 15:17-21; 17:8).

3. Abraham himself was to be greatly blessed (12:2; 22:15-17).

4. Abraham's name would be great (12:2).

5. Abraham would be a blessing to others (12:2).

6. Those who bless will be blessed (12:3).

7. Those who curse will be cursed (12:3).

8. In Abraham all will ultimately be blessed, a promise of Gentile blessing (12:3; 22:18).

9. Abraham would receive a son through his wife Sarah (15:1-4; 17:16-21).

10. His descendants would undergo the Egyptian bondage (15:13-14).

11. Other nations as well as Israel would come forth from Abraham (17:3-4,6; the Arab states).

12. His name would be changed from Abram to Abraham (17:5).

13. Sarai's name was to be changed to Sarah (17:15).

14. There was to be a token of the covenant—circumcision (17:9-14).

THE EXPANSION OF THE ABRAHAMIC COVENANT

John F. Walvoord (pp. 44–45) summarizes the foundational importance of the Abrahamic covenant in the study of Bible prophecy. He states: "The Abrahamic covenant contributes to the eschatology of Israel by detailing the broad program of God as it affects Abraham's seed....It is not too much to say that the exegesis of the Abrahamic covenant and its resulting interpretation is the foundation for the study of prophecy as a whole, not only as relating to Israel, but also for the Gentiles and the church. It is here that the true basis for premillennial interpretation of the Scriptures is found."

The Abrahamic covenant is important to any discussion of Bible prophecy, for it expresses many unconditional decrees that will be expanded upon in subsequent revelation and thus surely fulfilled in history. This expansion of a biblical theme in the later revelation of Scripture has been called "progressive revelation." We see this in God's dealings with the nation and people of Israel throughout the Bible.

ABRAHAMIC COVENANT

The Bible expands upon the three provisions of *land*, *seed*, and *blessing*. (See the chart above.) God enlarges these promises with new covenants: (1) the Land of Israel covenant (Deuteronomy 30:1-10), (2) the Davidic covenant (2 Samuel 7:4-17), and (3) the New Covenant (Jeremiah 31:31-34).

Land of Israel Covenant

The first expansion of the Land promise came after Abram left Haran and arrived in the Land of Canaan. Genesis 12:7 tells us that the Lord appeared to Abram in Canaan and said, "To your descendants I will give this land." The context shows that Abram understood the Lord to be referring to the Land of Canaan. The promise was clearly not just for Abram but for his descendants.

God further developed the Land promise just after Lot, Abram's nephew, separated from Abram. At this time the Lord said to Abram: "Now lift up your eyes and look from the place where you are, northward and southward and eastward and westward; for all the land which you see, I will give it to you and to your descendants forever" (Genesis 13:14-15). Again the promise emphasizes that God gave the Land to Abram and his descendants. The new element introduced is one of time—it is given *forever*. Much debate has occurred over this word. Generally its duration is determined by context. Unless otherwise indicated, it clearly refers to the duration of human history and can include eternity.

Genesis 15 provides the record of the actual covenant and describes the boundaries of the Land more precisely: "On that day the LORD made a covenant with Abram, saying, 'To your descendants I have given this land, from the river of Egypt as far as the great river, the river Euphrates'" (Genesis 15:18 NASB).

God promised not only to make Abram the father of a nation but also to provide a homeland for that nation. A nation cannot be a nation without a homeland of its own. Apart from its homeland a people lose their ethnic and national identity. Amazingly, Israel maintained a national identity even after 1800 years of separation from their national homeland.

Deuteronomy 30:1-10 expands this element of the Abrahamic covenant into the Land of Israel covenant (also called the Palestinian covenant). This passage teaches that all the Land promises that God has made to Israel will be fulfilled "when all of these things have come upon you, the blessing and the curse... and you return to the LORD your God" (Deuteronomy 30:1-2). God will fulfill this promise for national Israel after the Tribulation in conjunction with the Messiah's return and the millennial kingdom.

The Davidic Covenant

The second unconditional covenant between God and Israel was made more specifically with David. This is recorded in 2 Samuel 7:10-16. This covenant expands upon the seed provisions of the Abrahamic covenant. The Lord promises to establish David's kingdom, house, and throne forever.

> When your days are complete and you lie down with your fathers, I will raise up your descendant after you, who will come forth from you, and I will establish his kingdom. He shall build a house for My name, and I will establish the throne of his kingdom forever. I will be a father to him and he will be a son to Me; when he commits iniquity, I will correct him with the rod of men and the strokes of the sons of men, but My lovingkindness shall not depart from him, as I took it away from Saul, whom I removed from before you. Your house and your kingdom shall endure before Me forever; your throne shall be established forever (2 Samuel 7:12-16).

These three words—"kingdom," "house," and "throne"—all refer to the political future of Israel. God has clearly promised in this covenant to make Israel an independent political entity forever. This guarantees Israel's protection as a people and eventually as a nation. God will fulfill this promise in the messianic kingdom when the Lord Jesus Christ as the greater Son of David rules from David's throne. This has not taken place yet but points to Israel's future as a nation (see Ezekiel 36:1-12; Micah 4:1-5; Zephaniah 3:14-20; Zechariah 14:1-21). To interpret the future for Israel as anything other than a unique, distinct future for God's special people would be to make God a liar and a covenant breaker.

These promises and prophecies clearly show that (1) Israel has never possessed all the land God promised, (2) God promised not to change His mind, (3) God recognized that Israel would be scattered among the nations, (4) God will return them to their Land and reunite them as a nation, and (5) Israel will serve the Lord under the Messiah in the Land in the future.

The church has never been scattered among the nations, so we cannot apply to the church the concept of being reunited. Phrases like "their own land" and "the mountains of Israel" clearly refer to the geography of the Promised Land and not to the church. Further, the context clearly indicates that God was referring to a future for ethnic, political Israel, so to say that God intended to fulfill these promises in the church would mean that God intentionally deceived Israel. God is faithful and true, so these promises do not apply to the church.

The New Covenant

The next unconditional covenant between God and Israel is the New Covenant. The covenant is new because it replaced the Old or Mosaic Covenant. Israel was unable to keep the Mosaic covenant, so God graciously promised to give them a new covenant as well as a new heart to obey God. This covenant is recorded in Jeremiah 31:31-34:

> "Behold, days are coming," declares the LORD, "when I will make a new covenant with the house of Israel and with the house of Judah, not like the covenant which I made with their fathers in the day I took them by the hand to bring them out of the land of Egypt, My covenant which they broke, although I was a husband to them," declares the LORD. "But this is the covenant which I will make with the house of Israel after those days," declares the LORD, "I will put My law within them and on their heart I will write it; and I will be their God, and they shall be My people. They will not teach again, each man his neighbor and each man his brother, saying, 'Know the LORD,' for they will all know Me, from the least of them to the greatest of them," declares the LORD, "for I will

forgive their iniquity, and their sin I will remember no more."

Notice that God makes this covenant "with the house of Israel and with the house of Judah." This statement clearly refers to the ethnic nation of Israel. Second, the statement "not like the covenant which I made with their fathers in the day I took them...out of the land of Egypt" again clearly restricts the meaning of the statement to the physical descendants of Abraham through Isaac and Jacob. Third, this covenant has in view a future restoration of the people not only as God's people but as a people who were forgiven, regenerated, and serving the Lord.

When the Lord Jesus Christ went to the cross, He established the New Covenant. We remember that in the celebration of the Lord's table, Christ said, "This cup which is poured out for you is the new covenant in My blood" (Luke 22:20). The New Testament clearly teaches that the church is a beneficiary of the spiritual benefits of the New Covenant because of its relationship to Christ.

The covenants that God made with Israel in the Old Testament promised that Israel would have an eternal kingdom in the location of the Land God promised to Abraham. While God warned them time and again that because of their disobedience they would be removed from the Land, at the same time He promised that He would restore them to the Land as His people under the rule of the Messiah, and they would serve Him. Israel has never completely controlled the land God promised, and they have never returned to the Land under the conditions of the covenant, so the Old Testament promises and prophecies clearly foretold a future for Israel as an ethnic, political entity with a special status as God's people. This will be fulfilled when Israel submits to God spiritually.

PERMANENCE OF THE ABRAHAMIC COVENANT

The Abrahamic covenant is directed to Abraham, Isaac, Jacob, and their descendants. It is repeated to them about 20 times in Genesis (12:1-3,7-9; 13:14-18; 15:1-18; 17:1-27; 22:15-18; 26:2-6,24-25; 27:28-29,38-40; 28:1-4,10-22; 31:3,11-13; 32:24-32; 35:9-15; 48:3-4,10-20; 49:1-28; 50:23-25). The Abrahamic covenant has been in force throughout the years and is still a basis upon which God acts, even in our own day. Genesis 12–50 records the beginning of the historical outworking of the Abrahamic covenant. When people bless Abraham and his descendants, God blesses them. When people curse Abraham and his descendants, God curses them. The outworking of the Abrahamic covenant continues throughout the rest of the Old Testament.

Scripture demonstrates God's integrity in history through His relationship with His chosen people Israel. As He promised in the Abrahamic covenant, God uses His dealings with Israel to leave His mark throughout history. Through Israel God gave His law, founded a nation, caused His presence to dwell among them, mediated His Word, and sent the Savior of the world. Through Israel God will work to preach the gospel throughout the whole world, invoke the second coming, and reign for a thousand years in Jerusalem, the place of His eternal glory. Without Israel, the second coming cannot take place, since the nation must be present for this glorious event to occur. Thus, God's promise to Israel is that they have an eternal permanence in history and throughout eternity (Jeremiah 31:35-36).

> Thus says the LORD, who gives the sun for light by day and the fixed order of the moon and the stars for light by night, who stirs up the sea so that its waves roar; the LORD of hosts is His name: "If this fixed order departs from before Me," declares the LORD, "Then the offspring of Israel also will cease from being a nation before Me forever." Thus says the LORD, "If the heavens above can be measured and the foundations of the earth searched out below, then I will also cast off all the offspring of Israel for all that they have done," declares the LORD.

The Abrahamic covenant is the springboard through which every promise of blessing originates, whether to the Jews, the Gentiles, or the church of God. Just because God's promises have a wide-ranging scope does not mean that promises He made to Israel are not permanent and will not be kept. The force of the Abrahamic covenant is still in place today. God still blesses those who bless Israel and curses those who curse Israel. These promises will come to a climax during the events of the tribulation period, leading up to the second coming of Christ and His glorious reign from Jerusalem for 1000 years.

—Thomas Ice

BIBLIOGRAPHY

Dean, Robert L. "Theonomy, the Mosaic Law and the Nations" (unpublished paper).

Fruchtenbaum, Arnold. *Israelology.* Tustin, CA: Ariel Ministries, 1992.

Merrill, Eugene. "A Theology of the Pentateuch." In Roy Zuck, ed. *A Biblical Theology of the Old Testament.* Chicago: Moody Press, 1991.

Ross, Allen P. *Creation & Blessing.* Grand Rapids: Baker Books, 1988.

Walvoord, John F. *Israel in Prophecy.* Grand Rapids: Zondervan, 1962.

ACTS, ESCHATOLOGY OF

THE BOOK OF ACTS is a pivotal book in the New Testament. It records the transition from the Old Testament and the Gospels to the epistles, from a focus on Israel as God's chosen nation to the church—people whom God has chosen from all nations.

WHEN WILL GOD'S KINGDOM COME?

Acts 1:6-7 reveals that the apostles are expecting Jesus to fulfill the many prophecies of the Old Testament by establishing His kingdom on earth. Here they are anticipating neither heaven nor the church. Their words are definitive: "Lord, will you at this time restore the kingdom to Israel?" The word "restore" (Greek, *apokathistanō*) suggests four things:

1. The kingdom to which they are referring is that which Israel had at one time possessed. Israel became God's kingdom when they came out of Egypt as a nation (Exodus 19:6), and God was their King (1 Samuel 8:6-7; 12:12; Judges 8:23; Isaiah 43:15; Hosea 13:9-11).

2. This kingdom did not now exist at the time of this question by the disciples.

3. This kingdom will again exist with the nation of Israel.

4. This kingdom is the same kingdom that had been established with Israel, for "restore" means to bring back that which formerly existed.

Jesus mildly rebuked His disciples for their question, but He did not rebuke them for still anticipating the restoration of the earthly kingdom that God had established with the nation of Israel. He only rebuked them for making Israel's kingdom their present and primary concern. Christ's concern for that time was the establishment of His church (Acts 1:8). His admonition to the disciples that it is not for them to know the times or seasons (verse 7) may also be a warning for us not to speculate and theorize too much about future things that God has not chosen to reveal.

THE ASCENSION AND SECOND COMING OF JESUS CHRIST

The ascension of Jesus to the Father in heaven is significantly different from what had been occurring during the 40 days between His resurrection and ascension (Acts 1:9-11). On the former occasions He had instantly appeared and disappeared (Luke 24:31) and then reappeared on a later occasion. What happens here is different and final—their eyes behold His gradual ascension until a cloud obscures Him from their sight. This cloud may symbolize the shekinah glory and presence of God seen in the Old Testament (Exodus 40:34) and manifested on the Mount of Transfiguration (Matthew 17:5). While the apostles are entranced in the event, two "men" appear on the scene. That they are angels is evident by several facts.

1. Their white clothing fits that of angelic appearances (Matthew 28:3; John 20:12).
2. Their message fits that of angelic announcements (Matthew 28:5-7).
3. Angels are often described as men (Acts 10:3,30; Revelation 21:17).
4. Even the use of the rare pluperfect verb (*pareistēkeisan*—"stood") suggests a dramatic event (see Harrison, 41).

These two angels assure the apostles that Jesus will return in the same manner as He has just ascended.

1. He ascended visibly; He will return visibly (see Revelation 1:7).
2. He ascended bodily; He will return bodily to this very place—Mt. Olivet (Zechariah 14:4).
3. He ascended in the cloud of glory; He will return in the cloud of glory (Matthew 24:30; Mark 13:26).

Jesus' return has not yet happened and will not happen until the time when the Great Tribulation has come upon Israel and the whole earth (Matthew 24:29-30).

THE FULFILLMENT OF THE PROPHET JOEL

Peter seems to be saying in Acts 2:17-21 that Pentecost is the fulfillment of Joel's prophecy concerning the last days (Joel 2:28-32). But Joel quite clearly relates these events to the time of the Great Tribulation, for Joel, immediately after 2:32, states, "For behold, in those days and at that time..." and then goes on to describe the time of the Great Tribulation (3:9-16) and the kingdom of God on earth (3:18-21). So can Peter be seeing the fulfillment of Joel 2 on the Day of Pentecost? No, nor can he imagine its fulfillment. He has not seen the Spirit poured out on *all* flesh. When he preached this, he had just seen the Spirit poured out on only 120 people (Acts 1:15). But this is enough to convince him that this

is the beginning, the first phase, of that fulfillment (Bruce, p. 61).

THE RETURN OF JESUS AND RESTORATION OF ALL THINGS

If someone imagines that Peter was confused and spiritually dull when he asked Jesus about the restoration of the kingdom to Israel in Acts 1:6 prior to Pentecost and the indwelling presence of the Holy Spirit, then one can expect that after Pentecost, Peter's understanding should be much clearer. Yet in Acts 3:19-26, Peter's understanding of God's kingdom with Israel remains unchanged.

Peter says that Israel needs to repent and to turn to Jesus so that God may send Jesus back from heaven in order to bring the times of restoration and refreshing, the times proclaimed by all the Old Testament prophets (verse 21). The Greek noun translated "restoration" here is from the same root as the verb used in the apostles' question in Acts 1:6 concerning God restoring His kingdom to Israel at that time.

Peter rightly believes that God will restore His kingdom with Israel when Jesus literally returns from heaven to this earth (Matthew 25:31-32; Revelation 19:11–20:6) and that the nation of Israel must first repent (see Romans 11, especially verses 25-27; Zechariah 12:10-14; 13:8-9). Peter mentions two important points of eschatology in this sermon. On the positive side, Jesus will return and restore all that God had promised and Israel had lost. And on the negative side, those who do not hear and heed Jesus will be completely cut off from these millennial blessings (Fernando, p. 140).

AMOS' KINGDOM PROPHECY AND THE EARLY CHURCH

At the Jerusalem Council of Acts 15, James, the pastor at Jerusalem, quotes the Old Testament prophet Amos (9:11-12) to show that the salvation of many Gentiles during the days of the early church should not be surprising because the Old Testament prophets foretold it (Acts 15:15-17). Amos proclaims that these Gentiles will enter into God's kingdom. This leads some to believe that the church, therefore, is the fulfillment of the Old Testament promise of the kingdom of God.

James, however, does not say that Amos' prophecy is being fulfilled during his time in the early church. In fact, the evidence shows that James is saying that the prophecy will not be fulfilled until a later time, when Jesus returns to earth after this present age.

First, James says that "the words of the prophets *agree*" with what is happening in the early church (Acts 15:15). What God will do in the future millennial kingdom, that is, saving and including many Gentiles, He is already doing in the early church. James has carefully chosen the word "agree" rather than "fulfill." The conversion of Gentiles in the days of the early church is not the fulfillment of this Old Testament prophecy, but it is in harmony with what God will also do in His kingdom—He will include all nations.

Second, James changes the words of the Amos prophecy from "on that day" to "after this" to show that he understands that the prophecy refers to a time "after this" time of the first century. It refers to the time of the future millennial era.

Third, James adds the word "return" in his citation of this prophecy to allow for the fact that before Amos' prophecy will be fulfilled, Christ must come a second time to earth to restore His kingdom. James says, "*After this* I will *return* and will rebuild the tabernacle of David, which has fallen down. I will rebuild its ruins, and I will set it up; so that the rest of mankind may seek the Lord, even all the Gentiles who are called by My name, says the LORD who does all these things" (Acts 15:16-17). These two changes are not due to textual variations, as some propose, but due to James' interpretation.

Therefore, James bears witness to the fact that the church is not the promised kingdom but that this kingdom follows ("after this") this present church age.

THE RESURRECTION AND JUDGMENT OF ALL PEOPLE

In his address at Athens, Paul announced that the God who is creator of all is also judge of all. He has even fixed the day and appointed the Judge (Acts 17:30-32). The resurrection of this Judge, Jesus Christ, provides assurance that this judgment will occur. The first-century Athenians found it untenable to accept the notion of a physical resurrection because Neo-platonic philosophy regarded the physical realm as innately evil. Why would God raise man physically from death? Man, they thought, would live on only as a spirit. Yet Paul boldly proclaimed this eschatological resurrection and judgment as a central theme of the Christian gospel.

A NEW DISPENSATION

The book of Acts provides numerous examples of the dispensational transition from the Old Testament to the New Testament. For example, baptism is no longer a Jewish ritual but a distinctively Christian experience (Acts 19:1-5). Old Testament dietary laws are no longer applicable in the New Testament church (Acts 10:1-16). Gentile converts begin to outnumber Jewish converts as Jesus' prediction that He will build His church (Matthew 16:18) begins to come to pass and the gospel spreads to the "uttermost parts of the world" (Acts 1:8).

—JAMES FREERKSEN

BIBLIOGRAPHY

Bruce, F.F. *Acts* (NICNT). Revised edition. Grand Rapids: Eerdmans Publishing Company, 1998.

Fernando, Ajith. *The NIV Application Commentary: Acts.* Grand Rapids: Zondervan, 1998.

Harrison, Everett F. *Acts: The Expanding Church.* Chicago: Moody Press, 1975.

Kent, Homer A., Jr. *Jerusalem to Rome.* Grand Rapids: Baker Books/BMH, 1972.

Longenecker, Richard N. "Acts." In *Expositor's Bible Commentary*, Vol. 9. Grand Rapids: Zondervan, 1981.

AGES OF TIME

An IMPORTANT BIBLICAL PHRASE in Bible prophecy is "the age to come." An understanding of a related term, "the present age," is also necessary for properly interpreting biblical prophecy. "The present age" refers to the current church age that began almost 2000 years ago on the Day of Pentecost when the church was founded. It will end with the rapture of the church. "The age to come" is a reference to the millennial kingdom that will commence with the second coming of Christ and continue for 1000 years (Revelation 20:3).

THE MISUNDERSTANDING

Many amillennialists, postmillennialists, and preterists believe that "the age to come" refers to the current age in which we now live. Some say this began at Christ's first coming, while others say it began at Christ's supposed return in A.D. 70. Gary DeMar (pp. 69–70) says,

> The "end of the age" refers to the end of the Old Covenant redemption system with its attendant sacrifices and rituals.…The "end of the age" refers to the termination of the exclusive Jewish entitlement to the covenant promises and the inclusion of the Gentiles into the blessings of the covenant and the privileges of the gospel and kingdom (Matthew 21:41,43; 22:10). "End of the age" is a covenantal phrase. With the temple destroyed, there would be no way and no need to carry out the rigorous demands of the sacrificial system, a system that was predestined to pass away with the incarnation, death, resurrection, ascension, and enthronement of Jesus.

Preterists tend to believe that the phrase "present age" or "this age" refers to the approximately 40-year period between the earthly ministry of Christ and the destruction of Jerusalem in A.D. 70. Thus, as DeMar indicated, that means that after A.D. 70 we are in what

the Bible refers to as "the age to come." Full preterists (those who do not believe in a future second coming) believe that Jesus' reference to "this age" applies to the Mosaic age in which he was living, and the "age to come" is the Christian age. Thus, they view the church as already living in the "age to come."

THE PERSPECTIVES

Jewish Perspective of Bible Prophecy

The Jewish perspective of Bible prophecy divided history into two ages. The first was "this present age," the age in which Israel was waiting for the coming of the Messiah. The second was "the age to come," the age in which God would fulfill all His promises and covenants, and Israel would enter into her promised blessings as a result of Messiah's coming. "The present age" would end at the appearance of Messiah, and "the coming age" would begin with His advent. "The present age," then, would end in judgment, and "the coming age" would be preceded by this devastation.

The disciples questioned Jesus on the Mount of Olives (Matthew 24:3), linking His words of judgment about the destruction of the Temple with the invasion of Jerusalem that Zechariah predicted. The disciples believed this would precede the advent of the Messiah.

In Zechariah 14:4 (NASB) the prophet describes the advent of Messiah to institute His kingdom as follows:

> In that day His feet will stand on the Mount of Olives, which is in front of Jerusalem on the east; and the Mount of Olives will be split in its middle from east to west by a very large valley, so that half of the mountain will move toward the north and the other half toward the south.

This coming was to be preceded by an invasion and capture of Jerusalem (Zechariah 12:1-3; 14:1-3). However, Messiah would come from the Mount of Olives to deliver Jerusalem (Zechariah 14:4-5) and usher in the glory of the kingdom (Zechariah 14:14-15). This is when the "age to come" would arrive.

Christ's Perspective of Bible Prophecy

Jesus uses the same vocabulary in the same way when He says in Matthew 12:32, "Whoever speaks a word against the Son of Man, it shall be forgiven him; but whoever speaks against the Holy Spirit, it shall not be forgiven him, either in this age or in the age to come." Christ clearly distinguishes between the present age and the age to come. Meyer (vol. 1, p. 342) says, "'This age,' is the period previous to the coming of the Messiah...as Jesus understood it: *the time before the second coming*." He says "the age to come" is "the period that succeeds the coming of the Messiah...as Jesus understood it: *the time that follows the second coming*." Jesus says in Matthew 13:49, "So it will be at the end of the age; the angels will come forth and take out the wicked from among the righteous," as He continues to speak within the contemporary Jewish framework.

The disciples concluded that the judgment Christ had predicted was the one that would terminate this present age. After this judgment, the Messiah would come to introduce the age to come. Thus in Matthew 24:3 they asked their questions that precipitated the Olivet Discourse: "Tell us, when will these things happen, and what will be the sign of Your coming, and of the end of the age?" Later, after His resurrection and before His ascension, Jesus gave His disciples the Great Commission and said in Matthew 28:20, "Lo, I am with you always, even to the end of the age," continuing to speak within the framework of "this age" and "the age to come."

The Apostles' Perspective of Bible Prophecy

The apostle Paul uses the same language when he says in Ephesians 1:21 that New Testament believers have been given a position in Christ "far above all rule and authority and power and dominion, and every name that is named, not only in this age, but also in the one to come." Paul tells us in Galatians 1:4 that Christ "gave Himself for our sins so that He

might rescue us from this present evil age, according to the will of our God and Father." Paul also tells Christians that God's grace instructs us to "deny ungodliness and worldly desires and to live sensibly, righteously and godly in the present age" (Titus 2:12).

Paul continues to use the phrases "this age" and "the age to come" in the way that Christ used them. Even though Jesus had come, Paul still views the current church age as the time leading up to the coming of the Messiah. Thus, we are still in "the present age." This means that the "age to come" has not yet arrived and will come at the second coming, a time which is still in our own day a future event.

Even after a post-resurrection, 40-day period of instruction by Christ to the disciples "of the things concerning the kingdom of God," they ask Jesus in Acts 1:6, "Lord, is it at this time You are restoring the kingdom to Israel?" Jesus did not rebuke or correct the nature of their question as illegitimate. Instead He said, "It is not for you to know times or epochs which the Father has fixed by His own authority." This clearly implies there will be a future kingdom, as they thought...but not yet. "The kingdom" is a reference to the age to come. Our Lord then told His disciples to go preach the gospel throughout the world.

In Acts 3, Peter is preaching the gospel to Israel and says that his Jewish brethren and their rulers "acted in ignorance" when they demanded that Jesus be crucified. Then he says,

> The things which God announced beforehand by the mouth of all the prophets, that His Christ would suffer, He has thus fulfilled. Repent therefore and return, so that your sins may be wiped away, in order that times of refreshing may come from the presence of the Lord; and that He may send Jesus, the Christ appointed for you, whom heaven must receive until the period of restoration of all things about which God spoke by the mouth of His holy prophets from ancient time (Acts 3:18-21).

In a similar vein, we see in Acts 15:13-17 that James says to the Jerusalem Council:

> After they had stopped speaking, James answered, saying, "Brethren, listen to me. Simeon has related how God first concerned Himself about taking from among the Gentiles a people for His name. With this the words of the Prophets agree, just as it is written, 'After these things I will return, and I will rebuild the tabernacle of David which has fallen, and I will rebuild its ruins, and I will restore it, so that the rest of mankind may seek the Lord, and all the Gentiles who are called by My name.'"

James did not believe that "the age to come" or the kingdom had arrived, or he would not have made the above statement. It is clear that the New Testament writers of the epistles continue to use the phrase "this age" to refer to the time before the arrival of the Messiah, who will at that time bring with Him the kingdom, which is also still future to our own day.

THE IMPLICATIONS

The writers of the New Testament epistles present the current church age and the Tribulation as the last periods of history before the second coming of Christ and "the age to come." Three New Testament passages (Romans 16:25-27; Ephesians 3:1-13; Colossians 2:4–3:3) teach that the church age is a temporary mystery in the overall plan of God. Thus, the church age is a continuation of "this present age" from the time of Christ. Further New Testament revelation about the church age teaches that when it ends at the rapture and the Tribulation, "the age to come" will immediately follow—the time of Messiah's kingdom.

Urgency permeates the entire church age in which we now live. For example, Paul, speaking of the entire church age, calls it "the present distress" (1 Corinthians 7:26). Because Christ could return at any moment at the rapture, church-age believers are always to be ready and waiting for His return. Notice the following list of New Testament passages that teach this doctrine: 1 Corinthians 1:7; 16:22; Philippians 3:20; 4:5; 1 Thessalonians 1:10; Titus 2:13; Hebrews 9:28; James 5:7-9; 1 Peter 1:13; Jude 21; Revelation 3:11; 22:7,12,17,20.

Preterists see the end of the age occurring by A.D. 70, while others believe that it was inaugurated during the ministry of Christ at His first coming. Since the New Testament epistles were written to instruct believers in how to live until this present evil age comes to an end, it follows for preterists that all the doctrine and instruction applies only to the 40-year period that ended in A.D. 70. Logically, it is inconsistent for them to apply the teaching and instruction of the epistles to their lives because they believe that they are living in "the age to come." This applies as well to those who believe "the age to come" began at Christ's first coming. This explains why some preterists believe they are in the new heavens and new earth. But we are not living in the eternal state; we are still awaiting the any-moment return of our Lord Jesus Christ at the "end of the age."

—Thomas Ice

BIBLIOGRAPHY

DeMar, Gary. *Last Days Madness.* Powder Springs, GA: American Vision, 1999.

Guthrie, Donald. *New Testament Theology.* Downers Grove, IL: InterVarsity Press, 1981.

Meyer, H.A.W. "The Gospel of Matthew," 2 vols. In *Critical and Exegetical Commentary on the New Testament.* Edinburgh: T. & T. Clark, 1878.

Pentecost, J. Dwight. *Thy Kingdom Come.* Wheaton, IL: Victor Books, 1990.

AMILLENNIALISM

AMILLENNIALISM TEACHES THAT there will be no literal, future 1000-year reign of Christ on earth. Most amillennialists believe that a spiritual form of the kingdom is present now. Systematic amillennialism was the second of the three major eschatological views to develop; it was first taught within the church around the beginning of the fifth century.

Amillennialism teaches that there is no rapture. From the ascension of Christ in the first century until His second coming, both good and evil will increase in the world as God's kingdom parallels Satan's kingdom. Satan is currently bound, but evil increases. When Jesus Christ returns, the end of the world will occur with a general resurrection and general judgment of all people. This view spiritualizes the kingdom prophecies.

AMILLENNIAL SELF-DEFINITION

Floyd E. Hamilton (p. 129) describes *amillennialism* as the view "that Christ's millennial kingdom extends from His Resurrection from the tomb to the time of His Second Coming on the clouds at the end of this age." At no time will Christ reign on the earth in Jerusalem. "Christ's kingdom 'is not of this world,' but He reigns in the hearts of His people on earth. The thousand years are symbolic of the perfect, complete time between the two comings of Christ." After the second coming of Christ, believers from all of history will enter into heaven for eternity immediately following the final and single judgment of all mankind.

Kim Riddlebarger (pp. 31-32) defines amillennialism this way:

1. Amillennialism "can also be called 'present' or 'realized' millennialism." Riddlebarger sees the "present millennial age manifest in the present reign of Jesus Christ in heaven."

2. "Amillennialists hold that the promises made to Israel, David, and Abraham in the Old Testament are fulfilled by Jesus Christ and his church during this present age."

3. "The millennium is the period of time between the two advents of our Lord with the thousand years of Revelation

20 being symbolic of the entire interadvental age."

4. "At the first advent of Jesus Christ, Satan was bound by Christ's victory over him at Calvary and the empty tomb. The effects of this victory continued because of the presence of the kingdom of God via the preaching of the gospel and as evidenced by Jesus' miracles. Through the spread of the gospel, Satan is no longer free to deceive the nations."

5. "Christ is presently reigning in heaven during the entire period between Christ's first and second coming."

6. "At the end of the millennial age, Satan is released, a great apostasy breaks out, the general resurrection occurs, Jesus Christ returns in final judgment for all people and he establishes a new heaven and earth."

MILLENNIALISM AND THE EARLY CHURCH

We have no record of the presence of amillennialism in the earliest church. It appears to have risen first in opposition to premillennial literalism and then later developed into a positive system. In other words, the early church was premillennial, and then those who thought that early premillennialism was too materialistic began to teach what I will call "anti-millennialism." After a while, amillennialism arose out of anti-millennialism. Amillennialism came to dominate the church when the great church father and theologian Augustine (354–430) abandoned premillennialism in favor of amillennialism. The majority of the church's leadership has held to amillennialism for much of the church's history, including the majority of Protestant reformers during the fifteenth and sixteenth centuries.

The rise of figurative interpretation and Augustine's amillennial theory began to lay a foundation for the later development of postmillennialism. Walvoord (p. 19) notes that Augustine "held that the age between the first and second advents is the millennium of which the Scriptures speak and that the second advent would occur at the end of the millennium."

Historians and theologians readily and almost universally acknowledge millennial expectations in the early church. They also recognize the demise of these hopes and understand any later adherence to a millennial hope to be a false expectation based on mistaken exegesis. However, we can find an alternate explanation of its decline in the shift of accepted hermeneutical practices in the early and medieval church. Teachers moved from a normal, literal-grammatical interpretation to a strong reliance on allegory. Both the East and the West experienced a strong reaction against literal interpretation of the prophetic Scripture.

AMILLENNIALISM AND THE CHURCH FATHERS

In the East, Eusebius of Caesarea (263–339), the court theologian to Constantine and theological heir of Origen, was a strong leader in the rejection of apocalypticism. With the rise of Constantine and the adoption of Christianity as the empire's official religion, alternate perspectives fell into disfavor. Norman Cohn (p. 33) notes, "Millenarism remained powerful in the Christian Church so long as Christians were an unpopular minority threatened with persecution. When in the fourth century Christianity attained a position of supremacy in the Mediterranean world and became the official religion of the empire, the Church set out to eradicate millenarian beliefs." In the Latin West, Jerome (347–420) and Augustine also reacted strongly to prophetic interpretation. In his commentary on Daniel, written shortly before the year 400, Jerome argued that "the saints will in no wise have an earthly kingdom, but only a celestial one; thus must cease the fable of one thousand years."

Jerome was not alone in his attack on literal interpretation and millennial expectations. In *City of God*, Augustine repeatedly dismissed any hope for an earthly or physical millennial kingdom. Through the writings of men such as Jerome, Julian of Toledo, Gregory the Great, and most notably Augustine, literal interpretation of the Bible, and especially Daniel and Revelation, quickly faded. The Augustinian influence in the West eclipsed many perspectives, some orthodox and some unorthodox or heretical. Augustine's influence was so strong that it remained in force for centuries.

The dominance of allegorical interpretation in the West after the time of Augustine may best explain the seeming lack of a premillennial witness for so much of the church's history. But millennial thought did not completely cease, and it popped up occasionally upon an ocean of amillennial dominance. At the end of the sixteenth and the beginning of the seventeenth centuries, Johann Heinrich Alsted revived premillennialism and provided an alternative to the dominant amillennialism.

Since the early 1600s, amillennialism has remained the only significant view of eschatology within the Roman Catholic and Eastern Orthodox churches, while it has been in steady decline within Protestantism. However, today it still has a small following among some evangelicals and is the dominant view among those within the mainline denominations.

IS AMILLENNIALISM BIBLICAL?

The greatest problem with amillennialism is the fact that the Bible just does not teach it. The text of Scripture clearly teaches that Christ returns in Revelation 19, and then in Revelation 20, He sets up His reign upon the earth for 1000 years. Amillennialists cannot point to any specific passage that teaches their position. Lack of specific biblical support is fatal to amillennialism for any Bible-believing Christian. This explains why amillennialists typically first attack premillennialism and then present broad theological concepts that one must adopt in order to interpret biblical texts so that they "support" amillennialism.

Basic to amillennialism is its lack of a consistent hermeneutic. It must abandon the literal hermeneutic of the historical, grammatical, and contextual approach for some degree of allegorization. The amillennialist must supply ideas or concepts that one would not be able to find by simply reading the text. Allegorization, or spiritualization, brings a meaning from outside of a specific text to interpret it rather than basing the interpretation on what is written in that specific passage.

Nowhere does the New Testament teach that the kingdom of God came into existence at Christ's first coming. The New Testament does say that the kingdom was "near" during Christ's ministry, but it stops short of saying that it arrived during Christ's first coming. Furthermore, even though personal redemption is certainly an essential key to the kingdom, it does not negate equally clear teachings concerning the physical nature of this kingdom. It is a both-and, not an either-or issue.

The New Testament epistles, written to instruct the church during this current age, do not teach or assume that this age is the kingdom. The New Testament often refers to the kingdom as something that is future rather than present. Paul puts both the "appearing" of our Lord and "His kingdom" in the future in his charge to Timothy (2 Timothy 4:1). The kingdom arrives when the Lord appears at His second coming. Paul is confident the Lord will deliver him "from every evil deed, and will bring me safely to His heavenly kingdom" (4:18). Certainly this deliverance from every evil deed is future. And since it is, then so is His heavenly kingdom. McClain (p. 433) observed: "This expression is not a synonym for heaven, but rather indicates that the long-awaited Messianic Kingdom will be 'heavenly' in origin and character as contrasted with earthly kingdoms. It is the closest approximation to the familiar phrase 'kingdom of heaven' so frequently used in Matthew's Gospel."

After being persecuted in Derbe, Paul and Barnabas returned to some of the cities where they had won converts to Christ and sought to give them advice: "Through many tribulations we must enter the kingdom of God" (Acts 14:22). If they were *in* the kingdom,

this statement would make no sense. Since they were not in the kingdom, neither are we. They spoke of it as yet coming in the future.

Several New Testament passages speak of the church inheriting the kingdom in the future (1 Corinthians 6:9-10; 15:50; Galatians 5:21; Ephesians 5:5; James 2:5). McClain (p. 433) notes that "Paul not only sees this inheritance of the Kingdom in future time but definitely excludes it from the present age by placing it after the resurrection and rapture of the Church."

Christ is presently sitting victoriously at the Father's right hand (Revelation 3:21) and making intercession for the saints (1 John 2:1-3). Such language does not suggest that Jesus is currently on David's throne, which He will occupy for 1000 years in Jerusalem at His return. These are two separate thrones that He will occupy at two separate locations and times. Revelation describes Christ as personally present on earth during His millennial rule. Revelation 5:10 predicts the saints will reign with Him on the earth. At the end of 1000 years, the saints are still on earth, for this is where Satan comes to attack them (Revelation 20:9).

A SYMBOLIC INTERPRETATION

Amillennialism relies upon an unnatural, symbolic understanding of the 1000 years mentioned six times in Revelation 20:2-7. No one has demonstrated from ancient literature why the number 1000 should have any symbolic significance. In fact, neither the Old or New Testaments use the number 1000 symbolically. Whenever the Hebrew or Greek words for *year* are used with numbers, they always refer to literal years. Throughout the Bible, numbers convey mathematical quantities unless the text or context provides evidence to the contrary.

Is Satan Bound?

Amillennialism teaches that Satan was bound at some time during the first coming of Christ. Such a view has many problems, including this: The New Testament never indicates that Satan was bound in the past. How could Satan be bound and be so active at the same time? Affirming both of these contradictory realities defies logic and the testimony of Scripture. Christ returns to earth in Revelation 19:11-16, and Satan is bound in Revelation 20:1-3. Clearly Satan's binding takes place in the future.

If Satan is bound today, then why was he "dwelling in Pergamos" in Revelation 2:13? How is he wandering about like a roaring lion (1 Peter 5:8)? The binding of Satan is thorough and decisive, not progressive nor partial. The verbal actions "laid hold," "bound," "threw," "shut," and "sealed" are all in the aorist tense, indicating decisive, completed actions. Not one is in the imperfect tense, indicating continuous action in the past.

Israel and the Church

Amillennialism confuses Israel and the church. If the kingdom is present now, God's promises to Israel are fulfilled in the church. Jesus Christ has certainly fulfilled God's Old Testament promises to the church, but that does not mean that He will not fulfill God's promises for Israel as well. Modern amillennialism includes what is known as replacement theology or supersessionism. Thus, it denies that the modern state of Israel has any place in God's future prophetic plan. However, the New Testament never teaches that Israel has been replaced by the church. Paul says to these things, "God has not rejected His people [Israel], has He? May it never be!" (Romans 11:1). The church is certainly a partaker in the Abrahamic promises, but it does not usurp Israel's promises.

Christ's Revolutionary Rule

Amillennialism fails to account for the fact that the millennial conditions predicted in the Bible will occur only as a result of the revolutionary intervention of Jesus Christ at His second coming. We do not see the promised blessings of the kingdom in this present age. Only the personal presence of Jesus Christ

Himself and His rulership "with a rod of iron" will roll back the curse and create the wonderful conditions the Bible associates with the kingdom. Therefore, only the premillennial model describes a sequence of events necessary to implement a millennial golden age.

—THOMAS ICE

BIBLIOGRAPHY

Cohn, Norman. "Medieval Millenarism." In S.L. Thrupp, ed., *Millennial Dreams in Action.* The Hague: Moulton & Co., 1962.

Hamilton, Floyd. "Amillennialism." In *Zondervan Pictorial Encyclopedia of the Bible.* Grand Rapids: Zondervan, 1975. Vol. 1, p. 129.

McClain, Alva J. *The Greatness of the Kingdom.* Chicago: Moody Press, 1959.

Riddlebarger, Kim. *A Case for Amillennialsim.* Grand Rapids: Baker Books, 2003.

Walvoord, John J. *The Millennial Kingdom.* Grand Rapids: Zondervan, 1973.

ANGELS

THE BIBLE REFERS TO ANGELS more than 300 times as real, personal, created spirit beings. Many theologians believe that God created all angels on the first or second day of creation (see Psalm 104:4). Angels can be good or evil. Demons were once angels, but they joined Satan's rebellion against God and were cast out of heaven (see Revelation 12:4).

The Bible depicts angels as God's messengers, protectors of His people, and agents of His judgments. They have led God's people (Exodus 14:19; 23:20), called them (Judges 6:11), delivered them (Daniel 6:22), and prophesied to them (Matthew 1:20-23). In the book of Revelation, angels announce messages, assist God's people, and deliver God's judgments.

THE NATURE OF ANGELS

Angels are spiritual beings who can appear in human form (Genesis 18:1-8). They generally appear as males (Mark 16:5; Luke 24:4).

The only apparent exception is Zechariah 5:9, where two angels are described as women. In some cases, they appear as unusual "living creatures" (Revelation 4:6-8). At least two categories of angelic beings, *seraphim* and *cherubim,* have wings (Isaiah 6:2-6; Ezekiel 1:5-8). Several angels are described as flying (Daniel 9:21; Luke 1:19).

The Bible also describes angels as both sinless and sexless beings. They do not marry or have children (Matthew 22:28-30). They have individual personalities and names, such as Michael and Gabriel. Angels also appear to be localized beings with certain limitations (Daniel 10:10-14). They can be in only one place at a time. They are God's angels, but they are not divine and therefore do not exhibit the qualities of deity, such as omnipresence.

Angels walk, talk, and eat (Genesis 18:1-9), but their power exceeds that of human beings. They can excel in strength (2 Peter 2:11). They can limit human wickedness (Genesis 18:22) and execute human judgment (Genesis 19:1-11). Angels can also exert power and influence over nature (Revelation 9:14-15).

THE NAMES OF ANGELS

Angel is the transliteration of the Greek word *angelos,* meaning "messenger." It is similar in meaning to the Hebrew word *malak.* Fred Dickason (p. 61) states, "Depending on the context, these words may be used of a human messenger (1 Samuel 6:21) or of a supernatural, spiritual heavenly being who is employed by God as His messenger to make known His purposes (Luke 1:11)."

Minister refers to the nature of the angels as ministering spirits (Hebrews 1:14). The Old Testament uses the Hebrew word *mishrathim* (Psalm 104:4) in the same way the New Testament uses the Greek word *leitourgos* of the ministry of angels.

Host refers to God's angels as a heavenly army. "The Lord of hosts" is a title of God as the commander of the heavenly army. "A multitude of the heavenly host" appeared at the birth of Christ (Luke 2:13).

Watchers is the term Daniel 4:13,17 uses to show that angels watch over humans and observe their behavior. The Bible often depicts them as calling out to God to intervene in human affairs.

Sons of God is another term used of angels in the Old Testament. The Hebrew term, *bene elohim,* is used exclusively of angels (Job 1:6; 2:1; 38:7).

Holy Ones (Hebrew, *kadoshim*) means "separated ones" (Psalm 89:6-7). It reflects the character and nature of God's angels.

THE CLASSIFICATION OF ANGELS

The Bible describes several kinds of angels:

- *Cherubim* are the highest class of angels. They attend the glory, holiness, and majesty of God (Ezekiel 1:5-14).

- *Seraphim* are "burning ones" or angelic incendiaries who are ablaze with the glory of God and continually announce His triune holiness (Isaiah 6:3).

- *Living beings* (Hebrew, *hayoth*) is a general designation of the angels who both direct the worship of God and express His judgments (Revelation 4; 14).

- *Michael* is designated as the "archangel" in Jude 9. Dickason (p. 70) notes, "This title immediately sets him above the angels as the military leader of an army of angels in the battle with Satan" (Revelation 12:7).

- *Gabriel* is the messenger who announces the birth of John the Baptist to Zacharias (Luke 1:11-12) and the birth of Jesus to Mary (Luke 1:26-29). He also revealed several prophetic messages to Daniel (9:21).

THE MINISTRY OF ANGELS

Angelic beings minister to God and God's people in several ways:

- worshiping God (Revelation 4:6-11)
- serving God and His people (Hebrews 1:7,14)
- destroying evil (Genesis 19:1-13)
- protecting God's people (Daniel 6:20-22)
- delivering God's word (Revelation 2:1)

• executing God's judgment (Revelation 6)

Angels have different ranks (thrones, powers, rulers, authorities—Colossians 1:16; Ephesians 1:20-21; 3:10), and they are immortal. But we must remember they are not divine. Fascination with angels is often a vain attempt to fill the spiritual void that only Christ can fill. The Bible clearly instructs us not to worship angels (Colossians 2:18; Revelation 19:10; 22:9). They are merely the messengers of God to point us to Him.

—DAVID JEREMIAH

BIBLIOGRAPHY

Bietenhard, Hans. "Angel." In The New Testament International Dictionary of New Testament Theology. Vol. 1. Grand Rapids: Zondervan, 1986.

Bromiley, G.W. "Angel." In Evangelical Dictionary of Theology. Grand Rapids: Baker Books, 1984.

Davidson, M.J. "Angels." In Dictionary of Jesus and the Gospels. Downers Grove, IL: InterVarsity Press, 1992.

Dickason, Fred. Angels: Elect and Evil. Chicago: Moody Press, 1995.

Jeremiah, David. What the Bible Says About Angels. Sisters, OR: Multnomah, 1996.

Oropeza, B.J. 99 Answers to Questions About Angels, Demons and Spiritual Warfare. Downers Grove, IL: InterVarsity Press, 1997.

ANTICHRIST

BIBLICAL PROPHECIES CLEARLY predict the rise of the Antichrist in the end times and more than 100 passages of Scripture describe the Antichrist's origin, nationality, character, career, and global conquest. The term *Antichrist* may be applied both to an individual and to the system he represents.

Interestingly, the term *Antichrist* (*antichristos* in the Greek) appears only in 1 John 2:18-22; 4:3; and 2 John 7. The apostle John uses it both in the singular ("the antichrist") and in the plural ("many antichrists"). John indicates that his readers have already heard that *the* Antichrist is coming in the future. Then he surprises them by announcing that *many* antichrists have already come. He describes these lesser antichrists as liars who deny that Jesus is the Christ (2:22). In this sense, an antichrist is any false teacher who denies the person and work of Jesus Christ. Such teachers are truly *anti* (against) Christ.

In 1 John 4:1-3, John warns us to test the spirits to make sure they are from God. He warns that many false prophets (*pseudo-prophetes* in the Greek) have "gone out into the world." These are the people who do not acknowledge that Jesus is from God. In this sense, John announces that the "spirit of the antichrist...is already in the world."

SPIRIT OF THE ANTICHRIST

In this broad sense, we can say with certainty that the spirit of the Antichrist is already at work. This anti-Christian spirit does everything it can to reject, deny, and undermine the truth about Jesus Christ. This spirit has been at work since the first century A.D., actively opposing the work of Christ on earth.

The biblical writers undoubtedly believed the spirit of the Antichrist was alive and well in the first century A.D. Therefore, they were not surprised by opposition to Christianity, persecution, and even martyrdom. They were convinced that the spiritual war between Christ and Antichrist had already begun.

Numerous early Christian references to the Antichrist are included in the Apocalypse of Peter, the Didache, the Ascension of Isaiah, and the Pseudo-Titus Epistle, as well as in the writings of various church fathers, such as Irenaeus, Jerome, and Hippolytus. Irenaeus, who studied under Polycarp, who was discipled by the apostle John, said the Antichrist shall come as "an apostate," the very embodiment of "satanic apostasy."

From the very beginning of the Christian era, believers were convinced that a world ruler who was the embodiment of Satan would eventually come on the scene. Revelation 12–13 presents an "unholy trinity" that aligns Satan (vs. the Father), the Antichrist (vs. the Son), and the False Prophet (vs. the Holy Spirit). Thus, the real power behind the Antichrist is Satan. The "father of lies" is the source of the lie that will condemn multitudes to divine judgment (2 Thessalonians 2:11).

TITLES OF THE ANTICHRIST

The Bible uses several names and titles for the person we commonly call the Antichrist. Each of these provides a glimpse into a facet of his diabolical character and nature, and together they present an intricate portrait of the Antichrist. For example…

The Beast

> I saw a beast coming out of the sea. He had ten horns and seven heads, with ten crowns on his horns, and on each head a blasphemous name (Revelation 13:1 NIV).

The Antichrist

> Dear children, this is the last hour; and as you have heard that the antichrist is coming, even now many antichrists have come.…Who is the liar? It is the man who denies that Jesus is the Christ. Such a man is the antichrist (1 John 2:18,22).

A great deal has been written about the prefix *anti* in connection with the Antichrist. It can mean either "against" (in opposition to) or "instead of" (in place of). Is he the great enemy of Christ, or is he a false Christ? If he is the enemy of Christ and the head of a Gentile world government, then he is most likely to be a Gentile himself. If he is a false messiah who is accepted by the Jews, then it would stand to reason that he would be Jewish.

The one called *antichristos* (antichrist) denies the existence of Christ, whereas *pseudochristos* (false Christ) affirms himself to be Christ. The biblical picture is that he is *both*. Initially, he presents himself as the "savior" of Israel by making a covenant to protect her (Daniel 9:27). In this manner, he appears to be her long-awaited Messiah. But in reality, he is against all that the messianic prophecies foretell about the true Messiah.

Other titles for the Antichrist include "the man of lawlessness" and "the man doomed to destruction" (2 Thessalonians 2:3), "the lawless one" (2 Thessalonians 2:8), a little horn (Daniel 7:8), "the ruler who will come" (Daniel 9:26), and "the king [who] will do as he pleases" (Daniel 11:36).

THE ANTICHRIST'S NATIONALITY

The New Testament does not clearly state whether the Antichrist is a Jew or a Gentile. Most prophecy scholars believe he will be a Gentile for these reasons:

1. He leads the European union of Gentile nations (Daniel 7:8-24).

2. His covenant with Israel promises Gentile protection for Israel (Daniel 9:27).

3. His rule is part of the "times of the Gentiles" and their domination over Israel (Luke 21:24).

These passages make it clear that the Antichrist will lead the Western powers, but they do not specifically designate him as a Gentile. He could possibly be of Jewish origin or nationality and still be a European or American Jew who leads the final form taken by the one-world government of the last days. Daniel 11:37, which says he will not regard the "God of his fathers" (KJV), can also be translated "gods of his fathers" (NIV). This makes his background inconclusive. The exegesis of Daniel 11:37 usually focuses on the Antichrist's atheistic beliefs, regardless of whether he is a Jew or Gentile.

Both the books of Daniel and Revelation associate the Antichrist with a confederation of ten European nations that correspond in some way to the old Roman Empire. We see this confederation symbolized by the ten toes of the great statue in Nebuchadnezzar's dream, as described in Daniel 2:31-45. This confederation is also symbolized in Daniel 7:19-28 and Revelation 13:1-9 by the ten horns on the beast.

In Daniel's prophecies, the Antichrist is always associated with the final phase of the Roman Empire (the fourth kingdom). In Revelation 17:9, he is identified with a city that sits on "seven hills" (frequently interpreted as Rome). Daniel 9:25-27 states that he will come from among the people who will destroy the Second Temple—that is, the Romans.

With our world's current emphasis on international oneness and our need for a human leader who can guarantee a peaceful coexistence between nations, we can easily imagine a powerful world ruler coming on the scene in the immediate future.

THE ANTICHRIST'S GENIUS AND POWER

The Antichrist will be the most incredible political leader the world has ever known. On the surface he will appear to be the epitome of human genius and power. Arthur W. Pink (p. 77) writes, "Satan has had full opportunity afforded him to study fallen human nature.... The devil knows full well how to dazzle people by the attraction of power....He knows how to gratify the craving for knowledge....He can delight the ear with music and the eye with entrancing beauty....He knows how to exalt people to dizzy heights of worldly greatness and fame, and how to control that greatness so that it may be employed against God and His people."

Note the following list of the characteristics of the Antichrist as described in Scripture:

1. intellectual genius (Daniel 7:20)
2. oratorical genius (Daniel 7:20)
3. political genius (Daniel 11:21)
4. commercial genius (Daniel 8:25)
5. military genius (Daniel 8:24)
6. administrative genius (Revelation 13:1-2)
7. religious genius (2 Thessalonians 2:4)

Perhaps the most telling of his characteristics is depicted in Daniel 11:21, which tells us that he will come to power and "seize it through intrigue" ("flatteries," KJV). Here is a *master of deception,* empowered by the "father of lies." Many believe he will be Satan incarnate—thus his miraculous recovery in Revelation 13:3.

The contrasts between Christ and Antichrist show them as mirror opposites.

Christ	Antichrist
the truth	the lie
Holy One	lawless one
man of sorrows	man of sin
Son of God	son of Satan
mystery of godliness	mystery of iniquity
Good Shepherd	worthless shepherd
exalted on high	cast down to hell
humbled Himself	exalted himself
despised	admired
cleanses the Temple	defiles the Temple
slain for the people	slays the people
the Lamb	the beast

A simple survey of the characteristics of the Antichrist confirms that he is both a false Christ (*pseudochristos*) and against Christ (*antichristos*). He masquerades as an angel of light only to plunge the world into spiritual darkness. Like Satan, he is a destroyer, not a builder. Promising peace, he pushes the world into war. In every conceivable way, he is just like Satan, who indwells and empowers him.

IS THE ANTICHRIST ALIVE TODAY?

The spirit of Antichrist is alive and well—it is the Satan-inspired expression of lawlessness and rebellion against God, the things of God, and the people of God. It has been alive since Satan slithered his way around the Garden of Eden. It has been the driving force behind the whole terrible history of the human race—wars, murders, thefts, rapes, and the like. It is the ugly expression of the destructive nature of the great deceiver himself.

The New Testament authors assure us that the spirit of Antichrist was active in their day nearly 20 centuries ago. It has remained active throughout the whole of church history, expressing itself in persecutions, heresies, spiritual deceptions, false prophets, and false religions. Satan has battled the church at every turn throughout its long history, waiting for the right moment to indwell the right person—the Antichrist—as his final masterpiece.

Guessing whether certain contemporary figures might be the Antichrist, however, has always proven futile. Viewing the future through the eyes of the present led to some fantastic yet incorrect speculations in the twentieth century alone. The problem with these identifications is they are always tentative and are based on a limited perspective. Tragically, people guessing dates and selecting possibilities for the Antichrist are claiming to know more than the writers of Scripture.

The apostle Paul comments on this in 2 Thessalonians 2:1-12, where he tells us that the "coming of our Lord Jesus" will not happen "until the rebellion occurs" and the "man of lawlessness is revealed." Next, he tells us that "you know what is holding him back, so that he may be revealed at the proper time" (verse 6). Only after the rapture of the church will the identity of the Antichrist be revealed. In other words, you don't want to know who he is. If you ever do figure out who he is, you have been left behind!

Satan must prepare a man to be his crowning achievement in every generation, so we should not be surprised that several candidates have appeared on the horizon of human history only to vanish away. Satan must wait on God's timing, so he is already defeated before he ever begins his final assault on God. He can't make his move until God releases the restraining power of the Holy Spirit indwelling the church. Therefore, the Spirit is the agent and the church is the means by which God restrains Satan's diabolical plan until the Father calls us home to heaven.

In the meantime, Satan waits for his opportunity to destroy the whole world and the ultimate plan of God. He may be a defeated foe, but he has every intention of keeping up the fight to the very end. Even now he is moving about restlessly, searching for the right man to be the Antichrist.

TEN KEYS TO THE ANTICHRIST'S IDENTITY

The Bible gives us at least ten keys to identifying the Antichrist when he does come to power. They provide enough details to give a general idea of who he will be when Satan inspires him to make his move onto the world scene. These clues also make it clear that only one person in history will fit this description. Many prototypes have come and gone, but there will be only one Antichrist.

1. *He will rise to power in the last days:* "Later in the time of wrath [the time of the end]...a stern-faced king, a master of intrigue, will arise" (Daniel 8:19,23).

2. *He will rule the whole world:* "And he was given authority over every tribe, people, language and nation" (Revelation 13:7).

3. *His headquarters will be in Rome:* "The beast, which you saw, once was, now is not, and will come up out of the Abyss.... The seven heads are seven hills on which the woman sits" (Revelation 17:8-9).

4. *He is intelligent and persuasive:* "The other horn...looked more imposing than the others and...had eyes and a mouth that spoke boastfully" (Daniel 7:20).

5. *He will rule by international consent:* "The ten horns you saw are ten kings.... They have one purpose and will give their power and authority to the beast" (Revelation 17:12-13).

6. *He will rule by deception:* "He will become very strong...and will succeed in whatever he does....He will cause deceit to prosper, and he will consider himself superior" (Daniel 8:24-25).

7. *He will control the global economy:* "He also forced everyone, small and great, rich and poor, free and slave, to receive a mark on his right hand or on his forehead, so that no one could buy or sell unless he had the mark, which is the name of the beast or the number of his name" (Revelation 13:16-17).

8. *He will make a peace treaty with Israel:* "He will confirm a covenant with many for one 'seven.' In the middle of the 'seven' he will put an end to sacrifice and offering" (Daniel 9:27).

9. *He will break the treaty and invade Israel:* "The people of the ruler who will come will destroy the city and the sanctuary. The end will come like a flood: War will

continue until the end, and desolations have been decreed" (Daniel 9:26).

10. *He will claim to be God:* "He will oppose and will exalt himself over everything that is called God or is worshiped, so that he sets himself up in God's temple, proclaiming himself to be God" (2 Thessalonians 2:4).

The Bible gives many other details regarding the person we commonly call the Antichrist. But the general picture is that of a European who rises to power over the Western world. Whether he is Jewish or Gentile is not entirely clear. What is clear, however, is that he will control the last great bastion of Gentile world power. From his base in the West, he will extend his control over the entire world. He will administrate the world government and the global economy, assisted by the leader of the world religion (Revelation 13:11-18). Only time will reveal his true identity.

—ED HINDSON

BIBLIOGRAPHY

Anderson, Robert. *The Coming Prince*. London: Hodder & Stoughton, 1922.

Hindson, Ed. *Antichrist Rising*. Springfield, MO: 21st Century Press, 2003.

Hunt, Dave. *A Woman Rides the Beast*. Eugene, OR: Harvest House Publishers, 1994.

Jeffrey, Grant. *Prince of Darkness*. Toronto: Frontier Publications, 1994.

Pink, Arthur. *The Antichrist*. Minneapolis: Klock & Klock, 1979.

Price, Walter. *The Coming Antichrist*. Chicago: Moody Press, 1974.

APOCALYPTICISM

DISPENSATIONAL INTERPRETERS often categorize various prophetic books of the Bible, such as Ezekiel, Daniel, and Revelation, as "apocalyptic literature." In doing so, these interpreters simply mean that these books unveil or disclose God's future prophetic program. The Greek word *apokalypsis* simply means to unveil or disclose.

A NEW MEANING

However, some recent evangelical interpreters have begun to vest this term with a new meaning. When they use the term "apocalyptic literature," they are equating the books of Ezekiel, Daniel, and Revelation with a host of noncanonical, extrabiblical writings that flourished from the intertestamental period into the second century A.D. Examples include Enoch, Apocalypse of Baruch, Jubilees, Assumption of Moses, Psalms of Solomon, Testament of the Twelve Patriarchs, and Sibylline Oracles. These writings possess a common cluster of attributes. Such attributes include the extensive use of symbolism, vision as the major means of revelation, angelic guides, activity of angels and demons, focus on the end of the current age and the inauguration of the age to come, urgent expectation of the end of earthly conditions in the immediate future, the end as a cosmic catastrophe, new salvation and paradise, manifestation of the kingdom of God, a mediator with royal functions, dualism of God and Satan, spiritual order determining the flow of history, pessimism about man's ability to change the course of events, periodization and determinism of human history, other worldly journeys, and a final showdown between good and evil (Gregg, pp. 10–12; Murphy, pp. 130–33).

Ezekiel, Daniel, and Revelation share some of these characteristics—especially the book of Revelation, which was composed about the same time as the noncanonical apocalyptic writings. However, categorizing Revelation with the noncanonical apocalyptic writings significantly challenges the traditional dispensational interpretation of Revelation and alters the hermeneutical principles used to interpret the book.

LANGUAGE OF APOCALYPTIC LITERATURE

For example, the literal approach that one uses when interpreting Scripture is difficult to apply to the noncanonical apocalyptic writings. Gregg (p. 11) contends that although taking the text literally, unless it yields an absurd result, is a good rule of thumb to follow when dealing with other types of biblical material, this approach does not work in the case of apocalyptic literature where literalism is the exception and symbolism is the norm. Apocalyptic writings cannot be interpreted literally because they represent crisis literature (Collins, p. 38). In order to highlight the severity of the crisis, the apocalyptist spoke in exaggerated terms. Consider this statement: "My world has come to an end because my girlfriend has broken up with me." The world is obviously not literally coming to an end. Rather, the heightened language communicates the significance of a personal event. If John used the same methodology in Revelation, then statements such as half of the world's population being destroyed (Revelation 6:8; 9:15) and the greatest earthquake in human history (Revelation 16:18) cannot be construed literally. Rather, they similarly represent heightened language communicating a past event that the people of God experienced, such as oppression by Jerusalem or Rome. Understanding Revelation in such hyperbolic terms opens the possibility that John simply described a localized historical phenomenon with global language. This mind-set opens the door to historicism and preterism.

Also, apocalyptists sometimes used symbolic language to disguise the entity that was oppressing them. They sought to give hope to the oppressed people of God by predicting the cataclysmic destruction of their enemies. However, because of fear of retaliation, the apocalyptist was not free to identify the oppressor. Thus, he had to disguise the message in symbolic dress. For example, apocalyptic writings sometimes used Babylon as a code for Rome (Sibylline Oracles v. 143, 159–60, 434). If John was following this pattern, he also does not mean Babylon when he says Babylon. Instead, he is using the word "Babylon" as a symbolic disguise to identify an oppressor. He might have had in mind Jerusalem or Rome.

Multivalence is another hermeneutical characteristic of apocalyptic literature. The Jews' exile in Babylon furnished the paradigm for later crises, and Jewish apocalypses emphasized repetitious patterns rather than individual historical circumstances (Collins, p. 51). If John employs apocalyptic multivalence in Revelation, perhaps the events of the book are not anchored to one event but rather recur repeatedly throughout history. For example, some people maintain that Babylon refers not only to a future empire but to historical Jerusalem as well. Similarly, in this line of thinking, the beast of Revelation 13 might refer to both Nero and a future Antichrist.

LITERAL OR FIGURATIVE?

Categorizing Revelation as apocalyptic also influences how one interprets Revelation's numbers. Other apocalypses typically used numbers to convey concepts rather than count units (Gregg, pp. 11–12). Thus, categorizing Revelation as apocalyptic literature moves the interpreter away from a literal understanding of Revelation's numbers and more toward a symbolic interpretation. Many conclude that the number 1000 mentioned six times in Revelation 20 refers to an extended period of time rather than a literal 1000 years. Others show a similar reluctance to take the number 144,000 (Revelation 7) literally. Still others have questioned a literal interpretation of the numerical measurements of the eternal city described in Revelation 21–22.

Many futurist scholars believe that various numbers found in Revelation, such as 1260 days (Revelation 12:6) or 42 months (Revelation 11:2; 13:5), are direct references to the unfulfilled aspects of Daniel's 70 weeks prophecy (Daniel 9:24-27). The first 483 years (69 sevens) of this prophecy were exactly fulfilled to the day, so it stands to reason that the prophecy's unfulfilled aspects will also be fulfilled to the minutest detail. Thus, the numbers 1260 days and 42 months are not merely communicating concepts—they are specific count units. Revelation contains no verifiably symbolic numbers. Rather, nonsymbolic utilization of numbers is the norm.

SIMILARITIES AND DIFFERENCES

Opening these hermeneutical doors by categorizing Revelation with the apocalyptic books is unjustified. A closer scrutiny demonstrates that the differences between Revelation and the apocalyptic works outweigh any similarities between the two. For example, although apocalyptic literature was typically pseudonymous, Revelation bears the name of its author (Revelation 1:1,4,9; 22:8). Moreover, Revelation fails to share the pessimism of the apocalyptists, who despaired of all human history. Rather, Revelation reflects the optimism of God working redemptively through the Lamb presently as well as in the future. Furthermore, apocalyptic literature contains no epistolary material. By contrast, we find seven ecclesiastical epistles in Revelation 2–3.

In addition, noncanonical apocalyptic literature did not emphasize moral imperatives. Although there are occasional exceptions to this rule (1 Enoch 91:19), the apocalyptists are not generally motivated by a strong sense of moral urgency. The reason for this is the apocalyptists' conviction that they were part of the righteous remnant. They wrote in order to encourage the remnant to endure, remain faithful, and have hope rather than to persuade people to turn from sin. In contrast, Revelation utilizes moral imperatives. Christ's exhortations to the seven churches (Revelation 2:5,16,21,22; 3:3,19) emphasize humanity's need for repentance, and the exhortation to repent is found throughout the book as a whole (Revelation 9:20-21; 16:9,11).

Moreover, the coming of Messiah in apocalyptic literature takes place exclusively in the future. Revelation portrays Christ as having already come and laid the groundwork for His future coming through His redemptive death. Finally, Revelation makes numerous self-claims to be prophecy (Revelation 1:3; 22:7,10,18,19). In fact, Revelation employs the term *prophētēs* or its cognates 18 times. The following chart by Robert Thomas (*Evangelical Hermeneutics*, p. 338) summarizes these differences between Revelation and apocalyptic literature:

Apocalyptic Genre	Revelation
Pseudonymous	Not pseudonymous
Pessimistic about the present	Not pessimistic about the present
No epistolary framework	Epistolary framework
Limited admonitions for moral compliance	Repeated admonitions for moral compliance
Messiah's coming exclusively future	Basis for Messiah's future coming is past
Does not call itself a prophecy	Calls itself a prophecy

We can observe additional dissimilarities. For example, apocalyptic literature has a different view of suffering than does Revelation. In apocalyptic writings, suffering is an unfortunate byproduct of the conflict between good and evil. It is bad and should be avoided. In Revelation, however, suffering comes from the hand of God (Revelation 5:5). Therefore, at times, suffering can be good, and we should submit to it. Moreover, apocalyptic literature is pseudoprophecy or *vaticinia ex eventu*, which means "prophecies after the fact." In other words, apocalyptists typically portray a historical event as future prophecy. However, this is not so in Revelation, where John looks from his own day into the future (Morris, p. 94). In addition, Revelation is dominated by an "already but not yet" tension as John looked to the needs of his own day as well as to the distant future. This same tension is not evident in other apocalypses (Morris, p. 94).

PROPHECY OR APOCALYPTIC?

Revelation's heavy dependence upon Ezekiel and Daniel also raises questions as to whether the book should be categorized as apocalyptic. Ezekiel and Daniel prophesied 400 years before apocalyptic literature became prevalent in the intertestamental period. Also, Revelation 12:1 borrows imagery from Genesis 37:9-10, which took place in the patriarchal era nearly 1800 years before apocalypticism began to flourish. Finally, some apocalyptic writings fail to present a precise eschatological scheme (Collins, p. 56). Yet many have argued that Revelation 6–19, with its telescoping and fixed seven-year duration, does communicate a fixed eschatological scheme. Revelation 20–22 also seems to employ a chronology of events.

Although Revelation has many affinities with apocalyptic literature, it is difficult to classify the book as apocalyptic because the differences seem to outweigh the similarities. "Prophecy" is a better classification for the book than "apocalyptic." This classification best takes into account Revelation's numerous claims to be prophecy. It also takes into account Revelation's similarity to the pattern exhibited by the Old Testament prophets who not only called God's people to repentance but also comforted them through visions of victory to take place in the distant future (Isaiah 40–66; Ezekiel 36–48; Amos 9:11–15). Revelation fits this pattern by not only repeatedly calling the seven churches to repentance (Revelation 1–3) but also providing these oppressed churches with a prophecy to be fulfilled in the distant future regarding the believer's ultimate triumph (Revelation 4–22). Categorizing Revelation as prophetic also relates it to the book of Daniel, which it alludes to more than any other Old Testament book. Jesus specifically referred to Daniel as a prophet (Matthew 24:15). Because Revelation's content relies so heavily upon Daniel, it stands to reason that the material found in Revelation should also be categorized as prophetic. The Greek word *apokalypsis,* which appears in the opening verse of the book, does not disqualify Revelation from being categorized as prophecy. This word simply means "unveiling" and does not have the meaning that modern scholars attach to the term *apocalyptic.*

Categorizing Revelation as prophetic rather than apocalyptic significantly changes the hermeneutical landscape. If Revelation is prophecy, then we should interpret it just as we would any other prophecy. We should use the same literal, grammatical, historical method that we normally use for interpreting Scripture. No new set of hermeneutical principles is needed to properly interpret Revelation (Thomas, *Revelation* 1–7, p. 38). The previously described hermeneutical doors associated with apocalypticism are closed if the book is prophetic rather than apocalyptic. Instead, the interpreter is confined to literalism, which can be defined as attaching to every word the same meaning that it would have in normal usage.

LITERAL INTERPRETATION

A consistent application of a literal approach to Revelation logically leads the interpreter away from viewing the book's contents as being fulfilled in the past and instead leads to the futurist interpretation (Tenney, pp. 139, 142). A relationship exists between literalism and futurism because the ordinary import of Revelation's words and phrases makes it impossible to argue that Revelation's contents have already been fulfilled. The destruction of half of the world's population (Revelation 6:8; 9:15) and the greatest earthquake in human history (Revelation 16:18) obviously have never taken place.

By using the literal approach, the interpreter takes Revelation's content in its ordinary sense until he encounters some obvious clue in the text that alerts him to figurative or symbolic language. How does the interpreter recognize when such language is being used? Some overt textual indicators exist, such as Revelation 11:8 (NKJV), which notes that Jerusalem "is spiritually called Sodom and Egypt." Here, the use of the adverb "spiritually" is designed to alert the reader to an allegorical or spiritual application. Another clue involves the use of the word "sign" (*sēmeion*). John's use of this word alerts the interpreter that he is speaking figuratively or symbolically. For example, because John uses *sēmeion* to describe the woman in Revelation 12:1, the woman is obviously symbolic or representative of something. Another clue involves the words "like" (*homoios*) or "as" (*hōs*). When John employs such language, he is indicating a correspondence between what he saw in the vision and what he was trying to describe. For example, Revelation 8:8 says, "And something like a great mountain burning with fire was thrown into the sea...." The word "like" alerts the interpreter to the fact that John is simply using comparative language to describe what he saw, and the mountain is not to be interpreted literally.

Some figurative language in Revelation corresponds with identical figurative language in the Old Testament. Because the leopard, lion, and bear in Revelation 13:2 are also used in Daniel 7 to depict nations, the interpreter is alerted to the fact that John is employing symbolic language. Thus, the leopard, lion, and bear represent nations in Revelation 13 just as they did in Daniel 7. Figurative language also sometimes includes an interpretation in the immediate context. If something is interpreted for the reader, then the thing interpreted is obviously a symbol. The woman in Revelation 17 is obviously a symbol because the immediate context interprets her to be a city (17:18). Finally, we can also discern language to be figurative if a literal interpretation yields absurd results. For example, if the woman in Revelation 12:1 were literally clothed with the sun, the heat would destroy her. Because a literal interpretation yields an absurd result, symbolic language must be in use.

After one identifies figurative or symbolic language, how is such language to be understood? Sometimes the immediate context interprets the symbol. For example, Revelation 12:9 interprets the dragon of verse 3 as Satan. Prophecy scholar John F. Walvoord identifies 26 instances in Revelation in which a symbol is interpreted in the immediate context (Walvoord, pp. 29–30). Another method of interpretation is to see if the same symbol is employed elsewhere in the Old Testament. For example, the same symbol of the woman used in Revelation 12:1 is also used in Genesis 37:9-11 to depict Israel. Thus, the woman of Revelation 12 is symbolic of Israel. This strategy is useful because 278 of Revelation's 404 verses allude to the Old Testament. A final method for understanding Revelation's symbolic language is to note that John, through his use of "like" or "as," is attempting to describe futuristic events that are beyond his linguistic ability. Thus, he communicates through language of correspondence. In other words, in order to communicate the contents of his vision, he uses similes or language of comparison by equating things from his own world to the futuristic events that he sees in his vision.

In conclusion, probably the most significant decision that the interpreter can make regarding what hermeneutic he will use in interpreting the book of Revelation is that of determining if Revelation's character has more in common with the prophetic or apocalyptic genre. Viewing Revelation as apocalyptic opens numerous hermeneutical doors to matters such as code theories, multivalence, symbolic numbers, and viewing Revelation's global language as local language. Conversely, those who see Revelation as belonging to the prophetic genre are bound by the literal, grammatical, historical method of interpretation, which takes Revelation's words or phrases in their ordinary sense unless a convincing textual clue informs the reader to do otherwise. Revelation has some affinities with apocalypticism, but these similarities are overshadowed by vast differences between the two. The book has far more in common with prophecy. Thus, the similarities between Revelation and apocalypticism are not sufficient to cause the interpreter to dispense with a consistent application of literalism when deciphering the book.

—ANDY WOODS

BIBLIOGRAPHY

Collins, John J. The Apocalyptic Imagination: An Introduction to Jewish Apocalyptic Literature. Grand Rapids: Eerdmans Publishing Company, 1998.

Gregg, Steve, ed. Revelation: Four Views, A Parallel Commentary. Nashville: Thomas Nelson, 1997.

Morris, Leon. Apocalyptic. Grand Rapids: Eerdmans Publishing Company, 1980.

Murphy, Frederick J. Early Judaism. Peabody, MA: Hendrickson Publishers, 2002.

Tenney, Merrill C. Interpreting Revelation. Grand Rapids: Eerdmans Publishing Company, 1957.

Thomas, Robert L. Revelation 1–7: An Exegetical Commentary. Chicago: Moody Press, 1992.

———. Revelation 8–22: An Exegetical Commentary. Chicago: Moody Press, 1992.

———. Evangelical Hermeneutics: The New Versus the Old. Grand Rapids: Kregel, 2002.

Walvoord, John F. The Revelation of Jesus Christ. Chicago: Moody Press, 1966.

APOSTASY

DESPITE THE BEST INTENTIONS and desires of those who trust Jesus as Savior, a great departure from the truth will someday occur. The New Testament speaks often of this coming day. In 2 Thessalonians 2:3, Paul calls it the *apostasia*, translated "the apostasy" (NASB), "the rebellion" (NIV), or "the falling away" (KJV). He says that "some shall depart from the faith" in 1 Timothy 4:1 (KJV).

Paul's language suggests that the great departure will probably reach its fulfillment sometime just before the rapture of the church (2 Thessalonians 2:2,7-9; 2 Timothy 3:1). Paul also wrote that a form of this apostasy was already evident in his generation. These "departures" would continue throughout the ages of the church and climax in the last days (2 Thessalonians 2:7).

Whitlock (p. 70) defines apostasy as a "deliberate repudiation and abandonment of the faith that one has professed." He notes that apostasy differs from heresy in that the heretic denies some aspect of the Christian faith while continuing to profess to be a Christian. The apostate is one who has abandoned and denounced any Christian profession at all.

New Testament examples of apostates include Judas Iscariot, Demas, Hymenaeus, and Alexander (2 Corinthians 4:10; 1 Timothy 1:20). The Roman Emperor Julian "the Apostate" (A.D. 361–363) professed Christianity and later renounced it and attempted to reestablish paganism in the Roman Empire.

DEFINING APOSTASY

Only 2 Thessalonians 2:3 uses the word *apostasia* in its theological meaning with reference to the church. Here Paul writes, "Let no one in any way deceive you, for [the day of the Lord] will not come unless the apostasy comes first." Earlier in the New Testament, the Jewish believers in Jerusalem accused Paul of "teaching all the Jews who are among the Gentiles to forsake [*apostasia*] Moses" (Acts 21:21 NASB). We get an additional sense of the word from a related term, *apostasion,* which

is translated as "divorcement" in the Gospels (Matthew 5:31; 19:7; Mark 10:4).

Walter Bauer (p. 98) defines *apostasia* as "rebellion, abandonment." Liddell and Scott (pp. 218–19) suggest the meaning "to depart, to stand aloof, to detach, to forsake." Charles Ryrie (p. 140) writes that it is "a departure from truth previously accepted, involving the breaking of a professed relationship with God. Apostasy always involves willful leaving of previously known truth and embracing error."

Etymologically, the word is a compound of the Greek preposition *apo* ("away from") and the noun *stasis* ("stand"). Its literal meaning is "to leave or depart from" an established position.

WARNING OF COMING APOSTASY

In 2 Thessalonians 2:1-12, Paul describes the work of Satan and the Antichrist at the midpoint of the seven-year Tribulation. "In accord with the activity of Satan, with all power and signs and false wonders" (verse 9), the "man of lawlessness" will reveal his true colors and take "his seat in the temple of God, displaying himself as being God" (verses 3-4).

But the apostle Paul warns the believers in Thessalonica not to be disturbed because the day of the Lord, the Tribulation, has not come yet (verse 2). Before that day, the "departure" (*apostasia*) must take place first (verse 3). Paul tells the Thessalonian church that they may see an "apostasy" long before the Antichrist makes his move in the Tribulation. Blindness will overtake the professing church—the same blindness that has already darkened the moral and biblical senses of those who have rejected Christ.

In the final hours of the dispensation of the church, many who confess biblical truth and profess a relationship with God will simply be acting, living a lie, walking as religious charlatans. Apostasy will be intense in the final days before the rapture of the church.

The apostles John, Peter, and Paul all speak of apostasy existing in their own day and continuing into the last days. They refer to apostasy being both present and future in the church. Ryrie (p. 140) observes: "Apostasy is something that plagues the church in every generation, though at the end of the church age the great apostasy will come on the scene before the Day of the Lord."

In 1 Timothy 4:1-3, Paul writes that the Spirit explicitly speaks of a later falling away from faith. The words "falling away" come from the Greek verb *ephistemi* and can be rendered "they shall dismiss themselves" from the faith. These people are not believers in Christ. Paul adds that they will be "paying attention to deceitful spirits and doctrines of demons." Their consciences will be seared as with a branding iron.

In 2 Timothy 3:1-9, Paul speaks of "the latter days" in which difficult times will come. He writes of men being lovers of self and money. He calls the people of that future day revilers, boastful, arrogant, disobedient to parents, ungrateful, unholy, "lovers of pleasure rather than lovers of God." They are "holding to a form of godliness, although they have denied its power."

The apostle Peter describes false teachers who will "bring upon themselves swift destruction." He speaks of their sensuality, how they malign the truth and exploit with false words (2 Peter 2:1-3).

John the apostle (1 John 4:3) warns that the "spirit of antichrist" is coming, "and even now already it is in the world." In Revelation, John writes of apostasy that even then was choking the life from the churches. He speaks of the Nicolaitans (Revelation 2:15) and of the cult-like immorality of a "Jezebel" who was sapping the spiritual strength of churches such as Thyatira (2:20-23).

DEFENDING AGAINST APOSTASY

The epistle of Jude deals almost exclusively with the problem of apostasy. Jude urges Christians to stand for the faith "once delivered unto the saints" (verse 3) and to stand against the threat of apostasy. Lawlor (pp. 42-44) notes that Jude challenges believers to "contend earnestly," pointing out that this determination involves a willingness to fight for something the adversary desires to take away.

Jude defines apostates as those who turn the grace of God into license for excessive immorality and deny the lordship of Jesus Christ (verse 4). He explains that immorality is often the basis of apostasy. Apostates deny the faith because they have not been transformed by the grace of God.

Jude then lists several biblical examples of apostasy, including the fallen angels, the mixed multitude of the Exodus, and the people of Sodom and Gomorrah. Then he describes the character and conduct of apostates. They are "dreamers" and defilers (verse 8), living in perversion and delusion. They despise authority and blaspheme God. Jude closes his epistle (verses 20-25) by reminding true believers to edify themselves in the faith, pray in the Spirit, and focus on the love of God and the mercy of Christ, always reaching out to those who are about to perish.

STANDING TO THE END AGAINST APOSTASY

The New Testament is clear in its warning about the dangers of apostasy in every generation but especially in the last days before the rapture of the church. The apostles urge us to stand true to the faith until Jesus comes to call us home to be with Him. Minor deviations of doctrine or personal preferences are not primary concerns. Apostasy involves the deliberate abandonment and repudiation of Jesus Christ and the Christian faith.

—MAL COUCH AND ED HINDSON

BIBLIOGRAPHY

Bauer, Walter. "Apostasia." In *A Greek-English Lexicon of the New Testament.* Trans. Williams F. Arndt and F.W. Gingrich. Chicago: University of Chicago Press, 1979.

Couch, Mal. "The Coming Apostasy of the Church." In *The Fundamentals for the Twenty-First Century.* Grand Rapids: Kregel, 2000.

Gunn, George, and Ed Hindson. "Apostasy." In *The Dictionary of Premillennial Theology.* Grand Rapids: Kregel, 1996.

Lawlor, George. *The Epistle of Jude.* Philadelphia: Presbyterian and Reformed, 1976.

Liddell, H.G., and Robert Scott, *A Greek-English Lexicon of the New Testament.* London: Oxford University Press, 1990.

Ryrie, Charles C. *Dispensationalism.* Chicago: Moody Press, 1995.

Whitlock, L.G. "Apostasy." In *Evangelical Dictionary of Theology.* Grand Rapids: Baker Books, 1984.

ARK OF THE COVENANT

THE ARK OF THE COVENANT (Hebrew, *'aron ha-brit*) was Israel's most sacred ritual object. It was designed to contain the original tablets of the law, and it was where God manifested His shekinah glory. It was a box of acacia (Hebrew, *shittim*) wood overlaid with gold (Exodus 25:10-11), approximately three or four feet long and one or two feet high and wide. On top of the ark was the mercy seat (Hebrew, *kapporet,* literally "the covering"), a golden lid with sculpted figures. The figures on the mercy seat symbolized cherubim, the angelic creatures who guarded God's holy presence in the Garden of Eden (Genesis 3:24).

God promised Israel, "There I will meet with you; and from above the mercy seat, from between the two cherubim which are upon the ark of the testimony, I will speak to you about all that I will give you in commandment for the sons of Israel" (Exodus 25:22 NASB). The ark apparently served as the place between heaven and earth. As the visible footstool for the invisible throne of God, it was available when He "descended" to earth, as He did at Sinai, on the battlefield, or in a foreign land (such as Philistia). The ark enabled God to manifest His presence among the Israelites.

The Tent of Meeting, the Tabernacle, and finally the Temple were constructed to house the ark (see Exodus 25:8-22; 2 Chronicles 6:10-11). The ark disappeared when Babylonians destroyed the First Temple, and when the Hebrew exiles returned to Jerusalem to rebuild the Temple and restore its vessels (Ezra 1:7-11; Isaiah 52:11-12; Jeremiah 27:16-22), the ark was mysteriously absent.

PROPHETIC SIGNIFICANCE REVEALED

The prophets spoke of the ark as a symbol of God's discipline and His restoration of the Temple and national Israel. In Ezekiel's prophecy, the departure of the presence of God from the ark and the Temple foreshadowed the Temple's desecration and destruction (Ezekiel 10:4–11:23). In like manner, his prophecy of the return of God's presence to the final Temple, and presumably to the ark within it (Ezekiel 43:1-7), promises the Temple's rebuilding and rededication. When God restores Israel, He will set His glory among the nations and restore Israel's blessings (Ezekiel 39:21-26). This description seems to recall the functions of the ark: God's glory attended the ark (1 Samuel 4:21), and therefore it brought blessing to Israel (2 Samuel 6:11-12), securing Israel in its Land (Numbers 10:33-36).

Such language may imply that the ark will indeed be present in the last days. When God's glory previously filled the Temple, it followed the installation of the ark (1 Kings 8:4-12), constituting the Temple as God's throne (see 1 Samuel 4:4; 2 Samuel 6:2; 2 Kings 19:15; Isaiah 37:16; Psalm 80:1; 99:1) and the place where He would dwell forever with Israel (Psalm 132:7-8,13; Ezekiel 37:26-28). Where else would Ezekiel's audience have expected God's glory to have returned but to the ark (see Exodus 25:22)? Would they have considered the restoration program complete if the final Temple did not have what the First Temple lost? Even though the ark is not explicitly mentioned in Ezekiel's final Temple, it seems to be implicit in other statements that require its presence to properly fulfill ritual functions such as the day of atonement (included in the "all My appointed feasts" of Ezekiel 44:24). Other items of Temple furniture are mentioned, such as the priestly garments (Ezekiel 42:14), the altar of burnt offering (Ezekiel 43:13-27), and table of showbread (Ezekiel 41:22; 44:16), while others of importance are not (such as the altar of incense and the menorah). The inclusion of some furniture implies the inclusion of all because this Temple appears as a fully functioning Temple.

PROPHETIC PASSAGES EXAMINED
The Book of Revelation

The book of Revelation shows judgment coming from the heavenly Temple and ark in response to the desecration of the earthly Temple during the Tribulation period. Revelation 11:1-2 predicts that the earthly Temple's outer court will be trampled by the Antichrist (see Daniel 11:45). This desecration is apparently connected with the abomination of desolation prophesied by Daniel (Daniel 9:27; 12:11), Jesus (Matthew 24:15; Mark 13:14), and Paul (2 Thessalonians 2:3-4). In response to this act of desecration on earth, God's heavenly Temple opens, and the ark appears with signs of wrath (Revelation 11:19). This correspondence may imply that the Tribulation Temple will again house the ark, which would, like the Temple itself, be subject to ritual violation. Second Thessalonians 2:4 may also imply the existence of the ark in the Tribulation Temple.

"The wing of abominations" (Daniel 9:27) may suggest the precise place where the abomination of desolation occurs—near the winged cherubim on the ark. Paul's explanation of this desecration in 2 Thessalonians 2:4 shows the "man of lawlessness" (the Antichrist) seating himself in the innermost part of the Temple as an act of divine enthronement, "displaying himself as God." This act of self-deification in the Holy of Holies would only make sense if it followed the precedent of God's display of His divine presence at the ark (Exodus 25:22; Psalm 80:1; 99:1).

The Book of Jeremiah

The ark of the covenant also appears in Jeremiah's prophecy of the restoration of Jerusalem in the millennial kingdom in Jeremiah 3:16-17. Whatever his statement implies concerning the future existence of the ark, his point in this context is to relieve Israel's concern that their future could not be fulfilled without the central presence of the ark. Jeremiah explains that under the New Covenant, the ark would no longer have the central importance it had under the Old Covenant. In that day, all of Jerusalem would bear God's glory; the city will be a sanctuary (Isaiah 4:5; Ezekiel 43:12). In other words, in the millennium, the ark will not be needed as it was previously. Its loss will not prevent Israel's final restoration, so there should not be concern over its present fate.

Having said this, it should also be noted that Jeremiah 3:16-17 does not say that the ark will not be present, but only that it will not function as it did under the Old Covenant. Jeremiah's wording is that Israel will "no longer" refer to, be concerned for, remember, or visit the ark, suggesting that in the time before the millennium they may be doing these things.

The phrase "it will not come to mind" is better translated "neither shall it be taken to heart." This idiom means that the people should not worry about the ark in the future as they have in the past. Read in this light, the words of verse 16 are understandable.

However, the last words of verse 16, "nor will it be made again," require clarification to avoid contradiction of this proposal, for this translation implies the ark was destroyed and would not be remade. Therefore, the ark could not exist in the future. However, the translation "made again" can be rendered "used again." The Hebrew word 'asah usually means "to make" or "to do," but it also may mean "to use," and significantly one of the two instances in which the verb appears with this nuance concerns the materials "used" in the construction of the ark (Exodus 38:24; the other appearance is in 1 Samuel 8:16).

In this case the meaning is that the ark, in the time of the New Covenant, would not be used as it was under the Old Covenant. The ark will no longer be a witness to the law, and it will not be a conduit of God's power in warfare. Under the New Covenant, God's law will be internalized through the indwelling Spirit so that, as verse 17 records, "Nor will they walk anymore after the stubbornness of their evil heart" (see Jeremiah 31:33-34; Ezekiel 36:25-27). The tablets of the law within the ark will no longer be needed to bear witness against Israel of their violation of God's holiness, for they will be holy and live in obedience to God's will (Zechariah 14:20-21). Moreover, in the millennium, Israel and the nations will no longer learn war (Isaiah 2:4). The ark will no longer have to function as a symbol of God's protective power in war, since war will no longer exist. This interpretation is put forth in the textual notes of the current Israel Defense Forces standard issue Bible: "The Law of the Lord will be written in the heart, and there will be no need to keep it in the Ark. There will not be wars and there will be no need to take the Ark from place to place on the battlefield as it was in those former times."

Though this evidence is not conclusive, the ark of the covenant may have a role to play in the end time, returning to complete the prophetic program of a rebuilt Temple and the restoration of the glory of God to Israel and the nations in the millennium.

—RANDALL PRICE

BIBLIOGRAPHY

Bloomfield, Arthur. *Where Is the Ark of the Covenant and What Is Its Role in Bible Prophecy?* Minneapolis: Dimension Books, 1976.

Fruchtenbaum, Arnold. *Israelology: The Missing Link in Systematic Theology.* Tustin, CA: Ariel Ministries, 1992.

Lewis, David Allen. *Prophecy 2000.* Green Forest, AR: New Leaf Press, 1993.

Price, Randall. *In Search of Temple Treasures: The Lost Ark and the Last Days.* Eugene, OR: Harvest House Publishers, 1994.

———. *Searching for the Ark of the Covenant.* Eugene, OR: Harvest House Publishers, 2005.

ARMAGEDDON

ARMAGEDDON, THE LAST GREAT world war of history, will take place in Israel in conjunction with the second coming of Christ. The battle or campaign of Armageddon is described in Daniel 11:40-45; Joel 3:9-17; Zechariah 14:1-3; and Revelation 16:14-16. It will occur in the final days of the Tribulation, and John tells us that the kings of the world will be gathered together "for the war of the great day of God, the Almighty" in a place known as "Har-Magedon" (Revelation 16:14,16 NASB). The site for the converging of the armies is the plain of Esdraelon, around the hill of Megiddo. The area is located in northern Israel about 20 miles south-southeast of Haifa and 50 miles north of Jerusalem. This area was the scene of many battles in Old Testament times. The book of Judges records it is the location of Barak's conflict with the Canaanites (chapter 4) and Gideon's battle with the Midianites (chapter 7).

WHAT IS ARMAGEDDON?

The term *Armageddon* comes from the Hebrew tongue. *Har* is the word for "mountain" or "hill." *Mageddon* is likely the ruins of the ancient city of Megiddo that overlooks the Valley of Esdraelon in northern Israel, where the armies of the world will congregate.

According to the Bible, great armies from the east and the west will gather and assemble on this plain. The Antichrist will defeat armies from the south who would threaten his power, and he will destroy a revived Babylon in the east before finally turning his forces toward Jerusalem to subdue and destroy it. As he and his armies move upon Jerusalem, God will intervene and Jesus Christ will return to rescue His people Israel. The Lord and His angelic army will destroy the armies, capture the Antichrist and the False Prophet, and cast them into the lake of fire (Revelation 19:11-21).

When the Lord returns, the power and rule of the Antichrist will come to an end. Charles Dyer (pp. 237–38) states: "Daniel, Joel, and Zechariah identify Jerusalem as the site where the final battle between Antichrist and Christ will occur. All three predict that God will intervene in history on behalf of His people and will destroy the Antichrist's army at Jerusalem. Zechariah predicts that the battle will end when the Messiah returns to earth and His feet touch down on the Mount of Olives. This battle concludes with the second coming of Jesus to earth."

The campaign of Armageddon—actually at Jerusalem—will be one of the most anticlimactic events in history. Given the huge armies mustered on both sides, we would expect to witness an epic struggle between good and evil. Yet no matter how mighty someone on earth is, that individual is no match for the power of God.

WHAT ARE THE PURPOSES OF ARMAGEDDON?

As with many human events, two purposes are at work at Armageddon: a divine intent and a human rationale. The divine purpose is that the judgment at Armageddon prepares for the 1000-year reign of Christ on earth. The satanically inspired human purpose is to once and for all liquidate worldwide Jewry.

The Divine Purpose

Our sovereign Lord providentially superintends over all history. Thus, all history is the outworking of the decree of the Triune God. Nothing takes place that He did not actively plan. All through history, usually unknown to humanity, the battle rages between God and Satan, good and evil. The war of Armageddon is the culmination of a whole series of events that climax in this final act.

According to God's divine purpose, Armageddon will be the venue by which He will judge His enemies. Both satanic and human opposition will be focused on God's elect nation of Israel, and God will bring them to that location to bring down their foolish schemes of rebellion. The psalmist records God's response of laughter at the puny human plans to overthrow God Himself at Armageddon:

> Why are the nations in an uproar, and the peoples devising a vain thing? The kings of the earth take their stand and the rulers take counsel together against the LORD and against His Anointed, saying "Let us tear their fetters apart and cast away their cords from us!" He who sits in the heavens laughs, the Lord scoffs at them. Then He will speak to them in His anger and terrify them in His fury, saying, "But as for Me, I have installed My King upon Zion, My holy mountain" (Psalm 2:1-6).

The Human Purpose

The demented human perspective leading to the final march to Jerusalem appears to be motivated by these people's effort to solve what they believe to be the source of the world's problems—the Jews. As we follow the buildup to Armageddon in Revelation (11–18), the persecution of Israel begins at the midpoint of the Tribulation, builds, and culminates in the worldwide gathering of armies in Israel.

WHEN WILL ARMAGEDDON OCCUR?

Though today's popular culture often mentions the conflict of Armageddon, it will not take place tomorrow, next month, or next year. It is a military conflict that will occur after the rapture and at the end of the seven-year Tribulation. It will be the culmination of the Antichrist's reign and it will end with the second coming of Jesus Christ, who will destroy the Antichrist and his forces.

The conflict is the last major event on the prophetic timeline before the establishment of the millennial kingdom. Armageddon is not an event that any person should desire or anticipate with joy, for it will bring death and destruction to many people. It is, however, a definite future military conflict that no amount of negotiation will postpone.

The detailed sequence of events and the terms used in relation to Armageddon show that it is a campaign or a series of battles rather than a single battle. Rather than referring to it as the "final battle," we should refer to it as a campaign or a war. Armageddon is a whole series of conflicts that culminate at the second coming of Jesus Christ. The Greek word *polemos*, translated "war" in Revelation 16:14, usually signifies an extended war or campaign. The events of Armageddon are not a single battle and do not occur in a single day. They are carried out over a wide geographic area to the north and south of Jerusalem and as far east as Babylon. These events will occur over a period of at least several days, and more likely, several weeks.

WHO WILL BE INVOLVED IN ARMAGEDDON?

Scripture indicates that all the nations of the world will gather for war against Israel. This is a fitting climax to the Tribulation, during which the whole world is in rebellion against heaven (except for a remnant of believers). The Bible teaches that this war will involve not only the whole land of Israel but also all the nations of the world (Zechariah 12:3; 14:2; Revelation 16:14). Scripture mentions the kings (plural) of the East, who take a prominent role in the military buildup in preparation for the war of Armageddon. "The sixth angel poured out his bowl on the great river, the Euphrates; and its water was dried up, so that the way would be prepared for the kings from the east" (Revelation 16:12). The verse may emphasize the Eastern powers simply because that is where the largest masses of population reside.

When we consider the fact that the whole Tribulation will be a war between God and His opponents—Satan, the fallen angels, and unregenerate mankind—we should not be surprised that it will include a great number of military conflicts throughout. The biblical data leads us to believe that the Tribulation will be a time of great military conflict—so much so that we would not be incorrect to consider the entire Tribulation period as a world war.

WHAT ARE THE STAGES OF ARMAGEDDON?

A detailed study of all of the biblical passages pertaining to Armageddon reveals a very complex campaign. One of the most thorough studies of the campaign is that of Arnold Fruchtenbaum, who has divided the campaign into eight stages. Although other plans can just as readily be proposed, his evaluation seems to us to be the most logical and comprehensive. Fruchtenbaum (p. 314) writes:

The two climactic events of the Great Tribulation are the Campaign of Armageddon and the second coming of Jesus Christ. A considerable amount of data is given

about this time period in the Scriptures. One of the greatest difficulties in the study of eschatology is placing these events in chronological sequence in order to see what exactly will happen in the Campaign of Armageddon....The Campaign of Armageddon can be divided into eight stages, and this in turn will facilitate an understanding of the sequence of events.

Each of these eight stages serves a distinct purpose in the overall campaign. Although no single biblical passage provides a sequence of all the events, this plan seems to put all the pieces together in the most coherent and comprehensive way:

THE EIGHT STAGES OF ARMAGEDDON

1. The assembling of the allies of the Antichrist (Joel 3:9-11; Psalm 2:1-6; Revelation 16:12-16).

2. The destruction of Babylon (Isaiah 13–14; Jeremiah 50–51; Revelation 17–18).

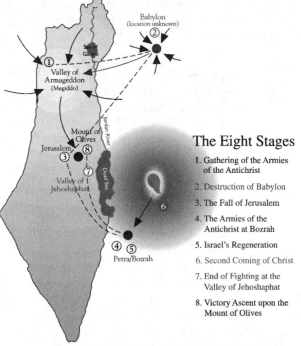

The Eight Stages

1. Gathering of the Armies of the Antichrist

2. Destruction of Babylon

3. The Fall of Jerusalem

4. The Armies of the Antichrist at Bozrah

5. Israel's Regeneration

6. Second Coming of Christ

7. End of Fighting at the Valley of Jehoshaphat

8. Victory Ascent upon the Mount of Olives

3. The fall of Jerusalem (Micah 4:11–5:1; Zechariah 12–14).

4. The armies of the Antichrist at Bozrah (Jeremiah 49:13-14).

5. The national regeneration of Israel (Psalm 79:1-13; 80:1-19; Isaiah 64:1-12; Hosea 6:1-13; Joel 2:28-32; Zechariah 12:10; 13:7-9; Romans 11:25-27).

6. The second coming of Jesus Christ (Isaiah 34:1-7; 63:1-3; Habakkuk 3:3; Micah 2:12-13).

7. The battle from Bozrah to the Valley of Jehoshaphat (Jeremiah 49:20-22; Zechariah 14:12-15; Joel 3:12-13).

8. The victory ascent upon the Mount of Olives (Zechariah 14:3-5; Joel 3:14-17; Matthew 24:29-31; Revelation 16:17-21; 19:11-21).

Stage 1: The Antichrist's Allies Assemble

The primary biblical reference to this first stage is Revelation 16:12-16, where the Euphrates River is dried up to prepare the way for the "kings of the east," culminating at Har-Magedon. The assembling of the armies begins at the same time as the divine judgment of the sixth bowl. At this time the Euphrates River will be dried up, providing for a faster and easier assembly of the armies of the "kings from the east." In the Bible, "east" refers to the region of Mesopotamia (Assyria and Babylon), and the drying up of the river will allow the forces of the Antichrist to assemble out of Babylon, his capital. The armies joining him will be those of the seven remaining kings out of ten described in Daniel 7:24-27 and Revelation 17:12-13. Their goal will be the final destruction of the Jews.

Stage 2: Babylon Is Destroyed

In this stage the activity shifts from the gathering armies of the Antichrist to the destruction of Babylon, which is his capital, by opposing forces. While the Antichrist is with his armies at Armageddon, his capital will be attacked and destroyed. The irony is that while Antichrist is gathering his armies in northern Israel for the purpose of attacking Jerusalem (God's city), God attacks the Antichrist's city—Babylon. In the Old Testament, Babylon was both the place of Israel's captivity and the originating site of idolatry. Known also as Shinar (Genesis 10:10; 11:2; Daniel 1:2; Zechariah 5:11), Babylon will be a worldwide economic and religious center of activity during the Tribulation (Revelation 17–18).

According to Isaiah 13:19 and Jeremiah 50:40, the destruction will be as devastating and complete as was that of Sodom and Gomorrah. Once the attack and destruction are finished, Babylon will be uninhabitable and will never again be rebuilt (Revelation 18:21-24). The Antichrist will be a world ruler, but his control will not be so absolute as to preclude rebellion or to squelch all opposition (Daniel 11:41). He will try, but it will be tactically impossible. The destruction will come as divine punishment for Babylon's long history of antagonism and evil against the people of Israel and the result will be the razing of the city.

> "But I will repay Babylon and all the inhabitants of Chaldea for all their evil that they have done in Zion before your eyes," declares the LORD. "Behold, I am against you, O destroying mountain, who destroys the whole earth," declares the LORD, "and I will stretch out My hand against you, and roll you down from the crags, and I will make you a burnt out mountain. They will not take from you even a stone for a corner nor a stone for foundations, but you will be desolate forever," declares the LORD (Jeremiah 51:24-26).

Stage 3: Jerusalem Falls

Although the Antichrist's capital will have been destroyed in the second phase of the campaign, his forces will not have been lost. Rather than moving eastward to confront the attackers of his capital, the Antichrist will move south against Jerusalem. We read of this move in Zechariah 12:1-3 and 14:1-2:

> The burden of the word of the LORD concerning Israel....Behold, I am going to make Jerusalem a cup that causes reeling to all the peoples around; and when the siege is against Jerusalem, it will also be against Judah. It will come about in that day that I will make Jerusalem a heavy stone for all the peoples; all who lift it will be severely injured. And all the nations of the earth will be gathered against it.

The Antichrist's forces will sweep down to Jerusalem, and once again the city will fall into Gentile control. Although Zechariah 12:4-9 and Micah 4:11–5:1 describe a temporary resurgence of Jewish strength and stiff resistance, Jerusalem will fall. The losses on both sides will be enormous, but the Antichrist's forces will prevail, and Jerusalem will fall. With the fall of Jerusalem the campaign's third stage will come to an end.

Stage 4: The Antichrist Moves South Against the Remnant

In the fourth stage, the campaign will shift into the desert and mountains, probably to a location about 80 miles south of Jerusalem to the area of Bozrah and Petra. At the beginning of the second half of the Tribulation, after the Antichrist breaks his treaty with Israel (Daniel 9:27; Matthew 24:15), many of the Jews will flee into the desert for safety. This will fulfill the words and exhortation of Jesus in Matthew 24:16-31. In verse 16, Jesus says of those who see the abomination of desolation, "then those who are in Judea must flee to the mountains." This flight for life is also described in Revelation 12:6,14.

After Jerusalem is captured the Antichrist will move south in an attempt to destroy those who fled in the previous 3½ years. In Micah 2:12 we read of God's gathering and protection of this remnant: "I will surely assemble all of you, Jacob, I will surely gather the remnant of Israel. I will put them together like sheep in the fold; like a flock in the midst of its pasture they will be noisy with men."

The area normally associated with this part of the campaign is that of Mount Seir, about 30 miles south of the lower end of the Dead Sea. Two sites are possibilities for the location of the fleeing Jews, Bozrah and Petra (see Isaiah 33:13-16 and Jeremiah 49:13-14). As the forces gather in the rugged wilderness of Mount Seir, the fourth phase will come to an end and the last few days of the campaign will begin.

Stage 5: The Regeneration of the Nation Israel

The campaign of Armageddon will culminate in the second coming of Christ. But before Christ returns, Israel will confess its national sin (Leviticus 26:40-42; Jeremiah 3:11-18; Hosea 5:15) and plead for the Messiah to return (Isaiah 64:1-12; Zechariah 12:10; Matthew 23:37-39). This will come as the armies of the Antichrist gather to destroy the Jews in the wilderness. According to Hosea 6:1-3, the Jewish leaders will issue a call for the nation to repent. The nation will respond positively and repent for two days.

Fruchtenbaum writes, "The leaders of Israel will finally recognize the reason why the Tribulation has fallen on them. Whether this will be done by the study of the Scriptures, or by the preaching of the 144,000, or via the Two Witnesses or by the ministry of Elijah, is not clearly stated. Most likely there will be a combination of these things. But the leaders will come to a realization of the national sin in some way. Just as the Jewish leaders once led the nation to the rejection of the Messiahship of Jesus, they will then lead the nation to the acceptance of His Messiahship by issuing the call of Hosea 6:1-3, which will begin the last three days before the Second Coming" (p. 337).

The fifth stage will come to completion on the third day of Israel's confession and prayer for Messiah's return. In the sixth stage, God, having heard their prayers, will answer them, fulfilling biblical prophecy and the hope of the ages.

Stage 6: The Second Coming of Jesus Christ

In the sixth stage the prayers of the Jews are answered, and Jesus Christ will return to earth to defeat the armies of the Antichrist at Bozrah and to begin the final portions of the campaign. He will return to earth in the clouds, in the same manner in which He departed (Matthew 24:30; Acts 1:9-11). The fact that Jesus returns first to the mountain wilderness of Bozrah is seen in Isaiah 34:1-7; 63:1-6; Habakkuk 3:3; and Micah 2:12-13. At His second coming, Jesus Christ the Messiah will enter battle against the Antichrist's forces, and He will miraculously defeat them.

According to Jude 14-15 and Revelation 19:11-16, Jesus will return with an angelic army and with the church saints (robed in white at the marriage of the Lamb) who had been raptured prior to the Tribulation. Revelation 19:11-16 makes it clear that the second coming will bring destruction to the enemies of Jesus Christ. These verses describe Him as treading the winepress of the wrath of God and ruling with a rod of iron.

At Israel's request, Jesus Christ will return to earth and enter the battle against the Antichrist and his armies. He will save the Jews in the wilderness from destruction and will then continue to Jerusalem to save the remnant there and conclude the campaign (Zechariah 12:7).

Stage 7: The Final Battle

In the seventh phase, Jesus the Messiah will fight alone on Israel's behalf, destroying the Antichrist and those who have come against the nation and persecuted it. In this phase the Antichrist will be slain by the true Christ (Habakkuk 3:13b; 2 Thessalonians 2:8). Among the very first casualties will be the Antichrist himself. Having ruled the world with great power and spoken against the true Son of God, the counterfeit son will be powerless before Christ. Habakkuk 3:13 says, "You went forth for the salvation of Your people, for the salvation of Your anointed. You struck the head of the house of the evil to lay him open from thigh to neck. Selah." Second Thessalonians 2:8 tells us, "Then that lawless one will be revealed whom the Lord will slay with the breath of His mouth and bring to an end by the appearance of His coming."

Beginning at Bozrah and moving back to Jerusalem and the Kidron Valley, also known as the Valley of Jehoshaphat, Jesus will engage

and destroy the Antichrist's forces (Joel 3:12-13; Zechariah 14:12-15; Revelation 14:19-20). In the Valley of Jehoshaphat, along the eastern walls of Jerusalem, the nations and armies that gathered against the Jews to destroy them will now find themselves being destroyed by Jesus Christ, the Messiah and King of the Jews.

Stage 8: The Ascent to the Mount of Olives

With the destruction of the Antichrist and his forces complete, the campaign will be over, and Jesus will go and stand upon the Mount of Olives in a symbolic victory ascent. When He does so, a number of cataclysmic events will occur, bringing the Tribulation to an end, as described in Zechariah 14:3-4.

> Then the LORD will go forth and fight against those nations, as when He fights on a day of battle. In that day His feet will stand on the Mount of Olives, which is in front of Jerusalem on the east; and the Mount of Olives will be split in its middle from east to west by a very large valley, so that half of the mountain will move toward the north and the other half toward the south.

Revelation 16:17 adds:

> Then the seventh angel poured out his bowl upon the air; and a loud voice came out of the temple from the throne, saying, "It is done." And there were flashes of lightning and sounds and peals of thunder; and there was a great earthquake, such as there had not been since man came to be upon the earth, so great an earthquake was it, and so mighty. The great city was split into three parts, and the cities of the nations fell.

The supernatural calamities that come upon the world at this time correspond to the seventh bowl judgment and include the greatest earthquake the world has ever known. As a result of the earthquake Jerusalem will split into three areas, and the Mount of Olives will split into two parts, creating a valley and means of escape from the earthquake for the Jewish inhabitants of the city (Zechariah 14:4b-5).

WHAT COMES AFTER ARMAGEDDON?

Armageddon will be the last great world war of history, and it will take place in Israel in conjunction with the second coming of Christ. The Bible is very clear that it is a certain and cataclysmic event yet to come. According to the Bible, great armies from the East and the West will gather and assemble to strike a final blow against Israel. There will be threats to the power of the Antichrist from the South, and he will also move to destroy a revived Babylon in the East before finally turning his forces toward Jerusalem to subdue and destroy it. As he and his armies move upon Jerusalem, God will intervene and Jesus Christ will return to rescue His people Israel. The Lord and His angelic army will destroy the armies, capture the Antichrist and the False Prophet, and cast them into the lake of fire (Revelation 19:11-21).

In a sense, Armageddon is a battle that never really takes place. That is, it does not take place in accordance with its original human intent. Its human purpose will be to gather the armies of the world to execute the Antichrist's "final solution" to the "Jewish problem." This is why Jesus Christ chooses this moment in history for His return to earth—to thwart the Antichrist's attempted annihilation of the Jews and to destroy the armies of the world. It seems only fitting, in light of mankind's bloody legacy, that a worldwide military conflict against Israel should precipitate the return of Christ.

—THOMAS ICE

BIBLIOGRAPHY

Dyer, Charles. *World News and Bible Prophecy*. Wheaton, IL: Tyndale House, 1991.

Feinberg, Paul. "The Mideast March to Megiddo." In William James, ed. *Foreshocks of Antichrist*. Eugene, OR: Harvest House Publishers, 1997.

Fruchtenbaum, Arnold. *Footsteps of the Messiah: A Study in the Sequence of Prophetic Events*. Tustin, CA: Ariel Press, 2003.

Hindson, Ed. *Approaching Armageddon*. Eugene, OR: Harvest House Publishers, 1997.

Jeffrey, Grant. *Armageddon: Appointment with Destiny*. New York: Bantam Books, 1991.

BABYLON

BABYLON IS ONE OF THE OLDEST cities of the ancient world. Located 50 miles south of modern-day Baghdad, it was the second most influential city on earth. Founded by a group of rebellious descendants of Noah approximately 100 years after the great flood, Babylon was a hotbed of idolatry and false religion. The Bible mentions it 280 times, second only to Jerusalem, which the Bible mentions more than 300 times.

Babylon could very well be called the city of Satan, for it quickly became the source of the world's religious evils. The city grew in influence and in rebellion against God, and in judgment, the Lord "confused the languages of all the earth" at the Tower of Babel and caused the people to scatter (Genesis 11:9 NKJV).

By 600 B.C., King Nebuchadnezzar had fashioned Babylon into the pagan empire of Babylonia, a center of religion, commerce, and government. Babylonia may have been the most powerful monarchy in the history of the world. God eventually brought the children of Israel to Babylonia as punishment for worshiping idols. There, through the prophet Daniel, God taught the world that "there is a God in heaven who reveals secrets." Israel's stay in Babylon once and for all cured the children of Israel of their bent toward idolatry.

But Babylon's control and influence would not last forever. Isaiah and Jeremiah predicted the end of its powerful reign over the world. Babylon fell in one night to the armies of Cyrus the Persian in 539 B.C. and ceased to be a world power. The city of Babylon eventually became a mound of ruins, just as the prophets had foretold.

THE TOWER OF BABEL

God's end-time program for Babylon is rooted in the historical account of the Tower of Babel (Genesis 11). This section of Scripture records humanity's first worldwide rebellion against God. God commanded mankind to scatter throughout the face of the earth following the flood (Genesis 9:7). Under the leadership of Nimrod (Genesis 10:8-12), mankind instead gathered in the land of Shinar (Genesis 11:2). There they built a city and a tower that was to reach into heaven (Genesis 11:4).

This was a spiritual rebellion. These early settlers probably designed the *ziggurat* as a temple for their worship of the stars (Hitchcock, p. 41). Babel is also the place of the origin of the infamous mother-child cult. According to extrabiblical tradition, Nimrod's wife, Semiramis, had a son named Tammuz through an alleged miraculous conception. According to tradition, Tammuz was killed by a wild animal and miraculously restored to life (Walvoord, p. 970). The legend of Semiramis and Tammuz eventually spread from Babel throughout the world, but their names were changed in different cultures. In Assyria, the mother was Ishtar and the son was Tammuz. In Phoenicia, it was Astarte and Baal. In Egypt, it was Isis and Osirus or Horus. In Greece, it was Aphrodite and Eros. In Rome, it was Venus and Cupid (Hitchcock, p. 42). Babylon became the "mother of harlotries" as the central influence in all following cultures (Garland).

According to Genesis 11:5-9, God frustrated this worldwide apostasy by confounding the builders' language, thus inhibiting them from communicating with one another. God's action had a purpose. Satan could lead humanity away from the truth more easily if only one government existed and this single government happened to fall into the hands of anti-God forces. However, with the existence of multiple nations, those nations that reject anti-God agendas can work together to restrain evil to some extent. Consequently, since the Tower of Babel incident, God has decreed that humanity be ordered according to national boundaries rather than global government (Deuteronomy 32:8; Acts 17:26).

However, Satan's purpose throughout history has been to subvert this divine ordering of nations and bring the world back together so that he once again can have unlimited control of it through one man (Hitchcock, p. 43). Thus, Satan's ambition may have always been to bring man back to Babylon under his authority. The fact that human rebellion could one day cycle back to where it all began comes as no surprise because of numerous parallel themes running through the books of Genesis and Revelation.

BABYLON IN REVELATION

Several theories exist about the identity of Babylon in the book of Revelation. Some scholars believe "Babylon" is a code word for Rome. A few (mostly preterist interpreters) assign the title to first-century Jerusalem. Other commentators see John's use of "Babylon" as a metaphor for a worldwide system of evil.

However, many Old Testament prophecies about the literal city of Babylon are not yet fulfilled. The present authors believe that in the coming Tribulation period, the Antichrist will rule the world from his headquarters in the literal, rebuilt city of Babylon on the Euphrates River in modern-day Iraq.

OLD TESTAMENT PREDICTIONS

Isaiah 13–14 and Jeremiah 50–51 depict Babylon's destruction. Although Babylon fell to the Medo-Persian Empire (Daniel 5:31) in 539 B.C., Babylon's historic fall does not match the cataclysmic language found in Isaiah and Jeremiah. For these prophecies to be accurately fulfilled, Babylon must be revived so that it can be destroyed again according to the specific details given by Isaiah and Jeremiah.

Zechariah 5:5-11 teaches that in God's providence, mankind's wickedness, commerce, and religion will once again return to the land of Babylon. Because Babylon had already fallen (539 B.C.) by the time this prophecy was given (519 B.C.), Zechariah's vision appears to predict a futuristic, rebuilt Babylon. Revelation 17–18 records the circumstances by which this vision will be fulfilled.

REVELATION 17–18

Revelation 17 features a woman with a title inscribed on her forehead, which reads, "Mystery, Babylon the Great, the Mother of Harlots and of the Abominations of the Earth" (Revelation 17:5). Of Revelation's 404 verses,

278 allude to the Old Testament. When the Old Testament uses the word "Babylon," the reference is always to literal Babylon. The same is likely true for Revelation. Human history will eventually cycle back to where it all began. In the same region where the first world emperor led mankind in a universal political and religious revolt against God, the future Antichrist will also lead the last collective revolt before Christ returns. However, "the Lamb will overcome them, for He is Lord of lords and King of kings" (Revelation 17:14). The political and economic world authorities will mourn for Babylon (18:9,11), but God will receive praise as the faithful cry out, "Alleluia! Salvation and glory and honor and power belong to the Lord our God!" (19:1).

—ANDY WOODS AND TIM LAHAYE

BIBLIOGRAPHY

Dyer, Charles H. *The Rise of Babylon*. Rev. ed. Chicago: Moody Publishers, 2003.

Garland, Tony. *"Revelation Commentary."* Accessed online at www.spiritandtruth.org on March 1, 2004.

Hitchcock, Mark. *The Second Coming of Babylon*. Sisters, OR: Multnomah Publishers, 2003.

Pink, Arthur. *The Antichrist*. Swengel, PA: I.C. Herendeen, 1923.

Thomas, Robert L. *Revelation 8–22: An Exegetical Commentary*. Chicago: Moody Press, 1992.

Walvoord, John F. "Revelation." In *The Bible Knowledge Commentary*, eds. John F. Walvoord and Roy B. Zuck. 2 vols. Colorado Springs, CO: Chariot Victor Publishing, 1983.

BEAST

There is no doubt that the beast of the book of Revelation is the Antichrist that the apostles Paul and John describe in their epistles. The word *beast* (Greek, *theerion*) means "wild animal," and Revelation first mentions this being in 11:7, where he comes from the abyss and kills the two witnesses of the Lord who convict the world of its evil. To say that he emerges from the depths may simply mean that his wicked motivations are inspired from the pits of Satan. Other passages of Scripture show him to be an evil and rational earthly being and not simply a demonic creature. When he arrives upon the world scene, he may become the most powerful and the most loathsome human being to reside on earth. He acts as the devil's arch tool for the physical and spiritual destruction of humanity.

The beast comes from the nations ("the sea," 13:1) and entices the world to follow after him (verse 3). The religious False Prophet, who is also called "a beast" (verses 11-12), leads the world in worshiping the first beast and even makes an image of him (verse 15). He is identified by a mysterious number: 666 (verse 18; 16:2). The exact meaning of this number has escaped the many speculations of scholars. When the events of the Tribulation take place, and the beast comes on the scene, true Christians will probably be able to recognize him by some feature that is identified by 666.

Toward the end of the Tribulation, the beast controls the last great rulers and kings of the earth (17:7-18). He leads them to overthrow and slay the great harlot of the book of Revelation, who "is the great city, which reigns over the kings of the earth." At the very end of the Tribulation, the beast leads the kings of the earth "to make war" against Jesus Christ, who comes against all of the nations that have assembled for the final conflict at the battle of Armageddon (19:11-19). The end of the beast is sudden, and at the end of the Tribulation he is seized with the false prophet and "thrown alive into the lake of fire which burns with brimstone" (19:20).

The ten horns of Revelation 17:7 coincide with the ten horns of Daniel 7:7. These are the leaders of the nations of the final great world empire, the revived Roman Empire. This is the same empire that Daniel envisions and is described as the "fourth beast," which is "dreadful and terrifying and extremely strong." This clearly relates to the beast of Revelation. However, it's important to observe that Daniel is describing a political and geographical entity while John, in Revelation, is referring to a personality. John's beast is not simply a force, nation, or power; the beast has all of the characteristics of personality. He is the other "horn," or the "little one" who comes out of the nations, as Daniel describes, who possesses "eyes like the eyes of a man, and a mouth uttering great boasts"—meaning he is worldly-wise and controls the nations by what he says (Daniel 7:8). This is the same beast John describes in Revelation.

The Antichrist is called "the beast" approximately 32 times in the New Testament—and only in the Apocalypse. However, the designation "Antichrist" is referred to in 1 John 2:18, though the apostle John speaks also of the spirit of Antichrist that fosters a denial of God the Father (verse 22), and an antichrist-like deception of what is true (4:3; 2 John 7). The apostle Paul mentions him in much detail in 2 Thessalonians 2 as the lawless one whose coming is energized "in accordance with the activity of Satan, with all power and signs and false wonders" (2 Thessalonians 2:9). (See also the articles on "Antichrist" and "False Prophet.")

—MAL COUCH

BIBLIOGRAPHY

Balz, Horst, and Gerhard Schneider. *Exegetical Dictionary of the New Testament.* 3 Vols. Grand Rapids: Eerdmans Publishing Company, 1994.

Couch, Mal, gen. ed. *A Bible Handbook to Revelation.* Grand Rapids: Kregel, 2001.

Froom, Leroy Edwin. *The Prophetic Faith of Our Fathers.* 4 Vols. Washington, DC: Review and Herald, 1954.

Hindson, Ed. *The Book of Revelation.* Chattanooga: AMG Publishers, 2002.

Pink, Arthur W. *The Antichrist.* Grand Rapids: Kregel, 1988.

Thomas, Robert L. *Revelation 8–22: An Exegetical Commentary.* Chicago: Moody Press, 1995.

Tucker, W. Leon. *Studies in Revelation.* Grand Rapids: Kregel, 1980.

Walvoord, John F. *The Revelation of Jesus Christ.* Chicago: Moody Press, 1966.

BIRTH PANGS

THE DOCTRINE OF THE BIRTH PANGS is extremely important in understanding Bible prophecy. It is first mentioned in Jeremiah 30–31. Here, Jeremiah prophesies about the Tribulation, the hatred of the nations for Israel, the New Covenant, and God's perpetual care for the Jewish people. In the Olivet Discourse (Matthew 24–25), Christ refers in some detail to the birth pangs and the Tribulation events. The apostle Paul also mentions the birth pangs and the day of the Lord in 1 Thessalonians, where he teaches that the church will not go through this terrible period.

JEREMIAH

In Jeremiah 30:6, the prophet writes, "Ask now, and see if a male can give birth. Why do I see every man with his hands on his loins, as a woman in childbirth? And why have all faces turned pale?"

Jeremiah sees a future day when men will groan and be in distress as if they were women with labor pains. This will take place when God "restore[s] the fortunes" of all the Jews (30:3) during the seven-year Tribulation. It is a period of "terror, of dread," and of no peace (30:5). The prophet adds, "For that day is great, there is none like it; and it is the time of Jacob's distress." Though many Jews will perish during these terrible times, the nation as a whole "will be saved from it" (30:7). The Hebrew particle *meen* means "out of, away from." The entire nation will be saved "away from" this time of final suffering. These things "shall come about on that day" (30:8)—the day of the Lord.

At the end of the birth pangs, the Lord "will restore the fortunes of the tents of Jacob and have compassion on his dwelling places" (30:18). Punishment "will burst on the head of the wicked" (30:23). Jeremiah explains how this period will end: "The fierce anger of the LORD will not turn back until He has performed and until He has accomplished the intent of His heart; in the latter days you will understand this" (30:24).

At the end of that time, when the millennial kingdom begins, the Jews will call out to each other, "Arise, and let us go up to Zion, to the LORD our God" (31:6). The scattered Jews will sing, "O LORD, save Your people, the remnant of Israel" (31:7). Then the nations will be told, "He who scattered Israel will gather him and keep him as a shepherd keeps his flock" (31:10).

JESUS' OLIVET DISCOURSE

Christ quotes Jeremiah 30 in His Olivet Discourse when describing the coming Tribulation. He tells His disciples that the day is coming when nation will rise against nation, with famines and earthquakes taking place in various locations (Matthew 24:7), and He then adds, "All these things are merely the beginning of birth pangs" (24:8). Jesus also says, "The one who endures to the end, he will be saved" (24:13). This is similar to what Jeremiah wrote in 30:7, as is Jesus' comment that "there will be a great tribulation, such as has not occurred since the beginning of the world until now, nor ever will" (Matthew 24:21).

Many dispensationalists apply the expression "great tribulation" (Greek, *megale thlipsis*) to the second half of this awful period, but when Jeremiah says in 30:7 "that day is great" (Hebrew, *ga'dol*) and that it is "Jacob's distress" (Hebrew, *za'rah*, tribulation), he seems to be describing the entire seven years of world terror.

PAUL AND THE THESSALONIANS

After Paul delivers his strong and detailed teaching on the rapture of the church (1 Thessalonians 1:9-10; 4:13-18), he assures the Thessalonians that they will not experience the "destruction [that] will come upon them suddenly like labor pains upon a woman with child" (5:3). "Upon them" could refer specifically to the trials of the Jewish people, or it may also refer to the terrible days that will fall upon the entire world. The broader interpretation seems to be correct because Jesus says "that day...will come upon all those who dwell on the face of all the earth" (Luke 21:34-35). Paul writes in 1 Thessalonians 5:3 that people will be saying, "Peace and safety!" just before the birth pangs begin. He calls this "the day of the Lord" (5:2). This is very similar to Jeremiah's statement that these things "shall come about on that day" (Jeremiah 30:8).

Paul calls the birth pangs "wrath" but assures his readers, "God has not destined us for wrath, but for obtaining salvation through our Lord Jesus Christ" (1 Thessalonians 5:9). This is good news for those of us living in this dispensation (the "church age" or the "age of grace"). The apostle exhorts his readers to "encourage one another [with this message of hope] and build up one another, just as you also are doing" (5:11).

What does Paul mean by "obtaining salvation"? Salvation (Greek, *soteria*) has three aspects: First, the believer is saved from the guilt of sin by the death of Christ. Second, the believer is enabled to overcome sin by the indwelling Holy Spirit. Third, here in 1 Thessalonians 5:9, the believer is delivered from the wrath, the birth pangs, that will fall on the unbelieving world.

FOR UNBELIEVERS

To summarize, it seems that the "birth pangs" include the entire period of the Tribulation. Jesus and Paul refer to this time as "the wrath." It is also the day of the Lord. It will fall upon unbelieving Jews and Gentiles, and it will take place as the Jews return to the Promised Land, the Land of Israel. The church will be raptured away from the horrors of this entire period.

The promise of deliverance from the birth pangs "is given without conditions: God, according to His own good will and pleasure, has decreed that we shall escape the outpouring of His wrath. No idea of sanctification nor of a partial rapture is found here. No believer who belongs to the body of Christ will be placed under this wrath" (Couch, p. 141).

—MAL COUCH

BIBLIOGRAPHY

Couch, Mal. *The Hope of Christ's Return*. Chattanooga: AMG Publishers, 2001.

Feinberg, Charles L. "Jeremiah." In *Expositor's Bible Commentary*. Frank E. Gaebelein, gen. ed. Grand Rapids: Zondervan, 1986.

Glasscock, Ed. *Matthew*. Chicago: Moody Press, 1997.

Holladay, William L. *A Concise Hebrew and Aramaic Lexicon of the Old Testament*. Grand Rapids: Eerdmans Publishing Company, 1974.

Thompson, J. A. *The Book of Jeremiah*. Grand Rapids: Eerdmans Publishing Company, 1989.

Toussaint, Stanley D. *Behold the King*. Sisters, OR: Multnomah Publishers, 1981.

Walvoord, John F. *The Prophecy Knowledge Handbook*. Wheaton, IL: Victor Books, 1990.

BLESSED HOPE

THIS EXPRESSION DESCRIBES the rapture of the church.

Paul wrote to his young Gentile helper, Titus, sometime during A.D. 63–65. He addresses how to live in this present age (2:12) and then says that the grace of God instructs believers to be "looking for the blessed hope and the appearing of the glory of our great God and Savior, Christ Jesus" (2:13 NASB). Paul urges believers to be looking for the blessed hope while living in this present age, the church age, which serves as an indication that the rapture must come before the Tribulation.

THE BLESSED HOPE

"The blessed hope" in Titus 2:13 might be better translated the "joyous anticipation" (Greek, *makaria elpida*). This hope will come to pass, and it can produce great joy as believers look forward to ultimate redemption. Those now being trained by God's grace eagerly anticipate the eschatological future of leaving this world before the horrors of the Tribulation come. Paul writes in 1 Thessalonians 1:9-10 that the believers in that church were waiting for Christ's return. This is surely a reference to the rapture. The believers were looking for this personal return of Jesus at any moment. This is to be the proper attitude of the child of God, who is ever ready to welcome the returning Lord.

THE APPEARING OF THE GLORY OF GOD

This "appearing" is also translated elsewhere as "brightness" as seen in Titus 2:11.

"Glory" in the Greek text is *doxa* and refers to God's reputation, honor, and radiance. Some render the passage as the "glorious appearing," but the "appearing of the glory" is more literal and points to Christ's glorification now in heaven. His glory *will* appear! The second instance of the article "the" is not in the Greek text, and the passage translates best without it: "the blessed hope, even appearing of the glory...." This implies that the reference is to one event viewed from two aspects. For believers, it is indeed the blessed hope and the longed-for consummation of that hope.

OUR GREAT GOD AND SAVIOR, CHRIST JESUS

This is a remarkable phrase in Paul's letter to Titus. It strongly supports the fact that Christ is God Himself, and it is an outstanding and important testimony to the doctrine of the Trinity. The Greek scholar Patrick Fairbairn says that the two expressions "great God" and "Savior" are attributive of the same person. He adds that many of the Greek and Latin church fathers refer to this passage and clearly understand the reference to God as speaking also of Christ (Fairbairn, p. 281).

Kenneth Wuest points out that the grammatical construction "that blessed hope, even appearing..." is the same in the phrase "glory of our great God, even Savior, Christ Jesus." He further argues that the god and savior of the Roman Empire was the emperor himself. The Christians' God and Savior is Jesus Christ, for whom we are looking to return from heaven. Paul could have been making a protest against Roman emperor worship. Wuest adds that "both expressions refer to the same individual. The deity of the Lord Jesus is brought out here by a rule of Greek syntax" (Wuest, vol. 2, p. 195).

Will God the Father make an appearance to rescue the church? No, He is Spirit and cannot be seen. The Son will be visible, and He is the great God. The deity of Christ is indisputable by the grammar. The New Testament never speaks of the appearing of God the Father but only of the Son. Paul says here that the appearing or epiphany of the glory of

Jesus Christ shall at last arrive. Then He who in His own person is "our great God and Savior" will come in all His glory, which will transcend all that we are able to imagine.

—Mal Couch

BIBLIOGRAPHY

Couch, Mal, ed. *A Pastor's Manual on Doing Church.* Springfield, MO: 21st Century Press, 2002.

Fairbairn, Patrick. *Commentary on the Pastoral Epistles.* Grand Rapids: Zondervan, 1956.

Knight III, George. *The Pastoral Epistles.* Grand Rapids: Eerdmans Publishing Company, 1996.

LaHaye, Tim. *The Rapture.* Eugene, OR: Harvest House Publishers, 2002.

Showers, Renald E. *The Pre-Wrath Rapture View.* Grand Rapids: Kregel, 2001.

Wuest, Kenneth S. *Wuest's Word Studies.* Grand Rapids: Eerdmans Publishing Company, 1998.

11 · BOOK OF LIFE

I saw the dead, small and great, standing before God, and books were opened. And another book was opened, which is the Book of Life. And the dead were judged according to their works, by the things which were written in the books (Revelation 20:12 NKJV).

God keeps a record of all of our thoughts, words, and deeds, ready to be recalled on the final day of judgment. "For God will bring every work into judgment, including every secret thing, whether good or evil" (Ecclesiastes 12:14).

Many people have the mistaken idea that because they have escaped the penalty for their sins in this world, those sins have somehow gone unnoticed. This is far from true. No act, word, or thought, good or bad, in public or in secret, eludes the all-seeing eyes of God—He has recorded each one.

Hebrews 9:27 states that "it is appointed for men to die once, but after this the judgment." Our status in Christ determines how we will be judged. Believers, in resurrected

form, will stand before the judgment seat of Christ immediately following the rapture. There they will receive rewards for the good works they performed while on earth. Their salvation is never in question. On the other hand, unbelievers, also in resurrected form, will appear before the Great White Throne judgment at the end of the millennium. Jesus Christ Himself will rule over the proceedings. He will judge their deeds according to the law because they chose not to accept Christ's free gift of salvation while on earth. No believer in Jesus will be judged during the Great White Throne judgment.

The New Testament refers to the Book of Life eight times (Philippians 4:3; Revelation 3:5; 13:8; 17:8; 20:12,15; 21:27; 22:19). Two of these references are to the "Lamb's Book of Life" (13:8; 21:27). The reference in 22:19 is disputed, thought by most scholars (based on manuscript evidence) to refer to the "tree of life" instead. Thus scholars hold two different views concerning how many "books of life" exist.

THE SINGLE BOOK OF LIFE VIEW

Many believe that the Book of Life refers only to the names of the elect of God, which have been recorded from eternity past (Walvoord, *Revelation,* p. 203; see Revelation 17:8). The reference in Revelation 3:5 to the possibility of having one's name blotted out of this book should not be understood as a threat but rather a promise not to do so (Walvoord, *Revelation,* p. 82). It may be viewed as a literary device known as *litotes,* whereby an assertion is made by denying its opposite, conveying the idea in 3:5 that there is no way in which a name written in this book would ever be blotted out. In addition, the Greek syntax of the passage contains "emphatic negation," implying that the names will "certainly not" be blotted out and emphasizing the firmness of the promise (Kessinger, pp. 189–90).

Others hold that the single Book of Life is actually a book of all the living, wicked as well as righteous (Wiersbe, p. 39), from which all unbelieving sinners' names are removed when they die and no longer have an opportunity to make a choice to believe (Kessinger, p. 191; see

Exodus 32:32; Psalm 69:28). If a person professes true saving faith in Jesus Christ, his name becomes permanent in the book, never to be erased. Revelation 3:5 is usually used as evidence for this view (Thomas, p. 165).

THE TWO BOOKS OF LIFE VIEW

In the view of the present author, there are two books—the Book of Life and the Lamb's Book of Life. The major difference between the two is that the Book of Life contains the names of all living people, whereas the Lamb's Book of Life includes only the names of those who have received eternal life from Jesus (the Lamb). One's name may be blotted out from the Book of Life, but not from the Lamb's Book of Life.

Once a person has entered the world, their name is automatically recorded in the Book of Life. If, by the time of their death, they have not called upon Jesus Christ for salvation, their name will be removed from the Book of Life. If they have accepted Christ and His forgiveness of sins, their name will remain in the Book of Life and be indelibly recorded in the Lamb's Book of Life, never to be erased. Their entrance into heaven is guaranteed (Revelation 21:27).

Those who appear before the Great White Throne judgment all died without accepting Christ's payment for their sins, so their works must be judged according to the law. This is where the books of man's deeds are opened. The inevitable outcome is that each person will be found guilty, "for all have sinned and fall short of the glory of God" (Romans 3:23). However, before the sentence is pronounced, the Lamb's Book of Life will be opened, but of course, the names of unbelievers will not be there. Finally, as one last double-check, the Book of Life will be opened. But once again, the names of unbelievers will not be found.

"Anyone not found written in the Book of Life [will be] cast into the lake of fire" (Revelation 20:15). This verse emphasizes the importance of making sure your name remains in the Book of Life. God's will is that none "should perish but that all should come to repentance" (2 Peter 3:9). To prevent your name from being blotted out from the Book of Life, you must make sure your name appears in the Lamb's Book of Life. To do that, simply accept Christ's payment for your sins, invite Him into your heart, and ask Him to be the Lord and Savior of your life (Luke 10:20). Your eternal destiny is at stake!

—Tim LaHaye

BIBLIOGRAPHY

Kessinger, Tony. *Come Out of Her My People*. Philadelphia: Xlibris, 2003.

Smith, J.B. *A Revelation of Jesus Christ*. Scottdale, PA: Herald Press, 1961.

Thomas, Robert L. *Revelation 8–22: An Exegetical Commentary*. Chicago: Moody Press, 1995.

Walvoord, John F. *The Prophecy Knowledge Handbook*. Wheaton, IL: Victor Books, 1990.

———. *The Revelation of Jesus Christ*. Chicago: Moody Press, 1966.

Wiersbe, Warren W. *Be Victorious*. Colorado Springs: Chariot Victor, 1985.

BOWL JUDGMENTS

THREE SEQUENCES OF JUDGMENT will fall on the earth during the Tribulation. The breaking of the seven seals begins the Tribulation (Revelation 5:1-5). With the breaking of the seventh seal (8:1-2) comes the sounding of the seven trumpets (8:2–9:21; 11:15-19). When the seventh angel sounds the final trumpet (15:8–16:1), the first bowl "of the wrath of God" is poured upon the earth. God's angels are the agents who bring about these judgments into the world.

THE INTENSITY OF THE SEVEN BOWLS

What is in the bowls? Though the Bible does not say, the descriptions of the terror that falls on the earth would indicate scalding water or liquid of some kind. The bowl judgments are the most intense of the sequences of judgment that fall on the world. "The difference between the trumpets and the bowls has to do with the more universal extent of the latter. And they come in rapid succession. As soon as God commands them to go, they move with swift abandonment. Each [angel] 'pours out' his bowl (cup or goblet) upon its destined target" (Hindson, p. 168).

DESCRIPTION OF THE SEVEN BOWLS

The *first bowl* causes loathsome (Greek, *pornon*) or possibly putrefied sexual sores to break out on those who have the mark of the beast (16:2). The word for "sore" is *helkos,* meaning abscesses or ulcers. The sores are also called "malignant" (Greek, *kakos*) to empha-size their severity.

The *second bowl* is poured upon the sea, and it becomes "blood," meaning that it turns to a coagulated vile and terrible soup, "and every living thing in the sea died" (16:3).

The *third bowl* is poured out upon the rivers and the springs of water, and they too become like blood or are terribly polluted (16:4-7). The angel of this judgment cries out that God is the Righteous One who ever lives and who is judging these things. He is judging not only the people of earth but also the earth itself, and specifically here, the waters of the planet. The apostle Paul reminds his readers in Rome that "the whole creation groans and suffers the pains of childbirth" because of sin (Romans 8:22). The Lord has subjected it to futility, and someday "the creation itself also will be set free from its slavery to corruption" (Romans 8:20-21). But there is more about this third bowl of judgment: John says that God has given men this pollu-tion (the blood) to drink because "they deserve it." The evil men on the earth during this Tribulation period "poured out the blood of saints and prophets" (Revelation 16:6). The martyrs near the heavenly altar cry out, "Yes, O Lord God, the Almighty, true and righteous are Your judgments" (16:7). The vast majority of people on the earth are more than deserving of what is coming upon the world because of their sins and their collective revolt against God and His Christ.

The *fourth bowl* of the wrath of God falls upon the sun "to scorch men with fire" and with fierce heat (16:8-9). Does this horror bring about repentance? No. The people of the earth "blasphemed the name of God who has the power over these plagues; and they did not repent so as to give Him glory." No matter how painful the tribulation, most people will not come to God, give Him honor, and repent of their sins. "Are they humbled and made repen-tant thereby? Are they crushed in spirit under the repeated and increasing severity of these judicial chastisements? No! They 'blasphemed the name of God.' What an answer on man's part to the expressed wrath of the Almighty! How incorrigibly bad and thoroughly corrupt is the will of man!" (Scott, pp. 328-29).

The *fifth angel* pours out his bowl upon the throne of the Antichrist and his kingdom (16:10-11). His kingdom, the vast empire that controls the peoples and the nations of earth, becomes "darkened; and [men] gnawed their tongues because of pain." Again there is no repentance. Instead, "they blasphemed the God of heaven because of their pains and their sores; and they did not repent of their deeds." Some think "'the kingdom of the beast' does not refer to the whole world but only to his own particular kingdom, the base from which he later will acquire control over all other kingdoms" (Morris, p. 306).

The *sixth angel* pours his bowl upon the great river Euphrates (16:12-16 NASB), "and its water was dried up, that the way would be prepared for the kings from the east." At this same time, three unclean spirits as loathsome as frogs proceed from the dragon (Satan), the beast (the Antichrist), and the False Prophet (see Revelation 13). "They are spirits of demons, performing signs, which go out to the kings of the whole world, to gather them together for the war of the great day of God, the Almighty" (16:14). This meeting place for the final conflict of the armies of the earth will happen in the Holy Land at the "Hill of Magiddo" (or Har-Magedon). This event will bring on one of the world's greatest battles (19:17-21). The leaders of the world will con-verge with their armies and be defeated by the Lord Jesus Christ when He returns at His second coming.

Why is the river Euphrates mentioned in 16:12? "Running for almost 2000 miles from Turkey through present-day Syria and Iraq to the Persian Gulf, the Euphrates River serves as a kind of cultural barrier to armies to the east. In places it is almost two-thirds of a mile wide. In the Tribulation, God will dry it up so that kings from the east will be able to cross it on their way to Israel" (Couch, p. 276). "When this judgment [falls] on the river Euphrates it [will be] to dry up its waters as a preparation for certain kings known as the 'Kings of the East.' They are coming! Zechariah also mentions this [gathering] and coming of kings and also the drying up of the river. (See Zechariah 10:10-11.) These kings may be designated as the 'Kings of the Sunrising.' They are the Kings of the East" (Tucker, p. 328).

When the *seventh angel* pours out the final bowl of wrath down upon the earth (16:17-21), a voice from the temple in heaven says, "It is done." After that comes lightning and thunder and a great earthquake "such as there had not been since man came to be upon the earth, so great an earthquake was it, and so mighty." A great city, either Jerusalem or Babylon, is split into three parts, and the Lord remembers Babylon for her evil. He gives her "the wine of His fierce wrath." The islands are moved, the mountains leveled, and huge hailstones fall from heaven. Do men repent? They do not. Instead, they "blasphemed God because of the plague of hail" and because of its severity.

With this seventh and final bowl, "not only does every city of the world come under terrible judgment as a result of the great earthquake which leaves all monuments of men's ingenuity in shambles, but the Scriptures also indicate great changes in the topography of the entire world. The sweeping statement is made in verse 20 that every island is affected and mountains disappear. The fierceness of the wrath of God in verse 19, literally the anger of His wrath, is manifested in the entire physical earth" (Walvoord, p. 241).

The seal, trumpet, and bowl judgments probably form the spine of the Tribulation events. "These seven angels, pouring out the seven bowls of wrath, are indeed a 'great' sign, for 'in them is finished the wrath of God.' We shall see them proceed 'from the temple of God in heaven'—all patience [from God] having been now exhausted" (Newell, p. 236).

—MAL COUCH

BIBLIOGRAPHY

Couch, Mal, gen. ed. *A Bible Handbook to Revelation.* Grand Rapids: Kregel, 2001.

Hindson, Ed. *The Book of Revelation.* Chattanooga: AMG Publishers, 2002.

Morris, Henry M. *The Revelation Record.* Wheaton, IL: Tyndale House Publishers, 1983.

Newell, William R. *Revelation.* Grand Rapids: Kregel, 1994.

Scott, Walter. *Exposition of the Revelation of Jesus Christ.* Grand Rapids: Kregel, 1982.

Thomas, Robert L. *Revelation 8–22: An Exegetical Commentary.* Chicago: Moody Press, 1995.

Tucker, W. Leon. *Studies in Revelation.* Grand Rapids: Kregel, 1980.

Walvoord, John F. *The Revelation of Jesus Christ.* Chicago: Moody Press, 1966.

CHURCH AGE

THE CHURCH AGE BEGAN on the Day of Pentecost in Acts 2 and will end with the rapture of the church before the beginning of the Tribulation. The church age is not characterized by historically verifiable prophetic events except its beginning on the Day of Pentecost and its ending with the rapture. But Bible prophecy does reveal the general course of this age.

Even most of the specific prophecy that is fulfilled during the church age relates to God's prophetic plan for Israel and not directly to the church. For example, the prophesied destruction of Jerusalem and the Temple in A.D. 70 relates to Israel (Matthew 23:38; Luke 19:43-44; 21:20-24). Prophetic preparations relating to Israel are already underway with the reestablishment of Israel as a nation in 1948 even though we still are living in the church age.

THE CHURCH AGE DESCRIBED

Matthew 13

The parables of Matthew 13 provide insight into this present age in its relation to the future kingdom. They cover the period of time between Christ's two advents—His first and second comings. This includes our present era (the church age), the Tribulation, the second coming, and the final judgment, though it bypasses the rapture.

Pentecost summarizes the description as follows:

> We may summarize the teaching as to the course of the age by saying: (1) there will be a sowing of the Word throughout the age, which (2) will be imitated by a false counter sowing; (3) the kingdom will assume huge outer proportions, but (4) be marked by inner doctrinal corruption; yet, the Lord will gain for Himself (5) a peculiar treasure from among Israel, and (6) from the church; (7) the age will end in judgment with the unrighteous excluded from the kingdom to be inaugurated and the righteous taken in to enjoy the blessing of Messiah's reign (Pentecost, p. 149).

This means that the church age is a time of constant preaching of the gospel. The church begins as a small band of individuals but becomes a global institution. As Christendom expands to fill the whole world, it will become increasingly apostate. This will result in global judgment after the rapture of the church.

Revelation 2–3

The letters to the seven churches also provide an overview of the course of this age (Revelation 2–3). This passage applies to the church and not to the future kingdom, as indicated by the often-repeated phrase, "He who has an ear, let him hear what the Spirit says to the churches" (Revelation 2:7,11,17,29; 3:6,13,22 NASB). These seven historical churches of the first century provide a pattern of the churches that will exist throughout church history.

Revelation 1:19 indicates a threefold division of the book of Revelation. "Write therefore the things which you have seen, and the things which are, and the things which will take place after these things." Revelation 1 corresponds to "the things which you have seen," which depict the resurrected Christ. Revelation 2–3 corresponds to "the things which are," the current church age. Revelation 4–22 corresponds to "the things which will take place after these things": the Tribulation, second coming, millennium, and eternal state.

What lessons do these seven epistles to the churches in Revelation teach us about the church age? Many scholars see the characteristics of all seven churches as existing continually throughout the church age. See the article "Seven Churches of Revelation" for an explanation of this approach. Other Bible students, such as G.H. Pember, believe that the seven churches "present a prophetic picture of the seven historical periods in which the visible church will develop" (Pember, pp. 494–95). This has been called "the historical-prophetical method of interpretation" (Fruchtenbaum, p. 38), and this method outlines the church age as follows (p. 36):

1. Ephesus: the apostolic church (A.D. 30–100)

2. Smyrna: the Roman persecution (100–313)

3. Pergamum: the age of Constantine (313–600)

4. Thyatira: the Middle Ages (600–1517)

5. Sardis: the Reformation (1517–1648)

6. Philadelphia: the missionary movement (1648–1900)

7. Laodicea: the apostasy (1900–present)

Of course, in this view only at the end of the church age would we be able to look back and correlate church history with the patterns revealed by our Lord's examination of those first-century churches.

The Epistles

A number of New Testament epistles speak of the condition within Christendom near the end of the age. Virtually all of these comments come from the epistles written shortly before the death of each author, as if to emphasize the dangers latent during the church's last days. The following is a list of the seven major passages that deal with the last days of the church: 1 Timothy 4:1-3; 2 Timothy 3:1-5; 4:3-4; James 5:1-8; 2 Peter 2; 3:3-6; and the tiny letter of Jude. Each of these passages emphasizes repeatedly that the outstanding characteristic of the final time of the church will be apostasy.

The English meaning of *apostasy* is "departure from one's faith." The Greek New Testament uses two words for apostasy. One is *apostasia.* This noun is a compound of the two Greek words *apo* ("from") and *istémi* ("to stand") and means "standing away from," or "departure from." The other is the verb *piptô,* which simply means "to fall" or "fall away from." When used abstractly of "falling away from the faith," it fits into the category of apostasy.

Apostasy occurs in two main areas: doctrine and behavior, or the way we think and the way we act. According to the New Testament, the professing church at the end of the age will be filled with denial about the truth and about godly living.

- Denial of God—2 Timothy 3:4-5
- Denial of Christ—1 John 2:18; 4:3
- Denial of Christ's return—2 Peter 3:3-4
- Denial of the faith—1 Timothy 4:1-2; Jude 3
- Denial of sound doctrine—2 Timothy 4:3-4
- Denial of Christian liberty—1 Timothy 4:3-4
- Denial of morals—2 Timothy 3:1-8,13; Jude 18
- Denial of authority—2 Timothy 3:4 (Pentecost, p. 155)

Scripture indicates that apostasy will characterize Christendom at the time of the rapture. The current church-age apostasy is preparation for even greater deception and apostasy led by the Antichrist during the Tribulation. Yet at the same time, as long as the church is on the earth, God the Holy Spirit will be at work bringing new people to Christ and enabling faithful believers to grow to maturity.

THE PROPHETIC DESTINY OF THE CHURCH

The Bible consistently warns church-age believers to be on guard against apostasy. This characteristic is a general sign of the end times. But what is the prophetic future of the church? To answer this question, we must separate the true church in particular from Christendom in general. The true church is made up of Jews and Gentiles who genuinely know Christ as their Savior and have their sins forgiven. Beginning on the Day of Pentecost in Acts 2 and continuing to the rapture, all believers are part of Christ's body, the church.

We call the realm of the professing church's influence *Christendom.* Christendom constitutes everything associated with the visible church, including all of its branches. Christendom includes true believers and mere professors, the wheat and the tares growing up together (Matthew 13:24-30). The true church and Christendom have very different prophetic destinies.

THE RAPTURE AWAITS THE CHURCH

The next event on the prophetic calendar for the true church is the rapture (John 14:1-3; 1 Corinthians 15:51-52; 1 Thessalonians 4:13-18). This event is described in 1 Thessalonians 4:17, which says it will be at a time in which all living and dead believers "will be caught up…in the clouds to meet the Lord in the air." This event could happen at any moment, without warning. While Christ is preparing a place for the church, the church is to remain faithful while constantly watching for His unannounced return. When the Father gives the signal, the shout will go forth, and the church age will be completed at the rapture, and we will always be with the Lord.

JUDGMENT AWAITS APOSTATE CHRISTENDOM

However, apostate Christendom will be left behind to enter the Tribulation period and serve as Satan's harlot—"the great harlot who sits on many waters" (Revelation 17:1)—who will help facilitate the great delusion of Antichrist. This apostate church will pave the way for a one-world religion—the worship of Antichrist and reception of the mark of the beast (Revelation 13:16-18). Revelation 13:11-18 presents the False Prophet (the head of the apostate church during the Tribulation) as the one who is advocating, on behalf of the Antichrist, reception of the mark of the beast. Just as the true church has as its role of declaring and making clear the truth of God, so Satan's harlot has a leading role in fostering his deception.

THE CHURCH IS SEPARATE FROM ISRAEL

The church is unique in the plan of God and separate from His plan for Israel. The church partakes of the spiritual promises of the Abrahamic covenant as fulfilled through Christ, but Israel—and not the church—will fulfill its national destiny as a separate entity. This will occur after the rapture and Tribulation, during the millennium. The New Testament teaches that the church was an unrevealed mystery in the Old Testament (Romans 16:25-26; Ephesians 3:2-10; Colossians 1:25-27), which is why she began suddenly and without warning in Acts 2, and why this age will end suddenly and without warning at the rapture. Therefore, the church has no earthly prophetic destiny beyond the rapture.

THE JUDGMENT SEAT OF CHRIST

The New Testament teaches that the church will be removed at the rapture before the Tribulation begins (1 Thessalonians 1:10; 5:9; Revelation 3:10) and taken by Christ to the Father's house (John 14:1-3). It will be in heaven during the Tribulation, as represented by the 24 elders (Revelation 4:4-11; 7:13-14; 19:4). There believers will stand before the judgment seat of Christ in preparation (Revelation 19:4-10,19) to accompany Christ at

His descent at the second coming (Revelation 19:14). The marriage supper of the Lamb will take place at the beginning of the millennium, after the second coming.

THE MILLENNIUM AND THE ETERNAL STATE

During the millennium, the church will reign and rule with Christ (Revelation 3:21). In Matthew 19:28, Jesus told His disciples, who are members of the church, that they would join Him in the kingdom and reign over the 12 tribes of Israel. In 2 Timothy 2:12, Paul writes, "If we endure, we will also reign with Him." The primary purpose of the millennium is the restoration of Israel and Christ's rule over it, but the church as the bride of Christ will be involved in millennial activities.

—THOMAS ICE

BIBLIOGRAPHY

Chafer, Lewis Sperry. *Systematic Theology.* 8 vols. Dallas, TX: Dallas Seminary Press, 1948.

Fruchtenbaum, Arnold G. *The Footsteps of the Messiah.* San Antonio, TX: Ariel Press, 1982.

Pember, G.H. *The Great Prophecies of the Centuries Concerning the Church.* Miami Springs, FL: Conley and Schoettle, 1984.

Pentecost, J. Dwight. *Things to Come.* Grand Rapids: Zondervan, 1958.

CHURCH IN PROPHECY

THE CHURCH IS NOT FOUND in the Old Testament. Rather, the Old Testament anticipates Messiah's kingdom (Isaiah 2; 4; 11; Jeremiah 23:5-6; Ezekiel 37:21-25). Abraham "waited for the city which has foundations, whose builder and maker is God" (Hebrews 11:10 NKJV). In the Davidic covenant, God promised David a perpetual line to rule Israel from an earthly throne (2 Samuel 7). Gabriel told Mary that her child would "be called the Son of the Highest; and the Lord God will give Him the throne of His father David. And He will reign over the house of Jacob forever, and of His kingdom there will be no end" (Luke 1:32-33).

John the Baptist preached that "the kingdom of heaven is at hand" (Matthew 3:2). Jesus announced the same, saying, "The kingdom of God is at hand" (Mark 1:14). Jesus chose and sent out the 12 with the exhortation, "Do not go into the way of the Gentiles, and do not enter a city of the Samaritans. But go rather to the lost sheep of the house of Israel. And as you go, preach, saying, 'The kingdom of heaven is at hand'" (Matthew 10:5-7). These references all apply to the kingdom, not to the church.

CHRIST PREDICTED THE CHURCH

But when the Jewish leaders and people rejected Christ's offer of the kingdom, especially as seen in Matthew 11–12, Jesus announced something new—the church. The word *church* occurs in the Gospels only in Matthew 16:18 and 18:19. At Caesarea Philippi, just six months before the crucifixion, Jesus used the future tense to prophesy something new. He said, "I will build My church, and the gates of Hades shall not prevail against it" (Matthew 16:18). Later, Jesus raised the possibility of one brother sinning against another, and He commanded that if the erring brother should ignore repeated efforts toward reconciliation, the offended brother should "tell it to the church" (Matthew 18:17).

THE CHURCH BEGAN AT PENTECOST

The church was a completely new entity that began at Pentecost (Acts 2). Even the disciples did not expect the church. After Christ's resurrection, the 11 asked Jesus, "Lord, will You at this time restore the kingdom to Israel?" (Acts 1:6). After all, that is what they had been waiting for. Journeying to Jerusalem for that final Passover, Jesus gave the parable of the ten pounds because His disciples "thought the kingdom of God would appear immediately" (Luke 19:11). The mother of James and John pled to Jesus for her sons to sit "one on Your right hand and the other on the left, in Your kingdom" (Matthew 20:21). The disciples repeatedly argued over which of them would be the greatest in the kingdom (Luke 9:46),

even during the Last Supper (Luke 22:24). Thus, they were surprised when Jesus told them not to worry about the kingdom (Acts 1:7) but to wait in Jerusalem until they were endued with power by the coming of His promised Holy Spirit (Acts 1:8).

THE CHURCH WAS COMPLETELY NEW

The apostle Paul describes the church as a body composed of both Jews and Gentiles. He teaches that Christ broke "down the middle wall of separation," alluding to the wall in the Jewish Temple that separated the Jews from the area open to Gentiles (Ephesians 2:11-18). Paul terms this a "mystery" (Ephesians 3:3-4). A mystery, in the biblical sense of the word, is something that was once concealed but later revealed. That was God's plan for the church. This mystery of the ages was "that the Gentiles should be fellow heirs, of the same body, and partakers of His promise in Christ through the gospel" (Ephesians 3:6). The church was planned by God, predicted by Christ during His earthly ministry, and initiated by the Holy Spirit at Pentecost.

THE CHURCH AND APOSTASY, FALSE TEACHING, AND IMMORALITY

The New Testament includes several prophecies about the church in general or about a local church in particular. Paul, in his address to the Ephesian elders, said, "For I know this, that after my departure savage wolves will come in among you, not sparing the flock. Also from among yourselves men will rise up, speaking perverse things, to draw away the disciples after themselves" (Acts 20:29-30). Paul exhorted these elders to "watch" because of the impending danger (Acts 20:31).

Likewise, the apostle Peter made a similar prediction about the churches he addressed in 2 Peter. Peter warned his readers that "there will be false teachers among you, who will secretly bring in destructive heresies, even denying the Lord who bought them" (2 Peter 2:1). He also indicated that "many will follow their destructive ways" and that the predicted false teachers "will exploit you with deceptive words" (2 Peter 2:3). Jude, writing a few years after Peter but with a message that was parallel to Peter's, noted that "certain men have crept in unnoticed…ungodly men, who turn the grace of our God into lewdness and deny the only Lord God and our Lord Jesus Christ" (Jude 4).

The New Testament repeatedly affirms that the church will always face the threats of apostasy, false teaching, and immoral conduct. This seems to be borne out in Jesus' own evaluation of the very church that Paul founded and warned in Acts 20. In His apocalypse, Jesus rebuked the Ephesian believers, saying, "You have left your first love" (Revelation 2:4). To the Thyatiran believers Jesus said, "You allow that woman Jezebel, who calls herself a prophetess, to teach and seduce My servants to commit sexual immorality and eat things sacrificed to idols" (Revelation 2:20). That was precisely what Peter predicted when he wrote to those same churches of Asia in 2 Peter.

THE RAPTURE OF THE CHURCH

Paul's exhortation for husbands to love their wives is rooted in this lofty comparison: "just as Christ also loved the church and gave Himself for her, that He might sanctify and cleanse her with the washing of water by the word" (Ephesians 5:25-26). Paul notes that Christ's purpose in that redemptive and cleansing process is "that He might present her to Himself a glorious church, not having spot or wrinkle or any such thing, but that she should be holy and without blemish" (Ephesians 5:27). Paul also predicts just when that presentation will occur. The rapture will take place "at the last trump" (1 Corinthians 15:57), at the same time that "the Lord Himself will descend from heaven with a shout, with the voice of an archangel, and with the trumpet of God" (1 Thessalonians 4:16). (For the timing of these trumpets with Matthew 24:31, see James A. Borland, "The Meaning and Identification of God's Eschatological Trumpets" in *Looking into the Future: Evangelical Studies in Eschatology*.)

This great prophecy about the church continues, "And the dead in Christ will rise first. Then we who are alive and remain shall be caught up together with them in the clouds to meet the Lord in the air" (1 Thessalonians 4:16-17). At that time the entire church will be presented to Christ perfect and without blemish. Paul explains, "For our citizenship is in heaven, from which we also eagerly wait for the Savior, the Lord Jesus Christ, who will transform our lowly body that it may be conformed to His glorious body, according to the working by which He is able even to subdue all things to Himself" (Philippians 3:20-21). The apostle John adds that "we know that when He is revealed, we shall be like Him, for we shall see Him as He is" (1 John 3:2). When we are made like Christ through that beatific vision, He will fulfill His presentation of the church to Himself "without spot or wrinkle." The church will be made perfect at that point.

CHRIST WILL JUDGE THE CHURCH

Following that event, every individual in the raptured church must "appear before the judgment seat of Christ, that each one may receive the things done in the body, according to what he has done, whether good or bad" (2 Corinthians 5:10; see also Romans 14:10). Christ's parable of the pounds or minas (Luke 19:12-27) and the parable of the talents (Matthew 25:14-30) will also be fulfilled. Paul refers to these judgments of the believer's works in 1 Corinthians 3:13, where he says, "Each one's work will become clear; for the Day will declare it, because it will be revealed by fire; and the fire will test each one's work, of what sort it is."

THE CHURCH WILL JUDGE ANGELS

The church will judge angels according to Paul in 1 Corinthians 6:3. This cannot mean judging the unfallen angels, for they are sinless. Paul must therefore be referring to Satan's host of fallen angels, the demons. And because of Paul's words, "Thus we shall always be with the Lord" (1 Thessalonians 4:17), we know that the church will also witness the judgments of others, such as occurs at the Great White Throne, when all the unsaved dead will be resurrected and stand before God for a final sentencing before being cast into the lake of fire (Revelation 20:11-15).

THE CHURCH WILL REIGN WITH CHRIST

Another result of the believer's union with Christ is that the glorified church will rule and reign with Christ. The church shares Christ's throne. Even Daniel 7 portrays the Son of Man, Christ, as giving His kingdom to His saints. "Then the kingdom and dominion, and the greatness of the kingdom under the whole heaven, shall be given to the people, the saints of the Most High" (Daniel 7:27). This shared rule with Christ initially takes place during the millennial reign of Christ (Revelation 20:4-5), but it will extend indefinitely. As long as Christ reigns, so does the church.

—JAMES A. BORLAND

BIBLIOGRAPHY

Borland, James A. "The Meaning and Identification of God's Eschatological Trumpets." In *Looking into the Future: Evangelical Studies in Eschatology*, ed. David W. Baker. Grand Rapids: Baker Books, 2001.

MacArthur, John, Jr. *The Church: The Body of Christ.* Grand Rapids: Zondervan, 1973.

Radmacher, Earl D. *What the Church Is All About.* Chicago: Moody Press, 1978.

Saucy, Robert L. *The Church in God's Program.* Chicago: Moody Press, 1972.

Walvoord, John F. *The Church in Prophecy.* Grand Rapids: Zondervan, 1964.

Wood, Leon J. *The Bible & Future Events.* Grand Rapids: Zondervan, 1973.

CONVERSION OF ISRAEL

THE RAPTURE OF THE CHURCH can happen at any time, but before Jesus' second coming, Israel must first repent and accept Him as the Messiah.

ISRAEL REJECTS JESUS AS THE MESSIAH

When Jesus preached to Israel, He proclaimed the kingdom of God. But the kingdom was preconditioned by Israel's accep-tance of Jesus as the messianic King. In Matthew 4–12, Jesus performed miracles to authenticate His person (that He is the Messiah) and His message (the gospel of the kingdom). When Israel rejected Jesus as the Messiah in Matthew 12:24, the purpose of His miracles and His whole ministry underwent a radical change.

The Pharisees had made their choice. They refused to accept Jesus as the Messiah because He did not fit their preconceived notion of what the Messiah was supposed to say and do (Luke 7:30-35). They declared that Jesus Himself was demon possessed—not by a common demon but by the prince of demons, Beelzebub. In Matthew 12:30-37, Jesus pronounced a judgment on those who arrived at this conclusion; they had committed the unpardonable sin.

In Matthew 12:38-40 (NKJV), Jesus announced His new policy regarding miracles:

> Then some of the scribes and Pharisees answered saying, "Teacher, we want to see a sign from you." But he answered and said to them, "An evil and adulterous generation seeks after a sign, and no sign will be given to it except the sign of the prophet Jonah. For as Jonah was three days and three nights in the belly of the great fish, so will the Son of man be three days and three nights in the heart of the earth."

Jesus continued to perform miracles after this event, but the purpose of His miracles had changed. No longer were they for the intent of authenticating His person and His message to get the nation to come to a decision about Him. That decision had now been made. Rather, His miracles would train the 12 apostles for the new kind of ministry they would need to conduct as a result of the rejection of Jesus as the Messiah. That generation would have no sign but one: the sign of Jonah, which is the sign of resurrection. This sign would come for Israel on three occasions: (1) at the resurrection of Lazarus, (2) at Jesus' own resurrection, and (3) at the resurrection of the two witnesses in the Tribulation. Israel rejected the first two. They will accept the third, for the resurrection of the two witnesses will lead to the salvation of the Jews of Jerusalem.

THE LEADERS SEAL THEIR REJECTION

At Jesus' triumphal entry into Jerusalem, thousands of Jews cried, "Blessed is the King who comes in the name of the Lord," which is a Jewish messianic greeting based on Psalm 118:26. The Jewish masses proclaimed His messiahship as He approached Jerusalem, but still the Jewish leaders refused Him, so Jesus pronounced words of judgment on the city of Jerusalem in Luke 19:41-44.

Matthew 23:1-36 is a denunciation and condemnation of the scribes and Pharisees, the leadership of Israel, for various sins. Two key passages in this condemnation are relevant here: The first is Matthew 23:13, where Jesus holds the Pharisees accountable not only for their rejection of Him but also for leading the entire nation to reject Him. The second is Matthew 23:29-36, where Jesus stated that the current generation would be accountable not only for the rejection of His messiahship but also for the blood of all the prophets of the Old Testament. The reason was that everything God intended to say concerning the Messiah had already been said by the Jewish prophets. The generation alive at the time of Jesus' proclamation possessed in their hands the entire Old Testament canon. Furthermore, they had heard John the Baptist announce the soon coming of the Lord. Finally, they had the physical manifestation and presence of Jesus the Messiah, who came with all the authenticating signs. Nevertheless, they rejected Him, following the example of their leaders. Thus, they would be held accountable for the blood of all the prophets who spoke about the Messiah.

So we see that the Jewish leadership rejected Jesus as the Messiah, accusing Him of being demon possessed, and led the nation to reject Him as well.

THE ONE CONDITION FOR BLESSINGS

In Leviticus 26, Moses predicted that the Jews would be scattered all over the world because of their disobedience to God's revealed will. According to the New Testament, this came as a direct result of their rejection of Jesus as the Messiah. By Leviticus 26:39, the world-wide dispersion is a fact. Up to this point, Leviticus 26 has been fulfilled. Then, in verse 42, Moses states that God intends to give Israel all the blessings and promises of the Abrahamic covenant, including the Promised Land. But before Israel can begin to enjoy these blessings of the Abrahamic covenant, they must first fulfill the condition of verse 40 and "confess their iniquity and the iniquity of their fathers." The word "iniquity" is in the singular and is specific. Israel must confess one specific iniquity before she can begin to enjoy all the benefits of the Abrahamic covenant. Their "fathers" or ancestors committed the iniquity, but a subsequent generation must now confess it.

Jeremiah 3:11-18 describes the blessings that God has in store for Israel in the messianic kingdom. Tremendous blessing and restoration will come to the Jewish people when their Messiah establishes His kingdom. But all these blessings are conditioned by verse 13, which explains that they must acknowledge or confess one specific iniquity that they committed against Jehovah their God.

Zechariah 12:10 further develops this theme. Chapters 12–14 are one prophetic revelation, a single unit of thought. Chapter 13 speaks of the national cleansing of Israel from their sin. Chapter 14 describes the second coming and the establishment of the kingdom. But the cleansing of Israel followed by the second coming and the messianic kingdom are all conditioned on Zechariah 12:10. Before Israel will receive the cleansing of her sin and before Messiah will return to establish His kingdom, Israel must first look to (not *on,* as in the NKJV) the One whom they have pierced and plead for His return. Once they do this, they will receive their cleansing and begin to enjoy the blessings of the messianic age.

Hosea 5:15 sheds even more light on this. God Himself is speaking, and He states that He is going to go back to His place. God's place is in heaven. Before God can go back to heaven, He must first leave it. The question is, When did God ever leave heaven? God left heaven at the incarnation in the person of Jesus of Nazareth. Then, because of one specific "offense" (the word is singular) committed against Him, He returned to heaven at the ascension from the Mount of Olives. This verse further states that He will not come back to the earth until Israel acknowledges their offense. What is the offense Israel committed against Jesus? It is not, as so many people think, that they killed Him. Gentile hands actually killed Jesus. A Gentile judge condemned and sentenced Him. Gentile soldiers crucified Him. But ultimately, all this is irrelevant, for regardless of Jewish acceptance or Jewish rejection, Jesus would have had to die anyway to become the sacrifice for sin. The national offense of Israel was their rejection of Jesus as the Messiah. According to Hosea 5:15, only when Israel acknowledges this offense will Messiah return to earth.

As we saw earlier, Matthew 23:1-36 describes Jesus' denunciation of the scribes and Pharisees, the Jewish leadership of that day, for leading the nation to reject Him as the Messiah. He was still speaking to them in verses 37-39. Speaking to the Jewish leadership, Jesus reiterates His original desire to gather them if they would only accept Him. Because of their rejection of Him, instead of being gathered, they are going to be scattered. Their house, the Jewish Temple, will be left desolate and will be destroyed, with nothing remaining. Then Jesus declares that they will not see Him again until they say, "Blessed is He who comes in the name of the Lord." This is a messianic greeting that will indicate their acceptance of the messiahship of Jesus.

SATAN'S STRATEGY AGAINST THE JEWISH PEOPLE

So Jesus will not come back to the earth until the Jews and the Jewish leaders ask Him to come back. For just as the Jewish leaders once led the nation to reject the Messiah, they must someday lead the nation to accept Him.

This explains Satan's war against the Jews throughout history in general and during the Tribulation in particular. Satan knows that once Messiah returns, his freedom ends. Satan also knows that Jesus will not come back until the Jewish leaders ask Him to come back. So if Satan can succeed in destroying the Jews once and for all before they come to national repentance, then Jesus will not come back and Satan's career is eternally safe. That is why once Satan is confined to his fourth abode and knows his time is short, he expends all of his satanic energies to try to destroy the Jews once and for all. Anti-Semitism in any form, active or passive, whether it is racial, ethnic, national, economic, political, religious, or theological, is all part of the satanic strategy to avoid the second coming.

THE NATIONAL REGENERATION OF ISRAEL

This, then, is the twofold basis of the second coming: Israel must confess her national sin (Leviticus 26:40-42; Jeremiah 3:11-18; Hosea 5:15) and then plead for Messiah to return, to "mourn for Him, as one mourns for an only son" (Zechariah 12:10; see also Matthew 23:37-39).

With the armies of the Antichrist at the city of Bozrah, the campaign of Armageddon will begin its last three days according to Hosea 6:1-3. This passage is actually a continuation of Hosea 5. The chapter division is unfortunate because it breaks the train of thought. Hosea 5:15 calls for repentance, and in Hosea 6:1-2, the Jewish leaders exhort the nation to repent and confess their national sin. Only then will God restore to Israel the physical blessings she once enjoyed (verse 3).

In those days, the leaders of Israel will finally recognize the reason why the Tribulation has fallen on them. This may happen through the study of the Scriptures, the preaching of the 144,000, the testimony of the two witnesses (the third sign of Jonah to which the Jews of Jerusalem had already responded), or the ministry of Elijah. Most likely, it will be a combination of these things. But the leaders will come to a realization of their national sin in some way. Whereas the Jewish leaders once led the nation to reject Jesus the Messiah, they will now lead the nation to accept Him by issuing the call of Hosea 6:1-3, which will begin the last three days before the second coming.

Israel will confess their national sin during the first two days. Isaiah 53:1-9 provides the actual words. In this confession, the people will admit that the nation had looked upon Jesus as nothing more than another man, a criminal who had died for His own sins. However, on this occasion they will recognize that He was no ordinary man—He was the perfect Lamb of God, the Messiah Himself. Furthermore, they will realize He did not die for His own sins but for theirs so that they would not be stricken for their sin.

Thus, the national regeneration will come by means of the national confession described in Isaiah 53:1-9. On the third of the last three days, the entire nation will be saved, fulfilling the prophecy of Romans 11:25-27. "All Israel" means just that—every Jew living at that point of time, meaning the third that are left from the original number of Jews living at the start of the Tribulation (Zechariah 13:8-9). Israel's national confession and regeneration will be accomplished within two days after the issuance of the call.

The second facet leading to the second coming is Israel's pleading for the Messiah to return and save them from the world's armies, who are intent on their destruction and are gathered outside of Bozrah. The pleading of the Jews for the Messiah to come and save them is the subject of much revelation. Zechariah 12:10–13:1 describes it. The pleading for the Messiah to return will not be confined to the Jews of Bozrah, but will include the Jews still in Jerusalem. They will confess their national sin, and then they will plead for Jesus' return to save them from the troubles described in the preceding context. They will plead for the One whom they have pierced. This will be the result of the outpouring of the Holy Spirit (12:10), Israel's mourning for the Messiah (12:11-14), and the cleansing of Israel's sins (13:1).

Another prophecy of this event appears in Joel 2:28-32. Regeneration is the work of the Holy Spirit, and the nation of Israel will be regenerated because of the outpouring of the Holy Spirit on the people, creating some dramatic manifestations in their midst (verses 28-29). The result of all this is that the Jews of Jerusalem, as well as the remnant of Bozrah, will be delivered and escape.

Zechariah 13:7-9 shows that the remnant comes to a saving knowledge of Jesus the Messiah by way of the fires of the Tribulation. Two-thirds of the Jewish population will die, but the remaining third will experience cleansing. By means of the national confession of their sin, they will be purified. God will then answer their pleading for Him to come and save them. They will once again be His people, and He will be their God.

Thus, Israel as a nation will be regenerated and saved after two days of national confession of sin. On the third day, Israel will plead for the second coming, and Christ will return to save Israel.

—ARNOLD FRUCHTENBAUM

BIBLIOGRAPHY

Fruchtenbaum, Arnold. *Footsteps of the Messiah.* Tustin, CA: Ariel Ministries, 1983.

———. *Israelology: The Missing Link in Systematic Theology.* Tustin, CA: Ariel Ministries, 1992.

Larsen, David. *Jews, Gentiles and the Church.* Grand Rapids: Discovery House, 1995.

Price, Randall. *Jerusalem in Prophecy.* Eugene, OR: Harvest House Publishers, 1998.

Walvoord, John F. *Israel in Prophecy.* Grand Rapids: Zondervan, 1962.

COVENANTS

GOD'S RELATIONSHIP WITH MAN is always mediated through one or more of the biblical covenants. God made six distinct covenants with promises: (1) the Noahic covenant (Genesis 6:18; 9:8-17), (2) the Abrahamic covenant (Genesis 15:1-21; 17:1-22; 26:2-5,24; 28:13-17),

(3) the Mosaic covenant (Exodus 19–20, 24), (4) the priestly covenant (Numbers 25:10-13), (5) the Davidic covenant (2 Samuel 7:12-16), and (6) the New Covenant (Jeremiah 31:31-34). Five are unconditional, irrevocable, everlasting, and by grace; only the Mosaic covenant was conditional, revocable, temporary, and by works.

The Bible never mentions a covenant of grace or covenant of redemption, nor does Scripture address the so-called Edenic and Adamic covenants as "covenants" in the over 280 uses of "covenant" in the Old Testament and over 30 appearances in the New Testament. (See the article "Dispensations" for an explanation of the "covenant" aspects of what God promised prior to Noah.) God has contracted to perform certain things in history, and prophecy focuses on how and when God will fulfill these promises.

THE DIFFERENT COVENANTS
Noahic Covenant

The term *covenant* first appears in the Old Testament in reference to the Noahic covenant (Genesis 6:18; 9:9-17). In the context of a universal flood expressing His wrath (6:1-7), God unilaterally covenanted with Noah to preserve the human race and living creatures from extinction and to prevent future, global death by promising never to repeat the experience. This covenant, not mentioned in the New Testament, is unconditional and everlasting, extending for the present earth's lifetime and signified by the rainbow (8:21-22; 9:11-17). This covenant's irrevocable quality illustrates the identical feature in the Abrahamic, priestly, and Davidic covenants (Jeremiah 33:20-26). God's common grace (Isaiah 54:9) is mercifully and compassionately expressed to the entire human race over their individual lifetimes (see Matthew 5:45; Acts 14:17; 17:25).

Abrahamic Covenant

God made the autonomous and sacred (Luke 1:72) Abrahamic covenant unilaterally (Genesis 15:7-17) with Abraham, Isaac, and Jacob (Exodus 2:24). He stated or reaffirmed

it at least eight times (Genesis 12:1-3; 13:14-17; 15:1-21; 17:1-21; 22:15-18; 26:2-5,24; 28:13-17; 35:10-12). This covenant was everlasting (Genesis 17:7-8,13,19), irrevocable (Hebrews 6:13-18), superior to the Mosaic covenant (Romans 4:13; Galatians 3:17), immediately conditional (Genesis 17:14; Leviticus 26:43) but ultimately unconditional (Leviticus 26:44; Deuteronomy 4:31). It was signified by circumcision (Genesis 17:9-14; Acts 7:8). This covenant promised: (1) Abrahamic descendants ethnically (Genesis 13:15; 15:18), (2) Abrahamic descendants redemptively (Romans 4:11; Galatians 3:7,26-29), (3) the Savior (Galatians 3:16), (4) a nation (Genesis 12:2; 17:4; 35:11), (5) land (Genesis 12:1; 13:15,17), (6) personal blessing and protection (Genesis 12:3; 28:15), and (7) blessings to the nations (Genesis 12:3; 17:4-6), especially redemption (Psalm 111:9; Romans 4:16-18; Galatians 3:8).

Mosaic Covenant

The unique, autonomous, and conditional Mosaic or Old Covenant (Exodus 19:5-6; Leviticus 26:1-46; Deuteronomy 7:12–8:20; 29:9,22-28) made at Mt. Sinai (Exodus 19–20) tested Israel (Exodus 20:20; Deuteronomy 8:2), who voluntarily entered this agreement (Exodus 19:8; 24:3-7; 34:27). It was signified by the Sabbath (Exodus 31:16-17). The ordinances lasted only for the covenant's effective life (Exodus 31:16; Leviticus 24:8; Numbers 18:19). The hopeless outcome (Deuteronomy 31:16,20) of this revocable, non-grace, and non-salvific covenant resulted from Israel's repeated violations (Leviticus 26:14-39; Deuteronomy 29:25-28; 31:16,20), which ultimately prompted God's voiding it (Ezekiel 44:7-14; Zechariah 11:10) so it no longer possessed authority (Romans 6:14-15; Galatians 3:23-25; Ephesians 2:14-16). It has been replaced by the New Covenant (Jeremiah 31:31-34; Hebrews 8:6-13; 9:11-22; 10:1-18) without negatively affecting the prior Abrahamic covenant (Galatians 3:15-22; 4:21-31). While faint hints of the Abrahamic (Deuteronomy 29:13; 30:5,20) and New (Deuteronomy 29:4; 30:6) covenants appear in Deuteronomy 29–30, the covenant made in Moab, that is, besides the earlier

Mosaic covenant at Horeb (Deuteronomy 29:1), most likely involves a reaffirmation in the sense of (1) at a later time, (2) in another location, and (3) by a new group. Thus, this covenant is not original or autonomous because the subsequent uses of "covenant" in Deuteronomy 29:9-25 point to the conditional (Deuteronomy 29:21,25,27; 30:19), bilateral (Deuteronomy 29:12) Mosaic covenant.

Priestly Covenant

The original Levitical and Aaronic priesthood, which was conditionally covenanted by God as part of the Mosaic or Old Covenant, would last only for the life of the covenant (see Exodus 29:9; 40:15; Leviticus 24:8-9; Numbers 18:8,19; Deuteronomy 33:8-11; Nehemiah 13:29; Malachi 2:4-5,8). However, the priesthood took on absolutely new dimensions in duration and direction with a unilateral (Numbers 25:12), autonomous, unconditional, everlasting (Numbers 25:13; Psalm 106:31), and irrevocable (Jeremiah 33:20-21) priestly covenant because of Phinehas' brave loyalty to God (see Numbers 25:10-13; Psalm 106:30-31). This promise to Phinehas' line (1 Chronicles 6:1-15) will continue in the millennium (Ezekiel 40:46; 43:19; 44:15; 48:11) through the seed of Zadok, who was the faithful high priest to David and Solomon (1 Kings 1:32-40).

Davidic Covenant

With ultimate unconditionality, God promised David that a descendant would be enthroned to rule over Israel and the world (2 Samuel 7:12-16; 1 Chronicles 17:11-14). This Davidic covenant is autonomous, unilateral (2 Samuel 23:5; 2 Chronicles 13:5; Psalm 89:3,28, 34), irrevocable (2 Samuel 7:15; 1 Chronicles 17:13), and everlasting (2 Chronicles 13:5; 21:7; Psalm 89:28,36). However, the covenant was immediately conditional (2 Samuel 7:14; 1 Kings 2:3-4; Psalm 89:30-32,39) since sinful descendants were disqualified. While the covenant is not explicitly named in the New Testament (see Acts 2:30), it appears clear that Jesus Christ is the specific Davidic seed (Matthew 1:1; John 7:42) whom God intends to enthrone (Matthew 19:28; 25:31; Luke 1:32;

John 18:37) for a future, earthly rule over Israel and the nations (Psalm 110:2; Zechariah 14:9; Luke 1:33; Revelation 11:15; 12:5; 19:15-16) during the millennial kingdom (Revelation 20:1-10).

New Covenant

The unconditional, unilateral (Ezekiel 20:37; 37:26), everlasting (Isaiah 55:3; 59:21; Jeremiah 32:40; Ezekiel 16:60; Hebrews 9:15; 13:20), and irrevocable (Isaiah 54:10; Hebrews 7:22) New Covenant assumes nullification, due to Israel's sin, of the conditional Mosaic or Old Covenant (Jeremiah 31:32; Ezekiel 44:7; Zechariah 11:10-11). Originally made with Israel (Jeremiah 31:31) and containing redemptive blessings of both salvation (Isaiah 49:8; Jeremiah 31:34) and subsequent life (Isaiah 49:8; Jeremiah 32:40-41), this autonomous covenant later allowed the New Testament church to be saved (see Romans 11:11-32) through Christ, the messenger (Malachi 3:1) and mediator (Hebrews 8:6; 9:15; 12:24) of a better covenant (Hebrews 7:22; 8:6), purchased with the blood and death of this unique High Priest (Zechariah 9:11; Matthew 26:28; 1 Corinthians 11:25; Hebrews 9:15; 10:29). Old Testament believers anticipated (Hebrews 9:15) Christ's life-giving sacrifice (2 Corinthians 3:6) involving (1) grace (Hebrews 10:29), (2) peace (Isaiah 54:10; Ezekiel 34:25; 37:26), (3) the Spirit (Isaiah 59:21), (4) redemption (Isaiah 49:8; Jeremiah 31:34; Hebrews 10:29), (5) removing sin (Jeremiah 31:34; Romans 11:27; Hebrews 10:17), (6) a new heart (Jeremiah 31:33; Hebrews 8:10; 10:16), and (7) a new relationship with God (Jeremiah 31:33; Ezekiel 16:62; 37:26-27; Hebrews 8:10). This covenant pictures Israel's new betrothal to God (Hosea 2:19-20) initiated by the same divine mercy as the Davidic covenant (Isaiah 55:3).

NATURE AND TYPES OF COVENANTS

Covenants in the Old Testament have certain components that are uniform among the various types. There was a solemn promise made binding by an oath. This oath could be a verbal formula or a symbolic action. The parties making the oath were obligated to

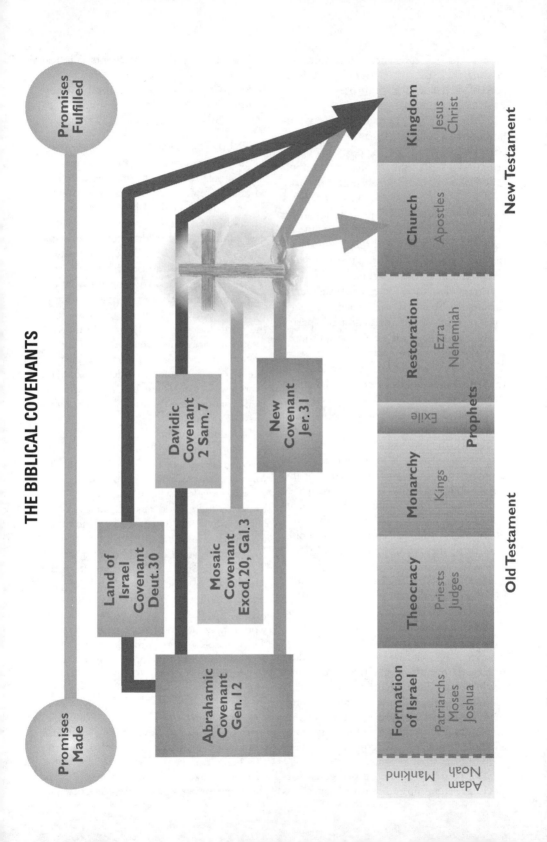

THE BIBLICAL COVENANTS

the contract. The covenant had legal force and became the basis for relationship between parties and defined the nature of ethical standards between them.

There are other important aspects of biblical covenants. First, covenants are contracts between individuals for the purpose of governing that relationship. God wants to bind Himself to His people to keep His promises so that He can demonstrate in history what kind of God He is. Second, relationships in the Bible, especially between God and man, are legal or judicial. This is why they are mediated through covenants. Covenants usually involve intent, promises, and sanctions.

There were three types of covenants in the ancient Near East: the royal grant treaty, the suzerain–vassal treaty, and the parity treaty. The royal grant treaty was a promissory type of covenant that arose out of a king's desire to reward his loyal servant. The reward usually involved grants of land, a dynasty, or a priesthood. Biblical examples of this kind of treaty include the Abrahamic and Davidic covenants.

Royal grant treaties or covenants are unconditional. This point is important for Bible prophecy because at stake is whether or not God is obligated to fulfill His promise specifically to the original parties of the covenant. For example, we believe that God must fulfill to Israel as a national entity those promises made to them through unconditional covenants like the Abrahamic, Davidic, and land covenants. If this is true, then they must be fulfilled literally.

A very popular form of covenant during the second millennium B.C. was the suzerainvassal treaty. This treaty bound an inferior vassal to a superior suzerain and was binding only on the one who swore. Biblical examples of this treaty form include Jabesh-Gilead serving Nahash in 1 Samuel 11:1 and the kings in the valley who served Chedorlaomer in Genesis 14. The most notable and perspicuous example, though, is the covenant between the Lord and Israel at Sinai.

The parity treaty bound two equal parties in a relationship and provided conditions as stipulated by the participants. Biblical examples include treaties between Jacob and Laban (Genesis 31:44-50), Abraham and Abimelech (Genesis 21:25-32), and Joshua and the Gibeonites (Joshua 9:3-27).

EXTENT OF THE COVENANTS

Suzerain–vassal treaties or covenants are conditional. This is important because it is within this framework that the Tribulation is first mentioned in the Bible as an event in Israel's history that will occur in "the latter days" and will lead to their repentance and conversion to the Messiah (Deuteronomy 4:30). An interesting aspect of Deuteronomy is that its covenantal structure provides the framework for Israel's history, past and future. In the historical prologue section (1:6–4:49) the Lord does not merely provide the customary history of the two contractual parties' dealings up to the time of the treaty. He goes one step further and provides a prophetic overview of Israel's entire future history. Deuteronomy provides a prophetic road map of Israel's history.

The unconditional covenants (such as the Abrahamic) provide humanity with God's sovereign decrees of where He is taking history. The conditional covenants (such as the Mosaic) provide us with the means He will use to get us there. God has said in the Abrahamic covenant that he will do certain things for the seed of Abraham, and the Mosaic covenant provides conditional stipulations that must be met before a decree from the Abrahamic covenant can take place. God decreed that Israel would receive certain blessings within the land of Israel, but that they would enjoy them only if they were obedient. Thus, Deuteronomy provides a prophetic road map covering the whole of history before Israel started down the road.

RESPONSE TO THE COVENANTS
Prophetic Patterns

As we move progressively through the Bible from the Pentateuch to the prophets, we find that the role of the prophets is similar to that of modern-day ambassadors who represent their government's positions and policy. The prophets provide divine commentary and rebuke to the nation on behalf of God, and always do so in terms of how the nation measures up to her Mosaic covenantal responsibilities.

By the time of the exilic and postexilic prophets, all hope that the nation will accomplish her destiny through corporate obedience has been abandoned. The hope for the nation, as well as for the entire Gentile world, is focused on the performance of a single individual—the Messiah. This prophetically prepares the nation for the first appearance of Messiah in the person of Jesus of Nazareth. Thus, Jesus and the New Testament writers follow the Mosaic and prophetic pattern of documenting specific violations of Israel's covenant (see Matthew 21–23), and this provides the basis for expulsion from the land and scattering among the nations. Thus, the ultimate rejection of God's Son Himself led to a more severe application of the ultimate curse upon the nation than it previously experienced during its first expulsion in the sixth century B.C. under the Babylonians.

Just as Israel was regathered after the Babylonian captivity and returned to the land, so it will be returned from its A.D. 70 diaspora from the nations. However, this time Israel will be regathered in preparation for a seven-year period we know as the Tribulation, which will serve to prepare her for conversion and ultimate covenantal blessing. Such a scenario is supported by an examination of passages from the Old Testament prophets that expand upon—but do not contradict—the Mosaic prophecy of the future Tribulation.

Our Confidence

God has bound Himself to keep the promises He made to the nation of Israel through the unconditional covenantal structure of the royal grant treaty. He also provided a prophetic road map for Israel's history through the device known as a suzerain–vassal treaty as constituted in the book of Deuteronomy. He deals with Israel through these covenantal mechanisms, and He has chosen to bind Himself through covenants. And because of His trustworthiness, we are confident that He will bring these things to pass in the future for both Israel and for all His redeemed people—the church.

—RICHARD MAYHUE AND THOMAS ICE

BIBLIOGRAPHY

Fruchtenbaum, Arnold. *Israelology.* Tustin, CA: Ariel Ministries, 1992.

Kline, Meredith. *The Structure of Biblical Authority.* Grand Rapids: Eerdmans Publishing Company, 1972.

Mendenhall, George. "Covenant." In *International Dictionary of the Bible.* Nashville: Abingdon Press, 1962, vol. 1, pp. 714-15.

Merrill, Eugene. *Deuteronomy.* New American Commentary. Nashville: Broadman & Holman, 1994.

CROWNS

A CROWN IS A CIRCULAR ornament, cap, turban, or wreath worn around the head to designate sovereignty, authority, achievement, or victory. A crown sets the wearer apart for a particular task or in view of some accomplishment. The term *crown* also refers to honor, glory, victory, or a reward.

OLD TESTAMENT

In the Old Testament, there are four different Hebrew words that translate into the English word *crown*.

1. *Netzer* means to be set apart or consecrated and is a cognate of the root for "Nazirite." This term designated the gold plate inscribed with "Holy to the Lord" that was affixed by a blue cord to the front of the turban worn by the high priest (Exodus 28:36-38; 29:6; 39:30; Leviticus 8:9). The king's royal crown was also described by this word (2 Samuel 12:30). Thus both the high priest's crown and the king's crown indicated a position endowed by God. The crowns of Gentile rulers were never described by this word in the Old Testament.

2. The generic term for "crown" (Zechariah 6:11) or "wreath" (Proverbs 4:9) was *'atara*. It designated crowns other than those of the king or high priest, that is, nobility (Esther 8:15), foreign kings (2 Samuel 12:30), a bridegroom (Song of Solomon 3:11), or someone worthy of honor (Proverbs 12:4; 14:24; Ezekiel 16:12; 21:26; 23:42).

3. *Kether* occurs only in Esther and describes the jeweled royal turban of the Persian monarch (Esther 1:11; 2:17; 6:8).

4. Another Hebrew word, *qodqod*, refers to the crown of one's head (Job 2:7).

NEW TESTAMENT

In the New Testament are two Greek words that translate to "crown"—*stephanos* and *diademos*. The *stephanos* was a crown or wreath given as an award in an athletic contest (1 Corinthians 9:25) or a decoration for some achievement in life. New Testament writers use the *stephanos* crown as a metaphor for the honor and rewards bestowed upon faithful believers at the judgment seat of Christ for their meritorious service and spiritual growth (1 Corinthians 3:10-15; 2 Corinthians 5:10). Christians earn these crowns through spiritual achievement, so the crowns do not reflect the believer's salvation or positional blessings, which are given through God's grace.

Four crowns are delineated as potential rewards for different categories of Christian service and devotion: the crown of righteousness (2 Timothy 4:8), the crown of life (James 1:12; Revelation 2:10), the crown of glory (1 Peter 5:4), and the crown of rejoicing (1 Thessalonians 2:19). Paul's reference to an imperishable crown (1 Corinthians 9:25) is a summary of reception of rewards.

Three other *stephanos* crowns also represent rule or sovereignty, especially prominent in the visions of the book of Revelation. The first is that worn by the locusts, the demon army led by Abaddon, the angel of the abyss (Revelation 9:7). The second is the crown of 12 stars worn by the woman who represents Israel (Revelation 12:1). The third is the crown of

thorns forced upon our Lord's head to deride His claims to royalty. In triumph, the risen, glorified Lord wears a golden *stephanos* wreath (Revelation 14:14; Hebrews 2:9).

The *diademos* describes only the headgear of royalty in the New Testament. *Diademos* is used only three times. The first two appearances (Revelation 12:3; 13:1) refer to the secular authorities that will comprise the political powers aligned with the Antichrist during the Tribulation. The third describes the crowns that will be worn by the King of kings and Lord of lords upon His victorious conquest of the earth (Revelation 19:12).

—ROBERT DEAN, JR.

BIBLIOGRAPHY

Benware, Paul N. *The Believer's Payday*. Chattanooga: AMG Publishers, 2001.

Bromiley, Geoffrey W., ed. "Crown." In *The International Standard Bible Encyclopedia*. Grand Rapids: Eerdmans Publishing Company, 1986.

Elwell, Walter A., ed. "Crowns." In *Evangelical Dictionary of Biblical Theology*. Grand Rapids: Baker Books, 1996.

Harris, R. Laird, Gleason L. Archer, Jr., and Bruce K. Waltke. "Nezer" and "'Atara." In *Theological Wordbook of the Old Testament*. Chicago: Moody Press, 1980.

DANIEL, ESCHATOLOGY OF

IN THE JEWISH RECKONING of the Old Testament books, Daniel is not found in the second division (the Prophets) but in the third division (the *Kethubhim*, the Writings). Some believe the reason is that Daniel was written much later than many of the other prophetic books, after the close of that section. In the narrow sense, Daniel was not a prophet but a statesman in the courts of the pagan monarchs of Babylon and Persia. He had the gift of prophecy but did not hold the office of a prophet. It is in this sense that Christ confirms Daniel's historicity and refers to him as a prophet (Matthew 24:15). Daniel is included among the minor prophets, but he is scarcely "minor" in his prophetic utterances. He stands alongside the major prophets of Isaiah, Jeremiah, and Ezekiel (Unger, *Commentary*, p. 1603).

ORTHODOX JEWISH VIEWS OF DANIEL

According to rabbinical scholar Judah J. Slotki, Daniel 7–12 shows "that the course of history is determined by a Divine plan, and it is part of that plan to end, in God's own time, the trials of the righteous" (Slotki, p. xv). He adds that the idea of the establishment of the kingdom of God and the final triumph of righteousness is not confined to Daniel. The same themes appear repeatedly in the earlier prophets, such as Isaiah, Jeremiah, Ezekiel, Hosea, and Amos. Jewish tradition interprets all these predictions as eschatological and does not recognize differences in kind between their prophecies of a universal kingdom of heaven and those of Daniel. Many biblical books imply the immortality of the soul, but the doctrine of the resurrection is explicitly enunciated in Daniel (Slotki, p. xv).

PROPER INTERPRETATION OF DANIEL

In order to correctly interpret Daniel, three assumptions are important. (1) Daniel is a genuine book penned by the prophet Daniel in the sixth century B.C. Many critics argue that Daniel is part of what is called *apocalyptic* literature, which did not arise until well into the Hellenistic period. Critics argue that false authorships and dates are part of such literary genre. But these rationalistic assumptions are unacceptable (Unger, *Commentary*, p. 1605).

The interpretation of any book labeled as apocalyptic does not require a special hermeneutic or interpretative system. To change one's hermeneutic is to place Bible prophecy outside of historic fulfillment. It is a liberal attempt to assign future prophecy to myth or fictional fancy. This destroys the prophetic message.

(2) Right interpretation depends upon the fact that predictive prophecy is not only possible but is actually the warp and woof of true and genuine biblical apocalyptic writings. Predictive prophecy has caused the so-called scholarly rejection of the genuineness of Daniel's visions. Many critics reject outright what is clearly predictive prophecy. The only way for such scholars to

account for Daniel's meticulously accurate prophecies is to explain them away by relegating them to a later time and another author (Unger, *Commentary*, pp. 1605–06).

(3) A correct interpretation of Daniel clarifies the scriptural revelation that God has a future for God's people Israel. Critical thinking about the prophetic message of Daniel creates a makeshift argument for the importance of the book. Such mishandling of the book removes the meaning of the prophecies and makes the writing of Daniel a travesty and a sham.

Daniel is the key to all biblical prophecy. Without Daniel, the far-distant eschatological revelations and the prophetic scope are unexplainable. The Lord's great prophecies in the Olivet Discourse (Matthew 24–25; Mark 13; Luke 21), as well as 2 Thessalonians 2 and the book of Revelation (which both speak of the Antichrist of Daniel 11), can only be understood with the help of Daniel's prophecies (Unger, *Commentary*, p. 1606).

PROPHECIES OF DANIEL
Nebuchadnezzar's Dream of a Statue

Daniel's first prophecy was to relate to King Nebuchadnezzar the details of a dream the king had, and also its interpretation. Daniel said to the king, "I will declare the interpretation to the king" (2:24 NASB), and then he proceeded to interpret for this powerful monarch his vision of an "extraordinary" (2:31) statue with a head of gold, breast and arms of silver, stomach and thighs of bronze, and legs of iron (2:32-33). This was a dream about future world powers. The head of gold is Babylon, the breast and arms represent the Medes and the Persians, the thighs of brass picture Greece, and the legs and feet stand for Rome in its primacy and decline. Finally, a "stone" would arise, representing Israel's Messiah, who would strike "the statue on its feet of iron and clay and [crush] them" (2:34). Then God will establish a kingdom "which will never be destroyed," referring to the far future messianic reign of Christ (2:44).

This prophecy spanned the full range of history and showed that aspects of all these nations would lead into the millennial kingdom. "The temporal aspect will merge into the eternal phase with the creation of the new heaven and earth" (Unger, *Commentary,* p. 1619). With Nebuchadnezzar's dream, God revealed through Daniel the full scope of all of history. No other prophet was given such a full and concise revelation.

The Writing on the Wall

During the reign of Belshazzar (553–539 B.C.), Daniel was summoned to interpret the writing that appeared one night on the wall of the king's banquet hall (Daniel 5). With divine boldness, Daniel declared to Belshazzar he was losing his kingdom because "the God in whose hand are your life-breath and your ways, you have not glorified" (5:23). The writing read, *MENE, MENE, TEKEL, UPHARSIN.* Daniel understood the full meaning behind these words and said, "God has numbered your kingdom and put an end to it....You have been weighed on the scales and found

deficient....Your kingdom has been divided and given over to the Medes and Persians" (5:26-28). That evening, by stealth Median soldiers slipped into Babylon and took over the capital city and the kingdom. "That same night Belshazzar the Chaldean king was slain. So Darius the Mede received the kingdom at about the age of sixty-two" (5:30-31).

Four Beasts

During the first year of the reign of Belshazzar, God revealed to Daniel another summary of the coming great world empires. Through a dream and night visions, Daniel saw the stirring of the sea (representing the peoples of the earth) and four great beasts coming forth, each "different from one another" (7:2-3). The animals were a lion, bear, leopard, and a nondescript beast that was "dreadful and terrifying and extremely strong" (7:7). Overlaying this prophecy with Nebuchadnezzar's statue, the animals represented Babylon (the lion), Medo-Persia (the bear),

DANIEL'S OUTLINE OF THE FUTURE

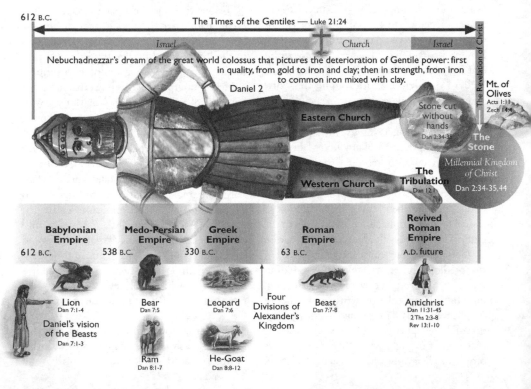

612 B.C.

The Times of the Gentiles — Luke 21:24

Israel   Church   Israel

The Revelation of Christ

Nebuchadnezzar's dream of the great world colossus that pictures the deterioration of Gentile power: first in quality, from gold to iron and clay; then in strength, from iron to common iron mixed with clay.

Daniel 2

Eastern Church

Stone cut without hands
Dan 2:34-35

Mt. of Olives
Acts 1:11
Zech 14:4

The Stone

Western Church

The Tribulation
Dan 12:1

Millennial Kingdom of Christ
Dan 2:34-35,44

Babylonian Empire	Medo-Persian Empire	Greek Empire		Roman Empire	Revived Roman Empire
612 B.C.	538 B.C.	330 B.C.		63 B.C.	A.D. future

Lion
Dan 7:1-4

Daniel's vision of the Beasts
Dan 7:1-3

Bear
Dan 7:5

Ram
Dan 8:1-7

Leopard
Dan 7:6

He-Goat
Dan 8:8-12

Four Divisions of Alexander's Kingdom

Beast
Dan 7:7-8

Antichrist
Dan 11:31-45
2 Ths 2:3-8
Rev 13:1-10

Greece (the leopard) with its four generals who divided the kingdom of Alexander the Great following his death, and Rome (the fourth beast). But a significant new element was added to this revelation.

The Son of Man

Daniel was given a heavenly vision of the Son of Man coming up before God Almighty, the Ancient of Days, and before His fiery and awesome throne of judgment (7:9-14). During the Upper Room Discourse, the Lord Jesus told His disciples that He (the Son of Man) would return back to His heavenly Father, who sent Him to the earth to die for humanity (John 14:1-6,28; 16:28). His departure back to glory was actually witnessed by these loyal followers. The angels told them that Jesus "has been taken up from you into heaven, [and] will come in just the same way as you have watched Him go into heaven" (Acts 1:11). Daniel was perhaps witnessing the Lord's ascension and entrance into the throne room of God after He had died for the sins of humanity. Daniel sees the Son of Man "coming, and He came up to the Ancient of Days and was presented before Him" (Daniel 7:13). Both the deity and the humanity of Christ are seen in these important designations of Jesus. He was the prophesied Son of God (Psalm 2:7) and Son of Man. The Son of Man designation shows that Christ was not only deity, but also a human being (Montgomery, p. 318).

To the Son of Man is given "dominion, glory and a kingdom, that all the peoples, nations, and men of every language might serve Him. His dominion is an everlasting dominion which will not pass away; and His kingdom is one which will not be destroyed" (Daniel 7:14). This is actually a fifth kingdom that will last for 1000 years during earth's history as we know it (Revelation 20:4-9). But this kingdom will transition into eternity with the new Jerusalem and the new heaven and earth, where peace and righteousness will prevail (Revelation 21–22).

Over this kingdom, the Messiah, the Highest One (Daniel 7:18,22,25,27) will reign: "The sovereignty, the dominion, and the greatness of all the kingdoms under the whole heaven will be given to the people of the saints of the Highest One; His kingdom will be an everlasting kingdom, and all the dominions will serve and obey Him" (7:27).

The 70 Weeks

Because of Daniel's piety and faithfulness, he is given one of the few timeline and calendar prophecies in all of the Scriptures. In 9:20-27 he receives the 70-weeks prediction of the rebuilding of the Temple and the city of Jerusalem that had been destroyed by the Babylonians. This prophecy also shows with remarkable accuracy the period and the very year of the rejection of the Messiah. And it also clearly predicts the seven-year worldwide Tribulation. (See "Seventy Weeks of Daniel.")

Other World Rulers

Daniel also predicted the rise of the "little horn," who was Antiochus Epiphanes, historically described in 1 Maccabees 1–6. In Daniel 8 the prophet sees a two-horned ram representing the Medo-Persian Empire. The ram pushes "westward, northward, and southward" (8:4) with furious intensity and expands the kingdom of the Persians. With keen prophetic insight Daniel foretells the harsh conquests of the Medo-Persians (539–331 B.C.). But then he sees a male goat that would be Alexander the Great (8:6-7). Daniel then predicts the breaking up of Alexander's Empire into four parts (8:8) and describes the coming of Antiochus (8:9-10,23-25).

The Antichrist

In 11:36-45 Daniel predicts the coming of the Antichrist. In chapter 7 the prophet also described him as "another horn, a little one… [with] eyes like the eyes of a man and a mouth uttering great boasts" (7:8). He is "the other horn" (7:20), the one whose dominion "will be taken away, annihilated and destroyed forever" (7:26). The apostle Paul picks up the description and calls this one "the man of lawlessness" and "the son of destruction" (2 Thessalonians 2:3) and the "lawless one" (2:8), who will someday in a rebuilt Temple in Jerusalem be "displaying himself as being God" (2:4). The apostle John refers to him in 1 John 2:18,22; 4:3; and 2 John 7. He especially mentions him in the book of Revelation, beginning in chapter 13.

The Resurrection

Daniel's final great prophecy has to do with the future resurrection of the Old Testament saints. "Many of those who sleep in the dust will awake, these to everlasting life, but the others [the lost] to disgrace and everlasting contempt" (Daniel 12:2). The righteous will shine forever like the stars (12:3). It is interesting to note that here, Daniel understands that both the righteous and the unrighteous exist into eternity. Those who have rejected God do not experience "soul sleep."

DANIEL'S INTERPRETATION OF PROPHECY

Daniel's prophecies contain much imagery, but what he envisioned and prophesied is to be taken in a full historical, normal, and literal sense. Behind Daniel's imagery is a literal fulfillment. As well, the imagery is about actual people or nations that either existed in the days of Daniel or would come on the world stage in the future.

In his prophecies, Daniel portrays the course of Gentile world power—"the times of the Gentiles" (Luke 21:24). And through the passage of history, we have seen many of these prophecies fulfilled. Still to come is the event in which great nations are destroyed by a fifth kingdom (the Messiah's), which is depicted as a stone cut out without hands (Daniel 2:34,45). Because of Daniel's great faithfulness, God promises him that he will enter into rest and will "rise again for [his] allotted portion [and reward] at the end of the age" (12:13).

—MAL COUCH

BIBLIOGRAPHY

Archer, Gleason L. A Survey of Old Testament Introduction. Chicago: Moody Press, 1994.

Freeman, Hobart E. An Introduction to the Old Testament Prophets. Chicago: Moody Press, 1969.

Leupold, H.C. Exposition of Daniel. Grand Rapids: Baker Books, 1969.

Montgomery, James A. A Critical and Exegetical Commentary on the Book of Daniel. Edinburgh: T. & T. Clark, 1989.

Neusner, Jacob. Dictionary of Judaism in the Biblical Period. Peabody, MA: Hendrickson, 1999.

Patai, Raphael. The Messiah Texts. Detroit, MI: Wayne State University Press, 1979.

Pusey, E.B. Daniel the Prophet. Minneapolis: Klock & Klock, 1985.

Slotki, Judah J. Daniel, Ezra, Nehemiah. New York: Soncino Books, 1968.

Unger, Merrill F. Unger's Commentary on the Old Testament. Chattanooga: AMG Publishers, 2002.

———. Introductory Guide to the Old Testament. Grand Rapids: Zondervan, 1981.

DAVIDIC COVENANT

THE DAVIDIC COVENANT is hinted at in God's covenant with Abraham (Genesis 12:1-3), stated clearly in Psalm 89 and 2 Samuel 7, and progressively developed throughout the rest of the Old Testament. It reveals God's eternal plan for His people, the nation of Israel.

The Lord said to Abraham, "I will make you a great nation" (Genesis 12:2 NASB). Later He said, "I will greatly bless you, and I will greatly multiply your seed as the stars of the heavens, and as the sand which is on the seashore" (22:17). From Abraham's seed (plural) would come a Seed (singular) who would secure the blessings for all of Abraham's descendants. The Seed is the Son of David, the Lord Jesus Christ.

The Davidic covenant includes many issues that are important in the study of Bible prophecy. Will a literal kingdom exist on the earth? Is the church the kingdom? Does the church replace the nation of Israel? Is Christ the Messiah of Israel in particular or simply the leader of the church in general? Will Israel be regathered and restored, and will David be coruler with the Lord Jesus?

A FAMILY OF KINGS

When God rejected Saul as king of Israel (1 Samuel 16:1), He said to Samuel, "I have selected a king for Myself among" the sons of Jesse, the father of David. Saul himself said to David, "You are more righteous than I" (24:17), and he concluded, "Now, behold, I know that you will surely be king, and that the kingdom of Israel will be established in your hand" (24:20).

After Saul's death, the Lord gave David a promise through His prophet Nathan. God said that David's son Solomon "shall build a house for My name, and I will establish the throne of his kingdom forever" (2 Samuel 7:13). The Lord added, "Your house and your kingdom shall endure before Me forever; your throne shall be established forever" (7:16). This promise is the basis of the Davidic covenant.

David's "house" is a reference to his family lineage. David's "throne" symbolizes his family's rulership over the kingdom of Israel. The "kingdom" included the people and their land. Subsequent generations of Israelites in both the Old and New Testaments knew this promise and accepted it literally: Only through the family of David would kings come to rule in Israel.

Psalm 89 rehearses the Davidic covenant. The Lord says, "I have made a covenant with My chosen; I have sworn to David My servant, I will establish your seed forever and build up your throne to all generations" (89:3-4). David is God's chosen (89:19), His servant, and His anointed (89:20). David would have a strong one (David's horn) who would come out of his loins and be exalted (89:24). This horn would cry to God, "You are my Father, My God, and the rock of my salvation" (89:26). He would be the Lord's "firstborn, the highest of the kings of the earth" (89:27). The Lord adds, "So I will establish [David's seed] forever, and his throne as the days of heaven" (89:29).

JESUS AND THE DAVIDIC COVENANT

The promises to the Davidic line continue into the future. God tells the kingly "house of David" (Isaiah 7:13) that it will receive a sign: "Behold, a virgin will be with child and bear a son and she will call His name Immanuel" (7:14). The Son of David will be the child, and God will give him to the Jewish people as a blessing (9:6). He has one long and unbroken name: "Wonderful Counselor, Mighty God, Eternal Father, Prince of Peace," and "there will be no end to the increase of His government or of peace. On the throne of David and over his kingdom, to establish it and to uphold it with justice and righteousness from then on and forevermore. The zeal of the LORD of hosts will accomplish this" (9:7).

About this Son of David, Unger (p. 1168) writes:

His rule as Prince of Peace will be universal in the earth and perpetual—the millennial Kingdom ultimately merging into the eternal Kingdom (1 Corinthians 15:24-28; Revelation 22:1-5)....He will reign as David's Son (humanity) and Lord (Deity), as the divine-human Redeemer (Revelation 19:16; 20:4-6) in fulfillment of the Davidic Covenant (2 Samuel 7:12-13; 23:1-5; Ezekiel 34:23; 37:24; Hosea 3:5; Amos 9:11; Luke 2:4; see also Acts 1:6)....[His] rule will be eternal, "forever," outlasting the earthly Kingdom age and merging into the eternal rule of the Lamb (Revelation 20:1,3).

The Gospels repeatedly refer to Jesus' relationship to David and to his covenant. Before the birth of Jesus, the angel Gabriel told Mary, "He will be great and will be called the Son of the Most High; and the Lord God will give Him the throne of His father David; and He will reign over the house of Jacob forever, and His kingdom will have no end" (Luke 1:32-33). Mary also learned that the child in her womb was the promised Son of God prophesied in Psalm 2 (Luke 1:35). In her prayer of thanksgiving, Mary realized that the birth of her Son was somehow related to the promises God made to Abraham. She cried out that God "has given help to Israel His servant, in remembrance of His mercy, as He spoke to our fathers, to Abraham and his descendants forever" (1:54-55).

In Zecharias' prayer of thanks for the birth of his son John (the Baptist), he quotes part of the Davidic covenant. He said that God had provided redemption for His people, "and has raised up a horn of salvation for us in the house of David His servant" (Luke 1:68-69). He is quoting part of the psalm of the Davidic covenant where the Lord speaks of David His "servant" (Psalm 89:20) and exhalts David's "horn" (89:24). Zecharias also ties the Davidic covenant to the Abrahamic promises. He prophesies the horn of salvation from David's house is salvation from Israel's enemies: "to show mercy toward our fathers, and to remember His holy covenant, the oath which He swore to Abraham our father" (Luke 1:69-72).

As Jesus ministered, even certain blind beggars understood He was the Son of David who fulfilled the messianic promises. The blind men cried out, "Have mercy on us, Son of David" (Matthew 9:27). Peter and the other disciples realized that the Davidic covenant included many doctrines about the Messiah. Peter told his fellow Jews that the Messiah, "by the predetermined plan and foreknowledge of God," was nailed to the cross and put to death for sins (Acts 2:23). He referred his hearers to David's prophecy that the Messiah would be the Holy One who would not suffer decay (Psalm 16:8-11; Acts 2:25-28). God had sworn to David that he would have a descendant who would someday sit on his throne; therefore, the resurrection was certain (Acts 2:30-31).

Peter argues that David could not have been prophesying about himself in Psalm 16 and in other psalms because David experienced death and had not ascended into heaven to sit at the right hand of God as did Jesus (Acts 2:34). Peter then quotes Psalm 110:1 and says about Christ, "The LORD said to my Lord, sit at My right hand, until I make Your enemies a footstool for Your feet."

A LITERAL INTERPRETATION

The Davidic covenant is to be interpreted literally. Five points confirm this in 2 Samuel 7 and Psalm 89: (1) The words and grammar convey a literal meaning. They give no indication that we are to spiritualize the promises. (2) The covenant is distinctly for the nation of Israel and not the church. (3) The covenant is called a perpetual covenant. Scripture gives no indication that it is to cease at some point in the future. (4) God confirmed the covenant with an oath (Psalm 89:3,4,33; 132:11). (5) God promised He will never break this covenant. "My covenant I will not violate, nor will I alter the utterance of My lips. Once I have sworn by My holiness; I will not lie to David. His descendants shall endure forever, and his throne as the sun before Me" (Psalm 89:34-36). God will fulfill the Davidic covenant when the Lord Jesus reigns on the throne of His father David for 1000 years.

In the book of Revelation, John the apostle reminds the church at Philadelphia that Christ is the one who fulfills the Davidic covenant.

John writes that Christ "is holy, who is true, who has the key of David, who opens and no one will shut, and who shuts and no one opens" (Revelation 3:7). Jesus is also the "Lion that is from the tribe of Judah, the Root of David" who has the authority to open the seven-sealed book that actually begins the Tribulation (5:5). And Jesus Himself says that He is "the root and the descendant of David, the bright morning star" (22:16). Jesus reminds the church of the Davidic covenant, but He never relates this covenant to the church! Christ's future kingly reign is not allegorized to refer to His leadership over the church.

ANSWERING THE PROGRESSIVE INTERPRETATION

Progressive dispensationalists argue that Christ is now on the Davidic throne in heaven because He is seated at the right hand of God in glory (Psalm 110:1-2). They argue this from several quotes in the epistles of Paul. "The description of Christ as 'seated at the right hand of God' in Colossians 3:1 appears in context with the phrase 'kingdom of His [God's] beloved Son' (1:13), a phrase that combines three features of Davidic promise—kingdom, abiding loving-kindness, and sonship—and applies them all to Jesus' present position and activity" in heaven (Blaising and Bock, p. 179). But Psalm 110 says Christ is seated not on His messianic throne but at the right hand of God (110:1). The verses in this psalm refer to His earthly rule and not His headship over the church.

Progressives emphasize Psalm 110:4: "The LORD has sworn and will not change His mind, You are a priest forever according to the order of Melchizedek." Is His Melchizedekian priesthood related to the Davidic covenant or to the New Covenant, which has to do with His sacrifice for sin and redemption? This verse is sandwiched between verses about Christ's future Davidic reign on earth, but the writer of Hebrews ties the Melchizedek relationship to the New Covenant and not to the Davidic.

The writer says that Christ "remains a priest perpetually" (Hebrews 7:3)—as a priest like Melchizedek, with no priestly tribal connections or priestly lineage. In this position He "has become the guarantee of a better covenant" (7:22), and He did this by offering Himself as a sacrifice (7:27). As a priest like Melchizedek, and one not after the Levitical priestly line, Christ brought about the initiation of the New Covenant, as the writer of Hebrews points out (8:8-13; Jeremiah 31:31-34). The author of Hebrews never indicates that Christ is now reigning on the throne of David in heaven!

Pentecost (p. 104) makes this conclusion:

> It can be shown that in all the preaching concerning the kingdom by John (Matthew 3:2), by Christ (Matthew 4:17), by the twelve (Matthew 10:5-7), by the seventy (Luke 10:1-12), not once is the kingdom offered to Israel anything but an earthly literal kingdom.... Christ anticipates such a literal earthly kingdom (Matthew 25:1-13, 31-46). The New Testament never relates the kingdom promised to David to Christ's present session.

The Davidic covenant will be fulfilled in the future when the Lord comes to earth and sits "on His glorious throne" (Matthew 25:31). As king, He will call all who are blessed of His Father and say, "Inherit the kingdom prepared for you from the foundation of the world" (25:34). Though this kingdom will last 1000 years, it is an eternal kingdom that will go on into eternity. Since the "throne," "house," and "kingdom" were all promised to David in perpetuity, Messiah's reign over David's kingdom from David's throne must never end. The Davidic covenant is therefore of vital importance to the understanding of future events.

—MAL COUCH

BIBLIOGRAPHY

Blaising, Craig A., and Darrell L. Bock, *Progressive Dispensationalism*. Wheaton, IL: Bridgepoint, 1993.

Couch, Mal, gen. ed., *Dictionary of Premillennial Theology*. Grand Rapids: Kregel, 1996.

Pentecost, J. Dwight, *Things to Come*. Grand Rapids: Zondervan, 1964.

Ryrie, Charles C., *Dispensationalism*. Chicago: Moody, 1995.

Thomas, Robert L., *Evangelical Hermeneutics*. Grand Rapids: Kregel, 2002.

Unger, Merrill F., *Unger's Commentary on the Old Testament*. Chattanooga: AMG Publishers, 2002.

DAY OF THE LORD

THE DAY OF THE LORD" is a key biblical phrase in understanding God's revelation about the future. The New Testament writers used this phrase according to their understanding of the Old Testament prophets. A survey of the prophets indicates the term was used in reference to both near historical fulfillment and far future eschatological events. The New Testament writers picked up on the eschatological usage and applied the phrase to both the judgment that will climax the Tribulation period and the judgment that will usher in the new earth.

The day of the Lord is one of the major strands woven throughout the fabric of biblical prophecy. Without a clear understanding of it, God's plan for the future is obscure.

"The day of the Lord" appears in four uncontested New Testament passages (Acts 2:20; 1 Thessalonians 5:2; 2 Thessalonians 2:2; and 2 Peter 3:10). However, the prophets actually wrote more about it and provided the basis for whatever Peter and Paul understood about it.

THE OLD TESTAMENT DATA

The phrase "the day of the Lord" appears 19 times in the Old Testament. The expression occurs in six minor and two major prophetic books.

Obadiah

Obadiah relates the family feud between Israel (Jacob) and Edom (Esau). The theme of this book is the day of the Lord experienced first by Edom and second by the nations (15-16) who walked in Edom's way. Obadiah 15 is the pivotal verse. The fact that the language of verses 1-14 is singularly applied to Edom warrants a near-future fulfillment—in all likelihood, Nebuchadnezzar's plunder. However, the language of verses 15-21 points to the far future and the establishment of God's kingdom.

Walter Kaiser (pp. 188–89) notes, "As for the fulfillment of this prophecy, Obadiah combined in one picture what history split into different times and events...having near and distant events, or multiple fulfillments, all being part of the single truth-intention of the author with its more immediate victory over Edom and the distant total victory of the kingdom of God."

To summarize, Obadiah makes several contributions to the biblical pattern. It combines the near view (with particular reference to Edom, verses 1-14) with the far view (involving all the nations, verses 15-21). It predicts judgment and destruction of all the godless (verses 15-16,18). The restoration of Israel is involved in the far view (verses 17-21) but is not evident in the near. The near is a preview, taste, and guarantee of what the far will involve in a lesser-to-greater logical flow. Finally, the day of the Lord ends with the establishment of God's kingdom (verse 21).

Joel

The day of the Lord is mentioned five times in Joel (1:15; 2:1; 2:11; 2:31; 3:14). The details in each passage are similar, but enough differences occur to suggest that Joel begins with a very narrow historical sample (a locust plague) and expands it to include a universal, eschatological application.

Joel uses themes in his description of the day of the Lord that other prophets pick up later:

Joel 1:15	Destruction	Isaiah 13:6
Joel 2:2	Day of Darkness	Zephaniah 1:15
Joel 2:2	Day of Clouds	Zephaniah 1:15; Ezekiel 30:3
Joel 2:2	Thick Darkness	Zephaniah 1:15
Joel 2:11; 2:31	Great	Zephaniah 1:14; Malachi 4:5
Joel 2:31; 3:15	Cosmic Disturbances	Isaiah 13:10
Joel 2:31	Terrible	Malachi 4:5

The locusts of Joel are real locusts or grasshoppers that had recently played havoc with Judah's countryside. They ravaged the fields and ruined the harvest. This vivid evidence of destruction is the basis for Joel to warn the nation to repent lest the day of the Lord soon come with even greater destruction (1:15). The message of Joel 1 is that natural disasters like locust plagues are harbingers of imminent divine destruction.

The warning of impending disaster and the past experience of the locusts in Joel 1 are used in Joel 2 to describe the future destruction caused by an invading human army. As Joel's prophecy proceeds, it grows in its intensity and scope. Joel 2:18-27 functions as a transition from the near view to the far view. The events that Joel predicts in 2:28-32 will be spectacular. God will pour out His Spirit on all mankind (2:28-29). Cosmic disturbances will flash God's greatness from the skies (2:30-31). Repentance will be available to everyone (2:32; see Obadiah 17).

Most significant in 2:31 (NKJV) is the statement that the great cosmic signs will be a prelude "before the coming of the great and awesome day of the Lord." This seems to limit the day of the Lord to the very end of the Tribulation if Joel 3:15, Matthew 24:29, and Revelation 6:12 refer to the same event. The day of the Lord at the end of the Tribulation will contain unmistakable manifestations of God's greatness. It will include both physical disturbances (see 2 Peter 3:10) and spiritual revival.

Amos

The prophecy in Amos 5:18,20 about the day of the Lord has an important historical setting. The prophet wrote to the northern tribes (7:10) and King Jeroboam, predicting their future exile to Assyria (5:27; 6:14; 7:9; 7:17). Amaziah, the priest of Bethel, accused Amos of conspiracy (7:10) and attempted to send Amos back to Judah. Amos' message of judgment conflicted with Amaziah's message of peace and prosperity.

These self-righteous Israelites mistakenly longed for the day of Yahweh's return, which they thought would bring them blessing and prosperity. Amos' description of the day of the

Lord was diametrically opposed to this view (5:18-20). According to Amos, it is not a day of delight but of darkness—a day of gloom, not gladness.

The day that Amos envisioned was the fall of Samaria in 722 B.C. (2 Kings 17). Amos stresses the inevitability of this destruction (5:19-20). He does not use "the day of the Lord" to portray the eschatological expression of God's judgment. However, Amos does anticipate God's intervention on behalf of Israel to reestablish His kingdom (9:11-15).

Isaiah

Isaiah 2:12 is the first mention of the day of the Lord in Isaiah's prophecy. This chapter emphasizes the future establishment of God's kingdom (2:2-4), the present sinful state of Israel (2:5-9), and the future day of reckoning (2:10-22). The prophet appears to look beyond the near and into the distant future in the judgment of 2:10-22, just as he had looked to the eschatological kingdom in 2:1-4. Several indicators of millennial conditions appear in 2:1-4 (see also Revelation 20:1-6). Mt. Zion will be the world capital, and all the nations will come to it (2:1-2) in order to seek God's word (2:3). God will judge between the nations, and war will be no more (2:4-5). This eschatological emphasis in 2:2-4 leads us to conclude that eschatological judgment is in view in 2:10-22.

Isaiah describes the day of the Lord as a time of universal humiliation for all who are proud (2:11-12,17). In contrast, God will display the splendor of His majesty, and the population will flee in terror to caves for protection (2:10,19,21). The Lord alone will be exalted (2:11,17). The timing and terminology of Isaiah 2:21 are strikingly similar to the description of the sixth seal in Revelation 6:16-17.

Isaiah 13:1-8 deals with God's use of Babylon as His instrument of indignation for the destruction of Israel (13:5-6). This reminds one of Habakkuk's dismay that God would do such a thing (Habakkuk 1:2-4). Isaiah had the day of the Lord in mind (13:6) even though it would not come for over 100 years, when Babylon destroyed Judah in 586 B.C.

However, Isaiah 13:9-16 speaks of implications for the far future: cosmic disturbances (13:10,13; see also Matthew 24:29; Revelation 6:12-13; Joel 2:31) and the universal judgment of mankind (13:11; see 2:11-12). The near emphasis returns in 13:17-22, where Isaiah describes the end of Babylon.

Zephaniah

This prophecy pictures Judah as the sacrifice (1:7) that is offered to God by the priest Babylon. Zephaniah begins with a broad, universal perspective (1:1-3) and then narrows his focus to the immediate situation of Judah (1:4-13). Finally he returns to the universal in 1:14-18.

In vivid terms, Zephaniah 1:14 portrays the day of the Lord as a day of wrath. He further describes it as characterized by trouble and distress, destruction and desolation, darkness and gloom, clouds and thick darkness, and trumpet and battle cry.

Ezekiel

Ezekiel wrote during the fulfillment of the near day of the Lord's judgment (13:5). He was taken captive to Babylon in 597 B.C. when Johoiachin was exiled (1:2). Ezekiel 13 was written in 592 B.C., six years after the second phase of the captivity. Here Ezekiel prophesied against false prophets (verses 1-16) and prophetesses (17-23). They had prophesied from their own hearts (13:2) and preached an imaginary peace when in fact there was no peace (13:10).

Ezekiel never explicitly makes the far eschatological application to all nations as Obadiah does in Obadiah 15-21. Yet Charles Feinberg (p. 173) suggests that we may assume such an application. The day of God's judgment on Egypt may be identified in principle with that day when He will call all nations to account.

Zechariah

Zechariah is the first postexilic prophet to speak explicitly of the day of the Lord. Because the Assyrian and Babylonian judgments were history, Zechariah's entire prophecy deals with the far eschatological expectation. His subject in chapter 14 is the day of the Lord and its subsequent results. The chapter states that things will get worse (14:2,5) before they get better (14:1,14). God will then intervene against the nations and fight on Israel's behalf (14:3-5,12-13). This pictures Christ's return at Armageddon (see Joel 3; Matthew 24; Revelation 19) to establish His millennial kingdom and to claim His rightful place on the throne of David.

Zechariah always describes the day of the Lord as a day of God's anger and wrath, not a day of God's blessing. Thus we may conclude that it is the time when God intervenes as the righteous Judge to impose and execute His decreed punishment. After the eschatological day of the Lord fulfills God's judgments, God will reign on earth and bless His people. The blessings that are tied to the day of the Lord are chronologically consequent to it, not inherent within it.

Malachi

The great and terrible day of Malachi 4:5 (see also Joel 2:11,31; Zephaniah 1:14) is described in 4:1-3. It is clearly a day of judgment, as the reference to furnaces, fire, chaff, and ash clearly show. It points to the end of the Tribulation, when the wrath of the Lamb and Almighty God will be poured out (see Revelation 6:16-17; 16:14).

THE PROPHETIC FULFILLMENT

God's servants the prophets spoke of the day of the Lord as both near historical and far eschatological events. Many passages contain a movement from the near to the far event. The prominent theme of every "day of the Lord" prophecy is God's judgment of sin. The blessings of God's reign are subsequent to and a result of the day of the Lord, but they are not a part of it.

R.V.G. Tasker (p. 45) observes, "The expression 'the day of the Lord' at the time of the rise of the great prophets of Israel denoted an event to which the Israelites were looking forward as the day of Jehovah's final vindication of the *righteousness of His people* against their enemies."

George Ladd (p. 68) adds, "The prophets viewed the immediate historical future against the background of the final eschatological consummation, for the same God who was acting in history would finally establish his Kingdom in the future."

"The day of the Lord" is a biblical phrase used by God's prophets to describe either the immediate future or the ultimate eschatological consummation. They used it to describe several events. Readers must interpret the appearance of it in its context to determine whether the prophet expected the immediate historical act of God or Yahweh's ultimate eschatological visitation.

Two periods of the day of the Lord are yet to be fulfilled on earth: (1) the judgment that climaxes the Tribulation period (2 Thessalonians 2:2; Revelation 16–18) and (2) the consummating judgment of this earth that ushers in the new earth (2 Peter 3:10-13; Revelation 20:7–21:1). The Old Testament's use of "the day of the Lord" provides a basis for a more accurate interpretation of Acts 2:20, 1 Thessalonians 5:2, 2 Thessalonians 2:2, and 2 Peter 3:10, which all have an eschatological emphasis.

G.M. Burge (p. 295) notes that the New Testament maintains a futurist expectation of the day of the Lord in relation to the second coming of Christ in judgment on the "day of Christ" (Philippians 1:10; 2 Thessalonians 2:2). Thus, the New Testament writers interpret this day in light of its eschatological fulfillment in the future.

—RICHARD L. MAYHUE

BIBLIOGRAPHY

Burge, G.M. "Day of Christ, God, the Lord," in *Evangelical Dictionary of Theology*. Grand Rapids: Baker Books, 1984.

Feinberg, Charles. *The Minor Prophets*. Chicago: Moody Press, 1976.

Kaiser, Walter. *Towards an Old Testament Theology*. Grand Rapids: Zondervan, 1978.

Ladd, George. *The Presence of the Future*. Grand Rapids: Eerdmans Publishing Company, 1974.

Price, W.K. *The Prophet Joel and the Day of the Lord*. Chicago: Moody Press, 1971.

Tasker, R.V.G. *The Biblical Doctrine of the Wrath of God*. London: The Tyndale Press, 1951.

DECEPTION

DECEPTION IS THE INTENTIONAL misleading of another person through word or deed. Though deception can be used for good purposes (such as when the Hebrew midwives deceived Pharaoh to save the lives of the newborn males [Exodus 1:19]), it is most often used to describe the unethical exploitation of another person or the teaching of erroneous doctrine.

THE USAGE OF DECEIT

Old Testament Usage

The primary Hebrew word for *deceit* is *ramah* and its related word group. *Ramah* is used to refer to personal and ethical deception. The verb form *(ramah)* is found eight times in the Old Testament and describes betrayal, deceit, or treachery. For example, the Gibeonites deceived Israel into making a treaty with them (Joshua 9:22). The noun form *(mirmah)* occurs 40 times in the Old Testament. It denotes one person's deceit of another. Because Shechem had raped their sister, Dinah, "Jacob's sons answered Shechem and his father Hamor with deceit" (Genesis 34:13 NASB). Amos condemns dishonest merchants who "cheat with dishonest scales" (Amos 8:5). Proverbs 11:1 says, "A false balance is an abomination to the LORD." The tongue of the wicked is said to be "deceitful" (Psalm 52:4). The "little horn," a reference to Antiochus Epiphanes, will use shrewdness and deceit to gain power, but then he will attempt to destroy God's people (Daniel 8:25) (Carpenter and Grisanti, pp. 1122-23).

The second Hebrew word for *deception* is *patah* and is translated by the Greek *apatao* in the Septuagint. The verb *patah* in the Niphal form means "to be deceived" (Job 31:9), in the Piel form, "to deceive" (2 Samuel 3:25; Proverbs 24:28), and in the Pual form, "to be deceived" (Jeremiah 20:7,10). Like *ramah*, *patah* refers to ethical and personal deception.

New Testament Usage

The New Testament uses several Greek words for *deceit: plane* (error), *dolos* (cunning or treachery), *apate* (deception, deceitfulness), and *paralogizomai* (deceive, delude).

The New Testament uses the active verb form *planao* almost exclusively in an apocalyptic sense (Gunther, p. 459). In Jesus' Olivet Discourse, He warns about false messiahs who would mislead many (Matthew 24:5; see also Mark 13:6; Luke 21:8). Paul predicts apostasy in the last days and warns that "evil men and imposters will proceed from bad to worse, deceiving and being deceived" (2 Timothy 3:13). John uses *planao* in an ethical and spiritual sense in 1 John 1:8: "If we say that we have no sin, we are deceiving ourselves and the truth is not in us" (see also 3:7). And like Paul, John warns about false teachers or antichrists "who are trying to deceive you" (1 John 2:26; 2 John 7). Paul, Peter, John, and Jude all use the noun *plane* to warn about the deceptive tactics of false teachers (2 Thessalonians 2:11; 2 Peter 2:18; 1 John 4:6; Jude 11-13). Jude's depiction of false teachers as wandering stars gives the primary idea of *planao*. Like stars that have moved out of their established place, false teachers have strayed from the truth and have attempted to persuade others to follow their erroneous ways. Thus, though *planao* has a spatial sense, the New Testament writers use it in a theological or ethical sense to describe those who have departed from the truth.

Deceit or *treachery (dolos)* is used primarily in an ethical sense. Jesus lists deceit *(dolos)* in a list of vices to emphasize that it is not what goes into the stomach but what comes out of the heart that corrupts a person (Mark 7:21-23). Paul condemns the Jewish sorcerer Elymas, declaring, "You who are full of all deceit and fraud, you son of the devil, you enemy of all righteousness, will you not cease to make crooked the straight ways of the Lord?" (Acts 13:10). Paul includes deceit *(dolos)* as one of the sins of depraved mankind (Romans 1:29). He calls false apostles "deceitful workers" (2 Corinthians 11:13). Peter urges believers to put aside "all malice and all deceit *(dolon)* and hypocrisy and envy and all slander" (1 Peter 2:1). In contrast to wicked, deceitful men, Jesus commended Nathaniel because he was a true Israelite, "in whom there is no deceit!" (John 1:47). Paul distanced himself from the deceitful ways of false teachers (1 Thessalonians 2:3). Peter praised Christ as a perfect example of one who suffered unjustly because He "committed no sin, nor was any deceit found in His mouth" (1 Peter 2:22). The arch-deceiver is Satan, whom the triumphant Christ will cast into the lake of fire (Revelation 20:10).

The New Testament uses *apatao* and *apate* both theologically and ethically. Paul cautions the Thessalonians not to be deceived by false teachers who claim that the day of the Lord has come (2 Thessalonians 2:1-4; see also Ephesians 5:6; Colossians 2:8). Jesus employs the word in its ethical sense to warn of the seductive attraction of riches (Matthew 13:22; see also Mark 4:19). Paul, Peter, and the unnamed author of Hebrews each use the term to expose the deceptive power of sin (Romans 7:11; Hebrews 3:13; 2 Peter 2:13). Paul uses it twice to refer to Satan's deception of Eve (2 Corinthians 11:3; 1 Timothy 2:14).

Paul uses *paralogizomai* (deceive, delude) to warn about persuasive arguments that might lead *(paralogizetai)* true believers astray (Colossians 2:4). James says that believers can deceive themselves by hearing the word but not doing it (James 1:22). Both passages contain the underlying idea of something that gives the impression that it is true or right when it is actually wrong.

THE SIGNIFICANCE FOR ESCHATOLOGY

Deceit is one of the sins of unbelievers (Mark 7:21-23; Romans 1:29). According to John, anyone who continues in sin fails the moral test for authentic faith (1 John 3:3-6). True believers cannot consistently engage in deceit. Thus, believers are urged to purify themselves in preparation for the return of Christ (1 John 3:2-3).

Jesus and the New Testament writers predicted that in the current age, false teachers would attempt to mislead believers by deceptive teaching. And apparently, as the present age approaches its end and the beginning of the Tribulation draws near, false teachers will proliferate, and their efforts to mislead uninformed unbelievers and gullible believers will intensify (2 Timothy 3:13).

The Antichrist (the beast out of the sea) and the False Prophet (the beast out of the earth) will work together to deceive people to worship Satan (the dragon) during the Tribulation (Revelation 13:1-18). But beware: Satan (who is the arch-deceiver), the beast, and the False Prophet are destined for the lake of fire (Revelation 20:10).

THE SERIOUSNESS OF DECEIT

Deceit, the deliberate misleading of another person, can serve good or evil purposes. When it is used for evil, it is a deadly sin. Eve disobeyed God because Satan deceived her, and all creation became captive to sin. Both the Old and New Testaments condemn ethical and theological deceit, warning of God's judgment on all who are deceitful.

—W.H. MARTY

BIBLIOGRAPHY

Braun, Herbert. "Planaõ" *Theological Dictionary of the New Testament*, vol. VI, ed. Gerhard Kittle and Gerhard Friedrich. Grand Rapids: Eerdmans Publishing Company, 1968.

Carpenter, Eugene, and Michael A. Grisanti. "Ramah." *The New International Dictionary of Old Testament Theology and Exegesis*, vol. 3, ed. Willem A. Gemeren. Grand Rapids: Zondervan, 1997.

Farr, F.K. "Deceit" and "Deceivableness." *The International Standard Bible Encyclopaedia*, vol. 1, ed. James Orr. Grand Rapids: Eerdmans Publishing Co., 1939.

Gunther, Walther. "Lead Astray, Deceive." *The New International Dictionary of New Testament Theology*, vol. 2, ed. Colin Brown. Grand Rapids: Zondervan, 1976.

Ryken, Leland, James C. Wilhoit, and Tremper Longman, III, eds. "Deception, Stories of." *Dictionary of Biblical Imagery*. Downers Grove: InterVarsity Press, 1998.

DEMONS AND UNCLEAN SPIRITS

THE SYNONYMOUS TERMS *demons* and *unclean spirits* refer to the fallen angels who followed Satan in his revolt against God (Matthew 12:24; Revelation 12:7). The real existence of these spirit beings is affirmed at least ten times in the Old Testament and by every writer of the New

Testament except the author of Hebrews. Jesus Christ recognized their existence by teaching about their reality (Matthew 12:27-28; 25:41; Luke 10:20; 11:18-20) and by casting demons out of individuals whom they indwelt.

THE TERMINOLOGY RELATED TO DEMONS
In the Old Testament

The Hebrew equivalent for *demon* is *shed*, used in two key passages (Deuteronomy 32:17; Psalm 106:36-37). These scriptures reveal the role of demons in promoting idolatry and false religion. The physical idols of metal, wood, and stone were representations of demons.

A second Hebrew word for demon is *sa'ir*. It occurs only in the plural (Leviticus 17:7; 2 Chronicles 11:15) and describes the goat demons (satyrs) worshiped by the pagan cultures that surrounded ancient Israel. Two other words, *Azazel* (Leviticus 16:8,10,26) and *Lilith* (also translated as owl in Isaiah 34:11) may be the names of demons.

The Old Testament also uses a more generic term—*spirit* (Hebrew, *ruach*)—to describe these creatures, suggesting their immaterial nature. *Spirit* is modified by *evil* seven times (Judges 9:23; 1 Samuel 16:14-16,23; 18:10; 19:9), emphasizing their character. In each of these cases the evil spirit is sent from God. A more detailed description of this is revealed in 1 Kings 22:19-23, where the prophet Micaiah relates how the sovereign Lord uses even the evil spirits to accomplish His purposes.

In the New Testament

The New Testament designates these fallen angels by three words: *demon* (*daimon* is used only in Matthew 8:31, but the diminutive form *daimonion* is used more frequently), *evil spirit* (*pneuma ponera*), and *unclean spirit* (*pneuma akathartos*). In some cases the adjectives *evil* (*ponera*, Matthew 12:45; Luke 7:21; 8:2; 11:26; Acts 19:12-16) or *deceptive* (*planos*, 1 Timothy 4:1) describe these spirits.

THE ACTIVITIES OF DEMONS
In the Old Testament

The Old Testament says little about the activities of demons. They are the reality behind false religion and idolatry (Deuteronomy 32:17; Psalm 106:37). As such, they play the role of Satan's emissaries, carrying out his schemes against the plan of God. They are not depicted as free agents, however. Ultimately, Satan and his demons are allowed to operate only under God's sovereign control (1 Kings 22:19-23).

God sometimes sent evil spirits to bring discipline and testing upon His people. After Gideon died, his son Abimelech sought to solidify his power by murdering Gideon's other sons. To punish him, God sent an evil spirit to create a schism with the citizens of Shechem in order to end Abimelech's rise to power.

God also sent an evil spirit to torment Saul as a part of divine discipline for Saul's disobedience (1 Samuel 16:14-23; 18:10-11; 19:9-10). Later, God used a deceptive spirit to lure Ahab into battle, where he met with military defeat, disaster, and death as part of God's discipline on the southern kingdom of Judah.

The first two chapters of Job depict an attack that Satan and his demons waged against the plan of God. There Satan seeks permission to test Job. In Daniel, God sends an angel to answer Daniel's prayer, but a "prince of Persia" delays the angel, indicating both organization and demonic opposition to God's plan in human history (Daniel 10:13).

In the New Testament

The biblical account describes more demonic activity during the ministry of the Lord Jesus Christ than at any other time. Though Jesus cast out demons on numerous occasions, the Gospels describe only eight specific instances:

1. Mark 1:23-28 (Luke 4:33-37)
2. Matthew 8:28-34 (Mark 5:1-20; Luke 8:26-40)
3. Matthew 15:21-28 (Mark 7:24-30)
4. Matthew 17:14-21 (Luke 8:2)
5. Mark 9:14-29 (Luke 9:37-43)
6. Matthew 12:22 (Luke 11:14)
7. Luke 13:10-17
8. Matthew 9:32-34

Two passages mention the disciples and the demonic: Matthew 10:1-8 (Mark 3:13-19; Luke 9:1) and Mark 6:7,13.

The book of Acts mentions demons or unclean spirits in only three contexts. The first mentions that the apostles healed people who were tormented by evil spirits (Acts 5:16). The second describes the ministry of Philip in Samaria and the fact that unclean spirits "came out" of many who were demon-possessed (Acts 8:7). And the third relates the failed attempt of unbelieving Jewish exorcists to perform their ritual in the name of Jesus (Acts 19:12-16).

The epistles say very little about demons. Paul recognizes that they are the power behind idols (1 Corinthians 10:20-21) and the ultimate source of false doctrine (1 Timothy 4:1). Paul also informs us that the demons have a hierarchical authority structure (Ephesians 1:21; 6:12). James recognizes that demons believe that God exists (James 2:19), but their wisdom contradicts God's (James 3:15). Peter and Jude both explain that God imprisoned some demons because of their disobedience at the time of the worldwide Noahic flood (1 Peter 3:19-20; 2 Peter 2:4; Jude 6).

The book of Revelation shows the activity of demons in the Tribulation. During that time, people will worship demons through idolatry (Revelation 9:20), and demons will be instrumental in gathering the armies of the world to battle against God at Armageddon. Their number is identified as one-third of all the angels (Revelation 12:4).

THE AFFLICTIONS DEMONS CAUSE

The New Testament describes certain people as being indwelt by demons. The common term to describe this is *demon possession,* a translation of the Greek participle *daimonizomai.* The New Testament also speaks of people *having a demon (echo daimonion).* Some debate the propriety of the term *possession* because it conveys the mistaken notion of ownership. However, *possession* can also convey the idea of indwelling, taking up residence without ownership, or internal control. This is what we see in the contexts that use *daimonizomai.* Those who

were demon-possessed had demons cast *out* of them, demons were seen to *enter into* people or *enter into* the swine, and they went *out of* people. This in-out terminology shows that demon possession occurs when a person has a demon indwelling his or her body.

The New Testament uses the Greek word *ekballo* to describe the removal of demons. This word describes Jesus' action of evicting the demons from their temporary domicile. Never does the word *exorcise (exorkizo)* apply to the actions of Jesus or His disciples. *Exorcism* describes the pagan rituals and incantations used to attempt demonic deliverance.

The power that indwelling demons exert over the human body is vast. Demons can impart incredible physical strength (Luke 8:29), cause blindness (Matthew 12:22), and induce a loss of speech (Matthew 12:22; Mark 9:17). They caused a boy to attempt suicide by throwing him into fire and water (Mark 9:22), gave a woman a crippling illness for 18 years (Luke 13:11-17), caused epilepsy (Matthew 17:15-18; Luke 9:37-42), and induced various mental and physical disorders (Matthew 9:32-33; Luke 8:26-35). The Jews of Jesus' day were not simply relating demon possession to disease. Although demons induced various physical maladies and diseases, Jesus healed some sickness and disease that was not associated with demonic activity (Matthew 4:24; Mark 1:32; Acts 5:16).

Debate continues over whether or not a Christian can be demon-possessed. Arguments in favor of this usually refer to anecdotes from the mission field. However, the strongest arguments against the possible demon possession of a believer are these: Believers' bodies become temples of the Holy Spirit at salvation (1 Corinthians 3:16), they are "in Christ" and Christ is in them, and the epistles include no warnings about possible demon possession and no instructions about casting out demons.

Perhaps the most insidious activity of demons today is the promotion of false doctrines and arrogant worldviews that oppose the teaching of Scripture (1 Timothy 4:1; James 3:15). This demonic influence can deceive Christians.

THE CATEGORIES OF DEMONS

Scripture includes three classifications of fallen angels.

Fallen Angels Presently Imprisoned in Tartarus

Evangelicals have debated the identity of the demons mentioned in Jude 6 and 1 Peter 3:19-20. These spirits' disobedience occurred at the time of the Noahic deluge. They "sinned" (2 Peter 2:4) by having sexual intercourse with a "different flesh" *(sarkos heteros)* and were imprisoned under bonds of deep darkness (Jude 6). These disobedient angels may be classified with the "sons of God" in Genesis 6, an Old Testament term that describes angels (Job 1:6; 2:1; 38:7).

Two other primary interpretations of "the sons of God" exist. The first of these identifies the sons of God with the godly descendants of Seth, but this lacks lexical support and suggests that all of Seth's descendants were saved and Cain's were not. It also implies that only the males in the Cain line married the females in the Seth line.

The second alternative is that the "sons of God" was an idiom for mighty warriors. This view again fails on lexical evidence, does not correlate with the passages in the New Testament, and does not explain how intermarriage between corrupt despots and commoners would corrupt the entire human race.

God will not release these imprisoned demons until the time of their final judgment, when He will send them to the lake of fire (Matthew 25:41).

Demons Active and Operating in the World Today

These are demons who operate unseen today, blinding the unsaved to the truth of the gospel (2 Corinthians 4:4), promoting false doctrine (1 Timothy 4:1), and distracting Christians from fulfilling God's plan of spiritual maturity for their lives.

Demons Confined in the Pit Until the Tribulation

This demonic army is currently confined to the abyss (Revelation 9:1). It will be released by the fifth angel in the fifth trumpet judgment of the Tribulation. Revelation likens these demons to locusts and their power to that of scorpions. They will inflict people with a painful torment so excruciating people will plead for death but not die (Revelation 9:6). Their leader, called *Abaddon* in the Hebrew, is the only named demon in the Bible. His name means "Destroyer."

The final judgment of all demons and fallen angels will apparently take place after Satan's failed final rebellion against God at the end of the millennium (Revelation 20:7-10). All demons will then be cast into the lake of fire and brimstone, along with their leader Satan (Matthew 25:41; Jude 6; Revelation 20:10).

—ROBERT DEAN

BIBLIOGRAPHY

Dean, Robert, and Thomas Ice. *What the Bible Teaches About Spiritual Warfare*. Grand Rapids: Kregel, 2000.

Lightner, Robert. *Angels, Satan, and Demons*. Nashville: Word, 1998.

Showers, Renald. *Those Invisible Spirits Called Angels*. Bellmawr, NJ: Friends of Israel, 1997.

Unger, Merrill F. *Biblical Demonology*. Wheaton, IL: Scripture Press, 1952.

DISPENSATIONALISM
(See also Dispensations)

MANY CHRISTIANS in conservative circles interpret the Bible dispensationally. They believe Scripture shows God relating to humanity through seven distinct dispensations or epochs. Salvation is by grace through faith in every dispensation, but God relates to people in different ways in each dispensation. Dispensationalists belong to many denominations, and they often identify with the *Scofield Reference Bible* and generally interpret the Scriptures according to its notes and outlines.

DEFINITION OF DISPENSATIONALISM

Dispensationalism is actually a multifaceted system of thought. Dispensationalists believe the following:

- The Bible is God's inspired and inerrant revelation to humanity. Scripture provides the framework through which we interpret the past and the future. God's written Word tells us of His plan for His creation, and His plan will surely come to pass.

- Because the Bible is God's literal Word and His plan for history, we should interpret it literally.

- The Bible reveals God's plan for history. God's plan includes different dispensations, ages, or epochs of history through which He tests His creatures (people and angels). God is instructing His creatures through history as His creation progresses from the Garden of Eden to the heavenly city.

- All humanity fell into sin, so each person must individually receive God's provision of salvation through the death and resurrection of Christ by believing the gospel. Thus, Jesus Christ is the only way to a relationship with God.

- Scripture teaches that because of mankind's fall into sin, all humanity is naturally rebellious toward God and the things of God. This is why only genuine believers in Christ are open to the teachings of the Bible. Thus, salvation through Christ is a prerequisite to properly understanding God's Word.

- God's plan for history includes a purpose for the descendants of Abraham, Isaac, and Jacob—that is, the nation of Israel. This plan for Israel includes promises that they will have the land of Israel, they will have a seed, and they will be a worldwide blessing to the nations. Many of the promises to national Israel are yet to be fulfilled. Therefore, God is not finished with Israel.

- God's plan from all eternity also includes a purpose for the church. However, this is a temporary phase that will end with the rapture. After the rapture, God will complete His plan for Israel and the Gentiles.

- God's main purpose in His master plan for history is to glorify Himself through Jesus Christ. Therefore, Jesus Christ is the goal and hero of history.

Lewis Sperry Chafer was right when he suggested that "any person is a dispensationalist who trusts in the blood of Christ rather than bringing an animal sacrifice" and "any person is a dispensationalist who observes the first day of the week rather than the seventh" (p. 9). Most students of Scripture would agree with dispensationalism in this broad sense as they distinguish between the features of the Old and New Testaments.

Summarizing the essential nature of dispensationalism, Charles Ryrie (p. 31) suggests, "Dispensationalism views the world as a household run by God. In this household-world God is dispensing or administering its affairs according to His own will and in various stages of revelation in the process of time. These stages mark off the distinguishably different economies in the outworking of His total purpose, and these economies are the dispensations. The understanding of God's differing economies is essential to a proper interpretation of His revelation within those various economies."

To understand the plan and objective of God throughout the ages, one must see the relationship between a dispensation and a covenant. A dispensation is a temporary period of time based on a conditional test to determine if humanity will be faithful to the conditions of God. Scofield (p. 5) defined a dispensation as "a period of time during which man is tested in respect of obedience to some *specific* revelation of the will of God." According to Ryrie (p. 29), "A dispensation is a distinguishable economy in the outworking of God's purpose. If one were describing a dispensation he would include other things, such as the ideas of distinctive revelation, testing, failure and judgment." Humanity has failed these various testings, so each dispensation ends in judgment.

A biblical covenant is an eternal agreement God makes with mankind, revealing what He will do for humanity. God made seven covenants with humanity throughout history. Each covenant reveals principles by which God will relate to man. Man has the free will to reject the covenant or principles of God, but when he violates the covenant, he suffers the consequences.

ESSENTIALS OF DISPENSATIONALISM

Ryrie (p. 41) has stated what he calls the three essentials or *sine qua non* (Latin, "without which not") of dispensationalism. "The essence of dispensationalism, then, is the distinction between Israel and the church. This grows out of the dispensationalist's consistent employment of normal or plain or historical-grammatical interpretation, and it reflects an understanding of the basic purpose of God in all His dealings with mankind as that of glorifying Himself through salvation and other purposes as well."

First Essential: Consistent Literal Interpretation

Ryrie's first essential of dispensationalism is not just literal interpretation, but more fully, a *consistent* literal hermeneutic. "The word *literal* is perhaps not so good as either the word *normal* or *plain*," explains Ryrie (p. 40), "but in any case it is interpretation that does not spiritualize or allegorize as nondispensational interpretation does." Literal interpretation is foundational to the dispensational approach to Scripture.

Second Essential: Israel and the Church Are Distinct

"A dispensationalist keeps Israel and the church distinct," declares Ryrie (p. 39). He also notes that anyone "who fails to distinguish Israel and the church consistently will

inevitably not hold to dispensational distinctions; and one who does, will." What does Ryrie mean by keeping Israel and the church distinct? Dispensationalists believe the Bible teaches that God's single program for history includes a distinct plan for Israel and a distinct plan for the church. God's plan for history has two peoples: Israel and the church. John Walvoord (p. 88) says that "dispensations are rules of life. They are not ways of salvation. There is only one way of salvation and that is by grace through faith in Jesus Christ."

Third Essential: God's Glory Is the Purpose of History

The third essential of dispensationalism is aptly summarized in this quote from Renald Showers (p. 53): "The ultimate purpose of history is the glory of God through the demonstration that He alone is the sovereign God."

A BIBLICAL PHILOSOPHY OF HISTORY

The dispensational view of the Bible provides a believer with a biblical philosophy of history. This is important for a Christian. Understanding God's purpose for each era of history helps us develop a worldview for living in accordance with God's will. A believer who has a divine perspective on the past, present, and future is able to know what God expects of him in every area of life in this present day.

In the current church age, the New Testament teaches us how to live privately and publicly. Dispensationalists, for example, do not live in this age of grace as if we were still under the rule of the Mosaic law. Instead, we understand that we are now under what the New Testament calls the law of Christ (1 Corinthians 9:21; Galatians 6:2). Current dispensational obligations combine with responsibilities from previous ages to provide a New Testament believer with a complete biblical framework for understanding how to please God in every area of our lives.

A BIBLICAL SYSTEM OF THEOLOGY

We believe that dispensationalism is a system of theology that has been properly developed from the Bible itself. Dispensationalism is essential to correctly understand the Bible, especially Bible prophecy. No one will be able to rightly divide God's Word without understanding these great truths. Instead of being a hindrance to correct understanding of God's Word, as critics contend, dispensationalism is a human label for the correct approach to and understanding of Scripture.

—**ELMER TOWNS AND THOMAS ICE**

BIBLIOGRAPHY

Bass, Clarence. *Backgrounds to Dispensationalism*. Grand Rapids: Eerdmans Publishing Company, 1960.

Chafer, Lewis Sperry. *Dispensationalism*. Dallas: Dallas Seminary Press, 1936.

Ryrie, Charles C. *Dispensationalism*. Chicago: Moody Press, 1995.

Scofield, C.I. *Scofield Reference Bible*. New York: Oxford University Press, 1917.

Showers, Renald. *There Really Is a Difference! A Comparison of Covenant and Dispensational Theology*. Bellmawr, NJ: Friends of Israel, 1990.

Walvoord, John F. "Biblical Kingdoms Compared and Contrasted." *Issues in Dispensationalism*. Chicago: Moody Press, 1994.

DISPENSATIONS
(See also Dispensationalism)

GOD ADMINISTERS THE AFFAIRS of the world according to His own will and in various stages. These stages are sometimes called dispensations. Understanding the difference between these dispensations helps us to properly interpret His revelation within each one. God introduces new promises and commands in each dispensation, but His plan for humanity's redemption and reconciliation remains the same throughout history.

WHAT IS A DISPENSATION?

The English word *dispensation* translates the Greek noun *oikonomía*, often rendered *administration* in modern translations. *Oikonomía* is a compound of *oikos*, meaning "house," and *nomos*, meaning "law." It pictures the man-

aging or administering of the affairs of a household.

A dispensation includes these elements:

- promises from God
- commandments from God that test humanity's obedience
- principles for humanity to live by
- humanity's failure to keep God's commands
- God's judgment
- progressive revelation of God's plan for history

THE SEVEN DISPENSATIONS

Some promises, commands, and principles continue from one dispensation into another, while others are annulled and replaced with fresh revelation. God has revealed seven dispensations in Scripture:

1. Innocence
2. Conscience
3. Human Government
4. Promise
5. Law
6. Grace or Church
7. Kingdom

(Note: The so-called Edenic and Adamic Covenants are not actually covenants, but can be discussed as such for the purposes of comparison to promises, judgments, etc.—see article titled "Covenants" for more on this.)

1. The Edenic Covenant and the Dispensation of Innocence

The first covenant involved man's physical existence on earth. Adam had no history and therefore no knowledge of how to care for his physical needs. Rather than leaving man to experiment with ways to provide for his necessities, God revealed to Adam how he should care for his human needs. Mankind's primary needs have not significantly changed through time.

When God created Adam sinless in the Garden, He gave Adam certain principles to

THE DISPENSATIONS—THE OUTWORKING OF GOD'S PLAN FOR THE AGES

	INNOCENCE	CONSCIENCE	HUMAN GOVERNMENT	PROMISE	LAW	GRACE	KINGDOM
Test	Do not eat of the tree of the knowledge of good and evil	Live by the knowledge of good and evil	Spread over the earth and form government	Live by faith	Obey the law	Accept Christ by faith	Based on God's faithfulness
Failure	Original sin	Man did only that which was evil	Tower of Babel	Left the land	Long record of disobedience	The apostate church	Final rebellion
Result	Expulsion from the Garden	The flood judgment	Confusion caused by multiple tongues	Bondage in Egypt	Exile and the cross	The Tribulation	Hell
Covenant	EDENIC COVENANT	ADAMIC COVENANT	NOAHIC COVENANT	ABRAHAMIC COVENANT	MOSAIC COVENANT	NEW COVENANT	DAVIDIC COVENANT
	1. Replenish the earth	1. Serpent cursed	1. Relationship of man to earth confirmed	1. Make Israel a great nation	1. Given to Israel	1. Better promises	1. Davidic house, prosperity of family
	2. Subdue the earth	2. First promise	2. Order of nature confirmed	2. Bless the seed	2. Three parts	2. A willing heart and mind	2. Throne—a royal authority
	3. Have dominion over animals	3. Changed state of woman a. Multiplied suffering in childbirth b. Motherhood sorrow	3. Human government established	3. Great name	a. Commandments reveal the righteousness of God	3. Personal relationship with Christ	3. Davidic kingdom—a rule
	4. Eat herbs and fruits	4. Earth cursed	4. No more universal flood—judgment by water	4. Be a blessing	b. Judgments reveal social requirements	4. Obliteration of sins	4. In perpetuity—forever
	5. Abstain from eating from the tree of good and evil	5. Inevitable sorrow of life		5. Bless them that bless you	c. Ordinances reveal religious life	5. Redemption accomplished	5. Christ will sit on the throne of David
	6. Penalty was death	6. Burdensome labor		6. Curse him that curses you	3. Revealed death	6. Perpetuity; conversion, blessing	
		7. Physical death		7. In Israel all the families of the earth will be blessed			
				8. Promised Land			

follow. If Adam kept these principles, he would prosper:

1. Replenish the earth with children (Genesis 1:28).
2. Use nature (subdue the earth) for food, shelter, and clothing (Genesis 1:28).
3. Have dominion over animal life (Genesis 1:28).
4. Eat fruit and vegetables (Genesis 1:29).
5. Work for sustenance (Genesis 2:15).
6. Obey God (abstaining from eating of the tree that God prohibited).

The Edenic covenant is tied to the dispensation of innocence, whereby God tested man to see if he would live by God's conditions. God told man not to eat of the fruit of the tree of the knowledge of good and evil (Genesis 2:17). The dispensation ended in man's failure—Eve was deceived (1 Timothy 2:14), and Adam deliberately disobeyed. As a result, the first man had personal and experiential knowledge of good and evil. What seemed like a simple, limited act of eating fruit ended in a broad, conscious knowledge of right and wrong. In the next dispensation, the descendants of Adam were responsible for this new awareness of sin.

Because Adam could not keep the conditions of the first dispensation, God judged him. The judgment was expulsion from the Garden. The first dispensation—and the others—reveals that natural man is incapable of obeying or pleasing God. Man lost the benefit of living in the innocent environment of Eden. But the covenantal principle would continue: Man was responsible to provide for his needs. As a result of man's failure, God placed cherubim at the entrance to the Garden to keep man from returning (Genesis 3:24).

2. The Adamic Covenant and the Dispensation of Conscience

The second covenant grew out of mankind's failure in the first dispensation. The Adamic covenant promised not only redemption for humanity but also judgment for the one who was responsible for the first

sin. The Adamic covenant included these promises and judgments:

1. God cursed the serpent, Satan's tool, and reduced it from a beautiful creature to a hated reptile.
2. God promised destruction for Satan in a future blow to the head (Genesis 3:15).
3. God promised that the woman would bear a seed, a Redeemer for mankind who would destroy Satan (Genesis 3:15).
4. Man would provide for the physical necessities of life through hard and despised physical work (Genesis 3:19).
5. God cursed nature (the creation). It reluctantly gives its fruit for man's necessities, and its beauty is veiled (Genesis 3:17-18).
6. The woman would have multiplied sorrow in childbirth and be in submission to her husband (Genesis 3:16).
7. The human race would experience physical death (Romans 5:12).

Because man failed to live up to the test of the dispensation of innocence, God gave him a second dispensational test. Mankind could not go back, so it went forward to its next test. As humanity entered a hostile environment outside the Garden, God gave a second set of conditions to live by. This dispensation of conscience is guided by the limited knowledge of right and wrong that Adam experientially accumulated. God introduced the Adamic covenant at the beginning of this dispensation.

During the dispensation of conscience, man enjoyed long life but was not able to follow his conscience. Humanity failed the test and revealed that it could not keep the general principle of good. Instead, "every imagination of the thoughts of his heart was only evil continually" (Genesis 6:5 KJV), and "it repented the LORD that he had made man" (Genesis 6:6). The dispensation of conscience ended in the judgment of the flood.

3. The Noahic Covenant and the Dispensation of Human Government

After the flood wiped out society and left only eight people alive, God introduced a new covenant with new promises. It came with a new dispensation and new tests. The principles of the first and second covenant continue (people must provide for themselves and live by their conscience), but now man no longer lives as a private individual, responsible only for himself. The Noahic covenant includes the institution of human government. Mankind is to live in a corporate society. Prior to this, people lived in extended families ruled by tribal heads. But as society became larger, people came to be organized under corporate government.

After the flood, God made a covenant with Noah and gave the rainbow as a sign: "This is the token of the covenant which I make between me and you" (Genesis 9:12). The Noahic covenant began the third period of time, the dispensation of human government. God no longer allows the conscience of individuals to be the sole basis of human life. Mankind failed to live according to personal conscience, so God punished mankind through the universal flood.

In the covenant of human government, God confirms elements of the previous covenants: Man is to subdue the earth and provide for his necessities (Genesis 9:3), and the physical laws of the universe will remain ordered (Genesis 8:22). And God also adds a new promise: The earth will never have another universal flood (Genesis 9:15). The core of the Noahic covenant was the judicial taking of life (Genesis 9:6), which is the ultimate expression of government.

The test of the dispensation of human government was for humanity to divide into nations or societies and govern itself. The Bible says very little about this dispensation and how man lived under its test. Most of written history records the generations of the different sons of Noah, so Genesis 10 is only representative of this lengthy and mysterious

period of time. However, the judgment that ends this era is well known.

Humanity's failure is evident from the divine judgment at the tower of Babel (Genesis 11:6-8). Even though mankind failed the dispensation of government, God did not dissolve the principles he gave to Noah. The principle of government and the principles from the first two covenants continued onward.

4. The Abrahamic Covenant and the Dispensation of Promise

When God called Abraham, the history of man experienced a dramatic turning point. God had previously dealt with all humanity in each of the dispensations. But with Abraham, God chose one man and planned to make from him a single nation as the center of His work. Through this single stream, God planned to save the world.

The Abrahamic covenant included these promises:

1. God would make out of Abraham a great nation—a nation that would influence the other nations, a nation that would continue while others disappeared.

2. God would bless this nation with financial and spiritual prosperity (Genesis 12:2).

3. God would make the name of Abraham universal and enduring.

4. God would bless Abraham (Galatians 3:13-14).

5. God would bless the nations that bless the seed of Abraham.

6. God would bless all the families of the earth through Abraham's seed, the Christ (Genesis 12:3).

7. God led Abraham to the Land (Genesis 12:1) and then promised to give it to him (Genesis 12:7). It is therefore called the Promised Land.

The most important aspect of God's covenant to Abraham is its promise. This fourth period, the dispensation of promise, tested God's people's willingness and ability to accept and live in light of the promise of God. They were to live in the Promised Land and trust God for the promised seed.

Each dispensation includes a test, and the fourth dispensation reflects man's inability to live by the promise of God. The descendants of Abraham refused to live in the land by faith, so they migrated to Egypt. This dispensation's final test and the failure of God's people (Israel) occurred when God attempted to bring them out of Egypt into the Promised Land. At Kadesh-Barnea, the people refused to trust God and enter the Promised Land. God judged them, and everyone who did not accept the promise of God died in the wilderness. Only those of faith (Joshua and Caleb) and those younger than 20 later entered the Promised Land.

5. The Mosaic Covenant and the Dispensation of Law

The covenant that God gave on Mount Sinai was the Mosaic covenant, and it included the law. The law demonstrated to each individual that he is a sinner before God. During the previous dispensations, man was a sinner even when he did not have knowledge of the law. Paul tells us, "Death reigned from Adam to Moses, even over them that had not sinned after the similitude of Adam's transgression" (Romans 5:14).

The Mosaic covenant had three parts: (1) the commandments expressing the righteous will of God, (2) the judgments expressing the social life of Israel, and (3) the ordinances directing the religious life of Israel. Jesus called all these "the law" (Matthew 5:17), and Paul explained that it was a "ministry of condemnation" (2 Corinthians 3:7-9). No one was ever saved by keeping the law—it was simply God's way of testing Israel. The nation's failure to keep the law ended in judgment, as did all the other dispensations.

The dispensation of law ended with Jesus Christ. He kept the law perfectly (Matthew 5:17) and then nailed the law to the cross (Colossians 2:14) and "abolished in his flesh the enmity, even the law of commandments contained in ordinances" (Ephesians 2:15).

And, just as principles from the previous covenants continue into the subsequent dispensations, so the principle of the law continues past the cross of Christ. He did not take away the wisdom of the law but rather the penalties of the law.

6. The New Covenant and the Dispensation of Grace

The Old Testament looked ahead to the New Covenant. "Behold, the days come, saith the LORD, that I will make a new covenant with the house of Israel, and with the house of Judah" (Jeremiah 31:31). The New Covenant, also called the New Testament, was accomplished at the death of Jesus Christ. It is also called the Second Covenant, in contrast to the Mosaic covenant of the law: "For if that first covenant had been faultless, then should no place have been sought for the second" (Hebrews 8:7). The New Covenant is "better" than the Old Covenant:

1. It is unconditional. "I will make [a covenant] with the house of Israel" and "I will be to them a God" (Hebrews 8:10).

2. God guarantees that men will keep its conditions. "I will put my laws into their mind, and write them in their hearts" (Hebrews 8:10).

3. It extends to all. "For all shall know me, from the least to the greatest" (Hebrews 8:11).

4. It will completely eradicate sins. "Their sins and their iniquities will I remember no more" (Hebrews 8:12).

5. It rests upon the sacrifice of Christ, the better Mediator, and assures eternal blessedness for those who accept it.

Christ predicted the New Covenant on the night of His death, when He instituted the Lord's Supper. "This is my blood of the new testament [covenant] which is shed for many for the remission of sins" (Matthew 26:28). The results of the New Covenant apply primarily to the dispensation of grace, but in the same way that the previous covenants have all had eternal applications to the *future* dispensations, the New Covenant provides the benefits of salvation for believers from *previous* dispensations.

The dispensation of grace does not test legal obedience. Rather, the question is this: What will a person do with Jesus Christ? The believers in this dispensation must accept Jesus Christ and live by grace. The dispensation of grace will end when the professing church rejects grace and slides into apostasy. The resulting Tribulation is God's judgment that ends the era of grace.

7. The Davidic Covenant and the Dispensation of the Kingdom

God's covenant with David is unique. An extended gap of time separates God's past revelation of the covenant to David from its future accomplishment. The Davidic covenant had immediate implications for Israel, but it was the basis for a future dispensation known as the kingdom age—the millennium—when David's son will sit on the throne of Israel and rule from Jerusalem.

Previously, God had promised Eve she would have a seed who would be the Redeemer (Genesis 3:15). God later narrowed the line of promise to the descendants of Shem (Genesis 9:26), then to the family of Abraham (Genesis 12:3), and finally to the tribe of Judah (Genesis 49:10). Now the focus narrows even more and the Redeemer-seed is promised to come from the descendants of David.

The Davidic covenant (Psalm 89:20-37) is unconditional and based on the nature of God. God established His nation through the Abrahamic covenant, He provided laws for the people of that nation through the Mosaic covenant, and He established a ruler over them in the Davidic covenant. The Davidic covenant has a fourfold promise (2 Samuel 7:13):

1. God will establish David's family line.
2. God will rule over His people through His Son, the Son of David.
3. God will establish His kingdom.
4. God will recognize David's reign forever.

This covenant is perpetual and unconditional: "My covenant will I not break...once I have sworn by my holiness that I will not lie unto David" (Psalm 89:34-35). When Israel disobeyed, God did not abrogate the covenant. He only chastised His people for disobedience. The chastisement came when the kingdom was divided under Rehoboam. God confirmed the Davidic covenant by an oath (Psalm 89), later confirmed it to the virgin Mary (Luke 1:31-33), and Peter repeated it on Pentecost (Acts 2:29-32). We can know with certainty that God will fulfill this covenant in a future kingdom. This seventh and last era of time to govern man's life on earth will follow the apocalyptic judgment at the end of the church age. Man will fail to please God even though he is given ample opportunity to do so. In this last dispensation, man will live in a perfect environment, Jesus Christ Himself will rule mankind, and God will remove the curse on nature. But even in these ideal circumstances, man will still fail to please God.

The "dispensation of the fulness of times" (Ephesians 1:10) is another name for this future kingdom, which David's son will rule (2 Samuel 7:8-17; Zechariah 12:8; Luke 1:31-33). This era will be filled with blessings:

1. Christ will take control of the kingdom (Isaiah 11:3-4) and put to an end all anarchy and misrule.

2. God will reward mankind and provide rest (2 Thessalonians 1:6-7).

3. God will glorify those who have suffered (Romans 8:17-18).

4. God will save all Israel (Romans 11:26), cure her blindness (2 Corinthians 3:14-17), and restore her (Ezekiel 39:25-29).

5. The times of the Gentiles will cease.

6. God will lift the curse on creation and nature will be magnified (Genesis 3:17; Isaiah 11:6-8; 65:20-25; Romans 8:19-21).

Even this last dispensation of ideal circumstances will end in judgment. The test will be for people to submit to the Son of David, Jesus Christ. He will rule with a rod of iron, which means He will be the absolute Ruler who will guide mankind with justice and equity. But at the end of 1000 years, a group will gather in rebellion against the King (Revelation 20:7-9). God will judge them along with Satan (Revelation 20:10). Then, at the final judgment of the ages (dispensations), those who rejected God will be cast into the lake of fire (Revelation 20:11-15).

Thus, God will have demonstrated that in every age (dispensation), under every circumstance or test, man could not or would not live according to the principles expressed in the covenants nor keep the requirements of the dispensations.

Those who live with God throughout eternity will do so because of the grace of God. Man has done nothing to merit salvation. Those who suffer eternal separation will realize that God gave mankind multiple opportunities and different tests through which to demonstrate faith in Him. And in every dispensation, humanity failed. Therefore, in future ages, no person will be able to say that God was unfair or unmerciful.

THE BEGINNING OF THE END

The dispensations enable us to correctly understand God's prophetic timetable for history. The current era focuses on the church as the instrument through which God now works, not on Israel. Yet for the rest of Daniel's prophecy (Daniel 9:25-27) to be fulfilled literally in the same way the initial 69 weeks were fulfilled, the church must be removed from the earth. This event is called the rapture. It could happen at any moment and will precede the last seven years of God's decree for Israel, known as the Tribulation.

—ELMER TOWNS AND THOMAS ICE

BIBLIOGRAPHY

Radmacher, Earl. "The Current Status of Dispensationalism and Its Eschatology." In *Perspectives on Evangelical Theology.* Grand Rapids: Baker Books, 1979.

Ryrie, Charles, C. *Dispensationalism.* Chicago: Moody Press, 1995.

———. "Dispensation, Dispensationalism." *Evangelical Dictionary of Theology.* Grand Rapids, Baker Books, 1984.

Showers, Renald. *There Really Is a Difference: A Comparison of Covenant and Dispensationalism Theology.* Bellmawr, NJ: Friends of Israel, 1990.

Willis, Wesley R., and John R. Master, eds. *Issues in Dispensationalism.* Chicago: Moody Press, 1994.

ELDERS (24)

THE 24 ELDERS APPEAR in Revelation 4:4,10-11; 5:8-10; and 19:4. They are part of John's vision of the future, of which he spoke in his outline of the book in 1:19 and which begins in 4:1. In 4:4, the elders are seated on thrones around a greater throne. They are clothed in white and are wearing crowns of gold, and in 4:10-11 they throw themselves to the ground, worshiping the Lamb and offering their crowns to Him. In 5:8-10 they have harps and fall down worshiping the Lamb and singing praises, and in 19:4, they leave their thrones to bow down and worship God, who is seated on the greater throne. The elders are in heaven during the Tribulation and respond to God's judgments with acts of worship.

FUNCTION OF THE ELDERS

In Revelation 5:8-10, the activities of the elders include having "golden bowls full of incense, which are the prayers of the saints" (NKJV). This heavenly scene pictures the importance of prayer on earth, especially during the Tribulation. "The role of the elders seems to be one of sympathetic presentation, not that of a mediator of earthly prayers" (Walvoord, p. 117). The symbolism of the bowls of incense representing prayers of believers is similar to David's words in Psalm 141:2: "May my prayer be counted as incense before You; the lifting up of my hands as the evening offering."

John does not specifically identify who the elders represent. The two major views regarding their identity each have three variations. The first view is that they represent people—either Israel and Old Testament saints, or the church, or both. The second view is that they are angelic beings and represent either the Old Testament priestly orders, the faithful of all ages, or a special class or order of angels (Thomas, pp. 344–45).

"The idea that they are a representative group finds its parallel from the Old Testament where the priesthood was represented by 24 orders of priests, each having one priest to represent the order. Similarly, the 24 elders are understood to be a representative body" (Walvoord, p. 106). The elders wear crowns of victory, not of rulership, though Revelation mentions both types of crowns. Significantly, the elders already have their crowns—they have already won the victory.

IDENTIFICATION OF THE ELDERS

The identification of the 24 elders in heaven is a major part of one's view of the rapture of the church. If the 24 elders represent church-age believers in heaven, and if the number of them represents the completed body of Christ in heaven, then church-age believers will not go through the Tribulation on earth but will be in heaven during that time.

In Revelation 4, we learn the following about this unique group: (1) They are called "elders," (2) they are sitting on 24 thrones, (3) they are clothed in white robes, and (4) they have crowns of gold on their heads.

In both Jewish and Christian history, *elders* refers to the key leadership of the congregation. They are the decision makers and the authorities for the people of God; they are to represent the people before the Lord and to carry out the Lord's will among His people. In the history of Israel, the priests played an important role in the people's worship and in representing them before God. In the New Testament church, all believers are "priests," and the leadership rests in the hands of the "elders."

A reference to "elders" in Revelation is more likely to refer to church leadership than to the leadership of the nation of Israel. This seems especially appropriate in that their first appearance follows the seven letters to seven churches. Israel was not a part of that vision, though it will be a factor later in the book.

An important footnote to the identity of the elders is a remark in Revelation 7. One of the elders inquires as to the identity of the great multitude who come out of the Tribulation. Obviously, this multitude is not to be identified with the 24 elders. In addition, "all the angels" of God are distinguished from the elders in Revelation 7:11, so the elders cannot refer to angels.

SYMBOLISM OF THE NUMBER OF ELDERS

The 24 elders are not likely to represent the completed nation of Israel because Revelation 7 speaks of 144,000 Jews on earth during the Tribulation, and Revelation 12 speaks of the nation's persecution by Satan during the Tribulation (as do many of the prophets in the Old Testament).

The only complete group of God's creatures left (excluding Israel, angels, and the great multitude who come out of the Tribulation) is the church. They are not mentioned as being on earth during the Tribulation. The Lord promised the church in Philadelphia, "Because you have kept my command to persevere, I also will keep you from the hour of trial which shall come upon the whole world, to test those who dwell on the earth" (Revelation 3:10).

But does the number 24 indicate a completed body? The Bible is the best source for understanding isolated words, verses, and passages found within its pages. Does the number 24 appear elsewhere?

In 1 Chronicles 24 we find a listing of the divisions of priests who come from the line of Aaron. His son Eleazar had sixteen "heads" of priestly families, and his son Ithamar had eight. Verses 7-18 name each of the 24 divisions and indicate that they were to serve in the Temple according to this order or listing. In 1 Chronicles 25, David organizes musicians in a similar fashion. Those who were highly skilled in music numbered 288. Their time for service in the Temple was based on the order listed in verses 9-31, which included 24 divisions of singers to match the 24 divisions of priests.

The number 24, when used of the priests and singers, represents the whole nation of

Israel. It is not mere speculation, therefore, to suggest that the 24 elders represent a completed body of people in heaven while the Tribulation is happening on earth.

Daniel 12:1-3 is quite clear in presenting the resurrection of Old Testament believers at the end of the Tribulation period. In addition, those who become believers during the Tribulation period and are killed during that time will be resurrected at the end of the Tribulation. All of which presents us with the problem of the 24 elders in heaven during the Tribulation on earth, for these elders are clothed in white robes, indicating that their resurrection has *already* taken place.

Perhaps the most important key for identifying these elders is the description of them in Revelation 4:4. As we noted earlier, these 24 elders sit on thrones, are clothed in white robes, and have crowns of gold on their heads. How fascinating to read in the letters to the seven churches that these are the promises given to the overcomers:

1. sitting on thrones (Revelation 3:21)
2. clothed in white robes (Revelation 3:5)
3. wearing crowns of gold (Revelation 2:10)

If Revelation 4:4 pictures a time before or during the Tribulation, then it is unlikely that the elders represent angels because their judgment occurs at the end of the millennium (Matthew 25:41; 2 Peter 2:4; Jude 6). The interpretation that the elders represent saints of all ages is also unlikely because the judgment of Old Testament saints does not occur until the end of the Tribulation at Christ's second coming (Daniel 12:1-3). Only the church, which has already been raptured and is receiving rewards, would at this point in the timeline be wearing crowns of reward and victory (1 Corinthians 3:10-15; 2 Corinthians 5:10). This would mean the elders are representative of church-age believers.

Therefore, we draw the conclusion that the 24 elders represent the complete body of Christ, the church, including all believers, both Jewish and Gentile, from the Day of Pentecost (Acts 2) until the rapture of the church (symbolized by Revelation 4:1 and clearly preceding the great Tribulation on earth).

—DAVID HOCKING AND
TIMOTHY J. DEMY

BIBLIOGRAPHY

Hocking, David. *The Coming World Ruler.* Portland, OR: Multnomah Press, 1988.

Jeremiah, David. *Escape the Coming Night.* Dallas: Word, 1990.

LaHaye, Tim. *Revelation Illustrated and Made Plain.* Grand Rapids: Zondervan, 1975.

Thomas, Robert L. *Revelation 1–7: An Exegetical Commentary.* Chicago: Moody Press, 1992.

Walvoord, John F. *The Revelation of Jesus Christ: A Commentary.* Chicago: Moody Press, 1966.

ESCHATOLOGY

ESCHATOLOGY IS THE AREA of systematic theology concerning the last things. The term is derived from the combination of the Greek words *eschatos,* meaning "last," and *logos,* meaning "word" (the English suffix *logy* denotes "doctrine, study, or science of"). Some contemporary writers are overly preoccupied with eschatology, and others avoid the topic altogether. Ideally, we want to establish a balanced eschatology somewhere between these two extremes.

Eschatology deals with such ultimate personal realities as death, the intermediate state, and glorification. However, it also touches on more general or cosmic issues, including the second coming of Christ, the millennium, the final judgment, eternal rewards and punishments, and the new heaven and new earth. Eschatology is both personal and general, individual and cosmic.

Even though eschatology deals with future events, it is rooted in Christ's historic life, death, and resurrection as well as His future return. As Berkouwer states, "It is not the unknown of the future but the known in the future that is decisive for eschatological reflection" (Berkouwer, p. 13). The real question is "whether the biblical expectation is dubious or sure, uncertain or immovable" (Berkouwer, p. 24).

PERSONAL ESCHATOLOGY

In 1 Corinthians 15:26 Paul writes, "The last enemy that will be destroyed is death" (NKJV). He is referring to physical death. Death, Paul says, is an enemy. For the believer, the fear of death is mitigated by the hope that is in Christ. Paul wrote to the Corinthians, "So when this corruptible has put on incorruption, and this mortal has put on immortality, then shall be brought to pass the saying that is written, 'Death is swallowed up in victory. O, Death where is your sting? O, Hades where is your victory?'" (1 Corinthians 15:54-55).

Human life consists of the material (body) and the immaterial (soul and spirit). At the moment of death, the immaterial aspect of the believer immediately enters God's presence. In 2 Corinthians 5:8 Paul writes, "We are confident, yes well pleased rather to be absent from the body and to be present with the Lord." Jesus expressed this same thought to the thief on the cross when He said, "Assuredly, I say to you, today you will be with Me in paradise" (Luke 23:43). At death, the physical body remains on earth to await that day when Christ will reunite soul and body to live eternally with Him in the New Jerusalem.

For the unbeliever, death is still an enemy. At death, the unbeliever's soul goes immediately to punishment in hades (Luke 16:19-31) to await the Great White Throne judgment of Revelation 20:11-15, whereupon hades will be cast into the lake of fire.

Because both the believer and the unbeliever will be in temporary surroundings, this is called the intermediate state. Here the soul will experience the presence or absence of God. It is not the final state of the soul, but a transition between death and resurrection.

GENERAL ESCHATOLOGY

One truth that almost all evangelical theologians agree upon is this: Jesus will come again. Christians base their hope on this promise. Christ makes the promise clear (Matthew 24:27-31). In the parables of the two servants (Matthew 24:45-51), the ten virgins (Matthew 25:1-13), and the talents (Matthew 25:14-30), Jesus taught with certainty that He would come again. His coming will be on the clouds of heaven (Daniel 7:13; Matthew 26:64; Revelation 1:7), in clear view (Matthew 24:30; 26:64; Revelation 1:7), in the same place from which He ascended (Zechariah 14:4; Acts 1:11), and at a time that only the Father knows (Mark 13:32).

Though Bible students generally agree that Jesus will return, they have different opinions about the details of the circumstances leading up to and immediately following Christ's return. These different opinions have to do with the sequence of end-time events, the Tribulation, the millennium, and the future of Israel.

THE SEQUENCE OF END-TIME EVENTS

Mark 13:32 indicates that only the Father knows the time of Christ's return. Matthew 24:42 states, "Watch therefore, for you do not know what hour your Lord is coming." Paul writes, "For you yourselves know perfectly that the day of the Lord so comes as a thief in the night" (1 Thessalonians 5:2). These Scriptures indicate that Jesus could return at any time, and they admonish us to be ready.

But other passages establish signs that precede Christ's return. Jesus Himself referred to signs that would accompany the end times. In Matthew 24:1-14 He details (1) false Christs, (2) wars and rumors of war, (3) nations rising against nations, (4) famines and pestilence, (5) earthquakes and cosmic disturbance, (6) tribulations, (7) apostasy, and (8) worldwide spread of the gospel. Paul provides two additional signs: the building of the Temple in Jerusalem and the enthronement of Antichrist in the Temple (2 Thessalonians 2:3-4). These Scriptures indicate that the watchful person will know from the signs of the times that Christ's appearance is near.

So could Christ come at any time, or must certain signs be fulfilled first? The answer may have to do with the two aspects of Jesus' return. First, Christ will return for His saints (John 14:1-3; 1 Corinthians 15:51-52; 1 Thessalonians 4:13-18) at the rapture of the church, where He will meet the believers who are alive and the resurrected saints in the air. Of the five rapture viewpoints, only the pretribulational rapture position teaches that Christ could return for His church at any moment. Later, Christ will personally, bodily, and visibly return to earth. The rapture and this second coming are separated by the Tribulation.

The Tribulation

The Old Testament refers to the Tribulation as the time of Jacob's trouble (Jeremiah 30:7), the day of the Lord (Isaiah 2:12; Zephaniah 1:7; Obadiah 15), the day of His wrath (Zephaniah 1:15), and the great and dreadful day of the LORD (Malachi 4:5). In the New Testament, Jesus describes it as a time of distress "such as has not been since the beginning of the world until this time, no, nor ever shall be" (Matthew 24:21). Revelation 3:10 calls it "the hour of trial which shall come upon the whole world." In Revelation 6:17, the people enduring this time say, "The great day of His wrath has come, and who is able to stand?"

Scholars have a difference of opinion as to whether (1) the Tribulation is happening now, (2) it is a future, literal seven-year period according to Daniel 9:24-27, or (3) it is a future, literal 3½-year period according to Daniel 7:25; 12:7; and Revelation 13:5. Some scholars believe the church will be removed from this hour of testing, and others believe the church will endure this time period but be protected through it.

The Millennium

Millennium is a Latin word that means "1000 years." The word itself is not found in Scripture. Revelation 20 mentions this period six times in its first seven verses. Bible students posit three positions regarding the millennium.

1. *Amillennialism.* The word means "no millennium." Those who favor an allegorical or symbolic interpretation of Revelation see the millennium as an indefinite period of time. It is spiritual, not physical, and it is either being fulfilled only in heaven or is fulfilled on earth in the present church age.

2. *Postmillennialism.* As the name implies, those holding this view see the second coming as occurring after the millennium. Postmillennialists believe the millennium is the entire period of time between the two advents of Christ.

3. *Premillennialism.* Those who interpret Revelation literally see the millennium as 1000 years that will begin after the second coming of Christ and will usher in a period of righteousness when Christ will rule the earth with a rod of iron.

The Future of Israel

Scholars debate two positions regarding the future of Israel.

According to the first position, God's promises to Israel in the Old Testament will be fulfilled in the church. The Jews rejected Christ as their Messiah and continue to do so, thereby forfeiting the right to be called people of God. Jewish believers will be absorbed into the church based on Paul's teaching that all distinctions between Jews and Gentiles ended in Christ. The Old Testament is to be interpreted in light of the New Testament. God's original plan was to establish Israel's earthly kingdom at the first coming of Christ.

According to the second position, God will yet fulfill His certain and irrevocable covenant with the nation of Israel. The New Testament is the climax of the plan God unfolded in the Old Testament. The New Testament cannot be understood without the Old Testament. According to Paul's statement in Romans 11:26, "All Israel will be saved."

Other subjects involved in general or cosmic eschatology include the resurrection, judgment, and the eternal state.

The Resurrection

The Bible promises the resurrection of believers and unbelievers. Daniel 12:2 refers to a future time when the dead will rise, some to everlasting life and others to shame and everlasting contempt. Jesus said, "Most assuredly, I say to you, the hour is coming, and now is, when the dead will hear the voice of the Son of God; and those who hear will live" (John 5:25). In one sense, believers have already bridged the gap between life and death. In another sense, a future time is coming when those who are dead will live. In John 11, Jesus said to Martha, the sister of Lazarus (whom He was about to raise from the dead), "I am the resurrection and the life. He who believes in Me, though he may die, he shall live" (John 11:25). The apostles taught the resurrection (Acts 4:2; 17:18; 24:15). Both Testaments speak of a resurrection of the just and the unjust (Daniel 12:2; John 5:28-29; Acts 24:14-15).

The Judgment

The second coming of Christ will include the immediate judgment that Jesus described in the parables of the wheat and the tares (Matthew 13:24-30,36-43) and the sheep and the goats (Matthew 25:31-46). However, Revelation 20:11-15 details an event that occurs after the 1000-year millennial period. This final judgment of the unbeliever is the Great White Throne judgment, also called the second death (Revelation 20:14). Those whose names are not found written in the Book of Life will be judged by their works. They will be found guilty and will be cast in the lake of fire to join Satan, the Antichrist, and the False Prophet. Here they "will be tormented day and night forever and ever" (Revelation 20:10).

The believer will stand before the judgment seat of Christ (Romans 14:10; 2 Corinthians 5:10). At this judgment the works of the believer will be assessed to ascertain whether or not they were of eternal value. Those works of the believer that were built on the proper foundation, which is Christ Jesus, are described as gold, silver, and precious stones. These works will be counted worthy of reward. On the other hand, those works built on a different foundation described as wood, hay, and straw will be burned up in the fire of testing, and no reward will be granted.

It is important to understand that this judgment likely occurs during the Tribulation period and does not entail the punishment of the believer. The believer's eternal destiny was decided the moment the believer submitted to the lordship of Jesus Christ. Paul writes, "There is now no condemnation to those who are in Christ Jesus, who do not walk according to the flesh, but according to the Spirit" (Romans 8:1).

The Eternal State

The eternal state of the believer is the New Jerusalem (Revelation 21:9–22:5). Revelation's description demonstrates the utter brilliance and majesty of being in the presence of God (Revelation 22:4). In His presence, believers will experience no more tears, sorrow, pain, or death (Revelation 21:4).

By contrast, the eternal state for unbelievers is the lake that burns with fire and brimstone. There they will remain forever, separated from the presence of God and "tormented day and night forever and ever" (Revelation 20:10).

—TONY KESSINGER

BIBLIOGRAPHY

Berkouwer, G.C. *The Return of Christ.* Grand Rapids: Eerdmans Publishing Company, 1972.

Grudem, Wayne. *Systematic Theology.* Downers Grove, IL: InterVarsity Press, 1994.

Kessinger, Tony. *Come Out of Her My People.* Philadelphia: Xlibris, 2003.

Pentecost, J. Dwight. *Things to Come.* Grand Rapids: Zondervan, 1958.

ETERNAL LIFE

CHRISTIANITY IS BUILT on the foundation of the resurrection of the body of Jesus Christ. And He promised His followers, "Because I live, you shall live also." Not surprisingly, no one in the Bible speaks more about the resurrection than Jesus Christ Himself.

> I am the resurrection and the life. He who believes in Me, though he may die, he shall live. And whoever lives and believes in Me shall never die (John 11:25-26 NKJV).

The Lord is saying that although those who believe in Him may die physically, the real person, which is the soul and spirit, will never die.

> Most assuredly, I say to you, he who hears My word and believes in Him who sent Me has everlasting life, and shall not come into judgment, but has passed from death into life. Most assuredly, I say to you, the hour is coming, and now is, when the dead will hear the voice of the Son of God; and those who hear will live. For as the Father has life in Himself, so He has granted the Son to have life in Himself, and has given Him authority to execute judgment also, because He is the Son of Man. Do not marvel at this; for the hour is coming in which all who are in the graves will hear His voice and come forth—those who have done good, to the resurrection of life, and those who have done evil, to the resurrection of condemnation (John 5:24-29).

We see in John 5:24-29 that both the righteous and unrighteous will be resurrected. Eternal life is therefore guaranteed for all. However, where and how that future will play out depends entirely on one's position in Christ. Presently, there are two places for the dead: Believers are instantly transported to heaven at the moment of death, and unbelievers are taken to the place of torment in Sheol (hades).

THE PROMISE OF HEAVEN FOR BELIEVERS

Believers who are in heaven (and those alive on the earth) will receive their new, immortal, resurrected bodies at the time of the rapture. Soon thereafter, they will stand before the judgment seat of Christ and receive rewards for their good works. While still in heaven, they will then participate in the marriage supper of the Lamb. And at the conclusion of the Tribulation, they will return with Jesus to the earth and rule with Him during the 1000-year millennial kingdom.

Joseph Stowell (p. 114) observes that we are "programmed for paradise." Therefore, we are to set our minds on things above. He says, "Eternity is primary. Heaven must become our first and ultimate point of reference....All that we have, are, and accumulate must be seen as resources by which we can influence and impact the world beyond" (p. 27). Stowell challenges us to focus on heaven as our ultimate goal, not just as a footnote to our Christian experience.

Henry Holloman reminds us that eternity in heaven is the grand destination of all believers. Beyond our experience in heaven prior to the rapture or even our experiences in the millennial kingdom, eternity awaits as God's ultimate blessing for the saved of all time. Holloman (p. 568) writes, "Eternity is more than quantitatively different from time; it is *qualitatively* different because it is another dimension of reality." God is eternal and transcends the temporal order of the universe. He alone is timeless. He existed before the creation of the universe, He exists now, and He always will exist. All our hopes of eternal life are bound in our relationship to Him. We will live forever because God, who is eternal, lives in us.

Theologians refer to our eternal existence as the "eternal state." Both human beings and angels will exist forever even though they had a finite beginning. In the eternal state the saved will live forever with God, whereas the unsaved will be condemned forever to suffer in the lake of fire.

THE CERTAINTY OF ETERNAL PUNISHMENT FOR UNBELIEVERS

Contrasting sharply with the glorious future that awaits each and every believer, the fate of the unbeliever is simply too horrifying to even imagine. Following death, the unbeliever is instantly taken to the place of torment in Sheol or hades. According to Revelation 20:11-15, immediately after the resurrection of the unbelievers, which occurs at the conclusion of the millennial kingdom, they will be brought out of Sheol to stand before Jesus Christ at the Great White Throne judgment. There, they will be judged according to their works. Since none have been born again, none will be able to see the kingdom of God. All unbelievers will then be cast into the lake of fire, where they will be tormented for all eternity. Had they only accepted Christ's free gift of salvation while they were alive, they would not have to endure eternal separation from God.

THE CHARACTERISTICS OF OUR GLORIFIED BODIES

Every born-again believer will receive an immortal, glorified body. This includes both those who are raptured or resurrected as well as those who live during the millennium in their human bodies. The redemption of the body is part of God's complete plan of salvation (Romans 8:23). At death, we are absent from the body but consciously present with the Lord (2 Corinthians 5:8). This presumes an intermediate state of some kind between the death of our physical bodies and their ultimate resurrection.

Holloman (pp. 574–76) lists 15 characteristics of our glorified bodies:

1. physical and material (1 John 1:1-2)
2. transformed (Philippians 3:21)
3. recognizable (Luke 16:19-31)

ETERNAL LIFE

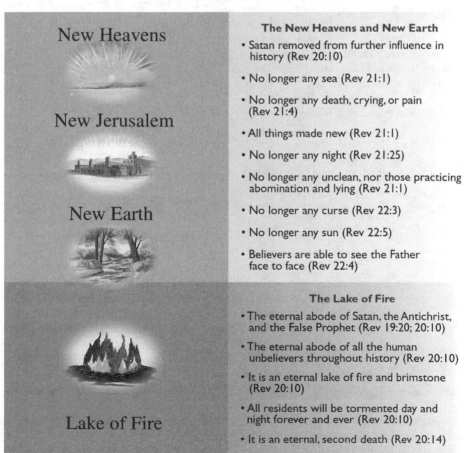

New Heavens

New Jerusalem

New Earth

Lake of Fire

The New Heavens and New Earth

- Satan removed from further influence in history (Rev 20:10)
- No longer any sea (Rev 21:1)
- No longer any death, crying, or pain (Rev 21:4)
- All things made new (Rev 21:1)
- No longer any night (Rev 21:25)
- No longer any unclean, nor those practicing abomination and lying (Rev 21:1)
- No longer any curse (Rev 22:3)
- No longer any sun (Rev 22:5)
- Believers are able to see the Father face to face (Rev 22:4)

The Lake of Fire

- The eternal abode of Satan, the Antichrist, and the False Prophet (Rev 19:20; 20:10)
- The eternal abode of all the human unbelievers throughout history (Rev 20:10)
- It is an eternal lake of fire and brimstone (Rev 20:10)
- All residents will be tormented day and night forever and ever (Rev 20:10)
- It is an eternal, second death (Rev 20:14)

4. imperishable (1 Corinthians 15:42)

5. immortal (1 Corinthians 15:53-57)

6. supernatural abilities (Luke 24:31,36)

7. sinless (Revelation 21:27)

8. glorified (Philippians 3:21)

9. unfailing (1 Corinthians 15:42-43)

10. spiritual (1 Corinthians 15:44)

11. heavenly (1 Corinthians 15:49-57)

12. radiant (Daniel 12:3)

13. unmarried (Matthew 22:30)

14. fully mature (1 John 3:2)

15. no negative effects (Isaiah 65:17)

THE GIFT OF OUR ETERNAL HOME

We receive the gift of eternal life as soon as we believe in Jesus Christ (1 John 5:11-12). Our eternal destination changes at that moment. From then on we are destined to heaven. The Bible pictures this destination as the eternal city of God. This city is called the New Jerusalem and reflects the glory of God. This city has no sickness, death, or sorrow. It is a place of eternal spiritual bliss. The tree of life, the river of life, and the throne of God are there, and so are all the saved of all time.

—TIM LaHAYE

BIBLIOGRAPHY

Holloman, Henry. "Eternity: The New Heavens and the New Earth." In Mal Couch, ed. *Fundamentals for the Twenty-First Century.* Grand Rapids: Kregel, 2000.

LaHaye, Tim. *Life in the Afterlife.* Wheaton, IL: Tyndale House, 1980.

MacArthur, John F. *The Glory of Heaven.* Wheaton, IL: Crossway Books, 1996.

Ryrie, Charles. *Basic Theology.* Wheaton, IL: Victor Books, 1986.

Stowell, Joseph. *Eternity.* Chicago: Moody Press, 1995.

EZEKIEL, ESCHATOLOGY OF

EZEKIEL WAS A PROPHET and priest who lived among the Jewish exiles in Babylon during the Babylonian captivity. He and his fellow Jews were cut off from the Temple, so many of his prophecies had to do with the Temple and its significance as the symbol of God's presence to Israel. His preaching included a wide range of issues and compelling imagery as he described both his present experiences and his future expectations.

As a prophet of God, Ezekiel foretold the coming destruction of Jerusalem and the First Temple, the resulting scattering (diaspora) of the Jews, and their ultimate return and restoration to the Promised Land. Ezekiel announces impending judgment for Israel, from whom the glory of God has departed. But he also foresees the return of the glory and the restoration of Israel's greatness in the messianic age.

Ezekiel's prophecies are expressed in four visions (chapters 1–3; 8–11; 37; 40–48), five parables (chapters 15; 16; 17; 19; 23) seven national judgments (against Ammon, Moab, Edom, Philistia, Tyre, Sidon, and Egypt, chapters 25–32), and 12 symbolic acts (chapters 3; 4; 5; 21; 24; 37). His major focus is on the holy people (Israel), the holy city, and the holy land. Despite his predictions of impending doom for unrepentant Judah, he also foresees a future redemption for Israel, which involves a new exodus, a new covenant, a restored Jerusalem, a regathered Israel, a revived Davidic dynasty, and a future messianic kingdom.

THE GLORY DEPARTS

Having described his inaugural vision (1–3) and having performed his initial symbolic actions regarding the coming siege of Jerusalem (4–7), Ezekiel turns his attention to the problem of the defilement of the Temple. He gives four reasons why God has chosen to depart and withdraw His shekinah glory from the Temple and the city of Jerusalem: the image of jealousy (8:3), idols of the house of Israel (8:10), women weeping for Tammuz (8:14), and 25 men worshiping the sun (8:16).

In response to this blatant spiritual and religious apostasy, God withdrew His presence in four distinct stages: The glory departed from the cherubim on the ark of the covenant (9:3), it moved to the threshold (10:4), it moved high above the cherubim, gradually departing from the Temple altogether (10:18), and finally moved to the Mount of Olives ("on the east side of the city"). From there it ascended back into heaven from the very same place where Jesus would later ascend into heaven (11:23; Acts 1:9-11). As a result, the Temple was left void of God's presence and vulnerable to attack and destruction by the Babylonians.

The departure of God's glory and the subsequent destruction of the Temple dominate Ezekiel's eschatology and prophetic anticipation of the return of the glory to a future Temple in the messianic age (40–48). But first, Israel must be regathered into her own Land, regenerated by her God, and rescued by His divine providence.

ISRAEL'S FUTURE RESTORATION

Ezekiel 36–37 focuses on the future regathering of the Jews into the Promised Land. This national restoration looks far beyond their initial return after the Babylonian captivity. It foresees a time when God will once again restore the nation to its intended greatness. It also predicts a time when the Jewish people will once again sanctify the name of God (36:23). God promises to give them a spiritual rebirth (a "new heart") and place His Spirit within them (36:26-27). As a result, they will "dwell in the land" (Israel), God will be their God, and they will be His people (36:28).

The prophecy reaches its crescendo in chapter 37 in the vision of the valley of dry bones. The scattered skeletal remains of the dispersed nation depict its hopeless condition without divine intervention. God raises the question, "Can these bones live?" and He clearly explains, "These bones are the whole house of Israel." In this well-known prophecy of the bones, God signifies the desperate condition of unregenerate Israel, predicts their ultimate regathering, and pictures their spiritual regeneration in the last days.

God reveals to Ezekiel that the Jewish people will no longer be divided into two nations (Ephraim and Judah) but will be "one nation" in the land of Israel (37:22). He reveals the eschatological picture of a regenerated Israel that will no longer "defile themselves" because, He says, "I will be their God" (37:23). David will rule over them, and the whole nation will live in peace (37:24-26).

THE INVASION OF GOG AND MAGOG

Chapters 38–39 predict a terrible and overwhelming invasion against regathered Israel in the "latter years" (38:8). In this amazing prophecy, Ezekiel foresees an alliance of enemy nations led by Magog and including Persia, Ethiopia, Libya, and others. This horde of invaders will sweep over the land like a storm cloud (38:9). But God will move against this enemy force with a great earthquake, pestilence, and an "overflowing rain" of fire and brimstone.

By the time this battle has ended, the invaders will be destroyed and Israel will be spared. Nothing in this prophecy corresponds with the details of Israel's invasion by either the Babylonians (586 B.C.) or the Romans (A.D. 70). Therefore, any literal fulfillment of this prophecy must yet be in the future. (See the article titled "Gog and Magog.") God says that as a result of His dramatic intervention, Israel will "know that I am the LORD their God" (39:22). The captivity of Jacob will finally end, and "the whole house of Israel" will reflect God's name and glory (39:25).

THE GLORY RETURNS

One of the most crucial texts for the futurist interpretation of prophecy concerning Israel is Ezekiel's vision in chapters 40–48. In this text the prophet presents God's instructions for the construction of a new Temple as part of the promise of Israel's restoration. The Second Temple, constructed by the Jewish remnant that returned from the exile (538–515 B.C.), did not implement Ezekiel's detailed plan, so futurism interprets the literal fulfillment of this prophecy eschatologically with the erection of a restoration Temple in the earthly millennial kingdom. This text is crucial to futurism. If a literal interpretation of this prophecy fails, then a literal interpretation of any Old Testament prophecy is suspect. This includes messianic prophecy, which is inextricably linked to the restoration prophecies.

Despite this caution, the symbolic interpretation of this portion of Ezekiel's prophecy is the dominant view advanced by critical scholars and conservative non-futurists (historicists, preterists, and idealists) based on their contention that prophetic visions employ apocalyptic language that uses the literary device of hyperbole (exaggerated speech) to convey idealistic or symbolic, rather than literal, concepts. Therefore, non-futurists explain that the reason the builders of the Second Temple did not follow Ezekiel's plans for the Temple was that the Jewish audience understood apocalyptic as symbolic rather than literal. However, the symbolic school of interpretation is divided on what this symbolism was intended to portray. Some interpreters believe it was meant to preserve the memory of the First Temple through an idealistic remembrance. Others say it idealistically describes the Second Temple, which was constructed upon the Jews' return to Judah after the exile. Still others see it illustrating a spiritual ideal (God's dwelling in holiness in the midst of His people) or a spiritual reality (heaven, the eternal state, or the church). The internal and external evidence supports the literal and eschatological interpretation of this section

LITERARY UNITY OF THE BOOK

Chapters 40–48 form an inseparable literary conclusion to the book. Although these chapters constitute a new vision in the prophecy, they are linked with chapters 1–39, repeating earlier themes in a more detailed fashion. This link is highlighted by the similarities between chapter 1 and chapter 40. For example, Ezekiel's vision of the presence of God in Babylon (Ezekiel 1:1; see also 8:1) finds its complement and completion in the vision in the Land of Israel (Ezekiel 40:2). In like manner, the problem created by the departure of God's presence in the opening section of the book (chapters 9–11) finds an anticipated resolution with its return in this section (Ezekiel 43:1-7). In fact, the concern for the presence

of God may be the uniting theme of the entire text of Ezekiel. Without chapters 40–48 there is no answer to the outcome of Israel in general and Jerusalem and the Temple in particular, no resolution to the nation's history of sacred scandal, and no grand finale to the divine drama centered on the chosen nation.

Ezekiel's prophecy of the future Temple shows the restoration of the presence of God to Israel (a physical as well as spiritual concern). It has a three-part focus: (1) prophecies of the Temple's desecration and destruction (Ezekiel 4–24), (2) prophecies of Israel's return and restoration (Ezekiel 33–39), and (3) prophecies of the Temple's rebuilding and ritual (40–48). If the literal First Temple was the subject of the first section of the book, the last section would logically deal with a literal Temple as well. The prophets saw the rebuilding of the physical Temple as essential to restoration (Daniel 9:20; 2 Chronicles 36:22-23; Ezra 1:2-11; Haggai 1:2–2:9; Zechariah 1:16; 6:12-15; 8:3). Would Ezekiel, a likeminded prophet (or God, the ultimate Author), have attempted to comfort his people's physical and spiritual loss with anything other than the literal restoration of a Temple to which God's presence could return?

THE CONTEXT OF THE TEMPLE'S RESTORATION

Chapters 40–48 open with a statement marking the specific date of Ezekiel's vision: "the tenth of the month [of Tishri]" (Ezekiel 40:1). The Jewish sages viewed the purpose of this chronological note as marking an eschatological context because the tenth of Tishri is reckoned as a Jubilee year (Hebrew, *yovel*), and the date of Ezekiel's vision was determined to be the first Day of Atonement (Hebrew, *Yom Kippur*) of the Jubilee year. Together, this date prefigured Israel's physical and spiritual day of redemption. Therefore, from the very first verse, the rabbis considered the context both eschatological and literal.

The restoration of God's presence in His sanctuary (Ezekiel 37:26-28) appears as the climactic event in the restoration described in Ezekiel 33–37. In chapters 40–48, God fills the Temple and consecrates it as His throne

(Ezekiel 43:1-7). Ezekiel 37 says this will happen when "David will [again] be king over them [Israel]," an "everlasting covenant of peace" will be established between God and Israel, "God's sanctuary will [again] be in their midst," and "the nations will know I am the Lord" (37:24-28). In particular, the "everlasting covenant of peace" (Hebrew, *shalom*) is unique. Ezekiel 34:25-29 describes it as Land-centered, completely eliminating harmful animals, guaranteeing security from any foreign invasion, and bringing unparalleled agricultural renewal accompanied by divinely sent seasonal rains (see Zechariah 14:17). Such a covenant was never enacted with Israel in the past and therefore must have its fulfillment in the eschatological age (the millennial kingdom).

The terms used to refer to the Temple in Ezekiel 37:26-28 likewise indicate an eschatological setting. The Temple is called a *mishkan*, the Hebrew word used formerly for the Tabernacle, and it is "in their midst," or more literally, "over them" (Hebrew, *'lyhm*). This pictures God's sheltering presence. The Temple is also called *miqdash* ("sanctuary"), emphasizing its holiness, and is said to be, like the covenant and the restoration of God's presence, eternal (37:26,28). Again, such a Temple could only find its fulfillment in the millennial kingdom, where the protective glory-cloud of God will return in the future.

THE DESCRIPTION OF THE TEMPLE

The Temple's precise measurements; the detailed design of its courts, pillars, galleries, rooms, chambers, doors, ornamentation, and vessels; and the careful instructions concerning the priestly service all show that an actual Temple is intended. Ezekiel 43:10-11 directs those Jews who will live in the time of the final restoration (when the prophecy will be fulfilled) to build the Temple according to Ezekiel's instructions. The same kind of architectural measurements as given for the Temple are given for the altar (43:13-27), to be followed "on the day it is built" (verse 18). Literary consistency (as well as logic) demands that if the altar of the Temple is to be built, then the Temple itself must be built as well.

OTHER OLD TESTAMENT PROPHETIC PASSAGES

As a restoration text, Ezekiel 40–48 should exhibit traits familiar to and consonant with other such texts in the prophetic corpus. For example, God commands Israel to build the Temple after "they are ashamed of all that they have done" (43:10-11). Ezekiel 36:22-38 already defined this national shame or spiritual repentance to be part of the regenerative work of the Spirit (verse 33). The prophets often referred to this national repentance (Isaiah 55:3-5; 66:7-9; Jeremiah 31:34; Hosea 3:4-5; Zechariah 12:10–13:2), as did Jesus (Matthew 24:30-31; Mark 13:26-27), Luke (Acts 3:19-21), and Paul (Romans 11:25-30). These passages reflect an ultimate hope for the nation, which must be projected into an eschatological kingdom.

PROGRESSIVE REVELATION

The departure of the shekinah glory from the physical Temple in Ezekiel 9–11 will be completed by its return to a physical Temple in Ezekiel 43:1-7. Ezekiel follows the return of the shekinah along the path of its previous departure, carefully describing the order of return to match the order of abandonment. It departs from the Holy of Holies, to the inner court, to the eastern gate, and to the east. It returns from the east, to the eastern gate, to the inner court, and finally to the Holy of Holies. This reverse progression was obviously intended to convey the restoration of what had been lost (the divine presence). None of Ezekiel's original audience would have understood these two events other than as complementary events, the latter resolving the former. If (as is universally accepted) the divine presence literally left the First Temple before its destruction, why should not it literally return to the Final Temple after its rebuilding?

Theological resolution also demands this be literally fulfilled. Nowhere in Scripture (or in extrabiblical Jewish literature) does the divine presence fill the Second Temple as it did the Tabernacle (Exodus 40:34-35) and the First Temple (1 Kings 8:10-11; 2 Chronicles 5:13-14; 7:1). Rather, Jewish sources (such as *Tosefta Yom Tov*) made a point of its absence and relegated such a hope to the eschatological period. Progressive revelation also requires that the theological dilemma created for Israel by divine judgment in a literal exile be resolved by a divine grace in a literal return and restoration. These are the two sides of prophetic prediction in the prophets, of which Ezekiel is a part. The rebuilding of the Temple and its dedication by the installation of the shekinah resolves the restoration program because it rejoins God to His people, restoring them to their chosen status as a holy nation and a kingdom of priests and light to the nations (Ezekiel 37:27-28). In order to consistently resolve the theological tension created by Israel's failure, there must be a return of her fortunes (both physical and spiritual). In this resolution the prophecy of Ezekiel's Temple figures prominently, concluding with the realization of restoration and the guarantee of its success by the declaration that "the Lord is there" (Ezekiel 48:35).

—RANDALL PRICE AND ED HINDSON

BIBLIOGRAPHY

Breuer, Joseph. *The Book of Yechezkel: Translation and Commentary.* Jerusalem: Phillip Feldheim Inc., 1993.

Feinberg, Charles. *The Prophecy of Ezekiel: The Glory of the Lord.* Chicago: Moody Press, 1969.

Greenberg, Moshe. "The Design and Themes of Ezekiel's Program of Restoration." *Interpretation 38.* 1984, pp. 181-208.

Price, Randall. *The Coming Last Days Temple.* Eugene, OR: Harvest House Publishers, 1999.

Schmidtt, John W., and Carl Laney. *Messiah's Coming Temple: Ezekiel's Prophetic Vision of the Future Temple.* Grand Rapids: Kregel, 1997.

FALSE PROPHET

THE ANTICHRIST WILL NOT RISE to power alone. His success will result from a worldwide spiritual deception perpetrated by the False Prophet. This religious leader's ability to perform miraculous signs will enable him to convince the public that the Antichrist is the leader for whom they have been looking. The ultimate deception of the end times will involve the worldwide worship of the Antichrist. This will be encouraged by the False Prophet (Revelation 19:20; 20:10), also known as the second "beast" (Revelation 13:11-17). Revelation does not clearly reveal his identity (nor the identity of the Antichrist), but it does give several clues.

THE IDENTIFYING FEATURES OF THE FALSE PROPHET

The False Prophet serves as the spokesperson for the Antichrist. Satan's program will culminate in the two beasts' corporate enterprise. The first beast will directly oppose Christ, and the second beast will assume the place of religious leadership that rightly belongs to Christ.

Revelation 13 presents ten identifying features of the False Prophet:

1. rises out of the earth (13:11)
2. controls religious affairs (13:12)
3. motivated by Satan (13:11)
4. promotes the worship of the beast (13:12)
5. performs signs and miracles (13:13)
6. deceives the whole world (13:14)
7. empowers the image of the beast (13:15)
8. kills all who refuse to worship (13:15)
9. controls all economic commerce (13:17)
10. controls the mark of the beast (13:17-18)

Some Bible scholars believe the False Prophet will be Jewish, while others believe he will be a Gentile. The biblical record itself is inconclusive. However, when we observe the relationship of the False Prophet to the great prostitute (Revelation 17), we immediately notice his connection to the city on "seven hills" (see 17:7,9) that rules "over the kings of the earth" (17:18). John seems to be referring to the city of Rome (famous for its seven hillls) by the terminology that he uses to describe the symbol of "Babylon the Great."

The Antichrist and the False Prophet are two separate individuals who will work toward a common, deceptive goal. Their roles and relationship will parallel those of ancient national rulers (Antichrist) and their high priests (False Prophet).

THE WORK OF THE FALSE PROPHET

Revelation depicts the False Prophet as one who uses miraculous signs and wonders to lure the world into worshiping the Antichrist. Even though this is yet a future event, we as Christians must always be on guard regarding spiritual deception, which takes place in our age and not just the end times.

A century ago, Samuel Andrews taught that the work of the False Prophet will be to extend his ecclesiastical administration over the whole earth by establishing the church of the Antichrist as the counterfeit of the true church. Andrews pictured an apostate religion bound together by a common hatred of Christianity and filled with demonic power. Thus, the False Prophet does not so much deny Christian doctrine as he corrupts it. Only in this way can the Antichrist sit in the Temple of God, demanding to be worshiped as God (see Isaiah 14:12-14).

When Satan tempted Christ in the wilderness, Satan appealed to Jesus for worship (Matthew 4:8-10). In fact, Satan offered to surrender the entire world to Christ if He would worship him. Therefore, we should not be surprised that the goal of the Satan-inspired False Prophet will be to inspire the whole world to bow down to the Antichrist, who is the personification of Satan himself.

Together, Satan (the dragon), the Antichrist (the beast of sea), and the False Prophet (the beast of earth) comprise an "unholy trinity" that is a counterfeit of the triune God. Satan opposes the Father, the Antichrist opposes the Son, and the False Prophet opposes the Holy Spirit. This ungodly alliance is Satan's final attempt to overthrow the work of God on earth.

The Bible explains their method. The Antichrist does not dare to appear until after the "rebellion" (NIV) or "falling away" (KJV) of apostasy (2 Thessalonians 2:3). In the meantime, the spirit of Antichrist (lawlessness) is already at work, attempting to pervert the gospel and to corrupt the true church. When this process is sufficiently established, the False Prophet will arise to prepare for the coming of the Antichrist.

THE SPIRITUAL PROSTITUTION BY THE FALSE PROPHET

Revelation 17 links the False Prophet with the "great prostitute" (apostate religion). Prostitution was often a part of pagan worship, but the adultery mentioned here refers to spiritual adultery. The woman is guilty of spiritual compromise and association with apostate religions.

Several scholars have noticed numerous parallels between the Antichrist and Antiochus IV Epiphanes, who persecuted the Jews in the second century B.C. The False Prophet is to the Antichrist what Menelaus was to Antiochus IV. Menelaus was responsible for enforcing many of the Hellenizing decrees of Antiochus IV upon his own people, the Jews.

John describes the False Prophet as having "two horns like a lamb, but he spoke like a dragon" (Revelation 13:11 NIV). He looks religious, but he talks like the devil. He counterfeits true religion in order to hide his real identity. Whereas the Holy Spirit's ministry is to bring people to Christ, the False Prophet's counterfeit work is to beckon people into a spiritual allegiance with the Antichrist.

The False Prophet deceives the world through apostasy, the renunciation of the true gospel. The spirit of Antichrist continues to work throughout church history, daring to deny the true Savior and His work on the cross that redeemed us from our sins.

THE RELIGIOUS APOSTASY SPURRED BY THE FALSE PROPHET

Puritan scholar John Owen observed that apostasy is brought about by the great apostate himself. He wrote, "The devil, that greatest of all apostates, has it as his chief desire to destroy Christ's church on earth, and failing that, to utterly corrupt it and so make it his church" (p. 135).

Owen pictures Satan's external attacks against the church as the ravages of a roaring lion and his internal attacks as the strikes of a poisonous serpent. "Once in, he secretly and gradually poisoned the minds of many by vain thought of power and ambition, with love for the praise and honor of the world, and with superstitions. Thus he turned them from the spiritual power and simplicity of the gospel....In this way, the 'mystery of iniquity' worked and was successful."

Owen goes on to list the danger signs of apostasy (pp. 148–150):

1. loss of all appreciation for the gospel
2. loss of conviction that the gospel is true
3. contempt for the promises of God
4. rejection of the true Christian religion
5. hatred for the people of God
6. hatred for the Spirit of God
7. hatred for Christ

Though Owen made these observations more than 300 years ago, they pinpoint exactly the nature of apostasy, both personal and ecclesiastical. When professing Christians turn against the truth, they often do so with a vengeance.

So we should not be surprised that the False Prophet represents the apostate religion of the end times. If his rise to power parallels that of the Antichrist, he will preside over apostate Christendom after the rapture of true believers to heaven. Those who aren't Christians will be left behind, and the False Prophet will have no problem deceiving them. The Holy Spirit will still be omnipresent in the world, but the removal of the church (the body of Christ) will bring His restraining ministry to an end.

THE GREAT LIE PROPOGATED BY THE FALSE PROPHET

The apostle Paul explained this process when he wrote, "The secret power of lawlessness is already at work; but the one who now holds it back will continue to do so till he is taken out of the way" (2 Thessalonians 2:7). After the rapture, the Holy Spirit will still convict people of sin, but His restraining ministry will be finished, and all of Satan's evil will break loose on earth. Then the lawless one

will be revealed. Paul said, "The coming of the lawless one will be in accordance with the work of Satan displayed in all kinds of counterfeit miracles, signs and wonders, and in every sort of evil that deceives those who are perishing" (2 Thessalonians 2:9-10). The rise of the Antichrist ("the lawless one") will parallel a general breakdown in religious and moral values, resulting in a decadent society that will believe "the lie" (verse 11) rather than the truth.

The apostle does not define "the lie" (Greek, *pseudei*), but he specifies that it is a particular lie, not just any lie. He could possibly be referring to a falsehood perpetrated to explain away the rapture. But more likely "the lie" is the official rejection of Christ and the acceptance of the deification and worship of the Antichrist.

Revelation presents the False Prophet as an individual who is empowered by Satan (Revelation 13:11-12), and the religious system that he represents is called the "great prostitute" (17:1) who is drunk with the "blood of the saints" (17:6). Therefore, the final phase of apostasy is both a religious system and the individual who leads it.

THE FINAL RELIGION ESTABLISHED BY THE FALSE PROPHET

A few observations are in order. First, the apostles were convinced that the spirit of Antichrist (1 John 4:3) and the mystery of iniquity (2 Thessalonians 2:7 KJV) were already at work in their own time. This means that the apostate spirit predates all modern churches as we know them today.

Second, if pretribulationists are correct in assuming the rapture of the true church will occur before the Tribulation begins, then all "Christian" churches that remain will be apostate regardless of their label. All these "pseudo-Christians" who are left behind may well align with one another in a common cause of unbelief (2 Thessalonians 2:8-12).

In summary...

1. The spirit of the Antichrist and the mystery of iniquity were already at work in apostolic times.

2. Apostasy has progressed throughout church history, predating the modern church.

3. A large segment of modern Christendom is already apostate. Unbelief is rampant in liberal circles.

4. After the rapture of true believers, all professing "Christians" who are left behind will be apostate believers regardless of their denomination.

5. The False Prophet will arise to lead apostate Christendom in its acceptance of the Antichrist.

In 2 Thessalonians 2:3-12, Paul indicates that this process will begin during the church age. The "falling away" (KJV; Greek, *apostasia*) will occur before the "coming of our Lord Jesus Christ" (2:1,3). But its final explosion as a form of worldwide unbelief will not occur until after the restraining ministry of the Holy Spirit (indwelling the true church) is removed at the rapture. This seems to indicate that we probably will not know who the False Prophet is prior to the rapture. Only those who are left behind to face the Tribulation will know his true identity.

—ED HINDSON

BIBLIOGRAPHY

Andrews, Samuel. *Christianity and Antichristianity.* Chicago: Moody Bible Institute, 1898.

Hindson, Ed. *Antichrist Rising.* Springfield, MO: 21st Century Press, 2003.

Lee, Richard, and Ed Hindson. *Angels of Deceit.* Eugene, OR: Harvest House Publishers, 1993.

Owen, John. *Apostasy from the Gospel.* Abridged by R.J.K. Law. Edinburgh: Banner of Truth, 1992.

Pentecost, J. Dwight. *Things to Come.* Grand Rapids: Zondervan, 1965.

Walvoord, John F. *Major Bible Prophecies.* Grand Rapids: Zondervan, 1991.

FALSE PROPHETS

SPIRITUAL DECEPTION BY false prophets (Greek, *pseudo prophetes*) is not a new phenomenon.

Moses raised the question to the children of Israel, "How can we know when a message has not been spoken by the LORD?" His answer was, "If what a prophet proclaims in the name of the LORD does not take place or come true, that is a message the LORD has not spoken. That prophet has spoken presumptuously. Do not be afraid of him" (Deuteronomy 18:21-22 NIV). A true prophet must...

1. speak in the name of the Lord and not some other god

2. have a message in accord with God's revealed truth in Scripture

3. give predictions of future events that come true exactly as stated

THEIR CHARACTERISTICS

The Bible describes false prophets in these ways:

1. *Self-deceived.* False teachers may be sincere, but they are still wrong. Some have deceived themselves into believing their messages are true. As Jeremiah 23:9-11 points out, their messages come psychologically from within their own minds and are not from God.

2. *Liars.* Some false prophets are deliberate liars who have no intention of telling the truth. The apostle John says, "Who is the liar? It is the man who denies that Jesus is the Christ. Such a man is the antichrist—he denies the Father and the Son" (1 John 2:22).

3. *Heretics.* False prophets preach heresy (false doctrine) and divide the church. Of them John said, "They went out from us, but they did not really belong to us" (1 John 2:19). The apostle Peter said, "There will be false teachers among you. They will secretly introduce destructive heresies....These men blaspheme in matters they do not understand" (2 Peter 2:1,12).

4. *Scoffers.* Some teachers do not necessarily promote false teaching but simply

reject the truth of God. Of them the Bible warns, "In the last days scoffers will come, scoffing and following their own evil desires" (2 Peter 3:3). The apostle Paul calls them "lovers of themselves...boastful, proud" (2 Timothy 3:2). Jude calls them "grumblers and faultfinders" (Jude 16).

5. *Blasphemers.* Those who speak evil of God, Christ, the Holy Spirit, the people of God, the kingdom of God, and the attributes of God are called blasphemers. Jude calls them godless men who "speak abusively against whatever they do not understand....They are wild waves of the sea...wandering stars" (Jude 10,13). The apostle Paul says that he himself was a blasphemer before his conversion to Christ (1 Timothy 1:13).

6. *Seducers.* Jesus warned that some false prophets will appear with miraculous signs and wonders to seduce or deceive the very elect, "if that were possible" (Mark 13:22). Our Lord's implication is that spiritual seduction is a very real threat even to believers. This would account for the fact that a few genuine but deceived believers may be found among the cults.

7. *Reprobates.* This term means "disapproved," "depraved," or "rejected." Paul refers to those who have rejected the truth of God and turned to spiritual darkness. Consequently, God has given them over to a "reprobate mind" (Romans 1:28-30 KJV). They have so deliberately rejected God that they have become "filled with every kind of wickedness." As a result, they are "God-haters." These people are so far gone spiritually that they know it and don't care. In Jesus' own prophetic message, the Olivet Discourse, He warned, "Watch out that no one deceives you.... Many will turn away from the faith.... And many false prophets will appear and deceive many people....For false

Christs and false prophets will appear and perform great signs and miracles" (Matthew 24:4,10-11,24). Our Lord warned His disciples of the possibility of spiritual seduction by false prophets.

THEIR DECEPTION

The Bible describes Satan as the "father of lies" (John 8:44) and pictures him as the ultimate deceiver. His name means "accuser," and he is depicted as the accuser of God's people (Revelation 12:10). He tempts men and women to sin against God's laws (Genesis 3:1-13). He denies and rejects the truth of God and deceives those who perish without God (2 Thessalonians 2:9-10). Ultimately, he inspires the false prophets and the very spirit of Antichrist.

The Bible clearly warns us that in the last days people will "abandon the faith and follow deceiving ['seducing,' KJV] spirits and things ['doctrines,' KJV] taught by demons" (1 Timothy 4:1). These false teachings will come through hypocritical liars whose minds have been captured by Satan's lies. Thus, the process of spiritual deception is clearly outlined in Scripture:

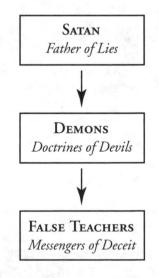

The term *angel* (Greek, *angelos*) means "messenger." God's angels are His divine messengers (Hebrews 1:14; Revelation 1:1), and

His true prophets and preachers are called the angels of the churches (Revelation 2:1,8,12,18; 3:1,7,14). By contrast, Satan is pictured as a fallen angel, the leader of other fallen angels, who deceives the world (Revelation 12:9). He is revealed as the ultimate power behind the Antichrist and the False Prophet, who deceives mankind with false religion (Revelation 13:14-15). Thus, the messengers (angels) of deceit are Satan-inspired false prophets and teachers whose messages are the very spirit of Antichrist.

Once a person accepts the premise of a false teaching, he closes his mind to the truth and throws away the key of logic. We live in a day when false teachings have become more and more rampant, and eventually the stage will be set for the ultimate False Prophet to perpetuate the final deception. So many people will be blind to the truth that they will no longer recognize deception for what it is. They will believe and do whatever they are told—even up to the point of worshiping the Antichrist.

—ED HINDSON

BIBLIOGRAPHY

Ankerberg, John, and John Weldon. *Cult Watch*. Eugene, OR: Harvest House Publishers, 1992.

Breese, Dave. *Marks of the Cults*. Wheaton, IL: Victor Books, 1984.

Enroth, Ronald. *A Guide to Cults and New Religions*. Downers Grove, IL: InterVarsity Press, 1983.

Horton, Michael. *The Agony of Deceit*. Chicago: Moody Press, 1990.

Hunt, Dave, and T.A. McMahon. *The Seduction of Christianity*. Eugene, OR: Harvest House Publishers, 1985.

Lee, Richard, and Ed Hindson. *Angels of Deceit*. Eugene, OR: Harvest House Publishers, 1993.

Mather, G.A., and L.A. Nichols. *Dictionary of Cults, Sects, Religions and the Occult*. Grand Rapids: Zondervan, 1992.

FEASTS OF ISRAEL

THE MOSAIC LAW PRESCRIBED seven annual feasts in Israel's ritual calendar. These feasts were divided into two groups: spring feasts and fall feasts. Each feast communicated a unique aspect of God's plan for Israel in human history and the coming of the Messiah (Hebrews 10:1).

The four spring feasts foreshadowed events in the saving work of the Messiah at the first advent and the founding of the church. These prophecies, or types, were fulfilled literally on the exact day of the feast. We can assume that God will fulfill the fall feasts just as literally. The spring feasts include Passover, the feast of Unleavened Bread, the feast of First Fruits, and Pentecost. The fall feasts include the feast of Trumpets, the Day of Atonement, and the feast of Tabernacles.

SPRING FEASTS

Passover was the first of these holy days and the first of three annual pilgrimage feasts requiring all Jewish males to celebrate at the Temple in Jerusalem (Exodus 12; 23:17; Leviticus 23:5; Deuteronomy 16:16). The Passover commemorated the historical deliverance of the Jews from slavery in Egypt and was observed on the fourteenth day of Nisan, the first month in the Jewish ritual calendar. Passover foreshadowed redemption through the crucifixion of the "Lamb of God who takes away the sin of the world" (John 1:29; 1 Corinthians 5:7). Christ was crucified on Passover eve as a substitute for the sins of the world (John 19:14).

The day after Passover, the fifteenth day of Nisan, the week-long feast of Unleavened Bread began. It continued through the twenty-first day of Nisan. During this week, Israel was to do no work. On the first and last day, the people offered sacrifices (Leviticus 23:6-8; Numbers 28:16-25; Deuteronomy 16:1-8). This feast emphasized Israel's separation from the world as a unique nation. The feast of Unleavened Bread also portrayed the impeccability of the humanity of Jesus Christ in hypostatic union, for Jesus Christ is called "the bread of life" (John 6:35). Because Christ was sinless, He was qualified to die on the cross for the sins of the world (2 Corinthians 5:21).

Israel observed the feast of First Fruits on the day after the Sabbath following Passover.

At this feast, which was dictated by the harvest, worshipers brought the first sheaf of barley into the Temple, and the priest waved it before the Lord. Then the priests threshed the barley, ground the grain into flour, and offered it to the Lord as a grain offering along with a quart of wine. The first fruits symbolized divine blessing and were a guarantee that the harvest would be bountiful (Leviticus 23:9-14). The feast of First Fruits portrayed the resurrection of Christ, "the first fruits of those who are asleep" (1 Corinthians 15:20). Like the feast of First Fruits, the resurrection of Christ anticipates and guarantees the harvest that is to follow (the resurrection of the saints).

Fifty days after the feast of First Fruits came Pentecost, the "Feast of Weeks" (Leviticus 23:15-22; Deuteronomy 16:9-12). It was the third annual pilgrimage feast and celebrated the wheat harvest, the arrival of God's provision. Pentecost represented the promise of God's Holy Spirit to Israel under the New Covenant. This was to be realized initially at the first advent. However, due to Israel's rejection of Jesus as Messiah, the arrival of the Holy Spirit presaged the judgment of God on the nation (fulfilled in A.D. 70) rather than the blessing of the messianic kingdom. Thus, the fulfillment of this feast will not occur for Israel until the people are regathered in the Land in the future millennial kingdom.

FALL FEASTS

The second stage of Israel's calendar occurs in the fall of the year, and the fall feasts foreshadow Jesus' second advent.

The feast of Trumpets occurs on the first day of Tishri (the seventh month in the Jewish ritual calendar) in the autumn (Leviticus 23:24; Numbers 29:1-6). This feast represents the preparation of Israel for national repentance and the acceptance of Jesus as Messiah. This feast will be fulfilled at the end of the Tribulation when the armies of the Antichrist attack Jerusalem. At this time, Israel will be prepared to turn to Jesus as Messiah and experience a national salvation.

The Day of Atonement, Yom Kippur ("day of covering," Leviticus 23:26-32), occurs on the tenth day of Tishri. This feast represents the

salvation of the nation and their recognition of Jesus as Messiah and Savior. The national expression of faith in Messiah's atonement on the cross comes at the close of the Tribulation. At this time national Israel will call upon the name of the Lord and ask Him to save them, initiating the second coming of Christ (Joel 2:32; Matthew 23:39; 24:30-31).

The feast of Tabernacles, also called *Succoth*, the feast of Booths, or Ingathering, takes place on the fifteenth to the twenty-first days of Tishri (Leviticus 23:33-43; Numbers 29:12-38). This feast occurred when the harvest was finally in and the people rejoiced that all was complete. It was a time of tremendous celebration (Deuteronomy 16:13-15) that lasted seven days, the first and last marked by sacrifices. The people gathered fruit and dwelt in booths made of branches and tree foliage to commemorate the complete provision of God and foreshadow the commencement of the millennium.

—ROBERT DEAN, JR.

BIBLIOGRAPHY

Fruchtenbaum, Arnold. *Israelology: The Missing Link in Systematic Theology.* Tustin, CA: Ariel Ministries, 1992.

House, H. Wayne, and Randall Price. *Charts of Bible Prophecy.* Grand Rapids: Zondervan, 2003.

McQuaid, Elwood. *The Outpouring: Jesus in the Feasts of Israel.* Chicago: Moody Press, 1986.

Scott, Bruce. *The Feasts of Israel: Seasons of the Messiah.* Bellmawr, NJ: The Friends of Israel Gospel Ministry, 1997.

FIG TREE

IN MATTHEW 24:32-33, JESUS told His disciples to learn a parable from the fig tree: "When its branch has already become tender and puts forth its leaves, you know that summer is near; so, you too, when you see all these things, recognize that He is near, right at the door" (NASB).

Many scholars understand the fig tree in this statement to be a symbol of Israel. Others see it as an illustration of the sequence of events immediately preceding Christ's second coming (Walvoord, p. 192). The time of the prophecy's fulfillment may refer either to Christ's second coming or to the destruction of Jerusalem in A.D. 70.

THE SIGNS

Jeremiah 24 and Hosea 9:10 are often used to equate the fig tree with Israel. However, in these texts, Israel is symbolized by the fig itself rather than the tree.

Jesus does seem to use the fig tree in Matthew 21:19-20 as a symbol of Israel. Elsewhere in the New Testament, though, the fig tree does not represent Israel. For instance, in Revelation 6:13, the fig tree is used as an illustration from nature of a cosmic catastrophe.

The parallel passage in Luke 21:29 provides the determinative clue for identifying the fig tree. Here Jesus refers not only to the fig tree but also to "all trees." The illustration is not limited to the fig tree alone but rather extends to trees in general and the seasonal cycle of new leaves coming with warmer weather. This type of analogy is also found in the Old Testament (Song of Solomon 2:11-13).

Further, if the fig tree symbolized Israel, one would expect to find other biblical uses of "summer" (rather than fall, winter, or spring) as a symbol for the prophetic season. However, Scripture never uses "summer" in this sense, and consequently the reference to summer actually weakens the idea that the fig tree symbolizes Israel.

The most convincing interpretation flows from an easily understood comparison. Jesus used this parable from nature to make the point that just as fig trees (or any other nonevergreens) bud in late spring and thus announce the coming of summer, so the appearance of signs (Matthew 24:4-28) precedes and portends the time when Christ is near.

THE SEASON

Does Matthew 24:32-35 refer to Jerusalem's demise at the hand of the Roman general Titus (A.D. 70), or does it speak of the second coming of Christ? Four lines of reasoning point to the latter.

First, as devastating as it was, Jerusalem's destruction in A.D. 70 did not begin to reach the scale pictured in Matthew 24:21. Thus, Matthew 24:32-35 necessarily looks beyond A.D. 70.

Second, according to Matthew 24:14, the gospel must reach the ends of the earth before the events of 24:32-35. That hardly happened before the first-century fall of Jerusalem.

Third, the immediately preceding context of Matthew 24:29-31 portrays the second coming of Christ. It is only logical to assume that the fig tree parable is to be understood in that same basic time frame.

Finally, and most convincing, there is the parallel passage in Luke 21:28: "When these things begin to take place, straighten up and lift up your heads, because your redemption is drawing near." Jesus told Israel that when these signs (pictured by the spring fig leaves) begin to take place, they would know that their redemption was near. It is impossible to equate the fall of Jerusalem with the redemption of Israel. Rather, Israel's redemption points incontrovertibly to the second coming of Jesus Christ (see Zechariah 14 and Revelation 19), when He will establish His righteous rule over Israel.

—RICHARD MAYHUE

BIBLIOGRAPHY

Blomberg, Craig L. *Matthew*. NAC. Nashville: Broadman Press, 1992.

Feinberg, Charles L. *Israel in the Last Days: The Olivet Discourse*. Altadena, CA: Emeth Publications, 1953.

Pentecost, J. Dwight. *Things to Come*. Grand Rapids: Zondervan, 1958.

Toussaint, Stanley D. *Behold the King*. Portland, OR: Multnomah Press, 1980.

Walvoord, John F. *Matthew: Thy Kingdom Come*. Chicago: Moody Press, 1974.

FINAL REVOLT

THE CLIMACTIC BATTLE of Armageddon, which will occur at the end of the Tribulation period, is often mistakenly referred to as the "last battle" between God and His archenemy, Satan. It is not. There is yet another engagement that, in many respects, surpasses the battle of Armageddon. It does so in the scope of the contest, in the total finality of the result, and certainly in what it reveals about mankind and the human condition.

That conflict is described in Revelation 20:7-9 (KJV):

> And when the thousand years are expired, Satan shall be loosed out of his prison, and shall go out to deceive the nations which are in the four quarters of the earth, Gog and Magog, to gather them together to battle: the number of whom is as the sand of the sea. And they went up on the breadth of the earth, and compassed the camp of the saints about, and the beloved city: and fire came down from God out of heaven, and devoured them.

THE BACKGROUND AND TIMING OF THE BATTLE

It is important to understand the prophetic setting for this conflict in order to fully understand the importance of the issues in this passage. The confrontation between human elements identified as "Gog and Magog" and the Lord will take place at the close of the millennium. During the millennial age, Christ will have returned, put down Satan, and judged the nations. He will reign for 1000 years on the throne of David in Jerusalem over those survivors of the Tribulation period who are believers. Only saved people will enter the kingdom age. Believers who were raptured prior to the Tribulation will return to the earth with Christ and, according to Scripture, "shall reign with him a thousand years" (Revelation 20:6). These believers who are reigning with Christ will not be susceptible to the lie that will cause millions of unbelievers (born during the millennium) to participate in the last revolt.

THE CENTRAL LESSON OF THE CONFLICT

Dwight Pentecost (p. 475), makes a telling point: "It [the final revolt] is necessary in order to provide a final test of fallen humanity.

Man will be placed under the most ideal circumstances. In spite of the visible presence of the King and all the blessings that come from Him, by rebellion at the termination of the millennium (Revelation 20:7-9), men will prove that the heart is corrupt."

THE IDENTITY OF GOG AND MAGOG

The identity of Gog and Magog in Revelation 20 is obscure. We simply are not given details as to who these people are, except to say that they will be gathered from "the four quarters of the earth" (Revelation 20:8). However, in regard to the final annihilation of the Babylonish system that will be destroyed in the conflagration of the Great Tribulation, we are told that "she shall be utterly burned with fire: for strong is the Lord God who judgeth her" (Revelation 18:8). Perhaps the implication we can draw here is that the Gog and Magog of Revelation 20 are a composite representation of mankind's debauchery in its entirety.

THE DEPRAVITY OF MANKIND

Satan will be removed from the scene during the millennium:

> I saw an angel come down from heaven, having the key of the bottomless pit and a great chain in his hand. And he laid hold on the dragon, that old serpent, which is the Devil, and Satan, and bound him a thousand years (Revelation 20:1-2).

Because Satan will be incarcerated throughout the millennium, whatever evil emanates from any human being will spring from his or her own fallen nature, not from outside influences, such as the voice of the devil. This extremely important truth emphatically illustrates, once and for all, that every person born on this planet—except one, the Lord Jesus—is born with a sinful nature inherited through Adam. In the final analysis, people do what they do because they are what they are—sinners by nature.

Consider also that during the millennium, the curse will be at least partially lifted, and the King will execute perfect justice. People will live in the peace they have longed for across the centuries and millennia. They will have what they want, when they want it, free of deprivation or the fear of repression. In other words, everything that mankind has said will satisfy and fulfill them will be theirs to enjoy. Will it be enough?

The answer is a resounding *no*.

EMBRACING DARKNESS

The rebels of the last revolt will be privileged above any generation of human beings since the fall of Adam and Eve in the Garden of Eden. The testimony of God's grace will emanate from the city of Jerusalem. The Holy City will be the place of the Messiah's throne and the center of worship for 1000 years.

Inexplicably, when living in the light of all that people could ask or think, millions of earth dwellers will join the final revolt. "And when the thousand years are expired, Satan shall be loosed out of his prison" (Revelation 20:7). Astonishingly, he will receive a tumultuous welcome from millions of people across the face of the earth. Scripture tells us that he will gather them "to battle: the number of whom is as the sand of the sea" (Revelation 20:8).

All of these people will be descendants of those who entered the millennium as saved individuals. Even though they lived under perfect conditions provided by the Creator and Sustainer of all the earth, they will choose to join Satan in his last grand push to depose God and His Christ.

We can observe from historical evidence that affluence has seldom contributed to mankind's drawing closer to God. To the contrary, it seems that under the best of conditions, people turn inward rather than to Him. This has been eloquently illustrated throughout the history of the nation of Israel. In the best of times, they seemed to drift further from the Lord. Most people cannot seem to abide sustained prosperity.

Therefore, when Satan arrives on the scene after 1000 years in the "bottomless pit," he will be received with open arms and hailed as a deliverer—so much so that he will successfully marshal a global military aggregation.

CALLING IT LIKE IT IS

Just as Satan and his minions rebelled against a benevolent God in the past, humanity will once again fall into the same iniquitous pit during the millennial kingdom. This seems incomprehensible, but in actuality, the story must be fully told. Without Revelation 20, the drama has no final chapter. What would happen, we might ask, if mankind finally experienced the opportunity they asked for: a society with justice, peace, prosperity, and the visible evidence of the existence of God? Would they remain rebellious? Or would they embrace the light of God? In short, are people, in essence, naturally good?

That question is forever answered when we see the grim realities of Revelation 20. People are not naturally good. They are inherently inclined toward evil. When given a choice, the majority—as in the case of "the sand of the sea" contingent—choose to do evil rather than good.

This final act of rebellion against God has a concluding exclamation point. With the millennium will come the last great act in the drama of redemption. Humanity will have been tested under every dispensation—innocence, human government, law, grace, and finally the messianic kingdom, to name a few. Under the test of every conceivable condition, mankind has failed. Therefore, no one can say that under the right conditions, mankind's goodness, like cream in a bottle, will rise to the top. No—God was right. Mankind is totally and wholly depraved.

And so, the book on the story of the nature of man closes on this dour note: "They went up on the breadth of the earth, and compassed the camp of the saints about, and the beloved city: and fire came down from God out of heaven, and devoured them" (Revelation 20:9).

THE GOOD NEWS

Although this may be the closing chapter on the story of mankind's rebellion against Christ, it is not the final chapter in the Bible.

In staccato-like fashion, the Scriptures chronicle the final demise of Satan (Revelation 20:10), the Great White Throne judgment (Revelation 20:11-15), and the entry of a new heaven and a new earth (Revelation 21–22).

Above all of these monumental events rings the great sounding bell of redemption. The case has been emphatically made for the necessity of the new birth. While some elements in the story of the total depravity of mankind may seem somewhat obscure, this can never be said of God's plan of redemption. Reading the entire account, from Eden to the last revolt of Revelation, creates only one conclusion: We desperately need a Savior—and thankfully, He has come.

—ELWOOD McQUAID

BIBLIOGRAPHY

Pentecost, J. Dwight. *Things to Come*. Grand Rapids: Zondervan, 1975.

Price, Randall. *Jerusalem in Prophecy*. Eugene, OR: Harvest House Publishers, 1998.

Ryrie, Charles. *The Basis of the Premillennial Faith*. Neptune, NJ: Loizeaux Brothers, 1953.

Walvoord, John F. *The Millennial Kingdom*. Grand Rapids: Zondervan, 1959.

FUTURE EVENTS

THE NEXT PREDICTED EVENT in God's prophetic calendar is the rapture of the church, which will bring about the completion of the body of Christ. Soon after that event, a series of Old and New Testament prophecies will be quickly fulfilled, including those relating to the Tribulation, the glorious appearing (second coming) of Christ, the judgments of God, the millennial kingdom, and the eternal state.

God designed these future events to fulfill both His promises and His warnings to the various groups with whom He has been working since the creation of the world, including mankind, Israel, and the church. Some events are predicted to occur in specific sequences (for example, the seal judgments, trumpet judgments, bowl judgments, and second coming of Christ), and others are to occur generally at the end of the age and lead into the conclusion of God's program for this earth. The following chronology represents what the Bible tells us about "things to come" (John 16:13).

1. Rapture of the Church

   John 14:1-3; 1 Corinthians 1:7-8; 4:5; 15:23,51-53; Philippians 3:20-21; Colossians 3:4; 1 Thessalonians 1:10; 2:19; 3:13; 4:13-18; 5:23; 2 Timothy 4:8; Titus 2:12-13; Hebrews 9:28; 10:25,37; James 5:8; 1 John 2:28; 3:2; Revelation 2:25; 3:10-11; 4:1

2. Judgment Seat of Christ

   Romans 14:10-12; 1 Corinthians 3:11-15; 9:24; 2 Corinthians 5:10; Galatians 6:7-9; Colossians 3:24-25; 2 Timothy 4:8; Hebrews 10:30; 1 Peter 1:7; 1 John 4:17

3. Appearance of the Antichrist and the False Prophet

   Daniel 7:24-25; 2 Thessalonians 2:2-3; Revelation 13:1,11-12

4. Organization of the Harlot Church

   1 Timothy 4:1; 2 Timothy 3:1-5; 4:1-4; 2 Peter 2:1; 1 John 2:18-19; Jude 4; Revelation 17:1-6

5. Revival of the Roman Empire

   Daniel 2:41; 7:23-24; Revelation 12:3; 13:1; 17:12

6. Antichrist's Seven-Year Peace Treaty with Israel

   Daniel 9:27

7. Ministry of the 144,000

   Matthew 24:14; Mark 13:10; Revelation 7:1-8; 14:1-5

8. Rebuilding of the Jewish Temple

   Daniel 9:27; Matthew 24:15; 2 Thessalonians 2:4; Revelation 11:1-2

9. Ministry of the Two Witnesses

   Revelation 11:3-6

10. Seven Seal Judgments
    Matthew 24:5-9; Mark 13:6-8,12,25; Luke 21:8-11,16; Revelation 6:2-14

11. Gog and Magog Invasion into Israel
    Ezekiel 38:1–39:12

12. Martyrdom of the Two Witnesses
    Revelation 11:3-7

13. Casting of Satan out of Heaven
    Revelation 12:9

14. Abomination of Desolation in the Temple
    Matthew 24:15-16; Mark 13:14-18; 2 Thessalonians 2:3-4; Revelation 13:11-15

15. Full Manifestation of the Antichrist
    Daniel 7:25; 11:36-37; 2 Thessalonians 2:8-10; Revelation 13:5-8

16. Worldwide Persecution of Israel
    Daniel 12:1; Zechariah 11:16; Matthew 24:21; Luke 21:20-22; Revelation 7:13-14; 12:13

17. Destruction of Religious Babylon
    Revelation 17:16

18. Seven Trumpet Judgments
    Revelation 8:7-12; 9:1-3,13-16; 11:15

19. Seven Bowl Judgments
    Revelation 16:2-4,8-12,17-21

20. Destruction of Economic and Political Babylon
    Isaiah 13:19-20; Jeremiah 51:8; Revelation 14:8; 18:1-2,9,18-21.

21. Battle of Armageddon
    Psalm 2:1-5; Isaiah 13:6-13; 24:1,19-20; 26:21; 34:2-3; 42:13-14; 63:6; 66:15-16,24; Joel 3:2,9-16; Micah 5:15; Zephaniah 1:14-17; 3:8; Zechariah 12:2-4,9; 14:1-3,12; Matthew 24:28; Revelation 14:14, 20; 16:6; 19:17-21

22. Second Coming of Christ
    Isaiah 11:12; 25:9; 40:5,10; 59:20; Ezekiel 43:2-4; Daniel 7:13-14; Habakkuk 3:3-6,10-11; Haggai 2:6-7; Zechariah 8:3; 14:4,8; Malachi 3:1; 4:2; Matthew 24:29-30; 26:64; Mark 13:26; 14:62; Luke 21:27; 22:69; Acts 1:11; 3:20-21; 15:16; Romans 11:26; 1 Corinthians 15:24; 2 Thessalonians 1:7-8; Revelation 1:7; 2:25; 19:11-13

23. Regathering and Judgment of Israel
    Isaiah 10:20-23; 11:12; 35:10; 40:5; 43:5-6; Jeremiah 16:14-15; 23:3; 24:6; 29:14; 31:8; 32:37-40; 46:27; Ezekiel 11:16-21; 20:33-44; 34:11-13; 36:25-28; 37:12-14; Hosea 1:10-11; 3:5; Amos 9:9-10,14-15; Micah 7:18-19; Zechariah 12:10; 13:1,8-9; Malachi 4:1; Matthew 24:31,48-51; 25:7-10,24-30; Mark 13:27; Luke 21:34-35; Romans 9:6

24. Judgment of the Nations
    Matthew 25:31-32; 13:40-41,47-49; 25:31-46

25. Judgment of Angels
    Mark 1:23-24; 1 Corinthians 6:3; 2 Peter 2:4-9; Jude 6

26. Resurrection of Old Testament and Tribulational Saints
    Job 19:25-27; Psalm 49:15; Isaiah 25:8-9; 26:19; Daniel 12:2-3; Hosea 13:14; John 5:28-29; 11:23-27; Hebrews 11:35; Revelation 6:9-11; 20:4-6

27. Casting of Satan into the Abyss
    Romans 16:20; Revelation 20:2-3

28. Marriage Supper of the Lamb
    Isaiah 61:10; Matthew 22:2; 25:1; Luke 12:35-36; Revelation 19:7-9

29. Millennial Reign of Christ
    Psalm 2:6-8; 98:4,9; Isaiah 2:2-4; 9:6-7; 11:9-6; 25:8; 29:18-19; 30:23-26; 35:5-10; 40:4-5,10-11; 42:16; 45:6; 49:10-11; 55:13; 60:1,3,11,19-20,22; 65:19-20,25; Jeremiah 23:5-6; Ezekiel 34:23-24; Daniel 2:44; 7:13-14; Joel 3:18; Amos 9:11,13; Micah 4:1-6; Habakkuk 2:14; Zephaniah 3:9,15,17; Zechariah 6:12-13; 8:3-5; 14:8-9,16,20; Matthew 19:28; 25:31; Luke

1:31-33; 22:30; Acts 2:30; Romans 8:21; 1 Corinthians 15:24-28; Philippians 2:10-11; 2 Timothy 2:12; Hebrews 1:8; Revelation 3:21; 5:13; 11:15; 19:15-16; 20:4

30. Satan's Final Revolt

Revelation 20:7-8

31. Great White Throne Judgment

Psalm 9:17; Ecclesiastes 12:14; Daniel 7:9-10; Matthew 7:21-23; 12:36-37; John 5:22,27; 12:48; Acts 10:42; 17:31; 2 Timothy 4:1; Hebrews 9:27; Revelation 20:11-12

32. Destruction of This Present Earth and Heaven

Isaiah 51:6; Matthew 24:35; Hebrews 1:10-12; 2 Peter 3:10; 1 John 2:17

33. Creation of a New Earth, New Heaven, and New Jerusalem

Isaiah 65:17; 66:22; 2 Peter 3:13; Revelation 21:1-2

—HAROLD L. WILLMINGTON
AND WAYNE A. BRINDLE

BIBLIOGRAPHY

House, H. Wayne, and Randall Price. *Charts of Bible Prophecy*. Grand Rapids: Zondervan, 2003.

Ice, Thomas, and Timothy J. Demy. *The Return*. Grand Rapids: Kregel, 1999.

Pentecost, J. Dwight. *Things to Come*. Grand Rapids: Zondervan, 1958.

Walvoord, John F. *Israel, the Nations, and the Church in Prophecy*. Grand Rapids: Zondervan, 1988.

———. *Prophecy in the New Millennium*. Grand Rapids: Kregel, 2001.

Willmington, Harold L. *Willmington's Guide to the Bible*. Wheaton, IL: Tyndale House, 1981.

FUTURE LIFE

CHRISTIANS AND NON-CHRISTIANS have very different lives in the future in God's prophetic plan. The redeemed of all ages receive eternal life with God, whereas the unredeemed will endure everlasting punishment and separation from God. And during the millennium, after the rapture and Tribulation, all those who are on earth will experience a partial lifting of the curse and of the effects of original sin on all of humanity and creation. This will not change the need for every person to believe in Jesus Christ for salvation, but it will affect creation.

LIFE IN THE MILLENNIUM

During the millennium, people will continue to age and die, and the complete effects of the Fall will not be lifted until the creation of the new heaven and new earth in the eternal state after the millennium (Revelation 22:3). However, the changes will be significant for daily life. Extensive descriptions of life during this period are found in Isaiah 11:6-9; 30:18-26; 35:1-10; 65:20-25; Jeremiah 31:3-14.

These scriptures show that in the millennium, people (and animals) will experience abundant rainfall, ample food supplies, cessation of predatory instincts and carnivorous appetites, longer life spans and increased birthrates, better health and eradication of much illness, and increased prosperity.

Unfortunately, even in the midst of such pristine conditions, human rebellion will still exist. Unbelievers will make a final revolt against the righteous government of Jesus Christ. This will occur at the end of the millennium when Satan is briefly released from bondage just prior to his final judgment and destruction (Revelation 20:7-10).

ETERNAL LIFE

Though life during the millennium will be very different from today, the most important aspect of future life for all people of any age is the potential possession of eternal life. Eternal life is a gift from God given to all who believe in Jesus Christ and have accepted His offer of salvation based upon His death and resurrection (John 3:15-16; 10:10; Ephesians 2:8-9). The recipient of this divinely bestowed gift lives forever in the blessedness of God's presence.

Eternal life stems from the character of God, who is eternal (Deuteronomy 33:27; Psalm 10:16; 90:2; Isaiah 26:4; Jeremiah 10:10). Because God is eternal, so also is God's Word, which is grounded in His being and will (Psalm 119:89). Other divine attributes, actions, and benefits that are eternal include God's love (1 Kings 10:9; Psalm 136), blessings (Psalm 21:6), covenants, reign, and rule (Psalm 9:7; 66:7), plans (Psalm 33:11), inheritance of His people (Psalm 37:18), faithfulness (Psalm 117:2), statutes (Psalm 119:152), and His name (Psalm 135:13). Especially noteworthy from a prophetic perspective is the fact that except for the Mosaic or Old Covenant, God's covenants are eternal—the Abrahamic covenant (Genesis 17:7, 13,19; 1 Chronicles 16:17; Psalm 105:10), the Davidic covenant (2 Samuel 23:5), and the New Covenant (Ezekiel 37:26; Hebrews 13:20).

Eternal life is a major theme in the Bible, and especially the New Testament, where it is mentioned more than 40 times. Eternal life emphasizes a quality of life—a quality that can only be imparted by God Himself to those who trust and serve Him. Yet it pertains not only to a *quality* of life in this age and the age to come but also to the *duration* of that future age—the eternal state. This quality of life does not, of course, make individual believers divine. The redeemed are and will always remain creatures. The Creator–creature distinction has no end.

Beyond the teachings of Jesus in the Gospels, eternal life is also emphasized in 1 John (1:2; 2:25; 3:15; 5:11,13,20) and in the letters of Paul (Romans 2:7; 5:21; 6:22-23; 1 Timothy 1:16; 6:12; Titus 1:1-2). Jude 2 (NASB) encourages readers to "Keep yourselves in the love of God, waiting anxiously for the mercy of our Lord Jesus Christ to eternal life." Paul teaches that the Christian has received the Spirit as a pledge of eternal life, but he awaits the redemption of the body (Romans 8:23; 1 Corinthians 15:53). This redemption, which began with the resurrection of Jesus from the dead (1 Corinthians 15:12-19), will continue with the resurrection of believers in the future.

The timing of the resurrection of these individuals depends upon whether they were Old Testament saints, Christians living before or at the time of the rapture, or Christian martyrs of the Tribulation. All of these in this "first resurrection" comprise the category "resurrection of life" as contrasted with those in the "second resurrection" or "resurrection of judgment" (1 John 5:29; Revelation 20:5-6).

Eternal life, as presented in the Bible, should not be confused with the endless or eternal existence that everyone will experience. Eternal existence will be common to the redeemed and the unredeemed, but the destinies will be very different (1 John 5:12). Christians will enter into heaven and the presence of God; unbelievers will be cast into the lake of fire.

The sure and lasting salvation of eternal life is repeatedly contrasted with the destruction of the non-believer in the New Testament. Those who believe in Jesus Christ the Son of God receive eternal life, but those who reject the Son have eternal life withheld (John 3:36), and as a result will suffer eternal destruction (Matthew 7:13; 2 Corinthians 4:3; 2 Peter 3:9). The future life of every person throughout history who has received eternal life will be filled with the glories and experiences of heaven. Revelation 21 provides a description of the New Jerusalem and the eternal state. In part, the experiences of life in heaven include no pain, no suffering, no hardships, no tears, and no death (Revelation 21:4).

—TIMOTHY J. DEMY

BIBLIOGRAPHY

Hahn, H.C. "Destroy, Perish, Ruin." In *The New International Dictionary of New Testament Theology*, ed. Colin Brown. Grand Rapids: Zondervan, 1975.

Ice, Thomas, and Timothy J. Demy. *Fast Facts on Bible Prophecy A to Z*. Eugene, OR: Harvest House Publishers, 2004.

———. *What the Bible Says about Heaven & Eternity*. Grand Rapids: Kregel, 2000.

Walvoord, John F. "Eternity." In *The Theological Wordbook*. Nashville: Word Publishing, 2000.

Yarbrough, Robert W. "Eternal Life." In *Evangelical Dictionary of Biblical Theology*, ed. Walter A. Elwell. Grand Rapids: Baker Books, 1996.

GENERATION, THIS

TRULY I SAY TO YOU, this generation will not pass away until all these things take place" (Matthew 24:34; Mark 13:30; Luke 21:32 NKJV). During the last 100 years, this has been one of the most controversial passages in Bible prophecy. Many prophecy teachers have used it to explain when they believe God will fulfill the prophetic events of the Olivet Discourse. What are the various views?

EXAMINING THE VIEWS
The Fig Tree View

One major view is that "this generation" refers to those who see the rebirth of the nation of Israel, which occurred in 1948. This view teaches that within a generation (40 years) of Israel's becoming a nation again, the Lord would return. Adding 40 to 1948, the proponents of this view erroneously came up with 1988 as the year of Christ's return. More recently, others have suggested using 1967 (when Israel took full possession of Jerusalem) as the starting date.

This is based upon the belief that "the fig tree" in Matthew 24:32 is a symbol for the reconstitution of Israel as a nation. Thus, the generation that saw Israel become a nation would also see the second coming. Unfortunately, this view has several problems. First, Jesus never indicates that the fig tree actually represents Israel. In Luke 21:29, Jesus refers to "the fig tree and all the trees" in the same illustration.

Second, this view takes Christ's illustration of the fig tree a step further than Jesus intended. In other words, Jesus used the appearance of leaves on a fig tree as an illustration about the signs of that time. Some have taken that illustration and turned it into a prophecy. The context clearly indicates that Jesus only intended to use the fig tree as an illustration and not to provide additional prophecy.

The Preterist View

Gary DeMar (pp. 66–67) says, "The generation that was in existence when Jesus addressed His disciples would not pass away until all the events that preceded verse 34 came to pass." In contrast with fellow preterist Kenneth Gentry, DeMar believes that this passage requires that all of Matthew 24 and 25 must have been fulfilled in some way by A.D. 70 through the Roman invasion and destruction of Jerusalem and the Temple. DeMar (p. 68) says, "Every time 'this generation' is used in the New Testament, it means, without exception, the generation to whom Jesus was speaking." But the phrase "this generation" does not have to refer to those who are alive at the time the term is used. For example, "this generation" in Hebrews 3:10 clearly refers to the generation of Israelites that wandered in the wilderness for 40 years during the Exodus.

FINDING THE CORRECT VIEW
The Context

But how is it that almost all of the other New Testament uses of "this generation" are considered to refer to Christ's contemporaries, whereas the usage in Matthew 24:34 is not? We determine this by examining how each is used in its context. For example, Mark 8:12 says, "Sighing deeply in His spirit, [Jesus] said, 'Why does this generation seek for a sign? Truly I say to you, no sign will be given to this generation.'" Why do we conclude that "this generation" in this passage refers to Christ's contemporaries? We know this because the referent in this passage is to Christ's contemporaries, who were seeking for a sign from Jesus. Thus, it refers to Christ's contemporaries because of the controlling factor of the immediate context.

DeMar and many preterists incorrectly interpret the phrase "this generation" in Matthew 24:34 to mean exactly the same as it does in Mark 8:12. However, each passage must be studied individually as well as in comparison with other texts. Context is the most important factor in determining the exact meaning or referent under discussion. That is how one is able to realize that most of the other uses of "this generation" refer to Christ's contemporaries.

Matthew 23:36 says, "Truly I say to you, all these things will come upon this generation."

To whom does "this generation" refer? In this context, "this generation" refers to Christ's contemporaries because of contextual support. "This generation" is governed or controlled grammatically by the phrase "all these things," which refers to the judgments that Christ pronounces in Matthew 22–23. Each time the New Testament mentions "this generation," the meaning is determined by what it modifies in its immediate context.

The Grammatical Relationship

DeMar insists that the near demonstrative pronoun "this" always ties the time when something will take place to the speaker's present moment. This is not the case. Greek grammarian Daniel Wallace (p. 325) says, "The near/far distinctions of *outos* [this] and *ekeinos* can refer either to that which is near/far in the (1) context, (2) in the writer's mind, or (3) in space of time of the writer or audience." Thus, Wallace notes that speakers can use a near demonstrative pronoun in at least three ways.

Just because Jesus spoke the phrase "this generation" in the first century does not mean that He always had His contemporaries in mind, as preterists presuppose. Instead, the grammatical use of "this" allows Jesus to speak in the first century but prophetically look ahead to a distant time. The phrase "all these things" governs the meaning of "this generation." Since the evidence demonstrates that none of those things were fulfilled in the A.D. 70 destruction of Jerusalem, then Christ was pointing to another time period.

EXPLAINING THE CORRECT VIEW

We know that "this generation" in Matthew 24:34 (see also Mark 13:30; Luke 21:32) does not refer to Christ's contemporaries because the governing referent to "this generation" is "all these things." Jesus is giving an extended prophetic discourse of future events, so one must first determine the nature of "all these things" prophesied in verses 4 through 33 to know what generation Christ is referencing. "All these things" did not take place in the first century, so Christ must be speaking of a future generation. He is saying that the generation that sees "all these things" occur will not cease to exist until all the events of the future Tribulation are literally fulfilled. Christ is speaking not to His contemporaries, but to the generation that witnesses the signs of Matthew 24. Darrell Bock (pp. 1691–92), in commenting on the parallel passage in Luke's Gospel, concurs:

> What Jesus is saying is that the generation that sees the beginning of the end, also sees its end. When the signs come, they will proceed quickly; they will not drag on for many generations. It will happen within a generation....The tradition reflected in Revelation shows that the consummation comes very quickly once it comes....Nonetheless, in the discourse's prophetic context, the remark comes after making comments about the nearness of the end *to certain signs*. As such it is the issue of the signs that controls the passage's force, making this view likely. If this view is correct, Jesus says that when the signs of the beginning of the end come, then the end will come relatively quickly, within a generation.

The preterist argument reverses the interpretative process by declaring first that "this generation" has to refer to Christ's contemporaries and then insisting that "all these things" had to be fulfilled in the first century.

"This generation" does not refer to first-century events, nor is it related to our own day. Christ used that statement to mean that the generation that sees the events of the seven-year Tribulation period would be the same generation that sees His second coming. This understanding fits the grammar and context of the passage, and furthermore, harmonizes with the rest of biblical teaching related to the events of the coming Tribulation period.

—THOMAS ICE

BIBLIOGRAPHY

Bock, Darrell L. *Luke 9:51–24:53*. Grand Rapids: Baker Books, 1996.

Carson, D.A. *Exegetical Fallacies*. Grand Rapids: Baker Books, 1984.

DeMar, Gary. *End Times Fiction*. Nashville: Thomas Nelson, 2001.

Wallace, Daniel. *Greek Grammar Beyond the Basics*. Grand Rapids: Zondervan, 1996.

Zuck, Roy. *Basic Bible Interpretation*. Wheaton, IL: Victor Books, 1991.

GLORIOUS APPEARING

THE GLORIOUS APPEARING of Jesus Christ at the time of His second coming to this earth to judge the world and establish His messianic kingdom is one of the most significant events predicted in the entire Bible. Many of the psalms and all of the prophets refer to it, as do the apostles and our Lord Himself on numerous occasions. All nine New Testament authors mention it, in 23 of the 27 New Testament books.

Several key doctrines of the Bible are absolutely dependent on this appearing of Christ in glory. It will accomplish the completion of the first resurrection of the dead. It will initiate the final phase of Christ's victory over Satan. Most importantly, it will vindicate His absolute trustworthiness because He promised so many times that He would return in the glory of His Father.

On the climactic night before Christ's death, for example, as the high priest and Sanhedrin of Israel interrogated Him about His claims to be Messiah and Son of God, Jesus said bluntly, "I say to you, hereafter you will see the Son of Man sitting at the right hand of the Power, and coming on the clouds of heaven." At this the high priest tore his clothes and shouted, "He has spoken blasphemy!" And the council answered, "He is deserving of death" (Matthew 26:64-66 NKJV). The second coming of Christ in glory is a central and essential element of Christ's own witness concerning Himself.

THE DISTINCTION BETWEEN FIRST AND SECOND COMINGS

First-century Jews commonly perceived the first and second comings of Christ as one event. They mistook the prophetic promises that the Messiah would overcome the world, set up God's kingdom, and bring world peace as predictions that would all be fulfilled when He came. The reason so many rejected Him was that they expected Him to free Israel from the shackles of their Roman oppressors, not realizing that prophecies relating to His future kingdom referred to a separate, second coming. The purpose of His first coming was to suffer for the sins of the world, die on the cross, and rise again, providing what is the only way for believers to receive eternal life. We today have the privilege of looking back and seeing which prophecies are yet to be fulfilled by His glorious, second appearing.

CHRIST'S RETURN IN GLORY

The second coming of Christ will occur in two phases: the rapture and the "glorious appearing." Revelation 19:11-20 describes the latter in detail. This event involving Christ's return to earth with His saints to set up His kingdom occurs at the end of the seven-year Tribulation period.

Compare the differences between the rapture and the glorious appearing (this same chart appears later in the article titled "Second Coming of Christ"):

RAPTURE	GLORIOUS APPEARING
Christ comes *for* His own in the air	Christ comes *with* His own to the earth
All Christians are translated into new bodies	There is no translation of bodies
Christians are taken to the Father's house	Resurrected saints remain on earth
There is no judgment upon the earth	Christ judges the inhabitants of the earth
The church will be in heaven	Christ sets up His kingdom on earth
It could occur at any minute (it is imminent)	It cannot occur until the end of the seven-year Tribulation period

RAPTURE	GLORIOUS APPEARING
There are no signs preceding it	There are numerous signs preceding it
It affects believers only	It affects all humanity
It is a time of joy	It is a time of mourning
It occurs before the day of wrath	It occurs after the Tribulation
There is no mention of Satan	Satan is bound in the abyss for 1000 years
Christians are judged at the judgment seat of Christ	There is no judgment seat of Christ
There is the marriage of the Lamb	His bride descends with Him to earth
Only Christ's own will see Him	Every eye will see Him
The Tribulation begins	The millennial reign of Christ begins

—TIM LAHAYE

BIBLIOGRAPHY

Couch, Mal, ed. *Dictionary of Premillennial Theology.* Grand Rapids: Kregel, 1996.

LaHaye, Tim, and Jerry Jenkins. *Are We Living in the End Times?* Wheaton, IL: Tyndale House, 1999.

Pentecost, J. Dwight. *Things to Come.* Grand Rapids: Zondervan, 1975.

Showers, Renald. *Maranatha: Our Lord Come!* Bellmawr, NJ: Friends of Israel, 1995.

Walvoord, John F. *Major Bible Prophecies.* Grand Rapids: Zondervan, 1991.

GOG AND MAGOG

EZEKIEL 38–39 CONTAINS one of the greatest prophecies in the Bible. It describes a massive invasion of Israel in "the latter years" by a great confederation of nations. The easiest way to understand this prophecy is to ask five questions about it: Who? Where? When? Why? What?

WHO WILL INVADE?

Ezekiel 38:1-6 lists ten proper names that help to identify the invading forces. Nine of these ten words describe geographical locations. "Gog" is the lone exception. *Gog* is not a geographical location or a personal name but a title, like Pharaoh, Caesar, or President. *Gog* means a high mountain, high, supreme, or a height. Gog will be the leader of this invasion, and he is also called a prince.

The names given by Ezekiel are the ancient geographical names of countries that existed in his day. These countries were all well known in his day but are totally foreign to us. Our task is to determine what countries today inhabit these ancient lands. This chart compares these ancient regions with our present-day political divisions. The names of these nations may change, but the geographical locations remain constant.

ANCIENT NAME	MODERN NATION
Rosh (ancient Sarmatians—known as Rashu, Rasapu, Ros, and Rus)	Russia
Magog (ancient Scythians)	Central Asia (Islamic southern republics of the former Soviet Union with a population of 60 million Muslims. This territory could include modern Afghanistan)
Meshech (ancient Muschki and Musku in Cilicia and Cappadocia)	Turkey (also southern Russia and Iran)
Tubal (ancient Tubalu in Cappadocia)	Turkey (also southern Russia and Iran)

ANCIENT NAME	MODERN NATION
Persia	Iran (name changed to Iran in 1935)
Ethiopia (ancient Cush, south of Egypt)	Sudan
Libya (ancient Put, west of Egypt)	Libya
Gomer (ancient Cimmerians—from seventh century to first century B.C. in central/western Anatolia)	Turkey
Beth-togarmah (Til-garimmu—between ancient Carchemish and Haran)	Turkey

This list shows that at least six key allies will come together for this end-time invasion of Israel: Russia, Turkey, Iran, Libya, Sudan, and the nations of Central Asia.

WHERE WILL THEY INVADE?

Ezekiel 38:7-9 explains that these nations will invade the land of Israel. The invasion will come to the "mountains of Israel."

WHEN WILL THEY INVADE?

Ezekiel gives three key clues concerning the timing of this invasion. First, Ezekiel actually tells us when this invasion will occur. He says specifically that this invasion will occur in the "latter years" (Ezekiel 38:8 NASB). This is the only occurrence of this exact phrase in the Old Testament.

Another similar phrase occurs in Ezekiel 38:16: "It will come about in *the last days* that I will bring you against My land" (emphasis added). This phrase is used in the Old Testament in reference to Israel's final time of distress or to Israel's final restoration to the messianic kingdom (see Isaiah 2:2; Jeremiah 23:20; 30:24; Hosea 3:5; Micah 4:1). Likewise,

in Ezekiel 38:16, the phrase "in the last days" is a technical term that refers to the end times. Therefore, Ezekiel is telling us that this invasion will occur in the final time of history in preparation for the establishment of the messianic kingdom of Christ. Also, we know that this invasion is still future because nothing even remotely similar to the events described in Ezekiel 38–39 has ever occurred in the past.

Second, Israel must be gathered to her land for this invasion to occur. Obviously, this gathering has taken place since the establishment of the nation of Israel in 1948.

Third, Israel must be at rest when this invasion occurs. This fact is emphasized three times in Ezekiel 38:

> But its people were brought out from the nations, and they are living securely, all of them (verse 8).

> I will go against those who are at rest, that live securely, all of them living without walls and having no bars or gates (verse 11).

> Thus says the Lord GOD, "On that day when My people Israel are living securely, will you not know it?" (verse 14).

Since 1948, Israel has never enjoyed a time of peace and safety when she could let her guard down. Modern Israel has never really had a time of peace—only brief respites of no war. Looking at the volatile situation in the Middle East today, we may wonder, *When will Israel enjoy a time of rest and security like the one described in Ezekiel 38?*

The Bible mentions only two times in Israel's future when she will be at peace. The first is a brief 3½-year period of peace during the first half of the seven-year Tribulation that will begin when the Antichrist makes a covenant or peace treaty with Israel (Daniel 9:27).

The second time of peace for Israel will be when the Prince of Peace, the Lord Jesus, returns to earth from heaven to destroy Israel's enemies and inaugurate His 1000-year kingdom of peace and joy centered in Israel. Isaiah 2:4 explicitly states this will be a time of peace: "He will judge between the nations, and will render decisions for many peoples; and they will hammer their swords into plowshares and their spears into pruning hooks. Nation will not lift up sword against nation, and never again will they learn war."

Putting all these clues together, the only time that fits the scenario described in Ezekiel 38 is the first half of the tribulation period, after the church has been raptured to heaven, when Israel is living under the peace and protection of her covenant with Antichrist (see Daniel 9:27).

WHY WILL THEY INVADE?

Russia and her allies will invade Israel for four reasons:

1. to cash in on the wealth of Israel (Ezekiel 38:11-12)

2. to control the Middle East

3. to crush Israel (the Islamic nations mentioned in Scripture hate Israel)

4. to challenge the authority of Antichrist (Daniel 11:40-45)

These four reasons are the human justifications for the invasion, but God's goal or purpose in this invasion is that He might be sanctified in the eyes of the nations (Ezekiel 38:14-16).

WHAT WILL HAPPEN WHEN THEY INVADE?

This invasion will look like the biggest mismatch in history. It will make the Arab invasions of Israel in 1967 and 1973 pale in comparison. When Russia assembles this last-days strike force, Israel will appear to be finished. But God will be in control of the entire situation. He will mount up in His fury to destroy these godless invaders: "'It will come about on that day, when Gog comes against the land of Israel,' declares the Lord GOD, 'that my fury will mount up in My anger'" (Ezekiel 39:18).

God will come to rescue His helpless people and will use four means to destroy Russia and her allies.

1. God will cause a great earthquake (38:19-20).

2. Infighting will break out among the troops of the various nations (38:21). In the chaos after the powerful earthquake, the armies of each of the nations represented will turn against each other. This will be the largest case of death by friendly fire in human history.

3. Disease will spread (38:22).

4. Torrential rain, hailstones, fire, and burning sulphur (38:22) will fall.

The Six-Day War occurred in Israel in June 1967. This will be the One-Day War or even the One-Hour War, when God supernaturally destroys this Russian-Islamic horde. Four key events will occur in the aftermath of this invasion:

1. The carnage that results from this slaughter will provide a great feast for the birds of the air and the beasts of the field (Ezekiel 39:4-5,17-20; see also Revelation 19:17-18). God refers to the carnage as "My sacrifice" and "My table" to which He invites the birds and the beasts as His guests.

2. Cleanup squads will set up markers throughout the land wherever they see a human bone. When the gravediggers come behind them, they will see the markers and take the remains to the Valley of Gog's Hordes for burial. The cleanup will be so extensive that a town will be established in the valley at the gravesites to aid those who are cleansing the land. The name of the town will be *Hamonah* (horde) (Ezekiel 39:11-12,14-16). The cleanup will take seven months.

3. This event will occur during the first half of the Tribulation, and the Israelites will continue to burn these weapons for 3½ years (Ezekiel 39:9-10).

4. In the midst of His wrath and fury, God will also pour out His grace and mercy. God will use the awesome display of His power against Russia and her allies to bring many Jews and Gentiles to salvation.

> You will come up against My people Israel like a cloud to cover the land. It

shall come about in the last days that I will bring you against My land, so that the nations may know Me when I am sanctified through you before their eyes, O Gog....I will magnify Myself, sanctify Myself, and make Myself known in the sight of many nations; and they will know that I am the LORD....And I will send fire upon Magog and those who inhabit the coastlands in safety; and they will know that I am the LORD. My holy name I will make known in the midst of My people Israel; and I will not let My holy name be profaned anymore. And the nations will know that I am the LORD, the Holy One in Israel....And I will set My glory among the nations; and all the nations will see My judgment which I have executed and My hand which I have laid on them. And the house of Israel will know that I am the LORD their God from that day onward (Ezekiel 38:16,23; 39:6-7,21-22).

Many of those who turn to the true God as a result of this demonstration of His power will undoubtedly be among the vast group of the redeemed in Revelation 7:9-14.

Ezekiel 38–39 is one of the most amazing prophecies in all of Scripture, and everything seems to be getting ready for its fulfillment in the near future. Russia and the radical Islamic nations surrounding Israel are the key players in this prophecy, and they will be the places to watch as the passage of time brings us closer to Christ's return.

—MARK HITCHCOCK

BIBLIOGRAPHY

Feinberg, Charles Lee. *The Prophecy of Ezekiel.* Chicago: Moody Press, 1969.

Fruchtenbaum, Arnold G. *The Footsteps of the Messiah,* rev. ed. Tustin, CA: Ariel Ministries, 2003.

Hitchcock, Mark. *After the Empire.* Wheaton, IL: Tyndale House, 1994.

———. *The Coming Islamic Invasion of Israel.* Sisters, OR: Multnomah Publishers, 2002.

Pentecost, J. Dwight. "Where Do the Events of Ezekiel 38–39 Fit into the Prophetic Picture?" *Bibliotheca Sacra* 114. October 1957, pp. 334-46.

GREAT TRIBULATION

JESUS WARNED HIS DISCIPLES that the last days before His second coming would include a period of time more horrific and traumatic than any other time in human history.

> Then there will be great tribulation, such as has not been since the beginning of the world until this time, no, nor ever shall be (Matthew 24:21 NKJV).

The disciples were familiar with this prophesied time of anguish, for many of the Hebrew prophets had warned Israel that such a period of intense suffering would come. Jeremiah called it "the time of Jacob's trouble" (Jeremiah 30:7). The Old and New Testaments refer to it by various names including the day of the Lord, the seventieth week, the day of desolation, the wrath to come, the hour of judgment, the Tribulation, and the Great Tribulation.

Both the prophet Daniel and the apostle John specified that this period will last seven years. The evil "prince who is to come" (the Antichrist, Daniel 9:26) will make a covenant with Israel, beginning the seven-year period. He will then break that covenant in the middle of the seven years by desecrating the rebuilt Temple in Jerusalem. The Tribulation will be the most terrible time of suffering and terror mankind has ever experienced, and although it will last only seven years, its devastations will seem endless to those who miss the rapture and are left behind on the earth.

Various prophetic Bible passages explain that the Tribulation will include...

1. judgment for those who reject the Savior

2. conclusion for those who rebel against God

3. decision for those who must choose between Christ and the Antichrist

4. chaos that will challenge man's false sense of security

5. unprecedented revival and the greatest soul harvest in history

When will the Tribulation take place? Although the Bible gives no exact date, it indicates in Matthew 24:29-30 that it must occur immediately before the glorious appearing of Christ, when Jesus Himself returns to earth to destroy the Antichrist.

A TIME OF MERCY

Those who view the Tribulation as only a time of wrath overlook the fact that it is also a time of mercy and grace. The Lord will not angrily heap catastrophes upon the heads of innocent men and women. The people who suffer the judgments of God during the Tribulation will not be innocent. These rebels will not only reject God and His free offer of salvation but also indulge in every vile sin known to man, including killing those who come to Christ during this period. Even then, God's hope is that they will at some point turn to Him. The Tribulation judgments therefore serve a dual purpose—to punish hardened sinners and to move others to repentance. The following passage in Joel exemplifies this truth:

> And I will show wonders in the heavens and in the earth: Blood and fire and pillars of smoke. The sun shall be turned into darkness, and the moon into blood, before the coming of the great and awesome day of the LORD. And it shall come to pass that whoever calls on the name of the LORD shall be saved (Joel 2:30-32).

Untold millions, possibly billions, will realize that although they missed the rapture because of their rejection of God and must now endure the terrors of the Tribulation, they still have the opportunity to be saved. The apostle John envisions this future event:

> After these things I looked, and behold, a great multitude which no one could number, of all nations, tribes, peoples, and tongues, standing before the throne and before the Lamb, clothed with white robes, with palm branches in their hands (Revelation 7:9).

THE TRIBULATION SAINTS

These "Tribulation saints," whose numbers are so large they can't be counted, come to the Lord precisely because of the Tribulation's trials. This demonstrates that our Holy God loves mankind beyond all human comprehension. No wonder the apostle Peter was able to write,

> The Lord is not slack concerning His promise, as some count slackness, but is longsuffering toward us, not willing that any should perish but that all should come to repentance (2 Peter 3:9).

In many respects, the rapture will set the stage for the coming Tribulation. Following the disappearance of millions upon millions of Christians, the world will not only be in shock but will experience mass chaos as well. This sets the stage perfectly for the rise of the Antichrist. He will come to power peaceably using diplomacy, as represented by the rider on the white horse—the first of the four horsemen of the Apocalypse (Revelation 6:1-2).

THE RISE OF THE ANTICHRIST

Daniel was the first prophet to write about the Antichrist's quest for a one-world government. During the last century, various groups such as the Council on Foreign Relations, the United Nations, the Club of Rome, and others have been working feverishly behind the scenes toward a united world government—all in the name of world peace. Such conditions will lay the foundation for the Antichrist's rise to power.

The spiritual vacuum left by the disappearance of millions of Christians will also enable the Antichrist to further his plan to establish a one-world religion. This pagan religion will unite all religions—with the lone exception of biblical Christianity—into one. However, through the work of the Holy Spirit operating in the 144,000 evangelists and the two witnesses in Jerusalem, countless numbers of people will come to Christ during the Tribulation despite the fact that such a choice will most likely result in martyrdom.

GLOBAL CONFLICT

On the heels of his peaceful ascension to power, the Antichrist will initiate what we might call World War III (Revelation 6:3-4) against three of the ten regional leaders who will be in power during this time. Death will come to earth on an unprecedented scale. This battle may possibly involve a nuclear exchange and will be followed by massive inflation, famine, and disease. Plagues will sweep across the land, and a fourth of the world's population will die (Revelation 6:5-8). All the while, the Antichrist will be carrying out his vengeance against those who have chosen to follow Christ instead of him (Revelation 6:9-11). The martyrdom of Tribulation saints will escalate as the world sinks further into chaos and despair.

DIVINE WRATH

Up to this point, the judgments that have come upon the earth during the Tribulation are largely the consequences of man's actions. But from here onward, however, the judgments are clearly supernatural. Revelation 6:12-15 describes a massive earthquake so large that "every mountain and island was moved out of its place." Massive volcanic eruptions seem to occur as well, causing the sky to turn black and the moon to appear red. The apostle John also writes of objects like meteorites crashing to the earth. The people of earth will be fully aware that they are witnessing the hand of God at work.

> The kings of the earth, the great men, the rich men, the commanders, the mighty men, every slave and every free man, hid themselves in the caves and in the rocks of the mountains, and said to the mountains and rocks, "Fall on us and hide us from the face of Him who sits on the throne and from the wrath of the Lamb! For the great day of His wrath has come, and who is able to stand?" (Revelation 6:15-17).

Then hail, fire, and blood will rain down from the sky, causing a third of the earth's trees and grass to burn up. Two more meteors will fall from the sky, killing a third of the sea life, destroying a third of the ships at sea, and poisoning a third of the earth's fresh water supply. Then darkness will fall across the land as the light from the sun and moon is dimmed by a third.

Revelation 9 describes a plague of locust-like creatures that sting people. For five months, these creatures will torment but not kill unbelievers.

DEMONIC HORDES

> Then out of the smoke locusts came upon the earth. And to them was given power, as the scorpions of the earth have power. They were commanded not to harm the grass of the earth, or any green thing, or any tree, but only those men who do not have the seal of God on their foreheads. And they were not given authority to kill them, but to torment them for five months. Their torment was like the torment of a scorpion when it strikes a man. In those days men will seek death and will not find it; they will desire to die, and death will flee from them (Revelation 9:3-6).

If that weren't enough, armies of demonic horsemen will kill another third of the world's population (Revelation 9:13-19).

THE MARK OF THE BEAST

The Antichrist will break his treaty with the nation of Israel, desecrate the rebuilt Temple in Jerusalem, and kill the two witnesses who have been proclaiming the gospel. He then will seize total control over the monetary system of the world, requiring all to carry his mark, the mark of the beast.

> He causes all, both small and great, rich and poor, free and slave, to receive a mark on their right hand or on their foreheads, and that no one may buy or sell except one who has the mark (Revelation 13:16-17).

Meanwhile, the judgments of God will continue to afflict the ungodly. Loathsome sores will break out upon those who have the mark of the beast. The sea and remaining fresh water will be turned into blood. Heat from the sun will scorch the unrepentant of the world, while darkness envelops the kingdom of the Antichrist headquartered in the rebuilt city of Babylon (Revelation 16:2-11).

THE BATTLE OF ARMAGEDDON

Then the Euphrates River will dry up, allowing the armies of the north to march on Israel and begin the battle of Armageddon. A tremendous earthquake will level the cities of the world as hailstones weighing about 135 pounds each smash into the earth. But does all this cause the ungodly of the world to repent? No.

> There was a great earthquake, such a mighty and great earthquake as had not occurred since men were on the earth. Now the great city was divided into three parts, and the cities of the nations fell. And great Babylon was remembered before God, to give her the cup of the wine of the fierceness of His wrath. Then every island fled away, and the mountains were not found. And great hail from heaven fell upon men, each hailstone about the weight of a talent. Men blasphemed God because of the plague of the hail, since that plague was exceedingly great (Revelation 16:18-21).

And with that, the judgments are over. The glorious appearance of Christ in the air brings death to the Antichrist and an end to the Tribulation. The establishment of the millennial kingdom of Christ on earth can now begin.

—TIM LAHAYE

BIBLIOGRAPHY

Couch, Mal. "The Great Tribulation," in Mal Couch, ed. *Dictionary of Premillennial Theology*. Grand Rapids: Kregel, 1996.

Hitchcock, Mark, and Thomas Ice. *The Truth Behind Left Behind*. Sisters, OR: Multnomah Publishers, 2004.

LaHaye, Tim. *The Rapture*. Eugene, OR: Harvest House Publishers, 2002.

Ryrie, Charles. "The Tribulation." In Joe Jordan and Tom Davis, eds. *Countdown to Armageddon*. Eugene, OR: Harvest House Publishers, 1999.

Walvoord, John F. *The Blessed Hope and the Tribulation*. Grand Rapids: Zondervan, 1976.

GREAT WHITE THRONE JUDGMENT

THE MOST SOBERING PASSAGE in the Bible is Revelation 20:11-15. Here unbelievers can see a glimpse of what their ultimate encounter with God will be like. These verses describe the Great White Throne judgment, which will occur at the end of the 1000-year millennial reign of Christ upon the earth.

> Then I saw a great white throne and Him who sat on it, from whose face the earth and the heaven fled away. And there was found no place for them. And I saw the dead, small and great, standing before God, and books were opened. And another book was opened, which is the Book of Life. And the dead were judged according to their works, by the things which were written in the books. The sea gave up the dead who were in it, and Death and Hades delivered up the dead who were in them. And they were judged, each one according to his works. Then Death and Hades were cast into the lake of fire. This is the second death. And anyone not found written in the Book of Life was cast into the lake of fire (Revelation 20:11-15 NKJV).

The Bible clearly states that some kind of judgment will follow death. Hebrews 9:27 tells us that "it is appointed for men to die once, but after this the judgment." Our status in Christ determines how we will be judged. Immediately following the rapture, the believer will stand before the judgment seat of Christ (2 Corinthians 5:10). There the resurrected saints will receive rewards for the good works they performed while on earth.

But this is far different from what will happen to the unbeliever, who will appear before the Great White Throne judgment at the end of the millennium. Revelation 20:11-15 depicts a scene of severe judgment. This event occurs after the 1000-year reign of Christ on the earth. Satan is released from his captivity in the bottomless pit and once more engages in battle against God. He deceives many into joining him in this futile attempt. Fire comes down from heaven and devours the followers of Satan, while Satan himself is cast into the lake of fire. Then the unsaved dead of all time appear before the Great White Throne judgment.

THE DESCRIPTION OF THE THRONE

In Revelation 20:11-15, John first describes a throne. This is not the first mention of a throne in Revelation, but John uses two unique adjectives to describe this throne. He calls it a "great" and "white" throne. The throne is great due to (1) the enormous size in contrast to those mentioned in Revelation 20:4, (2) the One who occupies the throne, and (3) the significance of the judgment that will issue from the throne.

The color of the throne also has several connotations. It signifies the purity of the One seated on the throne. It also pictures the equity with which justice will be administered. Finally, white connotes the righteousness of the judge and the verdict.

THE OCCUPANT ON THE THRONE

John does not directly identify the occupant of the throne. In Revelation, "the One who sits on the throne" frequently refers to God. However, John 5:22 states, "For the Father judges no one, but has committed all judgment to the Son." In Romans 2:16 Paul writes about "the day when God will judge the secrets of men by Jesus Christ." Revelation 3:21 speaks of Jesus sharing a throne with God. Perhaps Barclay (p. 421) gives the best solution when he states, "The unity of the Father and the Son is such that there is no difficulty in ascribing the action of the one to the other."

In the presence of this divine majesty, the earth and its immediate atmosphere vanish. Just as sinful man cannot remain in the presence of a holy God, the sin-corrupted earth and its environs flee. Second Peter 3:10 describes the heavens passing away with a great noise, the elements melting with fervent heat, and the earth being consumed by fire. No place is found for them because corruption has no place in the presence of a holy God.

THE PEOPLE WHO WILL BE JUDGED

"The dead, small and great" refers to those who have lived throughout history and, regardless of their stature or position, died without acknowledging and accepting Jesus Christ's payment for their sins. Whether in the earth or sea, in a grave or mausoleum, the ashes or remains of these deceased will be raised and united with their souls and spirits so that they can stand in a resurrected form before the Great White Throne.

After death, the soul continues to exist, and at the resurrection, the soul will receive a body suitable for eternal existence. Before the resurrection, the soul of the believer is in the presence of God awaiting eternal reward. The soul of the unbeliever is in hades, the place of the wicked dead, awaiting final judgment. At the Great White Throne judgment, all the unbelieving dead from all time will be resurrected. Daniel 12:2; John 5:28-29; and Acts 24:15 all describe a resurrection of the just and the unjust. Daniel and John further explain that at this resurrection the just will be raised to eternal life while the unjust will be raised to shame and condemnation. At the Great White Throne judgment, those unbelieving dead of all strata of society, all levels of intellect, all positions of power, all echelons of finance, have one thing in common. They all died without Christ. They will be raised from their graves, and hades will be emptied.

THE BASIS OF THE JUDGMENT

During this judgment, various books will be opened, revealing the records of every deed and thought, including those performed in secret, of every unbeliever. Ecclesiastes 12:14 reads, "God will bring every work into judgment, including every hidden thing, whether good or evil." It is sobering to think that each

THE GREAT WHITE THRONE JUDGMENT

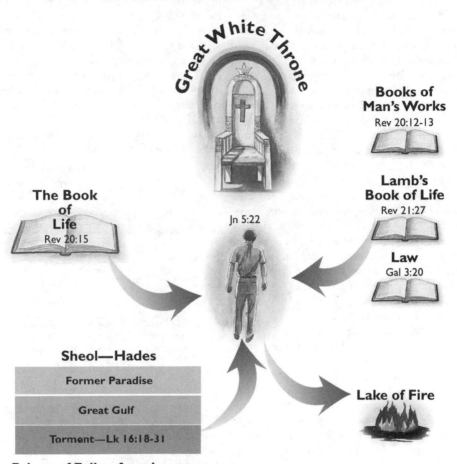

of us may have a recording angel tabulating our every thought, word, or deed. The actions and intentions of those who have foolishly chosen not to have their sins erased by the sacrifice of Jesus will be judged according to the law of the Old Testament. As Galatians 3:10 reveals, those who live under the law and not under Christ will be judged by the law. Unless we accept God's mercy made available in His Son, we cannot be found righteous, "for all have sinned and fall short of the glory of God" (Romans 3:23).

Hebrews 2:2 requires that "every transgression and disobedience [receive] a just reward." This is consistent with the justice of God and seems to indicate different levels of torment in hell. A relatively moral citizen who has lived a comparatively good life (though still short of the standard of God) would not be subjected to the same punishment as Adolph Hitler. Likewise, those who have never heard the gospel will be judged accordingly and certainly less severely than those who have heard the message repeatedly and rejected it. Matthew 11:21-24 reinforces this idea. In this passage of Scripture, Jesus explained that the people who heard His message and rejected it would be subjected to greater condemnation than the sinners who lived in the Old Testament cities Sodom and Gomorrah.

The judge sits on His throne, ready to give the verdict as He examines the books that are opened in the presence of the courtroom. These books record all the deeds of each defendant. Salvation is not the issue, for those in this judgment are described as dead, meaning that they are spiritually dead. Thus, their works, which cannot be pleasing to God (Romans 8:8), will be irrefutable evidence that they have no saving relationship with God. With no mediator (1 Timothy 2:5), they will be judged by their actions (Matthew 16:27). No defense attorney will plead the case of those standing before the throne. They will stand naked and open before the eyes of Him to whom they must give an account. Judgment will be entered, and the sentence is the lake of fire, a punishment of everlasting torment prepared for Satan, his angels, and all who refuse the offer of eternal life through Christ (Matthew 25:41,46).

Another book is opened. "Book" in this instance is singular, for there is only one. It is the Book of Life, which contains the names of God's elect, citizens of heaven. These people will experience no condemnation (Romans 8:1) or judgment. They are not among the dead, for they are alive. They have escaped the judgment and its consequent verdict, the second death. In John 6:50-51 Jesus stated that He was the bread of life and promised that anyone who ate of this bread would not die but would live forever. By making such a promise, Jesus didn't mean that a person would not die physically; He was referring to spiritual death.

In John 11:25, Jesus said to Martha, "I am the resurrection and the life. He who believes in Me, though he may die, he shall live." Creation is subject to physical death. But only unbelievers are subject to the second death, expulsion to the lake of fire. The resurrected Lord promised the church at Smyrna, "He who overcomes shall not be hurt by the second death" (Revelation 2:11). The Book of Life testifies against the unbelievers because their names are not found in it.

Paul writes in 1 Corinthians 15:26 that "the last enemy that will be destroyed is death."

Satan is destroyed and cast into the lake of fire in Revelation 20:10, joining the beast and the False Prophet, who had preceded him by 1000 years. The unbelieving dead are judged and cast into the lake of fire. Finally, death and Hades are defeated and cast into the lake of fire. Death is destroyed as God eliminates sorrow, causes crying to cease, and wipes away every tear. Death shall be no more (Revelation 21:4). "Death is swallowed up in victory. O Death, where is your sting? O Hades, where is your victory?" (1 Corinthians 15:54-55).

—TIM LaHAYE AND
TONY KESSINGER

BIBLIOGRAPHY

Barclay, William. *The Revelation of John*, vol. 2. Philadelphia: Westminster John Knox Press, 1976.

Johnson, Alan F. *Revelation*. Vol 12 of *The Expositors Bible Commentary*. Frank E. Gaebelein, ed. Grand Rapids: Zondervan, 1981.

MacArthur, John. *Revelation 12–22*, Chicago: Moody Press, 2000.

Mounce, Robert H. *The Book of Revelation*, Grand Rapids: Eerdmans Publishing Company, 1977.

Thomas, Robert L. *Revelation 8–22: An Exegetical Commentary*. Chicago: Moody Press, 1995.

HEAVEN

THE KING JAMES VERSION of the Bible employs the word *heaven* 582 times in 550 different verses. The Hebrew word usually translated "heaven," *shamayim*, is a plural noun form that literally means "the heights." The Greek word translated "heaven" is *ouranos* (the same word that inspired the name of the planet Uranus). It refers to that which is raised up or lofty. Scripture uses both *shamayim* and *ouranos* to refer to three different places. (This explains why in 2 Corinthians 12:2 Paul refers to being caught up into "the *third* heaven.")

THE KINDS OF HEAVEN
Atmospheric Heaven

The atmospheric heaven is the sky, or the troposphere—the region of breathable atmosphere that blankets the earth. For example,

Genesis 7:11-12 (KJV) says, "The windows of heaven were opened. And the rain was upon the earth forty days and forty nights." There, the word "heaven" refers to the blanket of atmosphere around the world, which is where the hydrological cycle occurs. Psalm 147:8 says that God "covereth the heaven with clouds." That is the first heaven.

Planetary Heaven

The planetary heaven, the second heaven, is where the stars, the moon, and the planets are. Scripture uses the very same word for heaven to describe this region. For example, Genesis 1:14-17 says,

> And God said, Let there be lights in the firmament of the heaven to divide the day from the night; and let them be for signs, and for seasons, and for days, and years: And let them be for lights in the firmament of the heaven to give light upon the earth: and it was so. And God made two great lights; the greater light to rule the day, and the lesser light to rule the night: he made the stars also. And God set them in the firmament of the heaven to give light upon the earth.

Third Heaven

The third heaven, the one Paul speaks of in 2 Corinthians 12, is the heaven where God dwells with His holy angels and those saints who have died. The other two heavens will pass away (2 Peter 3:10); this heaven is eternal.

Someone may ask, "If God is omnipresent, how can Scripture say heaven is His habitation? After all, how can an omnipresent being be said to dwell anywhere?" Solomon, when dedicating the Temple in Jerusalem, prayed, "Behold, the heaven and heaven of heavens cannot contain thee; how much less this house that I have builded?" (1 Kings 8:27).

"The heaven and heaven of heavens" certainly cannot contain God. He is omnipresent. His presence reaches every realm. The psalmist, exalting God's omnipresence, said,

"If I make my bed in hell, behold, thou art there" (Psalm 139:8).

So to say that God dwells in heaven is not to say that He is contained there. But heaven is uniquely His home, His center of operations, His command post. It is the place where His throne resides. And it is where the most perfect worship of Him occurs. In that sense, we say heaven is His dwelling place.

Scripture reveals that heaven is not confined to a limited height, width, and breadth. Heaven seems to span all those dimensions—and more. In Christ's message to the Philadelphian church, for example, He speaks of the eternal realm as "new Jerusalem, which cometh down out of heaven from my God" (Revelation 3:12). In the closing chapters of Scripture, the apostle John speaks of "that great city, the holy Jerusalem, descending out of heaven from God" (Revelation 21:10). The new heaven and new earth blend together in a great kingdom that incorporates both realms. The paradise of eternity is thus revealed as a magnificent kingdom where both heaven and earth unite in a glory that surpasses the limits of the human imagination and the boundaries of earthly dimensions.

THE PLACE OF HEAVEN

So heaven is not confined to one locality marked off by visible or measurable boundaries. It transcends the confines of time–space dimensions. Perhaps that is part of what Scripture means when it states that God inhabits eternity (Isaiah 57:15). His dwelling place—heaven—is not subject to the normal limitations of finite dimensions. We don't need to speculate about how this can be; we can simply note that this is how Scripture describes heaven. It is a real place where people with physical bodies will dwell in God's presence for all eternity, and it is also a realm that surpasses our finite concept of what a "place" is.

Heaven transcends normal space–time dimensions in another important sense. According to Scripture, a mysterious form of the kingdom of God—incorporating all the elements of heaven itself—is the spiritual sphere in which all true Christians live even now. The kingdom of heaven invades and begins to govern the life of every believer in Christ. Spiritually, the Christian becomes a part of heaven with full rights of citizenship here and now in this life.

That's exactly what Paul was saying when he wrote, "Our citizenship is in heaven" (Philippians 3:20 NASB). In a positional sense, we who believe are already living in the kingdom of God.

In Ephesians 1:3 the apostle Paul says that God "hath blessed us with all spiritual blessings *in heavenly places* in Christ" (emphasis added). Ephesians 2:5-6 likewise says, "Even when we were dead in sins, [God] hath quickened us together with Christ...and hath raised us up together, and made us sit together *in heavenly places* in Christ Jesus." Note that in both passages, the verbs are past tense. Paul is speaking of an already-accomplished reality. We aren't yet in heaven bodily. But positionally, we are seated with Christ in the heavenlies. Because of our spiritual union with Him, we have already entered into the heavenly realm. We already possess eternal life, and the spiritual riches of heaven are ours in Jesus Christ.

THE GLORY OF HEAVEN

Everything that is truly precious to us as Christians is in heaven.

The Father is there, and that's why Jesus taught us to pray, "Our Father which art in heaven, hallowed be thy name" (Matthew 6:9). Jesus Himself is at the Father's right hand. Hebrews 9:24 says, "Christ is not entered into the holy places made with hands, which are the figures of the true; but into heaven itself, now to appear in the presence of God for us." So our Savior is also in heaven, where He intercedes on our behalf (Hebrews 7:25).

Many *brothers and sisters in Christ* are there too. Hebrews 12:23 says that in turning to God we have come "to the general assembly and church of the firstborn, which are written in heaven, and to God the Judge of all, and to the spirits of just men made perfect." Our departed loved ones in the faith are there.

Every Old and New Testament believer who has died is now in heaven.

Our names are recorded there. In Luke 10:20 Christ tells His disciples, who were casting out demons, "Rejoice not, that the spirits are subject unto you; but rather rejoice, because your names are written in heaven." And by saying that our names are written in heaven, Christ assures us that we have a title deed to property there. This is *our inheritance.* First Peter 1:4 says we are begotten in Christ "to an inheritance incorruptible, and undefiled, and that fadeth not away, reserved in heaven for you."

"*Our citizenship* is in heaven," according to Philippians 3:20 (NASB). In other words, heaven is where we belong. We're just "strangers and exiles on the earth" (Hebrews 11:13). Our goals therefore should not include the accumulation of possessions here. Our real wealth—*our eternal reward*—is in heaven (Matthew 5:12). In Matthew 6:19-20 Jesus says that the only treasure we will possess throughout eternity is there.

In other words, everything we *should* love everlastingly, everything we rightly value, everything of any eternal worth is in heaven. Best of all, we can live in the glow of heaven's glory here and now, with our hearts already in heaven. This is to say that the Christian life is meant to be like heaven on earth. Believers regularly taste the sweetness of the same heaven to which someday we will go to dwell forever. Praising and loving God with all your being, adoring and obeying Christ, pursuing holiness, cherishing fellowship with other saints—those are the elements of heavenly life we can begin to taste in this world. Those same pursuits and privileges will occupy us forever, but we can begin to practice them even now.

THE NEW HEAVEN

Eternal heaven will be different from the heaven where God now dwells. In the consummation of all things, God will renovate the heavens and the earth, merging His heaven with a new universe for a perfect dwelling-place that will be our home forever. In other words, heaven, the realm where God dwells, will expand to encompass the entire universe of creation, which will be fashioned into a perfect and glorious domain fit for the glory of heaven. The apostle Peter described this as the hope of every redeemed person: "We, according to his promise, look for a new heavens and a new earth, wherein dwelleth righteousness" (2 Peter 3:13).

Clearly, a major cosmic remodeling has always been the plan of God. This was also God's gracious promise to His people through the Old Testament prophets. Speaking in Isaiah 65:17-19, God says,

> For, behold, I create new heavens and a new earth: and the former shall not be remembered, nor come into mind. But be ye glad and rejoice for ever in that which I create: for, behold, I create Jerusalem a rejoicing, and her people a joy. And I will rejoice in Jerusalem, and joy in my people: and the voice of weeping shall be no more heard in her, nor the voice of crying.

There God states that He will alter the present heaven and earth in a way that amounts to a whole new creation. Notice that in the new universe, New Jerusalem will be the focus of everything. The new heaven and new earth will be so glorious that it makes the first fade into insignificance ("The former shall not be remembered, nor come into mind"— verse 17). In the next and final chapter of Isaiah's prophecy, the Lord promises that this new heaven and new earth will remain forever, as will all the saints of God: "For as the new heavens and the new earth, which I will make, shall remain before me, saith the Lord, so shall your seed and your name remain" (66:22).

In the new heaven and earth nothing will make us afraid, and nothing will separate us from other people. The only water described in heaven is "a pure river of water of life, clear as crystal, proceeding out of the throne of God and of the Lamb" (Revelation 22:1). This crystal-clear river flows right down heaven's main street (22:2).

Revelation 21:3-7 outlines the most remarkable features of the new heavens and new earth:

> And I heard a great voice out of heaven saying, Behold, the tabernacle of God is with men, and he will dwell with them, and they shall be his people, and God himself shall be with them, and be their God. And God shall wipe away all tears from their eyes; and there shall be no more death, neither sorrow, nor crying, neither shall there be any more pain: for the former things are passed away. And he that sat upon the throne said, Behold, I make all things new. And he said unto me, Write: for these words are true and faithful. And he said unto me, It is done. I am Alpha and Omega, the beginning and the end. I will give unto him that is athirst of the fountain of the water of life freely. He that overcometh shall inherit all things; and I will be his God, and he shall be my son.

Here Scripture promises that heaven will be a realm of perfect bliss. Tears, pain, sorrow, and crying will have no place whatsoever in the new heaven and new earth. It is a place where God's people will dwell together with Him eternally, utterly free from all the effects of sin and evil. God is pictured as personally wiping away the tears from the eyes of the redeemed.

Heaven is a realm where death is fully conquered (1 Corinthians 15:26). There is no sickness there, no hunger, no trouble, and no tragedy. Just absolute joy and eternal blessings.

—JOHN MACARTHUR

BIBLIOGRAPHY

Baxter, Richard. *The Saints' Everlasting Rest,* abridged by John T. Wilkinson. London: Epworth, 1962.

Lane, Anthony, ed. *The Unseen World.* Grand Rapids: Baker Books, 1996.

MacArthur, John F. *The Glory of Heaven.* Wheaton, IL: Crossway Books, 1996.

Smith, Wilbur M. *The Biblical Doctrine of Heaven.* Chicago: Moody Press, 1968.

Stowell, Joseph. *Eternity.* Chicago: Moody Press, 1995.

HEBREWS, ESCHATOLOGY OF

THE BOOK OF HEBREWS IS unique in many ways. It is the only anonymous epistle in the New Testament. The writer addresses Hebrew Christians about five years before the fall of Jerusalem in A.D. 70. He demonstrates a tremendous knowledge of the Old Testament and its relationship to Jesus the Messiah, and his main point is that Jesus fulfills and is superior to Old Testament Judaism, and he demonstrates this by using the Old Testament itself. Christ fulfilled most of the prophetic references in Hebrews at His first coming, but some portions clearly refer to a future fulfillment.

WARNINGS OF JUDGMENT

In order to understand the eschatology of Hebrews we must first understand the author's purpose for writing. He warns Jewish believers (3:1,12-14; 6:9) not to abandon faith in Jesus as the Messiah (2:1) or to return to Judaism in order to escape increasing persecution (10:32-39). The letter includes five major warning passages (2:1-4; 3:7-14; 5:11—6:8; 10:19-39; 12:25-29) that outline the consequences of drifting away from faith in Jesus. Hebrews makes the case that Jesus is better in His person and priestly office than the Old Testament ministry, thus showing the superiority of New Testament Christianity to Judaism. The writer of Hebrews "wants to show them the superiority of the Messiah to the three pillars of Judaism: angels, Moses, and the Levitical Priesthood," notes Arnold Fruchtenbaum. "This he does by way of contrast. This is not a contrast between the bad and the good, for both are from God. The contrast is between the good and the better" (Fruchtenbaum, p. 951).

This epistle deals not only with individual Jewish believers' relationship with Jesus the Messiah but also with the judgment that the nation of Israel would undergo because of its first-century rejection of Jesus as its national Messiah. The Old Testament predicted this judgment (Leviticus 26:34-39; Deuteronomy 28:64-68; Daniel 9:26-27), and Christ Himself echoed the warning (Matthew 22–23; 24:1-2; Mark 13:1-2; Luke 19:41-44). However, those Hebrews who personally trusted Jesus as their Messiah would heed these prophecies, as did the Jewish Christians who fled to Pella as early as A.D. 62. This means that the five warning passages throughout Hebrews are intended in part to warn of the judgment in A.D. 70, which would be the application of the curses, because of disobedience, within the Mosaic covenant to national Israel. Thus, the author is warning Jewish believers that to return to the perceived comfort and ease of Judaism is to place oneself in the path of temporal judgment, which will have eternal consequences as well.

Hebrews deals with the immediate problem of Hebrew Christian apostasy, not the temptations and consequences of Christian apostasy as a whole. This twofold approach, presenting Jesus as superior to the Old Testament and warning readers about the danger of returning to Judaism, provides a rich context for insights into the prophetic future.

THESE LAST DAYS

The writer uses the phrase, "in these last days" in Hebrews 1:2 (NASB). Some commentators believe this is a reference to the prophetic last days of the Tribulation period. Although that phrase does sometimes refer to a future tribulation period (Isaiah 2:2; Jeremiah 23:20; 49:39; Ezekiel 38:16; Micah 4:1; Acts 2:17), the context has to determine the author's intent. In this context, the author has in mind the entire age between Christ's first and second coming. Thus, this is not an eschatological passage.

Verse 2 continues and says, "...whom He appointed heir of all things." Christ was victorious at His first coming and now sits at the right hand of God. However, when He returns to earth, He will rule over every aspect of heaven and earth. This is His destiny as "heir of all things."

CHRIST'S FUTURE REIGN

The rest of Hebrews 1 demonstrates from Old Testament citations that Jesus is the victorious God-Man who will one day reign over all creation. Even though Jesus is currently qualified to implement His rule, He is not yet reigning on David's throne. Only after His second coming will He defeat all His enemies and rule over all things in His millennial kingdom.

Hebrews 2:5-10 quotes the psalmist in order to show that Jesus fulfilled David's prophecy and will someday rule over angels and all creation. Angels will not rule over mankind in "the world to come" (verse 5). Psalm 8 indicates that for a little while, humanity has been made a little lower than the angels. Jesus, during His incarnation, also appeared lower than the angels. That, however, does not place Him under angelic authority. Rather, because of His victory, He will rule over angels in "the world to come."

Hebrews 7 explains that Jesus' priesthood was not like that of Aaron, which was locked in time and required repeated sacrifices. Instead, Jesus is like the mysterious character from early Genesis, Melchizedek, who appears to be timeless and to make intercession. Since Jesus' priesthood, like Melchizedek's, is eternal (7:17,24), it is superior to the temporal Mosaic priesthood. Thus, Jesus will be a high priest forever. Christ is currently making intercession for believers at the right hand of the Father.

SALVATION

We know that "at the consummation of the ages" (9:26) is a reference to Christ's first coming because the passage says, "He has been manifested to put away sin by the sacrifice of Himself." This reference to the first coming of Jesus prepares the way for the mention of His second coming in verse 28. Jesus "will appear a second time for salvation without reference to sin, to those who eagerly await Him." "Salvation" in this context refers not to spiritual salvation through faith in Christ (Ephesians 2:8) but to physical deliverance or rescue (Romans 13:11). When Hebrews 9:28 says Christ "will appear a second time," it is most likely referring to the rapture and not the second advent. This is evident from the phrase "to those who eagerly await

Him." The New Testament pictures the church-age believer who is awaiting the any-moment rapture of the church as eagerly awaiting Christ (Romans 8:19,23,25; 1 Corinthians 1:7; Galatians 5:5; Philippians 3:20; 1 Thessalonians 1:10; Jude 21).

THE DAY DRAWING NEAR

Hebrews 10:25 speaks of "not forsaking our own assembling together, as is the habit of some, but encouraging one another; and all the more as you see the day drawing near." The phrase "as you see the day drawing near" has been applied to the rapture, to the second coming of Christ, and to the approaching judgments included in the Roman destruction of Jerusalem and the Temple in A.D. 70. I believe that the latter reference is what the writer intended for the following reasons: First, the second generation of Jewish believers living in Judea would see the Roman army approaching Jerusalem in the late 60s. Second, the Bible never teaches that observable signs will attend the rapture of the church. It is always a signless event. This is why a church-age believer is constantly waiting for the rapture—no signs will precede it. Third, this statement is in the midst of the fourth warning passage to those who would return to Judaism, alerting them not only to eternal judgment but also to the soon-coming judgment of A.D. 70.

The book of Hebrews teaches the basic New Testament doctrine that believers should have an eternal perspective so that they will be motivated now to sacrificially serve the Lord. Such a mentality is illustrated in Hebrews 11, faith's hall of fame, where we read about many Old Testament saints who looked to the future and remained faithful in the present. A proper view of the future motivates believers to live for the Lord in the present. After presenting the many Old Testament examples in chapter 11, the author of Hebrews concludes,

> Therefore, since we have so great a cloud of witnesses surrounding us, let us also lay aside every encumbrance and the sin which so easily entangles us,

and let us run with endurance the race that is set before us, fixing our eyes on Jesus, the author and perfecter of faith, who for the joy set before Him endured the cross, despising the shame, and has sat down at the right hand of the throne of God (12:1-2).

THE TRIBULATION

The fifth and final warning passage contains comments that relate to eschatology (12:26-29). "His voice shook the earth then, but now He has promised, saying, 'Yet once more I will shake not only the earth, but also the heaven,'" says the writer of Hebrews in verse 26. The Old Testament quote comes from Haggai 2:6, which is a reference to the Tribulation. This fits the Hebrews meaning as well. The earlier reference to the Lord's voice shaking the earth points to the Exodus. The other shaking, this time of the earth and heavens, fits Revelation's description of the Tribulation. The "shaking" will be the judgment events of the Tribulation, which are designed to prepare the way for "a kingdom which cannot be shaken" (12:28). This kingdom is a reference to the millennial kingdom. Therefore, the believer is to "show gratitude, by which we may offer to God an acceptable service with reverence and awe" (12:28).

NOT A SYSTEMATIC ESCHATOLOGY

The eschatology of Hebrews does not provide a compressive view of New Testament future events. This is not surprising in light of the specific purpose of the epistle, which is to deal with Jewish Christian apostasy in light of the impending judgment of A.D. 70. Nevertheless, the writer mentions important prophetic events such as the rapture, the Tribulation, the second coming, the millennium, and the eternal state. The greatest eschatological emphasis is upon the present-day behavior of a believer in light of eternity.

—THOMAS ICE

BIBLIOGRAPHY

Fruchtenbaum, Arnold. *Israelology: The Missing Link in Systematic Theology.* Tustin, CA: Ariel Ministries Press, 1992.

Kent, Homer A. *The Epistle to the Hebrews: A Commentary.* Winona Lake, IN: BMH Books, 1972.

HELL

THE OLD AND NEW TESTAMENTS use 18 different words and figures to describe the doctrine of hell. Each of these contributes something to our understanding of the complete biblical teaching concerning hell. Even with these 18 descriptions of hell, our knowledge of this place necessarily remains limited. God, Creator of mankind, understands the psychological limit to man's ability to comprehend horror. Strong (p. 1033) refers to some of the 18 descriptions:

> The final state of the wicked is described under the figures of eternal fire (Matt. 25:41); the pit of the abyss (Rev. 9:2,11); outer darkness (Matt. 8:12); torment (Rev. 14:10-11); eternal punishment (Matt. 25:46); wrath of God (Rom. 2:5); second death (Rev. 21:8); eternal destruction from the face of the Lord (2 Thess. 1:9); eternal sin (Mark 3:29).

The fact that these and other descriptions of hell are graphic does not mean they are unreal. They may also represent other truths, but we have no biblical reason for disputing a literal interpretation of them.

BIBLICAL TERMS

1. *Sheol.* The derivation of the Hebrew term *sheol* is disputed among linguists, and we cannot be dogmatic on linguistic evidence alone, although most scholars prefer the meaning of "hollow" or "deep" place.

Some of the confusion over the meaning of "Sheol" is due to the fact that it often appears to refer merely to the grave, and at other times it refers to an existence, either positive or negative, after death. In part, this is due to theological rather than grammatical assumptions on the part of the biblical writers. Shedd (p. 34) suggests, "Sheol signifies the 'grave,' to which all men, the good and evil alike, go down. That Sheol should have the two significations of hell and the grave, is explained by the connection between physical death and eternal retribution." Summarizing the biblical usage of this term, Pentecost (p. 556) notes,

> The first is *Sheol,* which is used sixty-five times in the Old Testament, translated "hell" thirty-one times (cf. Deut. 32:22; Ps. 9:17; 18:5; Isa. 14:9), "grave" thirty-one times (cf. 1 Sam. 2:6; Job 7:9; 14:13), and "pit," three times (cf. Num. 16:30, 33; Job 17:16). This was the Old Testament word for the abode of the dead. It was presented, not just as a state of existence, but as a place of conscious existence (Deut. 18:11; 1 Sam. 28:11-15; Isa. 14:9). God was sovereign over it (Deut. 32:22; Job 26:6). It was regarded as temporary and the righteous anticipated the resurrection out of it into the millennial age (Job 14:13-14; 19:25, 27; Ps. 16:9-11; 17:15; 49:15; 73:24).

2. *Hades.* The translators of the Greek Septuagint generally used the word *hades* when translating *sheol.* Hades was also the designation of the underworld in Greek thought. Concerning the relation between these two words, Innes (p. 518) notes, "The Gk. *haidēs* represents the underworld, or realm of the dead, in the classics. In the LXX [Septuagint] it almost always renders *sheol,* and in the New Testament hades has an exclusively negative emphasis. It is used only to describe the place of retribution for the wicked."

The key passage in the New Testament describing hades is Luke 16:19-31. While some attempt to dismiss this account as a parable, Ironside (p. 510) observes:

> "There was a certain rich man." Was there, or was there not? He definitely declared that there was. He did not intro-

duce the story by saying, "Hear a parable," as on some other occasions; neither did He say, "The kingdom is as if there were a certain rich man and a poor beggar," or some similar language. But in the clearest, most definite way He declared, "There was a certain rich man."

If the rich man was real, then so is hell. The rich man went to hades at death and was tormented in real flames (Luke 16:24). The punishment of hades includes (1) burning, (2) separation and loneliness, (3) conviction by memory, (4) thirst, (5) falling, and (6) stench. The rich man could look across "a great gulf fixed" (Luke 16:26 KJV) and see where the saved were located. However, Scripture is silent as to whether the saved could see the torment of the unsaved. We do know that the rich man could not escape his torment.

The presence of the beggar in the relative proximity of the rich man suggests that originally both hades and paradise, or Abraham's bosom, were in the same place. At His death, Christ descended "into the lower parts of the earth" and "led captivity captive." He later ascended from that place (Ephesians 4:8-10). Many commentators believe paradise was, at that time, released from the regions of hades and taken to the third heaven.

3. *Tartaros.* Another biblical term describing hell is *tartaros* (Greek). It occurs only once in Scripture, and even there it is technically a related verb rather than the noun itself. Peter writes that God did not spare the angels that sinned, but "cast them down to hell" (2 Peter 2:4). Most agree the verb is based on a Greek noun describing the lowest of the nine levels of hell in Greek thought. God's punishment upon the fallen angels was such that He cast them to "the very bottom of hell."

4. *Gehenna.* A fourth biblical term translated "hell" is *gehenna* (Greek). This is the most severe word for hell in Scripture and one used almost exclusively by Jesus. Because of the severity of some of the statements and images concerning *gehenna,* those who argue against the existence of a literal hell, such as Jehovah's

Witnesses, are most likely to dispute the meaning of this term. The New Testament, however, describes hell by referring to a place in the valley of Hinnom where, in earlier days, human sacrifices were offered (2 Chronicles 33:6; Jeremiah 7:31). It is the name in Scripture for the lake of fire, the final and eternal abode of the lost (Revelation 19:20; 20:10,14-15).

The use of *gehenna* in the New Testament makes it clear that the word does not refer merely to a historical valley outside of Jerusalem, a garbage dump in that day. This term is associated with eternal fire, punishment, and torment. *Gehenna* is the place of eternal retribution, the final abode of the unsaved. All of the descriptions emphasizing the repulsiveness of hell—including the worm, fire, and gnashing of teeth—are descriptions of *gehenna.* Scripture probably does not describe the full horror of *gehenna* because of man's inability psychologically, mentally, and spiritually to comprehend such a place.

5. *Retribution.* Though the term *retribution* is absent in the KJV, the idea of retribution is fundamental to our understanding of God. The biblical ideas of punishment, vengeance, and wrath all suggest retribution as part of the judgment on sin. It is the judicial result of God's anger and wrath.

In addition, retribution in hell exists because the natural consequence of sin is destruction (see Proverbs 14:12; 16:25; Matthew 7:13; Romans 5:12). The corrupting nature of sin destroys all that it contacts. This does not minimize in any way the concept of divine wrath but rather identifies another of the sources of retribution. In one sense, hell is hell because it is the place where sin is unrestrained in its destructive passion.

6. *Prison.* On two occasions the Scriptures use the word "prison" in an apparent reference to hell (1 Peter 3:19; Revelation 20:7). Under Jewish law, imprisonment was not part of the penal code except when a prisoner found guilty was held until the execution of his sentence. Apparently, spirits in prison are awaiting a later execution of sentence. "Prison," there-fore, should be properly applied to hades rather than *gehenna.* Thus, "hell" is the equivalent to being held in jail while awaiting trial and sentencing to the penitentiary.

7. *Chains.* The image of chains is yet another biblical description of hell. In the Scriptures, chains appear to be reserved for angelic beings (2 Peter 2:4; Jude 6; Revelation 20:1). The third reference is to Satan being bound with a chain while he is locked in the abyss for 1000 years. This indicates that God is supreme even over satanic regions.

8. *Stripes.* Emphasizing the idea of degrees of punishment in hell, Jesus used the image of "stripes" to describe the judgment to come (Luke 12:48). Whatever else may be implied by Jesus' reference to stripes with reference to hell, it is certain He intended to emphasize the existence of degrees of punishment in hell. As not all sinners have equal light, nor have they engaged in their sin with equal intensity, so will the degree of suffering differ in hell. This does not in any way minimize the reality of suffering in hell. It will be of little comfort to one experiencing "few stripes" to know that somewhere else in hell, another is receiving "many stripes."

9. *Weeping and gnashing of teeth.* On several occasions Jesus used the expression "weeping and gnashing of teeth" to describe the personal anguish of individuals in hell (Matthew 8:12; 13:42,50; 22:13; 24:51; 25:30; Luke 13:28). The word "gnashing" is used to speak of grinding or striking together one's teeth in rage, pain, or misery of disappointment. In the Old Testament it represents rage, anger, and hatred. This expression seems to suggest the sorrow in hell will be caused by a sense of loss, anger, and despair.

10. *Abyss* or *bottomless pit.* Seven times in the final book of the Bible, John describes hell as a "bottomless pit" (9:1-2,11; 11:7; 17:8; 20:1,3). In each case the pit is closely associated with demons, and they are generally being released from or confined to the pit. The Old Testament

also uses the image of a pit to refer to the abode of the wicked dead. The word *abyss* refers to that which is deep and from which there is no escape.

11. *Outer darkness.* Another image of hell used by Christ was that of "darkness." In the eschatology of the New Testament, heaven is portrayed as a bright, well-lighted place. To be exiled from heaven was to be placed in outer darkness. Jesus' use of the word *skotia* to describe this place suggests extreme darkness as opposed to the gloominess of a cloudy or foggy day.

12. *Destruction.* On one occasion Paul used the expression "everlasting destruction from the presence of the Lord" (2 Thessalonians 1:9) to describe hell. Although "destroyer" is one of the many titles of Satan (see Revelation 9:11), Paul alone specifically identifies hell as the place of destruction. The idea was not foreign to Jewish thought and was believed to be the lot of the wicked. Paul, in this context, suggests it is the destiny of "them that know not God, and that obey not the gospel of our Lord Jesus Christ" (2 Thessalonians 1:8).

13. *Torments.* Hell is also described as a place of torment (Luke 16:23,28). Of the various words for suffering in the New Testament, this one may be the most severe. It denotes pain and anguish as extreme forms of human suffering, as is illustrated by the rich man who described hades as "a place of torments" (Luke 16:28).

14. *Worm.* Isaiah and Jesus both used the image of an undying worm in their descriptions of the fate of the wicked (Isaiah 14:11; 66:24; Mark 9:44,46,48). The worm properly belongs to the description of *gehenna* rather than *hades.* The image of the worm in *gehenna* would have been understood by Jesus' listeners as a horrifying picture of the judgment of God. This is the subject of the last verse of Isaiah (Isaiah 66:24).

15. *Fire.* Probably the best-known image of hell is that of fire. The rich man is described as tormented by the flame (Luke 16:24), and men are salted with fire (Mark 9:49), cast into the lake of fire (Revelation 20:15), and cast into a furnace of fire (Matthew 13:42). Further, fire and brimstone (Revelation 21:8) and the unquenchable flame (Mark 9:43,45-46,48) are used to describe hell. The use of fire to describe hell is not only descriptive but also emphasizes the continuous suffering of the lost.

16. *Second death.* The eternal abode of the lost is, as noted above, also designated as the second death, in contrast to physical death. Those who teach a view of annihilation or soul sleep often redefine this term to refer to a state of nonexistence or unconscious existence. In Scripture, however, death never refers to the cessation of life, but rather to the separation of something from that to which it belongs. The Scriptures identify a body without the spirit and faith without its evident works as dead (James 2:26). In the same way, the expression "second death" emphasizes the separation of a man from God. The consciousness of man is emphasized in the description of the second death at the final judgment.

17. *Wrath of God.* Hell is also described in Scripture in terms of the wrath of God. As an expression of His holiness, truth, and justice, God must punish sin. As sin is an offense against God personally, it should not, therefore, be surprising that God is offended and is therefore angry against sin. To deny the existence of this anger is to reject the necessity of Christ's reconciling work on the cross. According to Paul, the wrath of God can be revealed in nature (Romans 1:18). That wrath, which is today revealed in part against sin, will someday be expressed completely in hell.

18. *Eternity.* All the adjectives applied to hell give it a degree of suffering that is beyond the realm of human comprehension. Then add the word *eternity* to all the words that describe suffering, and the reality of hell is compounded far beyond human understanding. It

is one thing to be the object of God's wrath. It is another to be the object of that wrath for eternity. It is one thing to be in torment. It is something else to be eternally tormented. If hell were in any sense tolerable for its inhabitants, the concept of eternity makes it completely intolerable.

The two Greek words *aion* and *aionios* are the terms used to express time without end, or eternity. The New Testament's use of these terms is not limited to discussions of hell. If they do not mean "eternal" when applied to hell, they cannot mean "eternal" when applied to God, nor to the eternal salvation of God's people after death. Eternal punishment is the ultimate consequence of all who end up in hell.

—ELMER TOWNS

BIBLIOGRAPHY

Innes, D.K. "Hell," in J.D. Douglas, ed. *The New Bible Dictionary*. Grand Rapids: Eerdmans Publishing Company, 1982.

Ironside, H.A. *Addresses on the Gospel of Luke*. New York: Loizeaux Brothers, 1947.

Pentecost, J. Dwight. *Things to Come*. Grand Rapids: Zondervan, 1975.

Shedd, W.G.T. *The Doctrine of Endless Punishment*. Minneapolis: Klock & Klock, 1980.

Strong, Augustus H. *Systematic Theology*. Westwood, NJ: Fleming H. Revell, 1967.

Toon, Peter. *Heaven and Hell*. Nashville: Thomas Nelson, 1986.

HERMENEUTICS

HERMENEUTICS ARE the principles Bible students use to interpret biblical texts. Exegesis, or interpretation, is the implementation of those hermeneutical principles. Hermeneutics, then, are the rules of interpretation, and exegesis applies those rules to explain the meaning of a biblical text.

Evangelicals have traditionally used the grammar and historical context of a passage to arrive at its correct interpretation. This is the grammatical-historical or literal interpretation. Two important books that articulate this approach are *Biblical Hermeneutics: A Treatise on the Interpretation of the Old and New Testaments* by Milton S. Terry, and *Protestant Biblical Interpretation: A Textbook of Hermeneutics* by Bernard Ramm.

TRENDS IN EVANGELICALISM AND HERMENEUTICS

Through the first six decades of the twentieth century, literal interpretation prevailed among evangelicals. Some evangelicals, the dispensationalists, used the principles consistently in interpreting Scripture. Other evangelicals, the covenant theologians, followed grammatical-historical principles in all areas of doctrine except the doctrines of the church and of last things. That created a degree of unity between the two theological systems in most matters of doctrine such as the doctrine of Christ and the doctrine of salvation. But in the 1970s that unity began to disappear when some evangelicals started deviating from traditional principles of interpretation and embracing a more subjective hermeneutic. That change followed trends toward postmodernism that had already prevailed in nonevangelical theology, allowing the Bible reader to insert his own opinions into the interpretation instead of letting the biblical text speak for itself.

In the nineteenth century, Terry (p. 205) wrote, "A fundamental principle in grammatico-historical exposition is that the words and sentences can have but one significance in one and the same connection. The moment we neglect this principle we drift out upon a sea of uncertainty and conjecture." In contrast, a 1991 evangelical work on hermeneutics advocates double meanings in cases of single words. In fact, the work cites the Gospel of John as famous "for its widespread use of double meaning." Such a shift in principles of interpretation has had a huge impact on evangelical interpretation, and its impact will continue to grow if left unchecked.

This hermeneutical shift among some evangelicals has led to several new views within evangelicalism, such as progressive dispensationalism (PD). PD violates the traditional hermeneutical principle of single meaning. As a compromise between dispensationalism and covenant theology, PD finds multiple fulfillments of a single Old Testament passage. It proposes that God will fulfill His promises to national Israel in the future, but it also teaches that the church is currently fulfilling those same prophecies. What PD calls "complementary hermeneutics" clearly violates traditional principles of literal interpretation.

THE BOOK OF REVELATION AND APOCALYPTIC GENRE

Genre analyses divide the biblical books into groups based on comparisons with extrabiblical literature written immediately before, during, and immediately after the composition of the New Testament. These comparisons include such literary features as structure, style, content, and function. Some scholars place Revelation in a genre called *apocalyptic*. But no consensus exists as to a precise definition of genre in general or of apocalyptic in particular, so such classifications are at best vague.

Various interpretive approaches to Revelation have existed long before the recent attention given to apocalyptic genre, but most of the theories have adopted genre in order to promote their agendas more stringently. Interpreting Revelation in the apocalyptic genre, a typical *preterist* approach—one that says most of the book's prophecies were fulfilled by A.D. 70—views Revelation as a highly figurative book that cannot be interpreted with straightforward literalism. Because of the same apocalyptic assumption, an *idealist* view—one that sees the book as not referring to specific events but expressing the basic principles according to which God acts throughout history—interprets apocalyptic literature differently from other biblical literature. Idealists teach that Revelation presents basic principles of God's activity at every stage of history, a position that is completely out of accord with Revelation's analysis of itself as being prophetic rather than apocalyptic.

Only the *futurist* approach to Revelation accepts the book's self-claim of being a prophecy and interprets it literally. Embracing the premillennial return of Christ, it utilizes a normal hermeneutical pattern of interpretation based on the prophetic style, views the book as focusing on the last periods of world history, and outlines the various events and their relationships to one another. An opinion that an "exclusively prophetic interpretation usually insists on an impossibly literal hermeneutic which is therefore inevitably applied inconsistently" is to be expected from a person who does not consistently approach the book futuristically.

Most preterists and idealists interpret Revelation literally at times and see some futurist aspects in Revelation, but at the same time they create hermeneutical confusion. Such "eclectic" hermeneutical approaches to Revelation abound. A combination of *idealist* and *futurist* schemes is one example. Such a concept proposes that apocalypses spoke of the historical context in which they were written and can be transferred to new situations of later generations multiple times, with one final reference to real end-time tribulation.

Objectivity

New evangelical hermeneutics have opened wide doors for PD by trying to find a midpoint between covenant theology and dispensationalism.

Terry wrote, "We must not study them [the Scriptures] in the light of modern systems of divinity, but should aim rather to place ourselves in the position of the sacred writers, and study to obtain the impression their words would naturally have made upon the minds of the first readers" (p. 595). Traditional principles strongly emphasize the importance of letting the text speak for itself without imposing on it preconceived ideas of what an interpreter thinks it ought to teach.

Historical Interpretation

In order to appreciate the historical context of a passage, the interpreter should endeavor to take himself from the present and to transport himself into the historical position of the author, look through his eyes, note his surroundings, feel with his heart, and catch his emotion. Herein we note the import of the term "grammatical-historical interpretation."

By ignoring the way the original historical setting "freezes" the meaning of a text, PD creates a dynamic meaning—ever changing through the addition of new meanings. For PD, "historical" includes not only the situation of the original text but also ongoing conditions throughout the history of the text's interpretation.

Single Meaning

"Single meaning" is a principle that safeguards against deconstructionism and postmodernism. In the words of Bernard Ramm, "But here we must remember the old adage: 'Interpretation is one, application is many.' This means that there is only one meaning to a passage of Scripture which is determined by careful study" (p. 42). Deconstructionism and postmodernism allow for multiple interpretations of a single passage. PD is well on its way toward these nonevangelical ideologies.

When PD proponents concede that complementary aspects of meaning give an additional angle on the text, revealing an additional element of its message or a fresh way of relating the parts of a text's message, they fail to limit a passage to a single meaning. Changing the substance of something already written questions the credibility of its original meaning.

Sensus Plenior ("FULLER MEANING")

Violation of the single-meaning principle leads easily to PD's violation of the *sensus plenior* ("fuller sense") principle. To find a sense fuller than the grammatical-historical meaning of a passage clearly enters the realm of allegorical interpretation. Traditional grammatical-historical interpretation does not import new ideas into the text of Scripture, or new dogma to any words or passages. Yet recent evangelical interpreters have advocated such "fuller meanings." Such a practice is in total disharmony with traditional literal interpretation.

The New Testament Use of the Old Testament

The principle of single meaning requires that every Old Testament passage receives only its own grammatical-historical interpretation, regardless of how a New Testament writer uses it. An Old Testament passage must not receive multiple meanings by being read through the eyes of the New Testament. When the single-meaning principle is applied consistently, two kinds of New Testament usage of the Old Testament become evident. On the one hand, New Testament writers often abide by the grammatical-historical sense of the Old Testament. On the other hand, New Testament writers sometimes go beyond the grammatical-historical meaning to apply an Old Testament passage in its New Testament context so as to give it an additional sense.

In the former case, a New Testament writer adopts the Old Testament's literal sense. In the latter case, he follows a nonliteral use of the Old Testament. This nonliteral use may be called an "inspired *sensus plenior* application." Such a usage is "inspired" because the New Testament is inspired by God. It is *sensus plenior* in that it gives an additional or fuller sense than the passage has in its Old Testament setting. It is an application because it does not eradicate the literal meaning of the Old Testament passage but rather applies the Old Testament wording to a new setting. It is one thing for an inspired New Testament writer to do this, but it is quite another matter for a non-inspired postmodern interpreter to do it.

A Sure Guideline

Hermeneutical changes among evangelicals have had far-reaching effects on interpreting the book of Revelation and on the study of eschatology. If the current direction of evangelicalism continues, the movement will eventually reach the status of postmodernist and deconstructionist approaches to the Bible. The only remedy for this sickness is a return to traditional grammatical-historical principles of interpretation as our only sure guideline to understanding the true meaning of the biblical text.

—ROBERT THOMAS

BIBLIOGRAPHY

Couch, Mal. *An Introduction to Classical Evangelical Hermeneutics.* Grand Rapids: Kregel, 2000.

Ramm, Bernard. *Protestant Biblical Interpretation.* Grand Rapids: Baker Books, 1970.

Ryrie, Charles C. *Dispensationalism.* Chicago: Moody, 1995.

Terry, Milton S. *Biblical Hermeneutics.* Grand Rapids: Zondervan, 1974 (originally published 1890).

Thomas, Robert L. *Evangelical Hermeneutics: The New Versus the Old.* Grand Rapids: Kregel, 2002.

HOLY SPIRIT AND ESCHATOLOGY

DISPENSATIONAL PREMILLENNIALISM teaches that the Holy Spirit will have a different ministry in the future than He has today.

AT THE RAPTURE

He Will Complete the Church

When Christ ascended to heaven, He sent the Holy Spirit, as promised in John 16:7. Believers thus were first baptized in the Holy Spirit on the Day of Pentecost (Acts 2:1-4). Whenever a sinner in this church age believes in Jesus Christ for salvation, he is immediately baptized by the Holy Spirit into the body of Christ.

Jesus Christ will come someday to take the church to Himself (1 Thessalonians 4:13-18). When the last sinner is converted in this church age, the body of Christ will be complete, and the ministry of the baptism by the Holy Spirit will end at the rapture. Although people will be saved after the rapture, they will not become members of the body of Christ.

He Will Remove His Restraint of Sin

In Paul's correspondence with new believers in Thessalonica, he discussed these topics of eschatology: the rapture (1 Thessalonians 4:13-18), the day of the Lord (5:1-11), the man of sin, also known as the Antichrist (2 Thessalonians 2:3-4), and the return of Christ to the earth (2:8).

When will the Antichrist manifest himself? Paul explained, "Now you know what is restraining, that he may be revealed in his own time. For the mystery of lawlessness is already at work; only He who now restrains will do so until He is taken out of the way. And then the lawless one will be revealed, whom the Lord will consume with the breath of His mouth and destroy with the brightness of His coming" (2:6-8 NKJV). Someone or something is restraining the revelation of this future satanic leader. He or it must be more powerful than the Antichrist or Satan. The only one who is more powerful is God. In what sense, however, will He be taken away?

The phrase "what is restraining" is the translation of *to katechon,* a verbal participle of neuter gender. The phrase "he who restrains" is *ho katechon,* a verbal participle of the masculine gender. Apparently, both the work (neuter) and the person (masculine) of the restrainer are presented in this passage. The Greek New Testament uses both masculine and neuter pronouns for the Holy Spirit. The word *pneuma* ("spirit") is in the neuter gender, but the Spirit is an eternal Person.

The Spirit is the Restrainer, and He does His work of restraining through the church. When the church is removed from the earth at the rapture, the presence of the Spirit in church-age believers will also be removed. He will leave earth even as He came to the earth.

The Holy Spirit was present on earth before He came to fulfill distinctive ministries on the day of Pentecost. In the Old Testament era He convicted and regenerated sinners. After the rapture He will have a ministry similar to that in the age before the church began—He will continue to convict and regenerate sinners.

IN THE TRIBULATION

He Will Save Jews and Gentiles

The Tribulation is the entire seven-year period that will occur between the rapture of the church and the second coming of Christ to the earth. It is a synonym for the seventieth week of Daniel, the climax of God's program for Israel (Daniel 9:24-27). During this future time, the Spirit will do what He did in the ages before the church age.

In the Olivet Discourse, Christ described what would happen in the seven-year period just before His return to the earth (Matthew 24:24). In the parable of the sheep and the goats, the sheep represent the saved Gentiles of the Tribulation who will show kindness to the persecuted Jews (25:31-46). Modern Israelis would call them "the righteous Gentiles." In the parable of the virgins, the five wise virgins symbolize the saved Jews who will be ready to meet the returning Christ (25:1-13).

In John's visions recorded in the book of Revelation, he saw 144,000 sealed servants of God from the 12 tribes of Israel (Revelation 7:4-8). Through the ministry of the Spirit, God will save these Jews in the Tribulation period. John also saw "a great multitude which no one could number, of all nations, tribes, peoples and tongues, standing before the throne and before the Lamb" (7:9). This description includes both Jews and Gentiles. They are the saved ones who will "come out of the great tribulation, and [will have] washed their robes and made them white in the blood of the Lamb" (7:14). Because the Holy Spirit is God, He is omnipresent. So even though He will leave the world in the rapture, no longer indwelling the church, He will still be on earth, regenerating sinners as He did in prior ages.

He Will Energize God's Servants

No one can serve God out of his own energy. We are not sufficient to do so in ourselves (2 Corinthians 3:5). Thus the 144,000 Jewish servants in the Tribulation will serve by the power of the Spirit (Revelation 7:3-8).

God will also use two witnesses for a ministry of 3½ years (11:3-12). These anonymous witnesses will prophesy and perform miracles. In fact, they will do what Moses and Elijah once did: prevent rain from falling, turn water into blood, and smite the earth with plagues. Moses and Elijah were empowered by the Holy Spirit, so it is reasonable to assume that the two witnesses will have the same power of the Spirit. The two witnesses are likened to two olive trees and two lampstands, an analogy used of the priest Joshua and the leader Zerubbabel, who guided the returning Jews to rebuild the Temple (Zechariah 4:1-14). These two Old Testament leaders were encouraged by these words: "This is the word of the Lord to Zerubbabel: 'Not by might, nor by power, but by My Spirit,' says the Lord of hosts" (Zechariah 4:6). The two witnesses in the Tribulation will also minister by the power of the Spirit of God.

He Will Be Poured Out on Israel

Through the prophet Joel, God said to Israel, "It shall come to pass afterward that I will pour out My Spirit on all flesh; your sons and your daughters shall prophesy, your old men shall dream dreams, your young men shall see visions. And also on My menservants and on My maidservants I will pour out My Spirit in those days" (Joel 2:28-29). The outpouring will be accompanied by "wonders in the heavens and in the earth: blood and fire and pillars of smoke, the sun shall be turned into darkness, and the moon into blood" (2:30-31).

Peter quoted this prophecy from Joel in his sermon on the Day of Pentecost, so Pentecostals and charismatics claim that the prophecy was fulfilled on that day. However, the visible phenomena did not occur then. The outpouring of the Spirit on the Day of Pentecost simply manifested the power of the risen Messiah. In the future, God will pour out the Spirit on Israel at the end of the Tribulation period when Christ returns.

He Will Prepare Israel for the Coming of Christ

Israel will enter the seven-year Tribulation, also known as "the time of Jacob's trouble" (Jeremiah 30:7), in an unsaved condition. In that difficult time, two-thirds of Israel will die (Zechariah 13:8-9). Six million Jews died during the Nazi Holocaust, but even more will lose their lives at the hands of the Antichrist. Christ said this would be the worst period of persecution in the history of the world (Matthew 24:21).

Yet God will protect and save the surviving one-third (Jeremiah 30:7; Zechariah 13:9). The people of Israel will call on the name of the Lord and be saved (Joel 2:32; Zechariah 13:9), and will be delivered when they see Christ returning to the earth (Romans 11:26). They will exclaim, "Blessed is He who comes in the name of the Lord!" (Matthew 23:39).

Christ told Nicodemus that a person had to be born of the Spirit in order to enter the kingdom of God (John 3:3-8). Thus, Israelites will be born of the Spirit during the Tribulation and at the return of Christ in order to enter Christ's spiritual-political kingdom.

IN THE MILLENNIUM
He Will Energize the Reigning Christ

The words "one thousand years" occur six times in the Scriptures (Revelation 20:2-9). The English word *millennium* is based on the Latin *mille* ("one thousand") and *annus* ("year"). Though the words "one thousand years" do not occur in the Old Testament, there are prophecies in the Old Testament that describe the millennial period. When Jesus Christ returns to the earth after the seventieth week of Daniel (Daniel 9:24-27), He will destroy the Antichrist and the wicked nations at the battle of Armageddon (Revelation 19:17-21). He will then rule on the earth for 1000 years.

In a prophecy dealing with the blessings of the millennial kingdom, Isaiah wrote, "There shall come forth a Rod from the stem of Jesse, and a Branch shall grow out of his roots. The Spirit of the Lord shall rest upon Him, the Spirit of wisdom and understanding, the Spirit of counsel and might, the Spirit of knowledge and of the fear of the Lord" (Isaiah 11:1-2). The Spirit of God came on Jesus at His baptism and remained on Him throughout His earthly ministry. The Spirit still remains on Him today and will continue to be on Him throughout His future earthly reign.

He Will Indwell Believers

God promised to make a New Covenant with Israel (Jeremiah 31:31-37; Ezekiel 36:24-32), a covenant that will ultimately be fulfilled in the millennial kingdom. The blessings of that covenant include national restoration and unity in the Promised Land, the divine writing of God's law on the redeemed Israelites' minds and hearts, pure worship, forgiveness of sin, and material prosperity. In addition, God promised, "I will give you a new heart and put a new spirit within you; I will take the heart of stone out of your flesh and give you a heart of flesh. I will put My Spirit within you and cause you to walk in My statutes, and you will keep My judgments and do them" (36:26-27). In the millennium, all believers will be permanently indwelt by the Holy Spirit, who will enable them to obey all of God's commands.

IMPLICATIONS FOR US

First, we must realize that the present-day task of the Holy Spirit is to complete the formation of the church. Believers are to be involved in that divine task by witnessing and evangelizing. Since the rapture is imminent, we must be zealous in our attempts to win the lost.

Second, we must be holy channels through whom the Holy Spirit can restrain sin. We must be salt and light. We must not contribute to the moral decline of the world or the coldness of the church.

Third, we must pray for the peace of Jerusalem. We must love Israel, the covenant people of God. We must support the outreach of the gospel to the Jewish world.

—ROBERT GROMACKI

BIBLIOGRAPHY

Ferguson, Sinclair. *The Holy Spirit.* Downers Grove, IL: InterVarsity Press, 1996.

Gromacki, Robert. *The Holy Spirit.* Nashville: Word Publishing, 1999.

Ryrie, Charles C. *The Holy Spirit.* Chicago: Moody Press, 1997.

Unger, Merrill. *The Baptizing Work of the Holy Spirit.* Chicago: Moody Press, 1973.

Walvoord, John F. *The Holy Spirit at Work Today.* Chicago: Moody Press, 1973.

IMMINENCE

THE TERM *"imminence"* (or *imminency*) as applied to the rapture of the church means that Christ may return at any moment for His church, and no biblically predicted event must necessarily precede it. Those who believe that Christ will return for His church before the Tribulation normally hold that the rapture is imminent—that it may occur at any time and that it is the next predicted event in God's prophetic timetable.

THE QUALIFICATIONS

Other events may occur before an imminent event, but nothing else *must* take place before it occurs. In addition, one cannot know precisely when an imminent event will occur. Thus one should be prepared for it to occur at any moment. *Imminent* does not mean "soon"; the word *soon* implies that an event must occur within a short time or within a specified time, which destroys the concept of imminence. The rapture of the church has been imminent since the days of the New Testament, but it clearly was not "soon" at that time.

Some posttribulationists have responded to the doctrine of imminence by claiming that all the intervening signs have already occurred, and thus Christ's return can indeed occur at any time. Others deny that the Bible teaches imminence in any sense. Most simply redefine imminence to mean not necessarily "any moment" but that the return of Christ "*could* take place within any limited period of time" (Moo, p. 208). However, the following biblical passages clearly teach the imminence of the rapture.

John 14:1-3

When Jesus said, "If I go and prepare a place for you" (John 14:3 KJV), He was speaking of a literal departure, in which He went bodily from earth to heaven (see Acts 1:11). His next statement, "I will come again," likewise referred to a literal and bodily return from heaven, not a coming of Christ to individual believers in death or in the person of the Holy Spirit. When Christ returns, He will take believers to be with Him forever. John 14:2 clearly refers to heaven as "my Father's house," which is where the "mansions" (NASB, "dwelling places") must also be located. In verses 2 and 3, Jesus discusses an activity that He will carry out in His Father's house—He will "prepare a place" for believers. Sometime after He accomplishes that, He will "come again" and "receive" believers to Himself. Where will He take them? Jesus said He is preparing a place for them in heaven, so He must intend to take them to heaven—where He will be. Jesus' next statement, that the disciples knew the way where He was going, must still refer to heaven. Thus, Christ will go to heaven (His ascension), return literally and bodily to earth for His people, and take them literally to heaven with Him (at the rapture) to be with Him.

In the preceding context, the apostles began to show signs of fear in response to Jesus' statements about His departure. In answer to a question from Peter, Jesus said, "Where I go, you cannot follow Me now, but you will follow later," to which Peter replied, "Lord, why can I not follow You right now?" (13:36-37 NASB). This led Jesus to respond, "Do not let your heart be troubled." Christ clearly spoke of the rapture as an antidote to their fears and as a great hope and encouragement in light of His coming departure to heaven. No preceding signs are mentioned. It is purely a reunion of the apostles with their Lord, which issues in an eternal "at home-ness" with both Jesus and His Father.

Assuming a premillennial eschatology, this passage cannot refer to Christ's second coming to the earth because at that time, Christ will rule on earth rather than return to heaven with His people. In fact, at the second coming, no one is depicted as going from earth to heaven (Walvoord, *The Rapture Question*, p. 76). The events depicted in Matthew 25 and Revelation 20 are not possible in John 14:1-3, and John gives no hint of intervening events, such as the Tribulation.

1 Corinthians 1:7

In Romans 8:23, as Paul shows that the Christian's coming glorification is something that far outweighs the suffering he will experience in this life, he declares that believers "groan" within themselves, "waiting eagerly for…the redemption of our body." Two verses later, he explains that they "wait eagerly" for this hope with perseverance. The New Testament uses this verb, *apekdechomai*, to refer to Christian hope, and Paul uses it only in eschatological contexts (Fee, p. 42, note 36).

In 1 Corinthians 1:7, why did Paul, in the midst of a thanksgiving focusing on the Corinthians' wealth of spiritual gifts, remind them that they were eagerly looking forward to the revelation or unveiling (Greek, *apokalypsis*) of Christ? Paul intended to refocus their expectation on Christ rather than on themselves and their temporary gifts. This indicates he had in view an imminent rapture, eagerly expected at any moment, on which believers should focus their expectation.

The word *apokalypsis* can refer to either the rapture (Peter 1:7,13; 4:13) or the second coming (Romans 8:19; 2 Thessalonians 1:7) (Sproule, p. 18). In 1 Corinthians 1:7, where no signs are mentioned, an imminent rapture is not only possible but most likely. The concept of "seeing" an unveiled Christ as He really is coincides well with such clear rapture passages as 1 John 3:2, where John teaches that the church "will see Him just as He is."

Titus 2:13

In this passage, Paul describes Christ's return as "the blessed hope." The rapture is a totally positive and joyful expectation.

Some pretribulationists interpret this passage as referring to the second coming of Christ rather than the rapture because of Paul's use of the word *epiphaneia* (appearing). However, all four uses of the term in the pastoral epistles (1 Timothy 6:14; 2 Timothy 4:1,8; Titus 2:13) present the appearing of Christ as a joyous expectation apart from signs or tribulation and thus likely refer to the rapture.

Others have related Titus 2:13 to Christ's posttribulational second coming because it speaks of the appearing of the glory of Christ, which they reason must refer to the manifestation of an exalted and glorious Christ to the entire world (see Matthew 16:27; 19:28; 24:30; 25:31). However, although the world will not see Christ's glory until His second coming, the church will experience His glory when it meets Him in the air (Romans 5:2; 8:18,30; 1 Corinthians 15:43; Philippians 3:21; Colossians 1:27; 3:4; 1 Peter 5:1; 1 John 3:2; Jude 24). Nothing in the passage restricts this appearing to Christ's second coming (Walvoord, *The Rapture Question,* p. 157).

The fact that in Titus 2:13 Paul exhorts believers to look for the rapture as the blessed (happy) hope (confident expectation) for the church, without any mention of preceding signs or tribulation, strongly implies the imminence of this event—that it can occur at any time. The exhortation to watch or look for what is the hope *par excellence* of the church loses its significance if it may not arrive at any moment (Radmacher, p. 20).

1 Corinthians 16:22

Maranatha is an Aramaic word meaning "our Lord, come"—a petition to Christ that He should return now—at any moment. Paul used it in this letter to Greek-speaking (mainly Gentile) Christians in Corinth because it expressed an idea that had become universal in the early church. Christ could return at any moment, and Christians called upon Him to do so. The first part of verse 22 pronounces *anathema* on anyone who "does not love the Lord Jesus Christ" (NKJV), and the last part calls on Christ to come back now. It thus warns readers that at any moment they may have to answer to Christ as judge. The fact that believers (including the apostle Paul) petitioned Christ in this way strongly implies that they knew He could come at any moment.

1 Thessalonians 1:9-10

This passage describes three time periods in relation to the Thessalonian believers. First, when Paul visited them with the gospel, they "turned to God from idols." That is, they responded to Christ by faith and were born again. Second, they were now serving "the living and true God" (rather than the idols and false gods they formerly worshiped) as they waited for Christ to return from heaven. Third, one day Jesus would appear out of heaven and rescue them from "the wrath to come." Since Christ's appearance out of heaven is later described in 4:15-17 as the rapture, this "coming wrath" must be the same wrath described in 5:3,9, which is the wrath of the Tribulation (Harrison, p. 319). The general context of both Thessalonian epistles is the day of the Lord, especially that aspect of God's judgment that precedes and leads up to Christ's second coming. The fact that 1:10 calls it "the wrath to come" implies that the rescue is related to Christ's return.

Paul says that believers will be rescued from, out of, or away from the coming wrath. This points to a deliverance *before* wrath begins. First Thessalonians 1:9-10 summarizes Paul's eschatological teaching, which he expands and further explains in 4:13–5:11.

1 Thessalonians 5:4-9

Paul assured his readers that they knew "the times and the epochs" (5:1 NASB) and did not need any new information on the subject from him. They knew "full well" (accurately), for example, that "the day of the Lord will come just like a thief in the night" (5:2). The wrath of that day is the same as that of 1:10, coming as suddenly and unexpectedly as "labor pains upon a pregnant woman" (5:3 NKJV). Unbelievers will not escape.

The destruction described in verse 3 is the Great Tribulation as a whole and not the day of vengeance accompanying Christ's second coming (2 Thessalonians 1:7-9) or God's later judgment of the lost (Revelation 20:11-15). Those who suffer through this destruction are quoted as saying, "Peace and safety," just before the calamity suddenly and violently comes upon them (1 Thessalonians 5:3). It is unthinkable that people could be saying, near the end of the Tribulation or during the outpouring of

heavenly signs (Revelation 6–19) or at the time of God's final judgment, anything resembling "peace and safety" (Walvoord, *The Blessed Hope*, p. 117). Men's hearts will faint from fear during the Tribulation (Luke 21:25-27), and Christ's judgment will be no more comforting.

Beginning in 1 Thessalonians 5:4, Paul contrasts the situation of the believer with that of the unbeliever, inserting the pronouns "you" and "we" (5:4-5). The day of the Lord will overtake unbelievers "as a thief" because of their immoral state ("night," "darkness"). Believers, however, are of the "light" and "day" and will not be surprised (Feinberg, pp. 53–54). The contrast between "you" and "they" strongly implies that the church *will* escape, and that is one reason Paul has no need to discuss the "times and epochs" of the rapture (5:1).

Verses 6-8 include exhortations to be alert and sober (self-controlled), living in faith and love, and having confidence in salvation, since this is the lifestyle that is fitting for the day (see Romans 13:12-13). Drunkenness and sleep characterize the night, but alertness and soberness are appropriate for the daytime (Bruce, pp. 111–12; see 1 Peter 5:8). In verse 9, Paul reaffirms the fact that God has not destined believers to suffer this eschatological wrath but rather to obtain salvation through Christ. Verse 10 says this salvation includes eternally living together with Christ, thus showing that it is parallel to the rescue of 1:10 and the catching up (rapture) of 4:17.

According to verse 2, it is the "day of the Lord," not specifically the destruction, that will "come as a thief in the night." The destruction will be the evidence of the "day." This day of the Lord is apparently a literal period of time that stretches through the millennium to the new heavens and the new earth (2 Peter 3:7-13). It is this period of time that will begin in the night, like a thief. Both night and day are periods of time. The church, Paul says, is not of the night, but of the day (verses 4,5,8). Day and night cannot exist at the same time in the same way or in the same place. But here, one group (the church) is always of the day, and the other group (unbelievers) is trapped in the night and destined to suffer God's eschatological wrath. Paul presents salvation here as an alternative to the wrath of the Tribulation. The purpose of this salvation is that believers will live with Christ (5:10), which therefore has exactly the same results as the rapture in 4:17 ("we shall always be with the Lord"). Even the words of encouragement and comfort ("therefore encourage one another and build up one another," 5:11) are identical with those in 4:18 ("therefore comfort one another with these words"). Paul clearly teaches that a rapture will occur and that it will include all living believers (1 Thessalonians 4:17; 1 Corinthians 15:51). The fact that in 1 Thessalonians 5 Paul describes the rapture as part of the outworking of the salvation that will deliver the church from God's eschatological wrath (the Tribulation) shows that for Paul the means of saving the church from the wrath of the Tribulation (or day of the Lord) is specifically the rapture.

James 5:8-9

James wrote that "the coming of the Lord is at hand" (NKJV). A more literal translation of his words is "the coming of the Lord *has drawn near*." His choice of words indicates that Christ's coming "drew near" before James wrote his epistle and that His coming is still near (imminent) today. James warns Christians to stop grumbling because "the Judge is standing at the door." The language denotes that Christ as Judge was already "at the door," ready to return to earth, and is still "at the door" today. Christ can pass through the "door of heaven" at any moment; thus, believers need to be constantly ready and obedient.

1 John 3:2-3

In seeking to motivate Christians to purify themselves from sin and lawlessness (see 1 John 3:4-11), John reminds his readers that when Jesus appears, they will become just like Him. This is the Christian's hope, and everyone who has this hope in Christ and His return will purify himself now (in progressive sanctification) so that he may grow into the purity of Christ (see Romans 8:29). The hope is realistic and motivational in proportion to its

imminence. A Christian certainly has other motivations for purification and obedience than simply the imminent hope of the rapture, but the exhortation for Christians to purify themselves in light of Christ's return is most significant if His coming is imminent.

In 1 John 2:28, John hinted at the connection between an expectation of Christ's return and the purification of the believer's life. Now, in 3:2, John establishes a sequence of events: (1) Christ will appear, (2) we will see Him just as He is, and (3) we will be like Him. These three points describe the essential elements of the rapture. The phrase "when He appears" is exactly the same as that used to describe Christ's coming for believers in 2:28 and alludes to Jesus' coming to glorify the church. At the moment of Christ's appearing, all genuine believers will become or be revealed to be like Him—entirely conformed to the likeness of God's Son.

Such a character-changing vision of Christ cannot be isolated from individual Christian responsibility here on earth. The imminence of that future vision has practical implications here and now. The hope for the future is an incentive to purity in the present. In the verses that follow, this purity involves the rejection of sin. Keeping pure is endeavoring to stay free from sin (3:3). The hope of becoming like Christ when He appears should inspire Christlike character now. And it will, especially if that hope remains truly imminent, as this passage presents it.

Revelation 22:7,12,20

Three times in Revelation 22, Christ promises that He is coming quickly (see also 2:16 and 3:11). The Greek word *tachus* is an adjective meaning "quick" or "swift." The form *tachu*, a neuter singular, is used as an adverb, with two major types of meanings: (1) "quickly, without delay," and (2) "soon, in a short time." The meaning generally proposed for the occurrences in Revelation is "quickly." The major problem, of course, is that if we take Christ's promises literally, it may appear that He was off the mark when

He said He was coming back "quickly," or else He had an unusual view of the meaning of the word. Most likely the promises relate to the rapture as imminent and ready to occur "at any moment." The word *tachu* suggests the *suddenness* of Christ's coming, whenever it occurs. A related promise in Revelation is found at 16:15: "I am coming like a thief." The idea of a "swift, unexpected appearance" is indicated, especially with respect to the "possibility that Jesus could come at any time" (Beale, p. 1135). The promises thus assume imminence, and the probability of a reference to the rapture is strengthened by the reference to Christ's rewards in 22:12 (based on works, as at the judgment seat of Christ— 2 Corinthians 5:10-11).

THE ANTICIPATION

These passages teach or imply that the rapture of the church is imminent—it could occur at any moment. The purpose of these passages is either to encourage believers concerning the hope that awaits them or to motivate them to pursue holiness in anticipation of seeing Christ soon. As Feinberg says, "there is no mention of any signs or events that precede the Rapture of the church in *any* of the Rapture passages. The point seems to be that the believer prior to this event is to look, not for some sign, but the Lord from heaven" (Feinberg, p. 80).

—WAYNE A. BRINDLE

BIBLIOGRAPHY

Beale, G.K. *The Book of Revelation. New International Greek Testament Commentary.* Grand Rapids: Eerdmans Publishing Company, 1999.

Bruce, F.F. *1 & 2 Thessalonians. Word Biblical Commentary.* Waco, TX: Word Books, 1982.

Fee, Gordon D. *The First Epistle to the Corinthians.* Grand Rapids: Eerdmans Publishing Company, 1987.

Feinberg, Paul D. "The Case for the Pretribulation Rapture Position." In *Three Views on the Rapture.* Grand Rapids: Zondervan, 1996.

Gromacki, Robert. "The Imminent Return of Jesus Christ." *Grace Theological Journal* 6. Fall 1965, pp. 11-23.

Harrison, William K. "The Time of the Rapture as Indicated in Certain Scriptures—Part I," *Bibliotheca Sacra* 114/456. October 1957, pp. 316-25.

Moo, Douglas J. "The Case for the Posttribulation Rapture Position." In *Three Views on the Rapture.* Grand Rapids: Zondervan, 1996.

Radmacher, Earl. "The Imminent Return of the Lord." *Chafer Theological Seminary Journal* 4. July 1998.

Sproule, John A. *In Defense of Pretribulationism.* Winona Lake, IN: BMH Books, 1980.

Walvoord, John F. *The Blessed Hope and the Tribulation.* Grand Rapids: Zondervan, 1976.

———. *The Rapture Question.* Grand Rapids: Zondervan, 1957.

INTERPRETATION OF PROPHECY

BIBLE TEACHERS AND INTERPRETERS generally approach Bible prophecy in one of two ways: (1) with a literal hermeneutic, or (2) by allegorizing or spiritualizing the prophecies. Jewish orthodoxy generally interpreted the Old Testament literally. The Pharisees in Jesus' day also maintained that the prophecies about the Messiah and the kingdom would come to pass in history. Now, many amillennialists claim the Pharisees' acceptance of literalism is a good reason for us to reject it. But this is a fallacious argument. Christ never chided the Pharisees for their literal interpretation of prophecy. Rather, He criticized their legalism and pride.

Ramm points out that the literal meaning of a prophecy should guide its interpretation. To the Jew, "Zion" meant Zion, and "Canaan" meant Canaan. The first rule of the interpretation of prophecy should be to establish the literal meaning. That meaning is the prophet's meaning. Though the prophet may use symbols, readers should take literally the plain meaning of the passage. To interpret "Zion" or "Jerusalem" as the church is to destroy the Bible's teaching about Christ's literal return to earth and about the land promises to Israel. Those promises are not given to the church! (See Ramm, p. 46.)

John F. Walvoord rightly contends that the interpretation of Bible prophecy really falls into two distinct camps: the premillennial and the amillennial (Walvoord, chapter 5). Walvoord also focuses on the method of interpreting Scripture. Premillennialists use a "grammatical-historical" or literal interpretation, and amillenarians use a spiritual interpretation.

SPIRITUAL INTERPRETATION

The amillennial approach of interpreting Bible prophecy is not consistent. Amillennialists believe Christ's first coming was literal and historical, but His second coming and the attending events are spiritual. Most amillennialists would say that to take Christ's second coming in a literal manner is actually "Judaizing" the biblical text.

Philo (ca. 10 B.C.–A.D. 50)

Philo Judaeus was an Alexandrian Jew who was influenced by Hellenistic thinking and culture. Philo was a Platonist and a mystic. Most of the rabbis of his day rejected his writings, and because of this some Christian groups preserved his writings as defense against the legalism of the Jews. Philo employed an allegorical hermeneutic. The word *allegory* actually means "to say another thing," or to look for a hidden meaning. Allegory is the direct opposite of a literal interpretation. Philo interpreted the story of Cain and Abel, the laws of Moses, circumcision, and certain numbers in Scripture allegorically. Philo was loyal to his Jewish roots, but his thinking was Greek. Most evangelicals claim to have abandoned his Alexandrian school of allegory, but many still retain this approach to prophecy.

Origen (ca. 185–254)

Origen of Alexandria may be the first Christian theologian to challenge the premillennial orthodoxy of the early church. Scholars agree that the early Christians were distinctly premillennial.

Origen considered the literal method of interpretation to be too simple, though he allowed for the literal approach to be used alongside the typological and the spiritual. He taught that these three approaches were likened to the human being—body, soul, and spirit. Origen also allowed for multiple symbolic meanings and interpretations of the Bible. He employed mystical and speculative methods of interpretation to prophecy. Origen's allegorical interpretations, including his views about prophecy, gained acceptance in the early church. His influence, followed by Constantine's acceptance of Christianity and Augustine's teaching in the fourth century, helped amillennialism to become more dominant than premillennialism.

Augustine (354–430)

Augustine took an allegorical and spiritual approach to interpreting the book of Revelation. He spiritualized the millennium of Revelation 20, equating it with Christ's present reign with the saints in the church age. Augustine argued that during this church age, Satan is bound, or limited in power. Nevertheless, he still held to the 1000 years of Revelation 20 as some kind of literal period. Augustine's interpretation of prophecy persisted even after the Reformation; most of the reformers and their followers accepted Augustinian eschatology.

CONSISTENT, LITERAL HERMENEUTICS

Hermeneutics is a science of language study that follows set patterns of objective thinking. The term is most used in the field of theology and in relation to the approach one uses to interpret the Word of God. Bible readers should interpret prophecy the same way they interpret any other portion of Scripture. They should understand that (1) the Scriptures are the inspired and inerrant message of God, delivered through His appointed prophets and apostles, and that (2) such messengers did not simply record their own thoughts but were "men moved by the Holy Spirit [who] spoke from God" (2 Peter 1:21 NASB).

The message of the Bible unfolds from Genesis to Revelation. This is called *progressive revelation.* God did not reveal everything at once, so His revelation was not complete and final until the last book was written. Bible passages should be interpreted by the grammar, the history, the social context, and the religious background—that is, in a normal and literal way. "When we come to a prophetic passage, our commitment must be to understand that passage according to the accepted laws of language and not to seek some mystical or figurative interpretation." It is essential, therefore, "to have this literal mind-set as we approach the prophetic Word of God" (Benware, p. 20). A literal interpretation allows for the normal use of signs, symbols, figures of speech, parable, poetry, and the like. Yet all of these natural literary devices point to a literal idea. While some consider this a daunting interpretative task, in reality it is not. This does not mean that those who take the Bible in a more literal way never have interpretative problems. Yet a consistently literal approach to prophecy brings forth a clearer message of what is to come.

Benware provides us with some very important principles about the interpretation of prophecy:

- *Interpret prophecy literally.* Literal interpretation assumes that God wants people to understand His revelation, so He based it on the normal rules of human communication. Literal interpretation understands that in normal communication and in the Scriptures, figures of speech are valuable as communication devices.

- *Interpret by comparing prophecy with prophecy.* Prophecies weave their way from some of the earliest chapters in Genesis to the very end of Revelation. Thus, the interpreter of prophecy should compare Scripture with Scripture in order to ascertain the entire teaching on prophetic subjects. By so doing, a complete and accurate picture comes into focus of what God is going to do and perhaps how and why He is going to do it.

- *Interpret in light of possible time intervals.* Because the ancients did not fully understand the flow of time, sometimes the prophetic message compresses the time between events. This telescoping phenomenon is common in the prophets and reveals gaps in prophetic fulfillment. A key passage to illustrate this is Daniel 9:24-27, where such a gap is critical in properly understanding the prophecy. It is, of course,

only in the progress of God's revelation that we can see such intervals of time between prophetic fulfillments.

- *Interpret figurative language scripturally.* Look within the Bible for the interpretation of figurative language. Symbols and figures of speech need to be interpreted in light of (1) the immediate context, (2) the larger context, and (3) the historical-cultural context. (See Benware, pp. 19–29.)

Benware adds, "Prophecies that have been fulfilled completely have been fulfilled literally, and that gives us confidence to expect that those prophetic utterances that are not yet fulfilled (or completely fulfilled) will also end up being fulfilled literally. We believe that Jesus Christ will literally return to this earth and reign at His second coming because He literally came to this earth the first time, being born of the virgin Mary at Bethlehem" (Benware, p. 29).

COVENANT VS. DISPENSATIONAL HERMENEUTICS

Covenant theology is mainly amillennial in its origin. It is based on the so-called covenant of grace that becomes the main theme from Genesis to Revelation. Covenant theologians believe salvation is the main work of God in time. They also blend the various dispensations, blurring important distinctions in Scripture.

Dispensationalists interpret Scripture literally. Therefore, they keep the church distinct from Israel. The dispensation of the millennial kingdom is different from the theocracy of Israel or the church age. A normal hermeneutic brings these distinctions to the surface. "If plain or normal interpretation is the only valid hermeneutical principle and if it is consistently applied, it will cause one to be a dispensationalist. As basic as one believes normal interpretation to be, to that extent he will of necessity become a dispensationalist" (Ryrie, p. 90). With such an approach, the interpreter will come to understand other aspects of prophecy, such as the rapture, the Tribulation, and the second coming of Christ.

TYPOLOGY

Typology is one of the most difficult parts of interpreting prophecy. The word *type* (Greek, *tupos*) is used quite loosely in the New Testament. Sometimes it refers to a figure or a divinely intended resemblance. Typology illustrates the principle that prophetic utterances somtimes have a latent and deeper meaning than at first appears. Types prefigure coming realities, whereas prophecies delineate the future. The Passover lamb of the Jews is a type of Christ (1 Corinthians 5:7). This interpretation does not deny the historicity of Passover lambs vicariously slain in every Jewish home, but it finds a higher application of the Passover lambs in Christ, the Lamb of God.

Here are some rules about the use of types as explained by Paul Lee Tan:

- Typological interpretation is not a different method of interpretation. The interpretation of a type arises from the text and has a higher application of the same sense of that text.

- Typological interpretation is therefore the unfolding of the literal sense of the type, not the allegorization of that which is typified.

- When an Old Testament element is said to be a type of an element in the New, this does not mean that one equals the other.

- Some fanciful typologists see types lurking everywhere and anywhere in Scripture. Careful interpreters will avoid this.

- Some go to the other extreme and say that a type is not a type unless the New Testament specifically says so.

- Types must be based on either the explicit or the implicit teachings of Scripture. Imagination has no place in typology. (See Tan, pp. 169–71.)

Finally, some critics reject the prophetic teachings about a coming literal millennial kingdom. They argue a literal kingdom fails to recognize the truly spiritual nature of the kingdom, and that a literal kingdom would merely be an earthly political kingdom. However, the Old Testament predicts that the millennial kingdom will be the greatest outpouring of the Spirit, with joy, gladness, and peace in the Holy Spirit (Isaiah 35:10; 51:11; Ezekiel 11:19; Joel 2:18-32). Those who argue against a literal kingdom fail to recognize the difference between spiritualizing the kingdom and the kingdom being spiritual. Spiritualizing is equivalent to allegorizing. The Lord Jesus' reign and rule here on earth will be a spiritual kingdom empowered and refreshed by the work of God's Holy Spirit.

Interpreting the prophetic Word is not that difficult a task, but it has been clouded by contrary voices that have confused many earnest students of the Bible who wish to know what the Lord has said about the future. Our enthusiasm for understanding prophecy may begin with the words of the apostle John in Revelation 4:1. Looking upward, he wrote,

> After these things I looked, and behold, a door standing open in heaven, and the first voice which I had heard, like the sound of a trumpet speaking with me, said, "Come up here, and I will show you what must take place after these things."

—MAL COUCH

BIBLIOGRAPHY

Benware, Paul. *Understanding End Times Prophecy.* Chicago: Moody Press, 1995.

Cohn, Norman. *The Pursuit of the Millennium.* New York: Oxford University Press, 1970.

Couch, Mal, gen. ed. *An Introduction to Classical Evangelical Hermeneutics.* Grand Rapids: Kregel, 2000.

———. *Dictionary of Premillennial Theology.* Grand Rapids: Kregel, 1996.

Ramm, Bernard. *Protestant Biblical Interpretation.* Grand Rapids: Baker Books, 1982.

Ryrie, Charles C. *Dispensationalism.* Chicago: Moody Press, 1995.

Tan, Paul Lee. *The Interpretation of Prophecy.* Rockville, MD: Assurance Publishers, 1988.

Trigg, Joseph Wilson. *Origen.* Atlanta: John Knox Press, 1983.

Walvoord, John F. *The Millennial Kingdom.* Findlay, OH: Dunham Publishing Company, 1959.

Zuck, Roy B. *Basic Biblical Interpretation.* Colorado Springs: Victor Books, 1991.

ISAIAH, ESCHATOLOGY OF

ISAIAH HAS OFTEN BEEN CALLED the Prince of Prophets. His book stands at the peak of the Old Testament as the genius of classical Hebrew literature. It is the longest of the prophetic books and looks further into the future than any of its contemporaries. The prophet Isaiah predicted Christ's virgin birth, His earthly ministry, His substitutionary death, and His triumphal return. Isaiah's eschatology includes prophecies of the Tribulation, the millennium, and the new heavens.

Isaiah was one of the most prominent citizens of Jerusalem, having access to both royal and priestly leadership. His name, *Yesha Yahu*, means "the Lord is salvation." His name was appropriate, for he emphasized the coming of a divine Savior to bring salvation to both Jews and Gentiles.

The prophetic ministry of Isaiah extended over half a century, from the death of King Uzziah (740 B.C.) until some time after the death of King Hezekiah (686 B.C.). Many of the events described in his prophecies were fulfilled during his own lifetime, including the fall of Samaria and Damascus and the deliverance of Jerusalem from the Assyrian invasion of King Sennacherib. But several of his prophecies focused on the distant future, especially in regard to the first and second comings of Christ.

THE COMING MESSIAH

Jesus Himself quoted Isaiah 61:1-3 in Luke 4:17-21, saying, "Today this Scripture has been fulfilled in your hearing." Our Lord was claiming that He was indeed the fulfillment of Isaiah's messianic prophecies. When John the Baptist, facing execution, wanted assurance that Jesus was the Messiah, the Lord quoted from Isaiah 35 and 61 to assure John that the messianic signs were indeed being fulfilled in His ministry (Matthew 11:2-5).

Beginning with his prediction of the virgin birth (7:14), Isaiah portrays the coming Messiah with divine qualities, even calling Him the "mighty God" (9:6). The prophet's vision of this coming One is so clear that the early

Christians saw its immediate and obvious fulfillment in Jesus Christ (see Acts 8:26-35). Isaiah includes many prophetic pictures of Christ:

1. virgin birth (7:14)
2. Galilean ministry (9:1-2)
3. divine origin (9:6-7)
4. appeal to the Gentiles (11:10)
5. forerunner prepares the way (40:3)
6. incarnation (40:9)
7. Servant of the Lord (42:1-4)
8. Redeemer of Israel (44:6)
9. light to the Gentiles (49:6)
10. suffering Savior (52:13–53:12)
11. resurrected Lord (53:10)
12. coming King (66:15-18)

THE COMING TRIBULATION

Isaiah 24–28 has often been called the "little apocalypse." In these chapters, the prophet foresees a cataclysmic judgment coming upon the whole world in the future. His interchangeable usage of the Hebrew terms *'erets* ("land") and *tebel* ("earth") make it clear that this prophecy envisions a global conflagration of incredible magnitude such as will occur during the Great Tribulation (see Matthew 24:21-30).

Looking down through the corridor of time, Isaiah sees an era when the entire world will come under the judgment of God. As a result of the universal transgression of God's moral laws, the entire planet is practically obliterated. The universal nature of this eschatological judgment leaves the population of the earth "shaking" with fear (24:13). The foundations of the earth shake, and the planet is "shaken violently" (24:18-20). In each description of this judgment, a perfect verb follows an infinitive absolute, emphasizing the earthquake-like disaster that will shake the entire planet during the Great Tribulation.

THE COMING KINGDOM

Isaiah foresees not only the coming Tribulation period but also the coming kingdom age. He describes this period as a time when "all the nations" will flow into Jerusalem to worship the Lord (2:1-5). This will be a time when peace and salvation will reign all over the earth (26:1-4). The desert will blossom like a rose, and the glory of God will be resplendent in the earth (35:1-2). Holiness, righteousness, and the joy of salvation will bless the whole world (35:8-10).

The closing chapters of Isaiah (60–66) emphasize the peaceful nature of the coming messianic kingdom. God promises to keep His covenant agreement with Israel and send the Redeemer to Zion to bless His people. In these passages, Isaiah utilizes the Hebrew prophetic perfect because he is so confident of the fulfillment of these promises that he describes them as though they had already occurred.

Isaiah foresees a time when the Gentiles (Hebrew, *goyim*, "nations") will be attracted not to Zion but to the radiance of the Lord Himself shining on His people. Isaiah predicts that the nations will come from the remote mountains and islands of the earth to seek the Lord in the New Jerusalem, whose gates will be open continuously (60:11).

In the messianic age, Jerusalem will receive "double" (Hebrew, *misheneh*) of God's blessings to reverse the years that she was under the curse of judgment (61:7). This blessing will include "everlasting joy." God will bless Israel because of His "everlasting covenant" with them (61:8). In the days of this blessing they will wear the "garments of salvation" and the "robe of righteousness" (61:10).

One cannot read these chapters from a Jewish perspective and miss the fact that they are God's eternal promises to Israel. Attempts to apply these passages to the church as a spiritual "Israel" violate every normal principle of biblical interpretation.

Isaiah assures his hearers that God will keep His covenant promises to Israel during the time of His kingdom on earth. These promises were not fulfilled in ancient Israel, yet they are unique to Israel. Therefore, their ultimate fulfillment must be in the future, when the "redeemed of the LORD" will come to Zion with songs of peace and salvation for the whole world (62:12).

Isaiah 63–66 emphasizes the fact that divine judgment (the Tribulation period) will precede the kingdom age. The Messiah will trample the grapes of wrath in the winepress of God's judgment while He marches to victory at Armageddon (see Isaiah 63:1-6; Revelation 16–19).

Isaiah commands his readers to "rejoice with Jerusalem" because peace will flow "like a river" in the millennial age (66:10-16). Then the nations will declare the glory of the Lord in all the earth (66:19). The saved will participate both in the kingdom age and in the "new heavens and new earth" (66:20-22), when all the saved will come to worship the Lord.

THE ETERNAL STATE

Isaiah's prophecy ends with the stark reminder that there are only two destinies: heaven or hell (66:23-24). We have one lifetime in which to choose to follow God or suffer the consequences. From the glory of the gates of heaven comes the final warning of the reality of eternal condemnation. God sets before everyone the way of life and the way of death, and we must make our ultimate choice.

—ED HINDSON

BIBLIOGRAPHY

Delitzsch, F. *Biblical Commentary on Isaiah*, 2 vols. Grand Rapids: Eerdmans Publishing Company, 1949.

Hindson, Ed. "Isaiah." In *King James Bible Commentary*. Nashville: Thomas Nelson, 1999.

MacRae, A.A. *The Gospel of Isaiah*. Chicago: Moody Press, 1977.

Martin, Alfred. *Isaiah: The Salvation of Jehovah*. Chicago: Moody Press, 1962.

Watts, J.N.D. *Isaiah*, 2 vols. Waco, TX: Word Books, 1981.

Young, Edward J. *The Book of Isaiah*, 3 vols. Grand Rapids: Eerdmans Publishing Company, 1972.

ISRAEL IN PROPHECY

WHAT DOES BIBLE PROPHECY say about the future of Israel? There are at least five different perspectives, which we'll examine here, and along the way we'll examine the Scriptures carefully in order to determine what they say.

THE FIVE PERSPECTIVES
The First Perspective:
Replacement Theology

Replacement theology understands the modern Jewish state to be purely an accident of history that is totally unrelated to Bible prophecy. According to this first view, when Israel rejected Jesus as the Messiah, God rejected the Jewish people. Therefore, all of the prophecies about the Jewish people are already fulfilled, and no future final restoration is in store. God transferred all His covenantal promises from Israel to the church and will fulfill them in the church. The prophecies that speak of a worldwide gathering of the Jewish people are not to be taken literally. Rather, they refer to God bringing the elect into the church until the church is complete. Today's Jews can come to salvation in Christ, but they would simply be amalgamated into the church. God has no future restoration for Israel as an ethnic people. Nothing happening with Israel today is related to prophecy, and Israel has no prophetic future.

The Second Perspective:
Restoration but No Relevancy

The second perspective takes the opposite view. God will gather the Jewish people from around the world and restore them to the Promised Land. However, this interpretation does not accept the modern Jewish state as the fulfillment of Bible prophecy because Israel has not repented and received the Messiah. National repentance is to precede national restoration (Deuteronomy 30:1-5; Isaiah 27:12-13; Ezekiel 39:25-29). Israel will experience a future, final restoration, but the modern Jewish state is not relevant to Bible prophecy at all.

The Third Perspective:
A Gradual Process

The third perspective understands current events to be the beginning of the final restoration of Israel. More and more Jews will gradually return to the Land. At some point, they will undergo a national regeneration and salvation, and the Messiah will return.

This view applies the Tribulation prophecies to the Holocaust. The Tribulation has already passed, and what we are seeing today is the final restoration.

The Fourth Perspective:
Two Worldwide Gatherings

The first three perspectives fail to observe that when the Bible speaks of a worldwide gathering of the Jewish people, it actually speaks of two distinct events. The first will be a worldwide gathering in unbelief in preparation for judgment—the judgment of the Tribulation. The second will be a worldwide gathering in faith in preparation for blessing— the blessing of the messianic kingdom. This article will focus on those prophecies that clearly speak of a worldwide gathering in unbelief in preparation for judgment rather than the prophecies that speak of the worldwide gathering in faith in preparation for blessing. For more information on the second gathering, see the article entitled "Messianic Kingdom."

Three key biblical passages speak about the gathering in unbelief in preparation for judgment.

Gathering to the Land: Ezekiel 20:33-38

In these verses, Ezekiel compares this gathering with the Exodus, when God brought the entire nation of Israel out of the land of Egypt and into the wilderness of the Sinai Peninsula. God's plan and program for Israel at Sinai was to accomplish two things: First, they were to receive the law of Moses, and second, they were to build a Tabernacle through which they could maintain much of the law. With these two things accomplished, they were to press on into the Promised Land itself. But the people rebelled and murmured against the Lord, and at the oasis of Kadesh Barnea, which was on the border of the Promised Land, God judged His people. Those who came out of Egypt would now have to continue wandering throughout the wilderness for 40 years. All those who came out would die in the wilderness except for two righteous spies and those below the age of 20. Israel became a nation of free people, born not in slavery but in the wilderness.

This historical context is the backdrop for the future. But this time, Ezekiel prophesies, God will gather His people from all parts of the world. This will be a gathering out of wrath and for wrath. God gathered the Jews out of the wrath of the Holocaust. The events of the Nazi Holocaust, in which six million Jewish people died, created the world stage for Israel to become a state. It created the world stage for the gathering in unbelief.

And because it is a gathering in unbelief, it is a gathering for a future time of wrath. In that future time of wrath, God will once again judge His people and purge out the rebels among them. Those who remain will turn to the Lord; they will be brought into "the bond of the covenant"— specifically, the bond of the New Covenant (Jeremiah 31:31-34). Israel will experience a national salvation. Then it will be a new nation, a regenerate nation that will enter the Land under their King and Messiah for the final restoration.

In these verses, Ezekiel clearly describes a worldwide gathering in unbelief, from wrath and for wrath, in preparation for a specific period of judgment that will lead to a national salvation and final restoration.

Gathering to Jerusalem: Ezekiel 22:17-22

Ezekiel again describes a gathering, this time focusing upon the city of Jerusalem. This is also a gathering in unbelief because Israel is filled with the impurities of "bronze, tin, iron, and lead." They gather for a future time of wrath when God will melt and purify them. As a purified believing nation, they will then turn to the Lord.

Ezekiel again speaks of a worldwide gathering in unbelief in preparation for a specific future judgment, but the purpose of the judgment is to bring Israel to national repentance. Only then will Israel experience the final worldwide restoration in faith.

Gathering Before the Tribulation: Zephaniah 2:1-2

In Zephaniah 1:7-18, the prophet describes a period of time that he calls "the day of

Jehovah" or "the day of the LORD." This is the most common biblical term for the Tribulation. It describes a terrible period of time that Israel and the world will have to go through prior to the establishment of the kingdom.

Zephaniah 2:1-2 discusses an event that must occur *before* the day of the Lord. Four times the prophet says "before" (three times in the Hebrew text). Before the period of wrath described in chapter 1 comes, before the day of Jehovah comes, Israel must be gathered. But it is a gathering in unbelief, for the nation is not yet ashamed of its sins. The purpose of this period is to bring out that shame, to cause the nation to turn to the true God. This prophecy clearly specifies a gathering in unbelief in preparation for the judgment of the day of the Lord.

The Fifth Perspective: Isaiah 11:11–12:6

It shall come to pass in that day that the LORD shall set his hand again the second time to recover the remnant of his people who are left, from Assyria and Egypt, from Pathros and Cush, from Elam and Shinar, from Hamath and the islands of the sea. And he will set up a banner for the nations, and will assemble the outcasts of Israel, and gather together the dispersed of Judah from the four corners of the earth (Isaiah 11:11-12 NKJV).

The fifth view recognizes that Israel will be gathered twice: once in unbelief and once in faith. But this view goes on to say that we really cannot be sure that the present Jewish state, as we see it today, is a fulfillment of those prophecies that spoke of the gathering in unbelief. This view maintains that several gatherings in unbelief may occur before the specific one that fulfills the prophecies we have discussed. However, this passage in Isaiah shows that only two gatherings in unbelief can occur.

THE PERTINENT FACTS
Only Two Gatherings

Isaiah 11:11–12:6 is speaking of the final worldwide gathering in faith in preparation for blessing. It might appear to be irrelevant to our topic, but it *is* relevant because of the way Isaiah numbers the final worldwide gathering in faith in preparation for the messianic kingdom. In verse 11, he labels it as *the second* one. If the last one is the second one, how many can take place before that? Only one.

The Bible does not allow for several worldwide gatherings in unbelief. It allows for one worldwide gathering in unbelief, followed by one gathering in faith. This text only permits two worldwide gatherings from the four corners of the earth. Therefore, the present Jewish state is very relevant to Bible prophecy.

In addition to these passages that speak of a worldwide gathering in unbelief in preparation for judgment, three other corollary issues are relevant to the theme of the modern Jewish state in Bible prophecy.

The Start of the Tribulation

Daniel 9:24-27 records the famous vision of the 70 sevens, or the 490-year period that God has decreed over the Jewish people. By the end of verse 26, the first 483 years of this 490-year period have already been fulfilled in history, coming to an end at the first coming of the Messiah.

But seven years of this prophetic clock remain for Israel—the seven years of the Tribulation. What one event will begin the seven years of Tribulation, the seventieth seven of Daniel? The answer is found in Daniel 9:27:

> Then he shall confirm a covenant with many for one week; but in the middle of the week he shall bring an end to sacrifice and offering. And on the wing of abominations shall be one who makes desolate, even until the consummation, which is determined, is poured out on the desolate.

The pronoun "he" goes back to its nearest antecedent, which is found in verse 26: "the prince who is to come." In other words, "the prince who is to come" in verse 26 and the "he" who makes a covenant in verse 27 are one and the same, the individual better known in most Christian circles today simply as the Antichrist.

The last seven years, the seventieth seven, begin with one specific, decisive event: the signing of a seven-year treaty between Israel and the Antichrist. This is the event that starts the Tribulation. The rapture will not begin the Tribulation; the church will be raptured before the Tribulation starts. The rapture is an imminent event; it could happen at any time. The rapture could happen many years before the Tribulation. The starting point of the Tribulation is not the rapture but the signing of this seven-year covenant. Until this covenant is signed, the Tribulation cannot begin.

Isaiah 28:14-22 also mentions the signing of this covenant. It gives the reason Israel even bothers to make a covenant like this: military security. When Israel signs this covenant, she puts her trust in the Antichrist for her military security. This requires the existence of a Jewish state before the Tribulation.

The fulfillment of this prophecy presupposes two other things. One is not in place yet, and the other is. First, the fulfillment presupposes that the Antichrist is already in a position of high political power before the Tribulation. A sovereign state such as Israel would not sign a covenant with anyone of inconsequential power. This has not yet taken place but must come to pass before the Tribulation can begin. Second, a Jewish state must be in place. This has been true only since 1948. This is another way the modern state of Israel fits within Bible prophecy.

The Third Temple and the Abomination of Desolation

Four passages of Scripture (Daniel 9:27; Matthew 24:15-16; 2 Thessalonians 2:3-4; Revelation 11:1-2) describe the abomination of desolation, which takes place in the middle of the Tribulation when the Antichrist breaks the seven-year covenant with Israel. He will take over the Jewish Temple, seat himself in it, proclaim himself to be God Almighty, and call upon the whole world to worship him as God. Their acceptance of his deity will be signified by their taking his mark of 666.

For this to occur, Israel must be in control of the Temple compound. The fact that these events take place in the middle of the Tribulation means that the Temple is both standing and functioning by the middle of the Tribulation. The temple might be rebuilt during the first 3½ years of the Tribulation, or it might be rebuilt before the Tribulation starts. We cannot be more exact than that, but we know that by the midpoint of the Tribulation, the Temple is standing and has been functioning for a while.

That, in turn, presupposes Jewish sovereignty over the Temple compound area. Israel became a state in 1948, but the city of Jerusalem was divided for 19 years. From 1948 to 1967, the eastern part of Jerusalem, which is the biblical Jerusalem, the Old City where the Temple compound is located, was in Jordanian, not Jewish, hands. In 1967, one of the by-products of the Six-Day War was Jewish control of the Temple compound. This is another way the modern Jewish state fits into Bible prophecy.

The Israel of Ezekiel 38–39

Ezekiel 38–39 describes a confederation of nations located north and south of Israel that invade Israel from the north. Two items in this passage pertain directly to the modern Jewish state.

First, what kind of Israel is described in this passage at the time of this invasion? According to Ezekiel 38:8 and 12b, Israel has been gathered from the nations around the world and is rebuilding wasted cities that have been laying desolate for many centuries. The nation has been pursued by the sword—it is a gathering out of wrath. It is also a gathering in unbelief because Israel begins to believe only after this invasion.

In other words, Ezekiel is not describing what was true of Israel in ancient history. This has been true only since 1948. Regardless of one's view about the timing of this invasion, the main point to note is that this invasion could not have happened before 1948; before then, Israel did not fit this description.

The Place of the Destruction of the Invading Armies

The second item to note in this passage is the place in Israel where the invading armies

are destroyed. These armies will succeed in penetrating into the center of the country. Only then will God move to destroy them by His divine power. But where in the Land will they be destroyed? The location is revealed in Ezekiel 39:2 and 4a: "I will turn you around and lead you on, bringing you up from the far north; and bring you against the mountains of Israel....You shall fall upon the mountains of Israel."

When the prophet refers to "the mountains of Israel," he refers to the central mountain range that makes up the backbone of the country. In the Old Testament, these mountains were known as the hill country of Ephraim and the hill country of Judah. The famous biblical cities within these mountains include Dothan, Shechem, Samaria, Bethel, Ai, Ramah, Jerusalem, Bethlehem, Hebron, and Debir.

These armies will penetrate the central mountain ranges of Israel because their target, obviously, is the city of Jerusalem. However, from 1948 until 1967, these mountains were not in Israel—they were in Jordan. They are now in the region known as the West Bank. Jordanian forces took over these mountains in 1948 and annexed them to Jordan, leaving Israel only a small corridor of access to Jerusalem.

During the Six-Day War, not only did the Temple compound come under Jewish control, the central mountains also came under Israeli sovereignty. Therefore, the prophecy of Ezekiel 38–39 could not be fulfilled before 1948 or even 1967. This is yet another way the modern Jewish state fits within Bible prophecy.

THE FULFILLMENT AND THE FUTURE

The Bible speaks of two worldwide gatherings. The present Jewish state is not a fulfillment of those prophecies that spoke of worldwide gathering in faith in preparation for blessing, which is yet to come. Rather, it is a fulfillment of those prophecies that spoke of worldwide gathering in unbelief in preparation for judgment.

We must keep our balance. We must not see more fulfillment than is actually there.

But at the same time, we must not fail to see the fulfillment that does exist.

—ARNOLD FRUCHTENBAUM

BIBLIOGRAPHY

Fruchtenbaum, Arnold. *Footsteps of the Messiah.* Tustin, CA: Ariel Ministries, 1983.

———. *Israelology: The Missing Link in Systematic Theology.* Tustin, CA: Ariel Ministries, 1992.

Pentecost, J. Dwight. *Things to Come.* Grand Rapids: Zondervan, 1982.

Walvoord, John F. *Israel in Prophecy.* Grand Rapids: Zondervan, 1962.

JAMES, ESCHATOLOGY OF

UNLIKE THE EPISTLES OF PAUL, the epistle of James is not a communication of new revelation but an application of Old Testament teachings and the teachings of Jesus (see Matthew 24–25; Mark 13; Luke 17; 21). Therefore, James' eschatology doesn't include new information.

James speaks much of future judgment (2:13; 3:1; 5:5,9,12) and of death (1:15; 2:26; 4:14; 5:20). He refers to God's future kingdom (2:5) and to the second coming of the Lord (5:7-9). Three aspects of James' eschatology merit special attention: the kingdom, hell, and the return of the Lord.

HEIRS OF GOD'S KINGDOM

When James rebukes his Jewish Christian readers for showing favoritism to the rich and despising the poor, he reminds them that God often chooses the poor in the eyes of the world to become rich in faith and the heirs of His kingdom (2:5). This certainly involves the yet future millennial kingdom, which God promised through the Old Testament prophets and which Jesus promised to His disciples before He returned to the Father (Matthew 24:31; 25:31).

James does not suggest that all poor people go to heaven, but rather that they are at no disadvantage in becoming heirs of eternal life and of God's kingdom (see Luke 6:20; 1 Corinthians 1:26-29). James' readers favored the rich, but God honors the poor and accepts all people equally.

THE TONGUE IS SET ON FIRE BY HELL

The Old Testament teaches that the tongue is a fire (Psalm 120:3-4; Proverbs 16:27; 26:21). James intensifies this by identifying the source of this fire as hell (3:6). The word used here for "hell" is not the common Greek word for *hades* but the word for *gehenna*. This word is used only 12 times in the New Testament. Eleven of these are in the synoptic Gospels, where Jesus uses *gehenna* to describe the horror of the eternal lake of fire. The only other New Testament usage is this one by James.

In the Old Testament, Gehenna was the district on the southwest side of Jerusalem used in Ahaz' reign (c. 730 B.C.) as the site for human sacrifices to the pagan god Molech (2 Chronicles 28:3; 33:6). King Josiah (c. 630 B.C.) defiled the site of Gehenna (2 Kings 23:10), thus preventing any further human sacrifices.

By New Testament times, Gehenna had become the city dump for Jerusalem. The rubbish and filth burned continually. The stench from the maggots was unending (Mark 9:43-48). This provided a graphic illustration of the eternal lake of fire (see Revelation 19:20; 20:10,14,15).

THE COMING OF THE LORD

James, like the other apostles, was looking for the personal return of Jesus Christ. James (5:7-9) uses the Greek word *parousia* in reference to Christ's "coming." In secular Greek, *parousia* was used to speak of the arrival of a king or another dignitary. The early church consistently used the term to refer to the coming of Jesus Christ at the end of this age to judge the ungodly and to deliver the saints (Moo, p. 221; see 1 Corinthians 15:23; 1 Thessalonians 2:19; 3:13; 4:15; 5:23). This word emphasizes the coming and presence of the Lord with His people. It denotes a specific event, a hope well known to James' readers (Hiebert, p. 296).

The Greek word *parousia* is not used in the Greek translation of the Old Testament (the Septuagint), probably because this word is not associated with the Messiah until after His first advent on earth (Matthew 24:3,27,37,39). It is, however, used in the New Testament in relation to the future return of Christ (Hiebert, p. 296).

James clearly believes that Christ's return is imminent. He states that it is "at hand" and dramatically proclaims that Jesus, the Judge, stands "at the door." Thus, James exhorts his readers to be patient despite the injustices they face and to stop murmuring against one another in light of the imminent return of Jesus Christ.

—JAMES FREERKSEN

BIBLIOGRAPHY

Baker, William. *Books of James and 1 & 2 Peter*. Chattanooga: AMG Publishers, 2004.

Hiebert, D. Edmond. *The Epistle of James*. Chicago, IL: Moody Press, 1979.

Kent, Homer A., Jr. *Faith That Works: Studies in the Epistle of James*. Winona Lake, IN: BMH Books, 1986.

Moo, Douglas J. *The Letter of James*. Grand Rapids: Eerdmans Publishing Company, 2000.

JEREMIAH, ESCHATOLOGY OF

JEREMIAH, PROPHESYING during the last days before the fall of Jerusalem in 587 B.C., foretold that God would send Judah and Jerusalem into exile in Babylon as punishment for breaking the Mosaic covenant. However, he also foresaw a day when God would destroy the power of Babylon and other hostile nations and restore His people to the Land. At that time, God would establish a New Covenant relationship with reunited Judah/Israel, enabling them to obey Him perpetually. He would also reestablish Davidic rule and restore a purified Levitical priesthood. God would inaugurate all this at the end of the 70-year exile if the entire nation repented, and He would fully restore the kingdom to Judah/Israel if the nation continued to obey Him after the return. Jeremiah's prophecies were partially fulfilled in the return of the exiles under Zerubbabel in 536 B.C. and the rebuilding of the nation in the postexilic period. However, these events hardly lived up to the full glorious expectations of Jeremiah. The full realization of his prophecies await future eschatological fulfillment.

JEREMIAH'S DESCRIPTIONS OF FUTURE JUDGMENT

In chapters 2–29, Jeremiah foretold Nebuchadnezzar's coming subjugation of Judah, destruction of Jerusalem, and deportation of the people to Babylon. In chapters 30–33 he foresaw a future era when God would reverse the fortunes of Judah/Israel. At the end of 70 years, God would destroy Babylon (25:11-14) and restore the exiles to the Land (29:10-14).

JEREMIAH'S DESCRIPTIONS OF FUTURE RESTORATION

The fall of Babylon and the end of the 70-year exile would be followed by the restoration of God's people (25:12-14; 29:10,14). God would reverse the fortunes of Israel. He would restore the exiles to the Land in a glorious "second exodus," usher in a golden era of unparalleled blessing, inaugurate an eternal New Covenant with reunited Judah/Israel securing perfect obedience, reestablish the Davidic dynasty through a righteous "branch" of David, restore the Levitical priesthood, exalt a rebuilt and purified Jerusalem as the center of the worship of Israel and all nations, and bring about the redemption of repentant Gentile nations in response to witnessing God's mighty acts of blessing His people.

Conditionality is a central theme in Jeremiah's prophecies of both threatened judgment and promised blessing (18:1-11). Announced judgment could be avoided by repentance but made all the more certain by continued rebellion. Likewise, promised blessings would be fulfilled to reward obedience but revoked in response to sin. As even his contemporaries acknowledged, the judgment announced against Jerusalem in the days of Hezekiah (Micah 3:9-12) was averted when the city repented (Jeremiah 26:17-19). According to Jeremiah, the destruction of Jerusalem and the Babylonian exile could be avoided if the nation would repent. But if the nation refused to repent, its destruction would be all the more certain. Jeremiah announced that the exile would last 70 years, but the nation's restoration would not be automatic. It was contingent upon genuine national repentance: "Only when the seventy years of Babylonian rule are over will I again take up consideration for you. Then I will fulfill my gracious promise to you and restore you to your homeland" (29:10 NET).

In 536 B.C., a remnant returned to the Land in fulfillment of Jeremiah's prophecy of the 70-year exile (2 Chronicles 36:22; Ezra 1:1). However, Daniel informs us that Jeremiah's portrait of the kingdom's glorious restoration (Daniel 9:1-2) was not fully fulfilled in the sixth century B.C. but postponed until future eschatological fulfillment (Daniel 9:24-27). A remnant did repent, but the nation neither returned to God nor remained faithful during the postexilic period (Haggai 1:2-11; Malachi 1:6-14; 2:10-17; 3:6-7).

Return from Babylonian Exile: The "Second Exodus"

Jeremiah foretold the Babylon exile, but he also foresaw a day when God would restore the exiles. God would return the exiles of Judah and Israel, reuniting the nation. They would come seemingly from all directions and every nation, creating a great throng, including even those normally unable or unfit to travel, such as the blind, the lame, and pregnant women about to give birth (31:7-8). This mighty deliverance would be like a "second exodus" that would make the original deliverance from Egypt pale by comparison. Israel/Judah's arrival in Zion would inaugurate a golden age of eternal redemption and unparalleled blessing secured by their perfect obedience to God in an everlasting New Covenant.

Restoration, Purification, and Exaltation of Jerusalem

Jeremiah predicted the devastated city of Jerusalem would be reinhabited (30:17-20) and rebuilt (31:4,38; 33:7) to the extent that every building destroyed by the Babylonians would be rebuilt on its traditional site (30:18). Once defiled by sin, Jerusalem would be purified—even the unclean Hinnom Valley would be sanctified and included within the city's expanded borders (31:39-40). Jerusalem would live in perpetual safety and security under the Lord's protection (32:37; 33:16), never again to be torn down or destroyed (31:38-40). As the special object of God's blessing (31:23), the city's fame would spread among the nations and bring God glory (33:9). Pilgrimages to Jerusalem would again be made by the reunified people of Judah and Israel (31:6,12-14; 33:11) and the entire world (3:17). At that time, restored Jerusalem would be called "the LORD's throne" (3:17), "the holy mountain where righteousness dwells" (31:23), and "the LORD has delivered us" (Jeremiah 33:16; see Isaiah 1:26; 62:2-4; Jeremiah 23:6; Ezekiel 48:35; Zechariah 8:3).

Jerusalem was rebuilt and reinhabited, first on a small scale in the Persian period but on a grander scale during the Greek and Roman periods. Its condition and status, however, fell short of the holiness and glory pictured by Jeremiah. Zion became the center of Israel's worship—even Gentile proselytes worshiped there—but she was never the center of worship of all nations. Moreover, Jerusalem was neither perpetually safe nor secure, suffering the slaughter of Antiochus IV Epiphanes in 165 B.C. and the horrific destruction by Titus in A.D. 70. However, it was not Jeremiah's prophecies that failed, but Jerusalem herself. God had promised to "restore the fortunes" of Jerusalem on the condition of repentance (29:10-14) and perpetually bless the city contingent on its perseverance in obedience (31:31-34; 32:36-41; 50:4-5). Nevertheless, God will send the Redeemer to Zion in the future (Romans 11:27). God will send Christ from heaven to Jerusalem to fulfill all the covenant promises and ancient prophecies (Acts 3:19-21).

During the millennium, Christ will rule on His throne in "the beloved city" (Revelation 20:4-10). The ultimate fulfillment of Jeremiah's prophecies will culminate in the eschatological new Jerusalem of the future (Revelation 20:1-10; 21:2–22:5,14-15).

Reoccupation of the Land as an Eternal Possession

God had given the Land to Israel as an "eternal possession" (Genesis 17:8; 22:17; 48:4; 2 Chronicles 20:7), but continual and perpetual occupation was contingent on obedience (Deuteronomy 4:1; 6:1). The wicked generation of Jeremiah's day forfeited their eternal possession by sin (17:4; 32:23), but God would restore the Land to Israel as an "eternal possession" (3:18; 30:3; see 32:8). God would "plant" them in the Land, and they would flourish (31:27-28). Restored Israel would never again be uprooted from the Land (23:3-4; 24:6; 30:3) or subjugated by foreign rulers (30:8,19-20) but would live in the Land securely (32:37) and continue forever as a nation (31:36-37). Israel/Judah would resume possession of the Land after the exile if the nation would repent (29:10-14). They would retain possession of the Land forever if they remained obedient (7:3,7; 11:5; 25:5; 35:15).

Renewal of Covenant Relationship: New Covenant

The highlight of Jeremiah's portrait of Israel's future restoration was the promise of an eternal New Covenant (31:31-37; 32:36-41; 50:4-5). Jeremiah pictured the New Covenant's inauguration (31:31-37; 32:38-40; 50:4-5) when God would return the exiles from Babylon. As Moses anticipated long before (Deuteronomy 30:6), God would transform their hearts to secure genuine obedience: "I will give them a heart to acknowledge that I am the LORD" (24:7; see also 3:17). This covenant would be new in the sense that it would differ from the covenant established at Sinai. The difference would not lie in the basic demand of the covenant itself but in the people's capacity to obey it. The Old Covenant, engraved on tablets of stone, could only command but not instill obedience. The New Covenant would be written "on their hearts" (31:34) in stark contrast to Jeremiah's wicked contemporaries, whose hearts were engraved with sin (17:1) and whose capacity for evil was hopelessly ingrained (13:23). The Lord would continue to demand obedience, but this time He would impart the desire and ability to remain loyal to Him.

The New Covenant would so eclipse the Old Covenant that the former would be virtually forgotten by comparison (3:16-17). God would establish this New Covenant with Israel (31:31-37; 32:36-42; 50:4-5) in conjunction with His restoration of the exiles. This would be contingent on humbly seeking the Lord in godly sorrow and genuine repentance (50:4-5; see 29:10-14). Jesus inaugurated the New Covenant by His sacrifice as the New Testament quotations of Jeremiah 31:31-34 clearly affirm (Hebrews 8:8-10; 10:16). New Covenant blessings have been inaugurated for Jewish and Gentile believers in the church (Ephesians 1:13-14; 3:1-9), but the New Covenant promise of the redemption of Israel is yet future (Romans 11:25-27). This will occur when the ultimate Davidic King comes to Zion (Romans 11:27) and the kingdom is restored to Israel (Acts 1:6-8; 3:19-26).

Restoration of Covenant Blessings

Moses proclaimed God's promise to reward obedience with covenant blessings (Leviticus 26:1-13; Deuteronomy 28:1-14) and punish disobedience with covenant curses, culminating in exile (Leviticus 26:14-38; Deuteronomy 28:15-68). But God also promised to restore the nation conditioned on genuine repentance (Leviticus 26:39-45; Deuteronomy 30:1-10). In light of this covenant structure, Jeremiah portrayed the repentant nation's future blessings following the curse of Babylonian exile. These blessings would reverse the previous calamity (31:23), allowing the restored community to enjoy their former privileges (30:20).

God's promise to bless the repentant was partially fulfilled in reestablishment of the postexilic community. However, it was not enjoying the good things God promised to their fathers but was in great distress from foreign rulers (Nehemiah 9:36-37). The people of Israel often suffered covenant curses rather than blessings because of their disobedience to the Mosaic law (Haggai 1:7-11; Malachi 3:6-7). Through the New Covenant implemented by Christ, New Testament believers have been given all spiritual blessings (Ephesians 1:3) and are empowered to obey the law of Christ (Romans 8:3-4). When Israel turns to Christ, it will experience the fullness of covenant blessings (Romans 11:13-32). Ultimate fulfillment of these covenant blessings will occur in the eschaton as the reward for faith and obedience (Romans 8:20-24).

Restoration of the Eternal Davidic Kingship

With the exception of Josiah, the Davidic kings in the days of Jeremiah were wicked. But Jeremiah foresaw a day when God would restore godly leaders (3:15) and raise up a godly Davidic king to restore the dynasty (23:5-6; 30:9; 33:15-22).

God promised to establish an eternal succession of Davidic descendants on his throne (2 Samuel 7:12-16,25-29; 23:1-7; 1 Kings 2:1-4; 9:3-9; 1 Chronicles 17:7-14; 28:2-10; Psalm 89:3-4,19-37; 132:10-18), but He warned that unbroken succession of the dynasty would be conditioned on obedience (Psalm 132:12). So Jeremiah denounced the popular but mistaken belief that the Davidic throne was absolutely inviolable. God would hold individual wicked Davidic kings and the dynasty as a whole accountable (4:9; 21:11-14; 23:1-2). If they repented, the dynasty would continue from generation to generation, but if they refused to repent, the dynasty would be placed in jeopardy (17:19-26). However, Jeremiah foresaw a day when, after restoring the exiles to their homeland, God would restore the Davidic dynasty and raise up godly leaders ("shepherds") to properly lead ("shepherd") His people (3:15; 23:1-4). No longer would foreign kings rule over the nation, but one of their own countrymen would become their leader (30:21).

The dynasty would be restored through a "righteous branch of David," a godly Davidic descendant (23:5; 33:15). Some people view this ruler as David resurrected and ruling with Christ, but most believe this is a reference to Christ Himself. Jeremiah calls him "David" (30:9 NASB) not because He would be David resurrected but because He would rule in the spirit of His illustrious ancestor (see Ezekiel 34:23-24; 37:24; Hosea 3:5; Micah 5:2).

Restoration of the Levitical Priesthood

Although God judged the Levitical priests who were corrupt in Jeremiah's day (4:9; 6:13-15; 8:1; 13:13; 20:1-6; 23:34; 26:1-11), He would restore the Levitical priesthood (31:14; 33:11) to fulfill His promise of the "covenant of eternal priesthood" to the Levites, that their descendants would always serve as priests before God (33:18-22; see Numbers 18:19; 25:1-13; Deuteronomy 33:8-11; Psalm 106:30-33). According to Jeremiah, God would restore an eternal succession of Levitical priests to minister in the Temple just as He would restore an eternal succession of Davidic descendants to the throne.

Jeremiah's words were partially fulfilled when the priesthood was reestablished with Jeshua the high priest in 538 B.C. (Ezra 3:2,8-13). However, the perpetual succession and ministry of the Levitical priests was broken off when the Temple was destroyed in A.D. 70. The New Testament proclaims that the otherwise eternal Levitical priesthood was superseded by the Melchizedekian priesthood of Messiah, not for moral failure by the Levites but due to the superior efficacy of Christ's all-sufficient sacrifice. Some theologians believe the Temple must be rebuilt again and the Levitical priesthood reestablished to literally fulfill the prophecies of Jeremiah and other Old Testament prophets (particularly Ezekiel 40–48).

Restoration of Temple Worship

Jeremiah denounced the popular but mistaken belief that the Temple on Zion was absolutely inviolable (7:2,4,14; 26:6,9; 27:16; 28:6). Judah's sin had defiled the Temple (11:15; 23:11), so like the ancient sanctuary at Shiloh, it would be destroyed (7:14; 26:6,12; 27:18,21; 39:8). However, Jeremiah pictured a restored Temple in the future era after the exile. Jeremiah did not explicitly proclaim the Temple would be rebuilt, much less provide the kind of plan found in Ezekiel 40–48, but he did say lavish sacrifices would once again be offered on its altars (31:12,14; 33:11; see 17:26) and both reunited Israel/Judah and the entire world would make pilgrimages to the Temple to worship the Lord (3:17; 31:6,12-14; 33:11).

Future Gentile Salvation and Blessing: One People of God

Jeremiah foresaw a day, after God's judgment of the Gentile nations and His restoration of Israel from exile, when the Gentiles would repent of idolatry and embrace Yahweh alone (16:19-20). This Gentile salvation would be in response to God's restoration of repentant Judah (4:2). The nations would give God praise and honor in response to seeing His deliverance and blessing of restored Jerusalem (33:9). He also promised to restore the fortunes of Moab (48:47), Edom (49:7), and Elam (49:39). Babylon, however, is not offered future hope because its crimes were excessive—so much so that she is pictured elsewhere as representative of all the hostile nations that oppose God and His people (Revelation 14:8; 16:9; 17:5; 18:2,10,21).

Jeremiah also announced that after judging numerous hostile Gentile nations, God would relent and have pity on them as well, contingent upon their repentance (12:14-17). Jeremiah announced that the Lord would include repentant Gentiles among the people of God. Thus, Jeremiah anticipated the future inclusion of Gentile believers along with Jewish believers in the New Covenant, creating one people of God, fully revealed only in the New Testament. Thus, New Covenant realities are fulfilling Jeremiah's Old Covenant expectations. Jeremiah had anticipated that God's mighty deliverance of repentant national Israel would lead to the conversion of onlooking multitudes of Gentiles. Redemption of the remnant of Israel has led to the present conversion of a worldwide multitude of Gentiles, which will one day bring national Israel into New Covenant salvation as well (Romans 11:11-27).

—**GORDON H. JOHNSTON**

BIBLIOGRAPHY

Brueggemann, Walter. *A Commentary on Jeremiah: Exile and Homecoming*. Grand Rapids: Eerdmans Publishing Company, 1998.

Chisholm, Robert B. "A Theology of Jeremiah and Lammentations." In Roy Zuck and Eugene Merrill, eds. *A Biblical Theology of the Old Testament*. Chicago: Moody Press, 1991.

Feinberg, Charles. *Jeremiah: A Commentary*. Chicago: Moody Press, 1981.

Kaiser, Walter. "Evidence from Jeremiah." In D.K. Campbell and J.L. Townsend, eds. *A Case for Premillennialism*. Chicago: Moody Press, 1992.

McConville, J. Gordon. *Judgment and Promise: An Interpretation of the Book of Jeremiah*. Winona Lake, IN: Eisenbrauns, 1993.

JERUSALEM IN PROPHECY

JERUSALEM OCCUPIES A CHOSEN PLACE in God's plan for the ages, as the psalmist says: "The LORD loves the gates of Zion more than all the other dwelling places of Jacob" (Psalm 87:2 NASB). This is the city to which God descended, as the psalmist again declared: "The LORD has chosen Zion; He has desired it for His habitation. This is My resting place forever; Here I will dwell, for I have desired it" (Psalm 132:13-14). Consequently, Jerusalem attained a status as both the holy city and the city at the center of the world (Ezekiel 5:5). This privileged position explains why Scripture mentions Jerusalem more than any other city—more than 800 times (in 660 verses in the Old Testament and 142 in the New Testament).

Jerusalem appears in two-thirds of the books of the Old Testament and almost one-half of the books of the New Testament. *Jerusalem* is its most common appellation, but the Bible uses other names, such as Zion, Salem, and Ariel. The Bible also gives Jerusalem symbolic and allegorical names, such as

"Hagar [and] Mount Sinai in Arabia" (Galatians 4:25) and "Sodom and Egypt" (Revelation 11:8). Of the biblical references, 465 in the Old Testament and 24 in the New refer to prophecies of Jerusalem subsequent to the time of their utterances.

PROPHETIC SIGNIFICANCE

In the Bible, Jerusalem occupies a strategic position in two major prophetic periods: "the times of the Gentiles" (Luke 21:24) and the 70 weeks of Daniel (Daniel 9:24-27). The city prophetically marks the beginning and ending of the times of the Gentiles, which stretches from the Babylonian destruction of Jerusalem (587 B.C.) to the second advent of Christ. Events in Jerusalem likewise determine the beginning and ending of the 70 weeks, and they affect the parenthesis in time between the sixty-ninth and seventieth week.

During the time of the First Temple, Jerusalem became the focal point of prophecy as foreign invaders sought to capture the holy city. At one such occasion the prophet Isaiah prophesied Jerusalem's deliverance while declaring God's covenantal pledge to preserve it for the future: "I will defend this city to save it for My own sake and for My servant David's sake" (2 Kings 19:34).

Jerusalem is at the heart of messianic prophecy and redemptive history. In fact, God's plan required its presence (Luke 13:33). Jerusalem was indispensable to the preparation of Christ's first coming, being restored from ruin (Isaiah 52:7-12) to fulfill its role in the messianic advent as the city of the great king. Indeed, Jesus was sent to Jerusalem (Matthew 23:37), and the city served to mark defining moments in Jesus' earthly life and ministry: His dedication (Luke 2:22-38), His dialogue with the teachers in the Temple (Luke 2:41-49), His temptation by the devil (Luke 4:9-12), and His confrontation with the money changers (Matthew 21:12-27).

Jerusalem was where Jesus gave several signs of His messiahship (John 5:19; 7:14-29; 8:2-12), endured His trial and crucifixion (Matthew 25–27), and experienced His resurrection and ascension (Luke 24; Acts 1:9-11). Jesus commanded that the witness to the nations begin in Jerusalem. The church began in the city (Acts 2:1-13), the apostles performed miracles there (Acts 3), the Jerusalem Council met there (Acts 15:1-29), and from there Paul began his climactic trip to Damascus (Acts 9:1-6) and later experienced the conflict that led to his imprisonment and death.

FUTURE DESTINY

Jesus predicted Jerusalem's destruction because of its rejection of Him and its persecution of the church: "They will not leave in you one stone upon another, because you did not recognize the time of your visitation" (Luke 19:44). Yet Jesus' prediction included the future hope of Jerusalem's restoration when it repents and receives Him as Messiah (Matthew 23:39; Acts 3:19-21) at the second advent. Jesus even revealed the duration of its desolation—that the city would be "trampled underfoot by the Gentiles until the times of the Gentiles be fulfilled" (Luke 21:24). Thus, Jerusalem will experience escalating troubles until the Tribulation period, which culminates with Christ's deliverance at His second coming (Matthew 24:21-31).

Daniel's prophecy of the seventieth week (Daniel 9:27) influenced Jesus' prophetic discourse on the Mount of Olives (Matthew 24; Mark 13; Luke 21), Paul's prophetic instruction to the Thessalonians (2 Thessalonians 2:4), and John's prophetic vision of the city's invasion by the nations (Revelation 11:1-2). These scriptures refer to a time when the armies of the Antichrist will occupy the city, desecrate the Temple, and usurp the place of God (see also Daniel 11:45; Revelation 13:6,15).

Zechariah's prophecy chronicles this period of distress for the city, detailing the gathering of all nations against Jerusalem (Zechariah 12:2-3; 14:2) and the battles. At the climax of the campaign of Armageddon, the final assault on Jerusalem takes place (Zechariah 12–14). The Lord will bring about Israel's national repentance beginning with "the inhabitants of Jerusalem" (Zechariah 12:8–13:2), and Christ will defeat the invading armies of Antichrist

(Zechariah 14:3,12-15). He will deliver the Jewish remnant in the city by an earthquake (Zechariah 14:3-4) and there set up His millennial reign (Zechariah 14:9), transforming the city's topography (Zechariah 14:8,10), rebuilding the Temple (Zechariah 6:12-15), purifying and glorifying the city (Zechariah 8:3; 14:11,20-21; see also Isaiah 4:5-6; Jeremiah 3:17), and calling the nations to worship Him (Zechariah 14:16-19).

Isaiah, likewise, prophesies concerning Jerusalem in the millennial kingdom, declaring the elevation of the Temple Mount and its new position as the worship center for the world (Isaiah 2:2-3) and center of Messiah's rule over the nations, establishing universal peace (Isaiah 2:4). Isaiah also reveals the glorious reversal of Jerusalem's fortunes in the millennial restoration, announcing the divine declaration, "For behold, I create Jerusalem for rejoicing, and her people for gladness. I will also rejoice in Jerusalem and be glad in My people" (Isaiah 65:18-19). Jerusalem's restoration includes harmony in the created order to prevent the defiling of God's holy mountain in Jerusalem (Isaiah 11:6-9; 65:25). The nations will turn to Christ, becoming His people (Isaiah 11:10-12; 19:25) and beholding His glory in Jerusalem (Isaiah 66:18-20).

The prophet Ezekiel focuses on Jerusalem's millennial Temple and the city's extended sacred status (Ezekiel 40–48), depicting the Lord's return to dwell in Jerusalem (Ezekiel 43:1-7; see also 37:26-28) and conferring upon it a new descriptive title: YHWH Shammah ("The LORD is there," Ezekiel 48:35).

The final assault on the city occurs at the conclusion of the 1000-year reign of Christ when Satan, released from his imprisonment, deceives the nations and gathers an army to march against the Messiah enthroned in Jerusalem (Revelation 20:7-9). As He promised (2 Kings 19:34), the Lord defends Jerusalem and destroys these last adversaries of His holy city.

NEW JERUSALEM

With the creation of the new heavens and new earth for the eternal state, apparently the earthly Jerusalem will continue in relationship to the heavenly Jerusalem in fulfillment of its divine destiny as the place where God's name will remain forever (2 Chronicles 33:4; see also Psalm 48:8; 68:16; 132:14; Joel 3:20; Micah 4:7). In light of the position Jerusalem holds in the prophetic program, and how the hopes of the world are tied to its welfare, let us heed the command of the psalmist to "pray for the peace of Jerusalem" (Psalm 122:6).

—RANDALL PRICE

BIBLIOGRAPHY

Foos, Harold D. "Jerusalem in Biblical Prophecy." In *Dictionary of Premillennial Theology*, ed. Mal Couch. Grand Rapids: Kregel, 1996.

———. "Jerusalem in Prophecy." Th.D. dissertation, Dallas Theological Seminary, 1965.

Fruchtenbaum, Arnold. *The Footsteps of the Messiah: A Study of the Sequence of Prophetic Events*. Revised & enlarged edition. Tustin, CA: Ariel Press, 2004.

Hunt, Dave. *A Cup of Trembling*. Eugene, OR: Harvest House Publishers, 1995.

Olsen, Arnold. *Inside Jerusalem, City of Destiny*. Glendale, CA: Regal Books/Gospel Light Publications, 1969.

Pentecost, J. Dwight. *Things to Come*. Grand Rapids: Zondervan, 1958.

Price, Randall, *Jerusalem in Prophecy*. Eugene, OR: Harvest House Publishers, 1998.

JESUS CHRIST

JESUS CHRIST IS THE GREATEST person who has ever lived. No one even begins to compare with Him. His person, character, wisdom, integrity, and love outshine all others. The greatest men and women of history do not hold a candle to the blazing brilliance of His impeccable life. He stands like a mountain of granite against the sands of the seashore by comparison. Charles Spurgeon said of Jesus, "You may study, look, and meditate, but Jesus is a greater Savior than you think Him to be, even when your thoughts are at their highest."

Jesus is the focal point of the Bible. More than 100 messianic prophecies of the Old Testament point to His first coming. (See the article titled "Messianic Prophecy.") In addition, nearly 300 Old and New Testament prophecies point to His second coming. (See the article titled "Second Coming of Christ.") Together, these amazing predictions make it clear that Jesus is the main theme of prophecy. It is no wonder that Jesus Himself said, "All things must be fulfilled which were written in the Law of Moses and the Prophets and the Psalms concerning Me" (Luke 24:44 NKJV).

The Bible emphasizes the centrality of Christ in the unfolding plan of God for all things in heaven and earth. He is our Savior, Redeemer, Lord, and King. The Scriptures declare, "In Him we have redemption through His blood, the forgiveness of sins, according to the riches of His grace...that in the dispensation of the fullness of the times He might gather together in one all things in Christ, both which are in heaven and which are on earth—in Him" (Ephesians 1:7,10).

HIS PAST FULFILLMENT

Jesus launched His public ministry with powerful prophetic declarations. He proclaimed, "Repent, for the kingdom of heaven is at hand" (Matthew 4:17). Jesus clearly pictured Himself as the messianic King who had come to offer the fulfillment of the promise of the kingdom to the people of Israel. That He saw this as a fulfillment of biblical prophecy is made clear in Mark's Gospel, which records this: "Jesus came to Galilee, preaching the gospel of the kingdom of God, and saying, 'The time is fulfilled, and the kingdom of God is at hand. Repent, and believe in the gospel'" (Mark 1:14-15).

Jesus' view of the prophetic nature of His ministry is clear in His sermon in the synagogue of Nazareth (Luke 4:16-21). He read the messianic prophecy in Isaiah 61:1-2 and then declared, "Today this scripture is fulfilled in your hearing." He knew that God the Father had anointed Him to preach the gospel of salvation and offer the kingdom to Israel—contingent upon their acceptance of Him.

The Old Testament prophets had already predicted the coming of the Messiah. They had even gone so far as to predict the nature of His ministry—to preach the gospel to the poor, heal the brokenhearted, proclaim liberty to the captives, and give sight to the blind. Jesus did all of these things and more as evidence of His messiahship.

The list of prophetic fulfillments is impressive indeed:

- He was born of a virgin (Isaiah 7:14).
- He was born in Bethlehem (Micah 5:2).
- He began His ministry in Galilee (Isaiah 9:1-2).
- He worked miracles (Isaiah 35:5-6).
- He preached righteousness (Jeremiah 23:6).
- He rode into Jerusalem on a donkey (Zechariah 9:9).
- He was betrayed for 30 pieces of silver (Zechariah 11:12-13).
- He was crucified (Zechariah 12:10).
- He died for our sins (Isaiah 53:5-6).
- He rose from the dead (Psalm 16:10).

In all of human history, no one else has come close to fulfilling all these prophecies and 100 more like them. Jesus of Nazareth is the only person who has clearly fulfilled every one of these incredible predictions.

HIS PRESENT MINISTRY

In addition to serving as our heavenly High Priest, Jesus is also making preparations for our eternal future. The New Testament describes Him as our High Priest who is holy, harmless, and undefiled (Hebrews 7:26). "Therefore He is also able to save to the uttermost those who come to God through Him, since He always lives to make intercession for them" (Hebrews 7:25). He is also pictured as our "High Priest of the good things to come" (Hebrews 9:11) and the "Mediator of the new covenant" (Hebrews 9:15).

In fulfillment of His great prediction to build His church (Matthew 16:18), Jesus continues to function as Lord of the church during the dispensation of the church age (see Revelation 1:10-20). The New Testament teaches that the risen Christ is actively involved in the lives of His saints and in the growth and development of His church (see Acts 1:4-5; 2:47; 3:6; 4:12; 7:59; 9:5; 9:17; 16:31).

When Jesus met with the disciples in the upper room the night before the crucifixion, He explained that He was going to the Father's house to "prepare a place" for them (John 14:1-6). This promise was given only to the believing disciples. Judas had already left the room to make the final arrangements for the betrayal. Thus, Jesus promised to prepare a place in heaven for believers and then return one day to take them home to heaven. This is the first mention of the rapture in the New Testament.

In the meantime, Jesus is preparing His bride, the church. The New Testament pictures the spiritual relationship between Christ and His church as that of a husband and wife. The apostle Paul said, "Husbands, love your wives, just as Christ also loved the church and gave Himself for her…that He might present her to Himself a glorious church… holy and without blemish" (Ephesians 5:25,27). Revelation 19:7-9 describes the marriage of the Lamb in heaven. Christ is depicted as the Bridegroom whose wife (the church) has made herself ready for the wedding as the bride of Christ.

HIS FUTURE MINISTRY

Jesus Christ will continue building His church until the rapture calls us home to the Father's house (see Matthew 16:18; 24:14; John 14:1-6). The New Testament describes the future ministry of Christ in several facets related to His second coming.

1. *Rapture of the Church.* The first major event related to the second coming of Christ is the rapture of the church. At that time, Christ will descend from heaven "with a shout, with the voice of an archangel, and with the trumpet of God. And the dead in Christ will rise first. Then we who are alive and remain shall be caught up [Greek, *harpazo*] together with them in the clouds to meet the Lord in the air" (1 Thessalonians 4:16-17). This prophetic promise is accompanied by words of comfort, blessing, and encouragement. Thus, it is called "the blessed hope" (Titus 2:13). (See the article titled "Rapture.")

2. *Judgment Seat of Christ.* Every believer must stand before the judgment seat (Greek, *bema*) of Christ to receive his or her rewards (see 2 Corinthians 5:10). Jesus said, "The Father judges no one, but has committed all judgment to the Son" (John 5:22). Paul adds, "The Lord Jesus Christ…will judge the living and the dead at His appearing and His kingdom" (2 Timothy 4:1). The Great White Throne judgment involves only unbelievers and occurs at the end of the millennial kingdom, whereas the *bema* seat judgment involves believers and comes before the millennium. It is this judgment that determines the crowns and rewards of believers and prepares the bride of Christ to reign with Him on earth. (See the articles titled "Crowns" and "Judgment Seat of Christ.")

3. *Marriage of the Lamb.* Christ will be married in heaven to His bride, the church (Revelation 19:7-9). This spiritual union is depicted in Scripture as a marriage, followed by the marriage supper on earth. The 24 elders in Revelation 4:4, robed in white, symbolize the raptured church in heaven. Throughout the Apocalypse, the elders serve as a picture of the redeemed church, which has been rewarded with crowns of gold and robes of white. (See the article titled "Elders, (24).")

4. *Glorious Appearing.* The second coming of Christ is described as a glorious appearing (Greek, *epiphaino*) or epiphany. Second Thessalonians 2:8 refers to the "brightness of His coming." Jesus referred to this same event when He said, "Then the sign of the Son of Man will appear in heaven" (Matthew 24:30). He explained that all the tribes of earth would see Him coming "immediately after the tribulation of those days" (24:29). The glorious appearing, which occurs at the end of the Tribulation period, is a totally separate event

from the rapture of the church, which occurs at the beginning of the Tribulation period. (See the article titled "Glorious Appearing.")

5. *Triumphal Return.* Christ's second coming involves both His glorious appearing and His triumphal return. Revelation 19:11-16 describes this incredible event in which Jesus will appear on a white horse, in a blood-soaked robe, with eyes of flaming fire, leading His bride, the triumphant church, as He returns to earth to set up His millennial kingdom as King of kings and Lord of lords. He speaks the word and slays the army of the Antichrist. Then He casts the beast and the False Prophet into the lake of fire (see Revelation 19:19-21). (See the articles titled "Beast," "False Prophet," and "Lake of Fire.")

6. *Salvation of Israel.* Christ's return is depicted in the New Testament in connection with the salvation and deliverance of Israel. In Matthew 24:22-31, the days of the Great Tribulation are shortened, the elect Jews are spared, and the nation is saved. The Gentile nations (Greek, *ethnos*) are gathered before Christ and judged based upon their treatment of His "brothers" (Matthew 25:31-46). None of these events happened in A.D. 70 when Jerusalem fell to the Romans. All attempts to view these events as being fulfilled in the past simply do not fit with the facts; these events are yet to happen. (See the article titled "Conversion of Israel.")

7. *Binding of Satan.* Revelation 20:1-3 clearly indicates that Satan will be bound in the future in a manner that has never yet occurred in history. First, the prophetic picture of the binding of Satan follows the triumphal return of Christ in Revelation 19. This did not happen at the first coming of Christ. Second, the binding of Satan in Revelation 20 leaves him totally immobile. He is "cast into the bottomless pit" (Greek, *abysos*) where he is shut up, sealed in, and unable to deceive the nations. Attempts to argue that Satan is already bound by the power of the cross are ludicrous in light of clear biblical

statements to the contrary. Peter warned Christians to beware "because your adversary the devil walks about like a roaring lion, seeking whom he may devour" (1 Peter 5:8). Paul refers to Satan buffeting his body with a "thorn in the flesh" (2 Corinthians 12:7) and hindering his ministry (1 Thessalonians 2:18). The New Testament writers give every indication that Satan is an active foe whom we must resist until Christ returns to bind and immobilize him in the abyss. (See the article titled "Satan.")

8. *Millennial Kingdom.* The Old Testament prophets predicted a coming messianic age when the Messiah would reign over all on the earth. They depicted this time as an age of unparalleled peace, prosperity, and longevity (see Isaiah 60–66). Revelation 20:1-7 specifically refers six times to our Lord's earthly kingdom as lasting for 1000 years. For example, Satan will be bound in the abyss for 1000 years. The saints will reign with Christ 1000 years. The unsaved dead will not be resurrected until the end of the 1000 years. If John meant the number merely to be symbolic, he certainly would not have emphasized it in this way. Only after the 1000 years have passed will Satan be loosed and ultimately defeated and cast into the lake of fire (Revelation 20:10). (See the article titled "Messianic Kingdom.")

9. *Great White Throne Judgment.* After the 1000-year millennial kingdom of Christ on earth, the unsaved dead of all time will be resurrected to stand before Christ at the Great White Throne judgment (Revelation 20:11-15). Even death and hades will give up their dead to stand at this judgment. Condemnation to the lake of fire will be determined by whether or not one's name is listed in the Book of Life. The books of the works of individuals' lives will determine the severity of their punishment. To be condemned at this judgment is called the "second death" because it is permanent and eternal. (See the article titled "Great White Throne Judgment.")

10. *Eternal Reign.* Ultimately, even the millennial kingdom will fade in light of the eternal reign of Christ in the New Jerusalem (Revelation 21–22). The eternal city of God will be the home of the saved for all eternity. Every tear will be wiped away. There will be no more pain and suffering. The tree of life and the conditions of Eden will be restored, and there will be no sin, suffering, or death. Christ, the Lamb, will be the center of worship—the light and glory of the eternal city. (See the article titled "Eternal Life.")

—ED HINDSON

BIBLIOGRAPHY

Habermas, Gary. *The Historical Jesus.* Joplin, MO: College Press, 1996.

Hindson, Ed, and Ed Dobson. *Knowing Jesus Study Bible.* Grand Rapids: Zondervan, 1999.

LaHaye, Tim. *Why Believe in Jesus?* Eugene, OR: Harvest House Publishers, 2004.

Lee, Richard, and Ed Hindson. *No Greater Savior.* Eugene, OR: Harvest House Publishers, 1995.

Stott, John. *The Incomparable Christ.* Downers Grove, IL: InterVarsity Press, 2001.

JEWS IN PROPHECY, THE

DEUTERONOMY 32:8-9 (NASB) STATES, "When the Most High gave the nations their inheritance, when He separated the sons of man, He set the boundaries of the peoples according to the number of the sons of Israel. For the Lord's portion is His people; Jacob is the allotment of His inheritance."

God's prophetic program includes His plan for the church, His plan for the Gentile nations, and His plan for the nation of Israel. All three center on the Jewish people. Moses wrote that when God laid out what would become the boundaries of various nations, He took into account the number of Jews who would play a role in that nation's history, including those who would be alive during the Tribulation.

THE JEWS AND THE PURPOSE OF THE TRIBULATION

God has three purposes for the Tribulation. The first purpose applies equally to both the Jews and Gentiles. The second and third purposes of the Tribulation have a direct bearing on God's program for the Jewish people.

A Worldwide Revival

The first purpose of the Tribulation is found in Isaiah 13:9 and 24:19-20. It is to make an end of wickedness and wicked ones, both Jews and Gentiles. The second purpose of the Tribulation is to bring about a worldwide preaching of the gospel of Jesus the Messiah. In Matthew 24:14, Jesus said that the "gospel of the kingdom" will be proclaimed "to all the nations" before the end comes. Before the Tribulation can end, before the second coming can occur, the gospel must go out to all nations of that generation.

Revelation 7 is an exposition of Matthew 24:14. Revelation 7:1-8 tells us the means of this revival: Sometime after God raptures the church, He will save 144,000 Jews. They will proclaim the gospel to all the nations around the world. In Revelation 7:9-17 John describes the results of the preaching of the gospel by the 144,000 Jews—myriads and myriads of Gentiles standing before the throne of God. Verses 13 and 14 explain that these Gentiles responded to the gospel during the Tribulation.

Breaking the Will of the Holy People

Daniel 12:5-7 explains the third purpose for the Tribulation. In 11:1–12:4, Daniel sees a vision of what the Tribulation will be like for his people, the Jews. In 12:5-7, Daniel hears a question: "How long will it be until the end of these wonders?" The answer contains the third purpose of the Tribulation: The power of the holy people must be shattered. They must turn away from trying to establish their own righteousness and begin to seek the righteousness of God through Jesus the Messiah. This will lead to Israel's national regeneration.

Ezekiel 20:34-38 states exactly how God will accomplish this third purpose. At the

Exodus, God brought the entire nation of Israel out of the land of Egypt and into the wilderness of the Sinai Peninsula. However, the people repeatedly murmured against God's revealed will, and at Kadesh Barnea—right at the border of the Promised Land itself—the people refused to take possession of the Land, and God judged them. He sentenced the entire nation to continue wandering in the wilderness for 40 years. Everyone who came out of Egypt except for two men, Joshua and Caleb, and those under the age of 20, would die in the wilderness. Forty years later, Israel would be a new nation, born as free men in the wilderness and not as slaves in Egypt.

Ezekiel says that a similar event will occur in the future. God will regather His people from all parts of the world—a regathering which we have been observing with the present-day Jewish state of Israel. However, at some point God will enter into judgment with His people. By means of the Tribulation judgments, the rebels will be purged out and the unbelievers will be cleansed and regenerated. They will stop trying to establish their own righteousness and will seek the righteousness of God through Jesus the Messiah, and that will bring about their national regeneration. A new nation, a regenerate nation, will enter the millennial kingdom under Christ.

THE JEWS AND THE BEGINNING OF THE TRIBULATION

The second part of this study concerns the role of the Jews at the beginning of the Tribulation. Two passages of Scripture are particularly relevant here: Daniel 9:24-27 and Isaiah 28:14-22.

Daniel 9:24-27

In this passage, the prophet Daniel receives his famous vision of the 70 weeks, or better, the 70 sevens, the 490 years that God has decreed upon the Jewish people. By the end of verse 26, the first 483 years of this 490-year period has been fulfilled in history, ending with the first coming of Jesus the Messiah. However, seven years of this prophetic clock have yet to be fulfilled for Israel. These last

seven years, the seventieth week of Daniel, are the seven years of the Tribulation. What event will start the clock once again?

The last seven years, or the Tribulation, will begin when Israel and "the prince who is to come," the Antichrist, sign a seven-year covenant. Although the agreement is for the covenant to last for seven years, it will be broken at the halfway point: "In the middle of the week he will put a stop to sacrifice and grain offering." When this happens, desolations and abominations will fall upon the Jewish people.

Isaiah 28:14-22

The second passage gives God's view of those who make the covenant: "Therefore, hear the word of the LORD, O scoffers, who rule this people who are in Jerusalem..." (verse 14).

God's view of the Israelite leaders who enter the covenant is that they are scoffers, or fools. Why? Because of God's view of the covenant itself: "Because you have said, 'We have made a covenant with death, and with Sheol we have made a pact. The overwhelming scourge will not reach us when it passes by, for we have made falsehood our refuge and we have concealed ourselves with deception'" (verse 15).

The Jewish people will enter the covenant with Antichrist for security from further military invasions. God says they are fools for doing so, for this is not a covenant of life but "a covenant with death." In verses 17-18, we read that the covenant will be broken, and verses 19-22 go on to describe the desolations that will fall upon the Jewish people when the covenant is broken.

The Bible gives many names for the Tribulation, and verse 21 provides two: Jehovah's "unusual task," and His "extraordinary work." Why is it unusual and extraordinary? Verse 22 says, "For I have heard from the Lord GOD of hosts of decisive destruction on all the earth." When this covenant is signed, God will issue a decree of destruction upon all the earth.

So once again, the event that starts the Tribulation is the signing of the covenant. The Tribulation cannot begin until there is a seven-year covenant between Israel and the Antichrist.

WHAT HAPPENS TO THE JEWS DURING THE TRIBULATION?

The Bible has a great deal to say on this. However, for the sake of space, we will cover only four key passages.

Jeremiah 30:4-7

Jeremiah 30:7 calls the Tribulation "the time of Jacob's distress." Everyone will suffer during the Tribulation, but the Jewish people will suffer the most. This is because of the principle mentioned in Isaiah 40:1-2 that Israel receives "double for all her sins."

Matthew 24:15-22

Jesus gives a warning sign to those Jews alive at the middle of the Tribulation. When they see the abomination of desolation—when the Antichrist breaks the seven-year treaty with Israel, takes over the Temple, seats himself in it, and declares himself to be the one true god—they must get out of Israel fast!

Revelation 12:1-17

Revelation 12:6 speaks of the very same event as Matthew 24:15-22: "Then the woman fled into the wilderness where she had a place prepared by God, so that there she would be nourished for one thousand two hundred and sixty days." As in Matthew 24, so it is in Revelation 12: Suddenly the woman (Israel) is on the run, fleeing to a place the Bible simply calls the "wilderness." We know from passages such as Micah 2:12 that this wilderness is the land of Edom and the city of Petra.

Verses 7-12 explain why the woman is on the run. Satan is cast out of his present abode, the atmospheric heavens, and confined to the earth for the second half of the Tribulation. Once Satan is confined to the earth, he knows his time is short—3 ½ years. He is very angry and persecutes the Jews. He is the one who moves the Antichrist to break the treaty with Israel and begin his persecution of the Jews. This brings about the flight of Israel mentioned in Matthew 24 and Revelation 12.

During the second half of the Tribulation, Satan will fight an all-out war against the Jews, trying to destroy them once and for all.

Zechariah 13:8-9

To what extent will Satan and the Antichrist succeed in their program of Jewish annihilation? According to Zechariah, two-thirds of the Jewish population living at the beginning of the Tribulation will not survive it. At the second coming of the Messiah in the final days of the Tribulation, God will receive the remnant of Israel.

—ARNOLD FRUCHTENBAUM

BIBLIOGRAPHY

Fruchtenbaum, Arnold. *Footsteps of the Messiah.* Tustin, CA: Ariel Ministries, 1983.

———. *Israelology: The Missing Link in Systematic Theology.* Tustin, CA: Ariel Ministries, 1992.

Larsen, David. *Jews, Gentiles and the Church.* Grand Rapids: Discovery House, 1995.

Walvoord, John F. *Israel in Prophecy.* Grand Rapids: Zondervan, 1962.

JOHN, ESCHATOLOGY OF

RECENT CRITICAL STUDIES have raised serious questions regarding the relationship of John's teachings to the other writings of the New Testament. Theories have run the gamut from those of older scholars who saw John's teachings as the last word, changing the tradition, to those of younger scholars who understand it to be more likely the first word, changed by later tradition. Often when John's writings failed to fit such critical theories, scholars conveniently ignored the conflicting data as the work of a redactor or worse—the mistaken notions of the original authors.

Those committed to an inerrant text dismiss such conclusions as incompatible with the nature of Scripture. Nonetheless, even a strict inerrantist must acknowledge the uniqueness of John's content, style, and purpose when comparing his Gospel, his three epistles, and the Apocalypse to other New Testament writings.

A VERTICAL PERSPECTIVE

Following the insights of some critical scholars, but from an evangelical perspective, G.E. Ladd speaks of a twofold theological perspective in the New Testament writers. This he describes as a "two-fold dualism" (Ladd, p. 338 and following). John rather graphically illustrates a vertical (cosmic) perspective in John 1:51, and we see a horizontal (eschatological) perspective in 12:25. John emphasizes the vertical but does not ignore the horizontal. The contrast is rather striking when one compares, for example, the Olivet Discourse (Matthew 24–25) with the Upper Room Discourse (John 13–16). Whereas the other three Gospel writers are concerned with the horizontal sequence of eschatological events, John focuses on the sending of the Holy Spirit. Rather than talking about Christ's coming on clouds of glory in some future time, John wants the reader to understand that throughout the present age, Christ will be ever present in intimate fellowship through the indwelling of the Holy Spirit. John does not reject the truth of His future glorious appearance any more than the other writers reject the present ministry of Christ through the Holy Spirit. Rather, he writes to encourage his readers with this latter, more immediate truth (for example, see 1 John 2).

ETERNAL LIFE

Another way one may observe this duality in the New Testament writers is in the "already" and the "not yet" of the kingdom promises. This is seen especially in John's discussion of eternal life. Eternal life bespeaks a present reality as much as it does a future state of enduring life in the presence of God (John 3:16; 4:36; 12:25; 14:1-3; 1 John 1:2; 2:17; 3:1-3; 5:13). As does Paul, John gives a clear promise of a home in heaven (John 14:1-3; 2 Corinthians 5:1-8), but for both writers, the future (the "not yet") extends back into the present (the "already"). In the upper room, John records Jesus' statement to the disciples that while He is going away to "prepare a place" for them, they are to remain to receive the promise of the Paraclete and to do the "greater works" (14:7-17).

Paul exhorts his readers in much the same way as he links the promise of an "earthly tent...eternal in the heavens" with the coming of the Spirit, judgment, the new creation, and the ministry of reconciliation (2 Corinthians 5:1-21 NASB). This is seen again in John's first letter as he exhorts his readers to "abide in Him, so that when He appears, we may have confidence and not shrink away from Him in shame at His coming" (1 John 2:28). Again, "Beloved, now we are children of God, and it has not appeared as yet what we will be. We know that when He appears, we will be like Him, because we will see Him just as He is" (1 John 3:2). What we "will be" is what we already are—the children of God. And yet there is more. While John does not record the event of Christ's transfiguration (Matthew 17:2; Mark 9:2), one cannot help but consider that it was this manifestation of His glory, which he witnessed along with Peter and James, that John has in mind in this text. When He appears, the children of God will become "like Him"—gloriously transfigured. Eternal life is manifested in His first coming (1 John 1:2), but its fullness is not manifested until His second coming (1 John 3:1-3). In Philippians 3:20-21, Paul articulates much the same eschatological hope.

ANTICHRIST

This duality of future eschatological reality breaking into the present is also seen in John's teaching regarding the Antichrist. This duality is succinctly stated in 1 John 2:18: "Children, it is the last hour, and just as you heard that antichrist is coming, even now many antichrists have appeared; from this we know that it is the last hour." The mention of the Antichrist recalls the opposition of God's rule and God's people personified in Antiochus Epiphanes in Daniel 8 and 11. This opposition will reach its apex in the emergence of a demonically inspired personage, like Antiochus, who will come upon the scene in the end times—*the* Antichrist. From the perspective of John as well as other New Testament writers (2 Thessalonians 2:3-11), this one has not yet come.

Nevertheless, some people already pretend to be followers of Christ but are "not of us," as evidenced by the fact that they have "gone out from us" and are not in possession of the truth (1 John 2:19-22). These anticipate the work and wickedness of the Antichrist (1 John 2:18; 2 John 7). In the spirit of the Antichrist, they speak lies, do not acknowledge that Jesus is the Christ, and deny the Father and the Son (1 John 2:22-23).

DEATH, RESURRECTION, AND JUDGMENT

Since it is already true that the one "who believes in the Son has eternal life" (John 3:36), it is also true, as Jesus instructed Martha and Mary at the grave of Lazarus, that "he who believes in Me will live even if he dies, and everyone who lives and believes in Me will never die" (John 11:25-26). Martha was looking ahead to the future resurrection, but Jesus makes it clear that what will be the portion for those who are His is already true. For the believers, physical death—the separation of the spirit from the body—is a mere episode on the way to glory. But the dreadful reality for those who are not His is equally true—both now and in the future. The one who does not "obey the Son will not see life, but the wrath of God abides on him" (John 3:36).

Judgment, often thought of as exclusively eschatological, is already pronounced upon those who reject the only source of life. "He who believes in Him is not judged; he who does not believe has been judged already....This is the judgment, that the Light has come into the world, and men loved the darkness rather than the Light, for their deeds were evil" (John 3:18-19). And so judgment, like resurrection and glory, is pressed back into the present. Yet the apostle does not neglect to remind his reader that this is not yet the end (see John 5:24-29).

The final judgment will ultimately reveal the present judgment, and in doing so it will confirm it for all of its fiercesome reality. The lost live today in a fool's paradise of denial, but those who are Christ's abide, even now, in His love (see 1 John 4:17-19). The believer's destiny is to be loved by Him, to be like Him (John 17:22-26; 1 John 3:1-3), to be with Him (John 14:3; 1 John 1:2-3; Revelation 21:1-7), to be protected by Him (John 17:11-12; 1 John 5:18), and to worship Him forever (John 17:3; Revelation 7:15; 22:3).

—DANIEL R. MITCHELL

BIBLIOGRAPHY

Barrett, C.K. *The Gospel According to St. John*. London: SPCK, 1978.

Beasley-Murray, George R. *Gospel of Life: The Theology in the Fourth Gospel*. Peabody, MA: Hendrickson, 1991.

Ladd, George E. *A Theology of the New Testament*. 2d ed. Grand Rapids: Eerdmans Publishing Company, 1993.

Marshall, I. Howard. *The Epistles of John*. NICNT. Grand Rapids: Eerdmans Publishing Company, 1978.

Ryrie, Charles C. *Biblical Theology of the New Testament*. Chicago: Moody Press, 1959.

Stott, John R.W. *The Epistles of John*. TNTC. Rev. ed. Grand Rapids: Eerdmans Publishing Company, 1988.

JUDGMENT OF THE NATIONS

THE SCRIPTURES DESCRIBE several distinct eschatological judgments, including the "sheep and the goats" judgment, the judgment seat of Christ, and the Great White Throne judgment. These judgments occur at different times and apply to different groups. The psalmist referred to one such event when he declared, "Arise, O LORD, do not let man prevail; let the nations be judged before You" (Psalm 9:19 NASB). The Bible explains the time and place of this judgment of the nations. It also describes the participants, the basis of the judgment, and God's purposes in it.

THE TIME OF THE JUDGMENT

In Relationship to the Second Coming

According to the prophet Joel, this judgment of the nations takes place in connection with the "great and awesome day of the LORD," which makes it clear that Joel places this judgment near the end of the Tribulation and the beginning of the messianic kingdom (Joel 2:31). More specifically, Joel says that this judgment will take place when Judah and Jerusalem have their "fortunes restored" (Joel 3:1-2). Statements about the restoring of the fortunes of Israel are often used in reference to the millennial kingdom, which is established after the Lord Jesus Christ returns to this present earth in power and great glory (see Ezekiel 39:25; Amos 9:14-15). This places the judgment as occurring after the second coming because it is only after that event that Israel will receive the blessings spoken of here.

In His prophetic Olivet Discourse, the Lord Jesus also tied this event to His second coming. He said that the gathering of the nations for judgment would take place after He comes in His glory with the holy angels and is seated on His throne (Matthew 25:31-32).

In Relationship to the Millennial Kingdom

The judgment of the nations takes place prior to the start of the millennial kingdom. The results of the judgment of the nations determine participation in the millennial kingdom. Daniel 12:11-12 refers to a period of up to 75 days between the second coming and the actual start of the millennial kingdom. In these verses, Daniel declared that the one who perseveres to day 1335 would be wonderfully blessed. This blessing, we understand, is a reference to the privilege of entrance into Messiah's kingdom, which begins at that point. Because the judgment of the nations occurs before the millennial reign, it is not to be confused with the Great White Throne judgment, which takes place after the 1000-year reign of Christ is completed (Revelation 20:11-15).

THE PLACE OF THE JUDGMENT

The judgment of the nations takes place after the second coming, so it will evidently occur on the earth because that is where Christ will have come. The Lord Jesus placed the judgment after His return to the earth (Matthew 24:27-31; 25:31-32). The prophet Joel specifically stated that the nations would be gathered for judgment into the "valley of Jehoshaphat" (Joel 3:2,12). Some have identified this with the Kidron Valley, next to Jerusalem. Others see it as the location where God brought deliverance to King Jehoshaphat by defeating a coalition of enemies (see 2 Chronicles 20).

Most likely the name (which means "Jehovah judges") is intended to be symbolic. This will be the place in Israel where the recently returned Lord Jesus will gather the nations in order to judge them. It probably refers to a future site that will come into existence in connection with the topographical changes that will take place in Israel at the second coming (Zechariah 14:4). It will probably be near the city of Jerusalem.

THE PARTICIPANTS IN THE JUDGMENT

The One Who Judges

The Judge who carries out all judgments in the end times is the Lord Jesus Christ. According to the Lord Jesus Himself, the Father has committed all judgment to the Son. He will judge fairly and according to the will of the Father (see John 5:21-23,27).

The Ones Being Judged

Both Joel 3 and Matthew 25 state that the "nations" are gathered before the Lord. The word translated "nations" also means "Gentiles" and is translated that way the majority of times in the New Testament. It usually refers to people who do not belong to the chosen nation of Israel. So it would probably be clearer to speak of this as the "judgment of Gentiles" because these are set in contrast to the covenant people of Israel in both of the primary texts.

This judgment does not, however, include all Gentiles who have ever lived, but rather, only those who are living when Christ returns at the second coming. The word *Gentile* is not used of the dead but of living people. The passages that discuss this judgment do not mention the dead or a resurrection. The Gentiles who are alive at the second coming will be judged for the deeds they perform immediately before Christ's return (see Joel 3:2-3; Matthew 25:35-40).

THE BASIS OF THE JUDGMENT

When people stand before the Lord Jesus, their eternal destiny is not being determined. Their presence in or absence from the kingdom of God is settled during their earthly life and not at the time of judgment before the Lord Jesus Christ. Jesus clearly communicated to Nicodemus that entrance into the kingdom comes by the new birth (John 3:5). Entering the kingdom (salvation) is never by means of good works (Titus 3:5; Ephesians 2:8-9) but is always by faith alone in Christ (John 3:16; Romans 3:20-30; Galatians 2:16). Salvation is always as a gift from God, received by trusting in Christ.

During the seven years of the Tribulation, everyone on this earth will hear the truth of the gospel of Christ (Matthew 24:14). Although the 144,000 will probably take the lead in proclaiming the gospel message, millions of believers will give testimony of their faith in Jesus Christ (Revelation 7:4-17). So when the living Gentiles appear before the Lord Jesus at the time of this judgment, we can confidently conclude that they have already heard and have either received or rejected the offer of salvation.

The internal, spiritual condition of the Gentiles is revealed externally by the way they treat Israel during the Great Tribulation. This is valid proof of true righteousness because of the intense persecution that Israel will endure during the second half of the Tribulation period. Jews forced to flee death and destruction will have no means of caring for themselves. The righteous Gentiles, at great risk to themselves, will provide food and shelter for the covenant people and will show many other acts of kindness.

Jesus refers to these Gentiles as righteous (Matthew 25:37). The good deeds they do to Jesus validate that designation. However, these righteous Gentiles (the "sheep") were confused because they did not recall doing any good deeds to Jesus. But the Lord instructs them that when they did good deeds to "these my brethren," they did them to Jesus Himself (Matthew 25:40). Jesus' "brothers" is not a reference to mankind in general but rather to the Jews who are true believers and the objects of the satanically inspired persecution.

The righteous Gentiles will be welcomed into the millennial kingdom by the King. They are righteous because they were saved by grace, but they expressed their righteousness through their care for Jesus' "brothers" during those terrible days.

In like manner, the deeds of the unrighteous ("goats") reveal their true spiritual condition. Their unbelief of the gospel message is seen by their anti-Semitism. Jesus also will indict them on their refusal to give aid and assistance to His "brothers" during the Great Tribulation (Matthew 25:45). Their negative treatment of Jesus' "brothers" is proof that they are not righteous and, therefore, are to be excluded from entrance into the millennial kingdom.

THE PURPOSES FOR THE JUDGMENT

To Demonstrate the Character of God

Man must finally see and acknowledge that God is God. The judgments recorded in Scripture reveal that all creatures eventually will bow the knee and accept their rightful place of submission to their Creator God (Philippians 2:9-11; see also John 5:22-23). When the judgments are completed, no creature will challenge or speak against the character of the one and only God. The judgment of the Gentiles will contribute to that significant end.

To Grant Entrance to the Righteous

The righteous Gentiles will be welcomed into the kingdom of Jesus the Messiah when He tells them to "inherit the kingdom" (Matthew 25:34). These saved Gentiles are received with joy into Messiah's kingdom. In the Scriptures, "inheriting the kingdom" is conditioned upon an individual's good works after salvation and includes not only entrance into the millennial kingdom but also rewards.

The Judging of the Unrighteous

As with the righteous "sheep," the deeds of the unrighteous "goats" reveal their true spiritual condition (Matthew 25:41-46; Joel 3:2-3). They are refused entrance into the Messiah's glorious kingdom and sent away to eternal punishment. These will enter into a punishment of unending duration—the eternal fire that has been made for Satan and his angels (Matthew 25:41).

The "goats" reveal their rejection of the gospel message by their refusal to give aid and comfort to Jesus' "brothers" during the Great Tribulation. They are responsible for bringing great distress to the Jews as they drive them out of their Land, divide up the Land, and enslave the people. At judgment, these unrighteous Gentiles will have to bow the knee to the One they have rejected and treated with contempt.

GOD SEES AND KNOWS

Men are accountable to the Lord God for what they do with His truth and His people. Some people might think that God is not watching, but the Scriptures reveal that God knows everything man does and says. Man will be rewarded or punished in accordance with the standard of God's truth. This holds true for the Gentiles who are alive during the Great Tribulation. They will stand before the King at His second coming, and they will either be welcomed into or excluded from the messianic kingdom.

—PAUL BENWARE

BIBLIOGRAPHY

Benware, Paul. *The Believer's Payday.* Chattanooga: AMG Publications, 2002.

Dillow, Joseph. *Reign of the Servant Kings.* Hayesville, NC: Schoettle Publishing Company, 1993.

Fruchtenbaum, Arnold. *The Footsteps of the Messiah.* Tustin, CA: Ariel Ministries, 1993.

MacArthur, John F. *The Second Coming.* Wheaton, IL: Crossway Books, 1999.

Pentecost, J. Dwight. *Things to Come.* Grand Rapids: Zondervan, 1975.

Walvoord, John F. *Major Bible Prophecies.* Grand Rapids: Zondervan, 1991.

JUDGMENT SEAT OF CHRIST

SCRIPTURE TEACHES that every member of the human race is accountable to God (Jeremiah 17:10; 32:19). God will judge both the unbeliever and the believer. The judgment of unbelievers will take place at the Great White Throne judgment, described in Revelation 20:15. This judgment takes place after the millennial reign of Christ and is the final judgment prior to eternity future. Paul affirms the judgment of every believer in 2 Corinthians 5:10 (NASB): "For we must all appear before the judgment seat of Christ, so that each one may be recompensed for his deeds in the body, according to what he has done, whether good or bad."

That all are judged will justify the justice of God before all creatures. That any will be saved will be the greatest demonstration of God's grace the world could ever know. The judgment of the wicked will confirm their rejection of God's provision of salvation in His Son and will result in eternal condemnation. The judgment of the righteous will confirm their security in Christ and will determine their eternal rewards. The judgment of the wicked will result in suffering that is proportional to their wickedness (Matthew 10:15; 11:23-24; Luke 19:27). The judgment of the righteous will result in more or less rewards in proportion to their faithfulness (Luke 19:11-27). Unbelievers will stand before the Great White Throne, and believers will stand before the judgment seat of Christ.

THE BACKGROUND OF THE WORD *BEMA*

Paul refers to the seat of judgment as the *bema* (2 Corinthians 5:10). The *bema* was a step or a platform used in political and athletic arenas. Earthly *bemas* were raised platforms on which rulers or judges sat when making speeches (Acts 12:21) or adjudicating cases (Acts 18:12-17). In the Isthmian games (the forerunner to the Olympic games), the umpire presided from a raised platform called the *bema* (judgment seat). From there he watched the games and awarded the winners. The New Testament uses a variety of judicial and athletic metaphors for the judgment seat.

A WORD ABOUT THE JUDGE

God has committed all judgment to the Son (John 5:27). This is what makes all of His judgments just. Revelation 4–5 demonstrates Jesus' authority to judge. He is both the Lion from the tribe of Judah and the Lamb of God who died and rose again. He who was judged has the right to judge all humanity because He is both the Sovereign and the Savior. The Bible says that Jesus is the "righteous Judge," and therefore all judgments will be fair and final (2 Timothy 4:8). Like the Father, Jesus will also judge "without respect of persons" (1 Peter 1:17 KJV). The attributes of Jesus Christ as the Son of God guarantee that all the evidence will be gathered and carefully evaluated.

WHO WILL BE JUDGED AT THE *BEMA*?

The judgment seat of Christ will not determine whether we are believers—that is, whether we will enter heaven. Whoever appears before the judgment seat of Christ is already in heaven. Any person who has trusted in Jesus Christ for his salvation will never be condemned for his sins (Romans 8:1). Justification by faith results in peace with God through Jesus Christ (Romans 5:1). Redemption forever accomplishes forgiveness and assures reconciliation with a holy God. The punishment that everyone deserves was already borne by Jesus when He shed His blood and died on the cross. He was made to be sin with our sin so we could be made righteous with His righteousness (2 Corinthians 5:21). Therefore, sin and its relationship to eternal punishment will not be evaluated at the judgment seat of Christ.

The New Testament reveals who will be judged at the judgment seat of Christ. First,

only believers will be judged. Every passage that directly mentions or indirectly alludes to the *bema* assumes that those who will be judged will be believers. Second, *every* believer will stand before the judgment seat of Christ. The Bible says, "We must all appear..." (2 Corinthians 5:10). Finally, this judgment is not optional—every believer *must* appear for judgment. The judgment is obligatory and unavoidable, so believers are wise to be ready for such an evaluation.

WHEN AND WHERE WILL THE JUDGMENT TAKE PLACE?

Scripture seems to indicate that the judgment of believers will take place in heaven between the resurrection and rapture of the church and the personal return of Christ from heaven at the second advent. The elders in heaven, who may be representatives of the church age (see Revelation 4:4-10), already have their crowns in place.

In addition, the church as the bride of Christ is already clothed when she accompanies the Lord at His second coming to the earth (Revelation 19:7-9). The return to the earth is for the wedding banquet. Evidently, when Christ returns in judgment, the marriage and rewarding of the church will have already taken place. The rewarding of believers and the wedding between Christ and His bride are heavenly events before the throne. Jesus describes the marriage feast with all the invited guests as taking place on earth (Matthew 25:1-13).

Believers are not judged immediately at the time of their death. First Corinthians 4:5 seems to teach that before believers can be judged, Jesus must come back for His church. Therefore, after the Lord returns for the church and before He comes back to the earth to rule and reign, every saint of the church will stand before the *bema* of Christ for their judgment and rewards.

WHAT WILL BE JUDGED?

The purpose of the judgment of believers at the judgment seat of Christ is to determine the worthiness or worthlessness of their works. The judgment applies only to believers, for even if they suffer loss, they will be saved. Also, all who are judged have built their lives on the true foundation, Jesus Christ Himself (1 Corinthians 3:11-12). Christ will evaluate the works Christians do in their lifetime. Because we have been saved unto good works that God has prepared for the believer (Ephesians 2:10), we should expect Him to examine our faithfulness in service.

The New Testament affirms that the judgment seat of Christ will evaluate various elements of the believer's life and work. All of our sin was judged at the cross. Those sins God "will remember no more" (Hebrews 10:17). The second coming will not be in reference to the believer's sin (Hebrews 9:28). Therefore the judgment seat of Christ is not a judgment to determine salvation; it is a judgment of the saved with reference to their works. The evaluation of the believer's works will include the works themselves, the quality with which they have been done, and the motivation of the heart.

The Works

What one does for God really does count. Malachi 3:16 speaks of a "book of remembrance" in which God keeps track of all that has been done for Him. Scripture promises specific rewards for differing works. Suffering insults, persecution, and false testimony for the sake of Christ and the cause of righteousness will bring great rewards in heaven (Matthew 5:11-12; see Luke 6:21-22).

Luke 14:12-14 records Jesus' instruction to reach out to the underprivileged. He includes this promise: "You will be repaid at the resurrection of the righteous." Although certain works are singled out in various passages, the implication is that God will reward believers for all their works that have eternal value or merit.

The Quality

Christ will test the genuineness or character of believers' works. Paul wrote that the fire of God's judgment "will test the quality of each man's work" (1 Corinthians 3:13). The imagery of gold, silver, and precious stones as opposed

to wood, hay, and stubble reveals that the quality of the works themselves will be tested. What distinguishes one from the other is its eternal value. Works that have no eternal significance do not merit eternal recognition. In Paul's illustration, an adequate foundation, the quality of the materials, and the proper methods of building are the symbolic components for quality work for God. Works will be judged to be either good or bad (Greek, *agathos* or *phaulos*) at the judgment seat.

Good Works. Good works *(agathos)* may be defined as those that have been "manifested as having been wrought in God" (John 3:21). These may also be categorized as "work of faith" (1 Thessalonians 1:3). As defined by God, good works are designated by gold, silver, and precious stones. They are produced by a believer who is walking in fellowship with God and who is controlled by the Holy Spirit. Good works are also called "the fruit of righteousness which comes through Jesus Christ, to the glory and praise of God" (Philippians 1:11). The power to produce good works comes directly from God, not from within man (see Philippians 2:13).

Bad Works. Bad deeds *(phaulos)* are worthless in the sight of God. These could be called dead works or works of the flesh. The danger of producing works of the flesh is that the believer's labor is in vain (1 Corinthians 15:58), empty (1 Timothy 6:20; 2 Timothy 2:16), and worthless (Galatians 4:9; Titus 3:9; James 1:26). Bad works do not measure up to the standard and therefore are characterized as wood, hay, and stubble—commodities of little worth or durability. These are deeds produced in the energy of the flesh, apart from the power of the Spirit. Bad works also spring from wrong motives.

The Motivation

The motivation for our works will also be revealed at the judgment seat of Christ. Jesus said, "There is nothing covered up that will not be revealed, and hidden that will not be known. Accordingly, whatever you have said in the dark shall be heard in the light, and what you have whispered in the inner rooms shall be proclaimed upon the housetops" (Luke 12:2-3). Purposes give birth to behavior. The purpose or motivation of the heart validates or invalidates the actions of one's life.

An example from the Sermon on the Mount will illustrate the principle of motivation. Jesus said what appear to be two contradictory statements. On the one hand, He exhorted believers to let their lives shine as lights in order to be seen by others who, in turn, will glorify the Father in heaven (Matthew 5:16). On the other hand, Jesus taught that activities such as prayer, offerings for the poor, and fasting should be done in secret to be seen by God alone and not before others lest one lose his reward in heaven (Matthew 6:1-21). Believers do not lose eternal rewards when other people see their good deeds, but they lose rewards when they do their works so that others might see them. First Corinthians 4:5 says that the hidden counsels of the heart will be exposed. What Jesus thinks about our works is more important than what anyone else thinks. Revelation 2:23 reminds us that God searches both minds and hearts in order to determine our reward.

WHAT WILL BE THE RESULTS OF THE JUDGMENT?

Believers will gain or lose rewards at the judgment seat of Christ. Works enduring through the fire of God's judgment will be rewarded (1 Corinthians 3:14). Works that do not survive the fire of judgment will lose their value.

Losing Rewards

Several scriptures indicate that rewards can be lost. John wrote about the possibility of being ashamed at the coming of Christ (1 John 2:28). The grammar of this passage suggests the self-realizing embarrassment of shame at the appearing of the Lord rather than any punitive shaming from the Lord. Believers will not be condemned (Romans 8:1). John also taught that one could lose rewards for unfaithful living (2 John 8). He wanted his readers to get the "full reward" that was available to them for their faithful service. Paul also spoke of being "disqualified" by failing to live a faithful life (1 Corinthians 9:24-27). In Paul's analogy of the house that is burnt, the works are consumed, but the builder escapes with his life. Rewards are lost but the person is not. Believers can lose the recognition and reward that they could have received had they done their works according to God's standards.

Even though ministry done for the wrong motives may result in the forfeiture of rewards, it may still have eternal effects (Philippians 1:14-19). God's Word does not return void and may have an effect in spite of the person who may have been doing their duty in the power of the flesh.

Gaining Rewards

The distribution of rewards will take place at the judgment. The rewards are never given to satisfy the believer's ego but to bring praise and glory to Christ, who empowered the believer to serve (see Philippians 1:11). Rewards are promised for faithful service. Good works, the fruits of righteousness, glorify the One who graciously imputed His righteousness to believers (see John 3:21).

The New Testament mentions a series of crowns as motivations for godly behavior. The Bible speaks of two kinds of crowns in general: One is the diadem that rulers wear. The other is the victory crown (Greek, *stephanos*) awarded to those who achieve great accomplishments. The latter term is used to speak of the crowns of reward that are promised to the believer for successful service for the Lord. With the imagery of the winners' crowns handed out in the sporting events and military ceremonies of the first century, the New Testament writers use the crowns to picture the commendations to come to the Christian at the judgment of their works. Athletes' crowns were woven vines or wreaths made of withered, wild celery. As Paul says in 1 Corinthians 9:25 (KJV), "They do it to obtain a corruptible crown; but we an incorruptible." Scripture mentions four such crowns.

The Crown of Life. This is the crown awarded to those who remain faithful through trials (James 1:2-3,12; see Revelation 2:10; 3:11). Believers are to joyfully receive trials as opportunities from the Lord for growth and stability. They are also to be motivated by their love for the Lord. Israel was guilty of wrongly responding to their wilderness trials and forgetting God's powerful deliverance throughout their history (Psalm 78:11,42). Their unfaithful response to trials caused them to doubt God's redeeming care. Spiritual forgetfulness robs believers of their joy and calls the sincerity of their love into question.

The Crown of Righteousness. This crown is reserved for all who anxiously await the Lord's return. In his later years, Paul was more concerned about standing before the court of heaven than the court of Rome.

> I am already being poured out as a drink offering, and the time of my departure has come. I have fought the good fight, I have finished the course, I have kept the faith; in the future there is laid up for me the crown of righteousness, which the Lord, the righteous Judge, will award to me on that day; and not only to me, but also to all who have loved His appearing (2 Timothy 4:6-8).

Loving the appearing of the Lord assumes a lifestyle of obedience. Such faithfulness provides a platform of confidence as one awaits the soon return of the Lord.

The Crown of Glory. This crown is promised to those who shepherd the flock of God with right motives (1 Peter 5:2-4). Godly shepherds worthy of reward are those who serve willingly rather than under compulsion. They model godly living and don't simply mandate it to their sheep. They recognize theirs is an entrusted stewardship for which they will give an account to the Chief Shepherd. Jesus, of course, is the ultimate model— the Good Shepherd who laid down His life for the sheep (John 10:11) and has become "the Shepherd and Guardian" of the souls of all

believers (1 Peter 2:25). By the negative example of Israel's failure, Ezekiel taught that the real work of the shepherd toward the sheep was to feed them, care for them, restore them, and search out the lost (Ezekiel 34:2-4). Such is the nature of the pastoral ministry (see Acts 20:27-30).

The Crown of Rejoicing. This crown is the soul winner's crown. Paul wrote to the Thessalonians, "Who is our hope or joy or crown of exultation? Is it not even you, in the presence of our Lord Jesus at His coming? For you are our glory and joy" (1 Thessalonians 2:19-20). To the Philippians he said, "Therefore, my beloved brethren whom I long to see, my joy and crown, in this way stand firm in the Lord, my beloved" (Philippians 4:1). Evangelism of the lost is a deep desire of God, and He has promised to reward those who will seek the lost on His behalf. In John 4, Jesus taught that those believers engaged in active evangelism are gathering fruit for eternal life. The effort is a team ministry: "One sows, and another reaps" (John 4:37). The teamwork in evangelism among believers is designed by Christ so that "he who sows and he who reaps may rejoice together" (John 4:36).

THE GLORY OF THE CROWNS

Believers will one day use their crowns to praise and worship the Lord as they lay them before the throne of heaven (Revelation 4:10). Rewards also imply future responsibilities and privileges. Though believers will cast their crowns at Christ's feet, He might give them back as He assigns faithful believers with privileged positions of responsibility and rulership.

TWO PRINCIPLES TO REMEMBER

The parable of the talents (Matthew 25:14-30) and the parable of the pounds (Luke 19:13-27) illustrate an important and balancing set of principles in God's reward program. The talents illustrate that in some ways, believers receive unequal stewardship responsibilities in proportion to their ability. Not all believers enjoy the same natural talents, spiritual giftedness, intellect, educational opportunities, or sovereignly designed opportunities. They may, however, receive equal commendations and rewards from the Lord for their faithfulness. On the other hand, the parable of the pounds illustrates that in some ways all believers share an equal entrustment before the Lord. Each one has one life to live and give to God, the Scriptures, a common faith, and the gospel message. Differing assignments in God's kingdom are awarded according to proportionate faithfulness. Therefore both God's grace and human faithfulness play a part when Christ rewards believers.

THE METAPHORS OF JUDGMENT

The Bible uses several metaphors to describe the judgment seat of Christ. These word pictures are designed for both meditation and application. Biblical illustrations allow one to keep the truths in mind and to probe deeper into their implications. In addition, each image illustrates what one needs to do to successfully prepare for the coming judgment.

—MARK BAILEY

BIBLIOGRAPHY

Benware, Paul. The Believer's Payday. Chattanooga: AMG Publications, 2002.

Buchanan, Mark. Things Unseen: Living in Light of Forever. Sisters, OR: Multnomah Publishers, 2002.

Pentecost, J. Dwight. Things to Come. Grand Rapids: Zondervan, 1975.

Walvoord, John F. Major Bible Prophecies. Grand Rapids: Zondervan, 1991.

Wilkinson, Bruce. A Life God Rewards. Sisters, OR: Multnomah Publishers, 2002.

Metaphors of Judgment

METAPHOR	IMAGE OF EVALUATION	APPLICATION	SCRIPTURE
Building	Quality of material	Building well	1 Corinthians 3:12
Athletic race	Reward stand	Strict training Running hard	1 Corinthians 9:24-27
Marriage	Bridal beauty and purity	Eliminating flaws Staying faithful	2 Corinthians 11:2
Auditor's report	Record of good works	Producing good works	2 Corinthians 5:10
Work	Reimbursement	Heartfelt service	Colossians 3:24
Farming	Harvest	Being fruitful	John 4:36
Investment	Return on money	Wise stewardship	Luke 16:1-14
Favors	Return of favor	Dedicated service	Ephesians 6:8
Battles of war	Celebrated return	Being victorious	2 Corinthians 2:14-17
Working	Earned wages	Working hard	Revelation 22:12
Stewardship	Service to master	Being faithful	1 Corinthians 4:2
Boxing match	Winning the fight	Defeating an opponent	1 Corinthians 9:24-27

JUDGMENTS OF THE NEW TESTAMENT

THE IDEA OF A SINGLE general judgment at the end of time is inconsistent with biblical revelation. Paul Van Gorder (p. 1) observes, "The popular belief that there will be one final judgment in which all humanity will stand is a concept that is foreign to the teaching of the Word of God. Coming judgment? Certainly! A general judgment? Absolutely not!" Throughout the Old Testament, the judgment of God is associated with the flood, the destruction of Sodom, and the falls of various nations, including both Israel and Judah. In the New Testament, judgment is rendered in eight areas.

The subject of judgments is a large one in the Word of God. Three of the eight judgments are not related to God's eschatological program. They include the judgment of the cross (John 5:24; Romans 5:9, 8:1; 2 Corinthians 5:21; Galatians 3:13; Hebrews 9:26-28; 10:10,14-17), the judgment on the believer in chastening (1 Corinthians 11:31-32; Hebrews 12:5-11), and the self-judgment of the believer (1 Corinthians 11:31; 1 John 1:9). The other five judgments have eschatological implications: the judgment of the believer's works at the judgment seat of Christ (2 Corinthians 5:10), the judgment of the nation of Israel (Ezekiel 20:37-38; Zechariah 13:8-9), the judgment of the nations (Isaiah 34:1-2; Joel 3:11-16; Matthew 25:31-46), the judgment on fallen angels (Jude 6), and the Great White Throne judgment (Revelation 20:11-15).

1. *The Cross.* On Calvary, Jesus experienced the judgment of God upon the sins of the world. He died in the sinner's place as a substitute. "Christ hath redeemed us from the curse of the law, being made a curse for us: for it is written, Cursed is every one that hangeth on a tree" (Galatians 3:13 KJV). The cross was a judgment by God upon the sins of the world.

2. *Self-Judgment.* Before God judges Christians for sin in their lives, He first gives them the opportunity to deal with the problem. In explaining the reasoning for the sickness and death among church members in Corinth, Paul pointed to the judgment of God upon sin (1 Corinthians 11:30). He then explained, "If we would judge ourselves, we should not be judged" (1 Corinthians 11:31).

3. *Chastisement.* While problems such as physical sickness or adversity are often not the result of sin in a believer's life, they sometimes are. The Scriptures speak of these events as God's chastising of His sons (Hebrews 12:5-11). Believers can sometimes avoid this judgment by practicing self-judgment.

4. *The Judgment Seat of Christ.* This is sometimes called the *bema* judgment seat, using the Greek word *bema.* "For we must all appear before the judgment seat of Christ; that every one may receive the things done in his body, according to that he hath done, whether it be good or bad" (2 Corinthians 5:10). At the *bema,* God judges the believer's works, not his sins. Jesus has completely atoned for every believer's sins, and God remembers them no more (Hebrews 10:17). At the *bema,* every work will be evaluated for both faithfulness and results. Since God is just, He cannot overlook our works—good or evil. The judgment seat of Christ is often discussed as the doctrine of rewards for Christians. This is not a judgment to determine if Christians will enter into heaven, but to determine the quality and quantity of our past service on this earth. As a result of faithfulness to Christ, Christians will receive a reward.

Not everyone will obtain the same reward, and faithful service will be tested by God to determine the extent of the reward. Some may have very little with which to enter heaven except their salvation (1 Corinthians 3:12-15). The Bible also teaches that we can lose part of our reward that we had previously accrued. Therefore, it is important that a believer continue to be faithful in his service for Christ even after he has earned a prize (2 John 8). These rewards are sometimes identified as "crowns" in the Bible. (See the article titled "Crowns.")

THE BELIEVER'S REWARDS	
1. Incorruptible crown	1 Corinthians 9:25
2. Crown of righteousness	2 Timothy 4:8
3. Crown of life	Revelation 2:10
4. Crown of glory	1 Peter 5:4
5. Crown of rejoicing	1 Thessalonians 2:19

Often the judgment seat of Christ is pictured as a place of tears and remorse for some believers because of their unfaithfulness and sin. However, even those who are minimally rewarded will rejoice. Paul reminds us to "judge nothing before the time, until the Lord come," because then all believers will rejoice: "Then shall every man have praise of God" (1 Corinthians 4:5).

5. *Judgment of the Gentile Nations.* At Christ's second coming, all the nations of the world will pass before Him to be judged (Matthew 25:32). This scene is described in terms of a separation of sheep and goats. The basis of their judgment is in relation to their treatment of those identified by Christ as "these my brethren" (Matthew 25:40,45). These brethren may be (1) Israel, (2) the church, or (3) the oppressed.

A. *Israel.* Some believe Jesus was referring to the treatment of the Jews as the basis of His judgment. If that is the case, people of those nations that have sought to protect the Jews will be sheep. The others, who have sought to harm the Jews or simply ignore their plight, will be goats. This interpretation is in keeping with the promise of blessing in the Abrahamic covenant to those who bless the seed of Abraham (Genesis 12:1-3; 15:1-3).

B. *The Church.* Some commentators argue that the brethren of Jesus are really the church. Jesus said, "Whosoever shall do the will of my Father which is in heaven, the same is my brother, and sister, and mother" (Matthew 12:50). In this case, the treatment of churches and Christians in those churches will be the basis of the judgment.

C. *The Oppressed.* Throughout the Bible, God is portrayed as a defender of those who cannot defend themselves. Some have suggested God will judge the nations based upon their protection of the oppressed and defenseless members of their

THE COMING JUDGMENTS

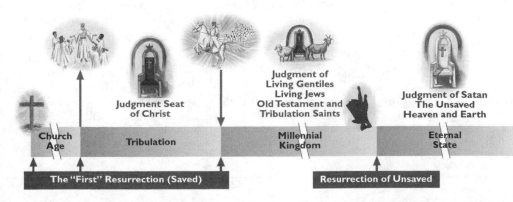

THE JUDGMENTS

Judgment	Judge(s)	Subjects of Judgment	Motive of Judgment	Time of Judgment
The cross	The Father	Christ and those "in Christ"	God's love for sinners	About A.D. 30 Passover 9 A.M. to noon
Self-judgment	Individual Christians	Individual Christians	Christian's desire to partake in Lord's Supper	Often in the Christian experience
Chastisement	The Father	Individual Christians	God's love for sons	During Christian life when needed
Judgment seat of Christ	The Lord Jesus	Individual Christians	The awarding of crowns	Soon after the rapture
Tribulation	God	"Earth dwellers"	Prayers of the martyred saints	Between the rapture and the Revelation of Christ
Gentile nations	The Lord Jesus	Gentile nations	The Lord's identification with "My brethren"	At the revelation of Christ in His glory
Great White Throne	God through the Son	Those not recorded in the Book of Life	Harmony of the love and holiness of God	End of the millennial reign of Christ
Angels	Christians, probably as a group with Christ	Angels, especially fallen angels	Rebellion of some angels under the leadership of Satan	Sometime after the rapture of the church, probably toward the end of the millennium

THE JUDGMENTS

Place of Judgment	Basis of Judgment	Purposes of Judgment	Penalty	Benefits of Judgment
Golgotha	Holiness of God	To provide an atonement for man's sins and thereby make possible reconciliation	Death	Salvation to those who believe
At the Lord's Table	The Scriptures	To avoid partaking unworthily	Sickness and death	Renewed fellowship
In body or experience of Christian	Sin in the life of the Christian	To demonstrate the existence of a relationship and develop a closer fellowship	Grievous at the time	Yields peaceable fruit of righteousness
Heaven, perhaps in the throne room	Quality of stewardship	To evaluate the works of Christians and award rewards	Loss of some rewards	Purification of some rewards
Judged in heaven, penalty inflicted on earth	Vengeance of God particularly directed toward those who oppose His work	To release the wrath of God on wickedness and bring about the repentance of some	Sufferings accompanying the seals, trumpets, and vials of wrath	Repentance of some
Before the throne of His glory	The gentile nations' concern or lack thereof for "My brethren"	To effect a separation of sheep and goat nations	Everlasting fire	Inheritance of a kingdom
Before the throne of God	Individual responses to Christ and their works (the degree of their opposition)	To ensure punishment for sin and determine the degree of that eternal punishment	Lake of fire, second death	Lesser degree of eternal suffering for some
Probably heaven	Sovereignty of God	To evaluate the angels	Everlasting fire	Marks the end of evil

society. This would include the very young and very old, the poor, and the unborn.

6. *Tribulation.* During the Great Tribulation, God will release three major sets of judgments upon the world (the seals, the trumpets, and the bowls). The first of these accompanies the breaking of the seven seals on a scroll which may be the title deed of the world. The second series of judgments accompanies the sounding of seven trumpets, while the final series of judgments occurs as seven angels pour out bowls of the wrath of God upon the world. (See the articles titled "Seal Judgments," "Trumpet Judgments," and "Bowl Judgments.")

7. *The Great White Throne Judgment.* At the end of the millennial reign of Christ, the unsaved dead will stand before the throne of God to be judged. "I saw the dead, small and great, stand before God; and the books were opened: and another book was opened, which is the book of life: and the dead were judged out of those things which were written in the books, according to their works" (Revelation 20:12). This judgment does not suggest these people may enter into heaven or hell on the basis of their works. All those who are judged at the Great White Throne are consigned to hell because they have rejected God. The Great White Throne judgment will determine the degree of punishment the rejecters will endure, based upon the nature of their evil work. When the books of works are opened (Revelation 20:12), a sentence of the severity of their punishment will be determined. All those sentenced will be consigned "into the lake of fire" (Revelation 20:14), where they will suffer according to their personally assigned sentences.

8. *Angels.* The Bible also teaches that fallen angels will be judged. Paul asked the Corinthians, "Know ye not that we shall judge angels?" (1 Corinthians 6:3). Toward the end of the age, Christians will represent God in the role of judge. It may be that during the Tribulation, the millennial kingdom, or eternity to follow, Christians will serve as judges similar to the judges who ruled before Israel's first king.

—Elmer Towns

BIBLIOGRAPHY

Pentecost, J. Dwight. *Things to Come.* Grand Rapids: Zondervan, 1975.

Thomas, Robert. *Revelation 8–22: An Exegetical Commentary.* Chicago: Moody Press, 1992.

Towns, Elmer. *Theology for Today.* Fort Worth: Harcourt & Brace, 2001.

Van Gorder, Paul R. *The Judgments of God.* Grand Rapids: Radio Bible Class, 1972.

Walvoord, John F. *The Revelation of Jesus Christ.* Chicago: Moody Press, 1966.

KINGDOM OF GOD

God is sovereign. He rules eternally in a kingdom in which He is the absolute authority. In order to understand the biblical teaching regarding the kingdom, we must recognize that it includes these elements: the right to rule, a realm in which to rule, and the actual exercise of authority.

THE KINGDOM IN ETERNITY

The Bible presents two aspects of God's kingdom: the eternal and the temporal. The eternal kingdom is characterized by four essential truths: (1) It is timeless, (2) it is universal, (3) it is providential, and (4) it is miraculous.

In eternity past, before the creation of the angels, the earth, and man, a kingdom existed in the sphere of "the heavenlies" because of the relationship among the members of the Trinity. God the Father was sovereign. God the Son, although equal in person, was subordinate to the Father. God the Holy Spirit was the active executor of the will of the Father (Genesis 1:2-3). Thus, in eternity past there was a kingdom, involving the right to rule as well as the sphere in which the right operated and the rule was exercised. Indeed, all the elements essential to a kingdom were present. This kingdom arises from the character of God and reaches from eternity past to eternity future.

God's kingdom was displayed in the angelic realm before it was developed on the earth. The created angelic hosts in that kingdom were subject to the Sovereign, and they worshiped Him and obeyed Him. This continued until the fall of Lucifer and the angels who followed him in rebellion.

THE KINGDOM ON EARTH (PRE-ABRAHAMIC)

God ordered this earthly sphere as the place where He would demonstrate His right to rule. He populated it with creatures who were responsible to recognize that right, submit to it, and give the Ruler that which was due Him. Our sovereign God, in every period of theocratic administration, has ruled through those to whom He assigned His authority. It was the responsibility of administrators to subjugate all to God's authority, to reward those who do good, to punish evildoers, and to provide an atmosphere in which the subjects of the King might live in peace. In the Garden, Adam was the theocratic administrator whose responsibility was to subject all creation to himself, so that through him creation might be subject to the authority of God. When this form of administration failed, God brought a judgment and expelled Adam and Eve from the Garden.

God instituted a new form of theocratic administration in which He wrote His law in the hearts of men and subjected man to His law. That law was man's conscience (Romans 2:15), and as men subjected themselves to the rule of conscience, they were in subjection to the authority of God. But that too failed. And when men rebelled against that form of theocratic administration, God wiped the human race off the face of the earth by a flood.

God then inaugurated yet another form of theocratic administration in which authority was given to human government (Genesis 9:6). It was the responsibility of human government to curb lawlessness and to bring man in subjection to the authority of God. Again man failed miserably.

THE KINGDOM IN ISRAEL

From Abraham to Jesus

With the call of Abraham, God introduced a new form of theocratic administration. He instituted the Abrahamic covenant, which promised Abraham a land, seed, and blessing. Throughout the Old Testament—through that expanding covenant program—God administered His theocracy here on earth.

The kingdom program was then developed with the nation Israel through the covenants God made with them: the Abrahamic (Genesis 15:18), the Davidic (2 Samuel 7:14), the New (Jeremiah 31:31-34), and the Palestinian (Deuteronomy 28–30). These eternal, unconditional, irrevocable covenants determined the ultimate form of the kingdom of the God of heaven on earth.

While the covenants promised a kingdom here on earth, it was the prophets who described the glories of that kingdom. The prophets of the Old Testament had proclaimed a message of hope that caused Israel to eagerly anticipate the fulfillment of God's covenants and promises to them. David's Son, the Messiah, would come to bring peace, righteousness, and prosperity to the nation. He would come as a Savior to redeem and as a Sovereign to reign. The nations that had persecuted Israel would be subjugated to Him, and Israel would know the promised peace that the Prince of Peace would bring. Her accumulated sins would be put away and she would experience forgiveness and life in righteousness. Such was the hope of Israel.

Centuries passed before the prophesied forerunner, John the Baptist, heralded his message to the nation: "Repent, for the kingdom of heaven is at hand" (Matthew 3:2 NASB). When Jesus began His ministry, He made the same proclamation (Matthew 4:17). The call to repentance shows that this was a contingent offer and that the blessings of the kingdom depended on the nation's response. This does not mean, however, it was not a genuine offer. The reference to the kingdom needed no explanation; it was the covenanted kingdom under David's Son, the Messiah, of which the prophets had so clearly spoken and for whom the nation was waiting. The nation was plunged into a great debate concerning His person. Who is this Jesus of Nazareth, who claims to be the Son of David and the Son of God? Is He what He claims to be? If so, He truly is the promised and covenanted Messiah. If not, He is a blasphemous impostor who is worthy of death. Jesus made His claims concerning His person very clear. He validated those claims convincingly by His miracles, and He challenged people to accept His claims and to put faith in Him, so as to receive a righteousness from Him that would enable them to enter His forthcoming kingdom.

From the inception of Jesus' ministry, two responses to His presentation were evident. John says: "He came to His own [things], and those who were His own did not receive Him. But as many as received Him, to them He gave the right to become children of God, even to those who believe in His name" (John 1:11-12). There were those who, on the basis of the evidence He had presented about Himself as the Son of David, the Messiah, expressed their willingness to accept Him as the Messiah. But there were also those who rejected the evidence and sought to explain it away so they would be guiltless for their rejection. There were two supernatural powers who could perform miracles: Satan and God. If the leaders acknowledged that Jesus performed miracles by God's power, they would be without excuse for their unbelief; but if He performed miracles by Satan's power, they could justify their rejection. Thus they sought to dissuade those who believed by saying, "This fellow does not cast out demons except by Beelzebub, the ruler of the demons" (Matthew 12:24 NKJV).

JESUS' JUDGMENT UPON ISRAEL

Jesus viewed the explanation by the leaders as indicative of the course that generation would follow. The message that He began to proclaim was no longer "Come to Me, all who are weary and heavy-laden, and I will give you rest" (Matthew 11:28), but rather, it was a message of judgment. From this time onward Jesus spoke of the judgment to come.

In the parable of the wicked vinedressers (Matthew 21:33-44), after the leaders kill the heir, the owner (God) would destroy those wicked men miserably. So, too, "the kingdom of God will be taken from you [that generation in Israel] and given to a nation [or generation] bearing the fruits of it. And whoever falls on this stone will be broken; but on whomever it falls, it will grind him to powder" (Matthew 21:43-44 NKJV). This signifies the withdrawal of the offer of the covenanted kingdom to Israel and its postponement to the future.

This same judgment is depicted in Matthew 22:1-7, where the guests (the nation Israel), who had been invited to a wedding banquet (Messiah's kingdom) but refused to come, suffered the consequences of rejecting the king's invitation. The king "sent out his armies, destroyed those murderers, and burned up their city." This parable reveals the form of judgment: Roman armies, under Titus, would attack the city of Jerusalem, destroy it, and either kill or disperse its inhabitants. Another specific prediction of the coming judgment is given in Matthew 23:37–24:2. Jesus declared He had sought to provide peace and security for Israel, but it was not experienced because "you were not willing." As a consequence, "Your house is left to you desolate" (Matthew 23:37-38).

Luke is specific in recording Jesus' message of judgment. In Luke 19:11-27 the nobleman declared, concerning the unfaithful, "Take the mina from him.…But bring here those enemies of mine, who did not want me to reign over them, and slay them before me." In this parable it is significant that judgment fell on those who refused to submit themselves to the One who had the right to reign. This was the sin of that generation in Israel. Once again, the judgment is predicted forcefully (Luke 21:20-24).

Thus the message of Jesus was initially one of hope, blessing, and salvation. But after the announcement by the leaders that Jesus received His power from Satan, and so was a blasphemous impostor, His message turned to one of judgment on that generation in Israel. This announcement did not cancel the covenants and promises given to Israel concerning the earthly kingdom of David's greater Son, but only postponed the realization of those hopes. Yet it did consign that generation to a physical and temporal judgment (Luke 19:27). Thus the kingdom program for Israel, which began with such high hopes at the beginning of Jesus' ministry, ends with the somber note of judgment and postponement.

THE KINGDOM IN THE PRESENT AGE

In light of all this, the following questions arise: What happens to God's kingdom, of which the Davidic millennial kingdom is only an earthly form, in this present age, when the millennial kingdom has been postponed? What form does the kingdom take in this present age? What are the essential characteristics or features of God's kingdom in this age?

Some scholars believe that the kingdom of God does not exist at all during the church age because it has been removed from Israel and will be reestablished on earth at Christ's second coming. In the view of the present author, however, when Jesus referred to "the mysteries of the kingdom" in Matthew 13:11, He was not referring to the Davidic, or millennial, kingdom. What the Old Testament had not revealed was that an entire age would intervene between the offer of the kingdom by the Messiah and Israel's reception of the King and enjoyment of full kingdom blessings. The time period covered by the parables in Matthew 13 extends from Israel's rejection until its future reception of the Messiah. Thus this new program began while Christ was still on the earth, and it will extend until His return to the earth in power and great glory.

This period includes the time from Pentecost, in Acts 2, to the rapture; that is, the age of grace (which we also call the age of the Holy Spirit or the church age). Although this period includes the church age, it extends beyond it, for the parables of Matthew 13 precede Pentecost and extend beyond the rapture. Thus, these parables do not primarily concern the nature, function, and influence of the church. Rather, they show the previously unrevealed form in which God's theocratic rule would be exerted in a previously unrevealed age, made necessary by Israel's rejection of Jesus Christ.

Matthew 13 includes seven parables, each one providing an essential characteristic of the kingdom in this present age. As we survey them, we find that in light of Israel's rejection of Christ, He foresaw postponement of the millennial form of the kingdom. He announced the introduction of a new form of the kingdom, one that would span the period from Israel's rejection of Christ until Israel's future reception of Christ at His second advent.

This present age is characterized by the sowing of the Word, to which there will be varying responses depending on the soil's preparation (the parable of the soils). Concurrent with the sowing of the Word is a false counter-sowing (the parable of the weeds). The new form of the kingdom had an insignificant beginning, but it will grow to great proportions (the parable of the mustard seed). The power in the kingdom is not external but internal (the parable of leaven hidden in meal). God will gather a peculiar treasure to Himself through this present age (the parables of the hidden treasure and the pearl of great price). The present form of the kingdom will end in a judgment to determine who are righteous and therefore eligible to enter the future millennial form of the kingdom, as well as who are unrighteous and thus to be excluded from the millennial kingdom to come. (See also "Kingdom Parables" and "Matthew, Eschatology of.")

This revelation of the new form through which the theocracy would be administered in this present age was followed by a specific prophecy: "I will build My church" (Matthew 16:18). The Gospels do not explain the nature and function of the church, but the book of Acts reveals its historical development, and the epistles explain its doctrines.

THE KINGDOM IN ACTS

The book of Acts shows that the kingdom of God in this present age, formed through the preaching of the gospel, is made up of Jews, Samaritans, and Gentiles. This was made clear to Peter in the vision given to him in Acts 10. Peter felt free to proclaim the gospel of the death and resurrection of Jesus Christ to the Gentiles assembled in Cornelius' house. In response to their faith, "The Holy Spirit fell upon all those who were listening to the message" (verse 44). They showed their identification with Jesus Christ and the company of believers by being baptized.

Later in Acts, Paul's life was also dedicated to the preaching of the grace of God, which he equated with proclaiming the kingdom of God (see Acts 28:23,30-31). As we survey Paul's ministry in the book of Acts, we see him as an ambassador of the kingdom of God, but his message was salvation through the death and the resurrection of Jesus Christ. No reference is made to support the notion that the earthly Davidic kingdom had been established. Rather, the message concerns entrance into a present form of the kingdom of God by faith in Jesus Christ.

THE KINGDOM IN THE EPISTLES

The New Testament epistles include many references to the kingdom, but on closer examination we find the term *kingdom* used in several different ways.

It is used of the future earthly Davidic kingdom to be established at the second advent of Jesus Christ (2 Timothy 4:1). Paul writes, "Christ the first fruits, after that those who are Christ's at His coming, then comes the end, when He hands over the kingdom to the God and Father, when He has abolished all rule and all authority and power" (1 Corinthians 15:23-24). Here Paul outlines a resurrection program that began with the resurrection of Christ and will continue with the resurrection of those who are Christ's at the rapture and at His second advent. The completion of the resurrection program does not come until after the reign of Christ here on earth. At the conclusion of that resurrection program, Christ will have delivered up the kingdom to God. The kingdom referred to here is therefore the millennial kingdom over which Christ reigns on earth, following His second advent. Thus, the idea of a future earthly Davidic kingdom is not at all foreign to the apostle's thinking.

Besides the future earthly Davidic kingdom, we also find that the future eternal kingdom is referred to in the epistles. In 2 Timothy 4:18 Paul declared, "The Lord will rescue me from every evil deed, and will bring me safely to His heavenly kingdom." Paul was anticipating the eternal reign of Christ in His eternal kingdom (see 1 Corinthians 15:50; 2 Peter 1:11).

While the term *kingdom* is used in these two senses in the epistles, its third and most common use is in reference to the present form of the kingdom, that into which a believer enters by faith in Jesus Christ. Paul stated that God "has rescued us from the dominion of darkness and brought us into the kingdom of the Son He loves, in whom we have redemption, the forgiveness of sins" (Colossians 1:13-14 NIV). Here the phrase "the kingdom of the Son He loves" is equated with the redemption and the forgiveness of sins received by faith in Jesus Christ.

Believers are exhorted to live lives worthy of God, who calls them into His kingdom and glory (1 Thessalonians 2:12). Paul told the Corinthians, "The kingdom of God is not a matter of talk but of power" (1 Corinthians 4:20 NIV). In other words, if those in Corinth were actually saved and in the kingdom of God, they would demonstrate that by manifesting the power of the kingdom in their daily lives. Mere profession was not a sufficient demonstration of salvation or participation in the kingdom of God; that relationship must be established and demonstrated by the work of the Holy Spirit, who is the power in the present form of the kingdom of God. According to Colossians 4:11, Paul considered himself a laborer on behalf of the kingdom of God, and he saw those faithful servants who worked with him as fellow workers in the kingdom.

From this survey, then, we see that the most frequent reference to the "kingdom" or the "kingdom of God" in the epistles is a reference to the present form of the kingdom, in which individuals by faith in Jesus Christ, and because of His death and resurrection, receive salvation and the gift of eternal life. All these are a part of the kingdom of God.

We conclude that the church is a part of a kingdom of the God of heaven, falling in the inter-advent period. It was an unrevealed mystery in the Old Testament, but it was necessitated by Israel's rejection of the Messiah, which caused the postponement of the promised and covenant form of the kingdom, which will be inaugurated by the appearance of the King of kings and Lord of lords at His second advent.

THE KINGDOM IN ETERNITY

While the major emphasis in the epistles is on the present form of the kingdom, there is an anticipation of the merger of the present form of the kingdom into the Davidic kingdom to be established at the second advent of the Messiah, and the eventual merger of that Davidic kingdom into the eternal kingdom over which Messiah will rule by divine appointment. According to 1 Corinthians 15:27-28, at the end of Christ's earthly rule, when all has been brought into subjection to the Father, either willingly or through judgment, the Father will assign rulership over the eternal kingdom to the Son. Thus, for the unending ages of eternity, God's right to rule will be recognized. All in that kingdom will be in submission to Him and will join in worship of the Sovereign forever.

—J. DWIGHT PENTECOST

BIBLIOGRAPHY

Fruchtenbaum, Arnold. *Israelology: The Missing Link in Systematic Theology.* Tustin, CA: Ariel Ministries, 1992.

McClain, Alva J. *The Greatness of the Kingdom.* Chicago: Moody Press, 1959.

Pentecost, J. Dwight. *Things to Come.* Grand Rapids: Zondervan, 1958.

———. *Thy Kingdom Come.* Wheaton, IL: Victor Books, 1990.

Walvoord, John F. *Major Bible Prophecies.* Grand Rapids: Zondervan, 1993.

———. *The Millennial Kingdom.* Grand Rapids: Zondervan, 1959.

KINGDOM PARABLES

JESUS DEVOTED MUCH of His earthly ministry to teaching His disciples. One way He taught was through parables, which enabled Him to address a large group and, at the same time, speak to a smaller group that would understand the real message of the parable. Matthew 13 records seven such parables in which Jesus sought to teach His disciples "the mysteries of the kingdom of heaven" (Matthew 13:11 NASB).

THE COURSE OF THE AGE IN MATTHEW 13

	Verses	
Parable of the Sower	1-23	There will be a sowing of the gospel throughout the world, with a variety of responses.
Parable of the Tares	24-30	There will be a counter-sowing by Satan.
Parable of the Mustard Seed	31-32	There will be an outward growth of Christendom.
Parable of the Leaven	33-35	There will be a permeation of the gospel into all areas of life.
Parable of the Hidden Treasure Parable of the Pearl of Great Price	44 45-46	God will gather to Himself a special people.
Parable of the Dragnet	47-51	God will end the age in judgment.

The Jews of Jesus' day expected the political Messiah to be a conquering king who would drive the Romans into the sea. After the Jews began to reject Jesus and His kingdom, He offered Himself as a spiritual King to rule the hearts of His subjects. During the church age, Jesus would conquer the inward lives of His followers; He would rule by inward peace and inward values. The church was not to be a political army but an evangelistic army. The Great Commission would conquer individuals and ethnic groups of people. Matthew 13 introduces this different stage of the kingdom, explaining what the King would do during the period when He was physically absent. Matthew 13 gives a sequence of events between His first and His second comings. The mysteries of the kingdom, accordingly, deal sequentially with events between the first and second advents of Christ and not the millennial kingdom.

The seven parables prophetically describe the course of this age. The record of church history reflects the accuracy of these predictions. The preceding chart summarizes the course of this age as seen in the kingdom parables of Matthew 13. (See articles titled "Kingdom of God" and "Matthew, Eschatology of."

—ELMER TOWNS

BIBLIOGRAPHY

Gaebelein, A.C. *The Gospel of Matthew: An Exposition.* New York: Publication Office, Our Hope, 1910.

McClain, Alva J. *The Greatness of the Kingdom.* Grand Rapids: Zondervan, 1959.

Pentecost, J. Dwight. *Things to Come.* Findlay, OH: Dunham, 1958.

Toussaint, Stanley D. *Behold the King.* Sisters, OR: Multnomah Publishers, 1980.

Walvoord, John F. *Matthew, Thy Kingdom Come.* Chicago: Moody Press, 1974.

LAKE OF FIRE

THE PHRASE "LAKE OF FIRE" appears five times in the New Testament, all in Revelation (19:20; 20:10,14,15; 21:8). In Revelation 19:20, the beast and the False Prophet are thrown into the lake of fire alive, denoting a conscious punishment. This description is missing from the other occurrences, but John likely intended his readers to remember it. This becomes a problem for those who hold to an annihilation view of final judgment (a view that is also contrary to Matthew 25:46).

"Lake of fire" is one of several biblical terms or phrases used in relation to hell and the eternal punishment of unbelievers and enemies of God, including Satan, the beast, and the False Prophet. According to Revelation 20:11-15, unbelievers will be cast into the lake of fire after the Great White Throne judgment at the end of the millennium and remain there forever.

At present, no one is in the lake of fire. The present location of all dead unbelievers since creation is called "sheol" in the Old Testament and "hades" or "hell" in the New Testament. According to Luke 16, this place is very similar to the lake of fire but not identical. After the Great White Throne judgment, all fallen angels and unbelieving humanity will spend eternity in the lake of fire. Believers, however, will enter heaven and eternal life in the presence of God. Those cast into the lake of fire incur a "second death" (Revelation 2:11; 21:8). This death is not identical in nature to the first, physical, earthly death. The first death is a cessation of earthly existence, but the second one brings no cessation. Instead, it includes a conscious awareness of eternal punishment (Osborne, pp. 723–24). Those who reject God's call and whose names are not written in the Book of Life will face a terrible judgment and future. "If heaven is many degrees greater than the portrait in 21:1–22:5, then eternal damnation is also many degrees worse than the portrait here [20:13-15]" (Osborne, p. 725).

The imagery of the "lake of fire" may be derived in part from the fire and sulfur coming from heaven to destroy Sodom and Gomorrah (Genesis 19:24; Luke 17:29-30). There is also the connection with *gehenna*, another word for eternal punishment used 12 times in the New Testament. It was originally the site where Ahaz and Manasseh sacrificed their children to the pagan god Moloch during the Old Testament era (2 Kings 16:3; 21:6; 2 Chronicles 28:3; 33:6). The site was condemned and became a symbol for future final punishment (Isaiah 66:24; Jeremiah 7:30-33; 19:6). During the time of Jesus, Gehenna (located in the Valley of Hinnom on the south slope of Jerusalem) was a garbage dump, a place where refuse was continually burned. Thus, Gehenna served as a symbol of eternal punishment (Matthew 3:12; 25:41-46; Mark 9:44-48).

The Old and New Testaments repeatedly stressed the ideas of catastrophic destruction and eternal punishment, so the readers of John's words would have been well acquainted with the concepts. The imagery of the "lake of fire" is vivid and well attested to in the Bible (Osborne, pp. 690–91).

Three important ideas emerge from John's use of the term "lake of fire." First, at a future date the wicked will be permanently separated from God and experience the "second death" (Revelation 20:14; 21:8). Second, the fire denotes the searing holiness of God through which He exacts retribution for sin and rejection (Hebrews 10:30; Revelation 14:9-11). Third, this is an unquenchable fire that portrays hell and separation from God as eternal (Mark 9:43-48; Revelation 20:10) (Phillips, p. 460).

—TIMOTHY J. DEMY

BIBLIOGRAPHY

Ice, Thomas, and Timothy J. Demy. *Fast Facts on Bible Prophecy from A to Z.* Eugene, OR: Harvest House Publishers, 2004.

———. *What the Bible Says about Heaven & Eternity.* Grand Rapids: Kregel, 2000.

Osborne, Grant R. *Revelation.* Grand Rapids: Baker Books, 2002.

Phillips, Timothy R. "Lake of Fire." In *Evangelical Dictionary of Biblical Theology.* Ed. Walter A. Ewell. Grand Rapids: Baker Books, 1996.

Walvoord, John F. *The Revelation of Jesus Christ: A Commentary.* Chicago: Moody Press, 1966.

LAMB OF GOD

ONE OF THE MOST IMPORTANT doctrines of the Old Testament pertains to sin and sacrifice. The Lord Himself slew the first innocent animal in order to cover the nakedness of Adam and Eve following their sin (Genesis 3:21). This sacrifice set the pattern for the rest of the Old Testament blood offerings. The sacrifice of an innocent animal prefigured the sacrifice of the Messiah, the ultimate and final sin-bearer for all of humanity.

God indicated that the sacrifices themselves could not take away sin. He said, "I delight in loyalty rather than sacrifice, and in the knowledge of God rather than burnt offerings" (Hosea 6:6 NASB; see Matthew 9:13).

THE PURPOSE OF SACRIFICE

All the various sacrifices given before and within the law of Moses pointed to the coming of Christ. The Lord Jesus would be the ultimate and final offering for sins. The sacrifices also taught Israel several important lessons: (1) By the blood shed when a sacrifice was made, the Jewish people could experience something of the awfulness of sin. (2) The sacrifice illustrated the idea of substitution. The innocent animal became a substitute onto which a person's sins would pass. (3) By the slaying of the sacrificial animal itself, the people could get a glimpse of the wrath and anger of God toward sin. (4) And finally, by the offering of sacrifice, the people came to realize they could receive the forgiveness of sin.

The story of the Passover further shows the importance of the sacrificial lamb (Exodus 12). The people offered an innocent animal in order to be liberated from the oppression of Pharaoh. Passover's importance is reflected in the fact that it became the most celebrated Jewish feast. On the night of deliverance, each Jewish family was to offer a lamb "for each household." Unknown to the Jews at the time, this offering of the "unblemished male" animal would signify and picture the Lord Jesus, who became the true Lamb, unblemished and spotless, and who offered up His own blood for sinners (1 Peter 1:19-20). On the night of Passover *(pas'ach)*, the Jews were to eat all of the roasted lamb with unleavened bread (picturing sinlessness) and bitter herbs (Exodus 12:8). This would be a "memorial" throughout all the generations of the Jewish people. It was a feast to be celebrated as "a permanent ordinance" (12:14). The blood of the sacrifice was to be marked on the lintel of the door of each house. Seeing the blood, the Lord said,

"I will pass over you" (12:13). The children of Israel were spared and delivered, but the Egyptians were judged with the loss of their firstborn sons. With the marking of the blood of the Passover, "the LORD will pass through to smite the Egyptians; and when he sees the blood on the lintel and on the two doorposts, the LORD will pass over the door and will not allow the destroyer to come in to your house to smite you" (12:23). The apostle Paul connects this important event with the crucifixion and writes, "For Christ our Passover also has been sacrificed" (1 Corinthians 5:7).

The book of Leviticus gives ample illustrations of the sacrifice of an innocent animal. When sin was committed, the individual became guilty (Leviticus 4:27). He or she brought an innocent animal to the priests, who laid their hands on the head of the sacrifice, signifying that the sins of the people were passed onto the offering (verse 29). The sacrifice was "presented" to God by the smearing of the animal's blood on the horns of the sacrificial altar (verse 30). Therefore atonement (*kah'phar*, "a covering") was made to satisfy the Lord. "Thus the priest shall make atonement for him in regard to his sin which he has committed, and he will be forgiven" (verse 35).

In reality, these sacrifices were but visual examples of what the coming Messiah would do. God clearly demonstrated through the example of Abraham that justification before the Lord came only by faith (Genesis 15:6).

THE SACRIFICIAL DEATH OF CHRIST

One of the most poignant Old Testament chapters on the substitution and sacrifice of the Messiah for sins is found in Isaiah 53. This prophecy is about the suffering servant, who is "forsaken of men," "smitten of God, and afflicted," and then "pierced through for our transgressions." Further, "the LORD has caused the iniquity of us all to fall on Him" who "like a lamb that is led to slaughter…did not open His mouth." The crucifixion of Christ is in view when the prophet predicts He would be assigned with wicked men and would be with a rich man "in His death." By this death,

God's Servant "will justify the many, as He will bear their iniquities."

The prophet Zechariah also alludes to the "piercing" of the Messiah and connects this directly to the second coming of the Son of God, who brings deliverance to the Jews and the city of Jerusalem (12:10).

John the Baptist had Isaiah 53 in mind when he cried out to the Jews upon seeing Jesus, "Behold, the Lamb of God who takes away the sin of the world!" (John 1:29,36). By becoming a sacrifice for sin as an innocent Lamb, Christ became a high priest (Hebrews 9:11) who would obtain for sinners an "eternal redemption" (verse 12), whereas animal sacrifices were but the predictive illustrations of what Christ would do at the cross. As the perfect and holy sacrifice, the Lord would become "the mediator of a new covenant" to give "the promise of the eternal inheritance" (verse 15). Psalm 40:6-8 predicted that Christ would offer His body as a sacrifice and a burnt offering. The writer of Hebrews focuses on this great prophecy and quotes it in some detail in Hebrews 10:5-7. When Jesus had "offered one sacrifice for sins for all time, [He] sat down at the right hand of God" to forever make intercession for those He redeemed (verse 12).

The apostle Peter further develops the sacrificial work of Christ as the Lamb of God. He says that believers are not redeemed with perishable things, "but with precious blood, as of a lamb unblemished and spotless, the blood of Christ" (1 Peter 1:19). In 2:21-25 Peter alludes specifically to the prophecy of Isaiah 53 and quotes directly, or by paraphrase, many of the verses. Thus, Christ suffered for us, "and He Himself bore our sins in His body on the cross, so that we might die to sin and live to righteousness; for by His wounds you were healed" (verse 24).

THE LAMB OF GOD

The book of Revelation closes with references to the exalted Lord Jesus as the Lamb of God. On into eternity, this imagery will be sustained, reminding us that we have eternal life because He gave up Himself as a Lamb for our sins. Also, as the Lamb of God, the doctrine of the Trinity is emphasized. For example,

God Almighty and the Lamb are together seen as the temple in the new eternal Jerusalem (Revelation 21:22). This "holy city, Jerusalem, coming down out of heaven from God" (verse 10) is called "the bride, the wife of the Lamb" (verse 9). The glory of God illumines the city, but also the Lamb of God is its lamp (verse 23). In the city the eternal water of life comes down "from the throne of God and of the Lamb" (22:1). In the new city "the throne of God and of the Lamb shall be in it" (verse 3).

Substitution for sin is the prevailing idea behind the imagery of "the Lamb of God." Concluding on the idea of *substitution*, Lightner (p. 115) writes:

> [Christ] did not die merely to demonstrate bravery in the hour of death. He did not die simply for the benefit of mankind. Nor did He die as a victim of His persecutors. Rather, He died in the place of sinners. His death was vicarious in that He was the sinless vicar intervening for humans. The Savior took the sinner's place and thus acted as the sinner's substitute. The certainty and finality of this substitution is true whether anyone ever appropriates it by faith or not.

—MAL COUCH

BIBLIOGRAPHY

Briggs, Charles A. *Messianic Prophecy.* Peabody, MA: Hendrickson, 1988.

Hengstenberg, E.W. *Christology of the Old Testament.* Grand Rapids: Kregel, 1970.

Lightner, Robert P. *Sin, the Savior, and Salvation.* Grand Rapids: Kregel, 1991.

Soltau, Henry W. *The Tabernacle.* Grand Rapids: Kregel, 1972.

Walvoord, John F. *Major Bible Prophecies.* Grand Rapids: Zondervan, 1991.

White, James R. *The God Who Justifies.* Minneapolis: Bethany House, 2001.

Witmer, John A. *Immanuel.* Nashville: Word, 1998.

LAST DAYS

THE BIBLICAL TERM "LAST DAYS" and the popular term "end times" do not always refer to the same thing. "Last days" and "end times" can refer to the current church age, or they can refer to the future culmination of God's plan for Israel.

LAST-DAYS VOCABULARY

Several biblical expressions refer to the end times. The Bible teaches that this present age will end with the rapture, followed by the Tribulation, which will end with the second coming of the Messiah to the earth. We must distinguish between the last days of the church age and the last days of Israel's tribulation.

Note the following chart, which classifies and distinguishes between passages referring to the end of the church age and the last days for Israel:

END-TIMES TERMS (NASB)

ISRAEL	CHURCH
"latter days" Deuteronomy 4:30; 31:29; Jeremiah 30:24; 48:47; Daniel 2:28; 10:14	*"later times"* 1 Timothy 4:1
"last days" Isaiah 2:2; Jeremiah 23:20; 49:39; Ezekiel 38:16; Hosea 3:5; Micah 4:1; Acts 2:17	*"last days"* 2 Timothy 3:1; Hebrews 1:2; James 5:3; 2 Peter 3:3
"last day" John 6:39-40,44,54; 11:24; 12:48	*"last times"* 1 Peter 1:20
"latter years" Ezekiel 38:8	*"last time"* 1 Peter 1:5; Jude 18
"time of the end" Daniel 8:17	*"last hour"* 1 John 2:18
"end of time" Daniel 12:4	
"end time" Daniel 12:9	
"end of the age" Daniel 12:13	

When a verse references the last days, the context shows whether it is relating the term to Israel or the church.

Some Bible readers believe that specific signs relate to the end of the church age. However, this is too strong a statement. Instead, the Bible indicates what the condition of the church will be—the general course of the age—and then warns about some general trends toward the later part of the church age. Passages like 1 Timothy 4:1-5, 2 Timothy 3:1-5, and 2 Peter 3:3 most likely refer to the second half or latter part of the church age. These passages warn believers that worldly beliefs and lifestyles will become common in the church. They do not speak about the general moral decline of society but about a specific, predicted decline within the church as part of the increasing apostasy.

This decline is hard to quantify. No matter how bad things get today, they can always get worse tomorrow. We cannot possibly know how bad things must be to qualify as prophetic signs. With the general condition of the church, "evil men and impostors will proceed from bad to worse, deceiving and being deceived" (2 Timothy 3:13). Jude states that apostasy had already occurred in the church in the first century (verses 3-4). Thus, since the earliest times, apostasy within the church has been proceeding from bad to worse.

THE NEW TESTAMENT AND
THE CHURCH AGE

In several New Testament passages, "last days," "last times," and "last time" clearly refer to the entire present church age. The writer of Hebrews says, "God, after He spoke long ago to the fathers in the prophets in many portions and in many ways, in these last days has spoken to us in His Son" (Hebrews 1:1-2). The context of this passage shows that "last days" is a reference to the current church age. In the same way, Peter says, "He was foreknown before the foundation of the world, but has appeared in these last times for the sake of you" (1 Peter 1:20). "These last times" must refer to the last 2000 years. John adds support to the two previous writers when he says,

"Children, it is the last hour; and just as you heard that antichrist is coming, even now many antichrists have appeared; from this we know that it is the last hour" (1 John 2:18). Jude, speaking of things going on in his own day, says, "In the last time there will be mockers, following after their own ungodly lusts" (verse 18).

Though the New Testament certainly provides information about the end of the world, it also references the present age as the last days. The last days of what? The last days before the coming of the messianic age. In at least four clear references, New Testament writers use end-times vocabulary to refer to their own day and the entire church age. Thus, in that sense, we are clearly living in the last days because the entire church age is considered the last days. However, that is not what most people mean when they ask, "Are we living in the last days?" They want to know if God is fulfilling the final prophecies of Scripture in our time. To answer that, we need to look into the Old Testament's use of end-times terminology.

OLD TESTAMENT END-TIMES TERMINOLOGY

To the Jews, history consisted of two ages. The first was *this present age,* the age in which Israel was waiting for the coming of the Messiah. The second was *the age to come,* the age in which God would fulfill all promises and covenants, and Israel would enter into her promised blessings as a result of Messiah's coming. A time of judgment and devastation, leading up to the Messiah's advent and Israel's deliverance, was to terminate the present age and introduce the coming age.

When we look at the Old Testament usage of end-times terms, we see that it does not refer to the church age. The Old Testament uses end-times language to refer to the Tribulation period—the time leading up to the coming of the Messiah to set up His kingdom on earth.

A clear example of this is Deuteronomy 4:30, which says, "When you are in distress and all these things have come upon you, in the latter days you will return to the LORD your

God and listen to His voice." The English word "distress" translates the Hebrew word for tribulation—in this context, the Tribulation—which means that this text equates the Tribulation with the "latter days." Thus, the "latter days" are the Tribulation period, which we are not currently living in but may be on the brink of entering. (The church will be raptured before the world enters the Tribulation.) Deuteronomy 31:29 also uses "latter days" as a reference to the Tribulation when it says, "Evil will befall you in the latter days."

Jeremiah refers to the Tribulation as the "latter days" twice (30:24; 48:47). Daniel also uses it this way: "There is a God in heaven who reveals mysteries, and He has made known to King Nebuchadnezzar what will take place in the latter days" (Daniel 2:28). Daniel commences to reveal God's plan for the future, which includes events that will unfold in the Tribulation period. This is also true in Daniel 10:14: "Now I have come to give you an understanding of what will happen to your people in the latter days, for the vision pertains to the days yet future."

The prophet Daniel uses a whole cluster of other "latter day" terms that all refer to the Tribulation period, which prepares the way for the kingdom reign of the Messiah. Terms like "the end of time" (Daniel 8:17; 12:4), "the end time" (Daniel 12:9), and "the end of the age" (Daniel 12:13) speak of the end-time Tribulation period, which is yet to come. These terms are used three times in Daniel 12, which references "a time of distress [tribulation] such as never occurred since there was a nation until that time" (12:1). Thus, the entire context is once again a reference to the coming Tribulation.

Daniel 12:4 says the teachings about the end times in Daniel will be sealed up for the Jewish people until "the end of time." Many commentators have long believed that shortly before Christ's return, the world would experience an increase in the speed of travel and an explosion of information according to Daniel 12:4, which says, "Many will go back and forth, and knowledge will increase." No one would quarrel with the fact that the last 100 years has indeed witnessed an exponential increase in both the speed of travel and the accumulation of knowledge. This would seem to be a sign in our time that the end is near. But is this really what Daniel is saying in the passage? Probably not. The meaning of the Hebrew words and the grammar do not support such a view.

Charles Ryrie provides the correct interpretation of the passage in his *Ryrie Study Bible* when he says, "As the end approaches, people will travel about seeking to discover what the future holds" (Ryrie, p. 1332)—not just people in general, but the Jewish people in particular. This means that during the Tribulation, many Jews will study the book of Daniel to try to find out what is happening. Harry Bultema says, "The movement of to and fro may refer to that of the eyes through leaves....Thus considered, it seems to us that the text here speaks of the diligent search of the Scripture at the end of time" (Bultema, p. 349). Thus, the scope would be limited to the future time of the Tribulation and would not include our own day.

WHAT DAYS ARE WE IN NOW?

So are we living in the last days? Yes and no. We are currently living in the last days because we are in the church age, which is called the "last days," "last times," and "last time." However, we are not in the last days as the Old Testament speaks of Israel. The Old Testament terms "latter days," "last days," "latter years," "end of time," and "end of the age" all refer to a time when Israel is in her time of tribulation, known also as the seventieth week of Daniel. This is a future time that we could very well be on the verge of entering. Perhaps we are seeing the stage being set for last-days or end-time events of the Tribulation. But we are not yet in those times.

—THOMAS ICE

BIBLIOGRAPHY

Bultema, Harry. *Commentary on Daniel.* Grand Rapids: Kregel, 1988.

Ryrie, Charles C. *Ryrie Study Bible.* Chicago: Moody Press, 1978.

LAST TRUMPET

In 1 Corinthians 15:52 the apostle Paul teaches that the rapture will take place at the last trumpet. Opponents of pretribulationism say the "last trumpet" statement in this passage indicates that the rapture cannot take place before the Tribulation. They argue that this mention of the last trumpet relates to events at the end of the Tribulation. However, we will see that Paul's "last trumpet" statement harmonizes perfectly with pretribulationism.

TRUMPETS IN REVELATION

Some midtribulationists and posttribulationists attempt to equate the "last trumpet" in 1 Corinthians 15:52 with the seventh trumpet in Revelation 11:15-19. Revelation 11:15, however, does not say specifically "last trumpet." It says "the seventh angel sounded." The seventh trumpet is the seventh in a series of judgments. The seventh trumpet is the last in a series of trumpet judgments, but it is not the last judgment in the larger series; seven bowl judgments follow.

The "last trumpet" of 1 Corinthians 15:52 is singular, referring to one judgment, not a sequence of seven. Ellicott notes, "There are no sufficient grounds for supposing that there is here any reference to the seventh Apocalyptic trumpet (Rev. xi. 15), or to the seventh and last trumpet" (Ellicott, p. 325). Henry Thiessen agrees:

> If he had thought of this trumpet as one of seven, he would undoubtedly have said something like the following: "For when the trumpets will be sounded and the time comes for the last one to sound, the dead in Christ shall be raised." At any rate, there is no ground for identifying the "trump" in 1 Cor. 15:52 with the seventh trumpet in Rev. 11:15 (Thiessen, p. 56).

In addition, if the seventh trumpet in Revelation 11:15 and the last trumpet in 1 Corinthians 15:52 are supposed to reference the same thing, why do many more months of judgment follow the supposed last trumpet in Revelation 11?

TRUMPETS IN CORINTHIANS AND THESSALONIANS

In looking at 1 Corinthians 15:52, it is clear the context of this passage is the church age, while the context of Revelation 11 is judgment during the Tribulation. First Corinthians 15:52 better harmonizes with 1 Thessalonians 4:16 NASB, which says, "The Lord Himself will descend from heaven with a shout, with the voice of the archangel, and with the trumpet of God, and the dead in Christ will rise first." Both passages speak of the rapture, and judgment is absent from both. The trumpets in both are the last or final command that the Lord gives to the church, resulting in the translation of all believers. J. Dwight Pentecost cites the following reasons as to why the "last trumpet" in 1 Corinthians 15:52 and the "trumpet" of 1 Thessalonians 4:16 are different from any of the trumpet judgments in Revelation.

> (1) The trumpet of 1 Corinthians 15:52...sounds before the wrath of God descends, while...the chronology of Revelation indicates that the trumpet in Revelation 11:15 sounds at the end of the time of wrath....(2) The trumpet that summons the church is called the *trump of God*, while the seventh trump is an angel's trumpet....(3) The trumpet for the church is singular....(4) In 1 Thessalonians 4 the voice associated with the sounding of the trumpet summons the dead and the living and consequently is heard before the resurrection. In the Revelation, while a resurrection is mentioned (11:12), the trumpet does not sound until after the resurrection, showing us that two different events must be in view. (5) The trumpet in 1 Thessalonians issues in blessing, in life, in glory, while the trumpet in Revelation issues in judgment upon the enemies of God. (6) In the Thessalonian passage the trumpet sounds "in a moment, in the twinkling of an eye." In Revelation 10:7 the indication is that the seventh trumpet shall sound over a continued period of time, probably for the duration of the judgments that fall under it, for

John speaks of the angel that shall "begin to sound"....

(7) The trumpet in 1 Thessalonians is distinctly for the church. Since God is dealing with Israel in particular, and Gentiles in general, in the tribulation, this seventh trumpet, which falls in the period of the tribulation, could not have reference to the church without losing the distinctions between the church and Israel. (8) The passage in Revelation depicts a great earthquake in which thousands are slain, and the believing remnant that worships God is stricken with fear. In the Thessalonian passage there is no earthquake mentioned....

(9) While the church will be rewarded at the time of the rapture, yet the reward given to "thy servants the prophets, and to the saints" cannot be that event. The rewarding mentioned in Revelation 11:18 is seen to take place on the earth after the second advent of Christ, following the judgment on His enemies. Since the church is rewarded in the air, following the rapture, these must be two distinct events (Pentecost, pp. 189–91).

THE SIGNAL TO GATHER

The last trumpet in 1 Corinthians 15:52 is the final command that Christ provides for His church when He sends the signal to gather us together for the meeting in the sky that we know as the rapture. The view that equates the last trumpet in 1 Corinthians 15:52 with the seventh trumpet of Revelation does not harmonize in any way.

—Thomas Ice

BIBLIOGRAPHY

Ellicott, Charles J. *St. Paul's First Epistle to the Corinthians*. Minneapolis: James Family Christian Publishers, 1887.

Thiessen, Henry C. *Will the Church Pass Through the Tribulation?* New York: Loizeaux Brothers, 1941.

Pentecost, J. Dwight. *Things to Come*. Grand Rapids: Zondervan, 1958.

Walvoord, John F. *The Thessalonian Epistles*. Grand Rapids: Zondervan, 1967.

LAWLESS ONE

PAUL REFERS TO the "man of lawlessness" (NASB, NIV) or "man of sin" (KJV, NKJV) in 2 Thessalonians 2:3. Paul had taught the Thessalonians that believers (the church) would be caught up (raptured) to meet the Lord in the air prior to the Tribulation, which was part of the day of the Lord. The Thessalonians were alarmed because they had been erroneously informed by word of mouth and by letter that the day of the Lord had begun. Not so, says Paul. He informs them that two prophetic events must occur before the coming of the day of the Lord. First, Paul tells the Thessalonians that the day of the Lord will be preceded by religious apostasy. The visible church will abandon true faith. Second, Paul says that "the man of lawlessness" must be revealed before the coming of the day of the Lord.

The expression "man of lawlessness" is Semitic (Hebrew) in origin. It refers to a person, not a principle. This person is not called "lawless" because he is ignorant of God's law; he is "the lawless one" because he deliberately ignores and violates God's law. He is a ruthless rebel.

THE HISTORICAL BACKGROUND

The term "lawless one" may come from the brutal reign of Antiochus IV, predicted by Daniel the prophet in 8:23-26 and 11:21-35. He was the fourth and the most ruthless of the Syrian rulers to control Palestine. He attempted to unify the country with an aggressive policy of Hellenization combined with eradication of Judaism. He was so egotistical that he adopted the name "Theos Epiphanes," meaning "manifest god." After a humiliating confrontation with the Roman representative Popillius Laenas in Egypt, Antiochus ordered his army to attack Jerusalem on the Sabbath, knowing that pious Jews would not fight to defend themselves. His soldiers plundered and burned the city. In 167 B.C., he accelerated his plan to stamp out Judaism by prohibiting Jews from observing the Sabbath, celebrating religious holidays and festivals, and circumcising their children. He ordered copies of the Torah (the law) destroyed. The penalty for the violation of any of these restrictions was death. An aged scribe named Eleazar was flogged to death because he refused to eat swine's flesh. The ultimate outrage came on December 16, 167 B.C. when he set up pagan altars to Zeus and then offered swine's flesh as a sacrifice to the god Zeus on the burnt altar in the Temple. This despicable act was indeed an "abomination of desolation" and was the spark that ignited the Maccabean revolt. Antiochus Epiphanes was indeed a lawless and brutal dictator who despised and rejected the law of God.

THE BIBLICAL TEXTS

The Old Testament

Hundreds of years before Paul, Daniel predicted that the lawless one would reject God's perfect law and replace it with his own perverted law. In Daniel 7, Daniel identifies four world empires in the imagery of four terrifying beasts. Out of the fourth and most terrifying of the four beasts Daniel describes the growth of ten horns or ten kingdoms and an eleventh horn or final world empire. This eleventh horn or king is different from the previous ten. He is particularly evil and blasphemous and has the audacity to denounce God. "He will speak out against the Most High and wear down the saints of the Highest One, and he will intend to make alterations in times and in law; and they will be given into his hand for a time, times, and half a time" (Daniel 7:25). He will not, however, rule forever because at the end of the Tribulation, God will destroy the kingdom of this usurper and establish His everlasting kingdom (Daniel 7:26-27).

The lawless one or the Antichrist is also described in Daniel 11:36-45. Because the first part of the chapter gives a remarkably accurate and detailed account of Antiochus Epiphanes, some believe that verses 36-45 are a further description of Antiochus. However, though Antiochus is a foreshadowing of this "king," they are not the same individual. Antiochus is past; the king is future. The "king" of Daniel 11:36-45 is the lawless one who will rule over the final world empire. He is a godless despot who "will do as he pleases, and he will exalt and magnify himself above every god

and will speak monstrous things against the God of gods" (verse 36). Though he is successful in gaining dominion over the world, his end is certain. "He will pitch the tents of his royal pavilion between the seas and the beautiful Holy Mountain; yet he will come to his end, and no one will help him" (verse 45). Posing as Christ, the lawless one will make Jerusalem the headquarters for his evil empire, but the Lord Jesus Christ will destroy his kingdom when He returns at the end of the Tribulation to establish the millennial kingdom (Revelation 19:19-20).

The New Testament

In prophecy resources, the man of lawlessness is usually called the Antichrist. The term "antichrist" occurs only four times in Scripture, all in the epistles of John (1 John 2:18,22; 4:3; 2 John 7). John warns his readers that "many antichrists" have already come, and more are to be anticipated. Though John does not have in mind a specific individual, he seems to anticipate an individual who will be a deceiver and blasphemous opponent of Jesus Christ. Generally, anyone or even a movement that denies the full deity and true humanity of Christ is an antichrist. But the Antichrist is more specifically a person who asserts himself on the world scene at the end of the present age and establishes an evil, godless empire for seven years (the Tribulation).

Because of the similarities between "the man of lawlessness" (2 Thessalonians 2:1-12) and "the beast out of the sea" (Revelation 13:1-10), many believe that they are the same individual, the Antichrist. Both are empowered by Satan (2 Thessalonians 2:9; see Revelation 13:4). Both exalt themselves and seek the honor of being worshiped as God (2 Thessalonians 2:4; cf. Revelation 13:5-8). "The man of lawlessness" is called a "son of perdition (destruction)," and "the beast out of the sea" is destined for destruction (2 Thessalonians 2:3; cf. Revelation 17:8; 19:20). However, because the beasts of Daniel 7, which represent empires and not individuals, are combined in "the beast out of the sea" (Revelation 13:2), others argue that the beast out of the sea refers to a government that is antichristian (Hendricksen,

p. 171). It seems best, however, to identify "the beast out of the sea" as the Antichrist who serves Satan ("the dragon") as a counterfeit of Christ and His service to God. "The beast out of the earth" (Revelation 13:11-18) is a false prophet who serves the Antichrist in a way that mimics the ministry of the Holy Spirit on behalf of Christ. This trinity of evil—Satan, the Antichrist, and the False Prophet—comprises Satan's attempt to counterfeit the true Trinity of God the Father, God the Son, and God the Holy Spirit.

THE ADVERSARIAL CAREER

His Work

The mission of the man of lawlessness is subversive. His aim is to destroy and dominate the world. Second Thessalonians 2:4 describes three of his activities. He is the "one who opposes" God. Like his master, Satan, he is the adversary of the Lord. He will "exalt himself over every so-called object of worship." He demonstrates utter contempt for the gods and sacred objects of the world's religions. He "takes his seat in the temple of God, displaying himself as being God." The only god that he recognizes is himself. Paul completes the description of the activity of the man of lawlessness in verses 9 and 10. His coming will be with power, signs, and wonders. Empowered by Satan, he will possess extraordinary power (Greek, *dunamis*). He will perform supernatural signs *(semeia)* and wonders *(terata)*. His pseudo-miracles will be "signs" drawing attention to himself as a miracle worker. The third element in his ploy to deceive will be "wonders." The term "wonder" refers to the astonishing effect a miracle produces on those who view it. Through this impressive display of power, the Antichrist will deceive many. Paul exposes the Antichrist's sinister motives by informing the Thessalonians that his deception is inspired by "wickedness" or "unrighteousness." Unfortunately, the Antichrist will be successful in deceiving unbelievers, and they perish because they reject the truth and believe what is false. Not because he is a cruel tyrant but because He is a just God, the Lord will send a "deluding influence" on those who stubbornly refuse to believe the truth. Instead, they will believe the lies of the Antichrist.

The career of "the man of lawlessness" spans the entire seven-year Tribulation, from the signing of a treaty with Israel to the second coming of the Lord Jesus Christ. Yet his end will be swift and decisive. With symbolic language, Paul says that the Lord will destroy the lawless one "with the breath of His mouth and bring an end by the appearance of His coming" (2 Thessalonians 2:8). The verb *katargeo*, "bring to an end" (NASB), means to "render useless" or "make inoperative." The Lord is so powerful that He only needs to blow on the Antichrist to destroy him, and with His appearance the Lord will bring the godless kingdom of the man of lawlessness to an end.

His Identity

Who is "the man of lawlessness"? He is the Antichrist, the future adversary of Christ. He is "the little horn," bold and audacious enough to blaspheme God (Daniel 7). He is "the arrogant king" of Daniel 11, an egomaniac who temporarily establishes a worldwide kingdom of terror and evil during the Tribulation. He is "the beast out of the sea," who, empowered by Satan, deceives the inhabitants of the earth and forces them to worship Satan and himself. He is "the lawless one" because he despises and rejects the law of God, replacing it with his own godless system of law. He is a satanically inspired egomaniac, the personification of all that is evil, who stands in opposition to God.

—W.H. MARTY

BIBLIOGRAPHY

Benware, Paul. *Understanding End Times Prophecy.* Chicago: Moody Press, 1995.

Bruce, F.F. *1 & 2 Thessalonians. Word Biblical Commentary.* Waco, TX: Word Books, 1982.

Hendricksen, William. *I and II Thessalonians.* Grand Rapids: Baker Books, 1955.

Hubbard, D.A. "Antichrist." In *Evangelical Dictionary of Theology.* Grand Rapids: Baker Books, 1984.

Limbeck, M. "Ανομς." In *Exegetical Dictionary of the New Testament*, Vol.1. Eds. Horst Balz and Gerhard Schneider. Grand Rapids: Eerdmans Publishing Company, 1990.

Morris, Leon. *The First and Second Epistles to the Thessalonians.* NICNT. Grand Rapids: Eerdmans Publishing Company, 1959.

Pentecost, J. Dwight. *Things to Come.* Grand Rapids: Dunham Publishing Company, 1958.

Thompson, J.E.H. "Antichrist." In *The International Standard Bible Encyclopedia,* Vol. 1. Ed. Geoffrey W. Bromiley. Grand Rapids: Eerdmans Publishing Company, 1979.

Verhey, A.D. "Lawless." In *The International Standard Bible Encyclopedia,* Vol. 3. Ed. Geoffrey W. Bromiley. Grand Rapids: Eerdmans Publishing Company, 1986.

LITTLE SCROLL

John's vision of the little scroll provides a dramatic moment in Revelation's narration of the Tribulation events (Revelation 10). The Lord gives this vision to John as momentary relief from the traumatic panorama of the horrors coming on the earth. The expression "little book" or "little scroll" *(biblaridion)* is a diminutive of the Greek word *biblarion,* which comes from the word *biblion,* or scroll.

John has just received a vision of the events that take place on earth when the sixth trumpet is sounded (9:13-21). Revelation 10:1–11:14 is an interlude before the seventh trumpet announces that Christ is soon to reign on His throne (11:15-19). The nations are enraged when they realize that more of God's wrath and judgment is coming.

The vision of the little scroll begins with a strong angel coming from heaven clothed with a cloud and a rainbow (Greek, *iris*) upon his head. This powerful angelic being's face shines like the sun, and his feet like pillars of fire (representing judgment). With his feet positioned on sea and land, he cries out with a loud voice. Seven loud peals of thunder follow. One senses that more judgment is coming on the earth. This angel pictures the anger of God against sinful humanity. When John starts to write about claps of thunder, he is ordered to stop and to seal up the written record at this point. This "recalls the command given to Daniel to seal up his vision until the end (Daniel 12:4). However, this command for John to 'not write' about the peals of thunder differs from the command given to Daniel in that these utter-ances were not to be written at all, whereas Daniel's prophecies were written and were to be sealed until the end" (Couch, p. 251).

THE MYSTERY OF GOD

The angel stands on the sea and the land with his right hand reaching up to heaven. We get the picture that what comes next certainly will have to do with the entire world. By raising his hand to heaven, the angel may be beseeching God to move forward with the impending judgment because of the sins of the earth. Swearing by the God of heaven who lives forever and ever, and who created the heaven and the earth, the angel says, "There will be delay no longer" (Revelation 10:6 NASB). The mystery of God is now finished "as He preached to His servants the prophets" in the Old Testament. What is this mystery? John Walvoord (p. 172) wrote:

> The mystery of God which is declared as subject to fulfillment is unfolded therefore in the Old Testament in the many passages which speak of the establishment of the kingdom of God on earth. The prediction is related to the full manifestation of the divine power, majesty, and holiness of God which will be evident in the glorious return of Christ, the establishment of His millennial kingdom, and the creation of the eternal state which will follow.

The voice from heaven tells John to "take the book which is open" (verse 8) out of the hand of the angel and to eat it. John tells us, "I took the little book out of the angel's hand and ate it, and in my mouth it was sweet as honey; and when I had eaten it, my stomach was made bitter" (verse 10). This is similar to what happened to the prophets Jeremiah and Ezekiel (Jeremiah 15:16; Ezekiel 3:1-3).

The angel warned John, "It will make your stomach bitter, but in your mouth it will be sweet as honey" (verse 9). Being "bitter" in his stomach probably implies that he suffered indigestion from the message of judgment and wrath written in the scroll.

PREACH THE WORD

John was told he had to continue in his prophetic task. "You must prophesy again concerning many peoples and nations and tongues and kings" (verse 11). From this point the judgments in the book of Revelation continue, and the hearts of the people on earth grow even more hardened. Satan intensifies his rebellion, knowing the time of his final defeat is near.

"The testimony to which John is called is that of faithfully delivering the Word of God as it is committed to him" (Walvoord, p. 173). John's message was bittersweet. "It was sweet (Greek, *glukas*) to the believer because it offered hope. But it was bitter (Greek, *pikros*) to the unbeliever because it pronounced judgment" (Hindson, p. 118). The little scroll "is sweetness to know that soon all the promises of God made for ages unto His people in the Prophets will soon be fulfilled. It is sweet to know that soon the earth's rule will pass from the hands of the enemy to the hands of Christ. It is sweet to know that soon the evil age will be ended and the Sabbatic age will begin. O, how sweet and solacing!" (Tucker, p. 232).

—MAL COUCH

BIBLIOGRAPHY

Couch, Mal, gen. ed. *A Bible Handbook to Revelation.* Grand Rapids: Kregel, 2001.

Hindson, Ed. *The Book of Revelation.* Chattanooga: AMG Publishers, 2002.

Scott, Walter. *Exposition of the Revelation of Jesus Christ.* Grand Rapids: Kregel, 1982.

Swete, Henry Barclay. *Commentary on Revelation.* Grand Rapids: Kregel, 1977.

Thomas, Robert L. *Revelation 8–22: An Exegetical Commentary.* Chicago: Moody Press, 1995.

Tucker, W. Leon. *Studies in Revelation.* Grand Rapids: Kregel, 1980.

Walvoord, John F. *The Revelation of Jesus Christ.* Chicago: Moody Press, 1966.

MARK OF THE BEAST

SCRIPTURAL REFERENCES TO the mark of the beast are found in Revelation 13:16-18; 14:9-11; 16:2; 19:20; and 20:4. The purpose of the mark is for commerce and worship, and every person who receives the mark will receive the same kind of mark. According to Revelation 13:16-18, during the Tribulation, every person will be required to receive the mark (Greek, *charagma*) or name of the beast before "buying or selling"—that is, before they can conduct any business transactions. All private and public transactions will require that the parties have this mark. Those who do not have it will be subject to great difficulty, persecution, and death.

According to Revelation 13:16, the mark, a sign of allegiance, touches every part of society. John uses three couplets to emphasize this: the small and the great, the rich and the poor, and the free and the slaves. Every cultural category and subgroup of humanity will be affected. There are no favorites before God or the satanic realm, and no distinction is made between the haves and the have-nots (Osborne, p. 517).

THE PURPOSE OF THE MARK

Giving the mark will be a satanic counterpart to the "sealing" of believers by God in Revelation 7:2-4. Just as the 144,000 in chapter 7 are sealed upon their foreheads to receive divine protection, so in chapter 13 unbelievers are marked or sealed to receive the affirmation and protection of the Antichrist. The seal placed upon the 144,000 witnesses is most likely invisible and for the purposes of protection from the Antichrist. The word used for "seal" is not the same as the word used for "mark." Like everything else the Antichrist does, the mark of the beast is an imitation and mockery. It may also be a parody of the command by God in Deuteronomy 6:8 for the Jews to place the *Shema* on their hands and foreheads (though they were on the left rather than the right hands). Additionally, in Ezekiel 9:4, God required that the Hebrew letter *tau* be placed on the foreheads of all who repented of the nation's idolatry. This signified that those people once again belonged to God. So here in Revelation we see another imitation, parody, or mocking of God's actions by Satan.

To take the mark will signify one's commitment and devotion to the Antichrist, affirming belief by the wearer that Satan, rather than God, is the supreme deity. The mark will be a visible symbol (*on* the individual) of the immense power and worldwide authority and control of the Antichrist. According to Revelation 20:4, thousands of people will refuse to receive the mark and, as a result, will be beheaded. These Tribulation martyrs will be resurrected at the second coming of Christ at the end of the Tribulation and will reign with Him during the millennium.

THE NATURE OF THE MARK

The biblical word for *mark* is similar in meaning to the contemporary words *tattoo* or *brand*. Throughout the Bible, the word for *mark* is used to distinguish or indicate something by a sign. For example, it is used many times in Leviticus as a reference to a mark that renders the subject ceremonially unclean (see Leviticus 13:47-59; 14:34-39). In such instances, it is usually related to leprosy. We have seen that Ezekiel 9:4 uses the word *mark* much as it is used in Revelation: "The LORD said to him, 'Go through the midst of the city, even through the midst of Jerusalem, and put *a mark on the foreheads* of the men who sigh and groan over all the abominations which are being committed in its midst'" (NASB, emphasis added). In this instance, the mark was one of preservation, similar to the way the blood of the Passover lamb on the doorposts spared the Israelites from the death angel (Exodus 12:21-30). In Ezekiel the mark is placed on the forehead, which anticipates John's use of the term in Revelation.

All seven instances of the Greek word for *mark* occur in Revelation and refer to "the mark of the beast." Scholars have offered numerous and diverse suggestions for the nature of the mark, including an official stamp, a wearing of phylacteries, the letter *X* corresponding to the Greek letter that begins the name of Christ, an invisible mark (or some technological variation such as a microchip implant), and a branding implant.

Religious tattooing was widespread in the Roman Empire and the ancient world, and devotees of a particular god or goddess were often branded or marked to show their devotion. Third Maccabees 2:29 speaks of Ptolemy Philopator (222–205 B.C.) marking Jews with an ivy leaf mark, the mark of Dionysiac worship. The word *mark* was also used for the image or name of the emperor on Roman coins, as well as for the seals that were attached to official documents (Mounce, p. 262). Likewise, soldiers captured in battle and disobedient slaves were often branded or marked. None of these is identical to what is occurring in Revelation, but they show that the concept was prevalent.

THE NUMBER 666

The apostle John states in Revelation 13:17 that the mark is "the name of the beast or the number of his name." In verse 18, John writes, "The number is that of a man; and his number is six hundred and sixty-six." The number is that of the Antichrist's name and the numerical value is that of 666. John begins the verse by stating, "Here is wisdom"—that is, understanding and skill are necessary to solve the problem of the number. In a similar manner, Daniel was given instruction and insight into solving the enigmatic number 70 in relation to the prophetic 70 weeks (Daniel 9:22-27; see also 12:10). So during the Tribulation, believers will receive insight and understanding in order to unravel the mystery of the number (Thomas, p. 183).

Probably no other number in the Bible or in history has received as much attention and speculation as 666. There have been numerous competing historic and contemporary solutions for the identification and understanding of the mark and the number, including (1) the names of various world leaders such as the pope, different Roman emperors, Adolf Hitler, Benito Mussolini, and Henry Kissinger; (2) chronological calculations attempting to link the duration of the Antichrist's reign with an empire such as Rome, Islam, or Nazi Germany; (3) apocalyptic riddles that use symbolism and contrast the name of Jesus with the number of the beast; and (4) a symbol for the Antichrist and his forces in which 666 symbolizes rebellion and imperfection (Osborne, pp. 519–20).

Some commentators on Revelation (including recent preterist interpreters), rejecting a futurist view of the book, have argued that the individual referred to was Nero Caesar. The Latin form of his name, transliterated to Hebrew, adds up to 616. However, this view is contrary to the text, requires using a defective spelling, and lacks historical support (Thomas, pp. 184–85, 187–88).

The Bible does not identify the Antichrist or interpret the number. Instead, it says that when the Antichrist is revealed during the Tribulation, the number of his name—the name's equivalent in numbers—will be 666. Any speculation as to the identity of the Antichrist before he is revealed goes beyond the bounds of legitimate prophetic interpretation. The identification is simply not yet available.

When the Antichrist is revealed, the interpretation of the mark will come as a result of understanding five successive comments stated by John in Revelation 13:16-18: the name of the beast, the number of his name, the number of the beast, the number of a man, and the number 666. Following this logical progression, the number is the Antichrist's own name, which has a numerical value of 666 (Fruchtenbaum, p. 205).

The practice of associating numerical values with names and letters is part of an ancient practice called "gematria." In Hebrew, letters of the alphabet were also used as numbers in counting. The Hebrew alphabet has 22 letters, and in the use of gematria, the first nine letters corresponded to the numbers one through nine, the next nine letters corresponded to 10 through 90, and the last four letters to 100 through 400. Every Hebrew name or word had a numerical significance (Osborne, pp. 518–19). The name of the Antichrist, when revealed in the future, will be the numerical equivalent of 666.

In summary, while the Bible does not completely identify the Antichrist or his mark, it does give some precise details about the mark. The mark of the beast will be

1. the Antichrist's mark and identified with his person

2. the actual number 666 and not a representation

3. a mark like a tattoo, visible to the naked eye

4. on the person as opposed to in him or her

5. easily recognized and not questioned

6. received voluntarily and not given through trickery or stealth

7. used after the rapture and not before it

8. used during the second half of the Tribulation

9. necessary for conducting commercial transactions

10. universally received by non-Christians and rejected by Christians

11. a sign of worship and allegiance to the Antichrist

12. promoted by the False Prophet

13. a mark that leads to eternal punishment

The use of this mark by the Antichrist will be one of many attempts to mimic the importance, rule, and work of Jesus Christ during the Tribulation. In that regard, it is interesting to note the words of Paul in Galatians 6:17: "From now on let no one cause trouble for me, for I bear on my body the brandmarks of Jesus."

—TIMOTHY J. DEMY

BIBLIOGRAPHY

Fruchtenbaum, Arnold G. *The Footsteps of the Messiah.* Rev. ed. Tustin, CA: Ariel Ministries, 2003.

Ice, Thomas, and Timothy Demy. *The Truth About the Antichrist and His Kingdom.* Eugene, OR: Harvest House Publishers, 1996.

McGinn, Bernard. *Anti-Christ: Two Thousand Years of the Human Fascination with Evil.* San Francisco: Harper-Collins, 1994.

Mounce, Robert H. *The Book of Revelation.* Grand Rapids: Eerdmans Publishing Company, 1977.

Osborne, Grant. *Revelation.* Grand Rapids: Baker Books, 2002.

Thomas, Robert L. *Revelation 8–22: An Exegetical Commentary.* Chicago: Moody Press, 1995.

Walvoord, John F. *The Revelation of Jesus Christ: A Commentary.* Chicago: Moody Press, 1966.

MARRIAGE OF THE LAMB

THE BIBLE DESCRIBES many weddings. God Himself performed the very first wedding (Genesis 2:18-25). Other famous biblical weddings include that of Jacob to Leah (29:21-25), of Ruth to Boaz (Ruth 4), of Ahab and Jezebel (1 Kings 16:29-31), and the wedding in Cana at which Jesus Christ performed His first miracle (John 2:1-11).

The most wonderful wedding of all is yet to take place. Jesus predicted this wedding through parables (Matthew 22:2; 25:1; Luke 12:35-36), and John described what God showed him through a vision: "Let us be glad and rejoice and give him glory: for the marriage of the Lamb has come, and his wife has made herself ready" (Revelation 19:7 NKJV).

The host of this marriage will be God the Father. He is pictured as preparing it and then sending His servants out to invite the selected guests (Luke 14:16-23). The bridegroom is Jesus Christ, the Father's beloved Son (Matthew 3:17; 17:5). In John 3:27-30, John the Baptist referred to Christ as the bridegroom and to himself as the friend of the bridegroom. In Luke 5:32-35, Jesus, alluding to His coming death, said, "But the days will come when the bridegroom will be taken away from them; then they will fast in those days."

The identity of the bride is also clear. The apostle Paul wrote concerning the church, "For I have betrothed you to one husband, that I may present you as a chaste virgin to Christ" (2 Corinthians 11:2). Later, to the Ephesians he wrote, "Husbands, love your wives, just as Christ also loved the church and gave Himself for her" (Ephesians 5:25).

The New Testament pictures the relationship of Christ to the church according to the pattern of a typical Near Eastern marriage. It consisted of three separate stages.

THE BETROTHAL

First-century marriage contracts were often initiated by the groom's father when both parties were very young (sometimes even prior to birth). He would sign a legal enactment before the proper judge, pledging his son to a chosen girl. The father would then offer the proper dowry payment. Thus, even though the bride had never seen the groom, she was nevertheless betrothed or espoused to him. A New Testament example of this first step is the betrothal of Mary and Joseph (Matthew 1:18).

Thus, the betrothal stage consisted of two parts: the selection of the bride and the payment of the dowry. The marriage of the Lamb is still in its betrothal stage.

- The bride has been selected. "Just as He chose us in Him before the foundation of the world, that we should be holy and without blame before Him in love" (Ephesians 1:4).
- The dowry has been paid. "For you were bought at a price; therefore glorify God in your body and in your spirit, which are God's" (1 Corinthians 6:20; see 1 Peter 1:18-19).

THE PRESENTATION

At the proper time, the father would send servants carrying the proper legal contract to the house of the bride. The servants would then lead the bride to the home of the groom's father. When all was ready, the father of the bride would place her hand in the hand of the groom's father. The groom's father would then place her hand in that of his son. Applying this background to the marriage of the Lamb, the church still awaits this second phase, which will happen at the rapture. "'Let us be glad and rejoice and give Him glory, for the marriage of the Lamb has come, and His wife has made herself ready.' And to her it was granted to be arrayed in fine linen, clean and bright, for the fine linen is the righteous acts of the saints" (Revelation 19:7-8).

Like the betrothal stage, the presentation stage also consists of two parts: the presentation of the proper legal papers, and the procession of the bride to the house of the groom's father.

- The proper legal papers will be shown. "Nevertheless the solid foundation of God stands, having this seal: 'The Lord knows those who are His'" (2 Timothy 2:19).

• The bride will be taken to the Father's home. "In My Father's house are many mansions; if it were not so, I would have told you. I go to prepare a place for you. And if I go and prepare a place for you, I will come again and receive you to Myself, that where I am, there you may be also" (John 14:2-3).

THE CELEBRATION

After the private marriage service was completed, the public marriage supper would begin. Many guests would be invited to this celebration. It was during such a supper that Jesus performed His first miracle (John 2:1-11). Jesus later made reference to this third step when He said, "The kingdom of heaven is like a certain king who arranged a marriage for his son, and sent out his servants to call those who were invited to the wedding" (Matthew 22:2-3; see Luke 12:35-37; 14:16-17).

When does the wedding transpire? It would seem that the wedding service (the presentation stage) will be privately conducted in heaven, perhaps shortly after the *bema* judgment seat of Christ. The wedding supper (the celebration stage) will be publicly conducted on earth shortly after the second coming of Christ.

It is no accident that the Bible describes the millennium as occurring right after the celebration supper has begun (Revelation 19–20). In New Testament times, the length and cost of this supper was determined by the wealth of the father. Therefore, when His beloved Son is married, the Father of all grace (whose wealth is unlimited) will give His Son and the bride a celebration that will last for 1000 years! The marriage supper involves Israel on earth and is a "parabolic picture of the entire millennial age, to which Israel will be invited during the tribulation period" (Pentecost, p. 227).

This wedding will be totally different from all other earthly weddings. First, in an earthly wedding, there can be a last-minute refusal on the part of either the bride or groom. But this cannot happen with the heavenly marriage. The bridegroom has already expressed His great love for His bride (Ephesians 5:25), and He never changes (Hebrews 13:8). And by this time, the heavenly bride has already been

glorified and is sinless and therefore cannot be tempted into changing her mind or losing her love for the bridegroom (Ephesians 5:27; Hebrews 10:14).

Second, in an earthly wedding, a serious legal problem might arise, such as lack of age, or even a previous marriage—but not in the heavenly wedding (see Romans 8:33-39). In an earthly wedding the tragedy of death might intervene—but not in the heavenly wedding. The bride will never die (John 11:26), nor will the bridegroom (Revelation 1:18).

—HAROLD L. WILLMINGTON

BIBLIOGRAPHY

Pentecost, J. Dwight. *Things to Come*. Grand Rapids: Zondervan, 1958.

Thomas, Robert L. *Revelation 8–22: An Exegetical Commentary*. Chicago: Moody Press, 1995.

Walvoord, John F. *The Prophecy Knowledge Handbook*. Wheaton, IL: Victor Books, 1990.

———. *The Revelation of Jesus Christ*. Chicago: Moody Press, 1966.

Willmington, Harold L. *Willmington's Guide to the Bible*. Wheaton, IL: Tyndale House Publishers, 1984.

MATTHEW, ESCHATOLOGY OF

THE GOSPEL OF MATTHEW serves several purposes. It proves Jesus is the Messiah and King in fulfillment of the Old Testament, it explains why the promised kingdom has not yet arrived, and it teaches the church regarding righteous living and the role of the church in this age. The kingdom foreseen in the Old Testament is a major theme of Matthew, so this Gospel contains much prophecy.

THE INCARNATION AND INTRODUCTION TO THE LORD'S MINISTRY (1:1–4:25)

The first allusion to yet-to-be-fulfilled prophecies is found in 1:21, where an angel of the Lord tells Joseph to name the child conceived by the Holy Spirit "Jesus" ("Jehovah saves") because He would "save His people from their sins." This is an allusion to the

Old Testament promise of a son of David who would deliver Israel from its sins and consequent calamities (see Isaiah 9:3-7; 16:5; 22:22; 55:3-4,12-13; Jeremiah 23:5-6; 33:14-16; see especially Psalm 130:8). As the book of Matthew progresses, "Messiah's people" are enlarged to be more than Israel, but the context of Matthew 1:21 describes the Lord's people as the Jews. In the future, God will deliver Israel and make it a great nation.

The name "Immanuel" (1:23) means "God with us." Throughout history, God's desire has been to dwell with mankind. He will accomplish this in the coming kingdom (see Exodus 15:17-18; Psalm 68:16; 132:14). In eternity, the New Jerusalem will have no Temple, for God Himself will be present. The Lord Himself will dwell in the millennial Temple (see Ezekiel 43:1-9). Matthew 1:23 anticipates the coming kingdom. In the meantime, the Lord Jesus, by means of the Holy Spirit, has three present-day temples—the human body (1 Corinthians 6:19), the local church (1 Corinthians 3:16), and the universal church (Ephesians 2:21-22).

The reference in Matthew 2:6 to Micah 5:2 looks ahead to the time when Israel, who will have known only false shepherds, will be governed by the Good Shepherd, the Lord Jesus. This again anticipates the millennium. Even the worship of the magi anticipates the future day when all Gentiles shall acknowledge His dominion.

The eschatological outlook comes into full view in Matthew 3 with John the Baptist's proclamation, "The kingdom of heaven is at hand" (verse 2). Matthew has much to say about "the kingdom," a term he uses some 53 times. The clearest and simplest way to explain the terms *kingdom of heaven* and *kingdom of God* is to say they always look ahead to the coming millennial kingdom and eternity.

John the Baptist proclaimed that the promised kingdom was near. For it to come, Israel needed to repent (see Zechariah 12:10-14). God will not grant entrance to an unrepentant soul. Judgment must precede the coming of the kingdom. The axe was already lying (present tense in the Greek text) at the base of the tree, so the kingdom was near (Matthew 3:10).

The Father's divine pronouncement on the Son (Matthew 3:17) also has prophetic significance. "This is My beloved Son" comes from Psalm 2:7, a psalm that anticipates the Lord's future reign. Isaiah 42:1 is the passage behind the words, "My beloved Son, in whom I am well pleased." Both of the Old Testament references look ahead to the Messiah's millennial reign.

Matthew writes that the ministry of Christ at Capernaum fulfilled Isaiah 9:1-2 (Matthew 4:14-16). The word "fulfill" is used here in the sense of "confirm" because Isaiah 9:1-2 will yet be accomplished in the future. Isaiah goes on to describe the righteous reign of the Messiah in the coming kingdom.

The Lord Jesus sanctioned John's message by proclaiming exactly the same message, "Repent, for the kingdom of heaven is at hand" (4:17). The kingdom was ready to come if only Israel would repent.

THE SERMON ON THE MOUNT (5:1–7:29)

The famous Sermon on the Mount is an ethic for the Lord's adherents to follow until the kingdom will come. It is a guide in the interim. The beatitudes (Matthew 5:3-12) promise blessing on these people because they will enter the future kingdom. The comfort, the inheritance of the Land, seeing God, and the other blessings all portray the coming kingdom—the millennium and eternity.

The references to the kingdom of heaven in 5:19-20 refer to the future reign of the Messiah. Verses 29-30 allude to hell (Greek, *gehenna*) and anticipate the tragic judgment of the lost.

Matthew 6 deals with rewards for the saved. The Lord rewards only good deeds performed to please God the Father. Doing good deeds to win men's approval and applause will not bring rewards. The Jews highly esteemed the acts of righteousness mentioned here by Jesus—giving, praying, and fasting. These activities are representative of all good deeds (6:1).

Jesus continues the subject of prayer with a sample prayer (6:9-13). The first three requests are full of prophecy. "Hallowed be Thy name" should be translated, "Let Your name be hallowed" or "Make Your name to be revered" and looks back to Ezekiel 36:16-36, which anticipates the kingdom age, when the whole world will honor God. In other words, this is a request for God to bring in the age when His name will be honored on earth.

"Thy kingdom come" is a petition requesting God to bring His kingdom to this earth. Some explain this to mean God's kingdom is to come into the hearts of people, but the Scriptures consistently refer to people entering the kingdom, not vice versa.

"Thy will be done on earth as it is in heaven" is another petition for God's kingdom to come to this earth. In other words, the first three requests of this prayer are for the same thing—the reign of God on this earth. God's people today should be praying for this coming kingdom. In Matthew 6:11-13, Jesus prays for the needs of the Lord's followers until the kingdom comes.

John the Baptist said judgment would precede the kingdom, and the Lord refers to the same judgment (still future today) in Matthew 7:13-27. The saved will enter the kingdom, and the lost will go into destruction and fire.

JESUS' MANIFESTATION TO ISRAEL (8:1–11:1)

In Matthew 8–9, the Lord presents a series of miracles that authenticated His person. They also show what the kingdom will be like, for these miracles illustrate what Christ will do to bring about kingdom conditions. Matthew 8:10-12 looks to the future with an emphasis on Gentile salvation. The Lord also anticipated the present age, when many Jews would not believe and therefore would be shut out of the future kingdom.

More problematic is the quotation of Isaiah 53:4 in Matthew 8:17. The healings performed in 8:16 confirmed the ultimate fulfillment for people who will have glorified bodies in the coming reign of Christ. In eternity, all who trust in Christ will know this blessing. People are healed today not because of healing in the atonement but because God sovereignly grants healing. The healing in the atonement will be given to all believers when they receive their eternal bodies.

When Jesus cast demons out of two demoniacs (Matthew 8:28-34), the demons made a very telling statement: "Have you come here to torment us before the time?" The demons evidently knew the lake of fire was prepared for the devil and his angels (25:41), and they knew that time had not yet arrived. It is still future.

In Matthew 10, the Lord Jesus sent His 12 apostles to Israel (to the exclusion of Samaritans and Gentiles) with the same message that John the Baptist and Christ had proclaimed (3:2; 4:17; 10:7): "The kingdom of heaven is at hand." The kingdom was still near, and the contingency of its coming was in the hands of Israel. This explains why the Lord prohibited the apostles from going to the Samaritans and the Gentiles (see also 15:24).

In verses 10:16-25, two difficulties arise. First, Matthew gives no indication the apostles confronted opposition on this ministry tour to the extent Jesus describes. The only plausible answer seems to be that this looks ahead to the post-resurrection ministry of the apostles. During Christ's earthly ministry, they were not brought before governors or kings because of their association with the Lord.

The second problem is one of the most difficult in the Bible. It concerns the Lord's prediction of His return during the lifetime of the disciples. The best solution says this assumes the Lord would be rejected, crucified, and resurrected, just as it happened (the rejection is seen in verses 22,24-25,38). Because Israel continued to spurn Jesus as the Messiah, even after His resurrection, God postponed the kingdom and the seven-year Tribulation just preceding it. During that future Tribulation, Jews will once again minister to Israel, and the same promise will again be valid. The coming of the kingdom and the future Tribulation were contingent on Israel's response to the Lord Jesus.

OPPOSITION TO CHRIST (11:2–13:53)

Matthew 11 contains the Lord's recognition of Israel's rejection of Him as Messiah. Therefore, verses 20-24 predict future eternal judgment on that generation, which would be more severe than the future judgment awaiting

Tyre, Sidon, and Sodom. This passage is important because it shows degrees of torment for the lost. The greater the light, the more severe the judgment (see 12:41-42).

Chapter 12 shows the Lord Jesus would be manifest in weakness until He comes to establish His kingdom (verse 20). This passage also anticipates Gentile salvation (verse 21).

Matthew 10–12 records Israel's rejection of the Lord. In Matthew 13, the Lord responds with a series of parables that inform the disciples that the kingdom would come much later, with a previously unpredicted age preceding it. The first and last parables serve as an introduction and a conclusion.

The six parables intervening present mysteries (new truths) about God's kingdom program. The parable of the wheat and tares (verses 24-30,36-43) teaches the disciples that a new age would intervene before the coming of the kingdom. Good and evil would coexist in this intervening age. After this age, the judgment would take place to determine who would enter the kingdom and who would not (in contrast with John the Baptist's proclamation that this judgment was imminent).

The parable of the mustard seed (verses 31-32) taught the disciples that the number of the heirs of the kingdom would grow gradually, and they would prosper. The kingdom in this age would not suddenly burst in on the civilizations of the world as Daniel predicted. That will occur at the end of the age.

Though disputed, the brief parable of the leaven (verse 33) evidently describes the growth of sin and apostasy until it takes over the world during the Tribulation. Instead of the expected kingdom, evil will reign. Then the kingdom will come.

In verse 44 is the parable of the hidden treasure. The hidden treasure is perhaps the kingdom; Christ may be the one who finds the treasure. The parable portrays the nearness of the kingdom, its subsequent hidden state, and its eventual revelation. The Lord Jesus purchased the field by His death.

The parable of the pearl (verses 45-46) parallels the parable of the hidden treasure. Perhaps the pearl represents the redeemed of all ages. These will enter the future kingdom.

The dragnet (verses 47-50) represents the judgment at the end of the Tribulation preceding the millennium.

These parables teach new truths about the age preceding the coming of the kingdom. This intervening age came about because Israel rejected its Messiah, and God wisely responded to this sad state of affairs with a previously unpredicted age when the gospel would go to the whole world and meet with a mixed response (see Romans 11:25-36).

JESUS' REACTION TO OPPOSITION (13:54–19:2)

The famous prediction that Christ would build His church on the rock (16:18) includes an important prophecy about the future: "The gates of Hades will not overpower it." The term "gates of Hades" is a reference to death, the greatest earthly evidence of Satan's power. But this will be overcome by Christ's resurrection and the future resurrection of the church! Death itself will not overpower the church.

The transfiguration (16:28–17:8) assures the future coming of the Lord's kingdom. The promise of 16:28 is fulfilled in 17:1-8. Second Peter 1:16-18 confirms that this is the correct interpretation. The Lord is glorified, Moses and Elijah represent saved saints with the Lord in glory, and Peter, James, and John illustrate the earthly, physical bodies of those who will inherit Christ's earthly kingdom.

Elijah is going to come before the Lord appears (17:11). Potentially, John the Baptist was Elijah, but because he did not fulfill the prophecy of Malachi 4:5-6, he did not become the predicted Elijah. A future person in the spirit and power of Elijah will fulfill the prophecies about the coming Elijah (Isaiah 40:3; Malachi 3:1; 4:5-6).

JESUS' PRESENTATION TO AND REJECTION BY ISRAEL (19:3–25:46)

The parable of the laborers in the vineyard (20:1-16) illustrates future rewards for the Lord's followers who use their opportunities to serve Him (see 19:27-30), but that is not its primary emphasis. The great stress is on the equality of Jew and Gentile in this age (verse 11). Those who have the contracts illustrate

Israel with its covenants; those without an agreement are Gentiles. Thus the first are last and the last first (19:30; 20:16), so all are equal (see Ephesians 3:1-6).

Matthew 22:1-14 compares the future kingdom to a wedding feast, the culmination of the wedding process in Judaism. The second section of the parable (verses 11-14) shows that the Lord Jesus is going to demand proper apparel for entrance into the kingdom. Someone may assume from the wide-open invitation that any kind of dress would be appropriate, but everyone without God's imputed righteousness as clothing will not enter the future kingdom on earth.

The infamous conundrum presented by the Sadducees concerning marriage in heaven (22:23-28) gave the Lord an opportunity to discuss the future resurrection of the saints (verses 29-32). This is the crucial part of His reply: "I am the God of Abraham, and the God of Isaac, and the God of Jacob." This is not looking at the present state of Abraham, Isaac, and Jacob. Such an argument would prove their present spiritual existence but would not confirm their resurrection. Jesus' quote of Exodus 3:6 looks back to God's promise that He would give the land of Canaan to *them* and their seed. Of course, these promises were never fulfilled to the patriarchs personally, so they must be resurrected for God to keep His word. Jesus muzzled the Sadducees with his response.

In Matthew 22:43-45, the Lord quoted Psalm 110:1, which anticipates the Messiah's present session and future reign on earth. It indicates that the Messiah, David's Son, would be greater than David. This "Lord" is now at the right hand of the Father until the kingdom comes. It anticipates His future reign (see Hebrews 10:12-13).

After the scorching indictment of the scribes and Pharisees (Matthew 23:1-36) and His tragic lament (23:37-38), the Lord states, "I say to you, from now on you shall not see Me, until you say, 'Blessed is He who comes in the name of the Lord!'" These words are from Psalm 118:26 and anticipate Israel's response to the Messiah in the future. All of Israel's hopes rest on the adverb "until." One

day Israel will repent, and then the kingdom will come. The coming of the kingdom is contingent on Israel's repentance (see Zechariah 12:8-14).

Matthew 24–25 records the Lord's most extended prophetic discourse. It begins with a startling statement concerning the Temple: "Truly I say to you, not one stone here shall be left upon another, which will not be torn down" (24:2). This was perplexing and disconcerting to the disciples, and they asked Jesus, "Tell us when will these things be, and what will be the sign of Your coming, and of the end of the age?" To the disciples all three of these questions revolved around their viewpoint of the Lord's coming as prophesied in Zechariah 14:1-4. To the disciples, the destruction of Jerusalem and the coming of Yahweh to deliver Israel comprised one relatively brief movement of history because of that prophecy.

The Lord's response began with a warning against being deceived (24:4-6). The intervening age would be characterized by false teachers and wars, but those things did not mark the end of the age.

Verse 8 contains the next time marker: "the beginning of birth pangs." In other words, the end of this age will see an increase in wars between nations and between kingdoms, in famines and earthquakes throughout the world.

The final period of the Tribulation will include universal persecution of Christians (those who become saved *during* the Tribulation), hatred, false prophets, lawlessness, and the proclamation of the kingdom to the entire world (24:9-14). This paragraph is a simple thumbnail sketch of the final seven years before Christ's second advent.

The outstanding characteristic of the Tribulation will be the abomination of desolation, predicted in Daniel 9:27; 11:31; and 12:11 (see also 8:13). This abomination, in all probability, is an idol set up in the Temple by the man of sin. It is still future and is probably referred to in Revelation 13:14-15. As Paul notes in 2 Thessalonians 2:3-4, this is the clearest indication that the Great Tribulation has begun. The abomination will precipitate unprecedented tribulation, and the Lord orders His followers to flee for their lives when the abomination occurs.

False messiahs, though they will perform very convincing miracles, can be unmasked because the next appearance of the Son of Man will be so splendorous no one will miss it. It will be as startling as a sky-spanning lightning bolt (24:23-27).

The Lord will presage His return with cataclysms in stellar bodies and some special manifestations of Himself in the heavens (possibly the shekinah glory of the Old Testament Jehovah; see Zechariah 12:10).

Finally, in fulfillment of Daniel 7:13; Isaiah 27:10; and Zechariah 9:14, the Lord will return with the sound of a trumpet to regather His chosen ones to Himself on earth (Matthew 24:29-31).

During the Tribulation period, earthlings will be so preoccupied with activities of daily life that they will be as unprepared for the return of Christ as the generation of Noah was suddenly overwhelmed by the flood. The individuals being taken in 24:40-41 are not taken in the rapture but are removed by death from the earth, so they will not enter the kingdom after the end of the Tribulation. As the victims of the flood were taken in that cataclysm, so these will be removed in judgment (Matthew 24:37-41).

In Matthew 24:42–25:30, the Lord presents several parables to illustrate the judgment of saved and lost, focusing on who will enter the coming kingdom and who will be put to death and cast into hell. Some of these parables also picture rewards for the saved that will involve the blessing of responsibilities and position during the Lord's reign on earth.

The judgment described in 25:31-46 is not the Great White Throne judgment prophesied in Revelation 20:11-15. These are two distinct judgments separated by 1000 years. The Great White Throne assize takes place after the millennial reign of Christ when the lost in hades (hell) will be cast into the eternal flames of the lake of fire (Revelation 20:14-15). Matthew 25:31-46 predicts the judgment of Gentiles who will be alive at the end of the Tribulation. The judgment of living Jews will precede this

one (see Romans 2:9-10; Ezekiel 20:33-44; Luke 19:27).

Three groups are involved in this picture—sheep (saved Gentiles), goats (lost Gentiles), and "my brethren" (saved Jews). Anti-Semitism will be at such a fever pitch during the Tribulation that rendering aid to a Jew could be life-threatening, especially to a Jew without the mark of the beast. The destiny of the saved is the kingdom that God intended for man since the creation of the world (25:34).

THE CRUCIFIXION AND RESURRECTION (26:1–28:20)

Significantly, God's future kingdom for mankind was in the Lord's mind even when He instituted the Lord's table (Matthew 26:29). On this occasion, Christ referred to literal fruit that will be enjoyed in the literal future kingdom.

When the high priest confronted Jesus and put Him under oath (Matthew 26:63-64), Jesus again referred to Himself as the Son of Man, a messianic term derived from Daniel 7:13-14. Jesus then described Himself as sitting at the right hand of the Father in accordance to Psalm 110:1, a position He now occupies (Hebrews 10:12-13). From that position He will return in the clouds of heaven (Daniel 7:13). This coming is still future and precedes His reign on earth.

The final prophecy of the Lord Jesus in the Gospel of Matthew is implied in the last verse. In Matthew 28:20, Christ promised to be with His followers until the end of this age, strongly suggesting what He had clearly prophesied earlier: This age will conclude with His glorious return. Not surprisingly, the early church proclaimed, "Maranatha!"

—STANLEY D. TOUSSAINT

BIBLIOGRAPHY

Fruchtenbaum, Arnold G. *The Footsteps of the Messiah.* Tustin, CA: Ariel Press, 1982.

Larson, David. *Jews, Gentiles and the Church.* Grand Rapids: Discovery House, 1995.

McClain, Alva J. *The Greatness of the Kingdom.* Grand Rapids: Zondervan, 1959.

Pentecost, J. Dwight. *Things to Come.* Findlay, OH: Dunham, 1958.

Toussaint, Stanley D. *Behold the King*. Portland, OR: Multnomah Press, 1980.

Walvoord, John F. *Matthew, Thy Kingdom Come*. Chicago: Moody Press, 1974.

MERCY OF GOD

To fully trust or appreciate God, one must understand that He is a merciful God, full of compassion and love for His creation. Those who reject the free gift of salvation from His Son, or who take note only of His acts of judgment, can never truly understand God. For centuries the Hebrew prophets used God's own description of Himself to Moses to teach the people about His merciful nature.

> The LORD, the LORD God, merciful and gracious, longsuffering, and abounding in goodness and truth, keeping mercy for thousands, forgiving iniquity and transgression and sin…(Exodus 34:6-7 NKJV).

Anyone familiar with the Bible will realize that God wants man to know Him as merciful. David, who probably knew God better than most other writers of Scripture, used that term to describe Him hundreds of times in the Psalms. In fact, in Psalm 136 alone, David states "His mercy endures forever" 26 times!

Nowhere is that mercy seen more clearly than in the book of Revelation. That statement may come as a bit of a shock to those who may be familiar with some of Revelation's more horrendous passages that describe the various judgments that are to be unleashed upon the earth during the seven-year Tribulation. It is during this period that God will pour out His wrath upon those who refuse to believe in Him and who instead turn to the Antichrist and even Satan himself in worship. Yet simultaneously, the mercy of God will also be made abundantly clear.

God is fully aware that the decision we make concerning Him and His Son will determine our eternal destiny. And He also knows that it is His love and mercy that ultimately attract us to Him. During the time of the Great Tribulation, God will demonstrate His incredible mercy through a number of specific acts. Prior to the beginning of the Tribulation, Jesus will first rapture all believers up to heaven to His Father's house in order to protect them from the wrath to come—thus keeping the promise He made in John 14:1-3:

> Let not your heart be troubled; you believe in God, believe also in Me. In My Father's house are many mansions; if it were not so, I would have told you. I go to prepare a place for you. And if I go and prepare a place for you, I will come again and receive you to Myself; that where I am, there you may be also.

In Revelation 3:10 God reinforces the point that He will protect those who have accepted Jesus as their Lord and Savior from the trials of the Tribulation:

> Because you have kept My command to persevere, I also will keep you from the hour of trial which shall come upon the whole world, to test those who dwell on the earth.

Beginning in Revelation 4, as an illustration, the apostle John himself is "raptured" from the earth before the Tribulation begins and is able to view its sobering events from the safety of heaven.

Not only will God protect His church from the impending judgments as a result of the rapture, He has devised six remarkable ways to demonstrate His mercy to the men and women who suddenly find themselves left behind. God will intervene supernaturally in the affairs of the world in an attempt to make His message of salvation plain to all.

THE HOLY SPIRIT

According to the prophet Joel, there will be an outpouring of the Holy Spirit upon the earth, resulting in the salvation of a tremendous number of souls. This will occur simultaneously with the catastrophic events of the Tribulation.

> I will pour out My Spirit on all flesh; your sons and your daughters shall prophesy, your old men shall dream

dreams, your young men shall see visions. And also on My menservants and on My maidservants I will pour out My Spirit in those days. And I will show wonders in the heavens and in the earth: Blood and fire and pillars of smoke. The sun shall be turned into darkness, and the moon into blood, before the coming of the great and awesome day of the LORD. And it shall come to pass that whoever calls on the name of the LORD shall be saved (Joel 2:28-32).

THE 144,000

Revelation 7 indicates there will be 144,000 evangelists sent to the four corners of the world during the Tribulation. These evangelists will go out in power and preach God's message during the most chaotic period in earth's history. And what will be the results of their labors?

Behold, a great multitude which no one could number, of all nations, tribes, peoples, and tongues, standing before the throne and before the Lamb, clothed with white robes, with palm branches in their hands (Revelation 7:9).

As Revelation 7:14 indicates, this multitude that can't be numbered "come out of the great tribulation." Who but a loving, merciful God could plan in advance to raise up 144,000 evangelists for the purpose of procuring the largest soul harvest in history?

THE TWO WITNESSES

In addition to the 144,000 witnesses, two additional witnesses for the Lord who have extraordinary powers will appear before the world during the first three-and-a-half years of the Tribulation.

I will give power to my two witnesses, and they will prophesy one thousand two hundred and sixty days, clothed in sackcloth (Revelation 11:3).

These two men will not only prophesy but also call the world's attention to the choice every human being must make. Their supernatural powers will closely mirror those of Moses and Elijah, which leads many scholars to believe that these two individuals may actually be Moses and Elijah. In any event, their powerful testimony of the Lord, backed up by astonishing supernatural feats (see Revelation 11:5-6), will be seen and heard worldwide. This is just one more example of God's incredible grace and mercy as He moves to draw the unsaved to Him.

A PLACE FOR ISRAEL

As bad as the first half of the Tribulation is, the second half will be far worse. The Antichrist will take control of the world and will attempt to destroy the Jewish nation. So begins the worst persecution in history. But once again, God will step in. As He indicates in Revelation 12, God will supernaturally protect the Jews and lead them into the wilderness to protect them from the Antichrist's satanic attack. Many believe they'll head to Petra, the rock city in Edom. As they do so, God will make good on His promise to protect His people and in the process, once again, demonstrate His everlasting mercy.

AN ANGEL TO PROCLAIM THE GOSPEL

For the first time in history, God will send a powerful angel to preach the good news of Jesus Christ.

Then I saw another angel flying in the midst of heaven, having the everlasting gospel to preach to those who dwell on the earth—to every nation, tribe, tongue, and people—saying with a loud voice, "Fear God and give glory to Him, for the hour of His judgment has come" (Revelation 14:6-7).

In the past, God has chosen to present His message through people. But now, as the fiery Tribulation is drawing to a close, He sends an angel to do the work. Why? Because the millennial kingdom is just around the corner, and God wants to make sure everyone has an opportunity to hear the gospel and make a wise spiritual decision.

A WARNING TO FLEE BABYLON

At the very end of the Tribulation, just before the battle of Armageddon and the return of Jesus, God will do one more thing to demonstrate His mercy. He will warn those with ears to hear to leave Babylon before the sword of judgment falls:

> Come out of her, my people, lest you share in her sins, and lest you receive of her plagues (Revelation 18:4).

Babylon, the commercial and governmental headquarters of the Antichrist's regime, will be destroyed just before the return of Christ. Even at the eleventh hour, God will be inviting anyone who will hear, "Come to Me." All of these examples clearly demonstrate a God who does not revel in destruction, but rather, delights in mercy.

—TIM LaHAYE

BIBLIOGRAPHY

Hindson, Ed. *The Book of Revelation.* Chattanooga: AMG Publishers, 2002.

LaHaye, Tim. *The Merciful God of Prophecy.* New York: Warner Books, 2002.

Ryrie, Charles C. *The Grace of God.* Chicago: Moody Press, 1963.

Walvoord, John F. *The Revelation of Jesus Christ.* Chicago: Moody Press, 1966.

MESSIANIC KINGDOM

The prophecies regarding Israel's messianic kingdom are the high point of Old Testament prophecy. Every writing prophet except Jonah, Nahum, Habakkuk, and Malachi referenced it. To spiritualize and allegorize away such a great amount of Scripture is to ignore commonsense rules of interpretation. We have no reason to spiritualize any of these prophecies, just as we have no reason to spiritualize prophecies about the Messiah's virgin birth, His birth in Bethlehem, His crucifixion, or His physical resurrection.

ISRAEL'S REGENERATION

Israel's final restoration is based on four covenants. In Jeremiah 31:31-34, God promises the regeneration of Israel through the New Covenant.

Of the five Jewish covenants, only the Mosaic covenant was conditional. God faithfully kept His terms of the covenant, but Israel did not, so the Mosaic covenant was broken. The Mosaic covenant showed the standard of righteousness that the law demanded, but it could never impart the power to keep it. That problem will be rectified in the New Covenant through regeneration, which will provide individuals with the internal power necessary to meet and to keep the righteous standards of the law (31:33). The result of the New Covenant will be a total national regeneration of Israel. In the messianic kingdom, every Jew will know the Lord. The sins of Israel will be forgiven and forgotten. The kingdom will include Gentile unbelievers, but not Jewish unbelievers.

Israel's regeneration through the New Covenant is a common Old Testament theme (Isaiah 29:22-24; 30:18-22; 44:1-5; 45:17; Jeremiah 24:7; 50:19-20; Ezekiel 11:19-20; 36:25-27; Hosea 1:10–2:1; 14:4-8; Joel 2:28-32; Micah 7:18-20; Zephaniah 3:9-13), and the New Testament mentions it in Romans 11:25-27.

ISRAEL'S REGATHERING

In addition to restoring Israel, God will regather the Jewish people to their own land. This promise is based on the Land covenant of Deuteronomy 29:1–30:20. The passage begins with a clear statement that the Land covenant is distinct and different from the Mosaic covenant. The former is eternal and unconditional, while the latter is both temporal and conditional.

In the Land covenant, Moses summarizes Israel's 40 years of wilderness wandering and warns the people against turning away from the Lord. Then he proceeds to say that they will do exactly that, resulting in their dispersion out of the Land into the Gentile nations to endure a long period of many persecutions. But this dispersion will not be permanent. After the long period of persecution described in chapter 29, the Lord will regenerate and then regather Israel from all over the world.

The regathering of Israel is another high point of prophetic revelation (Isaiah 43:5-7; Jeremiah 16:14-18.)

ISRAEL'S POSSESSION OF THE LAND

The Abrahamic covenant promises that Israel will once again possess the Promised Land.

In Genesis 12:1-3, God initiated His covenant with Abram and told him to go to a land that God would show him. When he arrived, God again revealed Himself to Abram (Genesis 12:7) and promised that his seed would possess it. In Genesis 13:14-17, God promises that Abram personally (as well as Abram's seed) will possess the Land. Yet Abram died having never possessed any part of it except for a few wells and a burial cave, which he had to purchase. In order for God to fulfill His promise to Abram, two things have to occur: Abram must be resurrected, and the Land must be restored to Israel.

When God confirmed the covenant in Genesis 15:12-21, He gave exact boundaries. God confirmed the covenant again to Isaac in Genesis 26:2-5 and to Jacob in Genesis 28:13-15.

ISRAEL'S REESTABLISHMENT OF THE DAVIDIC THRONE

The fourth part of Israel's final restoration is the reestablishment of the Davidic throne. This is based upon the Davidic covenant in 2 Samuel 7:11-16 and 1 Chronicles 17:10-14. The emphasis in the first account is on David's son Solomon, but the emphasis in the second passage is on the Messiah. This descendant of David, the Messiah, will build God a Temple, the millennial Temple, and His throne will be established forever.

This fourth facet of the messianic kingdom is further developed by the Jewish prophets in Isaiah 9:6-7; Jeremiah 23:5-6; Amos 9:11-12; and Luke 1:32-33.

OTHER CHARACTERISTICS OF THE KINGDOM

The first four aspects of the messianic kingdom—Israel's regeneration and regathering, her possession of the Land, and the reestablishment of the Davidic throne—are all connected to specific covenants. Other characteristics of the kingdom are not necessarily connected to specific covenants. For example, first, Israel will be reunited as a nation, never to be divided into separate kingdoms again (Jeremiah 3:18; Ezekiel 37:15-23). Second, Israel will be the center of Gentile attention because of the great work that God will do to Israel (Isaiah 14:1-2; 49:22-23; 60:1-3; 61:4-9; Micah 7:14-17; Zechariah 8:23). And third, the messianic kingdom will include various characteristics of righteousness, holiness, peace, security, joy, and gladness (Isaiah 32:16-20; 35:5-10; 51:3; 55:12-13; 61:10-11).

THE DIMENSIONS OF THE KINGDOM

For the first time in Israel's history, the Jews will possess and settle in all of the Promised Land, and it will again be subdivided into the 12 tribal divisions. But these tribal divisions will be different than those described in the book of Joshua. Ezekiel 47:13–48:35 sets out the boundaries of the Land during the millennium. The northern boundary will extend from the Mediterranean Sea to the Euphrates River, incorporating much of modern-day Lebanon and parts of modern Syria. The eastern border will incorporate the Golan Heights and portions of Syria almost up to Damascus, continuing south to the Jordan River where it exits from the Sea of Galilee. The border will then run along the river to the southern end of the Dead Sea. The southern border will incorporate the Negev and parts of Sinai along the Brook of Egypt to the Mediterranean Sea. And the Mediterranean Sea will serve as the western border.

In the center of the country will be the millennial mountain of Jehovah's house. The mountain of the holy oblation will be situated at the south of Judah's border and will serve as the dividing line between the seven northern tribes and the five southern tribes. At that time Jerusalem will be given a new name: *Adonai Shammah*, which means "Jehovah is there," and the Messiah will personally reign from the city.

—ARNOLD FRUCHTENBAUM

BIBLIOGRAPHY

Fruchtenbaum, Arnold. *Israelology: The Missing Link in Systematic Theology.* Tustin, CA: Ariel Ministries, 1992.

Kaiser, Walter. *Towards an Old Testament Theology.* Grand Rapids: Zondervan, 1982.

Price, Randall. *Jerusalem in Prophecy.* Eugene, OR: Harvest House Publishers, 1998.

Walvoord, John F. *Major Bible Prophecies.* Grand Rapids: Zondervan, 1993.

MESSIANIC PROPHECY

JESUS CHRIST IS THE SOURCE and main subject of Bible prophecy. The most dramatic prophecies in all the Bible point to the Messiah—the Savior who would both suffer and reign. Many of these ancient prophecies have been precisely fulfilled and point to only one person—Jesus of Nazareth.

After His resurrection, Jesus told His disciples that "all things must be fulfilled, which were written in the law of Moses, and in the prophets, and in the psalms, concerning me" (Luke 24:44 KJV). Christ Himself then taught the disciples which Old Testament scriptures predicted His life and ministry. Luke 24:45 says, "Then opened he their understanding, that they might understand the scriptures."

The Lord Himself instructed the New Testament writers regarding biblical prophecies and their fulfillment. The threefold designation—law, prophets, and psalms—refers to the three major divisions of the Hebrew Bible. The entire Old Testament predicted Christ's life, ministry, death, and resurrection. Therefore, the preaching of the early Christian disciples was filled with references to Old Testament prophecies and their fulfillment in the person of Jesus Christ. Matthew's Gospel alone makes 65 references to the Old Testament, emphasizing its fulfillment in Christ.

The Hebrew word for *messiah* comes from the word *meshiach*, meaning to "anoint" for consecration and service. In Psalm 2, the Messiah (the anointed one) is pictured as both King of Israel and God's Son. This passage confirms the association of Jesus in the New Testament with the Messiah in the Old Testament. The Greek New Testament equivalent of the Hebrew *meshiach* is *christos* ("anointed"), transliterated "Christ." Jesus Christ is the Messiah.

THE MESSIAH IN PROPHECY

The Old Testament writers ascribe godlike characteristics to the coming Messiah, compelling the reader to see one who is more than a mere man. The Old Testament refers to Him as the Son of David and as the Son of God. Dr. Robert B. Girdlestone has pointed out that the Old Testament makes no definite statement that one person will fulfill all these references, but such is the natural conclusion. Nonetheless, the Old Testament came to a close without one man fulfilling these messianic hopes.

The New Testament based its entire apologetic on the fact that Jesus was the Messiah of the Old Testament and that He conclusively fulfilled many clear predictions. Jesus Himself was always aware that prophecy "must be fulfilled" in Him. He subjected Himself completely to God's direction, and He knew the details of His life and death had to take place because they were predicted in the Word of God. He saw Himself as the culmination of prophecy.

The purpose of messianic prophecy was to make the Messiah known after He had fulfilled the events foretold. It served as a preparatory device to signal His arrival. Bible readers do not all interpret prophecy or its fulfillment the same way. Although a double sense of fulfillment is not impossible, we should not look for a supernatural fulfillment when a common, natural fulfillment is available.

Nor should we look for a fulfillment where none is intended or needed. The New Testament provides the best guideline to determine whether or not a certain event is fulfilled. It tells us where the prophets spoke of Christ and indicates that the Old Testament messianic references refer totally to one person— Jesus of Nazareth.

PREDICTIVE NATURE OF MESSIANIC PROPHECY

Messianic prophecy generally assumes some type of prediction. This discussion uses the word *predict* in the ordinary sense of "foretell." The Greek prefix *pro* indicates both "for" and "before." The prophet tells "for" God, and he tells "before" events will happen. This usage is certified by the New Testament's parallel use of the words "foretell" and "foresee." Peter, in Acts 2:30, speaks of David as a "prophet" because of his "foreseeing" *(proidon)* the resurrection of Christ. It would not make sense to insist that this be translated "forthseeing."

We can see, then, that the prophets were not always restricted to a "local" or immediate fulfillment.

Predictive prophecy must predict the future as only God could know it and bring it to pass, and it must contain a degree of obscurity. This quality of obscurity necessitates a direct fulfillment. Only when prophecy becomes history do we realize that it has been fulfilled. We see its intent dimly at first, but it becomes clear with its fulfillment. The New Testament recognized the value of predictive prophecy and its fulfillment as apologetic evidence to prove the supernatural nature and credibility of Christianity.

THE CENTRAL MESSAGE OF THE OLD TESTAMENT

The messianic prophecies are not merely a "scarlet thread" that runs indiscernibly throughout the Old Testament. They constitute the main theme and underlie the history, the poetry, the prophetic preaching, the national worship, and all the sayings of wisdom. The entire Old Testament is the record of God's promises, and the New Testament is the record of their fulfillment.

After healing the lame man, the apostle Peter addressed the people who had witnessed the miracle and told them he had done this in the name and power of Jesus Christ, "which God before had showed by the mouth of all his prophets" (Acts 3:18). Then, Peter called upon them to "repent...and be converted, that your sins may be blotted out" (Acts 3:19).

According to Peter, the prophets spoke of the sufferings of Christ. Peter reasons that since these prophecies have been fulfilled, men should repent of their sins. Only in Israel had God intervened in human history to bring these prophecies to fulfillment.

When the early Christians began to preach, they declared that Jesus of Nazareth was the promised Messiah of the Old Testament prophecies. The New Testament record reports that they never failed to make these remarkable claims without proving they were true. They insisted that Jesus was the Christ on the basis of three essential arguments:

1. His resurrection
2. their eyewitness account
3. fulfillment of Old Testament prophecy

Within weeks of the resurrection, the early Christians proclaimed that the events in Jesus' life fulfilled specific prophecies. In the first Christian sermon, Peter announced, "This is that which was spoken by the prophet Joel.... David speaketh concerning him...[that] he would raise up Christ to sit on his throne; he seeing this before spake of the resurrection of Christ" (Acts 2:16-31).

This is the New Testament proof of the truthfulness of Christianity. The apostles repeatedly used this approach in much the same way that God's prophets had for centuries. They pointed to fulfilled prophecy as the ultimate proof of the truthfulness of God's Word. In so doing, the New Testament writers urged their listeners to believe the whole message of the gospel of Jesus Christ.

OLD TESTAMENT PROPHECIES FULFILLED IN CHRIST

The Old Testament is filled with prophecies about the human race, the nation of Israel, and future events in general. But the most important prophecies are those that point to the coming of Christ. These are not merely isolated "proof texts." The whole of the Old Testament points the way to a coming future Messiah.

The laws of the Old Testament established the divine principle of righteousness. The history of Israel shows how God was preparing His people for the coming of the Messiah and how desperately they needed a Savior. The institutions of Old Testament religion (the Temple, priests, and sacrifices) pointed to someone who would fulfill the reality of these symbols. The psalms were not only expressions of worship and praise but also prophecies of the coming Messiah and the messianic age. The Jews recognized many of these predictions were messianic long before Jesus was born. Here is a list of such prophecies:

MESSIANIC PROPHECIES

Old Testament Text	Subject	New Testament Text
Genesis 3:15	Enmity between Eve's seed and the serpent	Luke 22:53
Genesis 3:15	Eve's seed bruises the serpent	Hebrews 2:14; 1 John 3:8
Genesis 12:3; 18:18; 22:18; 26:4	All nations blessed through Abraham	Acts 3:25-26; Galatians 3:8
Genesis 13:15	Abraham's seed inherits his promise	Galatians 3:15-16,19
Genesis 14:18-20; Psalm 110:4	Priesthood like Melchizedek's	Hebrews 5:6; 7:1-28
Genesis 49:10	Ruler from Judah	Luke 1:32-33
Exodus 12:1-13	Passover Lamb	1 Corinthians 5:7; 1 Peter 1:19
Exodus 16:4	Bread from heaven	John 6:31-33
Exodus 24:8	Blood of the covenant	Hebrews 9:11-28
Leviticus 16:15-17	Atoning sacrifice of blood	Romans 3:25; Hebrews 9:11-28; 1 John 2:2
Numbers 21:8-9	Those who look at the one who is lifted up will live	John 3:14-15
Numbers 24:17	Ruler from Jacob	Luke 1:32-33
Numbers 24:17	Star from Jacob	Revelation 22:16
Deuteronomy 18:18	Prophet from God	John 6:14; Acts 3:22-23
Deuteronomy 21:23	Curse for hanging on a tree	Galatians 3:13
Deuteronomy 30:11-14	God's command is near	Romans 10:6-8
2 Samuel 7:14; 1 Chronicles 17:13; Psalm 2:7	God's Son	Matthew 3:17; 17:5; Mark 1:11; 9:7; Luke 3:22; 9:35; Acts 13:33; Hebrews 1:5
2 Samuel 7:16	David's Son	Luke 1:32-33
Psalm 2:9	Rod of iron	Revelation 2:27
Psalm 8:2	Children's praise	Matthew 21:16
Psalm 8:4-5	Lower than the angels	Hebrews 2:5-9
Psalm 8:6	All things under His feet	1 Corinthians 15:27-28; Ephesians 1:22
Psalm 16:8-11	Not abandoned to death	Acts 2:25-32; 13:35-37
Psalm 22:1	Forsaken by God	Matthew 27:46; Mark 15:34

MESSIANIC PROPHECIES

Old Testament Text	Subject	New Testament Text
Psalm 22:7-8	Mocked by a crowd	Matthew 27:29,41-44; Mark 15:18,29-32; Luke 23:35-39
Psalm 22:18	Casting lots for clothing	Matthew 27:35; Mark 15:24; Luke 23:34; John 19:24
Psalm 22:22	Brothers	Hebrews 2:12
Psalm 31:5	"Into Your hand I commit my spirit."	Luke 23:46
Psalm 34:20; Exodus 12:46; Numbers 9:12	No broken bones	John 19:31-36
Psalm 35:19; 69:4	Hatred without a cause	John 15:25
Psalm 40:6-8	Came to do God's will	John 6:38; Hebrews 10:5-9
Psalm 41:9	Betrayal by a friend	John 13:18
Psalm 45:6-7	Characteristics of the king	Hebrews 1:8-9
Psalm 68:18	Ascended and gave gifts	Ephesians 4:7-11
Psalm 69:9	Zeal for God's house	John 2:17
Psalm 69:21	Vinegar for thirst	John 19:29
Psalm 69:25; 109:8	Betrayer's desolation and replacement	Acts 1:20
Psalm 78:2	Parables	Matthew 13:34-35
Psalm 102:25-27	Eternal king	Hebrews 1:10-12
Psalm 110:1	"Sit at My right hand...your enemies a footstool..."	Acts 2:34-35; 1 Corinthians 15:25; Ephesians 1:20-22; Hebrews 1:13; 10:12-13
Psalm 110:1	Lord of David	Matthew 22:41-45; Mark 12:35-37; Luke 20:41-44
Psalm 118:22-23	Rejected cornerstone	Matthew 21:42; Mark 12:10-11; Luke 20:17; Acts 4:10-11; 1 Peter 2:7-8
Psalm 118:26	Comes in the name of the Lord	Matthew 21:9; Mark 11:9; Luke 19:38; John 12:13
Isaiah 6:9-10	Hearing without perceiving	Matthew 13:14-15; Mark 4:12; Luke 8:10; John 12:37-41

MESSIANIC PROPHECIES

Old Testament Text	Subject	New Testament Text
Isaiah 7:14	Virgin birth	Matthew 1:18-23; Luke 1:26-35
Isaiah 8:14; 28:16	A cornerstone and a rock to stumble over	Romans 9:32-33; 1 Peter 2:6-8
Isaiah 9:1-2	People in Galilee see a great light	Matthew 4:13-16
Isaiah 9:6-7; Jeremiah 23:5; 33:15; Ezekiel 37:24-25	David's Son	Luke 1:32-33
Isaiah 9:6	Mighty God	John 1:1,18
Isaiah 9:6-7; Micah 5:5	Prince of Peace	Ephesians 2:14-17
Isaiah 11:1-2	The Spirit of the Lord	Matthew 3:16; Luke 3:21-22
Isaiah 11:10	Root of Jesse rules the Gentiles	Romans 15:12
Isaiah 22:22	Jesus to receive the key of David	Revelation 3:7
Isaiah 35:5-6	Blindness and deafness healed	Matthew 11:4-6; Luke 7:22
Isaiah 40:3-5	Voice in the wilderness	Matthew 3:3; Mark 1:3; Luke 3:4-6; John 1:23
Isaiah 42:1-4	Servant of the Lord	Matthew 12:15-21
Isaiah 45:23	Every knee will bow	Romans 14:11; Philippians 2:10
Isaiah 49:6	Light to the Gentiles	Acts 13:46-47
Isaiah 50:6	Beating and spitting	Matthew 27:26-30; Mark 14:65; 15:15,19; Luke 22:63; John 19:1,3
Isaiah 53:1	"Who has believed our report?"	John 12:38; Romans 10:16
Isaiah 53:3	Rejected	John 1:11
Isaiah 53:4-5	Healing ministry of God's servant	Matthew 8:16-17; Mark 1:32-34; Luke 4:40-41; 1 Peter 2:24
Isaiah 53:7-8	Suffering Lamb of God	John 1:29,36; Acts 8:30-35; 1 Peter 1:19; Revelation 5:6,12
Isaiah 53:9	Sinless servant of God	Hebrews 4:15; 1 Peter 2:22
Isaiah 53:9	Buried in a rich man's grave	Matthew 27:57-60

MESSIANIC PROPHECIES

Old Testament Text	Subject	New Testament Text
Isaiah 53:12	Numbered with transgressors	Matthew 27:38; Mark 15:27-28; Luke 22:37; 23:33; John 19:18
Isaiah 55:3; Ezekiel 37:26	Everlasting covenant	Luke 22:20; 1 Corinthians 11:25
Isaiah 55:3	Blessings of David	Acts 13:34
Isaiah 59:20-21	Deliverer from Zion	Romans 11:26-27
Isaiah 60:1-3	Gentiles worship the Messiah	Matthew 2:11; Romans 15:8-12
Isaiah 61:1-2	Spirit of the Lord	Luke 4:18-21
Isaiah 65:1	Gentiles find the Lord	Romans 10:20
Isaiah 65:2	Israel rejects the Lord	Romans 10:21
Jeremiah 23:6; 33:16	David's Son saves His people	Matthew 1:21
Jeremiah 31:15	Rachel weeping for slain children	Matthew 2:16-18
Jeremiah 31:31-34; 32:40	New Covenant	Luke 22:20; 1 Corinthians 11:25; Hebrews 8:8-12; 10:15-18
Ezekiel 37:24-25; Micah 5:4	Good shepherd	John 10:11,14; Hebrews 13:20; 1 Peter 5:4
Daniel 7:13-14	Son of Man comes	Matthew 24:30; 26:64; Mark 13:26; 14:62; Luke 21:27; Revelation 1:13; 14:14
Daniel 7:27	Everlasting kingdom	Revelation 11:15
Daniel 9:24-26	Timetable for the Messiah	Galatians 4:4
Hosea 11:1	Jesus to return from Egypt	Matthew 2:14-15
Amos 9:11-12	Gentiles believe	Acts 15:13-18
Jonah 1:17	Three days and nights	Matthew 12:39-40
Micah 5:2	Ruler born in Bethlehem	Matthew 2:1-6
Micah 5:2	Eternal ruler	Luke 1:32-33
Zechariah 9:9	King on a donkey	Matthew 21:1-9; Mark 11:1-10; Luke 19:28-38; John 12:12-16
Zechariah 11:12-13	Thirty pieces of silver	Matthew 27:1-10
Zechariah 12:10	Looking on the pierced one	John 19:37; Revelation 1:7

MESSIANIC PROPHECIES

Old Testament Text	Subject	New Testament Text
Zechariah 13:7	Striking the shepherd; the sheep flee	Matthew 26:31,55-56; Mark 14:27,48-50
Malachi 3:1	The messenger	Matthew 11:7-10; Mark 1:2-4; Luke 7:24-27
Malachi 4:5-6	Elijah	Matthew 11:14; 17:11-13; Mark 9:11-13; Luke 1:16-17

The Old Testament included more than 100 distinct prophecies of Christ. They are like pieces of a puzzle. Each presents a distinct element of the Savior's life and ministry, but the whole picture they portray becomes clear only after their fulfillment. They remained obscure until Jesus came and put them all in clear relation to one another. The chance of all these prophecies being fulfilled in the life of one man is one in 84 followed by 131 zeros.

These fulfilled prophecies of Christ are overwhelming evidence of the divine origin of Scripture, the messiahship of Jesus, and the truth of Christianity. The impact of these prophecies and their fulfillment in the Gospels cannot be easily dismissed. The fulfillment of any one prophecy by itself might be explained away, but taken collectively, the evidence they comprise is overwhelming.

Biblical prophecies and their literal fulfillment may fascinate our curiosity and challenge our minds, but ultimately they are designed to bring us to a personal point of faith and decision. If the Bible predicted these things would happen and they actually did happen, then we must take Jesus' claims seriously. If He alone fulfilled these prophecies, then He alone is the Savior, the Son of God.

—Ed Hindson

BIBLIOGRAPHY

Beecher, Willis. *The Prophets and the Promise*. Grand Rapids: Baker Books, 1978.

Freeman, Hobart. *An Introduction to the Old Testament Prophets*. Chicago: Moody Press, 1968.

Hindson, Ed, and Ed Dobson, eds. *Knowing Jesus Study Bible*. Grand Rapids: Zondervan, 1999.

Payne, J. Barton. *Encyclopedia of Biblical Prophecy*. Grand Rapids: Baker Books, 1980.

Walvoord, John. *The Prophecy Knowledge Handbook*. Wheaton, IL: Victor Books, 1990.

Wood, Leon. *The Prophets of Israel*. Grand Rapids: Baker Books, 1989.

Young, Edward. *My Servants the Prophets*. Grand Rapids: Eerdmans Publishing Company, 1952.

MIDTRIBULATIONISM

According to the midtribulation rapture position, the rapture of the church will occur before the wrath of God falls upon the earth during the last half of the Tribulation period, and it happens after "man's wrath against man" during the first half. The rapture will fulfill Christ's promise in Revelation 3:10 to remove the church from the hour of trial that will come upon the whole world. It occurs in the middle of the seventieth week and is preceded by the initial signs of the Tribulation. Some proponents find their support for this theory in Revelation 11:11-15; others find it in Revelation 14:1. This view agrees with the pretribulation view teaching that God removes the church before pouring out His wrath. Midtribulationists and pretribulationists disagree over the timing of the rapture, the distinction between the wrath of God and man's wrath against man, and the issue of an imminent (at any moment) rapture of the church.

According to the midtribulation position, the seventieth week of Daniel (Daniel 9:24-27) will last seven years. At the beginning of that period, the Antichrist will enter into a treaty that guarantees freedom of religion to Israel, and he will keep that promise for three and one-half years. That first half of the Tribulation is known as the "beginning of sorrows" (Matthew 24:8). This period includes the chaos and tribulation of all seven seal judgments and the first six trumpet judgments of Revelation. It also includes two of the first three woes described in Revelation 9 and 11:14. The seals, the first six trumpets, and the first two woes are seen as excruciating agonies much like what the people of God have endured throughout the ages (Acts 14:22; Romans 8:18; 2 Corinthians 4:17; 1 Peter 1:6). The Lord Himself endured the cross (Hebrews 12:2), and according to tradition, both Peter and Paul suffered agonizing deaths. So too, believers alive at this time will suffer the consequences of what midtribulation rapturists believe to be man's wrath against man.

The adherents of this theory hold to the promise that the true believer will be saved from the wrath that is to come (1 Thessalonians 1:10; 5:9; Romans 5:9; Revelation 3:10). Citing Daniel 7:25; 12:7,11; and Revelation 13:5, midtribulationists contend that the wrath of God lasts not seven years but only 3½ years. Nothing that precedes this final 3½-year period is regarded as the wrath of God (Archer, p. 139; Walvoord, p. 100).

THE SEVEN SEALS

The midtribulationists' claim that the wrath of God begins at the seventh trumpet has several problems. First, in Revelation 5:1-10, the seven-sealed scroll is taken from the hand of Him who sits on the throne. The one taking the scroll is said to be the only one worthy to open it. The Lord Himself breaks the seals and unleashes the judgments. Therefore, they signal the wrath of God, not the

wrath of man. Second, those experiencing the sixth seal (Revelation 6:15-17) understand what is happening and from where the wrath emanates. The seal judgments precede the trumpet judgments, so the wrath of God has already begun. Third, the seal judgments are so calamitous that at least one-fourth of the world's population dies as a result of the fourth seal alone. By the time the sixth trumpet sounds, at least one-half of the world's population has perished as a direct result of the judgments. That means that by this time, less than half of the world's population remains. Subtract from that total the number of believers to be raptured, and the remainder would be left to face the wrath of God. This hardly fits with an "hour of temptation, which shall come upon all the world, to try them that dwell upon the earth" (Revelation 3:10 KJV).

THE 144,000 AND THE TWO WITNESSES

Gleason Archer, a proponent of midtribulationism, sees the rapture of the church occurring just prior to the wrath of God being poured out at the midpoint of the seven-year Tribulation. He cites Revelation 14, where the 144,000 are assembled on Mt. Zion, as the likely point of the rapture. He acknowledges that Revelation does not explicitly mention their rapture, but he contends that the description of their condition suggests it (Archer, p. 142). Norman Harrison, who popularized the midtribulation theory in 1941, sees the rapture in Revelation 11:1-13, where the two witnesses are resurrected and ascend to heaven. These two witnesses symbolize a larger company of witnesses—presumably the living church and the resurrected saints (LaHaye, pp. 190–91).

The weakness of this viewpoint is that the two witnesses are real people and not symbols of larger groups. They perform individual activities, and the Bible even describes their clothing. These witnesses are killed by the Antichrist and resurrected. If they were symbolic of a larger group of believers, the implication would be that all believers they symbolize would be martyred. In such a scenario, no believers would be left alive on earth to populate the millennial kingdom (see Matthew 25:31-34). This would also have implications for the 144,000 who have been sealed for protection as detailed in Revelation 7:1-8.

THE LAST TRUMP

J. Oliver Buswell identifies the rapture with the seventh trumpet (Revelation 11:15-19), equating it with 1 Corinthians 15:52 (Archer, p. 143). The connection of the last trump of 1 Corinthians 15:52 with the seventh trumpet of Revelation 11:15 presents difficulties. The trumpet of 1 Corinthians 15:52 heralds the call of Christ to the church to join Him in the air. It is a trumpet of blessing that the expectant church eagerly awaits. The seventh trumpet of Revelation 11:15 heralds anger, wrath, judgment, fear, and destruction. Aside from this distinction, the seventh trumpet of Revelation 11:15 is not the last trumpet. At the second coming, which occurs after the seventh trumpet, Christ will send His angels to gather together the elect. The signal for that event to occur will be a "great sound of a trumpet" (Matthew 24:31).

THE HOLY SPIRIT

Regardless of which passage represents the rapture, midtribulationists believe that when the rapture happens, the Holy Spirit will remove His influence, which is currently restraining unredeemed man from totally disregarding the moral law. The Holy Spirit will cease to strive with man, just as He did in the days of Noah, and society will degenerate over the seven-year Tribulation. Despite the downward spiral, an amazingly successful evangelistic outreach will cause countless Jews and Gentiles to come to a saving relationship with Jesus Christ (Archer, pp. 126–27).

SIGNS

Midtribulationists believe signs will accompany the rapture. Matthew 24:4-14 details eight signs: (1) false Christs, (2) wars and rumors of war, (3) famines, (4) earthquakes, (5) hatred, persecution, martyrdom, (6) apostasy, (7) survival of the remnant, and (8) the worldwide spread of the gospel. Second Thessalonians 2:3-4 adds two more signs: (1) the building of a Temple in Jerusalem and (2) the enthronement of the Antichrist in that Temple. The rapture cannot be expected until these events occur (Archer, pp. 122–26).

Because midtribulationists identify these ten signs or events as preceding the rapture, they do not look for an imminent appearing of Christ. They do acknowledge an attitude of expectancy that they trace back to the apostle Paul. In 1 Thessalonians 4:15 and 1 Corinthians 15:52, Paul uses the personal pronoun "we" to seemingly include himself among those expecting Christ to return in his lifetime. Midtribulationists believe that a 3½-year Tribulation creates a greater sense of expectancy of Christ's return than does a seven-year tribulation view (Grudem, p. 1133).

A MEDIATING VIEW

Midtribulationism is a mediating view between pretribulationism and posttribulationism. It attempts to address prophecies that some Bible scholars insist must be fulfilled prior to the rapture. At the same time, it provides comfort by claiming the promise that God will remove the church from earth prior to pouring out His wrath.

In contrast, the pretribulation rapture view teaches that God will pour out his wrath during the entire seventieth week of Daniel. He will remove the church from that hour of trial. Pretribulationists see the rapture as the next prophetic event on God's timeline and look expectantly for that blessed hope.

—TONY KESSINGER

BIBLIOGRAPHY

Archer Jr., Gleason L. "The Case for the Mid-Seventieth Week Rapture Position." In *The Rapture: Pre-, Mid- or Post-tribulational?* Grand Rapids: Zondervan, 1984.

Grudem, Wayne. *Systematic Theology.* Leicester, England: InterVarsity Press, 1994.

LaHaye, Tim. *The Rapture.* Eugene, OR: Harvest House Publishers, 2002.

Stanton, Gerald B. *Kept from the Hour.* Miami Springs, FL: Schoettle Publishing, 1991.

Walvoord, John F. "Premillennialism and the Tribulation—Part VIII: Midtribulationism." *Bibliotheca Sacra* 113, April 1956.

MILLENNIAL SACRIFICES

THE RELATIONSHIP BETWEEN the atoning work of Jesus Christ and the animal sacrifices in the Old Testament has raised many questions for Bible theologians. This is especially true in light of the book of Hebrews and Old Testament prophecies concerning worship during the millennium. The answer may have to do with distinct functions in the plan of God for the blood of sacrificial animals and for the precious blood of Christ. This distinction is especially significant for understanding the reinstatement of animal sacrifices during the future millennial kingdom of Christ.

The atoning work of Christ is infinite in value and therefore eternally sufficient and effective for those who put their trust in Him. The book of Hebrews especially emphasizes the contrast between the substitutionary work of Christ and the blood of bulls and goats in the Old Covenant (see Hebrews 7:19; 9:9; 10:1,4,11,18). The New Covenant is infinitely superior to the Old Covenant of Moses, which was "only a shadow of the good things to come" (10:1 NASB). However, neither Hebrews nor the rest of the New Testament teaches that Israel as a nation has been forever set aside by God. The Old Covenant given by God to Israel through Moses has ended, but the New Covenant (stemming from the Abrahamic covenant) is in place and will be applied to Israel during the millennium. The contrast in Hebrews is between the shadowy, insufficient nature of the Old Covenant and the sufficient, permanent nature of the New Covenant.

During the present age, national Israel has been "rejected" (Romans 11:15-22) because of "transgression," "failure," and "unbelief" (11:11-12,23). But that has not terminated Israel as a nation (11:11). Some day it will experience divine "fulfillment" (11:12) and "acceptance" (11:15). The church has not supplanted Israel in God's program, for "the gifts and the calling of God are irrevocable" (11:29).

The New Covenant promises a new heart through the Holy Spirit for the entire nation of Israel (Ezekiel 36:26-27), the restoration of the regenerated nation to its ancestral land (36:28), and a dynamic, functioning theocracy of 12 tribes with a great new city and Temple (Ezekiel 40–48; see Deuteronomy 30:1-4). When this covenant is fulfilled for Israel, its high priest will be the Messiah Himself, not a descendant of Aaron (Psalm 110:4; Hebrews 7).

MENTION OF ANIMAL SACRIFICES

Isaiah foresaw not only God's New Covenant with Israel but also a Temple in the holy land (2:2-3; 60:13). Animal sacrifices would be offered on its altar by Egyptians (19:21) and Arabians (60:7), through priests and Levites (66:21), at God's "holy mountain" with burnt offerings and sacrifices on God's altar (56:6-7; 66:19-20).

God revealed the expression "a new covenant" first to Jeremiah. This New Covenant included the offering of animals on the altar of a Temple in the holy land. God announced through him, "I will cause a righteous Branch of David to spring forth....David shall never lack a man to sit on the throne of the house of Israel; and the Levitical priests shall never lack a man before me" (33:15,17-18). Thus Jeremiah, while stating the total demise of the temporary Old Covenant (31:32) and anticipating the national regeneration provided in the permanent New Covenant (31:31-34; 32:38-40; 33:6-13; 50:5), included animal sacrifices offered by Levitical priests as permanent aspects of this New Covenant for national Israel.

Ezekiel also described the New Covenant, including a provision for "My sanctuary in their midst forever" (37:26,28). This sanctuary or Temple is described in great detail in chapters 40–48. Included in the description are the different types and characteristics and purposes of its animal sacrifices (40:38-43; 42:13; 43:18-27; 45:15-25; 46:2-15; 46:20-24). Other prophets who spoke of the future Temple include Joel (3:18), Micah (4:1-5), and Haggai (2:7,9).

We will consider the theological issues arising from these descriptions by answering three questions: (1) What was the true function of animal sacrifices in the Old Covenant? (2) What are the fundamental differences between Ezekiel's picture of the New Covenant system of worship and the Old Covenant system of worship? (3) Would a worship system involving animal sacrifices represent a step backward for New Covenant Israel during the millennial age?

FUNCTION OF ANIMAL SACRIFICES

Animal sacrifices could never remove spiritual guilt from the offerer (Hebrews 10:4,11). One major purpose of these sacrifices (as teaching symbols) was to prepare the people of Israel for their Messiah and His infinite atonement. Another purpose was to provide a temporal, finite, external, and legal "forgiveness" through an "atonement" (a ritual cleansing—Hebrews 9:10,13) made by a priest (Numbers 15:25-26). This was not merely a prophetic anticipation of Christ's atoning work. In the Old Covenant, God provided a highly complex and rigid structure for his "kingdom of priests." National transgressions would receive national forgiveness when legitimate priests offered appropriate sacrifices to God at the Tabernacle or Temple altar. This forgiveness was promised regardless of the spiritual state of either the offerer or the priest.

However, such sacrificial blood could never cleanse the conscience or save the soul (Hebrews 10:1-2), so God repeatedly sent prophets to call His people to love and obey their God from the heart. Apart from such genuine faith, all the ceremonially "kosher" animals in the whole world would avail nothing in the spiritual realm (Psalm 50:7-15; Isaiah 1:12-20; Jeremiah 6:20; 7:21-23; Hosea 5:6; Amos 4:4-5; 5:20-27; Micah 6:6-8). It has always been true that "it is impossible for the blood of bulls and goats to take away sins" (Hebrews 10:4). But it was also true then, under the Old Covenant, that "the blood of bulls and goats...sanctify for the cleansing of the flesh" (Hebrews 9:13).

In the Millennial Temple under the New Covenant, future sacrifices will have nothing to do with eternal salvation, which only comes through true faith in God. Future animal sacrifices will be "efficacious" and "expiatory"

only in terms of the strict provision for ceremonial (thus temporal) forgiveness for national Israel. Thus, animal sacrifices will be not only memorial (like the bread and cup in church communion services) but also temporally atoning for believing Israel (Ezekiel 43:20,26; 45:15,17,20). Hoekema notes, "If the sacrifices mentioned in Ezekiel are to be understood literally, they must be expiatory, not memorial offerings" (Hoekema, p. 204). The distinction between ceremonial and spiritual atonement is significant, for it is at the heart of the basic difference between the theocracy of Israel and the church, the body and bride of Christ.

ISRAEL'S WORSHIP IN OLD AND NEW COVENANTS

The Temple of the millennium will be vastly different from those of Solomon, Zerubbabel, and Herod. The outer court, gates, walls, grounds, locality, and furniture will all be different. The Temple will not have the ark of the covenant, no pot of manna, no Aaron's rod, no tables of the Law, no cherubim, no mercy seat, no golden lampstand, no showbread, no veil, no holy of holies, no high priest, no evening sacrifice (West, pp. 429–30), no feast of Pentecost, no feast of Trumpets, and no Day of Atonement. These modifications indicate that the millennial sacrifices will focus on sanctification grounded upon the reconciliation already provided by Christ.

NOT A STEP BACKWARD FOR ISRAEL

It is the conviction of the present author that consistent dispensationalism must teach the practice of animal sacrifices for a restored and regenerated Israel in the millennium. But would such a worship system represent a great step backward for New Covenant Israel? Israel will be under a New Covenant program, not the Old Covenant given to Moses, which was never designed to guarantee salvation. Millennial Israel will have the entire New Testament available to them, including the book of Hebrews. They will know about the full and finished work of Christ. They will see no conflict between Ezekiel and Hebrews, and they will understand the omission of a high priest in Ezekiel 40–48 as opening the door to the Melchizedekian High Priest of Psalm 110:4, Jesus Christ Himself.

Believing Jews will experience regeneration and sanctification just as Christians do today—by the grace of God through faith in the Lord Jesus. These future Jewish believers will not be glorified (they will be survivors of the Tribulation and their descendants). The New Covenant theocracy of Israel will retain its distinctive Israelite characteristics—a promised land, a temple, appropriate animal sacrifices, and an earthly Zadokian priesthood (subordinate to Jesus Christ).

These sacrifices, illumined by a corporate understanding of the true significance of the Lamb of God who took away the sin of the world, will be appreciated all the more for what they can and cannot accomplish for the offerer. For non-glorified millennial Israel and her Gentile proselytes throughout the world (see Psalm 87; Isaiah 60:1-14; Zechariah 8:20-23), the continued presence of a sin nature will call for constant instruction and exhortation in revealed truth. Not even a perfect government will automatically solve this deep, universal problem. In distinction from the perfection of the eternal state described in Revelation 21–22, Christ will "rule all nations with a rod of iron" (Revelation 2:27; 12:5; 19:15) and with strict controls, especially in religious practices (see Zechariah 14:16-21). Even though outward submission to these religious forms will not necessarily demonstrate a regenerate heart, it will guarantee protection from physical penalties and temporal judgments. Those who love Christ will exhibit a genuine spirit of submission to His government. But those who do not truly love Him will follow Satan in global rebellion at the end of Christ's righteous reign, and they will be destroyed in cosmic fire (Revelation 20:7-9).

FORM AND CONTENT OF WORSHIP

How can vital spiritual instruction be accomplished for citizens of the millennial kingdom through a system of animal sacrifices?

If it is theoretically possible for the church today to achieve a spiritual, symbolic, and pedagogic balance in the use of the bread and cup in communion, then it will be all the more possible for regenerated Israel to attain the divinely intended balance between form and content within the structures of the New Covenant. It is not only possible but prophetically certain (in the view of this author) that millennial animal sacrifices will be used in a God-honoring way (Psalm 51:15-19; Hebrews 11:4) by a regenerated, chosen nation before the inauguration of the eternal state. (See the article titled "Millennial Temple.")

—JOHN C. WHITCOMB

BIBLIOGRAPHY

Bruce, F.F. *The Epistle to the Hebrews. New International Commentary on the New Testament.* Grand Rapids: Eerdmans Publishing Company, 1964.

Hoekema, Anthony A. *The Bible and the Future.* Grand Rapids: Eerdmans Publishing Company, 1979.

Hullinger, Jerry M. "The Problem of Animal Sacrifices in Ezekiel 40–48." *Bibliotheca Sacra* 152 (July-Sept. 1995), pp. 279-89.

Kent, Homer A., Jr. *The Epistle to the Hebrews: A Commentary.* Winona Lake, IN: BMH Books, 1972.

Pentecost, J. Dwight. *Things to Come.* Grand Rapids: Zondervan, 1964.

Ryrie, Charles C. *The Basis of Premillennial Faith.* New York: Loizeaux, 1953.

Sauer, Erich. *From Eternity to Eternity.* Grand Rapids: Eerdmans Publishing Company, 1954.

Walvoord, John F. *The Millennial Kingdom.* Findlay, OH: Dunham, 1959.

West, Nathanael. *The Thousand Years in Both Testaments.* New York: Revell, 1880.

Whitcomb, John C. "Christ's Atonement and Animal Sacrifices in Israel." *Grace Theological Journal* 6.2 (1985), pp. 201-17.

MILLENNIAL TEMPLE

SEVERAL OLD TESTAMENT prophets predicted that during the millennium, Israelite believers will worship God in a way that requires a new Temple. Note the following references:

1. *The house of the Lord.* "It will come to pass in that day that the mountains shall drip with new wine, the hills shall flow with milk, and all the brooks of Judah shall be flooded with water; a fountain shall flow from the house of the LORD and water the Valley of Acacias" (Joel 3:18 NKJV).

2. *The house of the God of Jacob.* "Many people shall come and say, 'Come, and let us go up to the mountain of the LORD, to the house of the God of Jacob; He will teach us His ways, and we shall walk in His paths.' For out of Zion shall go forth the law, and the word of the LORD from Jerusalem" (Isaiah 2:3).

3. *The sanctuary of God.* "The glory of Lebanon shall come to you, the cypress, the pine, and the box tree together, to beautify the place of My sanctuary; and I will make the place of My feet glorious" (Isaiah 60:13).

The prophets also envisioned animal sacrifices for Israel during the millennium.

1. *Burnt offerings and sacrifices.* "Even them I will bring to My holy mountain, and make them joyful in My house of prayer. Their burnt offerings and their sacrifices will be accepted on My altar" (Isaiah 56:7).

2. *An altar in the house of glory.* "They shall ascend with acceptance on My altar, and I will glorify the house of My glory" (Isaiah 60:7).

3. *Burnt offerings, grain offerings, and sacrifices.* "For thus says the LORD: 'David shall never lack a man to sit on the throne of the house of Israel; nor shall the priests, the Levites, lack a man to offer burnt offerings before Me, to kindle grain offerings, and to sacrifice continually'" (Jeremiah 33:17-18).

4. *Feast of Tabernacles, altar, and sacrifices.* "This shall be the punishment of Egypt and the punishment of all the nations that do not come up to keep the Feast of Tabernacles.…The pots in the LORD's house shall be like the bowls before the altar. Yes, every pot in Jerusalem and Judah shall be holiness to the LORD of hosts. Everyone who sacrifices shall come and take them and cook in them" (Zechariah 14:19-21).

It is difficult to interpret these passages literally without concluding that the Messiah will establish a Temple in Israel for the millennium. This Temple will be distinct from any previous historical Temple. It will contain some of what was lacking in one or more of the first three Temples (Solomon's, postexilic, and tribulational): Gentile worshipers and the shekinah glory of God (Isaiah 2:2-4; 60:7,13; Jeremiah 33:18; Ezekiel 37:26-28; 43:1-7; Haggai 2:9; Zechariah 6:12-13; 14:20), as well as a distinct architecture on an expanded Temple Mount (Ezekiel 40–48).

EVIDENCE FOR A LITERAL MILLENNIAL TEMPLE

Ezekiel 40–48 contains the most extensive description of the predicted Millennial Temple. Five lines of evidence confirm that this passage should be interpreted literally.

First, a careful reading of Ezekiel 40–42 gives the strong impression of a literal Temple because of the immense number of details given concerning its dimensions, parts, and contents. If the Scriptures devote so much space to a detailed description of this Temple, we can assume that it will be as literal as the Tabernacle and the Temple of Solomon. The fact that its structure and ceremonies will have a symbolic and spiritual significance does not argue against its literal existence, for even the Tabernacle was a literal structure in spite of the fact that it was filled with symbolic and typical significance.

Second, Ezekiel was told to "declare to the house of Israel everything you see" (40:4), which seems strange if the Temple was to symbolize only general truths. Even more significant is the fact that the Israelites were to "keep its whole design and all its ordinances, and perform them" (43:11). This is an exact parallel to the pattern of the Tabernacle that

Moses saw on the mountain, which God commanded him to construct (Exodus 25:8-9).

Third, the Temple of Ezekiel 8–11 was clearly the literal Temple of Ezekiel's day, even though the prophet saw it "in the visions of God" (8:3) while he himself was still in Babylon (8:1). These four chapters mention "the door of the north gate of the inner court" (8:3), "the porch" (8:16), "the altar" (8:16), "the threshold of the temple" (9:3), and "the east gate of the LORD's house" (10:19). Chapters 40–42 give no indication whatsoever that they describe an ideal Temple instead of a literal Temple. In fact, one finds descriptive formulas that are similar, if not identical, to those in chapters 8–11: "in the visions of God" (40:2; see 8:3), "a gateway on the inner court" (40:27; see 8:3), "the porch of the house" (40:48; see 8:16), "the altar" (43:18; see 8:16), and "the gate that faces toward the east" (43:1; see 10:19), through which the glory of the God of Israel is seen returning exactly as He had departed in 10:19 and 11:23. If the Millennial Temple is not to be a reality, why insist that the return of the God of Israel will be a reality?

Fourth, God promised to the line of Zadok an everlasting priesthood (1 Samuel 2:35; see 1 Kings 2:27,35). This confirms God's promise of an everlasting priesthood to Zadok's ancestor Phinehas (Numbers 25:13), which confirms His promise of an everlasting priesthood to Phinehas' grandfather Aaron (Exodus 29:9; 40:15; see 1 Chronicles 6:3,50). Furthermore, God confirmed this promise of an everlasting priesthood through Jeremiah (33:17-22), who linked the perpetuity of the Levitical priests with the perpetuity of the Davidic kingship and the perpetuity of the earth's rotation on its axis! In view of these promises of God, confirmed again and again, it is highly significant that the Millennial Temple of Ezekiel will have the sons of Zadok as its priests (40:46; 44:15). The intrinsic probability of this being fulfilled literally is strengthened tremendously by the mention of 12,000 Levites who will be sealed by God during the yet future seventieth week of Daniel (Revelation 7:7). If these are literal Levites, it would hardly be consistent to maintain that the Temple is spiritual or figurative. And if God's promises to Aaron, Phinehas, and Zadok may be spiritualized, how can we insist that His promises to David (2 Samuel 7:13,16) will be fulfilled literally?

Fifth, the Bible teaches that although true Christianity does not require an earthly temple, altar, or sacrifices (John 4:21; Hebrews 7-10), such provisions will exist for Israel following the rapture of the church (Matthew 24; 2 Thessalonians 2:4; Revelation 11:1-2; see Hosea 3:4-5; Daniel 9:24,27). Furthermore, Revelation 20:9 indicates that Jerusalem, the "beloved city," will once again be "the camp of the saints" during the millennial age.

OBJECTIONS TO A LITERAL MILLENNIAL TEMPLE

Its Size

The area of the temple courts (about one square mile) of Ezekiel's Temple would be larger than the entire ancient walled city of Jerusalem, and the holy portion for priests and Levites (about 40 by 50 miles) would cover an area six times the size of greater London today. Some say that it could not possibly be placed within present-day Palestine between the Jordan River and the Mediterranean Sea (Ezekiel 47:18). The millennial Jerusalem would be about 40 miles in circumference and thus ten times the circumference of the ancient city.

However, Israel will have the only sanctuary and priesthood in the world during the millennium, so the temple courts and sacred area will need to be greatly enlarged to accommodate the vast number of worshipers and the priests who will serve them (Isaiah 2:3; 60:14; 61:6; Zechariah 8:20-23). Various Old Testament prophecies speak of great geological changes that will occur in Palestine at the time of Christ's second coming, so it is not impossible to imagine a 2500-square-mile area for the Temple and city fitted into a reshaped and enlarged land (see Isaiah 26:15; 33:17; 54:2; Zechariah 14:4-10). The latter passage speaks of new valleys, new rivers, and a flattening of portions of land "like the Arabah" (NIV) that "will be raised up." The entire Dead Sea region may be lifted up more than 1300 feet, above the present sea level, for it will contain fish "of the same kinds as the fish of the Great Sea" (Ezekiel 47:10). Revelation 16:20 states that toward the end of the Great Tribulation, gigantic earthquakes will cause islands and mountains to vanish. Both Testaments thus speak of topographical and geographical changes that will accompany the inauguration of the millennial kingdom. Jerusalem itself, the beloved city (Revelation 20:9), will be the capital of the world, and its size will surely be proportionate to its importance.

Animal Sacrifices

Some people cannot imagine why a system of animal sacrifices would be reinstituted after the one perfect sacrifice of Christ has been accomplished, especially in the light of Hebrews 7–10. This may be the most formidable objection to a literal interpretation of Ezekiel's Temple.

However, several considerations tend to modify the force of this objection. First, the millennial system of sacrifices described by Ezekiel differs profoundly from the Aaronic system. It is not simply a reinstitution of Mosaic Judaism. Pentecost points out that there will be no ark of the covenant, tables of the law, cherubim, mercy seat, veil, golden lampstand, or table of showbread (Pentecost, pp. 520–24). Instead of a high priest, a prince who has some royal or priestly powers will be on duty, but he will actually be neither king nor high priest. The Levites will have fewer Temple privileges, except for the sons of Zadok, who will serve as priests. The feast of Pentecost is omitted, as well as the great Day of Atonement and the daily evening sacrifice. The dimensions of the Temple and courts are changed, and they are removed from the city. The later rabbis, who lost the true significance of Old Testament prophecy, were deeply troubled by the contradictions between Moses and Ezekiel, and they hoped that Elijah would explain away the difficulties when he returned to earth.

Second, though animal sacrifices and priests have no place in Christianity, this does not mean that they will have no place in Israel after the rapture of the church. The Scriptures make a clear distinction between Israel and the church. The fact that God will have finished His work of sanctification in the church by the time of the rapture is no warrant for assuming that He will have finished His work of instruction, testing, and sanctification in Israel. In fact, one of the main purposes of the 1000-year earthly kingdom of Christ will be to vindicate His chosen people Israel before the eyes of all nations (Isaiah 60–61). People who are saved following the rapture of the church will not be members of the bride of Christ, though they will be "made perfect," like all the redeemed (Hebrews 12:23).

Third, even in the age of grace, God uses the symbolism of the bread and the cup of communion to remind Christians of the awful price that Jesus paid on the cross. Drinking of this "cup of blessing" (1 Corinthians 10:16) does not involve a re-offering of the blood of Christ in contradiction to the book of Hebrews, but it serves as a powerful "remembrance" of Christ and a powerful proclaiming of "the Lord's death until He comes" (1 Corinthians 11:25-26). Likewise, in the context of distinctive Israelite worship, the five different offerings, four of them with blood-shedding, will serve as a constant reminder to the yet unglorified millennial Jews of the awful and complete sacrifice that their Messiah, now present in their midst, had suffered centuries earlier to make their salvation possible. In view of the fact that bloodshed may exist nowhere else in the entire world (Isaiah 11:6-9), such sacrifices upon the Temple altar would be doubly impressive. However, such sacrifices will not be voluntary and purely memorial as is true of the Christian communion. Ezekiel says that God will "accept" people on the basis of animal sacrifices (43:27), and they are "to make atonement for the house of Israel" (45:17; see 45:15). In other words, just as in Old Testament times, the privilege of life and physical blessing in the theocratic kingdom is contingent upon outward conformity to the ceremonial law. Such conformity did not bring salvation, and this has been God's plan in every dispensation. It is a serious mistake, therefore, to insist that these sacrifices will be expiatory. They could not completely take away guilt (Hebrews 10:4) and thus cleanse the conscience of the Old Testament Israelite (Hebrews 9:9,14), nor will they in the millennial kingdom age. But these sacrifices will be effective (as they once were) in sanctifying millennial Israelites "for the purifying of the flesh" (Hebrews 9:13,23; see 9:10) as an essential purification ritual because of God's infinitely holy presence in their midst (Hullinger, pp. 287–89). For this reason, their symbolic and pedagogic value, unlike the communion service, will be upheld by a system of forced participation. For example, those who decide to neglect the annual feast of Tabernacles will be punished by a drought or a plague (Zechariah 14:16-19). The offerings will serve as effective vehicles of divine instruction for Israel and the nations during the kingdom age. (See articles titled "Ezekiel, Eschatology of" and "Millennial Sacrifices.")

—JOHN C. WHITCOMB

BIBLIOGRAPHY

Alexander, Ralph. "Ezekiel." In *The Expositor's Bible Commentary*, Vol. 6. Ed. Frank E. Gaebelein. Grand Rapids: Zondervan, 1986.

Feinberg, Charles L. *The Prophecy of Ezekiel*. Chicago: Moody Press, 1969.

Hullinger, Jerry M. "The Problem of Animal Sacrifices in Ezekiel 40–48," *Bibliotheca Sacra* 152 (July 1995), pp. 279-89.

McClain, Alva J. *The Greatness of the Kingdom*. Grand Rapids: Zondervan, 1959.

Pentecost, J. Dwight. *Things to Come*. Grand Rapids: Zondervan, 1958.

Sauer, Erich. *From Eternity to Eternity*. Grand Rapids: Eerdmans Publishing Company, 1954.

Walvoord, John F. *The Millennial Kingdom*. Grand Rapids: Zondervan, 1959.

MILLENNIAL VIEWS

THE OLD AND NEW TESTAMENTS include numerous references to the kingdom of the Messiah, the long-anticipated rule and reign of the Lord Jesus Himself upon the earth. In fact, it is one of the most frequently mentioned subjects in the Bible. In Matthew 6:10, when Jesus taught His followers to pray, "Thy kingdom come," He was referring specifically to the time of this earthly reign. In the most incredible kingdom in all of human history, Jesus, the anointed King, will have the nations for His inheritance (Psalm 2:8), "the wolf also shall dwell with the lamb" (Isaiah 11:6 NKJV), and "the earth shall be full of the knowledge of the LORD" (Isaiah 11:9).

Just how long will His earthly kingdom last? Only one chapter in the entire Bible reveals its duration—Revelation 20:

> Blessed and holy is he who has part in the first resurrection. Over such the second death has no power, but they shall be priests of God and of Christ, and shall reign with Him a thousand years (Revelation 20:6).

This kingdom is often referred to as the millennium, a name derived from the Latin words *mille* (meaning "one thousand") and *annum* (meaning "year"). Church history has seen three differing views of the millennial kingdom. Premillennialism is the belief that the second coming of Christ will occur prior to the millennial age. This is the view accepted by most biblical scholars who take the Scriptures literally and at face value whenever possible. Other scholars believe the world is going to become more and more "Christianized," and that the kingdom of Christ will gradually evolve. In this scenario, Jesus would return at the end of the millennium to an already righteous earth. This perspective is known as postmillennialism. A third viewpoint, known as amillennialism, is the result of a nonliteral or spiritualized interpretation of Scripture that teaches that the millennium is not an earthly kingdom at all but rather a description of Christ's current reign from heaven.

PREMILLENNIALISM

Early Christians were unquestionably premillennialists. The disciples and those they taught anticipated the return of Christ and the establishment of His kingdom on earth in their lifetime. Detractors of the premillennial view claim that it is a relatively new theory. But scholars have demonstrated that premillennialism was the dominant view held during the first three centuries of the early church.

Premillennialists believe that the rapture, the Tribulation, and the glorious appearance of Christ will all occur before the beginning of the millennium. And during the millennium, Satan will be bound for 1000 years and a theocratic kingdom of peace on earth will

MILLENNIAL VIEWS

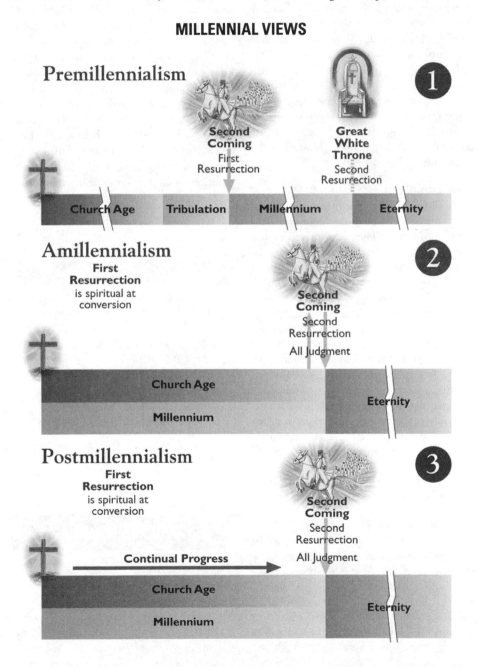

ensue, with Jesus as its King. The righteous will have been raised from the dead prior to the millennium and will participate in its blessings (Revelation 20:4).

Toward the end of the third century, an allegorical approach to Scripture began to dominate theological thought. Philosophy replaced the study of Scripture, and premillennialism fell into disrepute. Not until after the Reformation was there a revival of premillennial thought. Later, in the nineteenth century, Bible institutes and Christian schools across America began to emphasize a literal interpretation of the Bible, and with it, a return to premillennialism. Today, despite continued attacks, premillennialism is the dominant millennial view.

AMILLENNIALISM

Amillennialists do not believe in a literal kingdom on the earth following the second coming of Christ. They tend to spiritualize and allegorize the prophecies concerning the millennium and attribute yet-unfulfilled prophecies relating to Israel to the church instead. Those who hold to amillennialism also believe that Satan was bound at Christ's first appearance on earth 2000 years ago. Furthermore, its adherents differ as to whether the millennium is being spiritually fulfilled currently on earth or whether it's being fulfilled by the saints in heaven. However, they tend to agree that our current state of affairs is probably as good as it's going to get and that the eternal state (heaven), not the millennial kingdom, will immediately follow the second coming of Christ. Those who hold to this view do not adhere to a simple and plain literal interpretation of Scripture.

POSTMILLENNIALISM

Postmillennialism, the most recent of the three millennial views, was almost extinct by the middle of the twentieth century. Those who hold to this perspective believe that the world will continue to get better and better until the entire world is Christianized, at which time Christ will return to a kingdom already flourishing in peace. Although this view was popular at the beginning of the twentieth century, it was all but eliminated as a result of the World Wars, the Great Depression, and the overwhelming escalation of moral evil in society. Many who previously held postmillennial views adopted the amillennial position. However, postmillennialism is currently gaining some resurgence as a corollary to preterism and reconstructionism. It continues to promote the entrance of the kingdom prior to the return of the King.

The coming millennium will be the most incredible period in earth's history. It will be a time of unprecedented peace, when those who have accepted Jesus Christ as their Lord and Savior will be able to rule and reign along with their loving King. Only then will the kingdom of God finally be realized on earth. (See articles titled "Amillennialism," "Premillennialism," and "Postmillennialism.")

—TIM LAHAYE

BIBLIOGRAPHY

Bock, Darrell L., ed. *Three Views on the Millennium and Beyond.* Grand Rapids: Zondervan, 1999.

Clouse, Robert G., ed. *The Meaning of the Millennium: Four Views.* Downers Grove, IL: InterVarsity, 1977.

McClain, Alva J. *The Greatness of the Kingdom.* Chicago: Moody Press, 1959.

Ryrie, Charles C. *The Basis of the Premillennial Faith.* Neptune, NJ: Loizeaux Brothers, 1953.

Pentecost, J. Dwight. *Things to Come.* Grand Rapids: Zondervan, 1958.

———. *Thy Kingdom Come.* Wheaton, IL: Victory Books, 1990.

Walvoord, John F. *The Millennial Kingdom.* Grand Rapids: Zondervan, 1959.

MILLENNIUM

THE WORD *millennium* COMES from the Latin word *mille,* meaning "one thousand," and *annum,* meaning "year." The Greek word *chilias,* also meaning "one thousand," appears six times in Revelation 20, defining the duration of Christ's kingdom before the destruction of the old heaven and the old earth. The millennium therefore refers to 1000 years of Christ's future reign on earth, which will immediately precede eternity (Ryrie, pp. 145–46). During the millennium, Christ will reign in time and space.

POSITIONS ON THE MILLENNIUM

There are three different schools of thought with regard to the millennium: amillennialism, postmillennialism, and premillennialism. *Amillennialism* means "no millennium"—that is, there will be no literal kingdom on earth. The proponents of this perspective believe that millennial prophecies cannot be considered literal and thus would need to be fulfilled in nonliteral ways.

Postmillennialism states that the return of Christ will come after the millennium. This position became popular in the nineteenth century, suggesting that the millennium would occur during the last 1000 years of the present age with the whole world being won to Christ. Thus, the millennium would be that golden age lasting for 1000 years. With the coming of the World Wars, the postmillennial interpretation declined in influence. Today this position is being revived through a movement called Christian Reconstructionism (also known as Dominion Theology or Theonomy).

The *premillennial* interpretation teaches that the kingdom will follow the second coming of Christ and will be a literal 1000-year reign of Christ on earth. This position is not only based on the literal interpretation of the prophecies of the book of Revelation but also on abundant messianic prophecies from the Old Testament. It was also the dominant position of the early church (Larsen, p. 307).

God's promises in His covenants to Israel will come to pass when Jesus Christ comes to rule from Jerusalem. At that time, the Abrahamic covenant with its promises of the land and the seed (Genesis 13:14-17; 15:5,18-21; Isaiah 10:21-22; Jeremiah 30:22; Ezekiel 34:24; Micah 7:19-20), the Davidic covenant with its promises concerning David's house, his throne, and the kingdom (2 Samuel 7:16-19;

Isaiah 11:1-2; Jeremiah 23:5-8; Hosea 3:5), and the New Covenant with its promises of a new heart for God's law, the forgiveness of sins, and the indwelling of the Spirit for a converted nation (Jeremiah 31:31-34; Ezekiel 11:18-20; 36:24-28; Romans 11:26-29) will all be literally fulfilled. Fulfillment of these promises and covenants in the millennial reign of Christ will bring about God's purpose on earth for man.

The binding of Satan provides evidence that the millennial reign of Christ is yet a future event. Revelation 20:2 (KJV) says, "He laid hold on the dragon, that old serpent, which is the Devil, and Satan, and bound him a thousand years." Revelation 20:1-3 shows that God will prevent Satan from deceiving the nations. This passage teaches that Satan will not simply be restricted, but will be totally inactive during the millennium. This stands in stark contrast to his activity in the present age, of which the apostle Peter says, "Be sober, be vigilant; because your adversary the devil, as a roaring lion, walks about, seeking whom he may devour" (1 Peter 5:8).

Though Satan is not bound in this present age, he is under the sovereign restraints of God. This is evidenced by Satan's dealings with God concerning Job (Job 1:6-22). The binding of Satan during the millennial age does have a divine purpose: God will manifest His perfect righteousness and also give man an ideal state in which to live and worship the Messiah (see Pentecost, *Things to Come*, p. 477).

THE PERSONAGE OF THE MILLENNIUM

The central focus of the millennium is not Satan; it is the Savior, the Lord Jesus Christ. It is His time of manifestation, His time of revelation. Christ, in all of His glory, will institute His reign of righteousness and peace. During the millennium, the unveiled glory of Christ will shine forth in all of its fullness.

Psalm 2:6-9 reveals God's plan for Jesus Christ, His Son, to reign over the earth in spite of the rage of nations and their rebellion against God. His sovereign purpose will be realized. Daniel 7:13-14 also speaks of this event.

PRINCIPAL CHARACTERISTICS AND CONDITIONS OF THE MILLENNIUM

The millennium will be a time of both political and spiritual rule. Politically, it will be universal (Daniel 2:35), authoritative (Isaiah 11:4), and characterized by righteousness and justice, with assurances for the poor (Isaiah 11:3-5) and admonition and judgment for the violators of Messiah's rule (Psalm 2:10-12).

This literal earthly reign of Christ will also have spiritual characteristics. First and foremost it will be a reign of righteousness in which Christ will be the King, reigning in absolute righteousness (Isaiah 32:1). It will also be a time when the fullness of the Spirit and the holiness of God will be manifested (Isaiah 11:2-5). "In that day shall there be upon the bells of the horses, HOLINESS UNTO THE LORD....Yea, every pot in Jerusalem and in Judah shall be holiness unto the LORD of hosts" (Zechariah 14:20-21).

Everything from work to worship will be holy. Sin will be punished (Psalm 72:1-4; Zechariah 14:16-21) in an open, just way. The messianic age will also be characterized by a reign of peace (Isaiah 2:4; 11:5-9; 65:25; Micah 4:3). Isaiah's prophecy reveals many other conditions, including these:

- joy (Isaiah 9:3-4)
- glory (Isaiah 24:23)
- justice (Isaiah 9:7)
- full knowledge (Isaiah 11:1-2)
- instruction and learning (Isaiah 2:2-3)
- the removal of the curse on the earth and the elimination of sickness (Isaiah 11:6-9; 33:24)
- longevity of life (Isaiah 65:20)
- prosperity in work (Isaiah 4:1; 35:1-2; 62:8-9)
- harmony in the animal kingdom (Isaiah 11:6-9; 65:25)

Zephaniah 3:9 and Isaiah 45:13 predict that the millennium will have a pure language and pure worship. Pure worship will be possible because of the awesome presence of God (Ezekiel 37:27-28). The physical presence of the Messiah guarantees these blessings. Walvoord says, "The glorious presence of Christ in the millennial scene is of course, the center of worship and spirituality" (Walvoord, p. 307).

THE PLACE OF JERUSALEM IN THE MILLENNIUM

Although the reign of Messiah will be universal, the center of His government will be in Jerusalem: "Out of Zion shall go forth the law, and the word of the LORD from Jerusalem" (Isaiah 2:3).

Some believe that Jerusalem will again witness the presence of David, this time in his resurrected body, serving as a prince or regent under Christ and administering the millennial kingdom as it relates to Israel. According to Ezekiel, David will act as a shepherd over the people. "And I will set up one shepherd over them, and he shall feed them...and he shall be their shepherd. And I the LORD will be their God, and my servant David a prince among them; I the LORD have spoken it" (Ezekiel 34:23-24). These interpreters also see this concept of David ruling under Christ in Jeremiah 30:9; 33:15-17; Ezekiel 37:24-25; Hosea 3:5.

Many topographical changes will occur in Israel as Christ comes to set His feet on the Mount of Olives.

> His feet shall stand in that day upon the mount of Olives, which is before Jerusalem on the east, and the mount of Olives shall cleave in the midst thereof toward the east and toward the west, and there shall be a very great valley; and half of the mountain shall remove toward the north, and half of it toward the south (Zechariah 14:4).

Concerning these physical changes around Jerusalem, Larsen states:

> A great earthquake will rend the Mount of Olives (Zechariah 14:3,4) and the mount of the Lord will be sufficient size for the building of the millennial temple described in Ezekiel 40–48. From its summit will flow the life-giving

stream depicted in Ezekiel 47:1-12 which will reach to the Dead Sea with its rejuvenating qualities. Then, indeed, Jerusalem will be raised up and remain in its place and the promise will be kept. It will be inhabited. Never again will it be destroyed. Jerusalem will be secure (Zechariah 14:10-11) (Larsen, p. 314).

THE PARTICIPANTS OF THE MILLENNIUM

The people included in the millennial kingdom of Christ will be Old Testament saints (Daniel 12:1-2,6,13), Tribulation saints (Jews and Gentiles, both living and resurrected ones—Revelation 20:4), and the church of the Lord Jesus Christ (see Ryrie, pp. 149–50).

Although only the redeemed will go into Messiah's kingdom, the living saints from the Tribulation will enter into that kingdom in their natural bodies with the power of procreation. The children born to these saints during the millennium will be in need of salvation, and this salvation will be brought to them through Israel. As Pentecost says,

> During the millennial reign of Christ, Israel as a nation will fulfill the function for which they were originally set apart by God. They will become a kingdom of priests (Exodus 19:6) who are intermediaries between those who need to be saved and the King who provides salvation. They will become as they were originally appointed to be: God's lights to the world (Pentecost, *Kingdom*, pp. 316–17).

SATAN AND HIS LAST REVOLT

As Messiah's 1000-year reign of righteousness and peace comes to an end, Satan will be loosed for a season (Revelation 20:3). Why is Satan loosed? Why will he not remain in that bottomless pit forever? As Larsen says, "Lurking down in human hearts and expressed in many a treatise on the human condition is the notion that were only human beings economically self-sufficient, if only we were spared the graft, crookedness and prejudiceness of public officials, if only we did not have to face

the insecurity of hostile threat and war, we would do well" (Larsen, p. 320). The end of the millennium will reveal how unregenerate hearts will still be open to believe the lie of the devil and follow him in his final revolt against God. Again it will be evident that redemption through God's saving grace is the only answer for sin. For 1000 years, no one will be influenced by satanic or demonic activity, corrupt government, war, sickness, or bad weather. Still, people will rebel. All rebellion during the millennium will find its cause not in man's external circumstances but in his own internal corrupt nature. The loosing of Satan will demonstrate that no type of social order or environment in the world can possibly change the sinfulness of man's degenerate heart. Only by a personal relationship with Messiah through redemption can one resist not only his own evil human heart but also Satan himself.

After this final rebellion, Satan will be cast into the lake of fire (Revelation 20:10), and then will come the resurrection and the Great White Throne judgment of all unsaved dead of all ages of history with the result that they are cast into the lake of fire (Revelation 20:12-15). After that will come the ushering in of new heavens and a new earth with its eternal state (Revelation 21:1). What a glorious moment that will be!

FROM THE MILLENNIUM TO THE ETERNAL STATE

At the end of the millennium, what will happen to the reign of Jesus Christ? According to Pentecost, "While Christ's earthly theocratic rule is limited to 1,000 years, which is sufficient time to manifest God's perfect theocracy on the earth, His reign is eternal" (Pentecost, *Things to Come*, p. 493).

The millennial kingdom of Christ will usher in the eternal manifestation of the glory of the Lamb of God. Without the scriptural doctrine of the millennium, we would have no bridge between history and God's eternal order. This golden age will not only be God's way of linking history but also giving to man through the God-man, Jesus Christ, the dominion lost by the fall. And Messiah will be magnified as the Son of David coming to sit on the throne of David and reigning over the house of David from the city of David, Jerusalem.

—JOE JORDAN

BIBLIOGRAPHY

Bock, Darrell L., ed. *Three Views on the Millennium and Beyond*. Grand Rapids: Zondervan, 1999.

Clouse, Robert G., ed. *The Meaning of the Millennium: Four Views*. Downers Grove, IL: InterVarsity, 1977.

Larsen, David L. *Jews, Gentiles & the Church*. Grand Rapids: Discovery House Publishers, 1995.

McClain, Alva J. *The Greatness of the Kingdom*. Chicago: Moody Press, 1959.

Ryrie, Charles C. *The Basis of the Premillennial Faith*. Neptune, NJ: Loizeaux Brothers, 1953.

Pentecost, J. Dwight. *Things to Come*. Grand Rapids: Zondervan, 1958.

———. *Thy Kingdom Come*. Wheaton, IL: Victory Books, 1990.

Walvoord, John F. *The Millennial Kingdom*. Grand Rapids: Zondervan, 1959.

MYSTERIES

THE NEW TESTAMENT DEVELOPS many truths already revealed in the Old Testament. But it also reveals "mysteries"—truths not included in the Old Testament. In fact, the apostle Paul calls the entire church age a mystery (Ephesians 3:1-13). What are these mysteries, and what does the Bible teach about them?

OLD TESTAMENT ROOTS

The Bible does not use the word "mystery" as we would today when we speak of something like a mystery novel. "Mystery" in the Bible is not something that is mysterious or something that, with enough of the right clues, a sharp-minded person can figure out. In the Bible, a mystery is simply a secret. A mystery is something that you can learn only if someone tells you about it. Job says of God, "He reveals mysteries from the darkness, and brings the deep darkness into light" (Job 12:22).

Biblical mysteries are new information about God's plan that He reveals through revelation. We see this developed in the book of Daniel, which is the only other place that "mystery" is used in the Old Testament (NASB).

In Daniel 2, King Nebuchadnezzar had a dream. Rather than telling anyone about his dream, he kept the details a secret and demanded that his wise men and advisors tell him both the dream and its meaning. Nebuchadnezzar was apparently concerned that if he told these advisors the dream, they would simply make up an interpretation of his dream. Daniel stepped forward when "the mystery was revealed to Daniel in a night vision" (2:19). Daniel told the king, "As for the mystery about which the king has inquired, neither wise men, conjurers, magicians, nor diviners are able to declare it to the king" (2:27). Daniel said, "But as for me, this mystery has not been revealed to me for any wisdom residing in me more than in any other living man, but for the purpose of making the interpretation known to the king, and that you may understand the thoughts of your mind" (2:30).

So we see that Daniel understood this mystery because God revealed the meaning to him. This mystery pertained to a segment of God's plan for Gentile history as it related to Israel. King Nebuchadnezzar responded to the revelation of this mystery: "Surely your God is a God of gods and a Lord of kings and a revealer of mysteries, since you have been able to reveal this mystery'" (2:47).

NEW TESTAMENT MYSTERIES

The New Testament carries over Daniel's meaning of "mystery," but it adds a new twist. "Biblically a mystery is a divine truth that God had not disclosed in Old Testament times but did reveal to the New Testament apostles and prophets to proclaim freely to everyone who will listen," declares John Witmer (p. 250). Building upon the Old Testament usage of "mystery" as a revealed secret, the New Testament, especially Paul, adds the nuance that a mystery is a new, church-age revelation.

MAJOR MYSTERIES

The New Testament mentions many mysteries. However, few of these are major new revelations. Among them are the mystery of the nature of the church, the rapture of the church, the mystery of godliness, and the mystery of lawlessness. These are important to consider when one is attempting to systematize Bible prophecy.

The Mystery of the Church

Disclosed in the New Testament

Paul speaks in Ephesians 3:5 of a mystery "which in other generations was not made known to the sons of men, as it has now been revealed to His holy apostles and prophets in the Spirit." The mystery is identified by Paul to be "that the Gentiles are fellow heirs and fellow members of the body, and fellow partakers of the promise in Christ Jesus through the gospel." Charles Ryrie tells us, "The Old Testament does predict Gentile blessing for the millennial period (Isaiah 2:1-4; 61:5-6), but the specific blessings do not include equality with the Jews as is true today in the Body of Christ" (Ryrie, p. 134). Gentiles and believing Jews are fellow heirs and fellow members of the body of Christ. "This equality is the point of the mystery revealed to the apostles and prophets in New Testament times" (Ryrie, p. 34). Harold Hoehner explains:

> The mystery mentioned in Ephesians was hidden in God in ages past (3:9). It was something that could not be understood by human ingenuity or study. God revealed it to the apostles and prophets by the Spirit (3:4). Now that it is revealed, it is open to everyone and it is simple to understand and thus not relegated to an intellectual minority. Ephesians views God's sacred secret as believing Jews and Gentiles united into one body. In the OT Gentiles could be a part of the company of God, but they had to become Jews in order to belong to it. In the NT Gentiles do not become Jews nor do Jews become Gentiles. Rather, both believing Jews and Gentiles

become one new entity, Christians (Eph. 2:15-16). That is the mystery (Hoehner, pp. 433–34).

Paul teaches this same truth in Romans 16:25-27 and Colossians 1:24-29.

He says that the specific purpose of his ministry (Ephesians 3:7-8) is "to bring to light what is the administration of the mystery which for ages has been hidden in God, who created all things; in order that the manifold wisdom of God might now be made known through the church to the rulers and the authorities in the heavenly places" (verses 9-10). In previous ages—before New Testament times—God purposely hid His intentions from all, including the angelic world, because He wants to teach them something through this new organism known as the church. Thus, pedagogy is the reason for the progressive revelation of His plan.

Further, Paul states specifically that the church age "was in accordance with the eternal purpose which He carried out in Christ Jesus our Lord" (Ephesians 3:11). This is why dispensationalists have never taught the so-called plan A and plan B theory that critics suppose we hold. Dispensationalists have always taught that God has always had a single plan, carried out in stages. He previously revealed the portion relating to Israel, while He hid the portion relating to the church until after the birth of Christ's body. Verse 10 says it is "the manifold wisdom of God," meaning His many-sided wisdom. Nondispensationalist Ernest Best, commenting on Ephesians 3:5, said, "There is both continuity and discontinuity between the testaments: our passage stressed the discontinuity" (Best, p. 306). Thus, God's single plan has multiple aspects (dispensations) to it. Both unity and diversity are parts of God's plan. Dispensationalists recognize both God's single plan and its various stages.

A mystery is a secret that cannot be learned through reason. It must be revealed, as it was to Paul. This is why dispensationalists, and anyone who understands Paul's statement here, believe that the church age is unique and undisclosed in prior history.

Not Disclosed in the Old Testament

Paul says the mystery "in other generations was not made known to the sons of men, as it has now been revealed to His holy apostles and prophets in the Spirit" (Ephesians 3:5). In this verse, "as" denotes a comparison of *kind* rather than a comparison of *degree*.

Hoehner (pp. 339–40) provides five reasons why the "as" is used in this context as a comparison of kind. First, even though "as" is

NEW TESTAMENT USES OF "MYSTERY"

REFERENCE	PASSAGE
Matthew 13:11	"the mysteries of the kingdom of heaven"
Mark 4:11	"the mystery of the kingdom of God"
Luke 8:10	"the mystery of the kingdom of God"
Romans 11:25	"this mystery…a partial hardening has happened to Israel"
Romans 16:25	"the mystery which has been kept secret for long ages past"
1 Corinthians 2:7	"God's wisdom in a mystery, the hidden wisdom"
1 Corinthians 4:1	"servants of Christ, and stewards of the mysteries of God"
1 Corinthians 15:51	"I tell you a mystery; we shall not all sleep, but we shall all be changed"
Ephesians 1:9	"He made known to us the mystery of His will"
Ephesians 3:2-3	"the stewardship of God's grace…that by revelation there was made known to me the mystery"
Ephesians 3:4	"you can understand my insight into the mystery of Christ"
Ephesians 3:9	"the mystery which for ages has been hidden in God"
Ephesians 5:32	"this mystery is great…with reference to Christ and the church"
Ephesians 6:19	"the mystery of the gospel"
Colossians 1:26	"the mystery which has been hidden from the past ages and generations"
Colossians 1:27	"the riches of the glory of this mystery among the Gentiles, which is Christ in you, the hope of glory"
Colossians 2:2	"true knowledge of God's mystery, that is, Christ Himself"
Colossians 4:3	"the mystery of Christ, for which I have also been imprisoned"
2 Thessalonians 2:7	"the mystery of lawlessness"
1 Timothy 3:9	"holding to the mystery of the faith"
1 Timothy 3:16	"great is the mystery of godliness"
Revelation 1:20	"the mystery of the seven stars…are the angels of the seven churches"
Revelation 10:7	"the mystery of God is finished"
Revelation 17:5	"mystery, 'BABYLON THE GREAT'"
Revelation 17:7	"the mystery of the woman and of the beast that carries her"

commonly used as a comparison of degree, it is also used a number of times as a comparison of kind. Second, "Paul wrote in verse 9 that this mystery was hidden for ages in God." Third, "The verb in verse 5 means 'to uncover, unveil' something that has previously been completely covered or hidden. There is no indication of a partial uncovering of the mystery in the OT." Fourth, "The parallel passage in Col. 1:26 does not use the adverbial conjunction *as* but rather the adversative conjunction *but* and reads, 'the mystery which has been hidden for ages and for generations; but now was made manifest to his saints.' This corresponds with Romans 16:25-26, where Paul states that the mystery was kept secret for ages *but* now has been manifested." Finally, the adverb "now" agrees with Colossians 1:26 and Romans 16:26, marking the contrast between the past and present ages. "The same temporal adverb in Eph. 3:10 further substantiates this: 'In order that the manifold wisdom of God (which is the mystery of Jews and Gentiles united in one body) might *now* be made known to the rulers and authorities in the heavenly places through the church.' If the heavenly hosts in OT times did not know of this mystery, it is most unlikely that the people of that era would have known about it."

The Mystery of the Rapture

Paul speaks of the rapture as a "mystery" in 1 Corinthians 15:51-54. A mystery is a new truth that a New Testament writer reveals as part of God's plan for the church age. This supports the notion that the rapture is for the church and is a separate event from the second coming. The second coming was predicted in the Old Testament many times (Daniel 12:1-3; Zechariah 12:10; 14:4). Paul would not identify the rapture as a mystery if it was revealed in the Old Testament. Thus, because the rapture is called a mystery, it is a newly revealed event and is distinct from the second coming. This understanding supports the pretribulational rapture view, which places the rapture before the Tribulation and the second coming at the end of the Tribulation.

The Mystery of Iniquity

Paul says in 2 Thessalonians 2:7 that "the mystery of lawlessness is already at work; only he who now restrains will do so until he is taken out of the way." The next verse says that once restraint is removed, "the lawless one will be revealed." Since "mystery" means a secret, Paul speaks in this passage about Satan's plan for the "man of lawlessness" (verses 2,8), more widely known as the Antichrist, once he comes on the scene during the Tribulation. The emphasis upon "mystery" implies that we would not know or be able to figure out this satanic program without God's revelation of this evil plot.

Paul outlines the mystery of lawlessness, involving the man of lawlessness in 2 Thessalonians 2:1-12. The passage says that this satanic plan is already at work during the present time (the current church age), but its full development and implementation awaits removal of the restrainer, which will take place at the rapture. This event allows the man of lawlessness to bring his secret program onto the stage of history during the Tribulation.

The Mystery of Israel's Blindness

That partial blindness was to happen to the nation of Israel was no mystery. This partial blindness was revealed in the Old Testament (Isaiah 6:6-13). Romans 11:25 tells us, "I do not want you, brethren, to be uninformed of this mystery, lest you be wise in your own estimation, that a partial hardening has happened to Israel until the fullness of the Gentiles has come in." The new piece of information revealed here is the timing of Israel's release from blindness. Israel's blindness will be lifted when the full number of Gentiles are saved. When the fullness of the Gentiles has come in, according to the next verse (11:26), "all Israel will be saved."

The Mysteries of the Kingdom

Matthew 13 (see also Mark 4 and Luke 8) mentions "mysteries of the kingdom." This does not refer to a mysterious form of the kingdom, as some teach. In this passage, "of" means "concerning." In context, Jesus is teaching His disciples new truths concerning the kingdom of God in light of Israel's national rejection at His first coming.

The parables of Matthew 13 provide insight into the course of the current church age. Since Matthew 13 surveys this present age in its relation to the kingdom, the parables cover the period of time between Christ's two advents—His first and second comings. This includes the rapture, Tribulation, second coming, and judgment, but it also includes an important overview of our present era. What are these mysteries or new revelations about the kingdom that Matthew 13 depicts? J. Dwight Pentecost says,

> We may summarize the teaching as to the course of the age by saying: (1) there will be a sowing of the Word throughout the age, which (2) will be imitated by a false counter sowing; (3) the kingdom will assume huge outer proportions, but (4) be marked by inner doctrinal corruption; yet, the Lord will gain for Himself (5) a peculiar treasure from among Israel, and (6) from the church; (7) the age will end in judgment with the unrighteous excluded from the kingdom to be inaugurated and the righteous taken in to enjoy the blessing of Messiah's reign (Pentecost, p. 149).

The Mystery of the Faith

Paul says in 1 Timothy 3:9 that deacons should be "holding to the mystery of the faith with a clear conscience." In this context, "mystery of the faith" refers to the new revelations that God has given through the apostle Paul. In other words, it refers to church-age doctrine that is contained in the New Testament epistles. Paul wants deacons to be individuals who believe New Testament doctrine.

The Mystery of Godliness

In 1 Timothy 3:16 Paul mentions "the mystery of godliness." This too must be a New Testament revelation to the apostle Paul. What is it? It deals with the dynamics of living the

New Testament Christian life as taught in Paul's epistles.

—THOMAS ICE

BIBLIOGRAPHY

Best, Ernest. *Ephesians.* International Critical Commentary. Edinburgh: T & T Clark, 1998.

Hoehner, Harold W. *Ephesians: An Exegetical Commentary.* Grand Rapids: Baker Books, 2002.

Pentecost, J. Dwight. *Things to Come.* Grand Rapids: Zondervan, 1958.

Ryrie, Charles C. *Dispensationalism Today.* Chicago: Moody Press, 1965.

Witmer, John. "Mystery." In *The Theological Wordbook.* Eds. Don Campbell, Wendell Johnston, John Walvoord, and John Witmer. Nashville: Word, 2000.

NEW JERUSALEM

SCRIPTURE DESCRIBES the New Jerusalem as "the Jerusalem above" (Galatians 4:26), "the city of the living God, the heavenly Jerusalem" (Hebrews 12:22), and "the holy city" that "comes down out of heaven from God" (Revelation 21:2,10). The Old Testament refers to it as the abode of God; in the New Testament, it is also the heavenly home of the saints. The sacred structures within the heavenly city contributed the heavenly design for the earthly Tabernacle and Temple, and in its future descended form as the "tabernacle of God among men" (Revelation 21:3) it will constitute a celestial Temple that is both physical (Revelation 21:12-21) and spiritual (Revelation 21:22).

THE NEW JERUSALEM IN THE OLD TESTAMENT

The Old Testament prefigures the heavenly Jerusalem in the heavenly "mountain" and "sanctuary." Ezekiel refers to "the holy mountain of God" as well as "sanctuaries" in heaven (Ezekiel 28:14,16). Psalm 2 refers to "God who sits in the heavens" and "Zion, My holy mountain" (verses 4-5). The former refers to the place where God is enthroned in heaven, and the latter refers to the earthly Jerusalem, where God will enthrone His King after defeating the nations in the battle of Armageddon. Davidic psalms also refer to God being in His "house" or "Temple" (Psalm 11:4; 23:6; 26:8; 27:4; 138:2), even though the Temple was not built until after David's death. Such references must then be to the heavenly Temple, an identification that one psalm makes explicitly: "The LORD is in His holy Temple; the LORD's throne is in heaven" (Psalm 11:4). In this Hebrew parallelism, "holy Temple" and "throne in heaven" must refer to the same thing. Both Moses (Exodus 25:9,40) and David (1 Chronicles 28:11-19) were shown the heavenly Temple and used it as a pattern for the later construction of the earthly sanctuary (the Tabernacle and the First Temple). If there is a heavenly Temple, would there not also be a heavenly Jerusalem, since the earthly structures were copied after the heavenly (Hebrews 9:23)?

The Old Testament does not explicitly mention the New Jerusalem, but it speaks of the eternality and inviolability of Jerusalem. Psalm 125:1 says, "Those who trust in the LORD are as Mount Zion, which cannot be moved, but abides forever." However, the Old Testament prophets also predicted that neither the present earth nor heaven would continue (Isaiah 34:4). A New Jerusalem must be created to fulfill such prophecies. Some prophecies tie a restored Jerusalem to a new heaven and new earth. For example, Isaiah 65:17-18 says, "For behold, I create new heavens and a new earth; and the former things will not be remembered or come to mind. But be glad and rejoice forever in what I create; for behold, I create Jerusalem for rejoicing and her people for gladness." Isaiah 66:20-22 adds, "Then they shall bring all your brethren from all the nations...to My holy mountain Jerusalem....I will also take some of them for priests and for Levites, says the LORD. For just as the new heavens and the new earth which I make will endure before Me, declares the LORD, so your offspring and your name will endure."

Despite the association of Jerusalem with a new creation, some ambiguity remains. The context of Isaiah 65:17-25 reveals that the mil-lennial kingdom is in view because death (verse 20), decay (verse 22), and giving birth (verse 23) remain. However, the opening statement of the section (verse 17) concerns the new heavens and earth. This could be a general introduction with the millennial description following, but it is unclear. In Isaiah 66:10-24 the same period seems to be in view from verses 10-21, but the comparison to the new heavens and earth points to the eternal state (note the statement of eternal punishment in verse 24). Nevertheless, later Judaism apparently understood these implications and built upon them.

THE NEW JERUSALEM IN LATER JUDAISM

The goal of the restoration was conformity to the divine ideal, but the earthly restoration after the exile did not achieve this. After the Jews built the Second Temple, Jewish apocalyptic literature and the Jewish midrashim developed the concept of a heavenly restoration. These extra-biblical documents describe as the pinnacle of restoration a heavenly Jerusalem, perfect in every respect, which either replaces or transforms the imperfect earthly Jerusalem. The following Jewish apocryphal texts contain apocalyptic references to the New Jerusalem: Tobit 13:8-18; Testament of Dan 5:12-13; Sybilline Oracles 5:420-27; 1 Enoch 90:28-29; 2 Esdras 7:26; 10:25-28; 13:36; and 2 Baruch 4; 32:1-4. The Dead Sea Scroll documents contain an apocalyptic text known as The New Jerusalem. Extant only in a collection of fragmentary copies from four different caves, it records a vision of the New Jerusalem after the fashion of Ezekiel's vision of millennial Jerusalem and the Temple (Ezekiel 40–48). As in Ezekiel and Revelation, the dimensions of the New Jerusalem are much greater than those of the ancient city of Jerusalem. The language describing the city's construction is similar, including such details as the 12 gates of the city, each named for one of the 12 tribes, beautiful walls of pure gold, streets paved with alabaster and onyx, and living waters. In addition, this text notes that this New Jerusalem will appear after the final end-time battle in which Israel emerges victorious over the Gentile nations and is restored in glory. Because this structure appears to be of earthly construction and houses a new Temple, it may be the restored Jerusalem of the millennial kingdom. Even so, it bears witness to the New Jerusalem tradition in Second Temple Judaism. Jesus and the writers of the New Testament would have been well acquainted with this.

In the Talmudic age, the Jewish community had lost both its Temple and its city but not its promises. Therefore, even while retaining the hope of the restoration of the earthly Jerusalem, teachers emphasized that which could not be lost or destroyed—the heavenly Jerusalem. For example, we hear the rabbis explain, "Not only on the face of this earth is there a Jerusalem, called in Hebrew *Yerushalaim Shel Matta* ('Jerusalem the Lower'), but also in heaven is there such a city: *Yerushalaim Shel Maalah* ('Jerusalem the Upper')." According to the Judaism of the Second Temple and the Talmudic periods, the New Jerusalem appears as both present and future. For example, the Talmud teaches that although the heavenly city will be realized in the age of redemption, the righteous can already see it and receive inspiration from it in moments of grace. Therefore, Judaism understood that the New Jerusalem exists presently, will be realized in their millennial era, and will continue into the final age.

THE NEW JERUSALEM IN THE NEW TESTAMENT

The New Testament follows the Old Testament concept of the heavenly Jerusalem in such passages as Hebrews 13:14, which sets the heavenly city as the goal of the godly. Hebrews traces this hope back to Israel's beginning in Abraham: "By faith Abraham...was looking for the city which has foundations, whose architect and builder is God" (Hebrews 11:8-10). This text indicates that the heavenly Jerusalem was preexistent, and the righteous were at home with God there.

In like manner, the New Testament continues the Old Testament teaching that the earthly sanctuaries were constructed according to a divinely revealed pattern based on struc-

tures within the heavenly Jerusalem. Stephen's speech in Acts chapter 7 alludes to Exodus 25:8-9,40, and Stephen declares, "He who spoke to Moses directed him to make it [the Tabernacle] according to the pattern which he had seen" (Acts 7:44). The author of Hebrews compares the earthly and heavenly sanctuaries and refers to "the copies of the things in the heavens" (Hebrews 9:23). These same passages teach that "the Most High does not dwell in houses made by human hands" (Acts 7:48), but in "the greater and more perfect tabernacle, not made with hands...not of this creation" (Hebrews 9:11). These heavenly structures are not symbolic because the actual earthly structures were made according to them. This should be kept in mind when considering the texts in Revelation that depict the furniture of the heavenly Temple (Revelation 11:19; cf. 4:5; 5:8; 6:9; 8:3; 9:13; 14:18; 15:5-8; 16:7) and the structural elements and dimensions of the New Jerusalem itself (Revelation 21:12-21).

The New Jerusalem also appears in several New Testament texts. In Galatians 4:26, the apostle Paul speaks of "the Jerusalem above" in distinction to "the present Jerusalem" (verse 25). The author of Hebrews also understood the concept and contrasted the heavenly Jerusalem as a place of grace to the earthly Mount Sinai as a place of the law (Hebrews 12:18-22). He also described the inhabitants of the heavenly Jerusalem: "You have come to Mount Zion and to the city of the living God, the heavenly Jerusalem, and to myriads of angels, to the general assembly and church of the first-born who are enrolled in heaven, and to God, the judge of all, and to the spirits of the righteous made perfect, and to Jesus, the mediator of a new covenant" (Hebrews 12:22-24). This registry accords with Old Testament statements concerning the heavenly destination of believers (2 Kings 2:11; Job 19:25-27; Psalm 11:7; 73:24) and with descriptions of the heavenly court and the population of the New Jerusalem in Revelation (see below).

Hebrews 12:26-28 explains that the old creation will one day be removed, leaving that "which cannot be shaken" (the indestructible kingdom, the heavenly Jerusalem) as the eternal inheritance of the saints (see also Isaiah 65:17; 66:22). This agrees with Peter's description of the day of the Lord, which will climax in a cosmic dissolution and "a new heavens and a new earth" (2 Peter 3:10-13). Paul declares that "our citizenship is in heaven" (Philippians 3:20; see also Ephesians 2:19; Hebrews 12:1-2).

THE DESCRIPTION OF THE NEW JERUSALEM IN REVELATION

The term "New Jerusalem" (Greek *ten hagian Ierousalem*) is found only in Revelation. Because the book was written after the destruction of the Temple in Jerusalem, some commentators have suggested that the concept of a "new" Jerusalem developed in response to the loss of the "old" Jerusalem. However, the "old" Jerusalem was never entirely lost to the Jews. The concept had existed in the Old Testament, Jewish apocalyptic literature, and the New Testament letters long before the Temple's destruction. John, as a Jew, would have been quite familiar with these texts and traditions. For example, Revelation 21:22-23 closely parallels earlier Jewish midrashim on Isaiah 60:19 and Psalm 132:17. The similarities in these accounts do not mean that John borrowed his material from the Jewish midrashim, but that Jews and Jewish Christians arrived at similar conclusions concerning the New Jerusalem based on their interpretation of the same scriptural texts.

The most complete description of the New Jerusalem is in Revelation 21–22. John calls it "the bride, the wife of the Lamb" (Revelation 21:9), which has been "made ready as a bride adorned for her husband" (Revelation 21:2). The background of the marriage metaphor is the Jewish custom of the bridegroom husband leaving the bride at the betrothal to prepare a new house where they would dwell together once he returned to take away his bride. When the bridegroom returned, the bride was splendidly adorned, and the wedding took place. In the same way, the New Jerusalem will come down from God as the glorious place promised to the church.

The appearance of the New Jerusalem also finally fulfills the divine goal for the earthly Tabernacle and Temple (Exodus 25:8) and the church: It will be a "spiritual temple" (Ephesians 2:21-22) where the Creator and His creatures can enjoy a holy relationship. The New Jerusalem is therefore "the tabernacle of God" where God will forever "dwell" among His people (Revelation 21:3; 22:3-4) and a "temple" for "the Lord God, the Almighty and the Lamb" (Revelation 21:22). In this light, it is significant that the New Jerusalem is laid out as a "square" (Revelation 21:16). This design of a cube matches the unique cubical shape of the Holy of Holies in the Temple, in which the presence of God dwelt in the midst of Israel (1 Kings 6:20; 8:10-13; 2 Chronicles 3:8; 5:14–6:2). The New Jerusalem, then, completes the purpose of the temporary Holy of Holies by serving as the permanent and unrestricted meeting place for all the saints (as God's priests) and God.

Revelation compares the city's building materials to precious earthly stones. The brilliance and splendor of iridescent stones of every color and hue and streets of pure gold like transparent glass both speak of accommodation. In Exodus 24, when Moses and the elders of Israel were permitted to see the God of Israel, their vision of His heavenly court was of "a pavement of sapphire as clear as the sky" (verse 10). Ezekiel's vision of God's throne contained similar descriptions: "something like an expanse, like the awesome gleam of crystal," "something resembling a throne, like lapis lazuli in appearance" (Ezekiel 1:22,26).

This jeweled adornment of the city and the statement that the city is "the bride, the wife of the Lamb" (Revelation 21:9) have caused many interpreters to conclude that the whole description of the New Jerusalem is symbolic of the church. However, the language here is metaphorical, the use of an object for what it contains (the church *in* the city). Revelation 21:2 says the city is "made ready *as* a bride adorned for her husband," a clear use of simile, a literary device that makes a comparison between two separate things. Moreover, in Revelation 22:3 the church ("the bond-servants of the Lamb") is clearly separate from the city (in which they serve), so it cannot be a symbol of them. The city qualifies in every sense as a physical reality, with measurable architectural structures, planned design, building materials, rivers, trees, and human inhabitants. What appears to be an incredible description is intended to accommodate our present inability to grasp such heavenly realities. An eternal city designed for an eternal people is not of earth, and as the handiwork of an infinite God, we should not expect it to conform to human convention.

God's new creation (Revelation 21:5) bears many similarities with His original creation. The inner city has "a river of the water of life," "the tree of life," and "fruits" and "leaves...for healing of the nations" (Revelation 22:1-2). Although reminiscent of the Garden of Eden (Genesis 2:8-17), there is no reason to suppose the scene in either narrative is symbolic. Like the earthly Tabernacle and Temple, which were patterned after the heavenly originals, the earthly Garden of Eden could have been created as an archetype of the New Jerusalem.

The walls of the New Jerusalem reveal that Israel and the church share equally in the inheritance of the city. The names of the 12 tribes of Israel are inscribed on its 12 gates. The names of the 12 apostles are on its 12 foundation stones (Revelation 21:12-14). Even though these are all Jewish, they still represent the dispensations of Israel and the church (as in Hebrews 12:23).

The New Jerusalem has the glory of God (Revelation 21:11). This particular feature seems to have most impressed John, for he emphasized it in his description of the city. The supernatural illumination of the city, eliminating the need for the earthly cycle of day and night, derives from the presence of God and Christ (Revelation 21:23; 22:5). The illumination of the city also extends to the earth, allowing "the nations to walk by its light" (Revelation 21:24). This verse and verse 26 also state that the earthly kings will bring their tribute into the heavenly city. The prophets predicted that Gentiles would make pilgrimages to the earthly, millennial Temple and pay tribute to the Messiah (Isaiah 60:6-9; 66:18-21; Haggai 2:7; Zechariah 14:16-19). This may support the view that the New Jerusalem descends to earth over the earthly Jerusalem during the millennium so that the nations pay tribute to God in both the earthly and heavenly Jerusalem. The immediate objection may be that this context describes the eternal state, not the millennium (Revelation 21:1). However, John may be considering the position of the people (within and without the city) without regard to the position of the city itself (that is, in the millennium or in eternity).

Regardless of when the New Jerusalem descends from heaven, the prophetic promise of this eternal home of God's people compels the prayer of the saints, "Amen. Come, Lord Jesus" (Revelation 22:20).

—RANDALL PRICE

BIBLIOGRAPHY

Hayut-Man, Yitzhak. *Realizing the Heavenly Jerusalem.* Jerusalem: Academy of Jerusalem Monographs 3. March, 1995.

McClain, Alva J. *The Greatness of the Kingdom.* Winona Lake, IN: BMH Books, 1974.

Pentecost, Dwight J. *Things to Come.* Chicago: Moody Press, 1956.

Price, Randall. *Jerusalem in Prophecy.* Eugene, OR: Harvest House Publishers, 1998.

Smith, Wilbur M. *The Biblical Doctrine of Heaven.* Chicago: Moody Press, 1968.

Walvoord, John F. *The Revelation of Jesus Christ.* Chicago: Moody Press, 1966.

NUMBERS IN PROPHECY

SYMBOLIC NUMBERS in the Bible can be fascinating. Not all numbers in the Bible have a special meaning (such as the number of years each king reigned in Israel); many are simply statements of fact. On the other hand, certain numbers seem to appear repeatedly throughout the Bible. For example, Noah's deluge lasted 40 days, Moses was on the mountain 40 days, the Israelites were in the wilderness 40 years, and Christ's temptation lasted 40 days.

Symbolic and prophetic numbers are especially significant in the book of Revelation. However, these are also real numbers that point to real events. Revelation is woven around a series of threes and sevens. The triplet reveals the past, present, and future:

1. Past: "the things which you have seen" (chapter 1)

2. Present: "the things which are" (chapters 2–3)

3. Future: "the things which shall take place after these things" (chapters 4–22)

Revelation is built on seven groups of seven visions:

1. Seven churches (1:9–3:22)

2. Seven seals (6:1–8:1)

3. Seven trumpets (8:2–11:19)

4. Seven symbolic figures (12–14)

5. Seven bowls (15–16)

6. Seven judgments (17:1–19:10)

7. Seven triumphs (19:11–22:21)

Symbolic numbers are found everywhere in the Apocalypse. They include ½, 1, 2, 3, 4, 5, 6, 7, 10, 12, 24, 42, 144, 666, 1000, 1260, 1600, 7000, 12,000, 144,000, 100 million, and 200 million. The term *hour* is used ten times in Revelation (3:3,10; 9:15; 11:13; 14:7,15; 17:12; 18:10,17,19), always referring to a brief period of time (for example, "in one hour your judgment has come").

THREE

Three is the symbolic number of the Trinity. It is one of John's favorite numbers, and he constantly expresses himself in triplets: He blesses the one who reads, those who hear, and those who heed the prophecy (1:3). Jesus Christ is "the faithful witness, the firstborn of the dead, and the ruler of the kings of the earth" (1:5). Christ loved us, released us, and made us to be a kingdom of priests (1:5-6). The Lord God is and was and is to come (1:8). He is the living one, He was dead, and He is alive forevermore (1:18). Jesus knows the situation in Smyrna: the tribulation, the poverty, and the blasphemy (2:9). Christ exhorts the

believers in Sardis to remember what they received, to keep it, and to repent (3:3). The Laodiceans should buy gold, white garments, and eye salve (3:18). The book of Revelation includes scores of these triplets.

The number three also figures prominently in several passages referring to judgment. Revelation contains three main series of judgments: the seals, the trumpets, and the bowls. Judgment consists of basically three elements: fire, smoke, and brimstone. These elements kill a third part of mankind (9:17-18). A third of the earth is burned up, as well as a third of the trees (8:7), and a third of the sun, moon, and stars are darkened for a third of the day (8:12). A satanic trinity, the dragon, the beast, and the false prophet (16:13), oppose Christ's reign on earth. Finally, Satan suffers a threefold defeat—on earth (12:9), into the abyss (20:1-3), and into the lake of fire (20:10).

FOUR

When John describes the earth, he often uses four characteristics. For example, the earth has four regions (north, south, east, and west) and four seasons. The inhabitants of the earth include tribes, tongues, peoples, and nations (5:9; see also 10:11), and the New Jerusalem lies foursquare (21:16 KJV). Revelation describes four living creatures (4:6) as well as four angels at the four corners of the earth, holding the four winds (7:1). Four angels are bound at the Euphrates River (9:14-15).

SIX AND SEVEN

Six is the number of man, who was created on the sixth day. In Revelation 13:18 it represents the most wicked man, the Antichrist.

Seven is the most significant number in the Apocalypse. Revelation mentions seven spirits, seven churches, seven lampstands, seven stars, seven lamps of fire, seven horns, seven eyes, seven seals, seven trumpets, seven bowls, seven songs, seven angels, seven thunders, seven "worthys," seven heads, seven crowns, seven mountains, seven kings, and seven plagues. It includes a sevenfold description of Christ (1:14-16), a sevenfold message to each of the churches (chapters 2–3), sevenfold praise of the Lamb (5:12), a sevenfold result of judgment (6:12-14), and a sevenfold blessing (7:12). Seven thousand were killed (11:13), Christ accomplished a sevenfold triumph (11:19), and John sees seven "new things" (chapters 21–22). Revelation includes seven beatitudes (1:3; 14:13; 16:15; 19:9; 20:6; 22:7,14) and seven "I am" statements by Christ (1:8,17,18; 2:23; 21:6; 22:13,16). The frequent use of the number seven is part of the divine signature in the Apocalypse.

TWELVE

Twelve is the number of completeness. Israel has 12 tribes, Christ has 12 apostles, and 24 elders (a double 12) are seated around the throne. The tree of life has 12 types of fruit (22:2), the New Jerusalem has 12 gates guarded by 12 angels (21:12), and the city has 12 foundations (21:14). Twelve precious stones adorn the foundation stones and 12 pearl gates (21:19-21). John also includes multiples of 12: Each of the 12 tribes contains 12,000 people, making a total of 144,000 (12,000 x 12), and the city wall measures 144 cubits (12 x 12).

John uses these numbers to express the uniqueness and completeness of his prophecy of future events. All in all, the numerical structure of the Apocalypse makes it the most unique book in all of Scripture. Its symbolic numbers point us to God's perfect revelation of future events, one item at a time.

—ED HINDSON

BIBLIOGRAPHY

Cascione, J.M. *In Search of the Biblical Order.* Cleveland: Biblion Publishing, 1987.

Davis, John D. *Biblical Numerology.* Grand Rapids: Baker Books, 1968.

Hindson, Ed. *The Book of Revelation.* Chattanooga: AMG Publishing, 2002.

Metzger, Bruce. *Breaking the Code: Understanding the Book of Revelation.* Nashville: Abingdon Press, 1993.

Tenney, Merrill. *Interpreting Revelation.* Grand Rapids: Eerdmans Publishing Company, 1957.

OLIVET DISCOURSE

THE OLIVET DISCOURSE (Matthew 24–25; Mark 13; Luke 21; see Luke 17:20-37) is Jesus' longest prophetic sermon and one of the most important prophetic passages in all the Bible.

THE CONTEXTUAL SETTING

In the events leading up to Matthew 24, Christ presents Himself to the people of Israel as their Messiah, but they reject Him. Jesus rebukes them and exposes their hypocrisy and unbelief in Matthew 22 and 23. He notes that this present generation of Jewish leaders is like those from previous generations, who killed the prophets (23:29-36). Christ then tells the Jewish leaders, "Truly I say to you, all these things will come upon this generation" (23:36 NASB). What things? It will be the curse of judgment, which will come upon the Jewish people through the Roman army in A.D. 70. "All hope for a turning of Israel to God in repentance has gone," notes Stanley Toussaint (pp. 264–65). "The King therefore has no alternative but to reject that nation for the time being with regard to its kingdom program. The clear announcement of this decision is seen in these verses of Matthew's Gospel."

In spite of the fact that the Jewish people deserved the approaching judgment, Christ cries out, "O Jerusalem, Jerusalem, who kills the prophets and stones those who are sent to her! How often I wanted to gather your children together, the way a hen gathers her chicks under her wings, and you were unwilling" (23:37). Jesus wants to gather His people (as He prophesies in 24:31 that He will someday do), but instead, He will scatter them in judgment (Luke 21:24).

Jesus declares in Matthew 23:38, "Behold, your house is being left to you desolate!" To what does "your house" refer? In the context of this passage, it must be a reference to the Jewish Temple. Matthew 24:1-2 introduces a discussion between Jesus and His disciples about the Temple. Jesus startles them by saying, "Do you not see all these things? Truly I say to you, not one stone here shall be left upon another, which will not be torn down" (24:2). Both 23:38 and 24:2 refer to the same thing—the Temple, to which Jesus bids farewell until He returns in triumph at His second coming.

THE DISCIPLES' QUESTIONS

While sitting on the Mount of Olives, the disciples asked Jesus the following questions: "Tell us, when will these things be, and what will be the sign of Your coming, and of the end of the age?" (24:3). Are these two questions or three? Commentators disagree. If the disciples asked two questions, then surely the second question contains two parts. I believe the grammar of the passage shows that it contains two basic questions. This means that "Your coming" and "the end of the age" are closely related to one another in the mind of the disciples.

Clearly the first question relates to the destruction of the Temple, which happened during the Roman invasion and destruction of Jerusalem in A.D. 70. Equally clearly, the two parts of the second question have yet to be fulfilled in history. However, the disciples thought that all three events were related to a single event—the return of the Messiah (Zechariah 14:4). They were right to think of Zechariah 12–14. However, they were wrong to tie the impending judgment of Jerusalem and the Temple to the return of Messiah.

The disciples may have merged these events, but Christ did not. Matthew and Mark do not deal with the destruction of Jerusalem in their accounts of the Olivet Discourse. Their focus is upon the future Tribulation leading up to Christ's return. Only in Luke's account does Christ deal with the destruction of Jerusalem (21:20-24). But Luke also deals with the future Tribulation and Christ's return (21:25-36). For whatever reason, Matthew and Mark's entire focus is upon the last question: "What will be the sign of Your coming, and of the end of the age?"

The disciples first ask Jesus, "Tell us, when will these things be?" (Matthew 24:3). Christ had been speaking about the Temple and a time when "not one stone here shall be left upon another" (Matthew 24:2), so Jesus was clearly prophesying about the destruction of

the Temple in Jerusalem by the Romans in A.D. 70.

Luke 21:20-24 records Jesus' answer to the disciples' first question:

> When you see *Jerusalem surrounded by armies*, then recognize that *her desolation is at hand*. Then let those who are in Judea flee to the mountains, and let those who are in the midst of the city depart, and let not those who are in the country enter the city; because *these are days of vengeance*, in order that all things which are written may be fulfilled. Woe to those who are with child and to those who nurse babes in those days; for *there will be great distress upon the land*, and *wrath to this people*, and *they will fall by the edge of the sword*, and *will be led captive into all the nations*; and *Jerusalem will be trampled under foot* by the Gentiles until the times of the Gentiles be fulfilled (Luke 21:20-24, emphasis added).

Luke 21:20-24 clearly refers to the first-century Roman invasion of Jerusalem. The italicized words in the quote above identify key phrases that point to the A.D. 70 fulfillment. Yet this language is missing in Matthew 24 and Mark 13. Instead of "great distress upon the land, and wrath to this people," Matthew 24 speaks of the Son of Man sending His angels to rescue the Jewish people (Matthew 24:29-31).

So the disciples' first question in the Olivet Discourse relates to the destruction of Jerusalem in A.D. 70. Christ's answer is recorded only in Luke 21. Matthew 24–25 and Mark 13 deal only with the last question, which refers to events that have not yet occurred.

THE TRIBULATION PARALLELS

Matthew 24:4-41 refers to the seven-year Tribulation period (Daniel 9:24-27). The Tribulation is divided in half by the abomination of desolation, which Jesus mentions in verse 15. Thus, verses 4-14 refer to the first half of the Tribulation and are parallel to the first

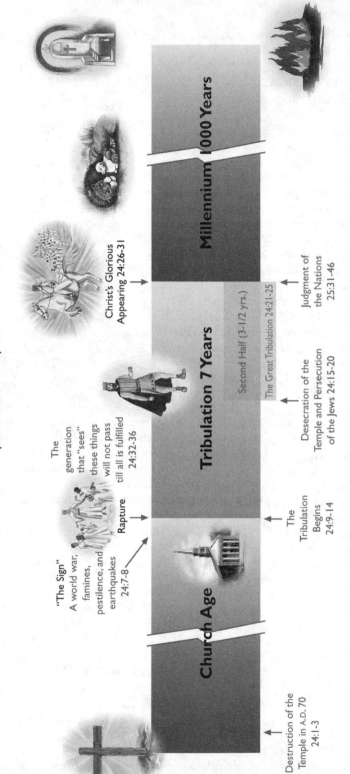

THE OLIVET DISCOURSE
(MATTHEW 24–25)

Destruction of the Temple in A.D. 70 24:1-3

"The Sign" A world war, famines, pestilence, and earthquakes 24:7-8

The generation that "sees" these things will not pass till all is fulfilled 24:32-36

Rapture

Christ's Glorious Appearing 24:26-31

Church Age

The Tribulation Begins 24:9-14

Tribulation 7 Years

The Great Tribulation 24:21-25

Desecration of the Temple and Persecution of the Jews 24:15-20

Second Half (3-1/2 yrs.)

Judgment of the Nations 25:31-46

Millennium 1000 Years

five seal judgments, which are described in Revelation 6.

Birth Pangs

Matthew 24:8 characterizes the events of verses 4-7 as "the beginning of birth-pangs." Most likely our Lord had in mind the Old Testament reference to birth pangs in Jeremiah 30:6-7 (see also Isaiah 13:8; 26:17-18; Jeremiah 2:32), which says, "Ask now, and see, if a male can give birth. Why do I see every man with his hands on his loins, as a woman in childbirth? And why have all faces turned pale? Alas! For that day is great, there is none like it; and it is the time of Jacob's distress, but he will be saved from it."

Do Not Be Deceived

Since the Tribulation begins with the arrival of the Antichrist, it is not surprising that this section also begins with a warning to believers about his arrival. Jesus begins answering the disciples' question with a warning about false messiahs: "See to it that no one misleads you. For many will come in My name, saying, 'I am the Christ,' and will mislead many" (Matthew 24:4-5). Spiritual deception will be the primary purpose of the Antichrist during the Tribulation, and Jesus warns His followers to make sure they are not misled. The emphasis in verse 5 is upon "many." The prophecy of many false messiahs obviously does not refer to events leading up to the A.D. 70 destruction of Jerusalem.

Wars and Rumors of Wars

The Greek word *polemos* is a general word for war and connotes the "whole course of hostilities" rather than just the individual battles that comprise a larger war campaign. This is a reference to actual wars against the future Jewish people.

Here we have the future parallel to Revelation 6:4 and the red horse judgment: "...to take peace from the earth, and that men should slay one another; and a great sword was given to him." The first seal judgment of Revelation 6:2 is the rider on a white horse, a counterfeit

PARALLELS BETWEEN THE OLIVET DISCOURSE AND THE SEAL JUDGMENTS OF REVELATION

	REVELATION 6	MATTHEW 24	MARK 13	LUKE 21
False Messiahs, False Prophets	2	5,11	6	8
Wars	2-4	6-7	7	9
International Discord	3-4	7	8	10
Famines	5-8	7	8	11
Pestilences	8			11
Persecution, Martyrdom	9-11	9	9-13	12-17
Earthquakes	12	7	8	11
Cosmic Phenomena	12-14			11

Christ who corresponds to Matthew 24:4-5. This means that the Antichrist begins the Tribulation with a false peace that soon turns into multiple wars all over the globe.

That Is Not Yet the End

People will tend to think that these wars signal the end, but such is not the case. In fact, this warning has been ignored down through church history. Too often many have thought that military conflicts were ushering in the end of the age. Thus, Christ is telling His disciples that when one sees the beginning of the birth pangs—the first few seal judgments of Revelation 6—the seven-year Tribulation period is just beginning. Many more events must unfold before people can "straighten up and lift up [their] heads, because [their] redemption is drawing near" (Luke 21:28).

Nations and Kingdoms on the Rise

The first half of Matthew 24:7 says, "For nation will rise against nation, and kingdom against kingdom." Immediately we notice a difference between our Lord's use of "nation" (Greek, *ethnos*) and "kingdom" (Greek, *basileia*). The use of these terms implies that national ethnic conflicts will escalate into international wars of a global magnitude.

Taking into account verses 6-7, this passage is describing events that will take place during the first part of the Tribulation. Matthew 24:6-7 is parallel to the second seal judgment in Revelation 6:3-4 and refers to the future Tribulation. Revelation 6:4 says, "Another, a red horse, went out; and to him who sat on it, it was granted to take peace from the earth, and that men should slay one another; and a great sword was given to him." Thus, early in the Tribulation, the Antichrist is involved in warfare against nations and kingdoms (see also Daniel 7:8,23-24).

Famines and Earthquakes

We know that the "abomination of desolation" (Matthew 24:15) occurs in the middle of the seven-year period (Daniel 9:24-27), so events prior to verse 15 will take place in the first half of the Tribulation. This is further confirmed by the correlation of the major events

of Matthew 24:4-8 with the first four seal judgments of Revelation 6:1-8. This would mean that the famines and earthquakes of Matthew 24:7 speak of a future time, which Revelation 6:5-8 expounds upon, not of any events that have occurred during the last 2000 years, nor of anything in our present day.

Tribulation

Since the Olivet Discourse focuses on Jerusalem, Matthew 24:7 likely has Jewish persecution in view. However, Christians of all stripes will receive similar harsh treatment during this time of Tribulation. This sentence appears only in Matthew's account of the Olivet Discourse—perhaps because of his Jewish orientation.

The Old Testament teaches that the Tribulation will be a time of great persecution toward the Jewish people (Jeremiah 30:7,11,22-24; Ezekiel 20:33-44; 22:17-22; Daniel 7:25; 12:1-3; Hosea 5:15; Zephaniah 1:7–2:3). The New Testament echoes this teaching as well (Matthew 10:17-22; 24:9,15-24; Mark 13:9-20; Luke 21:12-19; Revelation 13:7; 18:24). The entire chapter of Revelation 12 is devoted to depicting the future persecution of the Jewish remnant during the second half of the seven-year Tribulation by Satan himself and his partner in crime—the Antichrist, also known as the beast.

Martyrdom

The persecution that Matthew notes in 24:9 is a future one that will take place during the first half of the Tribulation. The verb "deliver" is the same one used of Judas' betrayal of Jesus (Matthew 26:15) and supports the notion that this future deliverance unto death will be a similar betrayal of the Lord's people. John MacArthur says, "*Paradidômi* (will deliver) has the basic meaning of giving over and was often used in a technical sense for arrest by the police or military (see Matt. 4:12)" (MacArthur, p. 23).

The reference to martyrdom in this passage is a parallel passage to the fifth seal in Revelation 6:9-11. Revelation 6:9 says, "When He broke the fifth seal, I saw underneath the altar the souls of those who had been slain because of the word of God, and because of the testimony which they had maintained."

Increased Lawlessness

The Greek word *anomia* is usually translated as "lawless" or "iniquity." It carries with it the idea of deliberately disobeying a specific standard. According to the context of this passage, God's standard will be ignored. Often the word "lawlessness" is used in opposition to "righteousness" or "good deeds" (Matthew 23:28; Romans 6:19; 2 Corinthians 6:14; Titus 2:14; Hebrews 1:9).

This time of lawlessness will surely be an unusual time in all human history. Our Lord has been expounding upon the spiritual condition of unbelievers that will characterize the Tribulation period, especially the first half. This description of lawlessness strikes a parallel to Paul's description of the "man of lawlessness" in 2 Thessalonians 2:3. Matthew 24 builds toward the abomination of desolation (24:15), which will be committed by the Antichrist in the middle of the Tribulation. Paul ties the man of lawlessness to the abomination of desolation when he says, "...the man of lawlessness is revealed, the son of destruction, who opposes and exalts himself above every so-called god or object of worship, so that he takes his seat in the temple of God, displaying himself as being God" (2 Thessalonians 2:3-4).

The Gospel of the Kingdom

Matthew 24:14 describes a future event and parallels Revelation 14:6-7. Both passages are set in contexts that tell us that this global evangelization will take place just before the middle of the seven-year Tribulation. They were no more fulfilled during the nativity of the church than was the Great Commission. Matthew 24:14, like all of those prophecies in that context, awaits a future fulfillment—specifically, during the future Tribulation.

The Abomination of Desolation

Matthew explains that the reader can understand the term "abomination of desolation" by referring to Daniel's writings. The key passages that mention the term "abomination of desolation" are Daniel 9:27; 11:31; and 12:11. This is a technical term; it has a precise and consistent meaning in all passages. The phrase refers to an act of abomination that renders the Temple unclean.

Daniel 9:27 says that this abomination is to take place in the middle of a seven-year period. The passage says, "In the middle of the week he will put a stop to sacrifice and grain offering; and on the wing of abominations will come one who makes desolate." In other words, the future prince will do at that time exactly what Antiochus did in the second century B.C. But Daniel goes on to say that the one who commits this act will be destroyed three and one-half years later. Daniel 12:11 provides the precise chronology: "From the time that the regular sacrifice is abolished, and the abomination of desolation is set up, there will be 1,290 days."

In addition to the three passages in Daniel, the two references by our Lord in Matthew and Luke, Paul's teaching in 2 Thessalonians 2:4, and John's vision in Revelation 13:14-15 also have this event in view. The abomination of desolation, which the reader is to understand, includes the following:

1. It occurs in the Jewish Temple in Jerusalem (Daniel 11:31; 2 Thessalonians 2:4).

2. It involves a person setting up a statue in place of the regular sacrifice in the holy of holies (Daniel 11:31; 12:11; Revelation 13:14-15).

3. This results in the cessation of the regular sacrifice (Daniel 9:27; 11:31; 12:11).

4. There will be a time of about three and one-half years between this event and the end of the time period (Daniel 9:27; 12:11).

5. It involves an individual setting up a statue or image of himself so that he may be worshiped in place of God (Daniel 11:31; 2 Thessalonians 2:4; Revelation 13:14-15).

6. The image is made to come to life (Revelation 13:15).

7. A worship system of this false god is thus inaugurated (2 Thessalonians 2:4; Revelation 13:14-15).

8. At the end of this time period, the individual who commits the act will himself be cut off (Daniel 9:27).

THE GREAT TRIBULATION

Previously, we saw that Matthew 24:15 describes an event that fixes the chronological midpoint of the seven-year Tribulation. Verses 16-20 describe the recommended response of the faithful who see the abomination of desolation in Jerusalem. They are to flee Jerusalem as fast as they can. Why? Because the second half of the Tribulation will be a time of persecution for the Jewish remnant. It is called the Great Tribulation in relation to the fate of the Jewish remnant in Israel. During the first half, they were protected by the covenant between the Antichrist and the nation of Israel. However, the second half will be a time of great persecution by the Antichrist.

Matthew 24:21 speaks about the Great Tribulation, or the last three-and-one-half-year period of the Tribulation, which will culminate in the second advent of Christ. Dr. John Walvoord (p. 188) says, "The great tribulation, accordingly, is a specific period of time beginning with the abomination of desolation and closing with the second coming of Christ, in the light of Daniel's prophecies and confirmed by reference to forty-two months. In Revelation 11:2 and 13:5, the great tribulation is a specific three-and-a-half-year period leading up to the second coming."

Jesus explains that the Great Tribulation will be the Jewish people's most difficult time in history. Mark 13:19 is even clearer. Our Lord says, "Those days will be a time of tribulation such as has not occurred since the beginning of the creation which God created, until now, and never shall." John MacArthur (p. 44) says, "No time or event in the history of Israel fits the description of the holocaust Jesus is here speaking of. Clearly, the events described by our Lord, by Daniel, and by John must refer to the same great holocaust at the end time, just before the millennial kingdom is established on earth."

WHO ARE THE ELECT?

Jesus uses the term "the elect" three times in the Olivet Discourse (Matthew 14:22,24,31; also in Mark 13:20,22,27). All three uses in both books refer to the same entity. They clearly refer, in context, to some group of believers during the Tribulation. Since the church has been raptured, the term "the elect" cannot refer to her. Rather, it refers to the Jewish remnant.

The New Testament epistles refer to church age believers (both Jews and Gentiles) as "the elect" (see Romans 8:33; Colossians 3:12; 2 Timothy 2:10; Titus 1:1). But this term is used in a variety of other ways. Christ most likely uses the term "the elect" because He is looking forward to those belonging to the Jewish remnant. Though not yet saved, they will yet receive Him and be converted. This is verified by a parallel passage in Daniel 12:1, in which the angel speaking to Daniel says, "Now at that time Michael, the great prince who stands guard over the sons of your people, will arise. And there will be a time of distress such as never occurred since there was a nation until that time; and at that time your people, everyone who is found written in the book, will be rescued."

A FUTURE EVENT

Preterists deny that Matthew 24:27-31 pictures a bodily, physical return of Christ. Their view is supported by only a few interpreters throughout church history. That Jesus speaks here of His bodily return is supported by the context. In contrast to Christ's coming in verse 27 are the false Christs and false prophets of verses 23-24, who are clearly individuals that can be physically seen. Christ's return is juxtaposed to them. Christ's return will be public and obvious to all. This cannot fit some "judgment-coming" through the Roman army. Regardless of what other biblical passages may teach in other contexts, the context of Matthew 24 supports a bodily return of Jesus, which has to be the future second coming.

The Greek word *parousia* is used in this verse and four times in Matthew 24. Bauer, Arndt, Gingrich, and Danker's Greek–English Lexicon says that *parousia* means "presence" or "coming, advent," of Christ, and nearly always of His messianic advent in glory to judge the world at the end of this age. It cites all four uses of *parousia* in Matthew 24 as references to Christ's second advent. Thus, *parousia* carries the idea of a "presence coming," not the preterist notion of a "non-presence coming," an invisible coming. Our Lord's use of *parousia* demands His physical, bodily presence.

GLOBAL, NOT LOCAL

Matthew 24:27, which says, "Just as the lightning comes from the east, and flashes even to the west, so shall the coming of the Son of Man be," emphasizes a global coming. This verse is set in contrast to the false teachers of verse 26, who say that the Messiah appeared locally. Preterists teach that Jesus came locally, through the Roman army, in A.D. 70. That view contradicts verse 27, which teaches that the Messiah's return will be global.

We see that this passage teaches that the second coming of Christ will be something that no human being—not even the Antichrist—will be able to counterfeit. It will be of such a nature that only God will be able to do it. It will be a global and miraculous event that does not in any way parallel the Roman destruction of Jerusalem in A.D. 70. Thus, it must be a future event because nothing like it has yet occurred.

IMMEDIATELY AFTER THE TRIBULATION

In Matthew 24:29, Christ's narrative transitions into a new emphasis, moving from events relating to the Tribulation to an event that will follow the Tribulation. Even though Jesus has already commented on the manner of His second coming in verse 27, He now focuses upon it in relation to the Tribulation. He has been speaking previously about Tribulation events (see Matthew 24:9,21; Mark

13:19) but now shifts to an event that will take place "immediately" after the Tribulation of those days. That event is the future, bodily return of Christ to planet earth, which is known as the second coming (verse 30). What Christ describes in a few verses (29-31), John explains in greater detail (Revelation 19:11-21). Thus, the second advent immediately follows the events of the Tribulation.

Eutheos is a Greek adverb usually translated "immediately," or "straightway, at once, directly." Thus, the events of verse 29 will follow the Tribulation immediately, at once, without any other events intervening, or without a time delay. This means that Matthew 24:29-31 will follow immediately the final bowl judgment found in Revelation 16:17-21.

THE SIGN OF THE SON OF MAN

One of the original questions that the disciples asked Jesus at the beginning of this discourse was, "What will be the sign of your coming?" He has been answering the question since verse 23. Having spoken of His coming in verse 27, Jesus now builds upon His previous point that He will not arrive clandestinely, but His return will be a clear, public event that will take place suddenly. Just such a glorious appearing is exactly what is described in verses 29 and 30. The word order of the Greek text in verse 30 is as follows: "And then shall appear the sign of the Son of Man in the heaven." The Greek text supports the probability that the sign of the Son of Man will appear in the heaven or sky. In summary, Matthew 24:30 describes a visible appearance of the Son of Man, the repentance of Israel, and the triumphant return of Christ to reign on planet earth.

AN ANGELIC GATHERING

In Matthew 23:37 Jesus weeps over Jerusalem as He pronounces the A.D. 70 judgment and declares, "How often I wanted to *gather* your children together, the way a hen *gathers* her chicks under her wings, and you were unwilling." Now in chapter 24, this same Jesus is returning after the Great Tribulation when Jerusalem is again in peril. But this time the Jews respond positively to the messiahship of Jesus, so our Lord sends out His angels to *gather* His elect (saved Jews at the end of the Tribulation) from around the world and bring them to Jerusalem, instead of scattering them as in A.D. 70 (Luke 21:24). Just such a regathering was predicted in the Old Testament:

> Then the LORD your God will restore you from captivity, and have compassion on you, and will gather you again from all the peoples where the LORD your God has scattered you. If your outcasts are at the ends of the earth, from there the LORD your God will gather you, and from there He will bring you back (Deuteronomy 30:3-4).

FIVE PARABOLIC ILLUSTRATIONS

Upon the completion of His discourse about the Tribulation and second coming, Jesus provides five parables that illustrate what He has just taught. These include the fig tree illustration (24:32-35), the days of Noah illustration (24:36-39), a comparison of two men and women (24:40-41), the faithful house holder illustration (24:42-44), and the wise servant illustration (24:45-51). All of these relate to Christ's teaching in the previous section of Matthew 24.

The parables within the Olivet Discourse all relate to the second coming and not the rapture of the church. This is evident from the fact that the entire Olivet Discourse was given to Israel and relates to her persecution and Christ's return at the end of the Tribulation. The truths relating to the rapture of the church are revealed later, in the New Testament epistles, with the exception of Christ's initial unveiling of the church's hope in the Upper Room Discourse (John 14:1-3).

—THOMAS ICE

BIBLIOGRAPHY

Enns, Paul. "Olivet Discourse." In *Dictionary of Premillennial Theology.* Ed. Mal Couch. Grand Rapids: Kregel, 1996.

Gaebelein, Arno C. *The Gospel of Matthew: An Exposition.* Neptune, NJ: Loizeaux Brothers, 1961.

MacArthur, John. *The New Testament Commentary: Matthew 24–28.* Chicago: Moody Press, 1989.

Toussaint, Stanley. *Behold the King: A Study of Matthew.* Portland, OR: Multnomah Publishers, 1980.

Walvoord, John F. *Matthew: Thy Kingdom Come.* Chicago: Moody Press, 1974.

ONE HUNDRED FORTY-FOUR THOUSAND

THE GREATEST REVIVAL the world has ever known will not occur during the church age but immediately following, during the first 21 months of the Tribulation. According to Revelation 7, while the Antichrist is busy orchestrating his political advances, the Holy Spirit, working through a group referred to as the 144,000, will move in the hearts of millions of people. He will lead them into a saving knowledge of Jesus Christ, resulting in the largest soul harvest in earth's history.

Who are these 144,000? Various religious groups and cults have contributed much speculation and widespread confusion regarding these supernaturally protected servants of God, but their identity becomes clear if we make a habit of taking the Bible literally whenever possible.

> I heard the number of those who were sealed: one hundred and forty-four thousand of all the tribes of the children of Israel (Revelation 7:4 NKJV).

This group will be comprised of 12,000 Jews descended from each of the 12 tribes of Israel, making a total of 144,000. An angel will "seal" these Jewish evangelists at the beginning of the Tribulation, and they will embark on their ministry of preaching the gospel to those who have been left behind. These servants of God will faithfully communicate God's message of salvation through Jesus Christ and will experience incredible results. However, they will also experience personal persecution and the horrific trials of the Tribulation.

Just as the Antichrist will demand that his followers receive "the mark of the beast" on their right hand or forehead (Revelation 13:14-18), the 144,000 witnesses will receive their own seal from God on their foreheads. They will have an understanding of the book of Revelation and will be able to anticipate the events and duration of the Tribulation. These Jews will immediately put everything else in their lives aside and begin to preach to all those worldwide who have ears to hear. The biblical text does not specifically call them "witnesses," but the proclamation of the gospel of Jesus Christ is one of their primary functions.

The Antichrist and his soon-to-be followers will be delighted to discover millions of Christians suddenly removed from their midst as a result of the rapture. But other people who are left behind will be seriously shaken. The rapture will leave an unprecedented vacancy in nearly every legitimate profession, causing chaotic consequences. Those who are left behind will be fully aware of the supernatural aspect of the rapture, especially when they realize that all of the missing are believers in Christ. The Antichrist will distort the truth and cause many people to forget the impact of this unusual event, but many others will become motivated to know more about biblical prophecy. Such a mental climate will provide fertile ground for the 144,000 Jewish evangelists.

We know from 2 Peter 3:9 that God does not want anyone to perish. The Holy Spirit will work in the hearts of those who have been left behind. The total number of people who come to the Lord during the first part of the Tribulation could possibly exceed the number of those who have converted to Christ during the last 2000 years. Several factors could make this possible, including the size of the world's population, the chaotic conditions during the Tribulation, and the powerful work of the Holy Spirit through the tireless evangelism of the 144,000 witnesses.

> After these things I looked, and behold, a great multitude which no one could number, of all nations, tribes, peoples, and tongues, standing before the throne and before the Lamb, clothed with white robes (Revelation 7:9).

> These are the ones who come out of the great tribulation, and washed their robes and made them white in the blood of the Lamb. Therefore they are before the throne of God, and serve Him day and night in His temple. And He who sits on the throne will dwell among them (Revelation 7:14-15).

The identity of this "great multitude which no one could number" is clear. These are the saints who have all come out of the Tribulation after having made personal commitments to Jesus Christ. The fact that they are "before the throne of God" indicates that they have died. Anyone who accepts Christ during the Tribulation will apparently suffer intense persecution and probable death at the hands of the Antichrist and his followers. However, those who "endure to the end" will receive blessings and rewards beyond measure from the Lord in the life to come.

—TIM LaHAYE

BIBLIOGRAPHY

LaHaye, Tim. *Revelation Unveiled.* Grand Rapids: Zondervan, 1999.

Pentecost, J. Dwight. *Things to Come.* Grand Rapids: Zondervan, 1975.

Thomas, Robert L. *Revelation 1–7: An Exegetical Commentary.* Chicago: Moody Press, 1992.

Trites, Allison. *The Concept of "Witness" in John's Gospel.* Cambridge University Press, 1980.

Walvoord, John F. *The Prophecy Knowledge Handbook.* Wheaton, IL: Victor Books, 1990.

———. *The Revelation of Jesus Christ.* Chicago: Moody Press, 1966.

ONE THOUSAND YEARS

FOLLOWING THE SECOND COMING of Christ, Satan will be captured and bound with a great chain (Revelation 20:1-2). He will then be incarcerated in the abyss, which will be shut and sealed (20:3), and thus Satan will not deceive the nations for 1000 years. Meanwhile, the Tribulation martyrs will be resurrected to reign with Christ (20:4-6). When the 1000 years end, Satan will be released for a short time to once again deceive the nations (20:3,7-8).

Some believe that the 1000 years are already occurring figuratively and that Satan is already bound by the cross of Christ and the church. However, the New Testament never states that Satan has already been bound. Nor has Satan been incapacitated on earth as Revelation 20:1-2 describes. He still entices men to lie (Acts 5:3), he still blinds the minds of unbelievers to the glorious gospel of Christ, and he is called the god of this world (2 Corinthians 4:4). Satan currently disguises himself as an angel of light to deceive the church (2 Corinthians 11:2-3,13-15). The devil hinders ministers of God (2 Corinthians 12:7; 1 Thessalonians 2:18) and roams about the earth to devour its population (1 Peter 5:8). He has unbelievers under his dominion (Acts 26:18), he tempts believers (1 Corinthians 7:5), and he seeks to deceive them as he battles against them (Ephesians 6:11-12). He is at work in unbelievers to influence them to live as they do (Ephesians 2:2). He deceives and traps unbelievers and holds them captive to do his will (2 Timothy 2:26) and remain in his power (1 John 5:19).

Satan cannot be bound and so active at the same time. Clearly Revelation 20 looks forward to a future time when Satan will be bound.

NUMBERS AND TIME

The essential question is this: Does *chilia ete* (1000 years) in Revelation 20 really mean a literal 1000 years? A basic rule of hermeneutics states that numbers should be accepted at face value—that is, as conveying a mathematical quantity—unless the context includes substantial evidence to warrant otherwise. This rule holds true throughout the Bible, including the book of Revelation. A survey of numbers in Revelation supports this. For instance, the seven churches and seven angels in Revelation 1 refer to seven literal churches and their messengers. Twelve tribes and 12 apostles are actual, historical numbers

(21:12,14). Ten lamps (2:10), five months (9:5), one-third of mankind (9:15), two witnesses (11:2), 42 months (11:2), 1260 days (11:3), 12 stars (12:1), ten horns (13:1), 1600 stadia (14:20), three demons (16:13), and five fallen kings (17:9-10) all use numbers in their normal sense. Out of the scores of numbers in Revelation, only two (seven spirits in 1:4 and 666 in 13:18) are conclusively used in a symbolic fashion.

Numbers are generally to be taken at face value in Revelation, and this is more specially true with numbers referring to time. Revelation 4–20 includes at least 25 references to measurements of time. Only two of these should be understood figuratively. The "day of His wrath" (6:17 NKJV) would likely exceed 24 hours, and "the hour of His judgment" (14:7) seemingly extends beyond 60 minutes. However, nothing in the phrase "one thousand years" suggests a symbolic interpretation.

Never in the Bible is "year" used with a numerical adjective when it does not refer to the actual period of time that it mathematically represents. Also, the number 1000 is not used elsewhere in the Bible with a symbolic sense. One thousand and its varied combinations are used frequently in both Testaments. No one questions the literal interpretation of 5000 believers (Acts 4:4), 23,000 men killed (1 Corinthians 10:8), or 7000 killed (Revelation 11:13). Likewise, we find no exegetical reason to question the normalcy of 1000 years in Revelation 20.

THE TESTIMONY OF HISTORY

From the earliest post-apostolic era, the church understood the millennium of Revelation 20 as a literal 1000 years. Papias, Barnabas, Justin Martyr, Irenaeus, and Tertullian all gave evidence of this fact in their writings. The church taught nothing else until the fourth century. When some theologians distorted biblical teaching about the millennium and described it as a time for the enjoyment of man rather than for the glory of God, other teachers attempted to correct this error by proposing a more spiritual interpretation of the 1000 years.

In the fifth century, Augustine popularized this reaction, which reasoned that the church inherited the blessings promised to Israel and that those blessings are spiritual, not earthly. He taught that Revelation 20 referred to this time. However, even Augustine, called by many the father of amillennialism, understood from Revelation 20 that this period would last 1000 literal years. To not hold to a literal interpretation is to do injustice to the text.

An unmistakable bridge links the Old Testament promises of a restored earthly kingdom of Israel with the distinctive statements of Revelation 20. It is the rule and reign of Jesus Christ on the throne of David in the city of God (see 2 Samuel 7:12-16; Psalm 2:1-12; Isaiah 2:2-4; 9:7; Jeremiah 33:14-18; Ezekiel 34:23-24; Daniel 2:44-45; Hosea 3:5; Joel 3:9-21; Zephaniah 3:14-20; Zechariah 14:1-11; Revelation 20:4,6).

TEXTUAL CHRONOLOGICAL CLUES

Amillennialists and postmillennialists normally conclude that the resurrection of the dead, the last judgment, the destruction of this world, and the rise of the new heavens and the new earth will all occur at the time of the second coming. They leave no room for a literal 1000 years before or after the second coming (see Kuyper, p. 272). Furthermore, they allege, "The text only reveals the order in which John *saw* the visions, not necessarily the order in which the events were to take place" (Mathison, p. 131).

Both of these assumptions rest on faulty hermeneutics. The sequence of events in Revelation will also be the sequence of their prophetic, historical fulfillment. Walvoord says that this is "based on the natural sequence of events in chapter 20 following chapter 19, viewing them as sequential and as stemming from the second coming of Christ. Many passages speak of the second coming of Christ being followed by a reign of righteousness on earth" (Walvoord, *The Bible Knowledge Commentary,* p. 978).

With the exception of two verses (Revelation 20:5-6), every verse in chapter 20 begins with the connective "and" (Greek, *kai*). All but 5 of the 21 verses in chapter 19 use the same grammatical feature. The constant usage of the connective demonstrates the flow of narrative action. John saw one event after another unfold before his very eyes. The continuation of the connective from chapter 19 into chapter 20 gives the impression that the events of chapter 20 follow those recorded in chapter 19. To conclude that the events of chapter 20 precede those in chapter 19 is to violate the hermeneutical principle of observation before interpretation and the normal grammatical usage of the connective in a narrative passage.

In addition, the usage of the adverb "no more" (Greek, *eti*) in the purpose clause of Revelation 20:3 strongly suggests that the events described in 20:1-3 follow those described in 19:11-21. The use of the adverb indicates an interruption of something that was already taking place—namely, the deception of the nations by Satan. The action of binding Satan, thus, could not occur before the second coming.

The beast and the False Prophet are cast into the lake of fire at the second coming (Revelation 19:20). Satan is cast into the lake of fire 1000 years later (Revelation 20:10). In the lake of fire, Satan is reunited with the beast and the False Prophet. This narrative action makes no sense if Satan is cast into the lake of fire at the same time as the other two. In fact, the phrase "where the beast and the false prophet are" presupposes an earlier judgment upon the beast and the False Prophet (Revelation 19:20) and also suggests a chronological sequence of Revelation 20 events following those in chapter 19.

LITERAL INTERPRETATION

Some argue that (1) the time designator "thousand years" does not occur anywhere else in New Testament eschatological teachings; (2) Jesus did not mention it in the Olivet Discourse (Matthew 24–25); and (3) no epistle refers to the 1000-year reign of Christ on earth, so the reference to this length of time in Revelation 20 should be understood symbolically (see Kistemaker, p. 535). They further advocate that the book of Revelation is a book of symbols, and the numbers must also be understood symbolically. Kistemaker, for example, states that "one thousand is ten to the third power and denotes fullness. It is therefore more in line with the tone and tenor of Revelation to interpret the term metaphorically…to refer to an indefinite period between the ascension of Jesus and his return" (Kistemaker, pp. 535–36).

However, the normal, ordinary meaning of "1000 years" is 1000 years. This is the essence of literal interpretation. If the plain sense makes good sense, seek no other sense. As Walvoord observed, "This chapter presents the fact that Christ will reign on earth for a thousand years. If this chapter is taken literally, it is relatively simple to understand what is meant" (Walvoord, *The Bible Knowledge Commentary*, p. 977).

Besides, John knew how to describe an indefinite brief period of time as such. In 20:3 he wrote that Satan would be released from the abyss for "a little while" (Greek, *mikron chronon*). The Holy Spirit could have guided John to write that Christ and the saints would reign for "a long time" (Greek, *polun chronon*), the same phrase used in the parable of the talents to indicate the period of the master's absence (Matthew 25:19). But God led John to contrast a definite period ("thousand years") with an indefinite period ("a little while").

In fact, all time designations in the book of Revelation are literal, having significance only if their temporal meanings are accepted in the normal sense. The nonliteral view makes Revelation 20 to be the exception.

Occasionally, some will reference 2 Peter 3:8 and Psalm 90:4 in defense of a nonliteral meaning. Peter wrote "that with the Lord one day is a thousand years, and thousand years as one day." For this comparison to make sense, the time phrases must be taken literally. The infinite, eternal God does not view time as we do, but He does know the distinction between a 24-hour day and a millennium. Psalm 90:4 conveys the same idea.

Robert Thomas has noted that "no number in Revelation is verifiably a symbolic number" (Thomas, p. 408). All numbers should be accepted literally, at face value. The distinctions in numerical value must be maintained throughout the book. They remain a literal constant in a book of symbols and metaphors. (See the article titled "Millennium.")

—RICHARD L. MAYHUE
AND ROBERT GROMACKI

BIBLIOGRAPHY

Kistemaker, Simon J. *Exposition of the Book of Revelation. New Testament Commentary*. Grand Rapids: Baker Books, 2001.

Kuyper, Abraham. *The Revelation of St. John*. Grand Rapids: Eerdmans Publishing Company, 1963.

Mathison, Keith A. *Dispensationalism: Rightly Dividing the People of God*. Phillipsburg, NJ: P&R Publishing, 1995.

Thomas, Robert. *Revelation 8–22: An Exegetical Commentary*. Chicago: Moody Press, 1995.

Walvoord, John F. "Revelation." In *The Bible Knowledge Commentary*. John F. Walvoord and Roy B. Zuck, eds. Wheaton, IL: Victor Books, 1983.

———. *The Revelation of Jesus Christ*. Chicago: Moody Press, 1966.

Wiersbe, Warren W. *The Bible Exposition Commentary*. 2 vols. Wheaton, IL: Victor Books, 1989.

PARTIAL RAPTURE

SOME BIBLE COMMENTATORS have suggested that the rapture, spoken of in 1 Thessalonians 4:16-17 and 1 Corinthians 15:51-52, will only be a partial rapture, not a rapture of all who believe. They reason that participation in the rapture is not based upon one's salvation but rather is conditional, based upon one's deserving conduct.

This theory rests on New Testament passages that stress obedient watching and waiting (such as Matthew 25:1-13; 1 Thessalonians 5:4-

8; and Hebrews 9:28). In this view, only part of the church is raptured, and those who are not raptured endure a portion of or the entire Tribulation. However, these biblical texts are better understood as differentiating between true believers who are raptured and merely professing ones who remain behind. Texts that refer to Christ's second coming are often also used mistakenly to support the partial rapture theory.

THE BASIS OF THE PARTIAL RAPTURE VIEW

The rapture could occur at any moment and will include every believer (1 Thessalonians 4:13-17). Our faithfulness to Christ and our obedience to His Word definitely determine our reward, but Scripture never indicates that some Christians might be in danger of losing any part of their salvation (1 Corinthians 3:15).

Some people accept the partial rapture theory because they believe that sin or disobedience makes Christians unfit to go with Christ, so they must be punished during the Tribulation. Explaining this view, Waugh (p. 108) wrote,

> But there are not a few—some of them deep and prayerful students of the Scriptures—who believe that only a prepared and *expectant section* of believers will then be translated. They believe that a clear inference from Luke xxi. 36 is that those Christians who do *not* "watch" will *not* "escape all these things that shall come to pass," and will *not* be accounted worthy "to stand before the Son of Man." They gather from such passages as Phil. 3:20, Titus 2:12-13, 2 Tim. 4:8, Heb. 9:28, that those only will be taken who "wait," "look for," and "have loved His appearing."

One of the chief problems with this view is that it necessarily denies part of the value of the death of Christ. According to the partial rapturist, good works of a Christian give him a standing with God and make him eligible for the rapture. Some who hold this view base it on a Wesleyan view of full sanctification as the basic qualification for being

taken in the rapture. But the proper meaning of redemption is that Christ has paid the complete price for every sin. Because every sin has been punished and paid for, God will not punish sinning Christians again by omitting them from the rapture.

Partial rapturists appeal to other passages to prove their view (Matthew 25:1-13; Ephesians 2:21-22; 5:27,30; 1 Corinthians 15:23). However, when these Scriptures are understood in their contexts, they do not support a partial rapture view. After studying the principle proof texts of the partial rapturist, Dawson (p. 46) concluded, "These Scriptures clearly show that every member of the Church, which is His Body, every truly born again person, will be raptured at our Lord's return."

PROBLEMS WITH THE PARTIAL RAPTURE VIEW

The partial rapture theory fails to be convincing for numerous other reasons. First, 1 Corinthians 15:51 says that "all" will be changed. Second, a partial rapture would logically demand a parallel partial resurrection, which is nowhere taught in Scripture. Third, a partial rapture would minimize and possibly eliminate the need for the judgment seat of Christ. Fourth, it creates a "purgatory" of sorts on earth for those believers left behind. Fifth, a partial rapture is nowhere explicitly taught in Scripture. The rapture will be full and complete, not partial.

Dwight Pentecost (pp. 158–61) opposed the partial rapture because it rests on the following "misunderstandings":

1. The partial rapturist position is based on a misunderstanding of the value of the death of Christ as it frees the sinner from condemnation and renders him acceptable to God.

2. The partial rapturist must deny the New Testament teaching on the unity of the body of Christ.

3. The partial rapturist must deny the completeness of the resurrection of the believers at the translation.

4. The partial rapturist confuses the Scriptural teaching on rewards.

5. The partial rapturist confuses the distinction between law and grace.

6. The partial rapturist must deny the distinction between Israel and the church.

7. The partial rapturist must place a portion of the believing church in the tribulation period.

Many partial rapturists sincerely believe we need to urge other believers to be ready for the rapture and not just assume they are going, regardless of how they live. This caution is certainly needed, but it has nothing to do with determining who will or will not be raptured. The ultimate resolution of this issue rests upon a proper understanding of the doctrine of salvation and a clear exegesis of the biblical passages about the rapture.

—Elmer Towns and
Richard Mayhue

BIBLIOGRAPHY

Clouse, R.G. "Rapture of the Church." In *Evanglical Dictionary of Theology*. Ed. Walter Elwell. Grand Rapids: Baker Books, 1984.

Dawson, J.E.M. *Present Day Problems*. London: Pickering & Ingalls, 1940.

LaHaye, Tim. *The Rapture*. Eugene, OR: Harvest House Publishers, 2002.

Pentecost, J. Dwight. *Things to Come*. Grand Rapids: Zondervan, 1975.

Waugh, Thomas. *When Jesus Comes*. London: Charles H. Kelly, 1901.

PATMOS

THE SMALL VOLCANIC ISLAND of Patmos in the Aegean Sea, off the coast of Asia Minor, is mentioned only once in the Bible. In Revelation 1:9, readers are told that this 15-square-mile island, the northernmost in the Dodecanese archipelago, was the location where John's revelation occurred and where the book of Revelation was written. John states,

"I, John, your brother and fellow partaker in the tribulation and kingdom and perseverance which are in Jesus, was on the island called Patmos because of the word of God and the testimony of Jesus" (NASB).

The crescent-shaped island of Patmos is about 40 miles west of the coastal city of Miletus (Acts 20:15,17; 2 Timothy 4:20). Because of its natural harbor facing eastward, it was a safe haven for ships during storms. It was also strategically located along commercial sea lanes. Patmos was the last stopping place when traveling from Rome to Ephesus and the first for the return trip (Thomas, p. 87). During New Testament times, the island had a large administrative center, at least three pagan temples (one each for the gods Artemis, Apollo, and Aphrodite), and a hippodrome for horse racing. It was governed by the proconsul of Ephesus (Franz, pp. 115, 118).

By his own testimony, John was exiled there. But the nature of his presence on the island has been disputed, resulting in three interpretations of Revelation 1:9. Some argue that John was sent there by God specifically to receive the revelation. Others believe that he went voluntarily to Patmos to preach the gospel. Most understand his presence on the island to be the result of banishment by the Roman government because of his preaching of the gospel. This exile occurred during the reign of Domitian (A.D. 81–96) about the year A.D. 95 (Thomas, pp. 87–89).

Although John was in exile, he was probably not imprisoned on the island. Nor was he under house arrest as Paul was in Rome. Rather, he likely had free access on the island as a temporary exile. He was probably only there for about 18 months and allowed to go to Ephesus in a general amnesty by the emperor Nerva in A.D. 96 following the death of Domitian (Osborne, pp. 81–82). The early historian Eusebius of Caesarea (c. 260–340) states that "the sentences of Domitian were annulled, and the Roman senate decreed the return of those who had been unjustly banished and the restoration of their property....The apostle John, after his banishment to the island, took up his abode at Ephesus" (Lake, p. 241).

Passages throughout Revelation conform to and reflect aspects of daily life on Patmos. For example, weather phenomena like white clouds (14:14), thunder and lightning (11:19; 14:2), hail (8:7; 11:19; 16:21), and rainbows (4:3; 10:1) are common on Patmos. Revelation mentions the sea at least 22 times, and the island has one sandy beach that may correspond to Revelation 13:1. Volcanic activity and earthquakes have also been part of the island's history (Franz, Part 2, pp. 121–22).

—TIMOTHY J. DEMY

BIBLIOGRAPHY

Franz, Gordon. "The King and I: The Apostle John and Emperor Domitian," Part 1. *Bible and Spade* 12.2 (1999), pp. 45-51.

———. "The King and I: Exiled to Patmos," Part 2. *Bible and Spade* 12.4 (1999), pp. 115-23.

———. "The King and I: Opening the Third Seal," Part 3. *Bible and Spade* 13.1 (2000), pp. 9-11.

Lake, Kirsopp, ed. and trans. *Eusebius: The Ecclesiastical History*, Vol. 1. Loeb Classical Series. Cambridge, MA: Harvard University Press, 1980.

Osborne, Grant. *Revelation*. Grand Rapids: Baker Books, 2002.

Thomas, Robert L. *Revelation 1–7: An Exegetical Commentary*. Chicago: Moody Press, 1992.

PAUL, ESCHATOLOGY OF

THE APOSTLE PAUL WROTE extensively on many prophetic subjects in his letters. He wrote literally and historically, and his comments were extremely practical and addressed his readers' current concerns. Among the topics he addressed was religious apostasy.

THE APOSTASY OF THE CHURCH

Though some liberal scholars may disagree, Paul distinctly prophesies about a religious apostasy coming at the end of the church age. The word *apostasia* means "to stand or fall away from" and Paul uses it only once (2 Thessalonians 2:3). He says he is writing to the

Thessalonian church concerning "our gathering together to Him [probably a reference to the rapture of the church], that you not be quickly shaken from your composure...by...a letter as if from us, to the effect that the day of the Lord has come" (2:1-2 NASB). The Thessalonian Christians mistakenly thought the terrible Tribulation was imminent. Paul assured them, "Let no one in any way deceive you, for it will not come unless the apostasy comes first, and the man of lawlessness is revealed, the son of destruction." He is referring to the Antichrist. Some readers believe the "apostasy" (or "departing") may refer to the rapture of the believers to glory, but the larger consensus is that it has in view a spiritual turning away ("departing" from the faith) that takes place in the final stages of the church age.

In his letters to Timothy, Paul is specific about what constitutes this falling away. He writes, "The Spirit explicitly says that in later times some will fall away from the faith, paying attention to deceitful spirits and doctrines of demons, by means of the hypocrisy of liars seared in their own conscience as with a branding iron" (1 Timothy 4:1-2). Since he writes they "fall away from the faith," he implies that these apostates remain "religious" but deny the body of truth in the faith concerning Christ and salvation. "Fall away" here is a future, middle, indicative of the verb *aphieemi* and means to leave or depart. Thus, men will themselves depart from the truth and buy into the doctrine of evil spirits and the teachings of demons. Paul writes of this apostasy again in 2 Timothy 3:1-5. He says, "In the last days difficult times will come" with men loving self and money. They will be "lovers of pleasure rather than lovers of God." He speaks of this in the future tense, but he adds that such spiritual departure is already taking place within the church.

Ryrie (p. 140) says apostasy is "a departure from truth previously accepted, involving the breaking of a professed relationship with God. Apostasy always involves willful leaving of previously known truth and embracing error." In the final hours of the dispensation of the church, many of those who have confessed biblical truth and who have professed a relationship with God will simply be acting out, living a lie, walking as religious charlatans. Apostasy will be intense in the final days before the rapture of the church.

THE RESURRECTION OF THE CHURCH SAINTS

Because the Lord Jesus was raised from the dead, believers in Christ are guaranteed and promised the resurrection of the body as well. Christ was buried and then raised "according to the Scriptures" and then appeared to Peter, to the 12 apostles, to five hundred brothers "at one time," to James, and finally to Paul (1 Corinthians 15:4-8). We have no hope of our resurrection without the raising up of Christ from the dead (15:12-19). Paul continues his eschatological argument for the believers' resurrection through the rest of 1 Corinthians 15. The greatest victory of humanity is the bodily resurrection, as Paul proclaims: "The sting of death is sin, and the power of sin is the law; but thanks be to God, who gives us the victory [over death] through our Lord Jesus Christ" (15:56-57).

When the Lord returns for the church, God will bring with Him "those who have fallen asleep in Jesus" (1 Thessalonians 4:14). They will be raised first, and then those who are still living will be raptured. The saints who are alive "will be caught up together with them [those who have died in Christ] in the clouds to meet the Lord in the air" (4:17). In this passage, Paul puts together the resurrection of the church saints and their rapture.

Other resurrections will take place for the Old Testament saints and for saints who die in the Tribulation, as well as for the lost, who will be judged at the Great White Throne judgment. However, Paul focuses here on the resurrection of the church, "the dead in Christ" (4:16).

THE RAPTURE OF THE CHURCH

Christ seems to allude to the rapture in John 14:1-3, but Paul is the one who gives the full doctrine and revelation about this event. He calls the rapture "a mystery," something hidden or not before revealed. He writes that those who have not died "will all be changed" (1 Corinthians 15:51-53). Paul prophesies that "in a moment" (Greek, *atoma*) at the blink of an eye, and at the last trumpet, we will be changed. And immediately the perishable will put on the imperishable.

Paul prophetically develops this truth: "For the Lord Himself will descend from heaven with a shout, with the voice of the archangel and with the trumpet of God, and the dead in Christ will rise first. Then we who are alive and remain will be caught up [Greek, *harpazo*] together with them [the resurrected] in the clouds." This is a blessed hope for those who have not died, as Paul writes: "Therefore comfort one another with these words" (1 Thessalonians 4:16-18).

Believers are to "wait for His Son from heaven...that is Jesus, who rescues us from the wrath to come" (1 Thessalonians 1:10), because "God has not destined us for wrath, but for obtaining salvation [deliverance] through our Lord Jesus Christ" (5:9). The child of God is to believe the prophecy and look for the "blessed hope and the appearing of the glory of our great God and Savior, Christ Jesus" (Titus 2:13). At His coming, He will usher believers into "the presence of our Lord Jesus" (1 Thessalonians 2:19) and present them unblamable in holiness "before our God and Father at the coming of our Lord Jesus with all His saints" (3:13). Paul's prophecy of the rapture is one of the unique features of his eschatology.

THE JUDGMENT OF CHRIST

Paul writes about Christ's rewards for the church saints. The judgment seat of Christ (Greek, *bema*) is the podium or throne from which "each one may be recompensed for his deeds in the body, according to what he has done, whether good or bad" (2 Corinthians 5:10). This judgment has been misunderstood. Too often it is seen only as a place of rewards. But Paul calls it a place of recompense (Greek, *komizo*, "receive to oneself"). The Lord is looking at what we have done whether good *(agathos)* or flawed *(phaulos)*. We receive back in return in relation to our works.

Paul earlier wrote of this judgment day for believers in 1 Corinthians 3:10-15. He says that believers are building upon the foundation of Christ and constructing their lives with either gold, silver, precious stones, wood, hay, or straw. These items represent the quality of the Christian's life and his or her service to Christ. These qualities will be tested by fire that will consume the worthless and leave that which honors Him.

THE TRIBULATION

Paul generally uses the word "wrath" (Greek, *orge*) to prophetically describe the seven-year period of tribulation on the earth. He says that at the rapture, Jesus will rescue us from the wrath to come (1 Thessalonians 1:10), and he states that "God has not destined us for wrath" (5:9). When Jesus comes to be glorified with His saints in the kingdom, He will execute a judgment of flaming fire, deal out retribution, and deliver "the penalty of eternal destruction, away from the presence of the Lord and from the glory of His power" (2 Thessalonians 1:7-9).

In 2 Thessalonians 2:3-4, Paul briefly describes the desecration of the rebuilt Tribulation Temple by the Antichrist, the "man of lawlessness...the son of destruction." The apostle refers to Daniel's prediction of the coming of the Antichrist (Daniel 11:36-45). Daniel predicts the self-willed king who speaks against the "God of gods" and who magnifies himself against God. Paul prophesies this Antichrist will be slain with the breath of the mouth of Christ at His second coming (2 Thessalonians 2:8).

During the Tribulation, God sends a deception on the unbelievers and mockers so that they do not receive the truth in order to be saved (2:9-10). God also sends a deluding influence so that those who "did not believe the truth, but took pleasure in wickedness" will believe what is false and be judged (2:11-12). Paul's warnings about rejecting Christ are sobering indeed.

THE MESSIANIC KINGDOM

Though Paul says little about the millennial kingdom, it is part of the backdrop of his eschatological discussions. He sees the church on the way toward the kingdom and someday enjoying the benefits of Christ's reign on earth.

As Paul and Barnabas went about preaching the gospel, they reminded believers that they would someday enter the kingdom "through many tribulations" (Acts 14:22). Paul preached the gospel in the Ephesian synagogue for three months, "reasoning and persuading them about the kingdom of God" (19:8). While under house arrest in Rome, Paul spoke to the Jewish elders of the city about Jesus, "testifying about the kingdom and trying to persuade them concerning Jesus" (28:23). Only those who are characterized as righteous and redeemed by the blood of Christ will be able to inherit the kingdom of God (1 Corinthians. 6:9). Christ will deliver up the kingdom to God the Father "when He has abolished all rule and all authority and power" (15:24). In God's divine view of all things, He has delivered the church saints out of the domain of darkness and has transferred us "to the kingdom of His beloved Son" (Colossians 1:13).

We should not confuse the dispensation of the kingdom with the dispensation of the church. Paul completely separates the kingdom from this present period of grace. The apostle makes this clear when he gives Timothy a charge "in the presence of God and of Christ Jesus, who is to judge the living and the dead, and by His appearing and His kingdom" (2 Timothy 4:1). Paul retains the Old Testament's view about the kingdom—a specific time period of the reign of Christ over the nation of Israel and the nations of the world. It is distinct from the church age. Paul does not replace the kingdom with the church, and He never calls the church the kingdom. The kingdom is still yet future; it will not come to earth until the King returns in person.

—MAL COUCH

BIBLIOGRAPHY

Couch, Mal, ed. *A Biblical Theology of the Church.* Grand Rapids: Kregel, 1999.

———. *The Fundamentals for the Twenty-First Century.* Grand Rapids: Kregel, 2000.

Enns, Paul. *The Moody Handbook of Theology.* Chicago: Moody Press, 1989.

LaHaye, Tim, and Thomas Ice. *The End Times Controversy.* Eugene, OR: Harvest House Publishers, 2003.

Ryrie, Charles C. *Dispensationalism.* Chicago: Moody Press, 1995.

PENTECOST

Pentecost IS THE GREEK NAME for the Old Testament Feast of Weeks (Exodus 34:22; Numbers 28:26; Deuteronomy 16:10). It is called the Feast of Harvest in Exodus 23:16. According to Leviticus 23:15-16, on the seventh Sabbath (seven weeks or 49 days) after Passover, the sons of Israel were to celebrate the harvest by bringing voluntary offerings to the Lord. In the New Testament this celebration was called Pentecost, which in Greek means "fiftieth," because this celebration landed on the day after the seventh Sabbath, or the fiftieth day after Passover.

EARLY HISTORY

During the Feast of Weeks, the primary offering was new grain consisting of "two loaves of bread for a wave offering, made of two-tenths of an ephah [approximately one bushel]; they shall be of a fine flour, baked with leaven as first fruits to the LORD" (Leviticus 23:17 NASB). The leaven came from the bread of the preceding barley harvest. Because the bread contained leaven it was not placed on the altar, but rather, was eaten by the priests. The second offering was a burnt offering of seven male lambs, a young bull, and two rams (Leviticus 23:18). A grain offering and drink offering were brought with the burnt offering (Leviticus 23:18). The people also brought a male goat for a sin offering and two male lambs for a peace offering (Leviticus 23:19). Portions of the lamb and the grain offering were waved before the Lord and then eaten by the officiating priest (Leviticus 23:20). The feast was a sacred occasion; no work was to be done on the day of observance (Leviticus 23:21).

PENTECOST AND THE GIVING OF THE LAW

After the Romans destroyed the Temple in A.D. 70, it was no longer possible to bring sacrifices to the Temple, and the purpose of the Feast of Weeks changed. Because of the close connection of the Passover and the Feast of Tabernacles with the period during which the Israelites were in the wilderness, the rabbis connected the Feast of Weeks with the giving of the law at Mount Sinai. Exodus 19:1 says that the children of Israel arrived at Mount Sinai in the third month, the same month that Pentecost is celebrated (see 2 Chronicles 15:10). Because of references to Pentecost in the Book of Jubilees (6:17-21) and perhaps in the Dead Sea Scrolls, Dunn concludes that the tradition is pre-Christian. He says, "But had Pentecost also become specifically the feast which celebrated the law-giving at Sinai? The answer is probably, Yes…the giving of the law at Sinai was the most important of the covenants. And the custom of reading Exodus 19 at the feast of Pentecost was probably already established in the century before Christ" (Dunn, p. 784). This is also the view of Witherington, who says that it is possible, but not certain, that associating the Feast of Weeks with the giving of the law is an earlier tradition. He cites a passage from Philo, who wrote before Luke, describing a phenomenon occurring at the giving of the law that was somewhat similar to the "tongues of fire" that were manifested at Pentecost (Witherington, p. 131).

Whether or not the transformation of the feast occurred before or after the first century is uncertain. In either case, at an early date Pentecost changed from a celebration of the first fruits of the harvest to a commemoration of the giving of the law. Jacobs (p. 1320) states that this remarkable transformation to "the anniversary of the giving of the Torah" was based on the reading of Exodus 19:1: "In the third month after the sons of Israel had gone out of the land of Egypt, on that very day they came into the wilderness of Sinai." Thus, in addition to the customary reading of the book of Ruth to celebrate the harvest, select portions of the Torah (the Pentateuch) were read to honor the law of Moses.

NEW TESTAMENT REFERENCES

In Acts 2:1, Luke states that Jesus fulfilled His promise to send the Holy Spirit on the Day of Pentecost (Acts 1:8; see also John 14:16-17; 15:26-27; 16:7,13). Luke's account of the events of the Day of Pentecost stresses the gift of the Spirit accompanied by the visible and audible sign of speaking in tongues (foreign languages), empowerment for the proclamation of the gospel, and the birth of the church. The coming of the Spirit on the small but faithful group of Jesus' followers is the actual beginning of the church, evident because Luke emphasizes that the 3000 who responded to Peter's message and submitted to baptism were "added" to the church.

On his second missionary journey, Paul bypassed Ephesus "in order that he might not have to spend time in Asia; for he was hurrying to be in Jerusalem, if possible, on the day of Pentecost" (Acts 20:16). Paul apparently intended to participate in Pentecost (the Feast of Weeks) with other Jewish believers. There is no evidence that the first-century church celebrated Pentecost, though there are two other references to Pentecost in the New Testament.

In 1 Corinthians 16:8 Paul informed the Corinthians that he planned to "remain in Ephesus until Pentecost." As in Acts 20:16, it is apparent that though he was a believer, Paul remained faithful to his Jewish heritage in practices not related to salvation.

PENTECOST AND THE CHURCH

The later church celebrated Pentecost on the fiftieth day after Easter. Since Easter always occurred on Sunday, Pentecost was always on Sunday as well. During the period between Easter and Pentecost, prayers were said standing rather than kneeling, and catechumens (people who were receiving instruction in Christianity) were baptized, but the Christians did not fast because Pentecost was a joyful occasion. Because the ascension had occurred shortly before Pentecost, many people thought Christ would return near the time of Pentecost. Later, Pentecost was observed as a commemoration of the giving of the Holy Spirit (Lohse, p. 827). The Roman Catholic church and churches that follow a liturgical calendar celebrate Pentecost for two days.

THEOLOGICAL SIGNIFICANCE

Some scholars have observed parallels between Jesus' reception of the Spirit at His baptism and the gift of the Spirit to Jesus' followers at Pentecost (Lincoln, p. 903; Longenecker, p. 269). The Spirit descended on Jesus while He was praying and was accompanied by visible and audible phenomena. The disciples were gathered in an upper room, probably praying (see Acts 1:14) when they received the Spirit, and there was something like the sound of a rushing wind and the sight of tongues of fire (Acts 2:2-3). Jesus received power for ministry with the coming of the Spirit (Luke 3:22; see also Acts 10:38), and Jesus' disciples received power for a universal witness when they received the Spirit (Acts 1:8).

Longenecker believes that the gift of the Spirit on the Day of Pentecost is not only parallel to Jesus' baptism experience but also demonstrates both continuity and contrast with the law. He says, "The Spirit's coming is in continuity with God's purposes in giving the law and…the Spirit's coming signals the essential difference between the Jewish faith and commitment to Jesus, for whereas the former is Torah centered and Torah directed, the latter is Christ centered and Spirit directed—all of which sounds very much like Paul" (p. 269). Though it is true that the church's life and mission were Christ centered and Spirit directed, it is unlikely that Luke's intention was to contrast the gift of the Spirit with the giving of the law. It was Paul, not Luke, who elaborated the differences between law and grace. Lohse is right when he concludes that "there is no evidence that this equation is made in NT days; the idea that the Christian Pentecost is a festival of the new revelation of God has no foundation" (p. 826).

It is almost universally agreed that the church was born on the Day of Pentecost. As the birthday of the church, Pentecost marks the end of the dispensation of the law and the beginning of the dispensation of grace (the church age). The 3000 who believed and were baptized were added to the first disciples of Jesus (Acts 2:41). As a new and Spirit-filled community, the church was energized for the universal proclamation of the gospel, a message of grace and an entirely new way of approaching God. Instead of law, people could now come to God through faith in the crucified, resurrected, and ascended Christ. The church age, which began at Pentecost, will continue until Christ returns for His own.

In his polemic against the Colossian heresy, Paul exhorts the Colossians not to be intimidated by those attempting to impose dietary restrictions or the observance of Jewish holy days on believers. He says that these are "a mere shadow of what is to come; but the substance belongs to Christ" (Colossians 2:16-17). Paul uses the same Greek word for "festival" as the Septuagint uses for "convocation" in Leviticus 23:1-4. Though Paul does not identify a particular feast, some believe that his statement is justification for interpreting the Jewish feasts typologically. The Feast of Weeks or Pentecost, with the ritual of the two loaves of bread for a wave offering, is considered typical of the union of Jews and Gentiles into one body (Ephesians 2:14-16). Since the loaves are made with leaven, the type fits the antitype precisely because Jews and Gentiles are contaminated with sin. According to Leviticus 23:19, the sin offering makes the loaves acceptable, just as Christ's death makes atonement for both Jews and Gentiles (Moorehead, p. 221).

RELATION TO JOEL 2

When Peter cited Joel 2:28-32 on the Day of Pentecost, was he signifying that Joel's prophecy was fulfilled on that day? No. On the contrary, we conclude that these Acts 2 quotations did not intend to communicate a then-fulfillment of Old Testament prophecies. Rather, the passage speaks of a still-future time.

In the course of the amazing events that transpired, the apostles were asked to give an account of what was taking place. The question posed by the mockers was whether the disciples were "full of sweet wine" (Acts 2:13). Peter answered this question by declaring that "these men are not drunk, as you suppose…but this is what was spoken of through the prophet Joel" (Acts 2:15-16). What does Joel describe in Joel 2:28-32? He describes the activity of God's Spirit at work in events surrounding a future second coming of Christ. Thus, Peter's point is that of *similarity* between what the Holy Spirit will do in the future with the nation of Israel and what He was doing almost 2000 years ago. This falls short of fulfillment at any point. The Spirit's activity in Joel cannot be separated from events that will transpire during the Tribulation; therefore, it could not have been fulfilled in Acts 2 unless the Tribulation had taken place at that time, which it had not. As noted in verse 16, the unique statement of Peter ("this is what") is the language of comparison, not fulfillment.

Not Fulfilled in Acts 2

Several observations confirm that the events described in Joel 2:28-32, even though mentioned by Peter in Acts 2, were not fulfilled at the founding of the church. First, when comparing the Joel and Acts texts, one immediately sees that Joel begins by saying, "It will come about after this" (Joel 2:28). Israel will experience the spiritual blessings noted in 2:28-29 after it experiences the material blessings described in 2:21-27. On the other hand, Peter begins with these words: "And it shall be in the last days…" (Acts 2:17). The context of the Joel passage is that of the Tribulation, which explains why Peter calls it "the last days." The phrase "last days" is always a description in the Old Testament for events taking place either during the Tribulation or in conjunction with the second coming (see Deuteronomy 4:30; 31:29; Isaiah 2:2; Jeremiah 23:20; 30:24; 48:47; Ezekiel 38:16; Daniel 2:28; 10:14; Micah 4:1). Both passages link the following events to the last days.

Second, Peter did not use a normal introductory formula to say that the Joel passage was fulfilled when he spoke. The normal "formula" for citing the New Testament fulfillment of an Old Testament prophecy is exemplified in Matthew 2:15, which says, "...that what was spoken by the Lord through the prophet might be fulfilled, saying, 'Out of Egypt did I call My Son.'" We know the departure from Egypt by Jesus and His family fulfilled an Old Testament prediction because the text says it was a fulfillment. There is no such language in Acts 2:16. Peter did not actually say that any of Joel's prophecy was fulfilled on the Day of Pentecost.

Third, the introductory phrase that Peter did use is "this is what." This is the only time in the entire New Testament that *this* is used to introduce an Old Testament quotation by a New Testament author. Why did Peter, under the inspiration of the Holy Spirit, say "this is what"? Peter uses "this is what" because he is making an application of similarity between the working of God's Spirit in the future—as noted in Joel—and what the Holy Spirit was doing in giving birth to the church. He is answering the assertion in verse 13 that these men were drunk. We can paraphrase Peter's response this way: "No, what you are seeing today is not caused by sweet wine; instead, it is produced by the Holy Spirit, just as we see Joel describing events that will also be a product of the Holy Spirit." Arnold Fruchtenbaum explains it this way:

> However, there was one point of similarity: an outpouring of the Holy Spirit resulting in an unusual manifestation. Acts 2 neither changes or reinterprets Joel 2 nor does it deny that Joel 2 will have a literal fulfillment when the Holy Spirit will be poured out on the whole nation of Israel. It is simply applying it to a New Testament event because of one point of similarity. In Joel the Spirit is poured out resulting in the unusual manifestation of prophetic dreams and visions; in Acts the Spirit is poured out

resulting in the unusual manifestation of speaking in tongues (p. 7).

Fourth, nothing that Joel prophesied actually took place in Acts 2. Clearly there were no "wonders in the sky above, and signs on the earth beneath, blood, and fire, and vapor of smoke" (2:19) at the time of Peter's sermon. Neither did the sun turn to darkness or the moon into blood (2:20) as Peter spoke. In fact, "the one thing that happened in Acts 2 (tongues) is not even mentioned by Joel" (Fruchtenbaum, p. 5). Robert Thomas says, "The phenomena on the Day of Pentecost were in no sense a fulfillment of Joel's prophecy, a prophecy that pertained to the people of Israel, not to the church....It is misleading to call them in any sense a fulfillment of Joel" (Thomas, p. 263).

Fulfillment Still Future

The fact that the events Peter quotes from Joel 2 were not fulfilled on the Day of Pentecost in Acts 2 has great implications for Bible prophecy. It means that the events of Joel 2 will be fulfilled in conjunction with the Tribulation and the second coming, as noted by Christ Himself in Matthew 24:29. It also means that one cannot legitimately argue that the kingdom of God arrived in Acts 2, whether spiritually or physically. The promised kingdom is not the church.

—W.H. MARTY AND THOMAS ICE

BIBLIOGRAPHY

Dunn, J.D. "Pentecost." In *The New International Dictionary of New Testament Theology.* Ed. Colin Brown. Grand Rapids: Zondervan, 1976.

Feinberg, Charles L. "Pentecost." In *Zondervan Pictorial Encyclopedia of the Bible.* Ed. Merrill C. Tenney. Grand Rapids: Zondervan, 1975.

Fruchtenbaum, Arnold G. "Rabbinic Quotations of the Old Testament and How It Relates to Joel 2 and Acts 2." Paper presented to the Pre-Trib Study Group, Dallas, TX: Dec. 2002.

Jacobs, Louis. "SHAVUOT." In *Encyclopaedia Judaica.* Ed. Geoffrey Wiyoder. Jerusalem: Keter Publishing House, 1971.

Lincoln, A.T. "Pentecost." In *Dictionary of the Later New Testament and Its Developments.* Eds. Ralph P. Martin and Peter H. Davids. Downers Grove, IL: InterVarsity Press, 1997.

Lohse, E. "*Pentekoste* [Pentecost]." In *Theological Dictionary of the New Testament* (Abridged). Eds. Gerhard Kittel, Gerhard Friedrich, and Geoffrey W. Bromiley. Grand Rapids: Eerdmans Publishing Company, 1985.

Longenecker, Richard N. "The Acts of the Apostles." In *Expositor's Bible Commentary*. Ed. Frank E. Gaebelein. Grand Rapids: Zondervan, 1981.

Moorehead, W.G. *The Tabernacle: The Priesthood, Sacrifices, and Feasts of Ancient Israel*. Grand Rapids: Kregel, 1957.

Thomas, Robert. *Evangelical Hermeneutics: The New Versus the Old*. Grand Rapids: Kregel, 2002.

Witherington III, Ben. *The Acts of the Apostles: A Socio-Rhetorical Commentary*. Grand Rapids: Eerdmans Publishing Company, 1998.

PETER, ESCHATOLOGY OF

For the apostle Peter, eschatology is the motivation for endurance through uncertain times of change, trials, persecution, mockery, and false teaching. It is the impetus for spiritual growth and the assurance of victory. The Father has called and chosen us (1 Peter 1:2,15), the Spirit of Christ is sanctifying us (1 Peter 1:2), and the promise of an imperishable and unfading inheritance awaits us (1 Peter 1:3-5). That mysterious salvation, which perplexed the prophets of old and astonishes the angels to this day, is ours to embrace fully and experience joyfully in the light of the glorious expectation of all that will be ours at the second coming of the Savior (1 Peter 1:5,7,13). In the simplest of terms, eschatology means that believers win even though every aspect of their present situation suggests otherwise. Eschatology is relevant for today and makes our toughest days livable and joyful (1 Peter 1:8).

ESCHATOLOGICAL TOPICS THAT ENCOURAGE

Peter refers to the following eschatological topics to encourage the saints to endure through difficulty and to do what is right and honorable before the Lord:

1. The living hope: a certainty of eternal life given to the believer through the resurrection of Jesus Christ (1 Peter 1:3; 3:15).

2. Salvation: a process through which God calls, sets apart, and transforms a person into the image of His Son. It is the secure process of redemption that begins at the cross through repentance and culminates at the second coming of Christ (1 Peter 1:2-9; 5:10).

3. An inheritance: a promised reward given to believers by the Lord that is imperishable, good, and without end (1 Peter 1:3-5; 3:9; 5:4).

4. Christ's return: for Peter, it is the moment when the purifying trials that accompany our earthly walk of faith finally result in the full praise, honor, glory, and exultation that believers have always longed to give the Lord (1 Peter 1:7; 4:13; 5:1). It is the moment when God's work of grace completes the salvation of the believer's soul (1 Peter 1:13; 5:1), and it is viewed as imminent—that is, the return of Christ could occur at any moment (1 Peter 4:7).

5. The promise of a holy nation: the building of a people whom God, through His great mercy, has chosen from among the peoples of the world to reflect His will and character (1 Peter 2:5-10).

6. Judgment: the promise that wrongdoing by any and every individual, such as inappropriate sensual pleasures and maligning of the righteous, will be held to account (1 Peter 4:3-5,17-18). Peter refers to God's final outpouring of His judgment as "the day of the Lord" (2 Peter 3:10,13).

7. Hell: it is likely that Peter had hell in mind when he discerned that "black darkness" is reserved for those who teach false doctrine (2 Peter 2:17).

8. New heavens and new earth: a period that is eagerly anticipated by believers and will bring an end to the day of the Lord (the last and terrible judgment of the world) and to sin and suffering. The new heavens and the new earth will

be a place where only righteousness dwells (2 Peter 3:13).

Peter does not address specific events that occur during the second coming, such as the rapture, the Great Tribulation, the second advent, the battle of Armageddon, the millennium, or the Great White Throne judgment. Rather, he sees Christ's return as a future and inevitable event that should encourage believers to stand firm in their faith.

ESCHATOLOGY FOR EVERYDAY ISSUES

Pursue God rather than the world (1 Peter 1:13-2:12).

Believers should devote each day of their lives to pursuing those traits and qualities that are consistent with their imperishable inheritance and not remain influenced by the perishable and fading things of the world (1 Peter 1:14; 2:1,11-12). As people of God, Christians are "aliens and strangers" in this world (1 Peter 2:11) whose ultimate destiny is a renewed heaven and earth in which only righteousness dwells. In keeping with this status, their behavior should be such that unbelievers who observe their values may find it difficult to slander them and hopefully be swayed into receiving the same mercy that God gives to all who repent (1 Peter 2:12).

Submit to authorities whether good or bad (1 Peter 2:13-25).

It is the responsibility of our authorities, whatever they may be (local, state, federal, military, business, church, or family), to ensure that justice is maintained, that our playing field is as even as possible. If during a Christian's interaction with these authorities he or she suffers inequities because of the authority's ignorance of injustice or unwillingness to fight it, then believers, as the servants of Him who sanctions their power within the sphere of His ultimate plan for all of humanity, must endure the consequence of seeking to do what is right in a bad situation. The Lord's suffering in His earthly life ended in resurrection and new life. And because of what He endured and accomplished on the cross, the Christians' earthly experience will end with complete spiritual healing (1 Peter 2:24) and the fulfillment of the living hope, for which they wait expectantly (1 Peter 1:3-5).

Give a blessing in the midst of trouble (1 Peter 3:1-22).

It is always the Christian's responsibility to offer a blessing—in other words, to bestow a gift through a word of praise, gratefulness, and support, or by a deed that benefits the seemingly unreceptive recipient. The salvation that God has promised believers and the inheritance that is guaranteed them free them to do good for others regardless of the context, for what lasting harm can the unjust bring to the just (1 Peter 2:6)? Nothing can separate the called from the Caller. The salvation of the believer is "signed, sealed, and delivered." Each believer has only to live out the salvation that God has provided in a manner that images the grace and love that God has for the cantankerous (1 Peter 3:8-9), whether that individual is a spouse (1 Peter 3:1-7), fellow believer, or enemy of the gospel.

Since a Christian has already received the greatest of all blessings—the guarantee of eternal salvation (1 Peter 1:2-9)—the believer is free to pursue godliness and to sacrifice whatever is necessary to bring that blessing to others. A knowledgeable eschatology emboldens the Christian to trust in and love the Christ he has not seen so that he or she can thoughtfully and with respect engage a world that does not see (1 Peter 3:15-16).

Live the rest of your life for the will of God (1 Peter 4:1-19).

No human being knows the time of the Lord's return. As far as can be known, it is always "near" or imminent (1 Peter 4:6). This fact compels Peter to encourage believers to get on with living for God (1 Peter 4:2). There is no time to waste pursuing those things that satisfy the natural lusts of sinful men, no time to be concerned about the mocking of those who pursue such lusts without you (1 Peter 4:4).

Those who choose to forsake the Lord and continue in self-gratification will receive judgment for their wrongdoing. Though the unrighteous choose to persecute the righteous, they have already lost the battle that matters—the battle between spiritual life and death, between the spirit and the flesh (1 Peter 4:5,17-18).

With the end always in sight, the believer is to recall that suffering with Christ identifies him or her as one who has ceased devotion to self for the benefit of others (1 Peter 4:1). Moreover, the return of Christ and the judgment to come stirs the heart of the Christian toward maintaining a sound mind that is focused on prayer, love and forgiveness, sharing of one's possessions (hospitality), and developing and using the gifts that God has given His saints to minister to one another and to others (1 Peter 4:7-11). The joy that a believer is able to muster while undergoing hardship for Christ will be transformed to exultation at the second coming (1 Peter 4:13). Those who suffer for doing the will of God entrust their eternal welfare to the care of the Creator whose promises of justice and joy are their daily expectation.

Let humility be the cement that unites God's family (1 Peter 5:1-14).

Though respect for authority and position in a church ensures order, position does not make one believer better or more valued than another. The awareness that a believer acquires regarding God's work in the salvaging of his or her wrecked soul can have no other impact than that of driving out any inkling of arrogance in favor of a heap of humility. Acceptance is all that people can bring to God's plan of salvation; everything else is the result of God's good graces. Understanding the past (chosen by God, 1 Peter 1:1-2), the present (sanctifying work of the Spirit and protection by the power of God, 1 Peter 1:2,5), and the future (an imperishable inheritance that is reserved in heaven, 1 Peter 1:4) aspects of the redemptive process makes it possible for leaders and lay people to work together for the benefit of the whole, each role serving the

other without jealousy or competition. In God's time, He will bring His children to their eternal glory where He will "perfect, confirm, strengthen, and establish" them (1 Peter 5:6-10). Humility recognizes that the future is in the control of a sovereign God, and therefore, those who possess it choose to ride out the storms that accompany faith in this life for the inexhaustible pleasure of living with Him in the next.

Heed the admonitions of an eyewitness (2 Peter 1:1-21).

Though eschatology is a great encouragement for enduring the difficulties that accompany living faithfully for the Lord in this life, eschatology alone is not enough to sustain a believer. Christian growth requires constant diligence, which over time will mature the divine nature, which by faith Christ has given to each believer, and assist him or her in overcoming the corruption of the world (2 Peter 1:2-4,9). The promises of God guarantee the completion of salvation for each believer (1 Peter 1:3-5,9,13), and the addition of Christian virtues into the life of the believer guarantees that the Christian experience is meaningful and that the life of the believer is useful and spiritually fruitful, having been shaped by the true knowledge of Christ (2 Peter 1:8-9). Without moral excellence, knowledge, self-control, perseverance, godliness, brotherly kindness, and love, the believer will live a nominal, unproductive, and unsuccessful Christian life (2 Peter 1:5-11).

The idea that Christians might fail in their faith is too intolerable for Peter to consider. It is clear in the text of 2 Peter that Peter's admonition to his audience is not the first (2 Peter 1:12-15). He is so concerned that they take him seriously that he reminds them over and over again that his understanding of the necessity of these essential Christian virtues comes from his being an eyewitness to the unveiling of Christ's honor and glory at the transfiguration, when God's audible approval of His Son thoroughly convinced Peter that Jesus' relationship with His Father is indeed unique (2 Peter 1:16-18). God's validation of His Son at the transfiguration made all the prophecies of the former prophets regarding Christ "more sure," giving instant and complete creditability to the Scripture (2 Peter 1:18-19). The knowledge of God's Word creates a committed, competent, and confident believer, one who will endure the tests of this time as he or she awaits the coming of the Lord at a later time (1 Peter 1:13; 2 Peter 1:16).

Remember that divine judgment of sin is certain (2 Peter 2:1–3:18).

There have always been periods of time throughout history when unrighteousness has been the order of the day; in fact, it is safe and right to say that ungodliness is a standard human pattern. Like David, who was weary from the onslaught and oppression of the unjust, believers today might appropriately cry out, "How long, O LORD, will the adversary revile, and the enemy spurn Your name forever?" (Psalm 74:10). However, it is important to remember that the Bible is rife with illustrations of God ensuring that the unrighteous will reap the consequences of the evil seed they have sown. Peter reminds his audience of God's judgment of fallen angels (2 Peter 2:4), His destruction of the ungodly in Noah's time (2 Peter 2:5), and the condemnation of Sodom and Gomorrah (2 Peter 2:6). Through the darkest times in history, God preserves the righteous (2 Peter 2:5,7-9) and condemns the wicked. Biblical history teaches that the end of all sin or false teaching is divine judgment. If He has judged the wicked in the past, He will certainly judge them in the future—His steadfast faithfulness requires Him to do no less.

Peter's message of encouragement is pure and simple: Stay faithful in the midst of false teaching. Protect yourself from its influence (2 Peter 2:17-22). God will not leave sin unchallenged indefinitely (2 Peter 2:17); in fact, at a time of God's own choosing, He will exact a judgment of global proportions (2 Peter 3:5-9) so encompassing that it will require the creation of new heavens and a new earth in which righteousness alone will shape the lives of all who dwell there (2 Peter 3:10-13).

Peter ends his second epistle in the same way that he begins the first: with the promise of a time when righteousness will reign unfettered by human sin. Knowing that victory is inevitable, believers should focus their life's energy on reflecting the moral excellence of their God (2 Peter 3:14), deepening their understanding of God's Word (2 Peter 3:2,16), and living obediently and free from the influences of the world (1 Peter 1:13-19).

—GARY P. STEWART

BIBLIOGRAPHY

Blum, Edward A. "1 Peter" and "2 Peter" in *The Expositor's Bible Commentary*, Vol. 12. Grand Rapids: Zondervan, 1981.

Fruchtenbaum, Arnold G. *The Footprints of the Messiah: A Study of the Sequence of Prophetic Events*, rev. ed. Tustin, CA: Ariel Ministries, 2003.

Gangel, Kenneth O. "2 Peter." In *Bible Knowledge Commentary: An Exposition of the Scriptures by Dallas Seminary Faculty, New Testament*. Eds. John F. Walvoord and Roy B. Zuck. Wheaton, IL: Victor Books, 1983.

Raymer, Roger M. "1 Peter." In *Bible Knowledge Commentary: An Exposition of the Scriptures by Dallas Seminary Faculty, New Testament*. Eds. John F. Walvoord and Roy B. Zuck. Wheaton, IL: Victor Books, 1983.

POSTMILLENNIALISM

STUDENTS OF ESCHATOLOGY usually hold one of three major views, depending on their understanding of the timing of the return of Christ and the millennial kingdom of God. The three systems are known as premillennialism, amillennialism, and postmillennialism.

John F. Walvoord (p. 845) describes his premillennial faith as "an interpretation that the Second Coming of Christ will occur before His literal reign of one thousand years on earth." After His victorious intervention into history, Christ will personally reign from Jerusalem, ushering in a time of peace, prosperity, and righteousness. Premillennialists see the present era as the church age, which is separate and distinct from God's plan for Israel. Christ's redemptive work is the only basis for salvation in every age.

Floyd E. Hamilton, a proponent of amillennialism, teaches that "Christ's millennial kingdom extends from His Resurrection from the tomb to the time of His Second Coming on the clouds at the end of this age." At no time will Christ reign on the earth in Jerusalem. On earth, Christ's kingdom "is not of this world," but He reigns in the hearts of His people on earth. After the second coming of Christ, believers from all of history will enter into heaven for eternity immediately following the final and single judgment of all mankind.

Norman Shepherd supports postmillennialism, "the view that Christ will return at the end of an extended period of righteousness and prosperity (the millennium)." Like amillennialists, postmillennialists see the current age as the kingdom of God. However, they see the reign of Christ not just in the hearts of believers today but also impacting society and bringing in the kingdom of God on earth. Postmillennialists believe that the kingdom was established at Christ's first coming and is currently expanding through the preaching of the gospel until an overwhelming majority is converted to Christ. Such gospel success will create a climate of reception to the things of Christ, including His mediated rule through the church of the entire world.

THE SIMILARITY OF AMILLENNIALISM AND POSTMILLENNIALISM

Walvoord (p. 6) has observed that "premillennialism is obviously a viewpoint quite removed from either amillennialism or postmillennialism." This is so because the premillennial view is consistently more literal in its hermeneutical approach than the other two views.

Some postmillennialists have noted their closer kinship with their amillennialist brethren as well. David Chilton links amillennialists and postmillennialists because of their common belief that the kingdom or millennium is the current age. Postmillennialism is an optimistic form of amillennialism. Also, the amillennial and postmillennial views do not interpret God's promises for national Israel literally. Rather, they apply them to the church.

A BRIEF HISTORY OF THE MILLENNIAL SYSTEMS

Premillennialism (known in the early church as chiliasm) is the oldest of the three systems. The other two systems developed in reaction to Ante-Nicene premillennialism.

Chiliasm

Premillennialism, or *chiliasm* as it was called in the early church, was the pervasive view of the earliest orthodox fathers. This is the consensus of both liberal and conservative experts of early church theology.

Church historians acknowledge that premillennialism or chiliasm was dominant through the middle of the third century. The great theologians who followed the second-century apologists (Irenaeus, Tertullian, and Hippolytus) were exponents of millenarianism. J.C. Ayer (p. 25) observes, "Primitive Christianity was marked by great chiliastic enthusiasm....By chiliasm, strictly speaking, is meant the belief that Christ was to return to earth and reign visibly for one thousand years. That return was commonly placed in the immediate future."

No orthodox church father contradicted premillennialism until the beginning of the third century, when Gaius (or Caius) first launched an attack. Gaius is the first person in recorded church history to interpret the 1000 years symbolically. He also rejected the book of Revelation, believing it was written by Cerinthus and should not be in the canon. Nonetheless, premillennialism was still very much the eschatology of the day.

Antimillennialism

Antimillennialism arose before amillennialism or postmillennialism. Hans Bietenhard (p. 30), after noting how the early church was solidly chiliastic in its interpretation of

Revelation 20 and other Scripture until the time of Augustine, says, "Today, it is admitted on all hands—except for a few Roman Catholic exegetes—that only an eschatological interpretation [in the context meaning chiliastic one] is consistent with the text. If the question is still open whether the hope is to be maintained or not, it will now be decided by other than exegetical and historical considerations."

Antimillennialism did not arise from the study of Scripture but rather as a result of the disturbed sensibilities of individuals who were already affected by pagan thought. The Alexandrian school in Egypt attacked premillennialism during the middle of the third century. In the East, Eusebius of Caesarea (263–339), the court theologian to Constantine and theological heir of Origen, was a strong leader in the rejection of apocalypticism. With the rise of Constantine and the adoption of Christianity as the empire's official religion, alternate perspectives fell into disfavor. As the Roman Empire embraced Christianity, chiliasm seemed an unnecessary option.

Historically, allegorical interpreters have commonly looked down on literal interpreters who rejected the "deeper" or "more spiritual" insights of the allegorical approach. A classic example of this attitude can be seen in Eusebius' comments about Papias' lack of intelligence because he interpreted the Bible literally.

Amillennialism

In the Latin West, Jerome (347–420) and Augustine (354–430) also reacted strongly to prophetic interpretation. In his commentary on Daniel, written shortly before the year 400, Jerome argued that "the saints will in no wise have an earthly kingdom, but only a celestial one; thus must cease the fable of one thousand years."

Jerome was not alone in his attack on literal interpretation and millennial expectations. In *City of God,* Augustine repeatedly dismisses any hope for an earthly or physical millennial kingdom. Through the writings of men such as Jerome, Julian of Toledo, Gregory the Great, and most notably Augustine, literal interpretation of the Bible, and espe-cially Daniel and Revelation, quickly faded. The Augustinian influence in the West eclipsed the original premillennial faith of the early church fathers.

Postmillennialism

Postmillennialism was the last of the three major views to develop. It is similar to amillennialism, but it adds a positive twist. Eschatological optimism does not necessarily relate to current events. The current revival of postmillennialism is fueled by the rise of New Age optimism in a postmodern culture.

Postmillennialism almost died out after the two world wars of the twentieth century. However, recent years have witnessed a renewed emphasis on postmillennialism. The Christian Reconstruction movement has been the primary catalyst for the recent resurgence of postmillennialism. "Indeed, it is no accident," declares Aiken Taylor (p. 11), explaining the recent rise of postmillennialism, "that both postmillennialism and theonomy...have sprouted in the soil of a strong Reformed revival."

This misguided optimism is a major error in postmillennialism. Evangelical postmillennialism is to be distinguished from the liberal form, but one should not overlook the role that postmillennialism played in the rise and development of the social gospel. Conversely, postmillenarians blame dispensationalism for creating a climate of retreat from social and political issues.

HERMENEUTICS AND PROPHECY

Dr. John Walvoord often predicted that the major theological challenge in the days ahead will be the hermeneutical problem of not interpreting the Bible literally, especially the prophetic passages. Amillennialists and postmillennialists do not interpret the entire Bible, especially prophecy, literally. Oswald Allis (p. 238) admits, "The Old Testament prophecies if literally interpreted cannot be regarded as having been yet fulfilled or as being capable of fulfillment in this present age."

A NATURAL INTERPRETATION

Amillennialists and postmillennialists both spend a lot of time explaining why they are opposed to premillennialism, especially dispensational premillennialism. Just as in the early church, modern amillennialists and postmillennialists often begin explaining their positions by attacking premillennialism.

A natural, literal, detailed exposition of the Scriptures shows that the Bible teaches premillennialism. Dr. Gerald Stanton summarizes premillennialism with the following points:

- The Bible should be interpreted consistently and literally.
- The Abrahamic covenant is unconditional.
- The Old Testament teaches a literal earthly kingdom.
- The kingdom is carried unchanged into the New Testament.
- Christ taught about an earthly kingdom.
- Scripture references multiple resurrections.
- Revelation 20 teaches premillennialism.
- The early church was premillennial.
- Premillennialism harmonizes the entire Bible.
- Only premillennialism provides a satisfactory conclusion to history.

SOUND THEOLOGY

The terms *premillennialism, amillennialism,* and *postmillennialism* exist because Revelation 20 speaks of a 1000-year reign of Christ that will take place after His return in Revelation 19. Sound theology should be developed from the Bible itself, and the Bible teaches only a single viewpoint on any issue. Amillennialism and postmillennialism are nowhere to be found, but premillennialism is found throughout the Bible. The strength of premillennialism is the text of Scripture.

—THOMAS ICE

BIBLIOGRAPHY

Allis, Oswald. *Prophecy and the Church.* Phillipsburg, NJ: Presbyterian & Reformed, 1952.

Ayer, J.C. *A Source Book for Ancient Church History.* New York: AMS Press, 1970.

Bietenhard, Hans. "The Millennial Hope in the Early Church." *Scottish Journal of Theology* 6, 1953.

Chilton, David. *Days of Vengeance.* Fort Worth, TX: Dominion Press, 1987.

Taylor, Aiken. "Postmillennialism Revisited." *Presbyterian Journal.* September 6, 1978.

Walvoord, John F. "Premillennialism." Floyd Hamilton. "Amillennialism." Norman Shepherd. "Postmillennialism." In *Pictorial Encyclopedia of the Bible.* Grand Rapids: Zondervan, 1975.

POSTTRIBULATIONISM

POSTTRIBULATIONISM TEACHES that the church will endure the Great Tribulation and be raptured at its conclusion. According to this view, the rapture and second coming of Christ are one and the same. Therefore, posttribulationists believe the Tribulation could be imminent, but the rapture is not.

Posttribulational writers suggest several "proofs" for their theory. Not every posttribulationist would agree with every argument listed below, but the following list identifies the major arguments by leading spokesmen in this theological camp.

POSTTRIBULATIONAL "PROOFS"

1. *The Historical Argument*

One argument advanced by posttribulational writers is that the early church held their view. For this reason they sometimes refer to themselves as historic premillennialists. This argument has both a positive and negative emphasis. The positive argument is stated by Gundry (p. 173): "Until Augustine in the fourth century, the early Church generally held to the premillenarian understanding of Bible eschatology. The chiliasm entailed a futuristic interpretation of Daniel's seventieth week, the abomination of desolation, and the personal Antichrist. And it was post tribulational."

It is questionable whether anyone can demonstrate a finely developed eschatological position taught by the early post-apostolic church. This means the early church was neither clearly pretribulational nor clearly posttribulational. Addressing this subject, Ryrie (p. 68) suggests, "The early church believed in tribulation, the imminent coming of Christ, and a Millennium to follow. The early church was clearly premillennial but not clearly pretribulational, nor was it clearly posttribulational when measured against today's developed pre- or posttribulation teachings."

The timing of the rapture was not an issue with early church fathers. They knew Christ's coming was imminent. Therefore, they were looking for Him to come potentially at any time to deliver them from persecution. Also, one does not find any concept in the church fathers that would indicate they would face the wrath of God in the Great Tribulation.

2. The Argument Against Imminence

One cannot read the New Testament and conclude the writers believed in anything other than an imminent return of Christ. They were convinced that Christ could return at any moment. Christians were exhorted to keep watching for His return (1 Thessalonians 5:1-8; 2 Peter 3:8-10) and wait for it (1 Corinthians 1:7; 1 Thessalonians 1:9-10; Titus 2:13). These commands were as meaningful and applicable to the first century as they are today. Even the implication of end-times signs does not conflict with the imminent return of Christ.

Posttribulational writers argue that the early church did not believe in the doctrine of imminence, nor do the Scriptures teach it. They claim the biblical injunctions to watch for the return of Christ do not necessarily mean it should be anticipated immediately. Posttribulationists argue that several things had to occur before Jesus could return, such as the fall of Jerusalem, Peter's death, the destruction of the Temple, the worldwide spread of the gospel, and the growth of the church.

Conservative scholars generally agree that the prophecy concerning Peter's martyrdom was recorded by John perhaps as much as 30 years after Peter was killed. How this could discourage the early Christians from believing in the imminent return of Christ is difficult to comprehend. The context in which this prophecy exists suggests some readers may have believed Christ would return even before the death of the aging apostle John (John 21:23).

Posttribulationists tend to ignore the distinction between the rapture and second coming. This biblical distinction is a major argument for the pretribulational view.

3. The Argument That the Church Is Promised Tribulation

Another posttribulationist argument is that the church will endure the Great Tribulation. Verses such as John 16:1-2,33 and Romans 12:12 predict tribulation for the Christian, not escape. Those holding this position argue that this tribulation is simply the trials experienced over the years by Christians, so they equate suffering with the Great Tribulation. Others agree there is a coming Tribulation and that Christians will suffer during this period, but they are not subject to the wrath of God. This appears to be the majority belief of contemporary posttribulational teachers. Gundry (pp. 46, 62) admits, "It is not a point of disagreement whether the Church will ever suffer God's retributive wrath. She will not (John 3:36; 5:24; Rom. 5:9; 8:1; Eph. 2:3; 5:6; 1 Thes. 1:10; 5:9). As now, the Church will suffer persecution during the tribulation, but no saint can suffer divine wrath."

But Pentecost (p. 170) notes, "It must be noticed that the term *tribulation* is used in several different ways in Scripture. It is used in a non-technical, non-eschatological sense in reference to any time of suffering or testing into which one goes. It is so used in Matthew 13:21; Mark 4:17; John 16:33; Romans 5:3; 12:12; 2 Corinthians 1:4; 2 Thessalonians 1:4; Revelation 1:9. It is used in its technical or eschatological sense in reference to the whole period of the seven years of tribulation, as in Revelation 2:22 or Matthew 24:29. It is also used in reference to the last half of this seven-year period, as in Matthew 24:21."

Scripture consistently describes the Great Tribulation as mostly Jewish and characterized not by the wrath of men but by the wrath of God. It is pictured as "the time of Jacob's trouble," not the church's trouble. It cannot begin until after the rapture of the church.

4. The Argument of the Historic Fulfillment of Daniel 9:24-27

Some posttribulationists hold to a historic fulfillment of Daniel 9:24-27, including the seventieth week of that prophecy. They believe the 70 weeks are a continuous, successive, unbroken period of years that ended with the death of Stephen or the destruction of Jerusalem. This is not the position of all posttribulationists, but those who do hold this view see no gap between weeks 69 and 70 of Daniel's prophecy. In contrast to this view, Gundry (p. 189), himself a posttribulationist, argues we cannot spiritualize Israel ("your people") to refer to a spiritual Israel inclusive of Gentiles without destroying the plain sense of the passage. The destruction of Jerusalem, for example, deals with Israel as a nation. In addition, "the finishing of Israel's transgression, the purging of her iniquity, and the bringing of her everlasting righteousness have not reached completion. Paul writes of these as still in the future for Israel (Rom. 11:25-27)."

5. The Argument That the Resurrection Occurs After the Tribulation

Posttribulationists argue that the doctrine of resurrection proves a posttribulation rapture. They argue that the first resurrection is associated with the coming of the Lord, the conversion of Israel, and the inauguration of the kingdom (Luke 14:14-15; Revelation 20:4-6). According to this argument, the rapture must be posttribulational because the resurrection occurs after the Tribulation.

This argument is based on the conclusion that the resurrection of Revelation 20:5-6, which is there called "the first resurrection," is the same resurrection referred to in 1 Thessalonians 4:16. The major weakness of this argument is the equating of "the first resurrection" or the resurrection of the Old Testament saints with the resurrection occurring at the rapture. The Scriptures identify at least four distinct resurrections, the first chrono-

logically being the resurrection of Christ (Matthew 28:1-7). The expression "first resurrection" can therefore be understood only within the immediate context of the passage since Christ's resurrection was first. The resurrection in Revelation 20:5-6 is "first" in that it comes 1000 years prior to the fourth and final resurrection, but it is also "third" in that it follows the resurrection of Christ and the resurrection of the saints at the rapture.

Walvoord (The Rapture Question, p. 154) observes: "The Old Testament saints are never described by the phrase 'in Christ.' The fact that the 'voice of the archangel'—Israel's defender—is heard at the rapture is not conclusive proof that Israel is raised at that time....The best answer is to concede the point that the resurrection of Old Testament saints is after the tribulation, but to divorce it completely from the translation and resurrection of the church....If the translation of the church is a different event entirely, [the argument] proves nothing."

Finally, perhaps the word "first" did not mean "first in time" but "first in kind," that is, the resurrection was of God's people (whether before or after the Tribulation). The "second of a different kind" involved the unsaved (Revelation 20:11-15).

6. The Argument of the Parable of the Wheat and Tares

The parable of the wheat and the tares is sometimes used to defend the posttribulational cause. Posttribulationists suggest that Christ spoke of the wheat and the tares growing together "until the harvest" (Matthew 13:30) and suggest a general judgment at the end of the age. Commenting on this text, posttribulationists generally argue that there will be no judicial separation of the righteous and the wicked until the final harvest. This, then, is taken to prove the fact that the rapture will not occur until the end of the Tribulation.

However, the purpose of the kingdom parables in Matthew 13 is to record not the history of the church but rather the history of the kingdom in mystery form—Christendom.

These parables clearly predict Israel's rejection of the Messiah (the King) and the present development of professing Christendom. They are not intended to illustrate the timing of the rapture or the final judgment.

7. The Argument of Fruit

Perhaps the weakest argument, from a theological position, is that based upon fruit—that is, the apparent results of a doctrinal teaching. Nevertheless, some posttribulationists have attempted to argue that pretribulationism is divisive and lacks a social conscience for the world. This, however, is convincingly refuted by the spiritual, moral, social, and political activities of pretribulationists such as Jerry Falwell and Tim LaHaye. In general, pretribulationists have shown evangelistic fervor, missionary zeal, social concern, and intense spiritual commitment in light of the fact that Jesus could come at any moment.

PRETRIBULATIONAL SUPPORT

The ultimate answers to the arguments of posttribulationism are the overwhelmingly affirmative reasons for believing in the pretribulational rapture:

1. the contrast of the events involving the rapture and the second coming

2. the need for time after the rapture for the judgment seat of Christ and the marriage of the Lamb in heaven

3. the necessity for the removal of the restrainer and the revelation of the man of sin—that is, the Antichrist

4. the uniqueness of the church as the body of Christ

5. God's promises to keep the church from the Great Tribulation

6. the absence of the church between Revelation 4:1 and 19:11

All these factors point to a pretribulational coming of Christ. "Even so come Lord Jesus" (Revelation 22:20).

—ELMER TOWNS

BIBLIOGRAPHY

Gundry, Robert H. The Church and the Tribulation. Grand Rapids: Zondervan, 1973.

Pentecost, J. Dwight. Things to Come. Grand Rapids: Zondervan, 1975.

Ryrie, Charles. What You Should Know About the Rapture. Chicago: Moody Press, 1981.

Walvoord, John F. The Blessed Hope and the Tribulation. Grand Rapids: Zondervan, 1976.

———. The Rapture Question. Grand Rapids: Zondervan, 1972.

PREMILLENNIALISM

PREMILLENNIALISM IS the eschatological view that Jesus Christ will return literally to establish His kingdom on earth for 1000 years. This will occur after the Tribulation period and before the establishment of the new heavens and new earth (Revelation 20).

Ryrie (p. 450) notes: "All forms of premillennialism understand that the Millennium follows the second coming of Christ. Its duration will be 1,000 years; its location will be on earth; its government will be theocratic with the personal presence of Christ reigning as King."

Within premillennialism in general exist a variety of views regarding the rapture of the church. These include pretribulational, midtribulational, and posttribulational premillennialism. In other words, premillennialists are divided over their views of when the rapture will occur in relation to the Tribulation and the millennium. (See articles on these views.)

1000 YEARS

Premillennialists believe the references to 1000 years in Revelation 20 are to be taken literally. Critics of premillennialism argue that the number appears only in this one passage, noting that the Old Testament gives no time frame for the future messianic kingdom. Others argue that Revelation is filled with symbols and suggest the 1000 years be interpreted symbolically to refer to a long period of time.

While it is true that the mention of 1000 years is found only in Revelation 20, it should be noted that it is mentioned six different times in this one passage. The point of such obvious repetition is to reinforce its significance. Attempts to dismiss the number as less than literal would lead one to dismiss all the numbers in Revelation as being merely symbolic as well. This would render the entire book a hopeless jumble of unintelligible symbols with no correspondence to reality.

The Old Testament clearly predicts a coming messianic kingdom in the future (Isaiah 2:2-4; 11:6-9; 65:17-25). Such a kingdom is necessary for several reasons:

1. It fulfills the promises of the Jewish covenants.
2. It fulfills the predictions of the Jewish prophets.
3. It brings the rule of God to earth.
4. It completes the perpetuity of the blessings of Christ.
5. It answers the disciples' question about the restoration of the kingdom to Israel (Acts 1:6).

The major contribution of Revelation 20 is that it makes clear who the messianic Ruler will be (Jesus Christ) and how long He will rule (1000 years).

A LITERAL KINGDOM ON EARTH

Premillennialists certainly acknowledge the spiritual benefits of the kingdom of God but are also insistent on the future literal aspects of Christ's rule on earth. We believe the basic text of Revelation describes God's timetable for the future:

1. the rapture of the church
2. the Tribulation period
3. the triumphal return
4. the defeat of the Antichrist
5. the binding of Satan
6. the millennial reign

If these events are not supposed to be interpreted as occurring sequentially and in order, why are they presented that way in the book of Revelation? All attempts to explain away the obvious order are inadequate at best and seriously distorted at worst.

These ten distinctive teachings summarize the primary tenets of premillennialism:

1. God has promised a literal kingdom to a restored Israel (Isaiah 11:9-16; 60:18-21).
2. God will give Abraham's descendants the land He promised to them forever (Genesis 17:7-8; Psalm 105:8-11).
3. God's covenant with Israel has never been forfeited or cancelled (Leviticus 26:40-44).
4. The nation of Israel will come back to inherit the land forever (Ezekiel 37:1-14; Jeremiah 31:35-37).
5. The second coming of Christ will result in the establishment of a literal kingdom on earth (Revelation 11:15).
6. The kingdom of Christ on earth will last 1000 years (Revelation 20:1-6).
7. The Temple of Ezekiel's vision will literally exist during the millennial reign of Christ (Ezekiel 40–48).
8. Redeemed Israel and the raptured church will reign with Christ on earth (Revelation 1:6; 5:10; 20:4-5).
9. God's promises concerning Jerusalem will be fulfilled literally (Psalm 132:13-14; Isaiah 62:1-2; 65:17-25).
10. The throne of David will be set up in Jerusalem with Jesus Christ, the Messiah of Israel, the Son of David, literally ruling upon it in His millennial kingdom (2 Samuel 7:12-16; Luke 1:32-33).

THE IMPORTANCE OF THE KINGDOM

The idea of the kingdom of God on earth is central to all biblical teachings. The Old Testament prophets predicted it. Jesus announced it. And the New Testament apostles foretold it again. The psalmist said, "God is my King" (Psalm 74:12 NKJV). Jeremiah said of the Lord,

"He is the living God and the everlasting king" (Jeremiah 10:10). John the revelator refers to Jesus Christ as "King of kings and Lord of lords" (Revelation 19:16).

The concept of the kingdom is closely associated with that of the King. Daniel wrote, "The Most High rules in the kingdom of men" (Daniel 4:17). The psalmist adds, "His kingdom rules over all" (Psalm 103:19). The primary meaning of the New Testament word for kingdom, *basileia*, is "reign" rather than "realm" or "people." In the general linguistic usage, *basileia* designates the character and the position of the King.

A kingdom cannot exist without a king. God has always chosen human representatives to mediate His kingdom on earth. The rule of God through such mediators is called a "theocratic" kingdom. Alva McClain (p. 17) defines such a kingdom as "the rule of God through a divinely chosen representative who speaks and acts for God."

The kingdom of God has always existed, and it will always exist. It is the sovereign rule of God from eternity past to eternity future. It has been mediated on earth through the dominion of man over the creation and through the divine institution of human government. In relation to the nation of Israel, the kingdom of God was to be administered by divinely appointed kings in the Davidic line (the line of the Messiah). But only with the coming of the Messiah will the hopes and dreams of a kingdom of God on earth be fully realized.

The millennial kingdom on earth is the ultimate expression of God's creative activity and His original plan for the planet. Hindson (p. 200) quotes William S. LaSor: "The triumph of God over the satanic dominion of this planet is necessary for the glory of God. If there were no messianic age, if God simply picked up the redeemed remnant and took them off to heaven, then we would have to conclude that God was unable to complete what He began."

The kingdom of God on earth reaches its apex during the 1000-year reign of Christ.

The term *millennium* comes from the Latin word *mille* ("thousand") and *annus* ("year"). Thus, it refers to the 1000-year reign of Christ. The Greek word for millennium comes from *chilias*, meaning "a thousand." The Greek term is used six times in the original text of Revelation 20 to define the duration of Christ's kingdom on earth.

THE MESSIANIC AGE

The Old Testament prophets foretold a golden era of peace and prosperity and the Messiah's rule on earth. Isaiah wrote, "It shall come to pass in the latter days that the mountain of the LORD's house shall be established...and all nations shall flow to it....For out of Zion shall go forth the law, and the word of the LORD from Jerusalem. And He shall judge among the nations....they shall beat their swords into plowshares, and their spears into pruning hooks; nation shall not lift up sword against nation, neither shall they learn war any more" (Isaiah 2:2-4).

God's promises to Israel include earthly and spiritual blessings. This explains why the disciples asked Jesus, "Lord, will you at this time restore the kingdom to Israel?" (Acts 1:6). This question was raised after the resurrection and before the ascension. It reveals that the Jewish disciples were still looking for the promised messianic kingdom. Little did they realize that Jesus was about to return to heaven and postpone that phase of the kingdom until the distant future.

"It is not for you to know the times or dates the Father has set by his own authority," Jesus replied (Acts 1:7 NIV). Now, He did not say there would be no future kingdom. Rather, He merely indicated that it would come later. In the meantime, He commissioned the disciples to go into all the world and preach the gospel.

During the church age, the kingdom of God does not come with "observation" (Luke 17:20). We become citizens of that kingdom by faith in Jesus Christ as our King. Thus, our citizenship is in heaven (see Philippians 3:20). In the meantime, we are Christ's ambassadors on earth, commissioned to proclaim the gospel to all nations.

As premillennialists, we look forward to the rapture of the church. We have no pretensions of being able to bring in the kingdom on earth by our own efforts. If the church must bring in the kingdom, we will be a long time awaiting its arrival. In fact, by all current measures, we are desperately falling behind.

Beyond the rapture, we look forward to the fulfillment of the messianic age. We believe the kingdom of God will come on earth when the King comes back to rule. In the meantime, we continue to declare Him as King and His gospel as the means of salvation. Jesus Himself told us to do this when He said, "This gospel of the kingdom will be preached in the whole world as a testimony to all nations, and then the end will come" (Matthew 24:14 NIV).

THE BINDING OF SATAN

Revelation 20 opens with an angel descending from heaven with the key to the abyss ("the bottomless pit"). He is carrying a "great chain" with which he bound Satan for "a thousand years" (Revelation 20:1). The angel cast Satan into the abyss and sealed it shut for that time.

Hindson (p. 201) quotes Robert Mounce: "The purpose of the confinement is not punishment. It is to prevent him from deceiving the nations. The elaborate measures taken to ensure his custody are most easily understood as implying the complete cessation of his influence on earth, rather than a curbing of his activities." This point is crucial to one's interpretation of the binding of Satan for 1000 years. Amillennial commentators try to say this is descriptive of the present age. They hold that Satan is currently "bound," and that his influence on earth is limited by the power of the gospel. In order to think this, they must view the 1000 years as figurative of the entire church age.

John Walvoord (p. 292) points out the problem with this viewpoint when he writes, "Opposed to the amillennial and postmillennial interpretation, however, is the uni-form revelation of the New Testament which shows Satan is a very active person. If anything, he is more active than in preceding ages and is continuing an unrelenting opposition to all that God purposes to do in the present age."

The epistles offer numerous examples of Satan's current activity:

1. He is the god of this world (2 Corinthians 4:4).

2. He blinds the minds of the lost (2 Corinthians 4:3-4).

3. He is the prince of the power of the air (Ephesians 2:2).

4. He appears as an angel of light (2 Corinthians 11:14).

5. He walks about like a roaring lion (1 Peter 5:8).

These passages show that Satan is anything but bound during the present age. All attempts to picture him otherwise seem ludicrous. Therefore, the binding of Satan must be a future event that has not yet occurred. Its relationship to the 1000 years indicates a literal, rather than symbolic, period of time, followed by the release of Satan, the deception of the last generation and, ultimately, Satan being cast into the lake of fire (Revelation 20:7-10). If the 1000 years are merely a symbol, when will these subsequent events take place?

Nothing in the text of Revelation 20 indicates that the 1000 years should be interpreted figuratively. Otherwise, all the other time indicators in Revelation would be meaningless. Harold Hoehner (pp. 249–50) writes, "The denial of a literal 1,000 years is not because of the exegesis of the text but a predisposition brought to the text."

Attempts to "spiritualize" the 1000 years as symbolic often go hand in hand with attempts to "spiritualize" the biblical promises of a glorious future to the nation of Israel. McClain (p. 463) quotes T.F. Torrance of the University of Edinburgh, Scotland, who says, "The historical particularity of Israel covenanted with God persists through the Christian era.

God has not cast off His ancient people (Romans 11); for the covenant with Israel as God's people remains in force, and cannot be 'spiritualized' and turned into some form alien to the stubborn historicity of its nature without calling into question the whole historical foundation of God's revelation."

RULING WITH CHRIST ON EARTH

Hindson (p. 202) quotes Beasley-Murray: "The essential element of the idea of the millennium is the appearing of the Kingdom of the Messiah in history, prior to the revelation of the Kingdom of God in the eternal and transcendent realm of the new creation." In this regard, Revelation 19 provides a transition from the fall of "Babylon" (city of man) to the arrival of the New Jerusalem (city of God).

There is no detailed description of the millennial reign here. For that we must rely on the Old Testament prophets. John focuses only on the fact that we will rule with Christ on earth—a promise he introduced earlier in Revelation 5:10. There the text says, "And hast made us…kings and priests: and we shall reign on the earth." Thus, the idea of a literal earthly kingdom has already been introduced as a future prospect. Now it is portrayed as a present reality.

John foresees the Tribulation martyrs ruling with Christ in the millennial kingdom. He also sees thrones and those seated on them to whom judgment was given. The scene is similar to the one described by Daniel (7:9-10,22). These may be the thrones of the 24 elders, but they are not specified as such (see Revelation 4:4; 5:8-10; 7:13; 11:15). Since Jesus promised the 12 apostles they would sit on thrones judging the 12 tribes of Israel (see Matthew 19:28; Luke 22:30), it seems likely that would be in view here during the earthly kingdom.

The total picture is much greater. The bride (church) has returned from heaven with Christ in chapter 19. Now the Tribulation saints (believers) are resurrected to rule with them. This is called the "first resurrection" (Revelation 20:5) to distinguish it from the second resurrection, in which the dead are brought to judgment after the 1000 years (Revelation 20:11-15).

The martyrs are those who were beheaded for the witness of Jesus and for the word of God. They had not worshiped the beast or his image nor received his mark (Revelation 20:4). The unsaved dead remain dead for the entire 1000 years. But the martyrs are resurrected to rule with Christ during the millennial kingdom. This privilege is the reward for their faithfulness to Christ in the face of unprecedented persecution. During this time, the damage of the Tribulation period will be reversed and the earth will prosper under the personal reign of Christ on the throne of David (see Zechariah 12:10; Isaiah 9:6-7). Without such a rule, the return of Christ would be only a "walk among the ruins" after the battle of Armageddon.

In one of the great surprises of the apocalyptic drama, Satan is loosed from the abyss after the millennium. John the revelator provides no specific details as to who accomplishes this, how, or why. He merely records, "When the thousand years are over, Satan will be released from his prison and will go out to deceive the nations" (Revelation 20:7-8 NIV).

Several facts are apparent in this account:

1. Some nations survive the Tribulation period and continue on into the millennium.

2. Children continue to be born to the people of earth during the millennium.

3. Christ rules during the millennium with a rod of iron.

4. Mankind rebels against Christ despite the blessing of the millennium.

5. Ultimately, the millennial kingdom is replaced by the eternal city—the New Jerusalem.

The final revolt is the ultimate proof of human depravity. Unredeemed minds will tolerate Christ's rule, but they will not bow their hearts to Him. As soon as Satan is loosed, they rebel against the rule of God. Even though Edenic conditions have been restored to earth, mankind once again falls prey to the deceiver.

While some are surprised—even shocked—by this revolt, we must remember two things have not changed: unrepentant Satan and unregenerate mankind. The devil is still the deceiver, the "father of lies." He will not cease from his destructive ways. He has not repented after 1000 years in the abyss. Therefore, God's only possible act of mercy to the rest of the world is to cast him into the lake of fire (Revelation 20:10).

The millennium will be a time of unparalleled peace and prosperity, but it is not heaven. It is earthly existence at its best—until the deceiver is loosed upon it. Thus, biblical prophecy points us ahead to the eternal state where deception, sin, and death will not exist in the eternal city—the New Jerusalem.

—ED HINDSON AND
DAVID HOCKING

BIBLIOGRAPHY

Couch, Mal, ed. *Dictionary of Premillennial Theology*. Grand Rapids: Kregel, 1996.

Hindson, Ed. *The Book of Revelation*. Chattanooga: AMG Publishers, 2002.

Hoehner, Harold. "Evidence from Revelation." In *A Case for Premillennialism*. Eds. D. Campbell and J. Townsend. Chicago: Moody Press, 1992.

McClain, Alva J. *The Greatness of the Kingdom*. Chicago: Moody Press, 1959.

Ryrie, Charles. *Basic Theology*. Wheaton, IL: Victor Books, 1986.

Walvoord, John F. *The Millennial Kingdom*. Grand Rapids: Zondervan, 1965.

PRETERISM

THE *preterist* (LATIN FOR "PAST") believes that most if not all prophecy was fulfilled by the time of the destruction of Jerusalem in A.D. 70. The *historicist* equates much of the current church age with the Tribulation period. Thus, prophecy has been and will be fulfilled during the current church age. *Futurists* usually believe that almost no prophetic events are occurring in the current church age but will take place in the following future events: the Tribulation period, the second coming, the millennium, and the eternal state. The *idealist* believes that the Bible does not indicate the timing of prophetic events and that we cannot determine their timing in advance. Therefore, idealists see prophetic passages as teaching great truths about God to be applied to our present lives.

WHAT IS PRETERISM?

Preterists believe that major prophetic portions of Scripture, such as the Olivet Discourse and the book of Revelation, were fulfilled in the A.D. 70 destruction of Jerusalem by the Romans. Preterists take such a view because Matthew 24:34 and its parallel passages say, "This generation will not pass away until all these things take place" (NASB). They interpret this to say the prophecies had to be fulfilled in the first century. Revelation, according to preterists, says something similar in the passages that state Christ is coming "quickly" or that His return is "at hand." If these prophecies had to take place in the first century, then the rest of the prophetic language must apply to a local fulfillment in Jerusalem instead of a worldwide fulfillment. Most preterists believe that we are currently living in a new heavens and new earth because they interpret the entire book of Revelation to have a first-century fulfillment.

THREE KINDS OF PRETERISM

There are at least three kinds of preterism. Mild preterism teaches that the book of Revelation was fulfilled during the first three centuries as God waged war on the two early enemies of the church: Israel and Rome. The first half of Revelation (up to chapter 11) teaches that Israel was defeated in A.D. 70, while the last half of Revelation (chapters 12–19) is about God's conquest of Rome in the fourth century, when Constantine declared the Roman Empire Christian. Thus, this earliest form of preterism teaches that Revelation was fulfilled in the first 300 years of the church's history.

Moderate preterists believe that Revelation 4–19 refers to the destruction of Jerusalem in A.D. 70. However, they believe that a few passages still teach a yet future second coming (Acts 1:9-11; 1 Corinthians 15:51-53; 1 Thessalonians 4:16-17) and resurrection of believers at Christ's bodily return.

Extreme, full, or consistent preterists, as they prefer to be known, hold that all Bible prophecy was fulfilled in the destruction of Jerusalem in A.D. 70. The second coming occurred in A.D. 70. If there is a future second coming, they say, the Bible does not talk about it. Extreme preterists deny a future, bodily return of Christ and a future bodily resurrection. This places them outside the realm of Christian orthodoxy.

THREE PRETERIST PROOF TEXTS

Preterists believe three major passages in Matthew demand a first-century fulfillment: 10:23; 16:27-28; and 24:34.

Matthew 10:23

Matthew 10:23 says, "Whenever they persecute you in one city, flee to the next; for truly I say to you, you shall not finish going through the cities of Israel until the Son of Man comes."

"Again, if we are correct in concluding that the coming referred to in this text is the parousia of Christ, then the primary timeframe for the parousia must be restricted to a forty-year period. It surely did not take the disciples much more than forty years to cover the boundaries of Palestine with the gospel message" (Sproul, *Last Days According to Jesus,* p. 56). Thus, preterists view this passage as promising the return of Christ in the lifetime of the disciples.

Is this what Jesus had in mind? Even J. Stuart Russell (p. 28) believes that there is "abundant warrant for assigning the important prediction contained in Matthew 10:23 to the discourse delivered on the Mount of Olives." Thus, to a large extent, a discussion of the time when Matthew 10:23 is to be fulfilled must be determined in light of Matthew 24.

Second, the vocabulary in Matthew 10:16-23 parallels the synoptic Gospels' versions of the Olivet Discourse (Matthew 24–25; Mark 13; Luke 17; 21). In fact, the *New Geneva Study Bible* (p. 1521), of which Sproul is the general editor, says of this passage, "The 'coming' is the Second Coming of Christ to judge the earth. This view fits most of the other occurrences of the phrase (24:30; 25:31; 26:64; but see 16:28)." This information supports the conclusion from the previous point that the timing of the fulfillment of this passage is tied to the Olivet Discourse.

Third, all agree that Scripture never indicates that the disciples experienced the kind of persecution mentioned in this passage before the crucifixion of Christ. J. Stuart Russell (p. 27) admits, "There is no evidence that the disciples met with such treatment on their evangelistic tour." This indicates that our Lord has a future time in mind when He speaks the words of this passage.

How should this passage be explained? Stanley Toussaint (pp. 141–42) states,

> The Messiah was simply looking past His death to the time of tribulation following. At the time the disciples would have the same message and possibly the same power. The narrow road leading to the kingdom leads through the tribulation (Matthew 10:16), and this persecution is to be of a religious and political nature....
>
> The Lord made no error and clearly had "the coming" for judgment in mind. However, the coming is contingent upon Israel's acceptance of its King. Because even after His resurrection, that nation refused Him, it became impossible to establish the kingdom (cf. Acts 3:18-26). In fact, the tribulation period did not come; if it had, the promise of the soon coming of the Son of Man would have been of great comfort to the apostles.

Matthew 10:23 does not support the preterist contention that the coming of the Son of Man occurred in A.D. 70 through the Roman Army. Instead, Christ was looking ahead to another time, the Tribulation leading up to the glorious second advent.

Matthew 16:27-28

"The Son of Man is going to come in the glory of His Father with His angels, and will then repay every man according to his deeds. Truly I say to you, there are some of those who are standing here who will not taste death until they see the Son of Man coming in His kingdom."

Preterists believe that Matthew 16:28 and parallel passages (Mark 9:1; Luke 9:27) predict the destruction of Jerusalem accomplished through the Roman army in A.D. 70. Many non-preterists believe Matthew 16:28 was fulfilled on the Mount of Transfiguration.

Matthew 16:27 is speaking of the future second coming, while verse 28 refers to the impending transfiguration. Why are these verses positioned in this way? Consider the line of thinking in this passage, beginning at verse 21. Christ reveals clearly His impending death to His disciples. Peter reacts to this suffering phase of Jesus' career, and Jesus responds to Peter with His famous "Get behind Me, Satan!" statement. Then Jesus provides a lesson to His disciples on denial of self. Christ is teaching that for Him and His followers to enter His kingdom, they must embrace the cross before the crown. Suffering precedes glory! But the glory will one day come at Christ's second advent, when each individual will be required to give an account of his actions during the time of suffering.

In order to encourage His followers, who would have to suffer the bitter pill of His impending death and their own suffering and eventual deaths for His sake, Christ provides a word of the promised future glory in 16:28 about some who will "see the Son of Man coming in His kingdom." "After Jesus predicted His own death, Peter and the other disciples needed reassurance that Jesus would ultimately triumph. His prediction that some of them would see the kingdom of God present with power must have alleviated their fears" (*Nelson Study Bible,* p. 1659.) Thus,

"verse twenty-seven looks at the establishment of the kingdom in the future, while a promise of seeing the Messiah in His glory is the thought of verse twenty-eight. They are two separate predictions separated by the words 'truly I say to you'" (Toussaint, p. 209).

All three instances of this parallel passage are immediately followed by the account of the transfiguration. This contextual relationship by itself is a strong reason to favor the pretribulational interpretation. In other words, Jesus made a prediction about a future event, and Matthew, Mark, and Luke each record the fulfillment of that prediction in the passage that follows. These passages are also connected grammatically. The conjunction with which Matthew 17 begins clearly establishes the unbroken continuity of thought between 16:28 and 17:1. The same is true in Mark and Luke, where no chapter division occurs.

Matthew's prediction of the actual, physical appearance of the Son of Man is clearly fulfilled in the transfiguration because Jesus was personally and visibly present. Matthew says, "He was transfigured before them; and His face shone like the sun, and His garments became as white as light" (17:2). The preterist interpretation does not meet Matthew's criteria because Jesus was not personally present in the later destruction of Jerusalem.

Mark's emphasis upon a display of the kingdom with power was certainly fulfilled by the transfiguration. No one could doubt that the transfiguration certainly fit the definition of a "power encounter" for the disciples. That Jesus appears dressed in the shekinah glory of God upon the mount (Mark 9:3) is further evidence to the disciples that He was God and acted with His power.

Luke's simple statement about some who will "see the kingdom of God" is vindicated also by his account (9:28-36). Twice Luke records our Lord describing the transfiguration with the term "glory" (9:31-32). Darrell Bock (pp. 859–60) asks, "Why exclude the reference to Jerusalem's destruction? Because Luke does not associate the kingdom's power with this event....Also, Jesus is not associated with Jerusalem's destruction directly, so it is not in view."

The transfiguration made such an impression upon John and Peter that both provided a description of the glorified Christ in later writings (Revelation 1:12-20; 2 Peter 1:16-21). Both describe the risen and glorified Christ in relation to His second advent (Revelation 1:7; 2 Peter 1:16). No one doubts that Peter has in mind the transfiguration in 2 Peter 1:16-18. Peter is encouraging believers to remain faithful when, as does Jesus, he looks to "the power and coming of our Lord Jesus Christ." Peter follows Jesus' pattern of supporting the future second advent by citing the past transfiguration. In this way, Peter's second epistle supports the futurist understanding of Matthew 16:28.

Matthew 24:34

Matthew 24:34 is the verse preterists most commonly use to support their position. The much-debated passage says, "Truly I say to you, this generation will not pass away until all these things take place" (see also Mark 13:30; Luke 21:32).

R.C. Sproul (Last Days According to Jesus, p. 158) says, "I am convinced that the substance of the Olivet Discourse was fulfilled in A.D. 70." Those who apply a consistently literal interpretation to the entire Olivet Discourse do not agree with Sproul's interpretation of "this generation." Christ is saying that the generation that sees "all these things" occur will not cease to exist until all the events of the future tribulation are literally fulfilled. Christ is not speaking to His contemporaries but to the generation that sees the signs of Matthew 24. Darrell Bock (pp. 1691-92), in commenting on the parallel passage to Matthew 24 in Luke's Gospel, concurs: "What Jesus is saying is that the generation that sees the beginning of the end, also sees its end. When the signs come, they will proceed quickly; they will not drag on for many generations. It will happen within a generation."

The context of a word determines the nuance of its meaning. It is true that every other use of "this generation" in Matthew (11:16; 12:41-42,45; 23:36) refers to Christ's contemporaries, but that is clear because of the context, not because of the phrase itself. The context of Matthew 24 does not point to A.D. 70, so the text must point to the future.

In fact, the Jews were not rescued in A.D. 70. Rather, the Jewish Christian community fled Jerusalem before the final siege. But Matthew 24 speaks of a divine rescue of those who are under siege (24:29-31). This could not have been fulfilled in the first century because no such rescue took place then.

THE PRETERIST VIEW OF REVELATION

Ken Gentry writes: "'Preterism' holds that the bulk of John's prophecies occurred in the first century, soon after his writing of them. Though the prophecies were in the future when John wrote and when his original audience read them, they are now in our past." In his commentary on Revelation (p. 43), the late David Chilton, also a preterist, said, "The Book of Revelation is not about the Second Coming of Christ. It is about the destruction of Israel and Christ's victory over His enemies in the establishment of the New Covenant Temple. In fact…the word coming as used in the Book of Revelation never refers to the Second Coming." The preterist view does not view Bible prophecy as "things to come" but rather as "things that came."

Preterists propose a first-century fulfillment of Revelation because they interpret it to say it will be fulfilled soon (just as they interpret the Olivet Discourse to say it will be fulfilled soon).

Preterist Gary DeMar (pp. 344–45) has collected what he calls the "time texts" in Revelation, which lead him to believe that the fulfillment of the Apocalypse had to occur during the first century.

1) The events "must soon [táchos] take place" (1:1).

2) "For the time is near" (eggús) (1:3).

3) "I am coming to you quickly [tachús]" (2:16).

4) "I am coming quickly [tachús]" (3:11).

5) "The third woe is coming quickly [*tachús*]" (11:14).

6) "The things which must soon [*táchos*] take place" (22:6).

7) "Behold, I am coming quickly [*tachús*]" (22:7).

8) "For the time is near" (*eggús*) (22:10).

9) "Behold, I am coming quickly [*tachús*]" (22:12).

10) "Yes, I am coming quickly [*tachús*]" (22:20).

In reality, these terms are more properly interpreted as *qualitative* indicators (not *chronological* indicators) describing *how* Christ will return, not *when* He will return. How will He return? He will come "quickly" or "suddenly."

Táchos and its family of related words can be used to mean "soon" or "shortly" as preterists believe (relating to time), or they can be used to mean "quickly" or "suddenly" as futurists contend. The *táchos* family is attested in the Bible as referring to both possibilities. The "timing interpretation" of the preterists teaches that the *táchos* word family used in Revelation means that Christ came in judgment upon Israel through the Roman army in events surrounding the A.D. 70 destruction of Jerusalem. How would the futurist understand the use of the *táchos* family in Revelation? Futurist John Walvoord (p. 35) explains:

> That which Daniel declared would occur "in the latter days" is here described as "shortly" (Gr., *en tachei*), that is, "quickly or suddenly coming to pass," indicating rapidity of execution after the beginning takes place. The idea is not that the event may occur soon, but that when it does, it will be sudden.

It is significant to note that the Septuagint (the Greek translation of the Old Testament) uses *táchos* in passages that even by the most conservative estimations could not have occurred for hundreds, even thousands of years. For example, Isaiah 13:22 says, "Her [Israel's] fateful time also will soon come." This was written around 700 B.C., foretelling the destruction of Babylon, which occurred in 539 B.C. Similarly, Isaiah 5:26 speaks of the manner, not the time frame, by which the Assyrian invasion of Israel "will come with speed swiftly." Isaiah 51:5 says, "My righteousness is near, My salvation has gone forth, and My arms will judge the peoples; the coastlands will wait for Me, and for My arm they will wait expectantly." This passage probably will be fulfilled in the millennium, but no interpreter would place it sooner than Christ's first coming—at least 700 years after it was given. Isaiah 58:8 says Israel's recovery will "speedily spring forth." If it is a "timing passage," then the earliest it could have happened is 700 years later, but most likely it has yet to occur.

One important issue relating to the preterist interpretation is the date of the writing of the book of Revelation. Preterists admit that if Revelation were written 25 years after the fall of Jerusalem, their entire labor would go up in smoke. Thus, if Revelation was given after the destruction of the Temple in A.D. 70, it could not have been a prophecy about that event as preterists contend. In reality, it was written around A.D. 95, thus rendering the preterist interpretation impossible. (See "Revelation, Date of.")

PRETERIST IMPLICATIONS FOR THE NEW TESTAMENT

Preterists such as Kenneth Gentry (pp. 86–89) believe that current history is identified as the new heavens and new earth of Revelation 21–22 and 2 Peter 3:10-13. It stretches credulity to think of the implications of such a conclusion. If we are currently living in the new heavens and new earth, then there is no Satan (Revelation 20:10), no death, crying, or pain (Revelation 21:4), no unclean persons, nor those practicing abomination and lying (Revelation 21:27), and no curse (Revelation 22:3).

The clear implication for preterists would be that Titus 2:12 no longer relates directly to the current age in which we live. Instead, it applied for three or four years, since Paul wrote Titus around A.D. 65. Preterists cannot logically use this or similar passages as doctrine, reproof, correction, and training in righteousness for believers, who are living in the new heavens and new earth. However, preterists regularly use and apply these passages in this way.

For preterists, the instruction of the New Testament on the issue of suffering only directly applied to believers until A.D. 70 because we would now be in the time of peace, not "the sufferings of this present time" Paul speaks of (Romans 8:18).

If preterists are correct, then most of the prophesied events in history are over. The current church age will then become increasingly successful, concluding with conversion of the world to Christ. By contrast, pretribulationalists believe the world will get worse as time goes on. For the preterist, the great apostasy happened in the first century. But Paul warns in 2 Timothy 3:1 that "in the last days difficult times will come." If "the last days" have already come and gone, we should expect that the persecution of the godly should be absent and "evil men and impostors" should not "proceed from bad to worse."

THE RESPONSE TO PRETERISM

Because of the current spread of preterism, pastors and teachers need to be prepared to defend orthodox eschatology from this attack. Those who believe that Christ came in A.D. 70 will certainly not be found looking for our Lord's any-moment return when He does rapture the church without any signs or warning. They can hardly obey our Lord's command to keep watching until He comes (Matthew 24:42).

—THOMAS ICE

BIBLIOGRAPHY

Bock, Darrell. *Luke 1:1–9:50*. Grand Rapids: Baker Books, 1994.

Chilton, David. *The Days of Vengeance*. Ft. Worth: Dominion Press, 1987.

DeMar, Gary. *Last Days Madness*. Atlanta: American Vision, 1997.

Gentry, Kenneth L. "A Preterist View of Revelation." Marvin Pate, ed. *Four Views on the Book of Revelation*. Grand Rapids: Zondervan, 1998.

Hitchcock, Mark. "The Stake in the Heart—the A.D. 95 Date of Revelation." In *The End Times Controversy*. Eds. Tim LaHaye and Thomas Ice. Eugene, OR: Harvest House Publishers, 2003.

Lang, G.H. *The Revelation of Jesus Christ*. Miami Springs, FL: Conley & Schoettle, 1985.

Nelson Study Bible. Nashville: Thomas Nelson Publishers, 1997.

Russell, J. Stuart. *Parousia*. Grand Rapids: Baker Books, 1999.

Sproul, R.C. *Last Days According to Jesus*. Nashville, Thomas Nelson, 1999.

———. ed. *New Geneva Study Bible*. Nashville: Thomas Nelson, 1995.

Toussaint, Stanley D. *Behold the King: A Study of Matthew*. Portland, OR: Multnomah Publishers, 1980.

Walvoord, John F. *The Revelation of Jesus Christ*. Chicago: Moody Press, 1966.

PRETRIBULATIONISM

THE PRETRIBULATIONAL VIEW of the rapture teaches that Christ will rapture His church to His Father's house prior to the seven-year Tribulation (John 14:1-3; 1 Thessalonians 4–5). The timing of the rapture is not a cardinal doctrine that should divide God's people, but those who interpret the Bible literally find many strong reasons to believe that the rapture will be pretribulational.

1. The pretribulational view offers the most logical interpretation of second-coming scriptures when they are taken for their plain, literal meaning. Indeed, Walvoord says, "The only view that interprets prophecy literally and consistently is that of the pretribulational, premillennial position" (Walvoord, *Prophecy*, p. 122). The pretribulational position has a logical explanation of every second-coming passage. Other views do not unless they jettison literal interpretation at one or more points.

2. Both Jesus and the apostle Paul promised believers they would be saved from the "wrath to come" (Matthew 3:7; Luke 3:7; 1 Thessalonians 1:10 NKJV) and kept from "the hour of trial which shall come upon the whole world,

to test those who dwell on the earth" (Revelation 3:10). Such a "trial" has not yet occurred. Paul gave the same promise in Romans 5:9 and 1 Thessalonians 5:9. All the other viewpoints contradict these scriptures by stating that at least a portion of the church will experience all or some of the Tribulation period.

3. The pretribulational position clearly and logically untangles the details of Christ's second coming. The Scriptures say that Jesus will come in the air to rapture (snatch away) His church, yet He will also come to the earth publicly to judge the earth. The coming of Christ in blessing for His church and His return to the earth in judgment are two distinct events separated by time. As Walvoord puts it, "The Rapture is a movement of the church from earth to heaven and is in sharp contrast to the church's return with Christ at the Second Coming, which occurs more than seven years later as a movement from heaven to earth" (Walvoord, *Prophecy*, p. 38). The book of Revelation and 2 Thessalonians 2 clarify what takes place between those two events.

4. The pretribulational rapture position is the only view that makes a clear distinction between Israel and the church. The lack of a proper understanding of the relationship between Israel and the church in prophecy is one of the major causes of confusion in the teachings of amillennialism and posttribulationism.

The church was born in Acts 2 on the Day of Pentecost. We know this because the church is the body of Christ (1 Corinthians 12:12; Ephesians 5:23; Colossians 1:18), believers become part of the body of Christ through baptism with the Spirit (1 Corinthians 12:13), and Spirit baptism commenced when the Holy Spirit came upon believers in Jerusalem on the Day of Pentecost (Acts 1:4-5; 2:1-4; 11:15-16).

The church was a "mystery" (it was not revealed) in the Old Testament (Ephesians 3:3-5,9; Colossians 1:26-27). Furthermore, the church could not have come into existence until Christ died (to provide atonement—Matthew 16:18-21), rose again (Ephesians 1:20-23), and ascended to heaven (Ephesians 4:7-11).

In fact, the Holy Spirit was not provided for believers until after Christ's ascension (John 16:7-13).

The apostle Paul calls the church "one new man" composed of Jews and Gentiles (Ephesians 2:15)—a completely new entity. It is distinguished from both Israel and the Gentiles, composed of members from both groups, and identified as the "church" and "one body" (Ephesians 2:16; 3:6). First Corinthians 10:32 distinguishes the church from both Israel and the Gentiles.

Also, the name Israel is never used of the church. In the New Testament, it refers either to Jews in general or Jewish believers in particular. The reference to the "Israel of God" in Galatians 6:16, so often taken by amillennialists as a synonym for the church, in fact refers only to Jewish believers in Christ.

In summary, there is no evidence that the church began before Acts 2, and much evidence that it began at that time as a new entity in the program of God. Therefore it must be kept distinct from Israel, and a pretribulational understanding of the rapture is the only means of doing this.

5. Pretribulationism is the only view that makes "the blessed hope" (Titus 2:13) truly a blessed hope. Few doctrines have brought more hope to grieving and persecuted souls during the past 2000 years than the doctrine of this blessed hope, which is the teaching that Christ will return for His church, resurrect the dead, and transport living believers to be with Himself while the world endures the Tribulation.

The midtribulational position destroys that hope by forcing Christians to anticipate the trauma of at least part of the Tribulation. Posttribulationism further destroys the hope by propelling Christians through the entire Tribulation period. No proper reading of Bible prophecy gives credence to the idea that the church will be on earth during that seven-year period. The judgment pictured in Revelation is clearly intended for Israel and the unbelieving world.

6. Pretribulationism allows sufficient time for important end-time events to occur. Christ

will take Christians to His Father's house and reward them at the judgment seat of Christ (Romans 14:12). The marriage of the bride of Christ in heaven occurs before He comes "with power and great glory" to the earth (Matthew 24:30; Luke 21:27). Other viewpoints are all too brief to allow time for the important events listed in Revelation.

7. Only the pretribulational view preserves the motivating power of the imminent return of Christ. In John 14:1-3; Acts 1:11; 1 Corinthians 15:51-52; Philippians 3:20; Colossians 3:4; and many other passages, the apostles taught that Christ could come at any moment. When the church loses this anticipation, it tends to become carnal and spiritually dead. (See the article titled "Imminence.")

8. Pretribulational Christians are looking for the coming of the Lord. In other views, Christians are awaiting the Tribulation, the Antichrist, and great suffering. In fact, only the rapture could occur as soon as today. The glorious appearing of Christ cannot occur for at least seven or more years (see Walvoord, *Prophecy in the New Millennium*, pp. 38–39).

9. Pretribulationism emphasizes the magnitude of the rapture. At least four passages of Scripture describe the rapture, so it must be a significant event. The posttribulational view trivializes the rapture, treating it as a quick trip up and right back down. The pretribulational view treats it as a dignified, blessed event commensurate with a heavenly bridegroom who comes to take His bride to His Father's house for their wedding.

10. Pretribulationism most clearly fits the flow of the book of Revelation (see Revelation 4:1-2). Further, this view explains why the church is so central in the first three chapters of Revelation but then disappears and is not mentioned again until 18:24. Pretribulationists insist that the church has already been raptured before the events of Revelation 4–18. Other views try to find the church in the Tribulation even though she is not mentioned in these chapters.

11. Pretribulationism preserves the credibility of Christ's word that Christians will be kept from the Tribulation. It is the only view that resolves the contrasting difficulties of Revelation 3:10 and 7:14.

12. The purpose of the Tribulation is not to prepare the church for glory but rather to prepare Israel for restoration in God's program (see Deuteronomy 4:29-30; Jeremiah 30:4-11).

13. The rapture of the church is not mentioned in any passage describing the coming of Christ following the Tribulation.

14. None of the Bible passages describing the Tribulation mention the church (see Jeremiah 30:4-11; Daniel 9:24-27; 12:1-2; Matthew 24:15-31; Revelation 4–19).

15. The church has not been appointed to wrath (Romans 5:9; 1 Thessalonians 1:9-10; 5:9; see Revelation 6:17).

16. When the church is raptured, believers will go to the Father's house in heaven (John 14:3). They will not immediately return to the earth, as posttribulationism teaches.

17. The exhortation in Titus 2:13 to look for Christ's return as a blessed hope is misleading if the Tribulation must come first. Believers would need to look for signs instead. On the contrary, the church is always exhorted to look for the Lord's coming. In the Tribulation, however, believers are told to look for signs (Matthew 24).

18. According to Old Testament texts, living Tribulation saints are not translated and glorified at Christ's second coming. They continue earthly human lives and occupations, including having children and raising crops (Isaiah 65:20-25). If all saints are translated and glorified (as described by the rapture) at Christ's second coming to the earth, this would be impossible. In addition, the separation of the "sheep" and "goats" described by Jesus in Matthew 25:32 would be unnecessary because it would already have occurred at the rapture before He even set up His throne of judgment (25:31).

19. God has often delivered believers (including, for example, Noah, Lot, and Rahab) before punishing the world for sin (see 2 Peter 2:6-9).

20. Jesus mentions the possibility of believers escaping the Tribulation in Luke 21:36.

21. Almost all scholars acknowledge that the early church believed in the imminence of Christ's return, which logically leads to pre-tribulationism.

(See article titled "Rapture.")

—TIM LAHAYE,
RICHARD L. MAYHUE,
AND WAYNE A. BRINDLE

BIBLIOGRAPHY

Archer, Gleason L., et al. *Three Views on the Rapture: Pre-, Mid-, or Post-tribulational?* Grand Rapids: Zondervan, 1996.

Hoyt, Herman A. *The End Times.* Chicago: Moody Press, 1969.

Pentecost, J. Dwight. *Things to Come.* Grand Rapids: Zondervan, 1964.

Walvoord, John F. *Prophecy in the New Millennium.* Grand Rapids: Kregel, 2001.

———. *The Rapture Question.* Grand Rapids: Zondervan, 1964.

PRE-WRATH RAPTURE

THE PRE-WRATH RAPTURE theory teaches that the day of the Lord, the time of divine wrath upon the earth, will begin sometime during the second half of Daniel's seventieth week and that the rapture of the church will immediately precede it (Rosenthal, p. 35). According to this view, the day of the Lord will be introduced by the cosmic disturbances associated with the sixth seal judgment and will begin with the opening of the seventh seal. The church will suffer persecution by Antichrist during the first 63 months of Daniel's seventieth week, yet proponents of this view assert that the presence of this persecution does not negate the blessed hope (Titus 2:13). In fact, the seals are the assurance of eternal security for believers who suffer martyrdom during this 63-month period. The Antichrist can harm their bodies but not their souls in much the same way as Satan treated Job (Rosenthal, pp. 144–45). This 63-month period is a time of man's wrath, which is to be distinguished from the final 21 months of the Tribulation, in which the world will experience God's wrath, or the day of the Lord.

According to this view's original proponents, the term *pre-wrath rapture* distinguishes this view from other rapture positions by affirming that the church will be rescued from the hands of the Antichrist before the wrath of God is poured out on the earth. It diverges from other rapture views in the timing of the rapture event and the definitions of events leading up to the second coming of Christ.

The pre-wrath perspective had its beginning in a series of discussions between Marvin Rosenthal and Robert Van Kampen beginning in 1986. In 1990, Rosenthal introduced his book, *The Pre-Wrath Rapture of the Church,* as a new understanding of the rapture, the Tribulation, and the second coming of Christ. In 1992, Van Kampen published *The Sign,* in which he attempted to harmonize end-time passages in both Testaments (Van Kampen, p. 13), and in 1997 he released *The Rapture Question Answered* as further argument for the pre-wrath position.

Pre-wrath rapturism teaches that the church will enter the seven-year period that precedes Christ's physical return to earth (the seventieth week of Daniel) and will encounter the tribulation of that period and the Antichrist himself. This seventieth week of Daniel (Daniel 9:24-27) contains three major features: the beginning of sorrows, the Great Tribulation, and the day of the Lord.

THE BEGINNING OF SORROWS

The first half of Daniel's seventieth week (3½ years) is initiated when Antichrist signs a covenant to protect Israel (Daniel 9:27). During this 3½-year period, the opening of the first four seals (Revelation 6:1-8) and the apostasy (2 Thessalonians 2:3-4) take place.

During this time period there will be wars and rumors of wars, nations will rise against nations, false messiahs will appear, and famines, earthquakes, and pestilence will occur in various places (Matthew 24:4-8).

THE GREAT TRIBULATION

At the midpoint of Daniel's seventieth week, the Antichrist will use Jerusalem as his command post in his ruse to protect Israel (Daniel 11:42-45). He will erect a statue to himself in the Temple (2 Thessalonians 2:3-4), and the Jews will realize his true character and identity. This event is known as the abomination of desolation (Daniel 9:27; 11:31; Matthew 24:15) and will initiate a period of such severe persecution that Christ Himself said, "Unless those days were shortened, no flesh would be saved, but for the elect's sake those days will be shortened" (Matthew 24:22 NKJV). This is a time of man's wrath against man when Satan energizes the Antichrist to attempt to extinguish the elect of God (Revelation 12:12-17). The opening of the fifth seal initiates the Great Tribulation, and the sixth seal brings it to a close (Revelation 6:9-17).

THE DAY OF THE LORD

This is the final expression of God's wrath, resulting in divine judgment. During the sixth seal, men flee to escape this wrath. The day of the Lord begins with the seventh seal. Angels blowing trumpets heralding God's wrath or pouring out bowls of wrath upon the earth initiate the resulting trumpet judgments. Pre-wrath rapturists see in this angelic activity a distinction between man's wrath against man in the opening of the seals and God's wrath against unrighteousness in the trumpet and bowl judgments. As the seventh seal is opened, the trumpet and bowl judgments are progressively carried forth and comprise a comprehensive outpouring of God's wrath.

According to the pre-wrath rapture advocates, the rapture occurs at the opening of the seventh seal in conjunction with the sound of the last trumpet (1 Corinthians 15:51-52). Thus, the seventh seal initiates both the rapture of the church and the day of the Lord. This coming of Christ is a singular event and occurs 21 months after the abomination of desolation (which occurs at the midpoint of Daniel's seventieth week). During the next 21 months the trumpet and bowl judgments are carried out and Christ is continuously on earth.

Both Rosenthal and Van Kampen argue that the restrainer Paul mentions in 2 Thessalonians 2:7 is Michael the archangel. The argument hinges on the Hebrew verb *amad* in Daniel 12:1. Rosenthal cites a French Jewish rabbi named Rashi who lived between 1040 and 1105 as his authority on the usage of the Hebrew word, which literally means "stand still." He contends that Michael in Daniel 12:1 will stand aside or be inactive in his special guardian relationship with Israel. Michael's inactivity constitutes the removal of the restraint currently limiting Satan's lawlessness (Rosenthal, pp. 256–57).

PRE-WRATH AND IMMINENCE

The doctrine of imminence holds that Christ can come to rapture His church at any moment. Believers in the early church, including the apostle Paul, believed that Christ could come in their lifetime (1 Thessalonians 1:10; 4:13-15; Titus 2:13). The church sees this doctrine as an incentive for ministry and godly living. Does this mean that Christ's return for His church will be at any moment, without any sign, and with no yet-to-be-fulfilled prophesied event to precede it? Pre-wrath rapturists argue that Christ could come in any generation but that signs will herald the general time. Those signs include (1) the emergence of Antichrist, (2) wars and rumors of war, (3) famine, (4) pestilence, and (5) cosmic disturbance. Pre-wrath rapturists emphasize Christians' expectancy of Christ's return rather than its imminence. This expectancy of Christ's return is the catalyst for holy living.

PRE-WRATH AND PRETRIBULATION

Because the pre-wrath theory is often described by some as pretribulational, it is important to note that the theory actually diverges from the pretribulational rapture view. Four areas are worthy of note:

The Wrath of Man and the Wrath of God

Pre-wrath's division of the seventieth week of Daniel into three sections is an arbitrary effort. It distorts the truth that the entire seventieth week of Daniel is a time of God's wrath. Pretribulationists consider the entire seven years as a time of God's wrath. Revelation 6:16-17 is a summary statement that the first six seals contain the wrath of the Lamb, under which the people ask, "Who is able to stand?" It does not say that the outpouring of God's wrath is yet to come, as pre-wrath adherents contend, but that the wrath is already being poured out. As a fulfillment of the promise of Revelation 3:10, the church has been removed from the "hour of trial," not subject to it as a time of lesser tribulation.

The Second Coming and the Rapture

Pre-wrath rapturists find the rapture in Matthew 24:40-41 and Luke 17:20-37. These passages are similar to recognized rapture passages (John 14:1-3; 1 Corinthians 15:51-53; 1 Thessalonians 4:13-18), but they do not describe the same event. At the rapture, believers meet Christ in the air; at the second coming, Christ's feet touch the Mount of Olives (Zechariah 14:4). At the rapture, the saints in heaven do not come to earth; at the second coming, Christ leads armies of heaven to earth (Revelation 19:11-16). At the rapture, believers are removed from the earth, leaving only unbelievers to enter the Tribulation; at the second coming, unbelievers are removed from the earth, leaving only believers to enter the millennial kingdom.

The Restrainer

The pre-wrath view holds to the rather inventive idea that Michael the archangel is the restrainer. This concept fails to take into consideration Michael's special protective ministry toward Israel. Pretribulationists usually see the Holy Spirit as the restrainer and understand that He remains on earth but allows Satan to cause the evil that prevails during the Tribulation period.

Imminence

Pretribulationalists hold that the rapture of the church is the blessed hope (Titus 2:13) to which believers look. It is an "any moment" event that need not be preceded by any other prophetic event. As a result, it is a catalyst for holy living and further expectation. Pre-wrath rapturists see at least five signs that must occur first, and they disparage the idea of an "at any moment" rapture, referring to expectancy rather than imminence.

Clearly the pre-wrath rapture position and pretribulational rapture position are different and distinct, and Scripture favors pretribulationism.

—Tony Kessinger

BIBLIOGRAPHY

LaHaye, Tim. *The Rapture*. Eugene, OR: Harvest House Publishers, 2002.

McLean, John A. "Another Look at Rosenthal's Pre-Wrath Rapture." *Bibliotheca Sacra* 148, October 1991, pp. 388-98.

Rosenthal, Marvin. *The Pre-Wrath Rapture of the Church*. Nashville: Thomas Nelson, 1990.

Stanton, Gerald B. "A Review of the Pre-Wrath Rapture of the Church." *Bibliotheca Sacra* 148, January 1991, pp. 91-112.

Van Kampen, Robert. *The Rapture Question Answered*. Grand Rapids: Fleming Revell, 1997.

PROGRESSIVE DISPENSATIONALISM

Dispensationalism is the theological system that recognizes God's dealings with humankind in different dispensations of time throughout history (see articles titled "Dispensations" and "Dispensationalism"). In general, dispensationalism rests upon a literal hermeneutic and a distinction between Israel and the church throughout the entire Bible. Dispensationalism is also the general theological framework for pretribulationalism.

In recent years, a new development has emerged from within dispensationalism that has come to be called "progressive dispensationalism." Adherents to this system consider themselves to be in the lineage of dispensational theology, but they have made numerous shifts toward a mediating position between dispensationalism and non-dispensationalism. Many elements of their interpretive approach are similar to those of non-dispensational historic premillennialists. Instead of following a traditional grammatical–historical system of interpretation, they advocate a historical–grammatical–literary–theological hermeneutic in explaining Scripture. So rather than allowing a text's original context and the author's original intent to determine the single meaning of a passage, progressive dispensationalism allows for the addition of other meanings that alter the author's original intent.

BASIC BELIEFS OF PROGRESSIVE DISPENSATIONALISM

Charles Ryrie (pp. 96–97) notes the following beliefs and emphases of progressive dispensationalism:

1. The kingdom of God is the unifying theme of biblical history (though the nature of this kingdom is not clearly defined).

2. Dispensational eras are limited to four: patriarchal, Mosaic, church, and Zionic. The prefall, postfall, and Abrahamic eras are blended into one. The Mosaic era ends at the ascension of Christ rather than His death, making the church (ecclesial) dispensation the inaugurated Davidic kingdom.

3. Christ has already inaugurated the Davidic reign in heaven. The throne of God is the throne of David. (This ignores the fact that Christ is seated on God's heavenly throne, not David's earthly throne. Ryrie further points out that Christ's present activity is that of our heavenly high priest. He will not function as a Davidic king on earth until He comes to rule in the millennial kingdom.)

4. The New Covenant is already inaugurated for Israel. Though its blessings will not be fully realized until the millennium, its effects are already guaranteed for Israel.

5. The distinction between Israel and the church must be abandoned. Progressives reject the concept of two purposes and two peoples of God. (However, the church is clearly distinct from Israel in the New Testament. The church has been baptized by the Holy Spirit [Acts 11:15-16]. It began at Pentecost and will continue until the rapture [1 Thessalonians 4:17]. It is indwelt by Christ [Colossians 1:27] and has been commissioned to evangelize the world. Israel, by contrast, is still pictured as a separate nation after Pentecost [see Acts 3:12; 4:8; 5:21,31,35; 21:28].)

6. Complementary meanings can be assigned to the Old Testament promises. In other words, progressive dispensationalists will spiritualize concepts found in the New Testament so as to make them complementary to promises. For example, literal hermeneutics dictate that the Temple in Revelation 11:1 is a literal building, but the complementary hermeneutic of progressive dispensationalists allows them to say it is a reference to a body of believers because the term is used in that manner elsewhere in the New Testament. This is one of the greatest problems with the progressive dispensational approach; it leaves the hermeneutical door open to a wide variety of interpretations.

7. God's plan of holistic redemption encompasses all people and all areas of human life. (While this is true in the ultimate sense of God's universal rule over all of life, it does not mean that universal priorities [social, political, ecological] should take precedence over the church and its mission to evangelize the world.)

PROBLEMS WITH PROGRESSIVE DISPENSATIONALISM

Progressive dispensationalists argue that they are merely attempting to revise dispensationalism. However, closer examination of their views reveals radical change rather than slightly nuanced developments. So much so that non-dispensationalists have publicly stated the obvious. Walter Elwell said in *Christianity Today* (September 12, 1994), "The newer dispensationalism looks so much like non-dispensational pre-millennialism that one struggles to see any real difference."

A truly dispensational position will exhibit two specific distinctions:

Israel and the Church

Ryrie (p. 39) sees this as a necessary element of true dispensationalism. He writes: "This is probably the most basic theological test of whether or not a person is a dispensationalist and it is undoubtedly the most practical and conclusive." He then continues: "Progressive dispensationalists seem to be blurring this distinction by saying that the concept is not in the same class as what is conveyed by the concepts Gentiles, Israel and Jews."

If Israel and the church are not distinct, why did the church cease to be under the law while Israel was always under it? If Israel and the church are not distinct, one must ask why those who had embraced the faith of Israel, such as John's disciples, needed to be baptized in the name of Jesus and receive the Spirit, or why the faithful at Pentecost had to identify with this new truth? The church seems to be a new reality. To be fair, progressive dispensationalists have created a hybrid, for they do not mean that the nation of Israel and the church are identical, or that the church is spiritual Israel, but rather, only that the faithful of Israel and the Gentiles make up the church. Progressive dispensationalists consider the church to be a continuation of people of Israel in the Old Testament who were believers. They have been united by Christ into one new body, and will all participate in the same resurrection and future reign in the Davidic kingdom during the millennium.

Literal Hermeneutics

The second *sine qua non* of dispensationalism is the consistent use of a literal hermeneutic. Ryrie (p. 40) says about this, "Consistently literal, or plain, interpretation indicates a dispensational approach to the interpretation of Scripture. And it is this very consistency—the strength of dispensational interpretation—that seems to irk the nondispensationalist and becomes the object of his ridicule."

But do progressive dispensationalists truly follow literal, grammatical, historical interpretation? They really prefer only the terms grammatical and historical, for supposedly it is difficult to know what is meant by *literal.* But most of us know what *literal* means in hermeneutics. This has been taught in the standard hermeneutics texts of the past. The obfuscation of this term so that it becomes merely the opposite of figurative is unnecessary.

When the Scripture speaks of the wolf dwelling with the lamb, is it speaking of some deeper meaning or higher truth like peace in the world, or does it mean in fact that the wolf and the lamb will exist without hostility? When the text tells us that the Messiah will actually descend to the Mount of Olives and that it will split in two, north and south, is this speaking of a higher principle of the Messiah's majesty, or will the real mountain east of Jerusalem split apart? When Zechariah the prophet spoke of a river flowing at the Temple that goes into both the Mediterranean and Dead Seas, complete with descriptions and boundaries, does this refer merely to some spiritual truth? Is Ezekiel's Temple only a vague description of Jesus as the temple of God? How we approach ideas such as these will reveal our commitment to a literal hermeneutic.

In dealing with literal interpretation, we speak of how a reader approaching a text would normally read the text, understanding the conventions of language such as idiom and figure, without added outside theology that could be superimposed on the text. This imposition is exactly what progressive dispensationalism does with complementary hermeneutics, in which fuller meaning found in the New Testament adds to the meaning found in the Old Testament text.

Thus, the methodology of progressive dispensationalism leaves the ultimate meaning of prophetic passages open to complementation.

Traditional dispensationalists view this as a dangerous practice that allows future interpreters to continue to read new meanings into the biblical text.

CONCERNS ABOUT PROGRESSIVE DISPENSATIONALISM

Many traditional dispensationalists are concerned that progressive dispensationalists are *blurring the distinction between Israel and the church*. In this regard the progressive approach begins to look more like covenant theology than dispensationalism.

When the distinct peoples of God (Israel and the church) are not distinguished, the function of these peoples within the plan of God becomes difficult to explain. This blurring took place rapidly in the fourth century. Certainly the earliest Christian leaders and apologists were Jewish Christians who still believed in a national future for Israel. But the Roman church's success in the fourth century led to triumphalism and a dramatic shift in the church's view of Israel's future.

A second concern is the *abandonment of a literal interpretation of Scripture*. Departing from literal, contextual, grammatical, historical exegesis eventually leads to innovative and inventive interpretations of Scripture. This, in turn, leaves the hermeneutical door open to multilevel methods of exegesis instead of sound exegesis of the text. Such an approach reads meaning into the text rather than allowing the text to speak for itself.

Most progressive dispensationalists do not view themselves as substantially deviating from classical dispensationalism. However, their innovative approach does seem to have that effect on those who follow their ideology. The so-called "complementary" method of interpretation very quickly and easily leads to the multilevel method supported by those who have gradually moved away from dispensationalism altogether.

We live in a time when the postmodern approach to truth is moving society away from objective truth and toward subjective truth. In light of this, do we not need to define the parameters of dispensationalism more clearly than ever before? Eroding the distinctives of dispensationalism in order to dialogue with covenantarians could ultimately lead to undermining the entire system of classical dispensationalism altogether.

—WAYNE HOUSE AND
ROBERT THOMAS

BIBLIOGRAPHY

Blaising, Craig and Darrell Bock. *Progressive Dispensationalism*. Wheaton, IL: Victor Books, 1993.

Ryrie, Charles. *Dispensationalism*. Chicago: Moody Press, 1995.

Saucy, Robert. *The Case for Progressive Dispensationalism*. Grand Rapids: Zondervan, 1993.

Thomas, Robert. "The Hermeneutics of Progressive Dispensationalism," *The Master's Journal* 6.2 (Spring 1995), pp. 79-95.

Willis, Wesley, and John Master, eds. *Issues in Dispensationalism*. Chicago: Moody Press, 1994.

PROPHETIC FULFILLMENT

THE OLD TESTAMENT PROPHETS spoke for God. They believed they were sent by God with a specific message. Whereas the priests represented the people to God, the prophets presented God to the people. Thus, the prophets spoke with divine authority and divine enabling. Prophets were called by God, accountable to God, and empowered by God. The people of Israel acknowledged them as "holy men of God" who spoke the word of God.

PROPHETIC PREDICTIONS

One of the most unique features of the true Old Testament prophets was their ability to predict future events with perfect accuracy. God Himself predicted Israel's bondage in Egypt and subsequent deliverance (Genesis 15:13-18). Moses predicted the Israelites' successful conquest of the Promised Land under Joshua (Deuteronomy 31:23). Samuel predicted the failure of Saul's dynasty (1 Samuel 15:28). Nathan predicted the consequences of David's sin and its effects on his own family (2 Samuel 12:7-12). Elijah predicted the deaths of Ahab and Jezebel (1 Kings 21:19-23). Isaiah predicted the deliverance of Jerusalem from the Assyrian invasion of Sennacherib (2 Kings 19:34-37). Jeremiah predicted the Jews' 70-year captivity in Babylon.

Samuel Schultz (p. 37) observes: "This predictive element was normal to the message of a prophet. Because his message had its origin with God, it was expected that future events would be included, since the past, present and future were all known to the eternal, omniscient and omnipresent God."

Jesus Himself came in the prophetic tradition (John 1:45) and was recognized as a "teacher come from God" (John 3:2 NKJV). In fact, Jesus clearly affirmed His commitment to "fulfill" the law and the prophets (Matthew 5:17). However, Jesus also clearly indicated that He was more than just a prophet. Unlike the prophets, Jesus boldly declared that He was one with God the Father. He also accepted worship (John 9:35-38) and proclaimed that He was the manifestation of God Himself (John 14:7-12).

Schultz (p. 148) adds: "Jesus came to fulfill the Scriptures. Without question He penetrated the multitude of conflicting interpretations of the Law...and spoke with authority concerning the true meaning and interpretation of God's will."

PROPHETIC LANGUAGE

The prophets delivered their messages in three basic ways: verbally, in writing, and through symbolic acts. They preached it, wrote it, or demonstrated it. Their verbal declarations were "the word of the Lord" (Hebrew, *debhar Yahweh*). The divine origin and inspiration of these declarations were presumed by their very nature. God said to Amos (7:14-16), "Go, prophesy to My people...now therefore, hear the word of the LORD."

Written prophecies were especially poignant because they often employed the Hebrew verbal form known as the prophetic perfect. Hobart Freeman (p. 122) notes: "In classical Hebrew there are no tenses indicating time. The time of a verb is determined by its context. Instead of tenses there are two states,

designated as 'perfect' and 'imperfect,' indicating complete or incomplete action respectively." Freeman goes on to point out that the Hebrew perfect state generally depicts past, completed action. However, one of the unique features of the Hebrew language is that the perfect state can also be used to refer to a future time that the prophet views as already having taken place.

The biblical prophets speak of future events as though they had already occurred. Thus, they foresee things yet to happen as though they were already in the present: The virgin is pregnant (Isaiah 7:14), the divine child is already born (Isaiah 9:6), the star of Jacob has already appeared (Numbers 24:17), Israel has already gone into captivity (Isaiah 5:13). These are but a few of the hundreds of examples of such language by which the prophet foresees the future and predicts its exact fulfillment with such certainty that he describes it as already having come to pass.

MESSIANIC PREDICTIONS

Among the many predictions of the prophets are a series of messianic prophecies, over 100 in all, that specifically pointed to Jesus Christ as the kingly Messiah, the Son of Man, the ideal Prophet, the perfect Priest, the sinless sacrifice, the servant of the Lord, and the coming Redeemer. (See the article titled "Messianic Prophecy.")

Hengstenberg (p. 10) points out, "The chief object of prophecy was to prepare the way for Christ, that when He should come, He might be identified by a comparison of the prediction with its fulfillment." While this should be evident to serious Bible readers, many evangelicals today are sliding on the slippery slope of liberalism by suggesting that many of these prophecies can only be interpreted as vague analogies to the person and life of Christ. Such thinking would have found little acceptance among the early Christians, who believed these scriptures to be specific prophecies about Jesus Christ.

Luke 24:44-45 goes so far as to state that Jesus Himself taught the disciples which prophecies were specifically pointing to Him.

Thus, the early Christians believed the viewpoint of the apostles and evangelists because their ideas came directly from the Savior Himself.

When Jesus read Isaiah 61:1-2 in the synagogue at Nazareth, He declared, "Today this Scripture is fulfilled in your hearing" (Luke 4:21). Jesus was undoubtedly declaring that He was the fulfillment of Isaiah's prediction. From the virgin birth in the town of Bethlehem (Matthew 1:23; 2:5) to the death of Christ as the servant of the Lord (Acts 8:28-35), we see Jesus pointing to these predictions and their literal fulfillments with great confidence.

PROPHETIC PATTERN

Girdlestone (p. 10) noted long ago that "although biblical prophecies are the utterances of many men and the product of many ages...when regarded as a whole they are found to be correlated. They form a vast series which extends through many generations." What the Old Testament prophets began, the New Testament writers project into the future. Thus, the "testimony of Jesus is the spirit of prophecy" (Revelation 19:10).

Freeman (p. 126) notes, "Messianic prophecy, in a real sense, may be regarded as the New Testament in the Old." The predictions of the prophets give us history in advance, and the New Testament authors help us understand the connection and application of these truths.

Ellison (p. 54) observes that the prophets were "not philosophers uttering eternal truths in the abstract. They were God's spokesmen in given historical situations. Their messages are still valid today because neither the character of God nor human sin has changed.... We must remember that God was speaking through the prophets in many and various ways (Hebrews 1:1). That means among other things that God's fulfillment is always more wonderful than the message itself."

The promise of the prophets was that God would fulfill His promises to His people, and the proclamation of the New Testament authors was that indeed He has done just that—literally and specifically. Therefore, we have great assurance that predictions of Christ's second coming will be fulfilled in the same manner—literally and specifically (Acts 1:11).

—ED HINDSON

BIBLIOGRAPHY

Ellison, H.L. *The Message of the Old Testament*. London: Paternoster Press, 1981.

Freeman, Hobart. *An Introduction to the Old Testament Prophets*. Chicago: Moody Press, 1968.

Girdlestone, R.B. *The Grammar of Prophecy*. Grand Rapids: Kregel, 1955.

Hengstenberg, E.W. *Christology of the Old Testament*. Grand Rapids: Kregel, 1970.

Schultz, Samuel. *The Prophets Speak*. New York: Harper & Row, 1968.

PROPHETIC POSTPONEMENT

Prophetic postponement IS A TERM used to communicate the delay of the messianic program of redemption for national Israel. The New Testament refers to first and second comings of the Messiah because of the judicial hardening of national Israel (Matthew 13:13-15; Mark 4:11-12; Luke 8:10; John 12:40; Acts 28:26-27; Romans 11:8-10). The postponement interrupted Israel's national restoration under the New Covenant (Jeremiah 31:31-37). In the Old Testament, Israel's national restoration included two inseparable elements: its spiritual regeneration (see Isaiah 49:1-7; 53-55; Ezekiel 36:25-27; 37:14,23) and its physical restoration to the Land (see Isaiah 49:8; 56:1-8; Ezekiel 36:24,28; 37:24-28).

The first messianic advent provided the basis for spiritual regeneration (Matthew 1:21; see Luke 2:11), which a Jewish remnant has experienced (Romans 11:1-5). It is a token of the later national experience that will happen after God completes His plan for the church (Romans 11:12-15,23,26,31). When Israel's leadership rejected Jesus as Messiah (Matthew 23:37-38; see Acts 3:13-15,17; 4:25-27), the restoration of the nation was postponed. This necessitated a second messianic advent in order to complete Israel's spiritual and physical restoration (Matthew 23:39; see Acts 1:6-7; 3:19-21; Romans 11:25-27).

The concept of prophetic postponement is crucial to a proper interpretation of several prophetic texts in the Old Testament. For example, in Daniel 9:27 an interruption in fulfillment occurs between the end of the first 69 weeks (fulfilled historically) and the beginning of the seventieth week (fulfilled eschatologically). This concept also helps us understand God's blessing on the church (as opposed to Israel) under the New Covenant (Genesis 12:3; Zechariah 8:22-23; Romans 11:17-32) as well as the purpose of Christ's second advent.

THE TERMINOLOGY OF POSTPONEMENT

The technical expression for this understanding of the gap in the messianic program for Israel is *apotelesmatic* interpretation. It is derived from the Greek verb *apotelo,* which means "to bring to completion, finish." *Telos,* ("end" or "goal") may here have the more technical idea of "the consummation that comes to prophecies when they are fulfilled" (Luke 22:37). With the prefix *apo,* which basically has the connotation of "separation from something," the idea is of a delay or interruption in the completion of the prophetic program. Therefore, *apotelesmatic* interpretation recognizes that some Old Testament texts present the messianic program as a single event, but they actually intend a near and far historical fulfillment, separated by an indeterminate period of time. Dispensational writers have referred to this as an "intercalation" or a "gap." However, *prophetic postponement* better expresses this concept. *Prophetic,* because we understand a purposeful, preordained act in the divine program, and *postponement,* because it retains the original idea of an interruption in fulfillment, while supplementing it with the notion that such a delay is only temporary.

Old Testament texts hinted at this postponement when referring to Israel's hardening (Isaiah 6:9-13; Zechariah 7:11-12) and judicial exile (Deuteronomy 4:27-30; 28:36-37,49-50,64-68), but the postponement was not fully revealed until the New Testament (John 12:37-

40; Acts 28:25-28; Romans 11:25-26). Accordingly, this postponement in the fulfillment of Israelite history is not so much an interruption of redemption as an extension of a predicted hardening (Romans 11:7-10). The exile, which was a punishment for national disobedience, has therefore been prolonged during the church age until the appointed time for Israel's national restoration (Acts 1:7; 3:21; Romans 11:25-27). So that none can question the infallibility of the divine promise to Israel (Romans 9:6; 11:29), individual Israelite redemption is presently being fulfilled within the church (Romans 11:1-5). This salvation of the remnant during the present age (Romans 9:8; 11:24,27) testifies to the ultimate salvation of all Israel in the age to come (Romans 11:26). This previously unrevealed aspect of the messianic plan (Romans 16:25-26; Ephesians 3:3-6) declares that Christ will redeem Israel (Romans 11:23) as surely as He is saving individual Jews and Gentiles now (Romans 11:12,15,23,31).

THE EXPRESSION OF POSTPONEMENT

The New Testament refers to the future fulfillment of Old Testament restoration texts. For instance, the Old Testament promised that the city of Jerusalem would be delivered from Gentile domination by messianic intervention (Zechariah 14:1-4). This has never happened, but Christ promised this would be fulfilled at His second advent (Luke 21:24-31). In this New Testament prediction of fulfillment, Jesus teaches that the destruction of the Temple (verses 20-23), the period of Jewish Diaspora (verse 24), wars on an international scale (verse 10), natural disasters (verse 11), persecutions (verses 12-19), and celestial and terrestrial phenomenon (verses 25-26) will all precede the national redemption brought by the second advent (verses 27-28).

When the Old Testament recorded that the Messiah would be born (Isaiah 9:6) and would rule on the throne of David and over his kingdom (Isaiah 9:7), it portrayed one messianic advent. However, in Acts 3:18-21, Peter explained that the second half has been postponed.

Therefore, one must ask why a second coming would be necessary if all the prophetic promises to Israel were fulfilled at the first advent (as preterists and historicists contend). Also, the apotelesmatic approach is different from the "already–not yet" dialectic, in that the latter would see a *partial* fulfillment of the *complete* promise, while the former would see a *complete* fulfillment of *part* of the promise. Jesus is not *partially* fulfilling the promise to reign on David's throne as Lord over the church (Acts 2:34-36; Hebrews 1:3; 12:2). This is postponed for a *future* earthly enthronement, which will completely fulfill the literal requirements of the Old Testament promises to national Israel (2 Samuel 7:16; Psalm 89:4; Matthew 19:28; 25:31).

QUALIFICATIONS FOR POSTPONEMENT

It is important to remember that the messianic prophecies were originally directed to national Israel and will ultimately be fulfilled *exclusively with Israel.* The church occupies a parenthetical period in the fulfillment of Israel's destiny, but the church has not been relegated to a parenthetical *position* (see Ephesians 1:12; 2:6-7; 3:9-10; 5:25-27; Colossians 1:26-27). The New Testament gives the church a distinct purpose in the messianic plan, alongside that of Israel. In the church, the elect (Jew and Gentile) have equal access to God (Ephesians 2:11-22) and a new revelation of God's saving grace through Israel's Messiah. This grace has incorporated Gentiles as fellow heirs of the messianic blessings (Ephesians 2:3-6), including the inheritance of the kingdom (1 Corinthians 6:10; Galatians 5:21; Ephesians 5:5; 1 Thessalonians 2:12; 2 Thessalonians 1:5).

Still, the restoration promises made to national Israel require a future fulfillment *in the same manner* as the redemptive promises have found past fulfillment. Messiah's first advent was originally directed to national Israel (Matthew 15:24) and fulfilled specific prophecies (Isaiah 53; Daniel 9:26). At the Messiah's second advent, He will restore national Israel (Acts 1:6; Romans 11:26-27; 2 Thessalonians 1:5-10; 2:3-12; Revelation 19:11–20:9). We know that these promises were not fulfilled at Jesus' first advent (as the historicist interpretation suggests) because Jesus in the Olivet Discourse (Matthew 24:30-31; 25:31) and Peter in Acts (Acts 3:19-21) tie their fulfillment to the second advent. And we know they were not fulfilled in A.D. 70 (as the preterist interpretation suggests) because "the times of the Gentiles" were not "fulfilled" (concluded), and Israel's fortunes were not restored. The only way to harmonize these discrepancies is to change the Old Testament prophets' meaning or to recognize a postponement of final prophetic fulfillment.

Apotelesmatic passages (prophecies that have intervals in their fulfillment) are common in the Bible. The length of an interval is inconsequential, and some predictions encompassed many centuries (such as the prophecy of the exodus and establishment in the Land in Genesis 15:13-16).

POSTPONEMENT AND CHRONOLOGICAL CONTINUITY

The apotelesmatic approach includes both an *extension* of Israel's exile and a *postponement* of Israel's restoration, with a *parenthetical* period incorporated to fulfill the messianic salvation promises for those (whether Jew or Gentile) who have accepted Israel's Messiah. Since Israel's hardening did not permit the promise of national repentance at the first advent (John 12:37-40), this will be fulfilled at the second advent. An objection to this concept of postponement, especially in prophetic passages where a definite measure of time or space is specified (such as Daniel 9:24-27), has been that in such cases the units of time or space must be understood to run continuously and successively.

Prophetic postponement does not affect the fulfillment of measured events. The same chronological events are fulfilled in the same temporal order as if no interruption occurred. Dispensational writers illustrate this by the imagery of a prophetic clock. If we reckon that this clock is keeping only "Israeli time," the hands on the clock froze in position during "times of the Gentiles." The clock will start again when "the times of the Gentiles are fulfilled." From the human perspective the clock has stopped, and the fulfillment may seem to have failed. From the divine viewpoint, however, nothing has changed, and all is proceeding according to schedule (because "the times of the Gentiles" was always an intended part of the fulfillment).

POSTPONEMENT AND THE PROPHETIC PERSPECTIVE

First Peter 1:10-12, a text addressed predominately to Gentile exiles (1:1; 2:11), explains that God had revealed to the prophets His intention to bring salvation to the Gentiles (see Isaiah 9:1-2; 19:21-25; 42:1-2; 56:1-8). These prophets knew that Israel's Messiah was to be a "light to the nations" (Isaiah 42:6; 59:6), and they diligently sought to discover the appointed time of the messianic advent, which for them combined both the first and second advents. But the prophets could not clearly discern when the Gentiles would receive mercy, for most of those promises were connected with the messianic age (Isaiah 11:10; 42:6; 60:3; Malachi 1:11).

JESUS' TEACHING OF PROPHETIC POSTPONEMENT

Jesus instructed His disciples concerning two phases of messianic advent (to accomplish redemption and restoration). He said, "Elijah *is coming* and will restore all things; but I say to you that Elijah *already came*, and they did not recognize him, but did to him whatever they wished. So also the Son of Man is going to suffer" (Matthew 17:11-12, emphasis added). Israel's response to John the Baptist foreshadowed its response to the Messiah and called for the postponement of its national restoration.

Just as the coming of the messianic forerunner has two phases, one as John the Baptist (for repentance) and one as Elijah the prophet (for restoration), so the Messiah's coming has two phases: one as Savior (to redeem) and one as Sovereign (to reign). Just as John the Baptist's rejection by Israel's leadership ended his prophetic ministry without the fulfillment of national repentance, necessitating a future messianic forerunner (Elijah), so Jesus' rejection by Israel's leadership ended His messianic ministry without the fulfillment

of national redemption and restoration, necessitating the future return of the Messiah.

Jesus also recognized the principle of prophetic postponement in His use of Isaiah 61:1-2 (Luke 4:16-21). He differentiates the time of fulfillment for two messianic events that follow one another immediately in the text. In Luke 4, Jesus went against Jewish tradition in public reading, abruptly ending His selected passage in mid-sentence. The rest of the sentence reads, "...and the day of vengeance of our God; to comfort all who mourn." If the Lord's purpose at the first advent was to redeem rather than to reign, then we can understand why He omitted the second half of this verse, which focuses on the second advent. He did not omit it, as some claim, in order to stress the grace of God, for He omitted words that also stress the grace of God. Rather, Jesus knew that the day of Gentile judgment was to be postponed, and so He read only that portion of the verse that pertained to the present fulfillment.

EARLY CHRISTIAN INTERPRETATION OF POSTPONEMENT

Early Christian theology clearly recognized this interruption in Israel's redemption. In Acts 3:18 we read of redemption and the first phase of Jesus' advent in the words, "But the things which God announced beforehand by the mouth of all the prophets, that His Messiah would suffer, He has thus fulfilled." This redemptive proclamation is then tied to restoration and the second phase of advent in verses 19-21: "Repent therefore and return, so that your sins may be wiped away, in order that times of refreshing may come from the presence of the Lord; and that He may send Jesus, the Christ appointed for you, whom heaven must receive until the period of restoration of all things about which God spoke by the mouth of His holy prophets from ancient time."

The phrases "times of refreshing" and "period of restoration of all things" picture the messianic era—the promised restoration of national Israel (see Isaiah 2:2-4; 4:2-6; 11:6-9; 62:1-12). These exact expressions appear only here in the New Testament and have no direct precedent in the Greek Old Testament, but parallel ideas do exist in the Jewish apocalyptic literature.

The Greek term *apokatastasis* ("restoration") in Acts 3:21 is derived from the verb *apokathistemi* ("to restore [to an earlier condition]") and appears in Acts 1:6 for "*restoring* the kingdom to Israel." In Matthew 17:11 and Mark 9:12 (see Malachi 4:5) it refers to Elijah's coming to "*restore* all things." Parallel expressions of this period of restoration in the New Testament (though broader in scope) include Jesus' use of "the regeneration" (Greek, *palinenesia*) in Matthew 19:28 and Paul's description of the future age of redemption in Romans 8:18-23. This term for restoration is especially related to national Jewish repentance because the two terms come from the same root and seem to be patterned after the prophetic condition for the restoration of the messianic kingdom: "Turn to Me [with a restored heart], and I will return to you [with restored blessings]" (Zechariah 1:3; Malachi 3:7; see Matthew 3:1-2; 4:17). This relationship between national repentance and the messianic advent for the nation, especially with the added requirement of Jewish witness and Gentile inclusion (Acts 1:8; 15:11-18), demands a parenthetical period before the final fulfillment.

PAUL'S INTERPRETATION OF POSTPONEMENT

Paul wrote that Israel's rejection of the promised Messiah brought a suspension in the fulfillment of the messianic promises to Israel (Romans 11:12,15,23,25-28,31). He explained that God would not fail in His promise to national Israel, and so the Gentiles, who presently share in Israel's Messiah during the church age, are also assured of God's promised blessings (Romans 9:6; 10:1; 11:11,29-32).

This means that despite Israel's national rejection of Jesus as the Messiah, the Abrahamic covenant has not been revoked. This does not secure their salvation apart from repentance (Matthew 3:8-9; Romans 2:17-29), but it does preserve the promise of the nation's future salvation once it repents (Zechariah 12:10–13:2; Matthew 24:30; Romans 11:25-27).

EXAMPLES OF PROPHETIC POSTPONEMENT

Many Old Testament eschatological prophecies have been partially fulfilled but await complete or ultimate fulfillment. Some apotelesmatic passages include both a near historical fulfillment and a far "day of the Lord" fulfillment.

ESCHATOLOGICAL "DAY OF THE LORD" TEXTS

Near Fulfillment	Far Fulfillment
Isaiah 13:6	Isaiah 13:9
Joel 2:1,11	Joel 2:31
Obadiah 1-14	Obadiah 15-21
Zephaniah 1:7	Zephaniah 1:14

Other Old Testament eschatological messianic texts reveal (in the light of the New Testament revelation) a distinction between a historical (first advent) and eschatological (second advent) fulfillment.

ESCHATOLOGICAL MESSIANIC TEXTS

Fulfilled Historically	Fulfilled Eschatologically
Genesis 49:10	Genesis 49:11-12
2 Samuel 7:15	2 Samuel 7:13,16
Psalm 2:7	Psalm 2:8
Isaiah 9:1-2	Isaiah 9:3-5
Isaiah 9:6	Isaiah 9:7
Isaiah 11:1-3	Isaiah 11:4-16
Isaiah 52:13–55:13	Isaiah 56:1-8
Isaiah 59:16	Isaiah 59:17-21
Isaiah 61:1-2	Isaiah 61:2-11
Daniel 9:26	Daniel 9:27
Micah 5:2	Micah 5:3-15
Zephaniah 2:13–3:7	Zephaniah 3:8-20
Zechariah 9:9	Zechariah 9:10
Malachi 3:1	Malachi 3:2-3
Malachi 4:5	Malachi 4:6

Many of the desecration–restoration texts in the prophets distinguish between a partial (near) fulfillment in the return to the Land and the rebuilding of Jerusalem and the Temple, and an ultimate or eschatological (far) fulfillment in national Israel's final regathering (Isaiah 11:11-12), its return to Jerusalem (Isaiah 2:2-3), and the rebuilding of the eschatological Temple (Ezekiel 37:26-28; 40–48) in the millennial kingdom.

PROPHETIC POSTPONEMENT AND DISPENSATIONALISM

Prophetic postponement is a tenet of classical dispensationalism. It was not created to keep the programs for Israel and the church separate. Rather, it is based on the observation that the New Testament keeps Israel and the church distinct when employing Old Testament messianic and restoration passages. The New Testament describes separate programs for Israel and the church. The following points may be made concerning prophetic postponement:

1. The present physical domination of Gentile powers and the present spiritual program of the church show that the literal historical fulfillment of national Israel's restoration and revival awaits a future age.

2. The evidence for prophetic postponement (apotelesmatic interpretation) is not restricted to any one text but is a characteristic of messianic and "day of the Lord" prophetic texts. It may be further supported by the restoration motifs of the prophets, which have not seen complete fulfillment in any subsequent age.

3. Prophetic postponement can be demonstrated in New Testament eschatological texts, especially the Olivet Discourse and Revelation 6–19.

4. The New Testament further demonstrates the acceptance of prophetic postponement through its continuation of the Old Testament restoration promises to national Israel (such as Acts 3:19-21; Romans 11:25-31). The second advent of Christ is uniquely associated with the fulfillment of these promises (see Matthew 24:30-31; Acts 1:6-7; 3:20; 2 Thessalonians 2:8).

Therefore, a distinctive tenet of the dispensational hermeneutic is apotelesmatic interpretation, or prophetic postponement. This phenomenon reveals the meaning of Old Testament "day of the Lord" or eschatological messianic texts in which some aspects of Israel's restoration are not yet fulfilled.

—RANDALL PRICE

BIBLIOGRAPHY

DeSanto, Pasquale. "A Study of Jewish Eschatology with Special Reference to the Final Conflict." Ph.D. dissertation, Duke University, 1957.

McLean, John A. "The Seventieth Week of Daniel 9:27 as a Literary Key for Understanding the Structure of the Apocalypse of John." Ph.D. dissertation, University of Michigan, 1990.

Pierce, Ronald. "Spiritual Failure, Postponement, and Daniel 9." *Trinity Journal* 10 NS (1982), pp. 211-22.

Price, Randall. "Prophetic Postponement in Daniel 9 and Other Texts." In *Issues in Dispensationalism*. Eds. Wesley R. Willis and John R. Master. Chicago: Moody Press, 1994.

PROPHETS

THE HEBREW PROPHETS were spokesmen for God. They wrote the books of history and the books of prophecy in the Old Testament. The prophetic books of history are followed in the Hebrew Bible by the prophetic books of prediction. The two categories of prophetic books form a unit in the middle of the Hebrew Scriptures under the common term "prophets" (Hebrew, *nebiyim*).

THE PROPHETIC OFFICE

The Hebrew term *nabiy* itself designates the prophet as a spokesman for God. While the prophet preached to his own generation, he also predicted events in the future. The twofold aspect of the prophet's ministry included declaring God's message and foretelling God's actions. Thus, the prophet was also called a "seer" (Hebrew, *roeh*) because he could see future events before they happened.

The Bible depicts the prophet as one who was admitted into the divine council chambers where God "reveals His secret" (Amos 3:7 NASB). The Hebrew text of 1 Samuel 9:15 pictures God "uncovering the ear" of the prophet (see KJV). By the process of divine inspiration, God revealed what was hidden (2 Samuel 7:27) so that the prophet perceived what the Lord had said (Jeremiah 23:18). This communion with God was essential for God's truth to be revealed by the process of prophetic inspiration. The word of the Lord was communicated to the prophet and mediated to the people by the Holy Spirit—with powerful conviction and precise accuracy.

The full picture of prophecy, then, is that it encompasses both a forthtelling of God's messages and a foretelling of God's actions. Through the Holy Spirit God energized the prophet to speak for Him. Isaiah, for example, was such a man, addressing himself to his own times as he brought God's direction to the kings of Judah, and also seeing far into the future of God's plans for His people.

THE PROPHETIC MINISTRY

The Hebrew term *nabiy* identifies the prophet as a preacher or proclaimer of God's word, as does the Greek term *prophetes*. Biblical prophets were both preachers of truth and predictors of the future. Prophecy has its roots in history, but it also extends into the future. In other words, the nature of predictive prophecy arises out of the prophet's historical context as the revelation of God points him toward the future as well as the present. Thus, the prophets speak both to their own generation and to future generations as preachers and predictors.

Ellison (p. 14) observes that the prophet's message "is derived neither from observation nor intellectual thought, but from admission to the council chamber of God, from knowing God and speaking with Him." The prophet is admitted to God's council chamber, where God "reveals" His secrets and shows him the future.

THE PROPHETIC MESSAGE

The Old Testament prophets foresaw the coming of a divine Messiah with God-like characteristics. The purpose of messianic prophecy was to clearly identify the Messiah, who would fulfill the specific events predicted about Him by God's prophets. Such predictions were so deliberate and specific that there could be no mistaking their intended designation. The best guideline for determining which prophecies refer to the predicted Messiah is the New Testament, which clearly applies these predictions to Jesus of Nazareth.

The New Testament uses predictive prophecy and its fulfillment to prove the supernatural credibility of Christianity. The prophets clearly predicted the coming of a divine being who would be born of a virgin (Isaiah 7:14) at Bethlehem (Micah 5:2) from the line of Abraham (Genesis 22:18) and David (2 Samuel 7:16). That person is none other than Jesus Christ. He alone clearly fulfills over 100 specific biblical prophecies about the coming Messiah. Jesus Himself said, "All things which are written about Me in the Law of Moses and the Prophets and the Psalms must be fulfilled" (Luke 24:44). Jesus willingly submitted Himself to the course that these prophecies had prescribed for Him and knew the details of His life and death had to take place because they were written in the Word of God. He saw the whole of prophecy culminating in Himself.

The New Testament also provides the best guideline for determining whether or not a certain event is fulfilled. It tells us where the prophets spoke of Christ. The New Testament clearly indicates that the Old Testament messianic references point to one person— Jesus of Nazareth. "Of Him all the prophets bear witness that through His name everyone who believes in Him receives forgiveness of sins" (Acts 10:43).

—ED HINDSON

BIBLIOGRAPHY

Beecher, Willis J. *The Prophets and the Promise*. Grand Rapids: Baker Books, 1975.

Ellison, H.L. *Men Spake from God*. Grand Rapids: Eerdmans Publishing Company, 1958.

Hindson, Ed. "Prophet." In *Tim LaHaye Prophecy Study Bible.* Chattanooga: AMG Publishing, 2001.

Wood, Leon. *The Prophets of Israel.* Grand Rapids: Baker Books, 1979.

Young, Edward. *My Servants the Prophets.* Grand Rapids: Eerdmans Publishing Company, 1965.

PSALMS, ESCHATOLOGY OF

THE KINGSHIP OF GOD

The eternal and absolute kingship of the Lord is the unifying theological concept of the Psalms. The Lord is the "great King over all the earth" (47:2 NASB), and His kingdom "is an everlasting kingdom" (145:13). His rule extends "above all gods" (95:3), and He is the "God of gods" and "Lord of lords" (136:2-3). The Psalms declare that the Lord established His right to rule at creation when He brought the world into existence (95:3-5; 96:4-10; 104:1-9; 146:6-10). Contrary to the claims of Canaanite religion, the Lord, not Baal, subjugated the sea and brought the forces of chaos under His authority (74:13-15; 89:9; 93:3-4). The Lord has also asserted His sovereignty in history by defeating His enemies and bringing Israel into the land of Canaan (9:5-7; 24:7-10; 66:6-7; 68:7-10,21-24; 77:16-20).

The eschatological hope of the Psalms is the consummation and universal recognition of the Lord's sovereignty. Though the Lord's kingship is an eternal reality, rebellious enemies still oppose God's rule and oppress His people. The Psalms display a tension between the fact of God's absolute rule and the evidence, which seems to suggest that the enemies of God have the upper hand. The nations conspire against the Lord and the Davidic ruler (2:1), and the forces of chaos that the Lord subjugated at creation continue to assert themselves (46:2-3).

The righteous suffer at the hands of their enemies, both national and personal (9:13; 17:8-12; 102:8). The psalmist is surrounded by enemies who are like ravenous beasts desiring to tear him apart (22:12-16). Instead of enjoying the security of the Lord as their Shepherd (23:1), Israel complains that they are "considered as sheep to be slaughtered" (44:22). Enemy armies who hurl their insults against the Lord have desecrated and burned His sanctuary (74:3-10). In the laments, the psalmists ask, "How long?" (6:3; 13:1; 119:84) until the Lord intervenes, and they call for God to "awake" and act in accordance with His character (7:6; 35:23; 44:23). The imprecatory psalms are angry and impatient cries for God to put an end to those who oppose His rule and His people (cf. 3:7; 58:6-10; 137:8-9).

THE LORD AS WARRIOR AND JUDGE

Despite the injustices of life, the Psalms reflect an unwavering confidence that the Lord will act as the Warrior and Judge to right these wrongs and deliver His people. The Lord will come to judge the earth (96:13; 98:9). As a result, the righteous are secure, like the well-watered tree, while the wicked are like chaff blown away by the wind of God's judgment (1:3-5). The Lord destroys the wicked with "fire and brimstone and burning wind" but rewards the godly deeds of the righteous (11:6-7). The wicked may prosper temporarily, but they will be swiftly and suddenly destroyed (73:18-20; 92:7-9).

Though the divine judgment anticipated in the Psalms is not explicitly eschatological in nature, the Psalms do look forward to a time when God will come to establish justice on a worldwide scale (cf. 67:7; 96:10-13; 98:9). The psalms of Zion promise that the Lord will defeat the hostile armies that attack the holy city of Jerusalem (46:5-7; 48:3-8; 76:2-6), and the Old Testament prophets speak of a final assault on Jerusalem in the great day of the Lord, when the Lord will purge Israel in judgment and then, once and for all, deliver His people from their enemies (Ezekiel 38–39; Joel 3:9-21; Zephaniah 3:6-20; Zechariah 14; see also Revelation 19:14-20; 20:7-9).

THE SALVATION OF THE NATIONS

The Psalms not only view the nations as objects of judgment but include the peoples of the world in God's plan of salvation. Israel enjoys unique privileges as God's covenant people, but the "lovingkindness" of the Lord extends to all the earth (33:5). God commanded Israel to proclaim the Lord's saving acts to the nations (96:1-4; 105:1), and the Lord's design was that His mighty acts in Israel and His providential blessings upon all of creation would cause the nations to submit to His rule (65:5-13; 98:3). The fact that the nations are called to praise the Lord for His saving acts on behalf of Israel (96:1-3; 98:1-3) shows that the nations themselves will eventually share in this salvation.

Ultimately, all nations will submit to the Lord and offer Him the worship that is due His name (22:27-30; 145:10-13). Psalm 47:9 even portrays the rulers of the nations assembling to worship "as the people of the God of Abraham," bringing to fulfillment the covenant promise that all people would be blessed in Abraham (Genesis 12:1-3). Israel's worship of God is the preview of the grander symphony of praise that all nations will offer to the Lord in the New Jerusalem (Revelation 21:22-27).

THE PSALMS AND MESSIAH

The eschatology of the Psalms is inextricably linked to the promise of a future Messiah because of the close connection between the reign of God and the rule of the Davidic king in Jerusalem. The Lord has established a covenant relationship with the house of David, promising David an eternal dynasty and stipulating that God will bless or punish individual rulers in the Davidic line according to their obedience to the Mosaic commandments (89:28-37; see also 2 Samuel 7:12-16).

The visible reign of the Davidic king is a reflection of the invisible rule of God. Because the Lord rules over the sea (89:9), He establishes the sovereignty of the Davidic king by setting "his hand on the sea" (89:25). The son of David is also a "son of God" not because the king is deified, but because the Lord has adopted him into this special relationship (2:7; 89:27). Like no other human ruler, the Davidic king enjoys a privileged position as servant of the Lord (35:27; 69:17; 89:3,20,39; 143:12). Psalm 45:6 declares, "Your throne, O God, is for ever and ever," with reference to the Davidic ruler (see verses 2-5) because of his status as God's unique human representative. The relationship between God and the house of David mirrors the relationship between God and Adam, where Adam is the "image of God" and serves as God's regent by ruling and having dominion over the rest of creation (see Genesis 1:26-28; Psalm 8).

Because of the covenant relationship between God and David, the Lord promises to protect the king in battle, defeat his enemies, and give him dominion over the nations (2:8-9; 18:35-45,50; 20:6-8; 72:8-11; 110:5-7). The Lord will bless the king with a long reign that brings blessing and prosperity to the people of Israel (72:1-7). The royal psalms were primarily prayers for the contemporary Davidic ruler, based on the special promises that God had made to the house of David. These psalms, for the most part, were not prophetic in the strict sense of the term because they expressed aspirations associated with every ruler in the Davidic line. However, these psalms take on a prophetic and eschatological significance because no Davidic king in the history of Israel and Judah realized the ideal they portray. Though the kings of subject nations brought their tribute to Jerusalem to honor the Lord (47:9; 2 Samuel 8:1-14; 1 Kings 10:1-15), no Davidic ruler ever established a dominion that extended to "the very ends of the earth" (2:8). The historic rulers of the Davidic dynasty all failed and were, at best, poor imitations of the ideal.

Only the Messiah, Jesus Christ, will fulfill the ideal the royal psalms envision. In perhaps the most directly prophetic reference to the future Messiah, David acknowledges the superiority of this future descendant by referring to Him as "my Lord" (110:1). Psalm 2:9 envisions Jesus establishing worldwide sovereignty by smiting the nations in judgment at His second coming (see Revelation 19:15). In fact, the fulfillment of the promises to David in

Christ goes beyond even the ideal language of the royal psalms. More than an adopted son of the Lord, Jesus is the Son of God in His very nature (Romans 1:3; Hebrews 1:2-3). He rules at the right hand of God not only from the earthly throne at Jerusalem but also from His exalted throne in heaven (110:1; see Acts 2:32-35; Hebrews 1:3; 8:1). Not merely part of an eternal dynasty, the Lord Jesus Himself shall rule for ever and ever (Luke 1:33; Revelation 11:15), literally fulfilling the hyperbolic language associated with the Davidic ruler in the Psalms (see 21:4-6; 72:5,17).

PERSONAL ESCHATOLOGY

The Psalms only hint at the details of life after death. The psalmist implores the Lord to cease from punishing him "that I may smile again before I depart and am no more" (39:13). Sheol, which includes both the grave and a dark and shadowy underworld, is the final destination of both the righteous and the wicked dead (89:48). It is a place where one can no longer remember or give praise to the Lord (6:5; 30:9; 115:17) and is associated with terror and fear (18:5; 116:3). The essential difference between the righteous and the wicked is that God preserves the lives of His faithful ones from untimely death, while the wicked are cast down to sheol swiftly and suddenly (that is, before their time) (see 37:35-36; 49:13-14; 55:15,23). However, certain passages in the Psalms promise eternal life in the presence of God. "You will not abandon my soul to Sheol" (16:10). "God will redeem my soul from the power of Sheol" (49:15). This hope bursts forth in greater detail in the prophetic literature (Isaiah 26:19; Daniel 12:2).

The Psalms express confidence in the permanence of the relationship between God and the righteous. In Psalm 23:6, the psalmist declares that he will "dwell in the house of the LORD forever." He will be part of the worshiping community for all his life. There are "pleasures forever" at the right hand of God (16:11), and the Lord is the psalmist's "portion forever" (73:26). These passages point to a relationship that cannot be confined to the boundaries of this life alone. While the Psalms do not clearly teach what is waiting on the other side, the confidence of an unending relationship with the Lord anticipates the sure hope of eternal life revealed in Jesus Christ.

ESCHATOLOGY AND THE ARRANGEMENT OF THE PSALTER

Recent studies have demonstrated that even the final shaping and arrangement of the Psalter seems to reflect an eschatological emphasis. Psalms 1–2, generally viewed as the introduction to the entire book, contain messages concerning a time of judgment and reckoning for both individuals (1:4-6) and nations (2:8-12). Similarly, Psalm 145 at the end of the Psalter focuses on the theme of God's kingdom rule (145:10-13) and calls on "all flesh" to bless His name (145:21). The concluding hallelujah psalms (146–150) offer praise to the Lord as the ruler over all. The Psalms as a whole reflect a movement from lament, the dominant genre in the first half of the Psalms (books 1–3 or Psalms 1–89), to hymns and praise, the primary forms in the last half of the Psalms (books 4–5 or Psalms 90–150). While God's people face times of crisis and distress in the present, they see through the eyes of faith the certainty of God's ultimate triumph.

Royal psalms appear at strategic points in the Psalter—Psalm 2 at the beginning of book one, and Psalm 72 and 89 at the beginning and end of book three. Psalm 89 deals with the crisis concerning the Davidic monarchy created by the exile and the absence of the king (89:39-51), leading to an affirmation of the Lord's kingship in Psalms 93–99. The Lord's kingship stands above and is not dependent upon the welfare of the Davidic line, though royal psalms in the latter half of the Psalms (110; 132) continue to affirm God's commitment to the house of David. The presence of a royal psalm promising the Davidic ruler's victory over the nations in the introduction to the book (2:8) and the inclusion of the royal psalms in the Psalter after the exile—when there was no king on the throne—testify to the tenacity of the messianic hope that is found in the Psalms, when the circumstances of history appear to have destroyed any such expectation.

—GARY YATES

BIBLIOGRAPHY

Brueggemann, Walter. *The Message of the Psalms.* Minneapolis: Augsburg, 1984.

Bullock, C. Hassell. *Encountering the Book of Psalms: A Literary and Theological Introduction.* Grand Rapids: Baker Books, 2001.

Chisholm, Robert. B., Jr. "A Theology of the Psalms." In *A Biblical Theology of the Old Testament.* Ed. Roy B. Zuck. Chicago: Moody, 1991, pp. 257-304.

Vincent, M.A. "The Shape of the Psalter: An Eschatological Dimension?" In *New Heaven and New Earth—Prophecy and the Millennium: Essays in Honor of Anthony Gelston,* eds. P.J. Harland and C.T.R. Hayward. Leiden, Netherlands: Brill, 1999, pp. 61-81.

Wright, Christopher J.H. *Knowing Jesus Through the Old Testament.* Downers Grove, IL: InterVarsity Press, 1995.

RAPTURE

THE RAPTURE OF THE CHURCH is one of the most compelling and exciting prophetic events in the Bible. It is clearly taught in 1 Thessalonians 4:15-18 (NKJV), where the apostle Paul provides us with these details:

> This we say to you by the word of the Lord, that we who are alive and remain until the coming of the Lord will by no means precede those who are asleep. For the Lord Himself will descend from heaven with a shout, with the voice of an archangel, and with the trumpet of God. And the dead in Christ will rise first. Then we who are alive and remain shall be caught up together with them in the clouds to meet the Lord in the air. And thus we shall always be with the Lord. Therefore comfort one another with these words.

This passage of Scripture delineates five stages to the rapture: (1) The Lord Himself will descend from heaven with a shout and with the sound of a trumpet, (2) the dead in Christ will rise first, (3) we who are alive and remain on the earth will be "caught up" (Greek, *harpazo*) together with them in the clouds, (4) we will meet the Lord, and (5) we shall always be with Him. The apostle Paul also unveiled what he called a mystery pertaining to the rapture. In 1 Corinthians 15:51-53, He explained that some Christians would not sleep (die), but their bodies would be instantly transformed.

> Behold, I tell you a mystery: We shall not all sleep, but we shall all be changed—in a moment, in the twinkling of an eye, at the last trumpet. For the trumpet will sound, and the dead will be raised incorruptible, and we shall be changed. For this corruptible must put on incorruption, and this mortal must put on immortality.

This is what will happen when the rapture takes place: Without warning, the bodies of all believers who have died since the day of Pentecost will suddenly be transformed into new, living, immortal, resurrected bodies. Even those whose bodies have long since decayed or whose ashes have been scattered out over the oceans will receive a new body. This new body will be joined together with the person's spirit, which Jesus will bring with Him. Then the bodies of those who have likewise accepted Christ as their Savior and are alive at that moment will also be instantly translated into new immortal bodies. Together, all believers will be instantaneously transported into the heavens to meet the Lord. Those who are alive and have rejected the salvation of Jesus Christ will remain behind on earth and will witness a miraculous event of astonishing proportions—the sudden mass disappearance of millions upon millions of people from the face of the earth.

THE BLESSED HOPE

The rapture is often referred to as "the blessed hope" (Titus 2:13) because it provides assurance to believers who are concerned about the coming Tribulation, and it offers comfort to those who long to be reunited

THE EVENTS OF THE RAPTURE

1. The Lord Himself will descend from His Father's house, where He is preparing a place for us (John 14:1-3; 1 Thessalonians 4:16).

2. He will come again to receive us to Himself (John 14:1-3).

3. He will resurrect those who have fallen asleep in Him (deceased believers whom we will not precede—1 Thessalonians 4:14-15).

4. The Lord will shout as He descends ("loud command," 1 Thessalonians 4:16 NIV). All this takes place in the "twinkling of an eye" (1 Corinthians 15:52).

5. We will hear the voice of the archangel (perhaps to lead Israel during the seven years of the Tribulation as he did in the Old Testament—1 Thessalonians 4:16).

6. We will also hear the trumpet call of God (1 Thessalonians 4:16), the last trumpet for the church. (Don't confuse this with the seventh trumpet of judgment upon the world during the Tribulation in Revelation 11:15.)

7. The dead in Christ will rise first (the corruptible ashes of their dead bodies are made

incorruptible and joined together with their spirits, which Jesus brings with Him—1 Thessalonians 4:16-17).

8. Then we who are alive and remain will be changed (or made incorruptible by having our bodies made "immortal" —1 Corinthians 15:51,53).

9. We will be caught up (raptured) together (1 Thessalonians 4:17).

10. We will be caught up in the clouds (where dead and living believers will have a monumental reunion— 1 Thessalonians 4:17).

11. We will meet the Lord in the air (1 Thessalonians 4:17).

12. Christ will receive us to Himself and take us to the Father's house "that where I am, there you may be also" (John 14:3).

13. "And so we shall always be with the Lord" (1 Thessalonians 4:17).

14. At the call of Christ for believers, He will judge all things. Christians will stand before the judgment seat of Christ (Romans 14:10; 2 Corinthians 5:10), described in detail in 1 Corinthians 3:11-15. This judgment prepares Christians for...

15. The marriage of the Lamb. Before Christ returns to earth in power and great glory, He will meet His bride, the church, and the marriage supper will take place. In the meantime, after the church is raptured, the world will suffer the unprecedented outpouring of God's wrath, which our Lord called "the great tribulation" (Matthew 24:21).

The Father's House

Marriage of the Lamb

⑫ ⑬ ⑭ ⑮

Judgment Seat
I Corinthians 3:9-15

John 14:1-3
① ②

⑪

Rapture
⑨ ⑩

I Thessalonians 4:16-17
I Corinthians 15:51-58

④

⑥ ⑤ ⑦ ⑧

③

Church Age

Tribulation 7 Years

Millennium 1000 Years

with their departed loved ones who share a faith in Christ.

The more than 300 biblical references to the second coming of Christ clearly show that His return has two distinct phases. The contrasting elements cannot be merged into a single event (see the article titled "Second Coming of Christ"). In the first phase, He will come suddenly to rapture His church in the air and take all believers to His Father's house in fulfillment of His promise in John 14:1-3. There, they will appear before the judgment seat of Christ (2 Corinthians 5:8-10). While the believers are in heaven, those left behind on the earth will experience the trials of the seven-year Tribulation period. In the second phase of Jesus' second coming (the glorious appearing), He will return to earth in great power and glory to set up His millennial kingdom. The entire second coming has been compared to a two-act play (the rapture and the glorious appearing) with a seven-year intermission (the Tribulation). The apostle Paul distinguishes between these two phases in Titus 2:13, where he refers to the rapture as "the blessed hope" and the return of Christ to the earth as "the glorious appearing."

WHAT DOES *RAPTURE* MEAN?

The English word *rapture* comes from the Latin word *raptus,* which in Latin Bibles translates the Greek word *harpazō,* used 14 times in the New Testament. The basic idea of the word is "to suddenly remove or snatch away." It is used by the New Testament writers in reference to stealing or plundering (Matthew 11:12; 12:29; 13:19; John 10:12,28-29) and removing (John 6:15; Acts 8:39; 23:10; Jude 23).

The New Testament employs a third use, which focuses on being caught up to heaven. It describes Paul's "third heaven" experience (2 Corinthians 12:2,4) and Christ's ascension to heaven (Revelation 12:5). Obviously, *harpazō* is the perfect word to describe God suddenly taking up the church from earth to heaven at the first part of Christ's second coming.

WILL THE RAPTURE BE PRETRIBULATIONAL?

The Church Is Not on Earth in Revelation 4–18

The common New Testament term for *church* (Greek, *ekklēsia*) is used 19 times in Revelation 1–3, which deals with the historical church of the first century. However, Revelation uses *church* once more—at the very end (22:16), where John returns to addressing the first-century church. Most interesting is the fact that nowhere during the Tribulation period is the term *church* used in reference to believers on earth.

John's shift from his detailed instructions for the church to his absolute silence about the church for many chapters is remarkable and totally unexpected if in fact the church continued into the Tribulation. If the church were to experience the Tribulation (the seventieth week of Daniel 9), then surely the most detailed study of Tribulation events would include instructions for the church. But it doesn't. The only explanation for this frequent mention of the church in Revelation 1–3 and total absence of the church on earth until Revelation 22:16 is a pretribulation rapture, which will relocate the church from earth to heaven prior to the Tribulation.

A Posttribulational Rapture Is Inconsequential

If God miraculously preserves the church through the Tribulation, why have a rapture? If it is to avoid the wrath of God at Armageddon (at the end of the Tribulation), then why would God not continue to protect the saints on earth (as is postulated by posttribulationism) just as He protected Israel (see Exodus 8:22; 9:4,26; 10:23; 11:7) from His wrath poured out upon Pharaoh and Egypt? Further, if the purpose of the rapture is for living saints to avoid Armageddon, why also resurrect the saints (who are already immune) at the same time?

If the rapture took place in connection with our Lord's posttribulational glorious appearing, the subsequent separation of the sheep from the goats (Matthew 25:31-46) would be redundant. Separation would have taken place in the very act of translation.

If all Tribulation-era believers are raptured and glorified after the Tribulation and just prior to the inauguration of the millennial kingdom, who then will be left to populate and propagate the kingdom? The Scriptures indicate that God will judge the living unbelievers at the end of the Tribulation and remove them from the earth (see Matthew 13:41-42; 25:41). Yet they also teach that children will be born to *believers* during the millenium and that these children will be capable of sin (see Isaiah 65:20; Revelation 20:7-10). This would not be possible if all the believers on earth were glorified through a posttribulational rapture.

A posttribulational rapture and the church's supposed immediate return to earth leaves no time for the *bema*—the judgment seat of Christ (1 Corinthians 3:10-15; 2 Corinthians 5:10). For these reasons, a posttribulational rapture makes no logical sense. A pretribulational rapture, by contrast, does not leave us with these insurmountable difficulties.

The Tribulation Is Not Impending

All through the New Testament epistles, God gave many instructions to the church, including warnings, but never once are believers warned to prepare for entering and enduring the Tribulation (Daniel's seventieth week).

The New Testament warns vigorously about coming error and false prophets (Acts 20:29-30; 2 Peter 2:1; 1 John 4:1-3; Jude 4) and against ungodly living (Ephesians 4:25–5:7; 1 Thessalonians 4:3-8; Hebrews 12:1). The New Testament even admonishes believers to endure in the midst of present tribulation (1 Thessalonians 2:13-14; 2 Thessalonians 1:4; and all of 1 Peter). However, the New Testament is absolutely silent about the church preparing for the Tribulation as described in Revelation 6–18.

The Scriptures would certainly not be silent about such a major and traumatic period of time for the church. If the rapture were to happen partway through or at the end of the Tribulation, one would expect the epistles to teach the presence, purpose, and conduct of the church during the Tribulation. However, we find none of this teaching whatsoever. Only a pretribulation rapture satisfactorily explains the lack of such instructions.

The Content of 1 Thessalonians 4:13-18

Let us hypothetically suppose for a moment that the rapture is not pretribulational. What would we expect to find in 1 Thessalonians 4? How does this compare with what we observe there?

We would expect the Thessalonians to be joyous over the fact that loved ones are home with the Lord and will not have to endure the horrors of the Tribulation. But we discover that the Thessalonians are actually grieving because they fear their loved ones have missed the rapture. Only the possibility of a pretribulation rapture accounts for this grief.

We would also expect the Thessalonians to be grieving over their own impending trial rather than over loved ones. Furthermore, we would expect them to be inquisitive about their own future doom. But the Thessalonians have no fears or questions about the coming Tribulation.

Finally, we would expect Paul, even in the absence of interest or questions by the Thessalonians, to provide instructions and exhortation for such a supreme test, which would make their present tribulation seem microscopic in comparison. But we find not even one indication of any impending tribulation of this kind. Given the scenario in 1 Thessalonians 4, only the possibility of a pretribulation rapture makes sense.

John 14:1-3 Parallels 1 Thessalonians 4:13-18

John 14:1-3 refers to Christ's coming again. It is not a promise to all believers that they will go to Him at death. Rather, it refers to the rapture of the church. Note the close parallels between the promises of John 14:1-3 and 1 Thessalonians 4:13-18. First, consider the promises of a presence with Christ: "…that where I am, there you may be also" (John 14:3), and "Thus we shall always be with the Lord" (1 Thessalonians 4:17). Second, note the promises of comfort: "Let not your heart be troubled" (John 14:1), and

"Therefore comfort one another with these words" (1 Thessalonians 4:18).

Jesus instructed the disciples that He was going to His Father's house (heaven) to prepare a place for them. He promised them that He would return and receive them so that they could be with Him wherever He was.

The phrase "wherever I am," while implying a continued presence in general, here means presence in heaven in particular. Our Lord told the Pharisees in John 7:34, "Where I am you cannot come." He was not talking about His present abode on earth, but rather, His resurrected presence at the right hand of the Father. In John 14:3, "where I am" must mean "in heaven," or 14:1-3 would be meaningless.

A posttribulation rapture would require that the saints meet Christ in the air and immediately descend to earth without experiencing what our Lord promised in John 14. Because John 14 refers to the rapture, only a pretribulation rapture satisfies the language of John 14:1-3 and allows raptured saints to dwell for a meaningful period of time with Christ in His Father's house.

The Rapture and the Return

A comparison of the rapture (1 Corinthians 15:50-58; 1 Thessalonians 4:13-18) with the glorious appearing (Matthew 24–25) reveals at least eight significant contrasts or differences. These differences demand that the rapture occur at a significantly different time from Christ's glorious appearing:

1. At the rapture, Christ comes in the air and returns to heaven (1 Thessalonians 4:17). At the glorious appearing, Christ comes to the earth to dwell and reign (Matthew 25:31-32).

2. At the rapture, Christ gathers His own (1 Thessalonians 4:16-17). At the glorious appearing, angels gather the elect (Matthew 24:31).

3. At the rapture, Christ comes to reward (1 Thessalonians 4:17). At the glorious appearing, Christ comes to judge (Matthew 25:31-46).

4. At the rapture, resurrection is prominent (1 Thessalonians 4:15-16). At the glorious appearing, resurrection is not mentioned.

5. At the rapture, believers depart the earth (1 Thessalonians 4:15-17). At the glorious appearing, unbelievers are taken away from the earth (Matthew 24:37-41).

6. At the rapture, unbelievers remain on earth. At the glorious appearing, believers remain on earth (Matthew 25:34).

7. Christ's kingdom on earth is not mentioned at the rapture. At the glorious appearing, Christ has come to set up His kingdom on earth (Matthew 25:31,34).

8. At the rapture, believers will receive glorified bodies (1 Corinthians 15:51-57). At the glorious appearing, survivors will not receive glorified bodies.

The Promise of Deliverance

In Revelation 3:10, Jesus promised, "I will keep you from [Greek, *ek,* "out of"] the hour of trial which shall come upon the whole world." This passage makes it clear that Christ's intention is to keep the church *out of* the Tribulation period.

The Greek preposition *ek* admittedly has the basic idea of emergence. But this is not always so. Two notable examples are 2 Corinthians 1:10 and 1 Thessalonians 1:10. In the Corinthian passage, Paul rehearses his rescue from death by God. Paul did not emerge from death but rather was rescued from the potential danger of death.

Even more convincing is 1 Thessalonians 1:10. Here, Paul states that Jesus is rescuing believers out of the wrath to come. The idea is not emergence out of, but rather protection from entrance into divine wrath.

If Revelation 3:10 means immunity or protection within as other positions insist, then several contradictions result. First, if protection in Revelation 3:10 is limited to protection from God's wrath only and not Satan's, then Revelation 3:10 denies our Lord's request in John 17:15.

Second, if Revelation 3:10 means total immunity, then of what worth is the promise in light of Revelation 6:9-11 and 7:14, where martyrs abound? The wholesale martyrdom of saints during the Tribulation demands that the promise to the Philadelphia church be interpreted as "keeping out of" the hour of testing, not "keeping within."

The church is to be delivered from the wrath to come. The apostle Paul tells us in 1 Thessalonians 1:10 that we should "wait for His Son from heaven, whom He raised from the dead, even Jesus who delivers us from the wrath to come." The context of this passage points to the rapture. The church must be removed from the earth before the Tribulation begins in order to be delivered from the wrath to come.

The church is not appointed to wrath. According to 1 Thessalonians 5:9, "God did not appoint us to wrath, but to obtain salvation through our Lord Jesus Christ." Once again, the context of this passage shows it is referring to the rapture. Because the Tribulation specifically involves God's wrath, and because Christians are not appointed to His wrath, the church must be raptured out of the way before the Tribulation begins.

If the church is raptured at the end of the Tribulation, no one will be left to populate the millennium. Just prior to the beginning of the millennium, all sinners (those who reject Jesus Christ as Savior) who survive the Tribulation will be cast into hell according to Matthew 25:46. Should the rapture occur at the end of the Tribulation, all Christians would be taken from the earth as well, leaving no one on earth with a natural body to repopulate the planet during the millennium. The "righteous" (the "sheep") who enter the millennium are the saints who survive the Tribulation—those who were unsaved at the time of the rapture but became believers during the Tribulation. Many of these saints will be martyred during this time, but those who survive the Tribulation will repopulate the earth during the millennium. For this to occur, the rapture must take place prior to the Tribulation instead of at the end.

QUESTIONS AND ANSWERS

1. *Since the phrase "to meet the Lord" in 1 Thessalonians 4:17 can refer to a friendly city going out to meet the visiting king and escorting him back to the city, does not this phrase point decidedly to a posttribulational rapture?*

First, this Greek term can refer to either meeting within a city (Mark 14:13; Luke 17:12) or going out of the city to meet and return back (Matthew 25:6; Acts 28:15). So the use of this particular phrase is not at all decisive. Second, remember that at the glorious appearing, Christ is coming to a hostile people in general who will eventually fight against Him at Armageddon. The pretribulational rapture best pictures the king rescuing, by a rapture, His faithful followers who are trapped in a hostile world and who will later accompany Him when He returns to earth to conquer His enemies and set up His kingdom (Revelation 19:11-16).

2. *Why does Paul write in 1 Thessalonians 5:6 for believers to be alert to "the day of the Lord" if they're not going to face it due to being raptured before the Tribulation?*

Paul exhorts believers in 1 Thessalonians 5:6 to be alert and living godly in a "day of the Lord" context just as Peter does in 2 Peter 3:14-15, where the "day of the Lord" experience is clearly at the end of the millennium (because the old heavens and earth will be destroyed and replaced with the new). In such passages are exhortations for true believers to live godly lives in the light of God's future judgment on unbelievers.

3. *Does not Matthew 24:37-42, where people are taken out of the world, teach a posttribulational rapture?*

In fact, Matthew 24:37-42 teaches just the opposite. First, it teaches that Noah and his family were left alive while the whole world was taken away in death and judgment. This is exactly the sequence to be expected at Christ's glorious appearing as taught in the parable of the wheat and tares (Matthew 13:24-43), the parable of the dragnet (Matthew 13:47-50), and the "sheep and goats" judgment of the nations (Matthew 25:31-46). In every one of these instances, at the glorious appearing, unbelievers are taken away in judgment, and the righteous believers remain.

4. *Does not a pretribulation rapture result in two second comings of Christ, whereas Scripture teaches there is only one second coming?*

Not at all. Regardless of the rapture position one holds, Christ's second coming is one event that occurs in two parts—Christ coming in the air to rapture the church and Christ coming to earth to conquer the world and set up His kingdom.

5. *If pretribulationism is true, why doesn't Revelation 4–19 mention the church in heaven?*

It is true that the Greek word for *church (ekklēsia)* is not used of the church in heaven in Revelation 4–19. However, that does not mean the church is invisible. The church appears in heaven at least twice. First, the 24 elders in Revelation 4–5 symbolize the church. Second, the phrase "you saints and apostles and prophets" in Revelation 18:20 clearly refers to the church in heaven. Also, Revelation 19 pictures the church (the bride of Christ) in heaven prior to her triumphal return. Which rapture scenario best accounts for the church being in heaven in these texts at this time? A pretribulation rapture.

6. *Why is Revelation addressed to the church if the church will not experience the Tribulation period due to the rapture?*

God frequently warned Israel in the Old Testament of impending judgment even though the generation who received the prophecy would not experience it. Both Paul (1 Thessalonians 5:6) and Peter (2 Peter 3:14-15) exhorted their readers to godly living by referring to a future judgment that their readers would not experience. John followed the same pattern in Revelation. He alerted the church to God's future judgments so believers would properly warn the unsaved world of judgment to come.

7. *Is the trumpet of 1 Thessalonians 4:17 and 1 Corinthians 15:52 the same as the trumpet of Joel 2:1; Matthew 24:31; and Revelation 11:15?*

A careful study of the almost 100 uses of "trumpet" or "trumpets" in the Old Testament quickly warns the student of Scripture not to equate the trumpets in any two texts without a great deal of corroborating contextual evidence. For example, trumpets are used for warning (Jeremiah 6:1), for worship and praise (2 Chronicles 20:28; Psalm 81:3; 150:3; Isaiah 27:13), for victory (1 Samuel 13:3), for recall (2 Samuel 2:28; 18:16), for rejoicing (2 Samuel 6:15), for announcements (2 Samuel 20:1; 1 Kings 1:34; 2 Kings 9:13), and for dispersal (2 Samuel 20:22), to name a few.

The trumpets in Joel and in the New Testament are used for several distinct purposes. The trumpet of Joel 2:1 is a trumpet of alarm that the day of the Lord is near (see Jeremiah 6:1). The trumpet of 1 Thessalonians 4:17 and 1 Corinthians 15:52 is a trumpet that announces the approaching king (see Psalm 47:5). The trumpet of Matthew 24:31 is a trumpet call to assembly (see Exodus 19:16; Nehemiah 4:20; Joel 2:15). The trumpet of Revelation 11:15 announces victory (see 1 Samuel 13:3). Scripture offers no compelling reason to equate the rapture trumpet with any of these other trumpets. Therefore, these texts cannot be used to determine the time of the rapture.

One of the chief characteristics of the rapture is that it will be sudden, unexpected, and surprising. "No man knows the day or the hour," so we should live so as to "be ready, for the Son of Man is coming at an hour you do not expect" (Matthew 24:44). Only a pretribulation rapture preserves an imminent ("at any moment") return of Christ. Throughout the ages, Christians have understood the rapture to be imminent. Nothing could be a better motivator to holy living than knowing that Jesus could come at any moment.

—TIM LAHAYE AND
RICHARD MAYHUE

BIBLIOGRAPHY

Hindson, Ed. *Earth's Final Hour.* Eugene, OR: Harvest House Publishers, 1999.

LaHaye, Tim. *The Rapture.* Eugene, OR: Harvest House Publishers, 2002.

Stanton, Gerald. *Kept from the Hour.* Miami: Schoettle Publishing, 1991.

Walvoord, John J. *The Blessed Hope and the Tribulation.* Grand Rapids, Zondervan, 1986.

———. *The Rapture Question.* Grand Rapids: Zondervan, 1967.

Wood, Leon. *Is the Rapture Next?* Grand Rapids: Zondervan, 1966.

RAPTURE, HISTORY OF

CRITICS OF THE PRETRIBULATIONAL rapture view often refer to its lack of historical support. For several years, opponents of the pretribulational rapture position have argued that it was invented by John Darby in the mid-1800s and was never mentioned before that. These arguments generally reason that because this teaching is less than 200 years old, it cannot be biblical, or Christians would have held to this view many years earlier. Ultimately, biblical truth must be determined by the clear teaching of Scripture, not how that teaching has been perceived throughout history. However, a substantial amount of evidence reveals a belief in a pretribulational rapture long before John Darby.

EARLY CHURCH FATHERS

The earliest documents of the ancient church (including the New Testament canon) reflect a clear premillennialism. However, minor controversy surrounds the relation of the rapture to the Tribulation. Pretribulationists point to the early church's clear belief in imminency as evidence that pretribulationism was held by at least a few from the earliest times.

As was typical of every area of the early church's theology, initial views of prophecy were undeveloped and sometimes contradictory, containing a seedbed out of which would develop various and diverse theological viewpoints. Finding clear pretribulationism spelled out in the early church fathers is difficult, but some pretribulational elements are clear. When systematized with their other prophetic views, these elements contradict posttribulationism and support pretribulationism. For example, the apostolic fathers clearly taught the pretribulational feature of imminence.

A cursory examination of the early church fathers reveals that they were predominantly premillennialists or chiliasts. Clear examples exist in the writings of Barnabas (ca. 100–105), Papias (ca. 60–130), Justin Martyr (110–165), Irenaeus (120–202), Tertullian (145–220), Hippolytus (ca. 185–236), Cyprian (200–250), and Lactantius (260–330). The early church fathers largely expected the church to be suffering and persecuted when the Lord returns. However, they also believed in the imminent return of Christ, which is a central feature of pretribulational thought. This lack of precision has led to debate among scholars as to how to interpret the early church fathers' writings.

Expressions of imminence abound in the apostolic fathers. Clement of Rome (90–100), Ignatius of Antioch (98–117), The Didache (100–160), The Epistle of Barnabas (117–138), and The Shepherd of Hermas (96–150) all speak of imminency. Their statements abound with exhortations to "watch," "wait," and "be ready" for the Lord's soon coming. Furthermore, The Shepherd of Hermas (1.4.2) speaks of escaping the Tribulation:

> You have escaped from great tribulation on account of your faith, and because you did not doubt in the presence of such a beast. Go, therefore, and tell the elect of the Lord His mighty deeds, and say to them that this beast is a type of the great tribulation that is coming. If then ye prepare yourselves, and repent with all your heart, and turn to the Lord, it will be possible for you to escape it, if your heart be pure and spotless, and ye spend the rest of the days of your life in serving the Lord blamelessly.

In the end, no one can produce a clear statement of patristic eschatology regarding the rapture. But we can conclude the following:

- They expected a literal coming of Christ followed by a literal 1000-year kingdom.
- They believed in the imminent coming of Christ with occasional pretribulational inferences.
- They were being persecuted by the Roman government but did not equate this with the future Tribulational wrath.

Larry Crutchfield (p. 77) rightly concludes,

> This view of the fathers on imminency, and, in some, references to escaping the time of the Tribulation, constitute what may be termed, to quote Erickson, "seeds from which the doctrine of the pretribulational rapture could be developed...." Had it not been for the drought in sound exegesis, brought on by Alexandrian allegorism and later by Augustine, one wonders what kind of crop those seeds might have yielded— long before J.N. Darby and the nineteenth century.

THE MEDIEVAL CHURCH

The period between Augustine and the Renaissance was largely dominated by "Augustine's understanding of the church, and his spiritualization of the Millennium as the reign of Christ in the saints." There were only "sporadic discussions here and there of a literal, future Millennium" (Hannah, pp. 315–16), making examples of pretribulationalism very rare. However, careful historical research has brought many long-neglected pretribulational statements to light.

Ephraem of Nisibis (306–373)

Ephraem was an extremely important and prolific writer. Also known as Pseudo-Ephraem, he was a major theologian of the early Eastern (Byzantine) church. His important sermon "On the Last Times, the Antichrist and the End of the World" (ca. 373) declares, "All the saints and elect of God are gathered together before the tribulation, which is to come, and are taken to the Lord, in order that they may not see at any time the confusion which overwhelms the world because of our sins."

In this sermon, Pseudo-Ephraem develops an elaborate biblical eschatology, including a distinction between the rapture and the second coming of Christ. It describes the imminent rapture, followed by a three-and-one-half-year-long Great Tribulation under the rule of Antichrist, followed by the coming of Christ, the defeat of Antichrist, and the eternal state. His view includes a parenthesis between the fulfillment of Daniel's sixty-ninth and seventieth weeks (Daniel 9:24-27). Pseudo-Ephraem describes the rapture as preceding the Tribulation and "imminent or overhanging."

Codex Amiatinus (ca. 690–716)

This significant Latin manuscript from England was commissioned by Abbot Ceolfrid of the monasteries of Jarrow and Wearmouth in Northumberland. In the title to Psalm 22 (Psalm 23 in the Vulgate), the following appears: "Psalm of David, the voice of the Church after being raptured." The Latin phrase *post raptismum* contains a verb from the root *rapio*, meaning "to snatch, or hurry away." This title is not carried over from Jerome's Vulgate and thus is likely the product of the Jarrow monastery. Though not conclusive and still in need of further study, it appears that Codex Amiatinus presents another example of pretribulational thought in the Middle Ages.

Brother Dolcino (d. 1307)

A recent study of the fourteenth-century text *The History of Brother Dolcino,* composed in 1316 by an anonymous source, reveals another important pretribulational passage. As leader of the Apostolic Brethren in northern Italy, Brother Dolcino led his people through times of tremendous papal persecution. One of the group wrote the following astonishing words:

> The Antichrist was coming into this world within the bounds of the said three and a half years; and after he had come, then he [Dolcino] and his followers would be transferred into Paradise, in which are Enoch and Elijah. And in this way they will be preserved unharmed from the persecution of Antichrist.

Thus, the writer of this *History* believed that Dolcino and his followers would be transferred to paradise, expressing this belief with the Latin word *transferrentur,* or "translation," a synonym for *rapture.* Dolcino and his followers retreated into the mountains of northern Italy to await their removal at the appearance of Antichrist.

It is believed that sects like the Albigenses, Lombards, and the Waldenses were attracted to premillennialism, but little is known of the details of their beliefs since the Catholics destroyed their works when they were found.

Francis Gumerlock is the individual who advocates the Brother Dolcino rapture find. Gumerlock (p. 80) wrote, "The Dolicinites held to a pre-tribulation rapture theory similar to that in modern dispensationalism." The significance of these early statements is that they clearly contradict those who have attempted to say that rapture statements did not exist before 1830. Gumerlock (p. 361) believes that this is a pretribulational rapture statement, and he concludes:

> This paragraph from *The History of Brother Dolcino* indicates that in northern Italy in the early fourteenth century a teaching very similar to modern pretribulationalism was being preached. Responding to distressing political and ecclesiastical conditions, Dolcino engaged in detailed speculations about eschatology and believed that the coming of the Antichrist was imminent. He also believed that the means by which God would protect His people from the persecution of the Antichrist would be through a translation of the saints to paradise.

THE REFORMATION ERA

After over 1000 years of suppression, premillennialism began to be revived as a result of at least four factors. First, the Reformers went back to the Bible and apostolic fathers. This exposed them to an orthodox premillennialism. Especially significant was the reappearance of the full text of Irenaeus' *Against Heresies,* including the last five chapters, which espouse a consistent futurism and cast the seventieth week of Daniel into the future.

Second, they repudiated much of the allegorization that dominated medieval hermeneutics by adopting a more literal approach, especially in the area of the grammatical and historical exegesis.

Third, many of the Protestants came into contact with Jews and learned Hebrew. This led them to ask whether passages that speak of national Israel were to be taken historically or allegorized in the tradition of the Middle Ages.

Fourth, beginning in the late fifteenth century, the translation of the Bible into the native tongues of the people for the first time since the days of the early church produced an explosion of Bible reading by the general public. This resulted in a general knowledge of the Bible, especially the Old Testament, for the first time in church history. Since the Old Testament speaks primarily of Israel, it took just a few decades for people to start thinking about Israel and its future. This also contributed to a revival of premillennialism.

Joseph Mede (1586–1638) is considered the father of English premillennialism, having written *Clavis Apocalyptica (Key of the Revelation)* in 1627 in which "He attempted to construct an outline of the Apocalypse based solely upon internal considerations. In this interpretation he advocated premillennialism in such a scholarly way that this work continued to influence eschatological interpretation for centuries" (Clouse, p. 646).

Increase Mather (1639–1723), president of Harvard College (1685), was a significant American Puritan. Concerning the future coming of Christ, he wrote that the saints would "be caught up into the air" beforehand, thereby escaping the final conflagration.

Others began to speak of the rapture. Paul Benware (pp. 197–98) notes:

> French Reformer Peter Jurieu in his book *Approaching Deliverance of the Church* (1687) taught that Christ would come in the air to rapture the saints and return to heaven before the battle of Armageddon. He spoke of a secret rapture prior to His coming in glory and judgment at Armageddon. Philip Doddridge's commentary on the New Testament (1738) and John Gill's commentary on the New Testament (1748) both use the term *rapture* and speak of it as imminent. It is clear that these men believed that this coming will precede Christ's descent to the earth and the time of judgment. The purpose was to preserve believers from the time of judgment. James Macknight (1763) and Thomas Scott (1792) taught that the righteous will be carried to heaven, where they will be secure until the time of judgment is over.

The clearest pre-Darby reference to a pretribulational rapture, if not the most developed, comes from Morgan Edwards (1722–1795), who saw a distinct rapture three and a half years before the start of the millennium. Edwards was a Baptist preacher, evangelist, historian, and educator who founded Rhode Island College (Brown University). During his student days at Bristol Baptist Seminary in England (1742–1744), he wrote an essay on Bible prophecy. The essay was published in Philadelphia in 1788 as *Two Academical Exercises on Subjects Bearing the Following Titles; Millennium, Last-Novelties*. Edwards wrote, "The distance between the first and second resurrection will be somewhat more than a thousand years... because the dead saints will be raised, and the living changed at Christ's 'appearing in the air' (1 Thessalonians 4:17)."

- He believes that more than 1000 years will transpire between resurrections.

- He associates the first resurrection with the rapture of 1 Thessalonians 4:17.

- He associates the meeting of believers with Christ in the air with John 14:2.

- He sees believers disappearing into heaven during the time of the Tribulation.

There is no doubt Morgan Edwards was a pretribulationalist nearly 100 years before Darby.

THE MODERN CHURCH

As futurism began to replace historicism within premillennial circles in the 1820s, the modern proponents of dispensational pretribulationism arrived on the scene. As early as 1818, William Witherby produced a work that had virtually all of the features of modern futurism. John Nelson Darby (1800–1882) claims to have first understood his view of the rapture as the result of personal Bible study during a convalescence stay at his sister's house from December 1826 until January 1827. He is the popularizer of the modern version of the doctrine of a pretribulational rapture.

The doctrine of the rapture spread around the world through the Brethren movement, with which Darby was associated. It appears that either through their writings or personal visits to North America, this version of pretribulationism spread throughout American evangelicals. Two early proponents of the view include Presbyterian James H. Brookes (1830–1897) and Baptist J.R. Graves (1820–1889).

The pretribulational position spread through influence of the Niagara Bible Conference era (New York, 1878–1909) and received wide exposure in the popular prophetic publications *The Truth, Our Hope, The Watchword,* and *Maranatha.* It was also carried forward in William Backstone's book *Jesus is Coming* (1909), C.I. Scofield's popular *Scofield Reference Bible* (1909), and other works. Prominent pretribulational Bible teachers articulated the position on the Bible conference circuit in the nineteenth and twentieth centuries, including Arno C. Gaebelein (1861–1945), A.J. Gordon (1836–1895), James M. Gray (1851–1935), R.A. Torrey (1856–1928), Harry Ironside (1876–1951), John F. Strombeck (1881–1959), Lewis Sperry Chafer (1871–1952), Alva J. McClain (1888–1968), Charles Lee Feinberg (1909–1995), J. Dwight Pentecost, John F. Walvoord (1910–2002), Charles Ryrie, and Tim LaHaye.

During the past 120 years, numerous schools, colleges, and seminaries were established expounding dispensational pretribulationalism. These include Moody Bible Institute, Biola University, Philadelphia Biblical University, Dallas Theological Seminary, Grace Theological Seminary, Liberty University, Bob Jones University, the Master's College and Seminary, and others. Pretribulationalism is also a major doctrinal position in many Baptist, Brethren, Presbyterian, Pentecostal, and independent Bible churches. On the popular front, nothing has done more to promote the pretribulational rapture position than Hal Lindsay's *Late Great Planet Earth* (1970) and Tim LaHaye and Jerry Jenkins' 12-volume Left Behind series (1995–2004).

—THOMAS ICE AND JAMES STITZINGER

BIBLIOGRAPHY

Benware, Paul. *Understanding End Times Prophecy.* Chicago: Moody Press, 1995.

Clouse, Robert G. "Joseph Mede (1586–1638)." In *The New International Dictionary of the Christian Church.* Ed. J.D. Douglas, rev. ed. Grand Rapids: Zondervan, 1978.

Crutchfield, Larry. "The Blessed Hope and the Tribulation in the Apostolic Fathers." In *When the Trumpet Sounds.* Eds. Timothy Demy and Thomas Ice. Eugene, OR: Harvest House Publishers, 1995.

Gumerlock, Francis. "A Rapture Citation in the Fourteenth Century." *Bibliotheca Sacra.* Vol. 159, no. 635 (2002).

Hannah, John. *Our Legacy: The History of Christian Doctrine.* Colorado Springs: NavPress, 2001.

Stitzinger, James. "The Rapture in Twenty Centuries of Biblical Interpretation." *Master's Seminary Journal,* 13.2 (Fall 2002), pp. 149-71.

RECONSTRUCTIONISM

THE CHRISTIAN RECONSTRUCTION movement began in the 1960s within a conservative branch of Reformed theology. Its goal is to reconstruct society in accordance with its understanding of certain New Testament principles and the Mosaic law. The founder of the movement was Rousas John Rushdoony. Prominent contributors include Gary North, Greg Bahnsen, Kenneth L. Gentry, Gary DeMar, and David Chilton.

Rushdoony's Chalcedon Foundation has composed "The Creed of Christian Reconstruction," listing Calvinism, theonomy, presuppositional apologetics, postmillennialism, and dominion theology as the distinctives of reconstructionism. None of these taken individually distinguishes one as a reconstructionist. Theonomy and postmillennialism are the two aspects that set adherents apart from most other traditions of Reformed theology and are most likely to classify them as Christian reconstructionists. People who adopt theonomy and postmillennialism have usually already accepted the other three beliefs.

CALVINISM

A Calvinist is not necessarily a reconstructionist. In fact, some of the strongest criticism of the movement comes from non-reconstructionist Calvinists. But it is hard to imagine a non-Calvinist as a reconstructionist. Calvinism is a broad system of thought, but one aspect of Reformed theology often featured by reconstructionists is covenant theology in general and replacement theology (that is, the church replaces Israel) in particular.

THEONOMY

The one feature that is unique to modern reconstructionism is theonomy (Greek, *theos*, "God," and *nomos*, "law"). For reconstructionists, the application of the Mosaic law will be the key to reconstructing America and eventually the entire world. Greg Bahnsen (p. 34), who coined the term *theonomy*, explains it this way: "The Christian is obligated to keep the whole law of God as a pattern for sanctification…this law is to be enforced by the civil magistrate where and how the stipulations of God so designate." The "whole law of God" includes the "the civil precepts of the Old Testament," which are a universal blueprint of perfect social justice. Bahnsen has argued that to reject his view is to embrace autonomy or antinominianism, a life and world without law. Rushdoony (p. 3) declares, "Man grows in grace as he grows in law-keeping, for the law is the way of sanctification."

Reconstructionists appropriate for the church (seen as the new Israel) the material blessings for obedience—and curses for disobedience—originally promised by God to now-defunct national Israel. Hence the urgent tone of their appeal to the rest of the church: To ignore the reconstructionist system of ethics is to fall miserably short in the area of sanctification. This quenches the Holy Spirit and blunts the intended blessings of God upon His church.

But theonomists believe the curses and blessings are not just for the church. They are for all of society as well. Sanctification therefore requires private obedience to the law, but it also dictates one's relationship to neighbors and the rest of society. This includes active stances on cultural norms and social, economic, and political issues. The theonomic goal for the Christian cannot stop at a godly personal life but must include a godly society where the government is an obedient minister of God's Old Testament justice. According to reconstructionists, this deliberate pursuit is the only way in which a believer can fully love his neighbors and truly obey the Great Commission. Every area of the Christian's personal life and every area of life in the Christian's society must become conformed to the whole law of God.

MOSAIC LAW CODE

Theonomists believe this conformity is demanded by God's sovereign commission of civil magistrates to restrain and punish municipal evil (law-breaking) while upholding public good. They argue that God appoints rulers to be His ministers of justice in society. When civic officials perform their tasks faithfully in deference to His law, citizens should obey them without exception. They are, in many cases, God's ministers of temporal wrath. Since theonomists use the Old Testament law to define standards of good and evil, they view this divine appointment of magistrates as a specific assignment to enforce that very code on a worldwide basis. Bahnsen cites what he terms "religious titles" given to civil rulers—Hebrew and pagan—as proof of their inherent theocratic purpose. He also contends that the pagan nations surrounding Israel were commanded in the Old Testament to obey the Mosaic law.

The reconstructionists' interpretation of man's original purpose also motivates them to institute the Mosaic civil code. They see the command to subdue the earth, given in Genesis 1 to Adam and Eve, as an eternally binding covenant that finds its paramount expression in the Mosaic law. The covenant is not merely with God's designated people, whether Israel or the church; it extends to all men. Only when every magistrate institutes the entirety of God's law, including the harshest Mosaic penal codes, will man be fully restored as God's vice-regent over the earth, exercising the dominion mandate lost by Adam in the Garden of Eden. God's law is "a plan for dominion" under Him, and "God's program for conquest."

The reconstructionist belief that the law of Moses is still in force today, in spite of the many New Testament statements to the contrary (Romans 6:14-15; 7:1-6; 1 Corinthians 9:20-21; 2 Corinthians 3:7-11; Galatians 4:1-7; 5:18; Ephesians 2–3; Hebrews 8:6-7,13; 10:9) cannot be supported from the Bible. Even during the Mosaic era, the law was given exclusively to Israel (Exodus 34:27; Deuteronomy 4:6-8; Psalm 147:19-20) for the purpose of separating and keeping Israel distinct from the nations (Exodus 19:5-6,10,14; Leviticus 19:2; Deuteronomy 7:6; 14:2). The New Testament church-age believer is not antinomian or lawless. Instead, he is under the law of Christ (Romans 8:2; 1 Corinthians 9:21; Galatians 6:2), which consists of hundreds of imperatives found in the New Testament, especially the epistles. Reconstructionists often speak of "biblical law" as if every law ever given by God always applies to all humanity regardless of jurisdictional factors. But the blessing and cursing sections of Deuteronomy 28 and Leviticus 26 are clearly given specifically to Israel. The New Testament teaches a different dynamic of sanctification for the church-age believer.

PRESUPPOSITIONALISM

The presuppositional apologetic of Cornelius Van Til is central to reconstructionism even though Van Til specifically distanced himself from many reconstructionist beliefs and emphases. Van Til's apologetic is a system to defend biblical faith, but reconstructionists believe that it gives them the philosophical basis for maintaining a distinctly biblical approach to every area of life. They believe that Van Til's epistemology should protect them from the inroads of humanistic thought that has so often plagued Christianity in the past. Van Til's thought is seen by many reconstructionists as a development that will enable the Christianization of the whole world as they seek to apply the Bible into every sphere of life without sinking into the pitfalls of humanism as was the lot of the Reformation and Puritan Christians before them. It is supposedly a tool that will facilitate the outworking of theonomy and postmillennialism. Many people who follow Van Til are not reconstructionists, but reconstructionists tend to be his most avid propagators and defenders.

POSTMILLENNIALISM

Conceiving of the Christian reconstruction movement without postmillennialism would be difficult. Without a doubt, postmillennialism provides the motivation and goal that drives the reconstructionist. The Calcedon Foundation vision of postmillennialism is as follows:

> Reconstructionists believe Christ will return to earth only after the Holy Spirit has empowered the church to advance Christ's kingdom in time and history. He has faith that God's purposes to bring all nations, though not every individual, in subjection to Christ cannot fail. The Christian Reconstructionist is not utopian. He does not believe the kingdom will advance quickly or painlessly. He knows that we enter the kingdom through much tribulation. He knows Christians are in the fight for the "long haul." He believes the church may yet be in her infancy. But he believes the Faith will triumph. Under the power of the Spirit of God, it cannot but triumph.

To the reconstructionist, premillennialism is unjustified pessimism. In fact, Rushdoony sees premillennialism as a heresy in the church because it impedes prescribed postmillennial progress. Reconstructionists tend to see contemporary downturns in society as a phase of God's judgment, out of which will emerge a growing remnant who will rebuild Christendom upon the current rubble. They support their view with their understanding that medieval Christendom and the Reformation advanced God's kingdom as they replaced pagan Rome and an apostate Christianity. With the aid of the Holy Spirit, they believe the church is already beginning to turn around, and society will eventually progress toward the millennium.

Such optimistic visions are not pictured in Scripture until after the return of Christ to reign and rule upon earth from Jerusalem. Postmillennialism confuses not only the timing of the millennium but also the agency. God is pleased to use the church to spread the gospel, but the progress of the millennium will not be through a similar agency. Postmillennialism romanticizes about this present age and the millennium because it improperly blends the age to come with this present evil age.

But equating this current age with the millennium ignores the fact that the interaction between groups, individuals, and the environment is so profound that a catastrophic alteration is required for the "perfect" social order. Even total regeneration of the human race would not be far reaching enough to establish the "millennial vision." The physical environment must be totally changed (Romans 8:19-22).

Only premillennial futurism interprets the Bible literally and describes the radical changes that Christ's kingdom will truly bring. Only according to premillennialism does the Bible speak of the future Eden in the same way that it pictures the original Eden in Genesis.

DOMINION

The Chalcedon Foundation Creed says, "The Christian Reconstructionist believes the earth and all its fullness is the Lord's: that every area dominated by sin must be 'reconstructed' in terms of the Bible." Premillennialists believe in man's dominion over creation but not in the same way as the reconstructionist. Premillennialists agree that Genesis 1:26-28 is the basis throughout history for cultural involvement. God gave this ordinance to all humanity. It has not been revoked. But the fall of Genesis 3 has caused man's dominion to be evil. Still, as David notes in Psalm 8:6, "You make him to rule over the works of Your hands" (NASB). Man is currently exercising dominion—an evil dominion that Christ will judge and replace with His rule at His second coming.

Dispensational premillennialism notes three factors that affect the dynamics of evil. First, the influence of regenerated and spiritually active people and the influence of unregenerate people conflict with each other. Second, the restraining ministry of the Spirit during the church age protects basic social structures from total evil domination. Third, Satan exercises some dominion over both the social order and its physical environment. The Spirit's ministry and Satan's influence are relatively stable. The basic variable is the impact of the church.

The unique contributions of premillennialism are the realistic upper and lower limits to satanic domination in the present social order. Regardless of how small the church is in the world, God will keep society from total Satanic control until the rapture. Satan's plans are held in temporary suspension while the human race is given opportunity to trust Christ (2 Peter 3:9). On the other hand, regardless of how many are won to Christ in the world, society will still remain under the influence of a corrupt physical environment. Christ must return to redeem physical creation. Thus, dispensational premillennialism provides a realistic picture of the working of evil in the social order today and explains why the perfect social order awaits supernatural intervention.

Dispensational premillennialists look forward to victory in every sphere of life. In fact, they believe in dominion theology! Just as salvation is accomplished immediately by Christ's work as the author of a whole new race, so will the consummation be immediate, not mediate as reconstructionists preach. Alva J. McClain (p. 531) notes the carryover of many accomplishments during the church age into the kingdom:

> The premillennial philosophy of history makes sense. It lays a Biblical and rational basis for a truly optimistic view

of human history. Furthermore, rightly apprehended, it has practical effects. It says that life here and now, in spite of the tragedy of sin, is nevertheless something worth-while; and therefore all efforts to make it better are also worthwhile. All the true values of human life will be preserved and carried over into the coming kingdom; nothing worthwhile will be lost. Furthermore, we are encouraged in the midst of opposition and reverses by the assurance that help is on the way, help from above, supernatural help—"Give the king thy judgments, O God....In his days shall the righteous flourish...all nations shall call him blessed" (Ps. 72:1,7,17).

The present age is not the kingdom, and the kingdom is yet future, so the biblical premillennialist is watching and waiting for our coming King, going about the tasks He has commissioned us to do while praying, "Come, Lord Jesus!"

INFLUENCE

Reconstructionism has greatly impacted the religious right in the development of their social and political direction. Reconstructionists have often been at the forefront of Christian schools and homeschools. They have also led a revival of postmillennialism and preterism. Reconstructionism has expanded beyond its Reformed beginnings and is making inroads into various aspects of the Charismatic movement. Reconstructionism has spread considerably throughout the English-speaking world and also has a number of British, German, and Dutch converts.

Christian reconstructionism is a deviant movement that attempts to prematurely deploy Christ's kingdom. Thus, some of its errors include replacing Israel with the church, spiritualizing the Bible at key points, putting believers under the Mosaic law, and teaching that Christ's return is not imminent but will occur only after the church has instituted millennial bliss.

—THOMAS ICE

BIBLIOGRAPHY

Bahnsen, Greg L. *Theonomy in Christian Ethics.* Phillipsburg, NJ: Presbyterian & Reformed Publishing Company, 1977.

Gentry, Kenneth L., Jr. *He Shall Have Dominion: A Postmillennial Eschatology.* Tyler, TX: Institute for Christian Economics, 1992.

House, H. Wayne, and Thomas Ice. *Dominion Theology: Blessing or Curse?* Sisters, OR: Multnomah Publishers, 1988.

Ice, Thomas. "Christian Reconstructionism." In *Dictionary of Premillennial Theology.* Ed. Mal Couch. Grand Rapids: Kregel, 1996.

McClain, Alva J. *The Greatness of the Kingdom.* Chicago: Moody Press, 1959.

Rushdoony, Rousas John. *The Institutes of Biblical Law.* Phillipsburg, NJ: Presbyterian & Reformed Publishing Company, 1973.

RESTRAINER

THROUGHOUT THE HISTORY of the church, people have offered various suggestions for the identity of the restrainer in 2 Thessalonians 2:6-9. Some of the church fathers held that the restrainer was the Roman Empire or some other form of law or government. Other people thought it might be the moral restraining influence of the church itself. Many people have held that the witness of the Christians restrains the Antichrist. Some people even see the work of Satan as a form of restraint on the appearance of the evil personality known as the "man of lawlessness" or "the son of destruction" (verse 3).

DETERMINING THE IDENTITY

Rome

Dispensationalists point to the fact that the restrainer must be a unique, divine individual who is capable of holding back the coming of the evil worker who will exercise great power and authority over the religions of the entire world (verse 4). This evil one would certainly be the Antichrist Paul describes in 2 Thessalonians 2:3-9. The Roman Empire would not qualify as the restrainer because it was itself a terror on the earth. Also, the Antichrist will actually rule and control the revived Roman Empire and use it to extend his rebellious authority worldwide. As John F. Walvoord writes, "The Tribulation period is revealed as an era of absolute government in which everything social, religious, and economic is regimented" by the new Roman power (Walvoord, p. 40).

The Church

In regard to the church, Gerald B. Stanton says, "The church is at best an imperfect organism, perfect in standing before God, to be sure, but experientially before men, not always blameless, not always beyond reproach. Similar to human government, the church is being used of God to hinder the full manifestation of the Evil One in this present age, but he who effectively restrains is certainly not the believer himself, but the One who empowers the believer, the indwelling Holy Spirit (John 16:7; 1 Corinthians 6:19). Apart from His presence, neither church nor government would have the ability to hinder the program and power of Satan" (Stanton, p. 61).

CLUES FROM THE GREEK

A closer look at the 2 Thessalonians 2 passage will help answer the question of the identity of the one who restrains. In 2:6 the Greek text is best translated, "and the thing now holding [him] down [or restraining him] you know, so that he [is] to be revealed in his own time." Verse 7 says, "For the mystery of this lawlessness is already working only until the one now holding [him] down [or restraining him] shall get out of the way." The Greek word *katecho* is a compound word formed from *kata* (down) and *echo* (to have, or to hold). From this comes the thought "to hold down or to restrain." *Katecho* can have the meaning "to hold back from action, to keep under control, to deprive of physical liberty, as by shackling, or arresting a criminal." The restrainer then is preventing the Antichrist from breaking out until his appointed time, which would be during or just before the beginning of the Tribulation.

In verse 6, *to katechon* is a neuter present participle, being translated "the thing now holding [him] down [or restraining him]," though in verse 7 the masculine present participle is used, *ho katechon,* and should be translated "the one now holding [him] down [or restraining him]." This grammatical difference would certainly exclude the church because *church* is a feminine word in Greek. Some think the neuter gender in verse 6 refers to the Roman Empire, and the masculine in verse 7 has to do with the Roman emperor. But this view is not plausible. The word "spirit" *(pneuma)* is in the neuter gender, but when referring to the Holy Spirit, the New Testament uses the masculine pronoun. John 14:26 calls the Spirit whom the Father will send in the name of Jesus the *paraclete* (the one called alongside, the counselor). *Paraclete* is a masculine noun, but *Spirit* is a neuter noun. "The purposeful change in grammar emphasizes the personality of the Holy Spirit. There would be no reason to change from the neuter to the masculine unless the Spirit was understood to be a person" (Enns, p. 249).

THE EVIDENCE OF THE SCRIPTURES

The point of the 2 Thessalonians 2 passage seems clear. The man of sin, the Antichrist, cannot come forth until this restraining power gets out of the way. By divine providence, and by all the evidence of the Scriptures, the Holy Spirit characteristically restrains and strives against sin (Genesis 6:3). The Spirit presently abides in the world in a special way in this age through the church. The failure to see the restrainer as the Holy Spirit is another sign of the inadequate understanding of the doctrine of the Holy Spirit in general and His work in relation to the larger providential movements of God in human history (see Walvoord, pp. 44–45).

One objection to naming the Holy Spirit as the restrainer has to do with the phrase at the end of 2 Thessalonians 2:7—"until he is taken out of the way." Many argue that taking away or removing the Spirit of God seems to be an awkward interpretation. But is this what the passage is saying? The Greek word translated "taken" is *genetai* and is an aorist middle subjunctive from *ginomai,* a deponent verb. Such verbs appear in the middle or passive form but are still translated as active, meaning the subject (which, in this case, is the restrainer) is doing the action. "The deponent verb does not denote removal by an outside force but rather a voluntary act on the part of the restrainer" (Hiebert, p. 207). "To be taken out of the way" should better read "to get out of the way" (Lenski, p. 421). The Holy Spirit is going to move out of the way. He is not going to be taken out of the way.

When the Holy Spirit moves aside, or out of the way, "then that lawless one [the Antichrist] will be revealed whom the Lord will slay with the breath of His mouth and bring to an end by the appearance of His coming; that is, the one whose coming is in accord with the activity of Satan, with all power and signs and false wonders" (verses 8-9 NASB). The Antichrist will remain active throughout the seven-year Tribulation, but at the second coming of Christ, he will be slain and thrown into the lake of fire (Revelation 19:20). Known as "the beast" in Revelation, the Antichrist, who required his followers to receive "the mark," will be tormented night and day with those who worshiped him and his image (14:9-11).

While it is probably correct to say the restrainer moves aside at the time of the rapture of the church so that "in his time [the Antichrist] may be revealed" (2 Thessalonians 2:6), the Holy Spirit will still continue the work on earth of bringing people to salvation. While the church is still here, He is active as the power working within the lives of believers.

—MAL COUCH

BIBLIOGRAPHY

Couch, Mal, gen. ed. *Dictionary of Premillennial Theology.* Grand Rapids: Kregel, 1996.

———. *The Hope of Christ's Return.* Chattanooga: AMG Publishers, 2001.

Enns, Paul. *The Moody Handbook of Theology.* Chicago: Moody Press, 1989.

Hiebert, D.E. *1 & 2 Thessalonians.* Chicago: Moody Press, 1992.

Lenski, R.C.H. *The Interpretation of St. Paul's Epistles to the Thessalonians.* Minneapolis: Augsburg Publishing House, 1966.

Stanton, G.B. *Kept from the Hour.* Miami Springs, FL: Schoettle Publishing, 1991.

Walvoord, John F. *The Rapture Question.* Grand Rapids: Zondervan, 1979.

RESURRECTION

ACCORDING TO THE New Testament, the resurrection of Jesus is the center of early Christian belief. First Corinthians 15:14-17 declares that this event is so foundational that the exercise of faith is actually vain or empty if Jesus did not rise from the dead.

Jesus Himself explained that it was the chief sign that He was God's Messenger (Matthew 12:38-42). Peter tells us that our heavenly hope is based on the resurrection (1 Peter 1:3-4). It was the event that marked Jesus as God's Spokesperson (Acts 2:22-24). Paul preached that the resurrection was the evidence indicating that everyone should repent and turn to Jesus (Acts 17:30-31). And significantly, the believer's resurrection is repeatedly based on Jesus' rising from the dead (1 Corinthians 6:14; Philippians 3:21; 1 John 3:2).

HISTORICAL EVIDENCES FOR THE RESURRECTION OF JESUS

We will first look at eight arguments that strongly support Jesus' resurrection. The first four are taken from Paul's writings. The remaining four are drawn from other New Testament sources.

1. Recent scholars agree that the apostle Paul is the major witness to Jesus' resurrection appearances. Having been an ardent opponent of Christianity (Galatians 1:13-14; 1 Corinthians 15:9; Philippians 3:4-7), Paul explains that his unbelief ended when he saw the risen Jesus (1 Corinthians 9:1; 15:8; Galatians 1:16).

Converted from Judaism to become one of Christianity's greatest scholars, Paul is certainly an excellent witness to the resurrected Jesus.

2. But as crucial as Paul's own eyewitness is, he contributes even more than his experience. In 1 Corinthians 15:3-7 Paul records a very ancient tradition that is actually pre-Pauline. It succinctly reports the gospel content of the early church: Christ died for our sin, was buried, was raised from the dead, and afterward appeared to many witnesses, both individually and in groups.

Paul specifically explains that the most important part of his message consisted of this gospel and that he was passing it on just as he had received it from others (15:3). Many textual indications show that these words were not originally Paul's. Many think that Paul first heard this report when he made his trip to Jerusalem in approximately A.D. 35, just three years after his conversion. There he spent time with Peter and James the brother of Jesus (Galatians 1:18-19). Speaking about the gospel (Galatians 1:11–2:10), Paul's language in Galatians 1:18 indicates that he was seeking information from these apostles. So it seems that Paul received an exceptionally early report about Jesus' resurrection appearances to others, providing additional evidence for these events.

3. But Paul did not stop after just a single trip to check out this apostolic testimony. He was so concerned about the truth of the gospel that he went back to Jerusalem 14 years later (Galatians 2:1-10). He explains that he did so in order to be absolutely sure that his message was not false (2:2). This time not only Peter and James were present, but so was John the apostle, and together they confirmed Paul's message (Galatians 2:9-10). Here we have an example of Paul doing some ancient research, consulting the three key Christian leaders in the early church. Are there four witnesses whose early testimony to the resurrection we would rather have? That Paul's gospel preaching was approved provides an incredible insight into the earliest Christian message.

4. But Paul adds still more confirmation. Not only did the other key apostles approve his gospel preaching, but Paul explains that he was well aware of their teaching on the resurrection appearances as well. They taught the same truth that he did (1 Corinthians 15:11). Together, they preached the message that they were witnesses of Jesus' appearances (15:12,15).

5. In addition to Paul's valuable eyewitness testimony, we have several other major evidences for Jesus' resurrection. One is that the sources indicate that Jesus' tomb was found empty, lending some credibility to the disciples' resurrection claim. There are many arguments supporting the fact of the empty tomb.

One strong argument is the unanimous agreement that women were the earliest witnesses. This report was potentially embarrassing, due to the widespread prejudice against the testimony of women, so it hardly would have been invented by the early Christians. Further, Jerusalem is the last place for the early apostolic preaching of the resurrection to begin unless the tomb was in fact empty, for a closed or occupied tomb would have been disastrous evidence against the apostles! Moreover, Paul's early report in 1 Corinthians 15:3-4 that Jesus died, was buried, and rose again implies that Jesus' place of burial had been vacated.

6. James, the brother of Jesus, was a skeptical unbeliever during Jesus' ministry (Mark 3:21-35; John 7:5). Some family members apparently even thought that Jesus was insane (Mark 3:21)! Just a short time later, however, James is the leader of the Jerusalem church (Acts 15:13-21; Galatians 1:18-19; 2:1-10). The intervening event, according to the pre-Pauline statement in 1 Corinthians 15:7, is that James witnessed a resurrection appearance of Jesus.

7. The disciples' convictions that they had seen the risen Jesus resulted in their radical transformation. They were more than willing to die for this certainty. Their metamorphosis

is unexplainable apart from an actual resurrection.

8. Many scholars believe that the book of Acts and many other portions of the New Testament contain early traditions like the one in 1 Corinthians 15. These succinct snippets of early preaching are located in a number of the Acts sermons. Key examples are found in 1:21-22; 2:22-36; 3:13-16; 4:8-10; 5:29-32; 10:39-43; 13:28-31; 17:1-3,30-31. Each statement centers on the gospel message of the death and resurrection of Jesus and is often dated very early.

Because of these data, almost all recent scholars conclude that Jesus' disciples truly believed they had seen Jesus alive again after His death by crucifixion. Together, they add up to a complementary set of considerations virtually unparalleled in ancient documents. From an array of angles, the disciples were deluged with reasons that convinced them that Jesus was alive and that they had seen Him.

THE NATURE OF JESUS' RESURRECTION BODY

While acknowledging Jesus' resurrection from the dead, some have questioned the *nature* of His new existence. One popular view is that Jesus was resurrected but in a non-physical body. This view says He appeared to His followers as a being of light, teaching a message of God's kingdom, hope, and a mission to the world.

Supporters of the non-bodily resurrection view often say that Paul took this position. They refer to 1 Corinthians 15:44, where Paul asserts that believers will be raised in a "spiritual body." Another favorite "proof text" is 1 Corinthians 15:50, where the apostle explains that "flesh and blood" cannot enter God's kingdom. If Paul thought that the believer is raised in a non-physical body, then, arguing backward, Jesus must have been raised similarly. Further, in the three Acts accounts of Paul's conversion (Acts 9:1-9; 22:6-11; 26:12-18), we are never told that Paul actually saw Jesus' physical body.

In response to this view, we will list here eight reasons for holding to the view that Jesus' resurrection body was literal and physical. Many of these reasons show that Paul affirmed a literal, bodily resurrection of Jesus, for those who hold to the opposing view think that this apostle thought that Jesus' resurrection was less than physical.

1. Recently, N.T. Wright (see the bibliography of this article) has argued very persuasively and at great length that among *both* pagans and Jews in the ancient Mediterranean world, the word *resurrection* almost always meant that the *body* would be raised. Even those who rejected the doctrine still used this definition for the term. Conversely, if they spoke about one's soul or spirit being glorified or living after death, they did not use the word *resurrection*.

2. Further, while some Jews about the time of Jesus did embrace other views regarding the afterlife (Matthew 22:23), the predominant first-century A.D. Jewish position was also a bodily resurrection of the dead. For example, the Pharisees held this view (Acts 23:8). The emphasis on a new life for the physical body was predominant.

3. The Gospels clearly embrace the view that although there were some changes, Jesus was raised in His own body. For examples, His resurrection body contained the scars from His crucifixion (Luke 24:39-40; John 20:20,25-27), He offered Himself for physical inspection (Luke 24:38-43; John 20:27), and He was actually touched (Matthew 28:9; see also John 20:17).

4. Paul classified himself with the predominant Jewish view, indicating that he had been a Pharisee (Philippians 3:4-6). According to Acts, Paul still identified himself as a Pharisee and specifically affirmed their view of bodily resurrection even after his conversion, causing the Pharisees who were present to agree with him, while the Sadducees disagreed (23:6-9). Moreover, this is probably why the Greeks in Athens sneered at Paul's resurrection message (Acts 17:31-32). They most likely believed that only the soul was immortal.

5. In agreement with the Gospel accounts, Paul also affirmed that Jesus appeared to groups of people (1 Corinthians 15:5-7; see Acts 13:30-31). This favors the view that Paul thought that Jesus had been raised bodily. After all, it would seem less likely that Paul meant that Jesus' glorified spirit was seen by over 500 people at once.

6. Paul's anthropology dictates that Jesus' body was raised from the dead. He used a Greek term in Philippians 3:11 *(exanastasin)* that literally means that Jesus was raised "out from among the dead ones" (see also 1 Corinthians 15:12). The implication here is that the body that was buried in the grave was the same one that was raised, although Paul clearly teaches that the body will be changed, too (1 Corinthians 15:35-55). Further, Christians will have resurrection bodies like Jesus' glorious body (Philippians 3:20-21). It is our mortal bodies that will be enlivened (Romans 8:11).

7. Paul's sociology also indicates his view that the body will be raised. The apostle always speaks of the resurrection of the dead in the plural—the dead ones. He again agrees here with the good Jewish theology (see John 11:23-24) that all believers will be raised corporately. Additionally, the earth will be renewed (Romans 8:18-23) and will be inhabited by our resurrected bodies. A corporate resurrection to occupy a new earth does not seem to apply to spirits!

8. Last, there are many strong evidences for the empty tomb. This alone would render very unlikely any view besides a bodily resurrection, for the point is that the tomb was found empty precisely because something happened to Jesus' *body*. We have said that Paul implies this, too, when he repeats the early tradition that the body that was placed into the tomb came out again (1 Corinthians 15:3-5).

What about the texts that cause some to think that Paul taught that Jesus was raised as a glorified spirit? In 1 Corinthians 15:44, Paul refers to the resurrection body as a "spiritual body." That's because it is imperishable, glo-

rious, and powerful, as he just said (15:42-43). It is changed. But we need to notice that it is still a spiritual *body*, not a spirit, which Paul could easily have said if he had meant the latter. We have to do justice to the terms "spiritual" and "body." In the same context, 15:12 is a strong reason for saying this.

Similarly, in 1 Corinthians 15:50, "flesh and blood" only rules out our *present* bodies from occupying God's kingdom. When this phrase is used elsewhere in the New Testament (Matthew 16:17; Ephesians 6:12), it refers to mortal humans. But we will not be mortal in eternity, but immortal, as Paul explains immediately in the second half of the verse and directly afterward (1 Corinthians 15:50-57).

In the Acts accounts of Paul's conversion, no description of Jesus is provided. But we must remember that Luke saw no discrepancy here, for he is the same author who taught that Jesus appeared bodily, ate food, and could be touched by His disciples (Luke 24:36-43). Luke also reports that Paul taught that Jesus was buried in a tomb and then raised from the dead (Acts 13:29-30), strongly implying that something happened to His *body*. Especially when combined with Paul's own teaching on the nature of Jesus' resurrection body, as well as that of the other Gospels, we must conclude that Jesus appeared bodily.

THE RESURRECTION OF BELIEVERS

We have concluded so far that Jesus was raised from the dead and that He appeared in a real body. What does that say to the prospect of believers being raised likewise?

Jesus' central message was clearly the reality of the kingdom of God, both in its present manifestation (Matthew 13:44-45; Mark 1:14-15) as well as its future fulfillment (Matthew 5:3-12; 6:10,33). Its present reality was inaugurated by the presence and preaching of Jesus (Luke 11:20; 17:20-21), while its future aspect included the offer of eternal life under God's rule (Matthew 25:31-46). The entrance requirements for the kingdom were based on an individual's response to Jesus (Mark 10:23-31; Luke 14:25-35; John 3:3,15-16). When Jesus stated His chief ministry purpose, He asserted that He had come to provide a path of salvation (Mark 2:17; 10:45; Luke 19:10).

Jesus' resurrection from the dead would have confirmed this central message above all else. The verification comes from at least two angles. First, since the resurrection requires God's action, we can only understand this event as God's confirmation that Jesus' central message was true. In other words, we know that Jesus' teachings concerning the kingdom are true because God would not have raised Jesus from the dead if He was mistaken, especially in this most crucial teaching.

Second, Jesus' resurrection, by its very nature, shows that eternal life is a reality. This event points beyond itself to another world—to God's future kingdom.

The New Testament makes a variety of similar points. Jesus taught that it was precisely because He would live after His death that His followers would also (John 14:19). Even death will not keep believers from eternal life, since Jesus is the resurrection (John 11:23-27). After He was raised from the dead, He taught His disciples that everything had to happen so that the gospel could be proclaimed around the world (Luke 24:46-49). There was a connection between Jesus' resurrection and His teaching of God's kingdom (Acts 1:3). This leads to Jesus' command to take His message to everyone (1:8).

So when the disciples obeyed Jesus and began preaching, they also proclaimed this connection between His resurrection and the resurrection of believers (Acts 4:2). The resurrection became their chief message (4:33). As Peter proclaimed later, it was Jesus' resurrection that secured heaven for believers, and this inheritance could never be diminished or taken away (1 Peter 1:3-4).

What a blessed proclamation! Because Jesus was raised, believers will be, too, and heaven will be the end result! Over a dozen times, the New Testament writers connect Jesus' resurrection to the resurrection of believers. For example, the same God who raised Jesus will also raise believers from the dead (1 Corinthians 6:14; 2 Corinthians 4:14; 1 Thessalonians 4:14). Jesus' resurrection body is the pattern for the future resurrection of the dead (1 Corinthians 15:44-57). We will be given glorious bodies like the one that Jesus had (Philippians 3:21; 1 John 3:2). Like Him, we will never die (1 Corinthians 15:42-44,53-57).

Jesus' resurrection body provides some important information related to the believer's eternal state. Incredibly, Jesus even taught that the kingdom of God also had a present aspect and that both spiritual blessings as well as eternal life begin now, in this earthly realm. Paul explains that Christians should live with a view toward eternity, because we are already citizens of heaven (Philippians 3:20)! These events are tied together so closely that all of the very strong historical evidence for Jesus' resurrection also evidences the believer's resurrection.

The early eyewitnesses who personally saw the risen Jesus came to realize this. When they saw Jesus, they witnessed more than a Man returning from the dead, as miraculous and reassuring as that must have been. But this Man had returned in an eternal body that would never again die. The early Christians learned that they would likewise be raised. The significance of this truth was too glorious to miss. In a very special sense, whether or not they realized it at the time, when they saw Jesus, they stared in the face of walking, talking, eternal life. To see the resurrected Jesus with their own eyes was to observe the reality of the afterlife; for 40 days they witnessed a little glimpse of heaven. Light from heaven had broken in and focused upon them. Paul would find later, when he saw Jesus, that this was literally true. No wonder their resurrection experience transformed their lives forever!

THE IMPACT OF CHRIST'S RESURRECTION ON BELIEVERS

The New Testament hope moves from the resurrected Jesus, alive in His immortal body, to the resurrection and immortality of believers. To be sure of the former is to have a solid basis for the latter. The resurrection of Jesus is enmeshed firmly in past history. Our resurrection constitutes our future, one that is confirmed.

For the earliest Christians, this truth was life-transforming. Similarly, the reality of heaven needs to be woven into our present lives. Both Jesus and the New Testament writers taught that a heavenly perspective should be applied to our daily beliefs, actions, and problems.

Our thoughts should center on heavenly truths rather than earthly ones (Colossians 3:1-3). Eternity should reorient our daily worries (Matthew 6:19-34) and redirect our worst fears (Matthew 10:28). Everlasting life means that we should love others as we do ourselves (Luke 10:25-37). It should give us a heavenly viewpoint on our possessions (Matthew 16:26) and help us determine how to spend our money (1 Timothy 6:17-19). It should even provide a unique perspective on death and dying (2 Corinthians 4:7–5:10). After all, the death of a saint is precious to God (Psalm 116:15).

—GARY R. HABERMAS

BIBLIOGRAPHY

Craig, William Lane. *The Son Rises: The Historical Evidence for the Resurrection of Jesus.* Chicago: Moody Press, 1981.

Davis, Stephen T. *Risen Indeed: Making Sense of the Resurrection.* Grand Rapids: Eerdmans Publishing Company, 1993.

Habermas, Gary R. *The Resurrection: Heart of New Testament Doctrine.* Joplin, MO: College Press, 2000.

——. *The Resurrection: Heart of the Christian Life.* Joplin, MO: College Press, 2000.

——. *The Risen Jesus and Future Hope.* Lanham, MD: Rowman and Littlefield, Publishers, 2003.

Longenecker, Richard N., ed. *Life in the Face of Death: The Resurrection Message of the New Testament.* Grand Rapids: Eerdmans Publishing Company, 1998.

Wright, N.T. *The Resurrection of the Son of God.* Vol. 3 of *Christian Origins and the Question of God.* Minneapolis: Fortress Press, 2003.

RESURRECTIONS

PHYSICAL DEATH DOES NOT end human existence. Jesus said, "Because I live, you will live also" (John 14:19 NASB). Without a doubt, one of the most comforting and reassuring parts of God's Word is the doctrine of the resurrection. Scripture describes a series of resurrections, and in each case one must ask who is being resurrected and when. Revelation 20:5 includes in "the first resurrection" the faithful martyrs who gave their lives for Christ during the Tribulation. The context implies that the second resurrection will be for unbelievers at the end of history. The "first resurrection" is thus a qualitative distinction that refers to the resurrection of believers. The "second resurrection" is likewise a qualitative description referring to the resurrection of the unsaved.

THE FIRST RESURRECTION

The first resurrection occurs at various times throughout history and the future.

The Savior. The resurrection of Jesus becomes the pattern and firstfruits for the first resurrection (Romans 6:8; 1 Corinthians 15:20,23; Colossians 1:18; Revelation 1:18).

Selected Old Testament Saints. At the death of Jesus, the tombs of selected Old Testament believers were opened. Then, after the resurrection of Jesus, these people appeared in the city to many people as a confirming sign that Jesus was the Messiah (Matthew 27:50-53).

The Saved Who Have Died. The redeemed of the Lord who will become the bride of Christ (2 Corinthians 11:2; Ephesians 5:23-32; Revelation 22:17) and have fallen asleep "in Christ" are resurrected at the rapture of the church. Paul says, "We shall not all sleep" (1 Corinthians 15:51), meaning that some will die, and those who do will be raised suddenly, silently, and selectively. We are not to grieve for our saved loved ones who have gone on to heaven before us, because we are confident they will be resurrected (1 Thessalonians 4:13-18).

The Two Witnesses. Revelation 11 recounts how two servants of the Lord will be witnesses in Jerusalem during the first half of the Tribulation. These two will ultimately be killed and resurrected for the entire world to see just three-and-one-half days later (Revelation 11:9-11).

Tribulation Martyrs. Revelation 20:4-6 identifies the martyred dead of the Tribulation as those who will be resurrected at the second coming of Christ in order to reign with Him for 1000 years.

Old Testament Saints. Daniel 12:1-2 makes it clear that these saints will be resurrected at the close of the Tribulation period in order to reign with Messiah in His kingdom.

THE SECOND RESURRECTION

The final resurrection of the unsaved occurs at the end of history (following the millennium). The lost of all ages will be collected from the place of the dead (hades) and brought before the Great White Throne (Revelation 20:11-15), where they will be condemned to spend eternity in the lake of fire.

This second resurrection is also taught in John 5:29 and involves only the unredeemed of all ages. The basis of their judgment is their rejection of God and of Christ.

In John's vision of the second resurrection (Revelation 20:12), the unredeemed are standing before the throne, an indication that they are about to receive judgment. It is validation of the principle found in Hebrews 9:27: "It is appointed for men to die once and after this comes judgment" (NASB). According to John, the unbelievers are judged according to their works. This is in accordance also with Matthew 25:31-46, where the nations are judged according to their works. In Revelation 20, it is not belief or unbelief that is apparently at issue, for that is already determined. Rather, it is the degree of punishment.

Revelation 20:13 states that the dead from the sea will also be raised. This emphasizes that it is not only those who received a normal burial in the grave, but all of the dead—regardless of the condition of their bodies—who will be resurrected. It is a reaffirmation of the fact of a universal resurrection of the unredeemed. The second resurrection includes no redeemed individuals—all are unsaved and destined for eternal punishment. This is a vivid contrast to the redeemed of the first resurrection, who will receive immortal and incorruptible bodies like the resurrection body of Jesus Christ. The unsaved receive no such body, but rather, a body suited for eternal punishment. Even though they are part of a group, every individual will be judged and made subject to the righteousness of God.

—GARY FRAZIER AND
TIMOTHY J. DEMY

BIBLIOGRAPHY

Fruchtenbaum, Arnold G. *The Footsteps of the Messiah.* Rev. ed. Tustin, CA: Ariel Ministries, 2003.

Habermas, Gary R. *The Resurrection: Heart of New Testament Doctrine.* Joplin, MO: College Press, 2000.

Hitchcock, Mark. *101 Answers to the Most Asked Questions about the End Times.* Sisters, OR: Multnomah Publishers, 2001.

Longenecker, Richard N., ed. *Life in the Face of Death: The Resurrection Message of the New Testament.* Grand Rapids: Eerdmans Publishing Company, 1998.

Walvoord, John F. *Major Bible Prophecies: 37 Crucial Prophecies That Affect You Today.* Grand Rapids: Zondervan, 1991.

———. *The Revelation of Jesus Christ: A Commentary.* Chicago: Moody Press, 1966.

REVELATION, BOOK OF

THE BOOK OF REVELATION (or the Apocalypse) primarily contains prophecies concerning the future. Revelation is a significant portion of biblical prophecy. It depicts the culmination of prophecies begun in the Old Testament and continued in the New Testament. Whereas Genesis tells of the creation of the heavens and the earth, Revelation foretells the end of the present heavens and earth and the beginning of the new heavens and the new earth.

TITLE OF THE BOOK

The apostle John wrote the book sometime around A.D. 95 while in exile on the small Mediterranean island of Patmos off the coast of Asia Minor. The resurrected Jesus appeared to him there and revealed information about the future. The very first word in the Greek text of Revelation, *apokalupsis* ("unveiling" or "uncovering"), refers to the revelation that God gave to Jesus to give to John. John's commission was to deliver this information to messengers from seven churches of the nearby

Roman province of Asia. The province was located in the western portion of modern-day Turkey.

SUBJECT OF THE BOOK

The subject of the book of Revelation includes "things which must shortly take place" (1:1 NKJV). At a key point in the last decade of the first century A.D., God saw fit to give John—through Jesus—the Bible's fullest revelation of what is to come in the history of the world.

Revelation 1:7, the book's theme verse, contains the main event of God's revelation for the future: "Behold, He is coming with the clouds, and every eye will see Him, even they who pierced Him; and all the tribes of the earth will mourn over Him. Even so, Amen." The return of Jesus Christ and all the events accompanying His return comprise the subject. He will be visible to all earth's inhabitants, many of whom will mourn over the judgment He will bring against sinful mankind.

OUTLINE OF THE BOOK

When instructing John to write the book, Jesus appeared to him in a glorified state (1:12-16) and gave him an outline of the prophecy to come (1:19). It included the vision of Jesus he had just seen, a message to each of seven churches in Asia (Revelation 2–3), and events that will transpire on earth after the faithful in the churches are taken away to heaven at the rapture (Revelation 4–22).

John's Initial Vision of Jesus (Chapter 1)

After issuing a greeting of grace and peace from God the Father, God the Holy Spirit, and God the Son (1:4-6), John tells of his initial vision of Jesus Christ, who commissioned him to write the Revelation (1:9-20). Overwhelmed at what he saw, he fell at the feet of Jesus as though he were dead. First, he saw seven golden lampstands, later identified as symbols of the seven churches to be addressed in Revelation 2–3. Then he saw in the middle of the lampstands a human form that reminded him of a messianic prophecy (Daniel 7:13).

The white head and hair in the vision represent the eternal preexistence of Christ as they do that of the Father in Daniel 7:9. Eyes like a flame of fire, derived from Daniel 10:6, speak of Christ's penetrating intelligence and His righteous wrath. The feet like burnished bronze emphasize Christ's purity as He moves among the seven churches (see Ezekiel 1:13,27; Daniel 10:6). The voice like the sound of many waters speaks of divine authority (Ezekiel 43:2). The seven stars—identified as the messengers of the seven churches—speak of His absolute authority over those messengers. The sharp two-edged sword proceeding from His mouth, an image taken from Isaiah 11:4, pictures a warrior defeating His enemies in battle and pronouncing His sentence of judgment upon them. "His face was like the sun shining in its strength" speaks of the overwhelming nature of the glory of the ascended Christ that John was privileged to witness not only here but also on the Mount of Transfiguration.

Messages to the Seven Churches (Chapters 2–3)

Two themes recur in Jesus' messages to the churches: warning and encouragement. Chapters 2 and 3 advise the churches about needed adjustments in their lives in view of the coming outpouring of God's wrath.

Each letter follows approximately the same pattern: (1) an address, (2) attributes of Christ, (3) Christ's knowledge about the people, (4) the state of the church, (5) a promise of Christ's coming, (6) a universal command to *hear,* and (7) a promise to the overcomer. The last four messages reverse the order of parts (6) and (7).

Ephesus, the church of loveless orthodoxy (2:1-7). Christ commends the Ephesian church for its stand for orthodox doctrine, but He reprimands the church for leaving its first love.

Smyrna, the church of martyrdom (2:8-11). The message to Smyrna is the only one of the seven that contains no promise of Christ's coming. This was a persecuted church, and the Lord's word to this church was, "Be faithful until death, and I will give you the crown of life."

Pergamum, the church of indiscriminate toleration (2:12-17). Christ commended the church at Pergamum for holding fast His name and not denying His faith, but He expressed displeasure with their toleration of those who hold to false teaching. He commanded them to repent of their indiscriminate tolerance or face the consequences of His judgment.

Thyatira, the church of compromise (2:18-29). Christ found the deeds, love, faith, service, and perseverance of this church worthy of commendation. Also, He complimented the growth of their good deeds. He had serious problems, however, with their toleration of a false prophetess who taught her followers to commit immorality and eat things sacrificed to idols.

Sardis, the church of complacency (3:1-6). Sardis was a church of false profession: Christ said, "You have a name that you are alive, but you are dead." They were complacent and about to die. They needed to wake up and repent. Their failure to do so would result in Christ's imminent judgment.

Philadelphia, the church of promised deliverance (3:7-13). Christ had nothing negative to say about the church at Philadelphia, just as He had no criticisms for the church at Smyrna. As a reward for this church's faithfulness, Christ promised the faithful that they will be kept from (Greek, *ek,* "out of") the imminent hour of trial that would overtake the rest of the world as part of His second advent.

Laodicea, the church of lukewarmness (3:14-22). Christ's charge against this church was that of being neither cold nor hot, a condition that He found nauseating. Christ urged them to turn to Him to remedy their serious spiritual deficiencies, repent in response to His reproof, and restore their fellowship with Him.

Events on Earth During and After the Tribulation (Chapters 4–22)

Jesus devotes the bulk of this revelation to describing judgments coming to an unrepentant world because of its rebellion against God. John is called up to heaven in a picture reminiscent of the rapture (4:1). There the prophet encounters the Father seated on His throne, the Lamb of God, and a seven-sealed book.

Seal Judgments

John sees the breaking of the first four seals (6:1-8) portrayed as a drama before his eyes. First came four different-colored horses with riders depicting peaceful conquest of the world, warfare and bloodshed, widespread famine, and death to one-quarter of the earth's population.

Then, with the opening of the fifth seal (6:9-11), John witnesses martyred saints in heaven praying for God to avenge their blood by punishing the people responsible for their deaths. The prayers of those saints will play a significant role in God's judgments of the rebellious world in the Great Tribulation.

Next, the sixth seal reveals various cosmic and terrestrial disturbances that signal unmistakably to earth's inhabitants that the seal judgments have initiated the predicted wrath of God against rebellious humanity (6:12-17). In His Olivet Discourse, Jesus had also predicted such disturbances when He spoke of coming earthquakes and cosmic signs (Matthew 24:7; Mark 13:8; Luke 21:11).

The Seventh Seal and the First Six Trumpets

The breaking of the seventh seal (8:1) results in the sounding of seven trumpets (8:7–11:15), seven physical judgments in addition to and more severe than those of the first six seals. The first trumpet predicts the burning up of a third of earth's vegetation. This judgment will be similar to the destruction of vegetation against the Egyptians in Moses' day (Exodus 9:25).

The sounding of the second trumpet brings a vision of the destruction of a third of sea life. The third trumpet signals an object falling from heaven that poisons a third of earth's fresh water. The fourth trumpet brings a darkening of a third of the heavenly bodies—the sun, moon, and stars. At this point in the trumpet series, an eagle flying in mid heaven brings a threefold "woe" to earth's inhabitants, a warning of the increased severity of judgment in the three remaining trumpets.

The fifth trumpet introduces a pain-inflicting demonic locust plague. The sixth trumpet brings death to a third of earth's inhabitants through another demonic visitation. A command from heaven charges the sixth angel to loose the four angels bound at the river Euphrates. When he does this, John sees horses whose riders have breastplates of fire and hyacinth and brimstone. These plagues kill one-third of all human beings. Still, men refuse to repent in spite of the plagues from which they suffer so severely.

An Interlude and the Seventh Trumpet

John gives additional data in 10:1–11:14. This section also serves as an introduction to the seventh trumpet. The first part of the preparation for the last trumpet is an announcement of "no more delay" in chapter 10. He connects fulfillment of the mystery of God with the sounding of the seventh trumpet (10:7).

The second part of seventh-trumpet preparation is the measurement of the Jerusalem Temple and its worshipers (11:1-14). The worshipers will be a godly remnant in Israel who will worship God in the rebuilt Temple, some of whom will come to faith in Christ through the ministry of the two witnesses described in 11:3-12. The two witnesses will be active in Jerusalem during the final 42 months (11:2) or 1260 days (11:3) before Christ's return. The two—probably Moses and Elijah—face the wrath of the beast from the abyss and eventually suffer martyrdom, but their visible resurrection results in a great revival in the city (11:13).

With the sounding of the seventh trumpet come two heavenly songs. Both songs anticipate a time at the conclusion of the trumpet series when God will have assumed active rule over the world.

Preparation for the Seven Bowls

Prior to describing the bowls themselves, John sees visions that prepare the way for the bowls (12:1–14:20). He first sees a vision of the woman, the male-child, and the dragon (chapter 12). The dragon—later identified as

Satan—is full of enmity against the male-child, the Messiah. The woman is a corporate symbol for ethnic Israel, who gave birth to the Messiah. The faithful remnant of the nation receives protection from the dragon's onslaught during the last half of the Tribulation period. Michael and his angels expel the dragon from heaven, and the dragon vents his wrath against the faithful remnant.

The next scene in preparation for the seven bowls takes John to a seaside where he sees "a beast coming up out of the sea." The scene portrays the beast's character and some of the beast's exploits (13:1-10). The dragon gave the beast his power, throne, and great authority, so the beast's activities are simply a continuation of the dragon's attempt to harm the rest of the woman's offspring mentioned in the previous chapter. This beast is obviously the Antichrist.

John then sees another beast coming up out of the earth whose task is to support the first beast (13:11-18). This second beast is the religious assistant of the first beast, who is the end-time false Christ. The role of the second beast is to capture all the world's organized religions and put them into the service of the first beast. Later, this second beast is identified as the False Prophet.

The next portion in preparation for John's description of the seven bowls comes as four climactic announcements (14:6-18). The first announcement is made by an angel proclaiming the eternal gospel, telling earth's inhabitants to fear God and give Him glory in order to escape the time of His judgment, which has now come. The second announcement tells of the fall of Babylon the Great as punishment for her excessive expressions of unfaithfulness to God. The third announcement describes the eternal torment of those who choose to worship the beast instead of God and His Son, Jesus. The fourth announcement pronounces blessing on those who remain faithful to the Lord.

The Seven Bowls

At this point John encounters seven new angels whose responsibility is to dispense the seven bowl judgments, also known as the seven last plagues (15:1). Revelation 15 is a sort of a celestial interlude to introduce the pouring out of the seven bowls of divine wrath in Revelation 16.

The seven angels are dispatched on their misery-inflicting mission. They pour out their bowls in rapid sequence, the first six bowls inflicting ugly and painful sores, bringing death to all sea life, transforming all fresh water into blood, scorching all people through the sun's intensity, darkening the beast's kingdom, and preparing for the doom of earth's kings (16:2-16). The seventh bowl is climactic and brings the destruction of Babylon (16:17-21).

John views seven scenes that continue to describe the seventh bowl's contents: (1) the second coming of Christ (19:11-16), (2) slaughter of Christ's human opponents (19:17-21), (3) Satan's imprisonment (20:1-3), (4) the millennial kingdom (20:4-10), (5) Satan's release and final defeat (20:4-10), (6) the Great White Throne (20:11-15), and (7) the introduction of the new Jerusalem (21:1-8). A detailed description of the new Jerusalem follows (21:9–22:5).

John's prophecy then describes the future millennial kingdom on earth, Satan's first imprisonment, and his assignment to the lake of fire. The sketch of the new Jerusalem presents a positive picture of existence in that city, but it also reflects the judgment of God against the unfaithful by mentioning their exclusion from that city (see 21:8,27; 22:15).

Epilogue (Chapter 22)

Revelation closes with an epilogue (22:6-21) that emphasizes three features already prominent earlier in the book. The three emphases are a confirmation of the genuineness of the prophecy (22:6-9,16,18-19), the imminence of Jesus' return (22:6-7,10,12,20), and an invitation to enter the new Jerusalem (22:11,14,17).

—ROBERT L. THOMAS

BIBLIOGRAPHY

Hindson, Ed. *The Book of Revelation*. Chattanooga: AMG Publishing, 2002.

LaHaye, Tim. *Revelation Unveiled*. Grand Rapids: Zondervan, 1999.

Thomas, Robert L. *Revelation 1–7: An Exegetical Commentary*. Chicago: Moody Press, 1992.

———. *Revelation 8–22: An Exegetical Commentary*. Chicago: Moody Press, 1995.

Walvoord, John F. *The Revelation of Jesus Christ*. Chicago: Moody Press, 1966.

REVELATION, DATE OF

THE MAJORITY OF SCHOLARS choose between two dates for the composition of Revelation: the early or Neronic date, during the reign of Nero (A.D. 64–67) and the late or Domitianic date, during the reign of Domitian (A.D. 95). To determine which of these views is correct, we must consider the external evidence (evidence from outside the book of Revelation) and the internal evidence (evidence from within the book of Revelation itself).

Both lines of evidence point to the late or Domitianic date (A.D. 95) as the correct view.

SUMMARY OF THE EXTERNAL EVIDENCE

WITNESSES FOR THE DOMITIANIC DATE (A.D. 95)	WITNESSES FOR THE NERONIC DATE (A.D. 64–67)
Hegesippus (A.D. 150)	
Irenaeus (A.D. 180)	
Victorinus (C. 300)	
Eusebius (C. 300)	
Jerome (C. 400)	
Sulpicius Severus (C. 400)	
The Acts of John (C. 650)	
Primasius (C. 540)	Syriac Version of NT (550)
Orosius (C. 600)	
Andreas (C. 600)	
Venerable Bede (C. 700)	
	Arethas (C. 900)
	Theophylact (d. 1107)

EXTERNAL EVIDENCE

Placing the external evidence side by side, we see that the first clear, accepted, unambiguous witness to the Neronic date is a one-line subscription in the Syriac translation of the New Testament in A.D. 550. Only two other external witnesses to the early date exist: Arethas (c. 900) and Theophylact (d. 1107).

The late date, on the other hand, has an unbroken line of support from some of the greatest, most reliable names in church history, beginning in A.D. 150. Moreover, Clement of Alexandria, Tertullian, and Origen all support the late date. They are not included in the chart above because they don't specifically say that John was banished by Domitian. The external evidence from church history points emphatically to the A.D. 95 date for the composition of Revelation.

INTERNAL EVIDENCE

Two key lines of internal evidence from within the book of Revelation favor the Domitianic date for the writing of Revelation.

The Condition of the Seven Churches

One of the key internal arguments for the late date of Revelation is the condition of the seven churches of Asia Minor in Revelation 2–3. The churches of Asia Minor show all the characteristics of a second-generation church. The period of Paul's great mission work seems to lie in the past. Let's consider the clues on the date of Revelation from three of the churches Christ addresses in Revelation 2–3.

The Church of Ephesus

If John wrote Revelation in A.D. 64–67, then the letter to the church of Ephesus in Revelation 2:1-7 overlaps with Paul's two letters to Timothy, who was the pastor of that church when Paul wrote to him. In fact, if John wrote Revelation in 64–66, then Paul likely wrote 2 Timothy after John wrote to the church. Yet Paul makes no mention of the loss of first love or the presence of Nicolaitans at Ephesus in his correspondence with Timothy. Neither does he mention these problems in his Ephesian epistle, which was probably written

in A.D. 62. Jesus' statement to the church of Ephesus in Revelation 2:2 that it had guarded itself well against error does not fit what we know of this church in Nero's day (Acts 20:29-30; 1 Timothy 1:3-7; 2 Timothy 2:17-18).

Those who support the early date often respond to this point by noting that error can erupt very quickly in a church. As an example they sometimes cite the churches of Galatia, whom Paul says were "so quickly deserting Him who called you by the grace of Christ, for a different gospel" (1:6 NASB).

But there is a great difference between the condition and maturity of the Galatian churches after Paul's brief visit there on his first missionary journey, and the church of Ephesus, where Paul headquartered for three years, where Apollos taught, where Priscilla and Aquila ministered, and where Timothy pastored for several years.

Moreover, Revelation 2:1-7 makes no mention of the great missionary work of Paul in Asia Minor. On his third missionary journey, Paul headquartered in Ephesus for three years and had a profound ministry there. If John wrote in A.D. 64–67, the omission of any mention of Paul in the letters to the seven churches of Asia Minor is inexplicable. However, if John wrote 30 years later to the second generation of individuals in the churches, the omission is easily understood.

The Church of Smyrna

Apparently, the church of Smyrna did not even exist during the ministry of Paul. Polycarp was the bishop of Smyrna. In his letter to the Philippians, written in about A.D. 110, Polycarp says that the Smyrnaeans did not know the Lord during the time Paul was ministering (11.3).

> But I have not observed or heard of any such thing among you, in whose midst the blessed Paul labored, and who were his letters of recommendation in the beginning. For he boasts about you in all the churches—those alone, that is, which at that time had come to know the Lord, for we had not yet come to know him.

Polycarp is saying that Paul praised the Philippian believers in all the churches, but that during Paul's ministry in the 50s and 60s, the church of Smyrna did not even exist.

The Church of Laodicea

The church of Laodicea is the only one of the seven churches (with the possible exception of Sardis) that receives no commendation from Jesus. In his letter to the Colossians, probably written in A.D. 60–62, Paul indicates that the Laodicean church was an active group (Colossians 4:13). He mentions the church three times in his Colossian letter (2:1; 4:13,16). For the church to depart so completely from its earlier acceptable status that absolutely nothing good could be said about it would certainly take more than two to seven years to take place.

John describes the church in Laodicea as flourishing economically. Jesus quotes the church as saying, "I am rich, and have become wealthy, and have need of nothing." Yet the city suffered devastation in the earthquake of A.D. 60. After the earthquake, the Laodiceans refused all aid and assistance from Rome, preferring to rebuild their devastated city from their own resources.

Tacitus, the Roman historian, in his *Annals* (14.27), describes this independent spirit. "In the same year, Laodicea, one of the famous Asiatic cities, was laid in ruins by an earthquake, but recovered by its own resources, without assistance from ourselves." The extent of the damage to Laodicea and the length of time it took to reconstruct the city are powerful evidence of the late date for Revelation.

Most of the main ruins that survive today in Laodicea are from buildings constructed during the time of earthquake reconstruction. The great public buildings destroyed in the earthquake were rebuilt at the expense of individual citizens and were not finished until about A.D. 90. The completion date of the stadium can be precisely dated to the latter part of A.D. 79, and the inscriptions on several other buildings indicate that they too can be dated to this same period. New gates and fortifications seem to have culminated the rebuilding of Laodicea. It is likely that the great triple gate (Syrian gate) and towers were not finished until A.D. 88–90.

Since the rebuilding of Laodicea after the earthquake occupied a complete generation, it is highly problematic to claim that Laodicea was rich, wealthy, and in need of nothing in A.D. 64–67. During those years the city was in the early stages of a rebuilding program that would last another 25 years. However, if Revelation was written in A.D. 95, the description of Laodicea in Revelation 3:14-22 would fit the situation exactly. By this time the city was completely rebuilt with its own resources, enjoying prosperity and prestige and basking in the pride of its great accomplishment.

John's Banishment to Patmos

Revelation 1:9 states that when John received the Revelation, he was exiled on the island of Patmos. Church history consistently testifies that both Peter and Paul were executed in Rome near the end of Nero's reign. Those who hold to the early date for the writing of Revelation maintain that during this same time, Nero banished the apostle John to Patmos. But why would Nero execute Peter and Paul and banish John? This seems inconsistent. The difference between Peter's and Paul's sentences and John's sentence seems to indicate that they were persecuted under different rulers. Moreover, we have no evidence of Nero's use of banishment for Christians.

Domitian was the second Roman emperor after Nero to persecute Christians, and banishment was one of his favorite modes of punishment. So John's exile to Patmos is much more likely to have taken place under Domitian's rule than Nero's.

CONCLUSION

Taking into account all the relevant evidence, both external and internal, we find the greatest support for the view that the apostle John wrote the book of Revelation in the year A.D. 95 while exiled to the island of Patmos by the Roman emperor Domitian.

—MARK HITCHCOCK

BIBLIOGRAPHY

Beale, G.K. *The Book of Revelation. The New International Greek Testament Commentary.* Eds. I. Howard Marshall and Donald A. Hagner. Grand Rapids: Eerdmans Publishing Company, 1999.

Eliot, E.B. *Horae Apocalypticae*, 2nd ed., 4 vols. London: Seeley, Burnside and Seeley, 1846.

Hemer, Colin J. *The Letters to the Seven Churches of Asia in Their Local Setting.* The Biblical Resource Series, gen. eds. Astrid B. Beck and David Noel Freedman. Grand Rapids: Eerdmans Publishing Company, 2001.

Schaff, Philip. *History of the Christian Church*, 3rd ed., vol 1. New York: Charles Scribner's Sons, 1910. Reprint, Grand Rapids: Eerdmans Publishing Company, 1979.

Thomas, Robert L. *Revelation 1–7: An Exegetical Commentary*, gen. ed. Kenneth Barker. Chicago: Moody Press, 1992.

REWARDS

The New Testament promises faithful believers that they will receive rewards in recognition of their faithful service and spiritual growth. These rewards will honor the achievements and works of believers and thus are not to be confused with salvation, which is a free gift of God not based on works or human merit.

THE EVALUATION

The believers' evaluation judgment, called the judgment seat *(bema)* of Christ (2 Corinthians 5:10), transpires in heaven after the rapture of the church, during the seven-year Tribulation on earth. At this judgment the believer's works are judged, not the believer himself. The issue is not salvation but rewards. The purpose of this evaluation of church-age believers is to reward faithful service and to purify and prepare the church, the bride of Christ, to rule and reign with our Lord in the millennial kingdom.

At the judgment seat of Christ, each believer will "receive" (KJV) or be "recompensed" for (NASB) the deeds done in the body. Recompense (Greek, *komizo*) entails earning or gaining back something that is due or that which is earned. This fits with the concept of reward (Greek *misthos*), which conveys the idea of remuneration for work done, or that which has been earned through one's actions. Neither of these ideas is consistent with the offer of salvation, which is a free gift based on divine grace and not human merit (Romans 3:24; Ephesians 2:8-9; Titus 3:5). Thus, rewards relate to achievement in the spiritual life after salvation.

The description of the evaluation at the judgment seat of Christ reveals that it is for believers only. Some believers will have spiritual production worthy of recognition and honor, and others will not. The foundation for every Christian's life is the salvation freely given through faith in the complete substitutionary atonement of Christ on the cross. On this the believer builds his spiritual life (1 Corinthians 3:11). In the process of spiritual growth, the Christian will produce a variety of deeds, some done in the flesh or sin nature (Galatians 5:16,19) and others done in the power of the Holy Spirit (Galatians 5:22-23). At the judgment seat of Christ, these deeds will be evaluated. The metaphor is of a refining process in which fire purifies the deeds by burning off the dross. The Christian's life is a combination of worthless effort and faithful service. After the impurities—the wood, hay, and straw—are burned off, the believer is rewarded for that which has eternal value—the gold, silver, and precious stones (1 Corinthians 3:12). He will then hear the Lord say, "Well done, good and faithful servant" (Matthew 25:21).

However, the dire warning is that some believers will not have rewardable service. Their efforts were marred by self-serving motivation, selfish ambition, or failure to even serve the Lord. These believers will suffer loss of rewards but not lose their eternal salvation (1 Corinthians 3:15).

The apostle Paul communicated the gravity of the believer's future evaluation through the metaphor of winning the prize in athletic games (1 Corinthians 9:24-27). Greek culture valued the sacrifice and dedication of the athlete. The Corinthians were well acquainted with the rigors and standards of the games. Every seven years one of the four Pan-Hellenic athletic events, the Isthmian Games, was held seven miles from Corinth at Isthmia. Rules and discipline were strictly enforced. If an athlete violated his diet or training regimen in any way, he was disqualified and could not compete in the games. For the believer, disqualification does not mean loss of salvation, but loss of rewards (2 Timothy 2:5).

At the conclusion of the contest the victors were awarded the prize by the judge, who sat on the judgment bench, the *bema*. Each of the differing games had its own award wreaths (Greek, *stephanos*) woven from various plants: wild olive at Olympia, fresh wild celery at Nemea, laurel at Delphi. But at Corinth, the "perishable" crown was a withered celery wreath. Thus, Paul uses this to contrast the self-discipline of the athlete working for a temporal, perishable wreath with the believer who is pursuing an imperishable crown.

THE AWARDS

Two distinct crowns are mentioned in Scripture: *diademos* and *stephanos*. The first is a royal crown, the second the reward for victory in athletic games, military valor, or celebratory feasts. These were woven from oak, ivy, myrtle, celery, or olive leaves. In contrast to these easily spoiled crowns, the believer pursues a crown that is indestructible. It will last for eternity.

Four of these imperishable crowns are delineated as potential rewards, but there may be more. These will be awarded for different categories of Christian service and devotion. Each of these crowns display the quality of the reward: "the crown consisting in life," "the crown consisting in glory," "the crown consisting in rejoicing," "the crown consisting in righteousness."

The crown of life (James 1:12; Revelation 2:10). James declares that those who steadfastly apply the Word of God during times of testing receive a specific reward related to life. This is not the eternal life that is the possession of every believer, but a special quality or enhancement of that life, both in time and especially

in eternity. Every believer faces numerous tests that provide opportunities to trust God and apply His Word. As he encounters these tests, he may endure in obedience or yield to the temptation to handle the test independently of God. Those who keep His commandments are those who love the Lord (John 14:15,21,23). For those who endure tests by showing their love for the Lord in obedience to Him, even when it costs them their life, there is the promise of this special reward in heaven. Every believer can gain this crown because all go through trials and tests.

The crown of glory (1 Peter 5:4). This crown has a special brilliance that will never fade away. Our Lord was crowned with glory for His faithful service culminating in His saving work on the cross (Hebrew 2:9). In like manner, those who faithfully serve Him in teaching and leadership ministries will receive due recognition.

The crown of rejoicing (1 Thessalonians 2:19; Philippians 4:1). Those who are faithful in witnessing and leading others to Christ will be honored with this special crown.

The crown of righteousness (2 Timothy 4:8). Every believer can earn this award as well. This crown does not describe the imputed righteousness of God, which every believer possesses, but his own righteous deeds produced by walking by the Holy Spirit. These are the deeds of gold, silver, and precious stones that comprise the practical righteousness lived out in the Christian life. When church-age believers return with Christ, they will be clothed with these righteous acts (Revelation 19:8). This crown is promised to those who love and anticipate our Lord's appearance. These are the ones who live in the light of eternity and the expectation of Christ's imminent return. So motivated, they will not be among those who will experience shame at Christ's coming (1 John 2:28). Those who prepare for Christ's return will finish the course and keep the faith and receive a commendation and reward from our blessed Savior (2 Timothy 4:7-8).

—ROBERT DEAN, JR.

BIBLIOGRAPHY

Benware, Paul N. *The Believer's Payday.* Chattanooga: AMG, 2002.

Broneer, Oscar. "Paul and the Pagan Cults at Isthmia." *Harvard Theological Review* 44. 1971, pp. 169-87.

Dillow, Joseph. *The Reign of the Servant Kings.* Miami Springs, FL: Schoettle, 1992.

Leafe, G. Harry. *Running to Win.* Houston: Scriptel, 1992.

Wall, Joseph. *Going for the Gold.* Chicago: Moody Press, 1991.

ROMAN EMPIRE

DANIEL 7 RECORDS a significant prophecy in the form of a dream or vision. In this prophecy God revealed the future course of Gentile world dominion from Daniel's time to the second coming of Messiah. The vision portrayed four great beasts coming out of a sea one after the other.

God used this imagery of beasts to reveal a progression of Gentile world powers. Babylon (represented in the vision by a winged lion in verse 4), the great power in Daniel's day, would be succeeded by Medo-Persia (represented by a bear in verse 5). Medo-Persia would be followed by Greece (represented by a four-winged, four-headed leopard in verse 6). And Greece would then be conquered by Rome (represented by a dreadful nondescript beast in verses 7-8).

The beast that represented the Roman Empire was so terrifying and ferocious that no known animal could represent it. Daniel noticed the overwhelmingly destructive power of this beast. With iron teeth it devoured and crushed everything in its way and trampled all else under its feet. This was an apt description of the ancient Roman Empire, for it was able to crush and shatter the ancient world in an unprecedented way through its great military strength.

This unusual beast had ten horns on its head. An angel told Daniel that the ten horns represented "ten kings" (verse 24). In the Ancient Near East, kings and their kingdoms were synonymous with each other (see Daniel 2:38-39 where Daniel equated King Nebuchadnezzar with his kingdom). Thus, the ten horns represented ten rulers and their realms. The fact that the ten horns were on the head of the fourth beast indicated that the ten rulers and their realms belonged to the Roman Empire.

The angel told Daniel that these ten rulers (and their realms) would arise out of the Roman Empire (Daniel 7:24). This statement implied that the Roman Empire would experience more than one phase of history. The first phase would be the beast or conquering phase (the ancient Roman Empire). A later phase would be the ten-ruler or ten-division phase.

The language of verses 8, 20, and 24 implies that the ten rulers would all be ruling at the same time. This, together with the fact that the ten rulers and their realms would belong to the Roman Empire, indicated that in this later phase of its history the Roman Empire would consist of a ten-division federation.

In a parallel prophetic dream that God gave to King Nebuchadnezzar of Babylon (Daniel 2), this later phase of the Roman Empire was portrayed as a mixture of iron and clay (verses 41-43). Daniel interpreted the iron and clay mixture as follows: Just as iron is strong, so the Roman Empire in this later phase would be strong. Just as iron and clay do not naturally mix with each other, so this later phase of the Roman Empire would be characterized by divisions. Different realms of people would federate together to have influential strength, but they would not completely integrate or adhere to one another.

The combination of Daniel 2 and Daniel 7 shows that this later phase of the Roman Empire's history would consist of a ten-division federation with ten equal rulers co-ruling at the same time. Ten realms would federate for the sake of strength in the world, but they would not integrate to the extent of losing their ethnic and cultural identities.

The Roman Empire has never consisted of a ten-division federation with ten equal co-rulers. That prompts the conclusion that this later phase of the Roman Empire is yet to come. In other words, a revived form of the Roman Empire will exist in the future.

REGROUPINGS OF THE EMPIRE

The western half of the ancient Roman Empire fell in A.D. 476. Over the centuries since that time, western European leaders have persistently held on to the dream of continuing or reviving the Roman Empire.

Between A.D. 768 and 800, Charlemagne, King of the Franks, brought more of Western Europe under his rule than had been under one man since A.D. 476. He appeared to be about to revive the Roman Empire. In fact, on Christmas Day, A.D. 800, the Pope crowned Charlemagne "Emperor of the Romans." However, Charlemagne's realm fell apart after he died in A.D. 814.

The idea of the Roman Empire was revived again in A.D. 962 when the German ruler, Otto the Great, started the Holy Roman Empire. This lasted until 1806 when Napoleon ended it.

Napoleon craved the restoration of the forms of Roman imperialism, considered himself to be a Roman, and wanted to be an emperor. He thought that Europe should be ruled by one emperor who would have kings under him (Ludwig, pp. 245–46). He laid plans "to reunite Europe in the bonds of an indissoluble federation" (Ludwig, p. 667), which he referred to as "a United States of Europe" (Ludwig, p. 514). On December 2, 1804, Napoleon crowned himself "Emperor" with a Roman crown of gold leaves (Ludwig, pp. 227–28). Later he said, "I am a Roman emperor, in the best line of the Caesars" (Ludwig, p. 566). But Napoleon's empire disintegrated after his defeat at Waterloo in 1815.

The idea of a Roman Empire was revived again when Bismarck, the Iron Chancellor of Germany, conquered France in 1870. In 1871 the Germans called their new empire "the Second Reich." They regarded it to be the continuation of the old Holy Roman Empire (A.D. 962–1806) (Shirer, p. 133). The emperor of the Second Reich, Wilhelm I, was given the title "Kaiser" (the German form of Caesar). The Second Reich ended, however, in 1918 after Germany's surrender to the allied forces of World War I.

On February 15, 1930, Winston Churchill published an article entitled "The United States of Europe" in *The Saturday Evening Post*. He encouraged a federation of European nations on the continent (Zurcher, p. 6).

Mussolini dreamed about a revival of the ancient glory of Rome (Fermi, p. 216). When his black-shirted troops occupied Rome in 1921, he said, "It is destiny that Rome again takes her place as the city that will be the director of the civilization of all Western Europe" (Mussolini, p. 130). On May 9, 1936, Mussolini proclaimed "the reappearance of the Empire on the fated hills of Rome" (MacGregor-Hastie, p. 237). Hitler declared that the Roman Empire had been resurrected through the efforts of Mussolini (Fermi, p. 361). But by 1943 the course of World War II had gone so strongly against Italy and Mussolini that he was dismissed from office and imprisoned by decree of King Victor Emmanuel on July 25 (Shirer, p. 1295). "So fell, ignominiously, the modern Roman Caesar" (Shirer, p. 1296).

In July 1944, national resistance movements of Europe issued a joint declaration stating, "Federal union alone could ensure the preservation of liberty and civilization on the continent of Europe" (Zurcher, p. 19).

In 1944 several German generals plotted to overthrow Hitler and Nazism. If successful, they planned to ask the western allies for an armistice and hoped for the establishment "of a 'constructive peace' within the framework of a United States of Europe" (Shirer, p. 1340).

On September 19, 1946, Winston Churchill talked about Europe's ills at the University of Zurich: "What is the sovereign remedy? It is to recreate the European family, or as much of it as we can, and to provide it with a structure under which it can dwell in peace, safety, and freedom. We must build a kind of United States of Europe" (Zurcher, p. 21).

From May 7 to May 10, 1948, 750 delegates from all over free Europe gathered at The

Hague and established the Congress of Europe for the purpose of unifying Europe (Zurcher, pp. 22–24).

On March 25, 1957, statesmen from six western European nations met on the Capitoline Hill in Rome and established the European Economic Community (more popularly known as the Common Market and later called the European Union). Western European leaders expressed the hope that the Common Market would become the nucleus of a future United States of Europe (Gunther, pp. 263–64).

Konrad Adenauer, chancellor of postwar West Germany, stated, "I want to stay alive longer for only one reason—to see a United States of Europe in my time" (Gunther, p. 18). "The integration of Europe must be achieved. I am convinced that it is the sole salvation for the Christian West" (Adenauer, pp. 49–50). "The necessity for union for economic, political, and military reasons is incontestable" (Adenauer, p. 53).

One observer of the movement for European unity stated that it "has reconceptualized and brought up-to-date the historic ideal of European unity, dating back to Roman times" (Zurcher, p. 172).

It is interesting to note how many leaders over the years have dreamed of a federation of nations in Europe (a federation very similar to that revealed in Daniel 2 and 7) and have associated that federation with a continuation or revival of the Roman Empire (just as Daniel 2 and 7 associated their federation with a later phase of the Roman Empire's history).

CURRENT PROSPECTS OF
A REVIVED EMPIRE

Developments within the European Union have increasingly made it a significant prospect to fulfill both the revelation in Daniel concerning a future revived Roman Empire and the dream of western European leaders over the centuries. A common economy is the forerunner of a unified political system. A Canadian television documentary entitled "Birth of a Superstate" gave the following evaluation of the direction of Western Europe: "Europe is moving to become the economic, political center of the world. It will also develop great military strength. One Europe, under one flag, will perhaps be the superpower that will challenge the world of the twenty-first century." With a common currency, one European Central Bank, and a strengthening political union, the stage is set for the complete fulfillment of the final prophecies of Daniel 2 and 7.

A COMING WORLD RULER

In the prophetic dream described in Daniel 7, an eleventh horn pushed its way up through the head of the fourth beast and uprooted three of the ten horns that were already there (verse 8). Verse 24 provides the interpretation of this imagery. It indicates that sometime after the establishment of the future ten-division revived Roman Empire, an eleventh ruler will rise to power from within it while the original ten rulers are co-ruling. This new ruler will overthrow three of those rulers. This implies that he will thereby gain the dominant position of authority over the empire and in essence become its emperor.

Daniel 7 and other prophetic passages signify that this ruler (now commonly called the Antichrist) will be an arrogant, blasphemous, absolute dictator during the last seven years prior to the second coming of Christ to earth. In the middle of that period he will set himself up as God in a new Temple in Jerusalem (Daniel 9:27; 11:36-37; 2 Thessalonians 2:3-4). Then he will severely persecute Israel and those who refuse to worship him (Daniel 7:21,25; 9:27; Revelation 13:4-8; 20:4). His goal will be to bring the whole world under his rule on behalf of his master, Satan (Daniel 11:38-45; Revelation 13:1-8; 16:13-16; 19:19).

UNDERSTANDING THE NUMBER TEN

Finally, the Bible consistently states that the future revived Roman Empire will consist of ten divisions (Daniel 7:7,20,24; Revelation 13:1; 17:3,7,12,16). By contrast, the European Union consists of more than ten member nations. In light of this, how can such an organization possibly lead to the fulfillment of the biblical revelation concerning a future revived Roman Empire? One possible solution is that some nations may drop out. A second solution may be found in the increasing focus in Europe on regions rather than separate nations. In other words, it may be that the biblical number ten is a reference to ten regions rather than ten nations. Only time will tell.

—RENALD E. SHOWERS

BIBLIOGRAPHY

Adenauer, Konrad. *World Indivisible, with Liberty and Justice for All.* New York: Harper and Brothers, 1955.

Christmas, Robin, producer. "Birth of a Superstate." Canadian television documentary, June 1990.

Fermi, Laura. *Mussolini.* Chicago: University of Chicago Press, 1961.

Gunther, John. *Inside Europe Today.* New York: Harper and Brothers, 1961.

Ludwig, Emil. *Napoleon.* New York: Boni and Liveright, 1926.

MacGregor-Hastie, Roy. *The Day of the Lion.* New York: Coward-McCann, 1963.

Mussolini, Benito. *My Autobiography.* New York: Charles Scribner's Sons, 1928.

Shirer, William L. *The Rise and Fall of the Third Reich.* New York: Fawcett Publications, 1962.

Showers, Renald E. *The Most High God.* Bellmawr, NJ: The Friends of Israel Gospel Ministry, 1982.

Zurcher, Arnold J. *The Struggle to Unite Europe, 1940–1958.* New York: New York University Press, 1958.

SATAN

THE HEBREW WORD *satan* means "adversary, accuser, opponent." The term occurs 26 times in the Hebrew Bible. The NKJV translates 18 of these as the proper name *Satan.* Eight times the word describes a human acting in an adversarial role. This title is affixed to the chief angel who instigated a revolt against God among the angels. In the New Testament, the Greek *satanas* transliterates the Hebrew and is equivalent to *diabolos;* both describe the same personage (Revelation 20:2). The Greek *diabolos,* "devil," is a title (always

occurring with the definite article) and occurs 33 times. It describes this creature as one who slanders or accuses those who trust God (Revelation 12:10).

Scripture also assigns Satan a number of other titles that describe his various character traits and roles: "accuser of the brethren" (Revelation 12:10), "serpent" (Genesis 3:1), "dragon" (Revelation 12:9), "the ruler of this world" (John 12:31; 14:30), "prince of the power of the air" (Ephesians 2:2), "god of this age" (2 Corinthians 4:4), "evil one" (Matthew 6:13; John 17:15; 2 Thessalonians 3:3), "tempter" (Matthew 4:3), "wicked one" (1 John 2:13-14; 5:19), "Belial" (2 Corinthians 6:15); "roaring lion" (1 Peter 5:8), "adversary" (1 Peter 5:8), "enemy" (Matthew 13:28,39), "liar" (John 8:44), and "deceiver" (2 Corinthians 11:3).

THE FALL OF SATAN

The Bible lacks a specific description of the primordial revolt of Satan and his angels against God. Many scholars, however, believe that the pronouncements against the king of Tyre (Ezekiel 28:12) and the king of Babylon (Isaiah 14:4) cannot be restricted to human figures. Phrases such as "you were in Eden, the garden of God," and "you were perfect in your ways from the day you were created, till iniquity was found in you," as well as the identification "the anointed cherub who covers" preclude identification of the king of Tyre with a human being (Ezekiel 28:12-15). Some scholars allege that this is simply imagery borrowed from the pagan mythology of Ezekiel's day and does not refer to the fall of Satan. However, nothing remotely similar has been discovered among any ancient neareastern mythologies.

The second passage that may describe the original sin of Satan is in Isaiah 14:12-15. It is here that the name *Lucifer* became attached to Satan, based on the Latin Vulgate translation of *helel ben shahar,* "morning star, son of the dawn" (NIV). This section of Isaiah figures into the future scene of the defeat of the king of Babylon. At the end of the seven-year Tribulation, the Lord Jesus Christ returns physically to the earth to vanquish the armies of Satan, the False Prophet, and the Antichrist. In Revelation 18 the kingdom of the Antichrist is identified as Babylon. Scholars debate whether this is a literal kingdom centered in Babylon or simply a symbol used to describe the human kingdom in revolt against God. Either way, it is this yet future time that is pictured in Isaiah 14. At that yet future time, the king of Babylon will be ridiculed as one who brought about the fall of nations. His sin of arrogance is typified by five statements, each beginning with "I will." The power behind the king of Babylon is Satan himself. Thus, these five statements summarize the sin that initiated Satan's original revolt against God.

SATAN IN THE OLD TESTAMENT

Satan initially appears in Scripture disguised as the serpent that tempted Adam and Eve in the Garden; only later is his identity confirmed as Satan (Revelation 12:9; 20:2). God curses the serpent for his role in the fall of mankind and announces his eventual defeat (Genesis 3:15). In this first promise of salvation, God announced that the seed of the serpent would inflict a powerful but not fatal wound on the seed of the woman. But the seed of the woman, an allusion to the Savior who was true humanity, would fatally destroy the serpent's seed.

Job 1 describes the first appearance of this angel under the title Satan. Along with the other angels, called "sons of God," he appears in regular convocations before the throne of God. He reports on what he observes as he roams about the earth (Job 1:7; 2:2; 1 Peter 5:8). As part of his intelligence-gathering operation, he brings accusations against believers and, as in the case of Job, seeks permission to bring adversity into their lives to invalidate their testimony. This episode in Job reveals that Satan can do nothing apart from divine permission. A picture of Satan as the prosecutor against believers is also found in Zechariah 3:1.

These limited depictions of Satan in the Old Testament reveal a creature in opposition to God who possesses enormous powers yet is restricted by the sovereign authority of God.

SATAN IN THE NEW TESTAMENT

The New Testament reveals a more complete picture of the person and operations of Satan. He is presented as the ruler of a vast kingdom of evil that extends from the fall of Adam to Satan's eventual defeat. As the ruler of this age, he vigorously opposes the plan of God, the appearance of the Savior, and the evangelism and ministry of church-age believers.

During the time of the Messiah's incarnation, this antagonism resulted in an intensified opposition manifested through numerous instances of satanic and demonic activity. Our Lord was the personal target of a series of temptations designed to discredit His character (Matthew 4:1). When Jesus was in the wilderness, Satan offered to Him the rulership of all the earthly kingdoms. It is important to note that Jesus did not dispute the legitimacy of Satan's offer or his claim to authority over these empires. However, Jesus rejected the temptation to take a shortcut to the kingdom by accepting these kingdoms from the hand of Satan.

Our Lord's victory over Satan's assaults qualified Him to go to the cross. There Satan appeared to have achieved his victory in preventing the establishment of a messianic kingdom, but ironically, this short-lived "victory" actually destroyed Satan's own kingdom. At the cross, the sins of mankind were completely paid for and the defeat of Satan was secured, though it will not be until the end of the millennium that he will be finally and permanently confined to the eternal lake of fire.

During the present age, Satan's strategy is to destroy the witness of believers, the expansion of the church, and the exploitation of Jesus Christ's strategic victory on the cross. As ruler of this present world system, which is organized according to the devil's own principles, procedures, and goals, he has devised numerous strategies to distract, confuse, and defeat the believer in his daily walk and advance to spiritual maturity (Ephesians 6:10-12). Satan works to blind the minds of the lost to their need for salvation (2 Corinthians 4:4), to lead Christians into sin (1 Corinthians 7:5), to entice believers to rebel against God, and to bring suffering and opposition into their lives to distract them from spiritual growth. Satan distracts believers through counterfeiting the truth of God's Word (2 Corinthians 11:13-15) and by counterfeiting the genuine teachers of truth. He disguises himself as an angel of light, and his demons are disguised as messengers of truth. In this way he deceives men into following the doctrines of demons (1 Timothy 4:1).

The solution to the devil's attacks against the believer is to resist him (James 4:7; 1 Peter 5:9). No scripture authorizes the believer to rebuke, bind, or attack the devil. Instead, we are to put on the full armor of God that we may stand against (or resist) him when under assault (Ephesians 6:10-18). The believer is to take up a defensive posture toward Satan in spiritual warfare, not an aggressive one. It is Jesus Christ who will eventually bind the devil, not the individual Christian (Revelation 20:2).

During the future Tribulation, God will permit Satan an almost free hand to affect the destinies of mankind and to do his utmost to advance his claims to rule as god. During this time the horrible consequences of sin and evil will become more exaggerated as the restraining influence of the Holy Spirit is removed. Satan will personally empower the future world ruler known as the Antichrist ("the beast of the sea," "the prince who is to come") to form a one-world government in opposition to the rule of God.

Revelation 12 provides an overview of the career of the devil and his hostility to the nation Israel. The "woman clothed with the sun" in this passage represents Israel. She gives birth to a child, the Lord Jesus Christ, who is persecuted by the dragon, Satan. Though Satan sought to devour the child, the child was caught up to heaven—a reference to the ascension of Christ after the resurrection. One result of Christ's victory over Satan is that the devil increases his promotion of anti-Semitism. His goal is to destroy the Jews before God can literally fulfill the promises He made to Israel in the unconditional Abrahamic, Land, Davidic, and New covenants. The devil's hope is that by accomplishing this he can prove himself more powerful than God and escape his eternal doom.

During the Tribulation, the warfare between the holy angels under Michael and the devil and his angels intensifies (Revelation 12:7). Satan and his demons are ejected from heaven and cast to the earth. In his wrath, the serpent seeks to destroy all living Jews during the second half of the Tribulation (Revelation 12:17). However, the believing remnant follows the Lord's command to flee into the wilderness, where God protects them.

When Jesus Christ returns physically to the earth at the second coming, He will destroy the armies of the Antichrist and the False Prophet and cast the two leaders into the lake of fire. God will then bind Satan in the bottomless pit for 1000 years (Revelation 20:2). At the end of that period, God will release Satan for a brief period of time, during which Satan will deceive the nations and lead a revolt against God. God will destroy him and his followers by fire from heaven, and Satan will finally meet his eternal destiny in the lake of fire (Revelation 20:10).

—ROBERT DEAN, JR.

BIBLIOGRAPHY

Dean, Robert Jr., and Thomas Ice. *What the Bible Teaches About Spiritual Warfare*. Grand Rapids: Kregel, 2000.

Lightner, Robert. *Angels, Satan, and Demons*. Nashville: Word, 1998.

Showers, Renald. *Those Invisible Spirits Called Angels*. Bellmawr, NJ: The Friends of Israel Gospel Ministry, 1997.

Unger, Merrill F. *Biblical Demonology*. Wheaton, IL: Scripture Press, 1952.

SEAL JUDGMENTS

THE SEVEN-SEALED SCROLL containing the seal judgments is first mentioned in Revelation 5. The scroll comes from the "right hand of Him who sat on the throne" and is a book written "inside and on the back, sealed up with seven seals" (5:1 NASB). The One on the throne is God Almighty, whom heavenly beings praise: "Worthy are You, O Lord our God, to receive glory and honor and power; for You created all things, and because of Your will they existed, and were created" (4:11). When the Lord breaks the first seal on the book, the horrors of the seven-year Tribulation period will begin. The breaking of the seals triggers the Tribulation events—things that "must take place after these things" (4:1), referring back to the great vision of Christ in heaven and the spiritual happenings in some of the churches on earth during the time of John (chapters 2–3).

What is the implication of the word "seal" (Greek, *sphragis*)? Even today, some official government documents have wax seals that guarantee the integrity of the document and show that it has not been tampered with. In ancient days, kings wore a signet ring bearing their official seal, which would be used to impress the wax used to seal and secure a document until it was to be formally opened. This sealed book in Revelation is to be opened only by the Lamb of God (6:1), who alone is "worthy to open the book or to look into it" (5:4). He is "the Lion that is from the tribe of Judah, the Root of David" (5:5), who has earned this right by His obedience unto death for the sins of humanity.

Revelation 6:1–8:6 describes the seven seals. When the final seal is broken, unleashing more Tribulation events on earth, seven trumpets will be sounded (8:7–11:19), and with the final trumpet, the "seven bowls of the wrath of God" will follow (16:1-21). From the broken seals to the final bowl of wrath, the events on earth become more and more terrible. These three stages of wrath form the basic outline of Revelation, though the apostle John often stops the progress of the narration and focuses on certain elements in the Revelation account, such as the 144,000 witnesses (7:1-8), the two witnesses (11:1-14), horrible wars on earth (12), the revelation of the beast and the False Prophet (13), Babylon the harlot (17), and the commercial Babylon (18), the second coming of Christ (19:1-16), the battle of Armageddon (19:17-21), the coming of the millennium

(20:1-3), and the events of the millennium (20:4-10).

THE TIMING OF THE SEALS

Where does the breaking of the seven seals fit in the chronology of the Tribulation? Most of the speculation follows these four views:

1. Some scholars hold that the seals will begin after the midpoint of the Tribulation and flow consecutively. John F. Walvoord writes, "There is some evidence…that the events pictured in the seals, trumpets, and vials [bowls] are instead a concentrated prophecy of the latter half of this [seven-year Tribulation], i.e., a period of three and one-half years, designated as a time of wrath and the great tribulation, and constituting the introduction to the second coming of Christ" (Walvoord, p. 123).

2. Some Bible teachers have placed the three phases of these judgments (seals, trumpets, and bowls) to run concurrently, overlapping each other. Tim LaHaye rejects this view and writes, "The problem with that idea is that it completely overlooks the fact that the opening of the seventh seal introduces the trumpet judgments of chapters 8 and 9, and the blowing of the seventh trumpet introduces the seven bowls of chapter 16. Therefore, we may conclude that the three judgments run chronologically and represent three succeeding periods of the Tribulation. The seal judgments cover approximately the first quarter of the Tribulation or the first twenty-one months" (LaHaye, p. 98).

3. Others view the trumpet and the bowl judgments coming out of the breaking of the seals; they see the trumpet and bowl judgments running simultaneously. This makes for a more complicated and repetitious pattern to the unfolding of the book of Revelation.

4. The most accepted view is that the seal judgments bring on the trumpet judgments, which in turn bring about the most ferocious of the judgments, the bowls of wrath. "The opening of the seven seals initiates the messianic judgments that comprise the whole of

Revelation 6–11 and 14–19" (Hindson, p. 79). The conviction that judgments must fall prior to the coming of the kingdom of God is rooted in the teaching of the Old Testament prophets concerning the day of the Lord (see the passages beginning at Isaiah 2:12; Amos 5:18; Zechariah 12:2.).

The Tribulation certainly begins with the opening of the seven seals that have kept the scroll closed. As they are opened, they generally follow the pattern of the Olivet Discourse (Matthew 24–25; Mark 13; Luke 21), the "Little Apocalypse." The similarities between the seal judgments and the Olivet Discourse are extremely close (Thomas, p. 416).

THE FOUR HORSEMEN

The first four seals reveal the riders on the four horses, who play a key role in the events that fall upon the earth. When the second seal is broken, a red horse comes forth, and its rider is personified as war. Peace is removed from the earth "that men would slay one another; and a great sword was given to him" (Revelation 6:4). Jesus seems to refer to this when He says, "Nation will rise against nation, and kingdom against kingdom" (Matthew 24:7). With the breaking of the third seal, a rider comes forth with a pair of balancing scales, and he is riding a black horse (Revelation 6:5). Famine and economic inflation is in view with the people on earth spending a denarius for about eight quarts of wheat or barley in order to survive. A denarius was a day's wage for a Roman soldier. When the fourth seal is broken, an ashen horse comes forth with a rider named "Death." Hades (the grave) is said to follow as a fourth of earth's population dies from "sword and with famine and with pestilence and by the wild beasts of the earth" (6:8).

These three seals seem fairly understandable, but what about the first seal and its rider on the white horse? Much speculation has been written about the identity of the one who holds a bow along with a crown with which "he went out conquering, and to conquer" (6:2). What are some of the views?

1. Because the other horsemen may be personifications, some claim that the rider on the white horse must also be a personification of government or authorities "in the last days in the hands of Gentiles" (Walvoord, p. 125; he notes this is not his view).

2. Another view, though not popular, is that the rider represents the aggressive and ancient Parthians.

3. Some who hold to a historicist view of Revelation take all of the seals as the history and the glory and decline of the pagan Roman Empire. This position is complicated and has been rejected by many.

4. Some have said that the rider on the white horse is Christ at His second coming because the white horse is a symbol of victory. This view, however, seems unlikely because Christ the Lamb is the one who just broke the first seal. Also, depicting Christ in this way at the beginning of the Tribulation would be odd. He will come on a white horse at the end of the Tribulation, not at its beginning (Couch, p. 234).

5. The view most widely accepted by premillennialists is that the white horse pictures the Antichrist. This rider carries a bow as an instrument of war, whereas Christ carries no weapon but the sword of His mouth (19:15). The rider has a crown, whereas Christ already has many crowns (19:12), and the rider's crown is called a *stephanos,* a "victor's wreath," whereas Jesus wears the *diadema,* the "royal crown." Ed Hindson observes:

> Since there is no point of similarity between Christ and this rider, other than the color of the horse, this must be an imposter—the Antichrist. He is called the "beast" in Revelation 13:1-18; 16:10-13; 17:3-14; 19:19-21; 20:10. Other biblical names include "man of lawlessness" (2 Thessalonians 2:3), "the son of perdition" (John 17:12), the king who does "as he pleases" (Daniel 11:36-45), and the "antichrist" (1 John 4:3). David Jeremiah calls him the "Dark Prince on a White Horse" (Hindson, p. 81).

The four horsemen parallel the horsemen in Zechariah 1:7-11, though the horsemen in Zechariah are sent only to patrol the earth rather than to inflict God's wrath. As animals of war, horses signify the ability to attack swiftly and with frightening results against an enemy's foot soldiers. And in ancient times, when an army general paraded through the streets of Rome after a victorious conquest in some other land, he rode a white horse. The Antichrist is a victor of evil and not a conqueror of righteousness (Couch, p. 234).

THE SOVEREIGNTY OF GOD

The authority of God and His providence in launching the Tribulation is clearly seen in certain words used in the text of Revelation. A crown "was given" to the rider on the white horse; to the rider on the red horse "was granted" the ability to take peace from the earth; and authority "was given" to Death to slay a fourth of earth's population. We can see, then, that the Tribulation cannot begin until Christ initiates it and allows it to happen. And the events of the Tribulation do not take place until after Christ begins to break open the seven seals on the scroll. So when it comes to the Tribulation, in the midst of all the chaos, "God is still in control. Jesus Christ is in charge of the opening of the seals, and the sovereign will of heaven prevails despite the inhumanity of a depraved and corrupt society" (Hindson, p. 85).

—MAL COUCH

BIBLIOGRAPHY

Couch, Mal, gen. ed. *A Bible Handbook to Revelation.* Grand Rapids: Kregel, 2001.

Hindson, Ed. *The Book of Revelation.* Chattanooga: AMG Publishers, 2002.

LaHaye, Tim. *Revelation.* Grand Rapids: Zondervan, 1980.

Seiss, Joseph A. *The Apocalypse.* Grand Rapids: Kregel, 1987.

Thomas, Robert L. *Revelation 1–7: An Exegetical Commentary.* Chicago: Moody Press, 1992.

Walvoord, John F. *The Revelation of Jesus Christ.* Chicago: Moody Press, 1966.

SECOND COMING OF CHRIST

THE SECOND COMING of Jesus Christ to this earth is one of the most significant events mentioned in the entire Bible. The New Testament alone includes 321 references to this awesome occurrence, making it the second most prominent doctrine presented in Scripture next to salvation itself.

Enoch was the first prophet to mention the second coming in Scripture, as recorded in Jude 14-15. The second coming is referred to in many of the psalms, by all of the prophets, by all of the apostles, and of course by our Lord Himself on numerous occasions. The New Testament teaches it in one out of every 30 verses and in every chapter of 1 and 2 Thessalonians, the first books written for the early church. Moreover, all nine New Testament authors mention it in 23 of their 27 books. Obviously God intended His church to be motivated to holiness, evangelism, and missionary concern by the study of the second coming of Christ.

Several key doctrines of the Bible are absolutely dependent on the second coming of Christ. For example, the resurrection of the dead cannot be fulfilled until Jesus comes again. Likewise, Christ's victory over Satan cannot be completed until He returns. Most importantly, His divine nature cannot be vindicated unless He comes to earth again since He promised so many times that He would. He would be guilty of fraud and deceit if He failed to return, and God simply cannot lie. John 14:3 quotes Jesus as saying, "I will come again." Therefore, the second coming of Christ is not only a certainty; it is a doctrinal necessity.

DISTINCTION BETWEEN FIRST AND SECOND COMINGS

The fact that the first and second comings of Christ were inadvertently perceived as one event explains why so many Jews did not accept Jesus as their Messiah 2000 years ago. His promises to overcome the world, set up

His kingdom, and bring world peace (promises that apply to His second coming) were mistakenly applied to His first coming. Therefore, the major reason many rejected Him was not because He worked incredible miracles and was the greatest teacher who ever lived. It was because the people wanted Him to free Israel from the shackles of their Roman oppressors, not realizing that prophecies relating to His future kingdom referred to His second coming, not His first. The purpose of His first coming was to suffer for the sins of the world, die on the cross, and rise again—without which there would be no eternal life. We who live in the church age have the benefit of being able to look back and determine which prophecies have already been fulfilled by His first coming and which have yet to be fulfilled by His second coming.

THE TWO PHASES OF THE SECOND COMING

The Rapture

Christ's first physical appearance on earth can be separated into several parts: His birth, ministry, death, resurrection, and ascension. The second coming can only be understood if one realizes it has separate phases as well. The many references to His second coming reveal that it is not just a singular event. The first phase involves the rapture of the church. It consists of our Lord coming from heaven in the air to take all believers back to His Father's house as He promised in John 14:1-3. The numerous references to this magnificent event include the apostle Paul's descriptions in 1 Corinthians 15:50-58 and 1 Thessalonians 4:13-18.

> The Lord Himself will descend from heaven with a shout, with the voice of the archangel, and with the trumpet of God, and the dead in Christ will rise first. Then we who are alive and remain will be caught up together with them in the clouds to meet the Lord in the air, and so we shall always be with the Lord. Therefore comfort one another with these words (1 Thessalonians 4:16-18).

The Return

The second phase of His second coming is known as the "glorious appearing" and is described in detail in Revelation 19:11-20. This event involving Christ's return to earth with His saints to set up His kingdom occurs at the end of the seven-year Tribulation.

THE RAPTURE AND RETURN ARE SEPARATE EVENTS

Problems arise when theologians attempt to dismiss the multiphase aspect of Christ's second coming and place both the rapture and glorious appearing at the end of the Tribulation. This is known as the posttribulational view of the rapture. In this scenario, Christians will be required to experience the horrors of the Tribulation. In order to hold this view, one must either spiritualize away or simply ignore numerous passages of Scripture. But a careful study of all biblical references to the second coming clearly shows that the rapture and the glorious appearing are two separate phases of His second coming. Compare the following differences (this same chart appears earlier in the article titled "Glorious Appearing"):

RAPTURE	GLORIOUS APPEARING
Christ comes *for* His own in the air	Christ comes *with* His own to the earth
All Christians are translated into new bodies	There is no translation of bodies
Christians are taken to the Father's house	Resurrected saints remain on earth
There is no judgment upon the earth	Christ judges the inhabitants of the earth
The church will be in heaven	Christ sets up His kingdom on earth
It could occur at any minute (it is imminent)	It cannot occur until the end of the seven-year Tribulation period

RAPTURE	GLORIOUS APPEARING
There are no signs preceding it	There are numerous signs preceding it
It affects believers only	It affects all humanity
It is a time of joy	It is a time of mourning
It occurs before the day of wrath	It occurs after the Tribulation
There is no mention of Satan	Satan is bound in the abyss for 1000 years
Christians are judged at the judgment seat of Christ	There is no judgment seat of Christ
There is the marriage of the Lamb	His bride descends with Him to earth
Only Christ's own will see Him	Every eye will see Him
The Tribulation begins	The millennial reign of Christ begins

REASONS FOR RECOGNIZING A TWO-PHASE SECOND COMING

Kept from God's Wrath

The second coming of Christ can best be viewed as encompassing the entire seven-year, multievent period that includes the rapture, the Tribulation, and the glorious appearing.

The rapture remarkably demonstrates God's incredible mercy for believers. He has promised that the church of Jesus Christ will not have to go through the Tribulation, which is one reason why the Bible calls the rapture the "blessed hope" in Titus 2:13. As 1 Thessalonians 1:10 says, we "wait for His Son from heaven, whom He raised from the dead, that is Jesus, who rescues us from the wrath to come." The context of this verse points to the rapture, and the "wrath to come" is the Tribulation. As Jesus Himself promises in Revelation 3:10, "I also will keep you from the

hour of testing, that hour which is about to come upon the whole world, to test those who dwell on the earth."

First Thessalonians 5:9 contains another strong indication that the believer will not pass through the Tribulation: "God did not appoint us to suffer wrath, but to receive salvation through our Lord Jesus Christ." Once again, the context of this chapter is the rapture. Similarly, the description of the Tribulation in Revelation 4–18 does not mention the church even once. Why? Because the church would have been safely taken out of the way via the rapture prior to the beginning of the Tribulation's horrors, which are described in Scripture as the wrath of the Lamb (Revelation 6) and the wrath of God (Revelation 16).

The Millennial Population Explosion

Another reason it's impossible for the rapture to occur at the conclusion of the Tribulation is because that would leave no believers on earth in a natural body who could populate the millennial kingdom. All the participants in the rapture will find themselves in glorified resurrected bodies that will no longer be involved in procreation (Matthew 22:30). And Matthew 25:41 indicates that all unbelievers will be sent into "the eternal fire," thus leaving no one with a natural body to enter the millennial kingdom. But we know from numerous Old Testament passages as well as Revelation 20:7-10 that there will be a huge population explosion during the millennium. Where do these people come from? Those who become Christians during the Tribulation (thanks to the preaching of the 144,000 Jews and the two witnesses) and survive to the end are the ones who will repopulate the earth. These people will not be raptured at the end of the Tribulation in some kind of posttribulation rapture, but rather will enter Christ's 1000-year millennial kingdom in their natural bodies.

—TIM LaHAYE

BIBLIOGRAPHY

Couch, Mal, ed. *Dictionary of Premillennial Theology*. Grand Rapids: Kregel, 1996.

LaHaye, Tim, and Jerry Jenkins. *Are We Living in the End Times?* Wheaton, IL: Tyndale House, 1999.

Pentecost, J. Dwight. *Things to Come.* Grand Rapids: Zondervan, 1975.

Showers, Renald. *Maranatha: Our Lord Come!* Bellmawr, NJ: The Friends of Israel Gospel Ministry, 1995.

Walvoord, John F. *Major Bible Prophecies.* Grand Rapids: Zondervan, 1991.

SEVEN CHURCHES

THE SEVEN CHURCHES LISTED in Revelation 1 and addressed by Christ in Revelation 2–3 were all located in western Asia Minor (modern Turkey) in a province the Romans identified as Asia. The apostle Paul and his fellow workers founded most of these churches during his third missionary journey (Acts 19:1,10,26). They were located in seven cities and are listed in a circular order that, geographically speaking, a messenger carrying the letters from Patmos (where John wrote the book of Revelation) would probably have followed. Sailing the 40 miles from Patmos on the Aegean Sea to the harbor of Ephesus, the messenger would have traveled overland 35 miles north to Smyrna, then north 55 miles slightly inland to arrive at Pergamum. From Pergamum the messenger would have journeyed 40 miles southwest to Thyatira, then 35 miles south to Sardis. Leaving Sardis, the messenger would have trekked another 35 miles southeasterly to Philadelphia. At the end of the route the messenger would have arrived at Laodicea, some 40 miles southwest of Philadelphia. The cities in which these churches were located were the wealthiest, most populous, and most influential in western Asia Minor.

REPRESENTATIVE CHURCHES

These seven churches seem to be representative of all churches throughout the church age, and they were not the only churches in Asia Minor at the time John wrote Revelation. Churches also existed in Colossae, Hierapolis, Troas, Pontus, Galatia, and Bithynia. However, the condition of the seven churches in Revelation reflected the varying spiritual conditions of all the churches, and it appears that Christ may have chosen to address only seven because the number seven in Scripture denotes completeness or perfection.

Another theory that is growing in popularity among those who take prophecy literally is that these seven churches represent the seven stages of church history. This is not a new theory; it originated in the late third century.

In my commentary on Revelation, *Revelation Unveiled,* I quote Dr. Gary Cohen, who wrote,

> The theory that the seven churches of Revelation 2–3 are prophetical, that they represent seven consecutive periods in ecclesiastical history, seems to have first been suggested by some of the words of the martyr Victorinus, Bishop of Pettau (died c. A.D. 303). This belief as held today does not deny that at the same time the seven churches are also historical and representative. It asserts that the prophetical elements is in addition to these other elements and wholly compatible with them. Thus it beholds the seven congregations (1) as historically existent at the time of John's writing in A.D. 95–96, (2) as representing the entire church through the seven types of local churches which shall exist throughout the dispensation, and (3) as prefiguring seven aspects of the professing church which would successfully rise into prominence before Christ's second coming.
>
> The seven periods are generally given approximately as follows:
>
> 1. Ephesus—Apostolic church (A.D. 30–100)
>
> 2. Smyrna—Persecuted church (A.D. 100–313)
>
> 3. Pergamos—State church (A.D. 313–590)

4. Thyatira—Papal church (A.D. 590–1517)

5. Sardis—Reformed church (A.D. 1517–1790)

6. Philadelphia—Missionary church (A.D. 1730–1900)

7. Laodicea—Apostate church (A.D. 1900–)

Although this time-honored belief that Christ's message to the seven churches includes a prophecy of the seven stages of church history has never been unanimous, it is held by most premillennialists. Even Phillip Schaff, the writer of the classic eight-volume set *History of the Christian Church,* accepts that position.

This theory explains why God chose these seven churches from among the hundreds of churches in the early days of Christianity or in A.D. 95 when Revelation was written. Their selection was based not only on the conditions at that time, but on the fact that they provided a glimpse of what that age would eventually be like.

The seven churches each had their own strengths and weaknesses, and the letters to the churches were both specific to a particular church and generic to the entire group. Each letter addresses specific challenges. The problems associated with Ephesus, Pergamum, Thyatira, Sardis, and Laodicea progressively worsen. Interspersed between these churches are Smyrna and Philadelphia, which have suffered physically but have a spiritual depth despite their persecution. The messages are to be read by each church as evidenced by the word "and" that appears before the salutation to each church after Ephesus. Additionally, the admonition "He who has an ear, let him hear what the Spirit says to the churches" has a cumulative effect in that "churches" is plural. Thus, what the Spirit says to one church is applicable to all the churches.

PROBLEMS IN THE CHURCHES

In Acts 20:29-30, the apostle Paul warned the Ephesian elders that savage wolves would appear in their midst. This attack would be on two fronts: those from within using deception and heresy, and those from without. The letters to the churches warn of the doctrines of the Nicolaitans and of Balaam as well as the treachery of Jezebel. From without, the churches suffered persecution from governing authorities and unbelievers.

The persecution these churches suffered took two forms. Foremost was the persecution associated with the Christians' refusal to participate in emperor worship. The Roman emperor Domitian, who ruled Rome at the time of the writing of the book of Revelation, was the first Roman emperor to demand to be worshiped as a god while he was still alive. Each year every person in the empire was required to publicly burn incense and utter the words, "Caesar is Lord." This was no problem for Roman citizens. Adding one more god to their pantheon was easy. For the Christians, however, this was not acceptable. To the Romans, this annual expression was an act of patriotic duty. Refusal by anyone to honor Rome and Caesar in this manner was considered unpatriotic. Jews were exempt from this requirement because of their favored status.

The Romans had no prosecuting officers to ensure compliance with the laws. They relied on a system known as *delation* to bring lawbreakers to justice. Private citizens could take someone to the Roman court if they knew he or she had committed a crime. Roman citizens exercised this right and were compensated for their efforts. Delation became a lucrative trade, and those who participated in it were known as *delators.* When Christians refused to offer incense to Caesar, delators would prosecute the Christians for their failure to abide by the law.

FORMAT OF THE LETTERS

The letters to the churches in Revelation 2–3 have a consistent format. Some commentators break the structure down into seven categories. This can be a valuable tool, but not all the letters addressed all seven categories. For our purposes here, it seems best to note two specific categories—encouragement and exhortation. The risen Lord instructs John to infuse the churches with fresh courage and to make an urgent appeal for change.

The seven churches had four things in common: (1) They each received a message from Jesus, (2) He knew the works of each church, (3) He gave a promise to the one who overcomes, and (4) He admonished each church, "He who has an ear, let him hear what the Spirit says to the churches."

The format of the message is another common characteristic:

- Christ addressed each church by name.
- He identified Himself according to the content of each message.
- He informed the church what He knew about it.
- He assessed the condition of the church.
- He gave an exhortation.
- He admonished each church to heed His exhortation.
- He made a promise to the one who overcomes.

The messages to the churches were addressed to the angels of the churches, symbolically referred to as stars in 1:16,20. Each angel functioned as though it were the church, like a surrogate. They were expected to communicate the content of the message to their respective congregations and heed the message's encouragement and exhortation. The word *angel* (Greek, *angelos*) has been a source of great debate; some say the word refers to typical angels—God's ministering spirits (Hebrews 1:14), and others say the word refers to messengers sent to deliver a message. Of the 175 times *angelos* is used in the New Testament, all but six usages refer to ministering spirits. This would reasonably lead one to conclude that the intended meaning is heavenly beings.

But the same word is used to describe John the Baptist in Matthew 11:10; Mark 1:2; and Luke 7:27. John's followers are referred to as messengers in Luke 7:24, using the same word. In Luke 9:52 the disciples are referred to as messengers. Finally, in James 2:25 the word is used to describe the two spies protected by Rahab in Jericho (Joshua 2:1-22). In each of these cases, the word refers to human agents.

That these angels be viewed as human beings rather than heavenly beings seems reasonable in that they represent each individual church and that they are expected to communicate Jesus' messages and heed His warnings, and that they are called to repentance along with the rest of the congregation. Heavenly beings, on the other hand, are exempt from sin and thus there would be no need to call them to repentance. These angels are therefore apparently human agents who may have had some leadership capacity in the churches. They may have visited John on Patmos and returned back to their respective cities with the messages.

THE CHURCHES AND THE MESSAGES

Ephesus

When John wrote Revelation, Ephesus was the largest of the seven cities, with a population of about 250,000. It was a harbor city that had been relocated at least five times during its long history because of the buildup of silt in its harbor. Christ encouraged this church because He knew their labor and because they disapproved of evil and tested those who aspired to be teachers. They hated the deeds of the Nicolaitans, which He also hated. Although doctrinally sound, this church had left its first love. It had become mechanically orthodox. If the Ephesians chose to ignore Jesus' exhortation, they would face the removal of their lampstand (church). To the ancients, Ephesus was "the Light of Asia." The exhortation was thus significant for the city's reputation. The overcomer in this church would receive eternal access to the tree of life.

Smyrna

This city had been destroyed by marauders in its early history, and after 400 years it was rebuilt as one of the most beautiful cities in the world. The residents took this as a source of great civic pride. Christ encouraged this church to be faithful despite the persecution they were then facing and would continue to face. They were in abject poverty, but their riches were spiritual, abundant, and overflowing in their relationship to Him. Christ promised this church the crown of life and protection from the second death.

Pergamum

The description of the sender, "He who has the sharp two-edged sword," would have evoked strong images in the minds of the recipients. The judgment of the sword would not have escaped their attention.

This city was situated at the base of a terrain that rose sharply in elevation to 1000 feet. Terraced into the terrain were three levels of construction. At the base was the temple of Asklepios, the god of healing. On the middle terrace was the famous altar of Zeus. On the highest level was the temple to the Roman emperor. Temples to Dionysius and Athena were also clearly visible in the city. The polytheism of the city aptly qualified it as a satanic stronghold, "where Satan's throne is." On one hand, Christ encouraged the Christians in that church when He said, "You hold fast to My name, and did not deny My faith." On the other hand, He chastised them because they tolerated those in the church who held to the doctrines of Balaam and the Nicolaitans. Unless they repented, the sword of His mouth would fight against them. The overcomer in this church would receive hidden manna and a white stone on which is written a new name given by Christ Himself.

Thyatira

This city was situated inland, approximately 45 miles southeast of Pergamum. It was a military outpost designed to serve as the first line of defense for Pergamum. Due to its lack of natural fortification, it could only stave off hostile forces temporarily until reinforcements arrived. In the letter to this church, Christ describes Himself as one who has eyes that pierce to the very heart and feet like brass, capable of executing the chastisement that was written. Those piercing eyes knew the works of the church and that the most recent works were greater than those done in the past. But Thyatira also tolerated false teaching. Jesus exhorted the followers of the false teacher, Jezebel, to repent of their deeds. The rest of the church was told to hold fast to what they had. The overcomer would receive the morning star and power over the nations.

Sardis

This city was situated in the fertile Hermus Valley and enjoyed a legendary reputation due to the notoriety of its most famous king, Croesus. Here, Christ identified Himself as "He who has the seven Spirits of God and the seven stars." He chastised the church because they, like their ancestors, were living on past reputation. They had a reputation for being spiritually alive when in fact they were dead. They failed to protect their entrustment and lost their spiritual vitality. Christ exhorted them to discard their apathy and to be on the alert, strengthening the little spiritual life that yet remained in them. He encouraged them to remember what the faith was about and how they came to receive it. He promised the overcomer permanent inclusion in the Book of Life and confession of his name before God and His angels.

Philadelphia

The city of brotherly love was also the city of the open door. Despite persecution and "the synagogue of Satan," this church took advantage of the opportunities it had to share the gospel message. The risen Lord encouraged this church by letting them know that He understood how dedicated they had been in sharing His message. Their works had not gone unnoticed. He reminded them that He had opened this door for them, and no one could shut it. He exhorted them to persevere, for they had little strength, but His was great. He promised this little church freedom from the hour of trial that would come upon those who dwell on the earth. Their lives might be unstable, but the overcomer would be as secure as the pillar in the Temple of God in the New Jerusalem with a new name emblazoned on it, the new name of Jesus Himself.

Laodicea

The wealthiest of all the seven cities, Laodicea was a center of finance, industry, and medicine. Though the city was decimated by an earthquake in A.D. 60, the people refused financial help, opting to rebuild their city from their own resources. They considered themselves self-sufficient and in need of nothing. This church had been deceived into self-sufficiency and needed a reprimand from the One who knows what is true, speaks what is true, and is Himself Truth. The Laodiceans were as useless as water that is neither hot enough for batheing nor cold enough to drink. They were under the impression that they needed nothing. They were self-sufficient. Jesus warned them that they were not what they thought, but instead were wretched, miserable, poor, blind, and naked. He exhorted them to accept from Him that which they desperately needed and could only obtain from Him. Their condition was so deplorable that He wanted to vomit them out of His mouth. He encouraged them to open the door as He stood outside of the church and their lives, continually knocking on the door of their hearts, desiring entrance. To those who opened the door, the overcomers, He promised a seat on the throne next to Him as He shares the throne of the Father.

There is widespread agreement that these seven churches were literal churches and that they also represent different types of churches. There is also a consensus that all seven kinds of churches have existed in every era of church history and that they will continue to exist as long as the church is on planet earth. There is a third area at which consensus breaks down: Although not explicitly stated in Scripture, there seems to be a downward regression of church history beginning with the loss of one's first love at Ephesus and ending with the lukewarmness of those at Laodicea. Some scholars see in this a key to the mystery of the seven stars.

—TONY KESSINGER

BIBLIOGRAPHY

Aune, David S. *Revelation 1–5.* Dallas: Word, 1997.

Barclay, William. *Revelation.* Vol. 1. Philadelphia: Westminster, 1976.

Hemer, Colin J. *The Letters to the Seven Churches of Asia.* Grand Rapids: Eerdmans Publishing Company, 1989.

Hindson, Ed. *Revelation.* Chattanooga: AMG Publishers, 2002.

Kessinger, Tony. *Come Out of Her My People.* Philadelphia: Xlibris, 2003.

LaHaye, Tim. *Revelation Unveiled.* Grand Rapids: Zondervan, 1999.

MacArthur, John. *Revelation 1–11: An Exegetical Commentary.* Chicago: Moody Press, 1999.

Thomas, Robert L. *Revelation 1–7: An Exegetical Commentary.* Chicago: Moody Press, 1992.

SEVENTY WEEKS OF DANIEL

NO PORTION OF THE Old Testament unlocks the mysteries of God's prophetic plan for Israel and the nations as much as the book of Daniel. In particular, Daniel's prophecy of the 70 weeks (Hebrew, *shavuah,* "sevens") in Daniel 9:24-27 provides the indispensable chronological key to Bible prophecy. This prophecy concerns both the beginning and ending of "the desolation of Jerusalem" (from the Babylonian conquest to the second advent of Christ) and defines that period as "the times of the Gentiles" (Luke 21:24), after which Israel's time of restoration will begin (see Isaiah 2:2-4; Zechariah 8:1-15; 14:3-21). The prophecy of the 70 weeks therefore belongs to the larger corpus of prophetic restoration texts given to Israel as a comfort in her captivity. These prophecies promise the messianic redemption through the Davidic dynasty in Jerusalem (Isaiah 40–66; Jeremiah 30–33; Ezekiel 33–48).

The 70-weeks prophecy is included in the part of Daniel that records visions of future earthly kingdoms, both human and divine (chapters 7–12). It provides a prophetic template for later eschatological revelations such as Jesus' Olivet Discourse (Matthew 24; Mark

13; Luke 21), Paul's "day of the Lord" discourse (2 Thessalonians 2), and the divine wrath section of the Apocalypse (Revelation 6–19). The New Testament writers used the 70-weeks prophecy to predict future events, so we too should interpret it futuristically.

THE CONTEXT OF THE PROPHECY

Daniel understood from Jeremiah's prophecies that the Babylonian exile would last for 70 years (Daniel 9:2; Jeremiah 25:11; 29:10). He recognized that the restoration depended on national repentance (Jeremiah 29:10-14), so Daniel personally interceded for Israel with penitence and petition. He prayed specifically for the restoration of Jerusalem and the Temple (Daniel 9:3-19). Daniel apparently expected the immediate and complete fulfillment of Israel's restoration with the conclusion of the 70-year captivity. However, the answer delivered to him by the archangel Gabriel (the 70-weeks prophecy) revealed that Israel's restoration would be progressive and ultimately fulfilled only at the time of the end (see also Daniel 12).

THE EXTENT OF THE PROPHECY

God decreed that He would complete His messianic redemption of the Jews and Jerusalem (which includes both advents of Christ) in 70 weeks. He listed six restoration goals that He would accomplish during this time: (1) "to finish the transgression," (2) "to make an end of sins," (3) "to make atonement for iniquity," (4) "to bring in everlasting righteousness," (5) "to seal up vision and prophecy," and (6) "to anoint the most holy place."

The 70 "weeks" are actually 70 weeks of years, or 490 years. They are divided into seven weeks (49 years), 62 weeks (434 years), and one week (7 years). Israel's full restoration would not be accomplished with the return of a remnant of the exiles after the 70 years. Rather, God would fulfill His promises for Israel's future after 490 years. Conservative Christian scholarship applies this prophecy to the coming and death of Jesus, the Messiah

(9:25-26) and to "the destruction of the city [Jerusalem] and the sanctuary [Temple]."

These events took place after the 7 weeks and the 62 weeks, or 483 years (according to the Jewish lunar calendar). The 483 years began with Artaxerxes' decree to Nehemiah to rebuild the walls of Jerusalem in 444 B.C. and ended with the death of Christ in A.D. 33. Futurists have classically interpreted the seventieth and final week (in verse 27) as beginning long after the end of the sixty-ninth week. Daniel 12 and the New Testament prophetic texts that are based on Daniel's 70-weeks prophecy show that the events of the seventieth week describe the Tribulation, including the revelation and destruction of the Antichrist. The Bible also calls this seven-year period the Great Tribulation, the day of the Lord, the day of wrath, the day of distress, the day of trouble, the time of Jacob's trouble, a day of darkness and gloom, and the wrath of the Lamb. The seventieth week accomplishes Israel's restoration in the end time (Daniel 12:4,9; see also 8:17), so it follows (and is distinct from) the church age (which is consummated by the rapture).

The chart of Daniel's 70 weeks on page 358 features the premillennial pretribulational perspective of the 70 weeks. That is, it shows the rapture occurring before the Tribulation and the second coming of Christ taking place before the millennium. Although not all evangelicals hold to a pretribulational rapture view (some favor, instead, a midtribulational or posttribulational view), they agree that the Antichrist will arise during the Tribulation. He may be in a position of power before the rapture, but people will not recognize him as the Antichrist until the Tribulation (2 Thessalonians 2:6,8).

THE INTERPRETATION OF THE PROPHECY

The 70-weeks prophecy will be fulfilled when its six restoration goals are met (Daniel 9:24). Non-futurists claim that the death, resurrection, and ascension of Jesus accomplished these goals. They therefore view the entire

Daniel's Seventy Weeks
(Daniel 9:24-27)

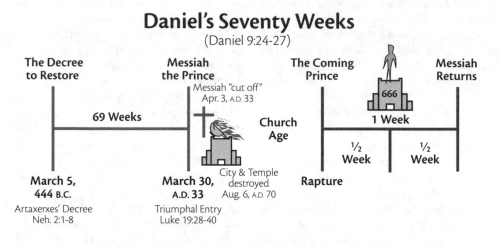

Explanation of Daniel's 70 Weeks of Years

69 weeks of years x 7 years in each week x 360 days per year = 173,880 days

March 5, 444 B.C. (Artaxerxes' decree) + 173,880 days = March 30, A.D. 33 (the triumphal entry)

Verification

444 B.C. to A.D. 33 = 476 years

476 years x 365.2421989 days = 173,855 days

+ days between March 5 (Artaxerxes' decree) and March 30 (the triumphal entry) = 25 days

Total = 173,880 days

Rationale for 360-Day Years

½ week (or 3½ years)—Daniel 9:27

1260 days—Revelation 11:3; 12:6

42 months—Revelation 11:2; 13:5

42 months = 1260 days = time, times, half time = half week

Therefore, one month = 30 days; one year = 360 days

prophecy as being fulfilled consecutively without interruption between the sixty-ninth and seventieth weeks. Some futurists agree that some of the redemptive goals may have been fulfilled in Christ's first advent, but they believe that other goals cannot be fulfilled apart from events that attend the second advent of Christ. For example, we do not yet

see the answer to Daniel's central concern—the final end of the captivity of the Jews and Jerusalem (Daniel 9:2).

The non-futurist view points to temporary Jewish revolts, but all of these were unsuccessful and ultimately led to the destruction of the city and the Temple and to further exile. This, of course, offers no solution to Daniel's specific petition for his people's return to Jerusalem and the rebuilding of the Temple (9:16-19). As a result, non-futurists generally depart from literal historical interpretation and resort to a symbolic fulfillment: a "spiritual restoration" coming through Christ's atonement.

Gabriel promised Daniel that the one who would desolate the Temple would be completely destroyed (9:27). This has never happened. Rather, the Roman general Titus, who destroyed the Second Temple together with his emperor father Vespasian, paraded the Temple vessels through the streets of Rome. The prophetic destruction of the Temple desolator in verse 27 must occur literally just as the destruction of the Temple in verse 26 occurred literally and the messianic references in verses 25-26 were fulfilled literally. This destruction is "decreed"—it will clearly be the result of divine judgment. Only the futurist interpretation that sees the Temple desolator as the Antichrist (2 Thessalonians 2:3-4; Revelation 11:1-2) with his destruction at the second advent of Christ (2 Thessalonians 2:8-9; Revelation 19:11-20) is in harmony with this.

THE PROGRESSIVE FULFILLMENT OF THE PROPHECY

Several other factors also point to a progressive future fulfillment of these goals. For example, according to Daniel 9:24, the 70-weeks prophecy is for national Israel and Jerusalem. In other words, this is not a universal promise. It predicts the future of the Jews in their historic Land.

In answer to Daniel's prayer, a Jewish remnant returned to Judah to resettle the Land and to rebuild Jerusalem and the Temple. Also, a Jewish Messiah came to the Land of Israel to "make atonement for iniquity" (9:24). In the same way that these events were fulfilled literally, the six prophetic goals of the 70 weeks should also be expected to be fulfilled literally. These six goals have not been fulfilled in the church in this age; rather, they apply to the Jewish nation in the age to come.

Messiah's Mission

The first three goals relate to the *sins* of national Israel, and the final three goals have to do with her *salvation*. The Messiah fulfills these goals in His first and second advents. Israel's return at the end of the 70 years did not "finish the transgression," "make an end of sin," or "make atonement for iniquity."

Jewish commentators also held that the final fulfillment of these goals had not been accomplished with the return and restoration under Zerubbabel in 538 B.C. According to the Jewish commentator Abarbanel, Israel's sin required not 70 years but 490 years because of the violation of the sabbatical law (2 Chronicles 36:21). Other Jewish commentators such as Rashi and Metzudos held that this referred to a period following the 490 years, which they believed ended with the destruction of the Second Temple.

Messiah's Death

Daniel's prophecy clearly reveals that the Messiah came and accomplished the first part of His mission (the first three goals) at the time predicted in verses 25-26—that is, 483 years into the 490 years. In verse 26, the Messiah is cut off, and Jerusalem and the Temple are destroyed. This occurred late in the Second Temple period. This was precisely when the rabbinic sources (see the Babylonian Talmud, tractate Sanhedrin 97a-b) expected the Messiah to arrive. The Messiah's death made an end of sin and made atonement for iniquity as predicted in verse 24. This act serves as the basis for Israel's future salvation at the second advent (Zechariah 12:10; Matthew 24:30-31; Luke 21:27-28; Romans 11:26-27). The words "cut off and have nothing" may mean "without inheriting the messianic kingdom" (verse 26). After Jesus' death and resurrection, He said that the kingdom was still future (Acts 1:6-7).

Messiah's Program

The fulfillment of the last three goals awaits the time of the end. The phrase "to bring in everlasting righteousness" refers to the millennial restoration or "age of righteousness" (see Isaiah 1:26; 11:2-5; 32:16-18; Jeremiah 23:5-6; 33:15-18). This eschatological restoration may also "seal up the prophetic vision." The final goal, "to anoint the most holy," must look to a future dedication of the Temple's Holy of

Holies. Rabbinic interpretation referred this to the Third Temple. According to Tosefta Sotah 13:2, the Second Temple had not been anointed because it lacked both the ark of the covenant and the *shekinah* (the divine presence). When Messiah returns in glory, He will build the millennial Temple (see Ezekiel 40–48), fill it with the divine presence (Ezekiel 43:1-7), and consecrate it for use throughout the messianic age (Isaiah 56:6-7; 60:7; Jeremiah 33:18; Ezekiel 43:11,18-27; 44:11-28; 45:13–46:15; Zechariah 14:16-21). Therefore, Daniel describes Messiah's mission to Israel beginning with His crucifixion as Israel's Savior and culminating with His reign as Israel's king. God will fulfill all the elements of Daniel's prayer in the coming age of Messiah's reign.

The signal event that leads to the completion of the messianic program for Israel in the concluding half of the seventieth week is the "abomination that makes desolate." A leader (called a "prince" like the messiah in verse 25) related to the people (the Romans) who destroyed the Second Temple would make a covenant with the leaders ("the many") of Israel. The specific nature of this covenant is unclear, but it relates to the rebuilding of the Temple in some way.

Jesus said that the future desecration of the Temple would be the unavoidable sign to Israel of the time of Great Tribulation (Matthew 24:15; Mark 13:14). The apostle Paul also used it as evidence for the unmistakable rise of the "man of sin" (the Antichrist) and of the judgment of God to come in the Tribulation (2 Thessalonians 2:9; Revelation 13:11-15). With the destruction of the Antichrist and his armies by Christ (Revelation 19:20), and the national repentance of Israel (Romans 11:26-27), the final restoration of Israel and the exaltation of Jerusalem and God's Sanctuary for which Daniel prayed will be accomplished (see Isaiah 2:2-3; 4:2-6; Jeremiah 3:17; Ezekiel 37:24-28; 48:35; Zechariah 8:3-8; 13:1-2; 14:8-20).

THE PURPOSE OF THE PROPHECY

Daniel had searched the prophets and prayed for an answer to the mystery that surrounded the desolation of the Temple in his day. He learned that the times of the Gentiles began with the captivity of his day and would end with an international empire headed by a coming wicked ruler. God revealed that this would occur in the end time and that the final act of Temple desolation would signal God's final judgment against the Gentile powers. Finally, God would fulfill all His promises to Israel (Daniel 2:44-45; 7:17-27; 12:1,7). In the 70-weeks prophecy, Daniel gives us the key to the prophetic puzzle of the end time so that we might know what to expect and have confidence in our own day.

—RANDALL PRICE AND THOMAS ICE

BIBLIOGRAPHY

Culver, Robert D. *Daniel and the Latter Days*. Chicago: Moody Press, 1977.

Ironside, H.A. *The Great Parenthesis*. Grand Rapids: Zondervan, 1943.

McClain, Alva J. *Daniel's Prophecy of the Seventy Weeks*. Grand Rapids: Zondervan, 1960.

Pentecost, J. Dwight. *Things to Come*. Grand Rapids: Zondervan, 1975.

Walvoord, John F. *Daniel: The Key to Prophetic Revelation*. Chicago: Moody Press, 1971.

SHEOL

THE OLD TESTAMENT USES the Hebrew word *sheol* to describe the abode of the dead 65 times. The Septuagint renders it in Greek as *hades*, and the New Testament refers to it several times (see Luke 16:23). In English translations of the Old Testament, it appears variously as "hell," "the pit," and "the grave." *Sheol* can have different meanings in different contexts. This has led to some confusion and differing interpretations regarding the exact nature of the meaning of *sheol*.

It can mean the grave (Job 17:13; Psalm 16:10; Isaiah 38:10), but it can also mean the place to which the departed dead go (Genesis 37:35; 42:38; Numbers 16:33; Job 14:13; Psalm 55:15). The redeemed will be rescued from *sheol* (Psalm 16:9-11; 17:15; 49:15), but the wicked will not (Job 21:13; 24:19; Psalm 9:17; 31:17; 49:14; 55:15). "Whether the grave or the netherworld is in view, *sheol* speaks of the deepest depths, the antithesis of the highest heavens (Job 11:8; cf. Proverbs 9:18)" (Merrill, vol. 4, p. 6). *Sheol* also refers to a place of punishment from which only God has the power of release (1 Samuel 2:6; Job 24:19; Psalm 30:9; Isaiah 26:19).

Some of the interpretive confusion has arisen because *sheol* is said to be a place where both good people (such as Jacob in Genesis 37:35) and bad people (such as Korah and Dathan in Numbers 16:30) go. This led some earlier interpreters of the Bible to assert a two-compartment theory—one for Old Testament saints and the other for the rest of Old Testament people. A different interpretation avoids some of these problems by suggesting a double meaning of the word: It originally meant "the grave" but became specialized for "hell." Yet another interpretation is that *sheol* is poetic language that refers primarily to the grave rather than an intermediate state (Harris, vol. 2, pp. 892–93). This last perspective is appealing, but it does not satisfy every usage in the Old Testament (Psalm 86:13; Proverbs 15:24).

The major focus of the Old Testament usage is on the place where the bodies of people go, not where their souls exist. The destiny of the souls of individuals in the intermediate state is not widely discussed in the Old Testament. Although there is some expectation in the Old Testament of deliverance of the righteous from *sheol* (Psalm 16:10; 49:15), the full doctrine of eternal destiny depends on the progressive revelation of the New Testament (see 1 Corinthians 15:50-58).

According to Revelation 20:11-15, unbelievers will be cast into the lake of fire after the Great White Throne judgment at the end of the millennium, where they will remain forever. It is an individual's choice that brings this terrible judgment and eternal punishment. Every person must decide whether to spend eternity in heaven or in hell; the choice is eternal punishment or eternal life (Matthew 25:46). (See the article titled "Hell.")

—TIMOTHY J. DEMY

BIBLIOGRAPHY

Harris, R. Laird. "Sheol." In *Theological Wordbook of the Old Testament*. Eds. R. Laird Harris, Gleason L. Archer, Jr., and Bruce K. Waltke. Chicago: Moody Press, 1980.

Ice, Thomas, and Timothy J. Demy. *What the Bible Says about Heaven & Eternity*. Grand Rapids: Kregel, 2000.

Merrill, Eugene. "Sheol." In *New International Dictionary of Old Testament Theology and Exegesis*. Ed. Willem A. VanGemeren. Grand Rapids: Zondervan, 1997.

Zuck, Roy B., ed. *Biblical Theology of the Old Testament*. Chicago: Moody Press, 1991.

SIGNS OF THE TIMES

THE END OF ALL THINGS is near. Therefore be clear minded and self-controlled so that you can pray" (1 Peter 4:7 NIV). Peter and the other apostles sensed that they had moved dramatically closer to the consummation of God's plan for this world. Peter's reference to the end is expressed by a perfect-tense verb in the Greek text. This means the action involved is a present reality with future consequences. We could just as appropriately read, "The end of all things has already begun." For Peter, the end of the age was already a present reality.

The first coming of Christ initiated the end of the age (see Acts 2:14-20; Hebrews 1:2), and His second coming will terminate the end of the age (Matthew 24:30). Therefore, the entire church age is the "last days."

Scripture also speaks of the end as a future event. The apostle Paul predicted, "There will be terrible times in the last days" (2 Timothy 3:1). The opening verse of the apocalypse refers to "what must soon take place" (Revelation 1:1) and goes on to warn us that "the time is near" (Revelation 1:3). Scripture also presents Christ's coming as an imminent reality. "Behold, I am coming soon!" Christ promised (Revelation 22:7). He will come suddenly—He could come for the church at any moment!

That leaves us asking this question: What time is it now? Peter wrote that "[Christ] was revealed in these last times" (1 Peter 1:20). But he also referred to the coming of Christ as a future event, "ready to be revealed in the last time" (1 Peter 1:5). He clearly viewed the last times as both a present reality and a future event.

The Bible affirms three basic facts about the coming of Christ and the end of the age.

First, we are living in the last days. Every generation of Christians has lived with the hope of the imminent return of Christ. We believe that He could return for us at any moment. No prophetic event remains to be fulfilled before He comes to rapture His church. In fact, certain events, such as the return of Israel to her land, indicate that we are close to the end.

Second, God's timetable is not our timetable. Peter told us that "in the last days scoffers will come," questioning the promise of Christ's second coming (2 Peter 3:3-4). They will reject the idea of God's intervention in human history and suggest that all things are moving forward at their own pace without God. These skeptics will also fail to anticipate God's coming judgment upon the world (2 Peter 3:8-9). But we dare not mistake the patience of God for a change in His plans. He is waiting, giving people time to repent. The Bible warns, "He who is coming will come and will not delay" (Hebrews 10:37).

Third, Christ's coming is always drawing closer. The Bible emphatically promises that Christ is coming again (Luke 12:40; Philippians 3:20; Titus 2:13; Hebrews 9:28). Scripture urges us to be watching, waiting, and ready for our Lord to return. Every day that passes brings us one day closer. Whether He returns next week or 1000 years from now, we are to be living as though He were coming today.

LOOKING AHEAD

Anticipation is the key to preparation. And if we really believe Jesus is coming, we will want to be prepared for Him when He comes. Jesus illustrated this in His own prophetic teaching with the story of the ten virgins (Matthew 25:1-13). Only those who were prepared for the wedding were invited into the wedding banquet. The others were left out. Jesus used this illustration to remind us to "keep watching" because we don't know the time of His coming. The rapture could happen at any moment.

WHAT DOES THE FUTURE HOLD?

The Bible predicts the major events of the future. It gives us the big picture of what is coming in the end times. The specific details are not always as clear, and we must be cautious about trying to speculate beyond what the Bible itself actually says. Our goal is to be balanced, not minimizing or maximizing the future. We must not try to make the Bible say more than it is saying.

Those who prefer a literal interpretation of prophecy foresee Israel returning to the land, the rebuilding of the Temple, the rise of a literal Antichrist, the making and breaking of a real peace treaty, and the ultimate invasion of Israel, leading to the battle of Armageddon. We do not believe that we can simply spiritualize away the basic statements of Bible prophecy. For us, the rapture means being "caught up" into heaven (1 Thessalonians 4:13-17), and the "thousand years" of Christ's reign means a literal 1000 years (Revelation 20:4). We do not discount the use of figurative or symbolic language in prophetic passages (such as "the Lamb," "the beast," and "the dragon"). But we believe the prophetic passages pointing to the second coming of Christ refer to specific people and events, as did the prophetic passages pointing to His first coming (such as Isaiah 53).

According to a pretribulational viewpoint, we believe that Jesus Christ will return to rapture the church prior to the Tribulation. In commenting on this spectacular event, the apostle Paul wrote, "For the Lord himself will come down from heaven, with a loud command, with the voice of the archangel and with the trumpet call of God, and the dead in Christ will rise first. After that, we who are still alive and are left will be caught up [Greek, *harpazo*, 'snatched away'] with them in the clouds to meet the Lord in the air. And so we will be with the Lord forever" (1 Thessalonians 4:16-17).

The picture of the future in biblical prophecy centers on 15 key predictions, many of which involve signs of Christ's return at the end of the Tribulation. Some of these prophecies are already fulfilled, so we are probably very close to the end because the rapture will precede Christ's final return to earth.

The Spread of the Gospel Message and the Growth of the Church

Jesus established the church and promised to continue to build it until He returns (Matthew 16:18). He also predicted that the gospel "will be preached in the whole world as a testimony to all nations" (Matthew 24:14). The growth of the church and world evangelism will continue until the body of Christ is complete. No prophecy tells us exactly how long the church age will last. It will continue until the Lord returns to receive the church at the rapture.

The Increase of Wickedness and the Spread of Evil

The Bible also predicts that the "increase of evil" will continue until the end of the age (Matthew 24:12). Paul predicted that "there will be terrible times in the last days" and then defined those days as a time of unparalleled greed, avarice, and selfishness (2 Timothy 3:1-5). Today, these prophecies are being fulfilled at a startling pace.

The Rise of False Prophets and Apostate Religion

Jesus Himself warned about the coming of "false Christs" and "false prophets" (Matthew 24:4,24). Peter predicted, "There will be false teachers" (2 Peter 2:1). Paul called them "false apostles, deceitful workmen, masquerading as apostles of Christ" (2 Corinthians 11:13). The Bible seems to indicate that false prophets and apostate religion will become worse as we get closer to the end (Jude 17-18).

The Return of Israel to the Promised Land

"I will bring you from the nations...where you have been scattered," wrote Ezekiel (20:34). "I will bring your children...from the ends of the earth," promised Isaiah (43:5-6). In 1948, these ancient prophecies were ful-

filled when Israel became a nation again after nearly 1900 years in exile. Ezekiel predicted a two-stage return: a physical regathering and a spiritual rebirth (Ezekiel 37:1-14).

Conflict in the Middle East

The general picture of the future is one of turmoil between the Jews and the Arabs in the Middle East. Jesus warned of "wars and rumors of wars" in the future (Matthew 24:6-7). The prophet Joel predicts the nations invading Israel in the last days—"multitudes, multitudes in the valley of decision: for the day of the LORD is near in the valley of decision" (Joel 3:2-14 KJV). Ezekiel (38:1-6) predicts a massive invasion of Israel in the "latter days" by a coalition of nations: Magog, Persia, Libya, Ethiopia, Gomer, and Togarmah. Collectively, the prophets foresee Israel back in the land but under constant threat of attack.

The Rapture of the Church

At some undated time in the future, Jesus will return to rapture the church (all believers) to heaven. When He was preparing to return to heaven, Jesus promised, "I will come back and take you to be with me" (John 14:3). Paul predicted that those who had died in Christ will rise first, and then the living believers will be "caught up" into the clouds and united with those who have been resurrected (1 Thessalonians 4:13-17). The rapture will happen "in a flash, in the twinkling of an eye, at the last trumpet" (1 Corinthians 15:51). The rapture precedes the Tribulation and fulfills the Lord's promise: "I will also keep you from the hour of trial that is going to come upon the whole world" (Revelation 3:10).

The Marriage of Christ and the Church in Heaven

After the rapture and prior to the return of Christ to the earth, the "wedding of the Lamb" will take place in heaven (Revelation 19:7-9). The marriage is followed by the "wedding supper," which appears to last for seven years during the tribulation period. Christ is the husband or bridegroom, and the church is the bride of Christ (see Ephesians 5:25-27;

2 Corinthians 11:2). Following the pattern of traditional Jewish weddings in biblical times, Jesus spoke of the promised engagement, followed by the departure of the groom to prepare a place for the bride, followed by the groom's sudden return "at midnight" to call the bride away (Matthew 25:1-6).

The Rise of the Antichrist and the False Prophet

Paul predicts the rise of the "lawless one" after the restrainer (the indwelling Spirit in the church) has been removed (2 Thessalonians 2:3-8). "Then the lawless one will be revealed," Paul writes. This seems to indicate that the identity of the Antichrist will remain a mystery until after the rapture. John calls him "the beast" in Revelation 13:1-10 and "the antichrist" in 1 John 2:22. John also pictures this last great political leader being assisted by the "False Prophet"—a deceitful religious leader (Revelation 13:11-18). Together, they deceive the whole world during the tribulation period.

The Development of a Global System

The book of Revelation clearly predicts the world of the future will combine a global economy (Revelation 13:16-17), a world government (13:8; 17:1-18), and a universal religion (13:8-12). The global economy is already a reality! The world government is already in the process of forming under the banner of democracy. At the present time, the United States is the major player in the attempt to ensure global peace and security. A consensus of world religion does not exist today, but it could easily develop after the rapture. In the meantime, the sentiment of apostate Christendom continues to favor a religion of universal tolerance.

The Tribulation Period

Despite efforts at world peace, the rule of the Antichrist will be marked by wars of mass destruction, environmental disasters, and divine judgments (Revelation 6:1-16; 9:16-18). Daniel (12:1) calls this period a "time of distress." Zephaniah (1:14) calls it "the great day of the Lord." Jeremiah (30:7) calls it "a time of trouble

for Jacob." John calls it the "wrath of the Lamb" (Revelation 16:16). Most pretribulationalists view the Tribulation as being simultaneous with the seven years of Daniel's seventieth week (Daniel 9:24-27). We believe the Antichrist will make a peace treaty with Israel during this period, but then break the treaty at the midpoint of the Tribulation (Daniel 9:27).

The Battle of Armageddon

The prophetic picture indicates a series of wars of mass destruction will happen in the future (Revelation 6–18). These will result in nearly half the population of the world being destroyed (Revelation 8:7; 9:16-18). Eventually, these wars will culminate in a final battle at "the place...called Armageddon" (Revelation 16:16). The mountains will be "soaked with blood" (Isaiah 34:3). "All the nations that fought against Jerusalem" will be destroyed (Zechariah 14:12-13). In the end, Christ Himself will return and conquer the beast and the False Prophet, casting them into the lake of fire (Revelation 19:11-20). Satan will be bound in the abyss for 1000 years (Revelation 20:1-2). Christ will win the greatest battle in the history of the world when He conquers the enemies of God by the power of His spoken word (Revelation 19:15,21).

The Triumphal Return of Christ

Jesus predicted that one day "the sign of the Son of Man will appear in the sky....They will see the Son of Man coming on the clouds of the sky, with power and great glory" (Matthew 24:30). Zechariah (14:3-4) predicted that "his feet will stand on the Mount of Olives" and it will "split in two" when He returns. Isaiah (63:1-4) pictures Christ marching in triumph in blood-splattered garments on the "day of vengeance." Revelation 19:11-16 describes Him coming on a white horse with the church, robed in white, at His side. He "judges" with eyes of "blazing fire" and "makes war" with the "sharp sword" of His spoken word. He treads the "winepress...of the wrath of God" when He come to rule as "King of kings and Lord of lords."

The Millennial Kingdom

The Old Testament prophets pictured the coming messianic age as a time of peace and prosperity for Israel, when "they will beat their swords into plowshares" and "nation will not take up sword against nation" (Isaiah 2:2-4). They also foresaw the Messiah reigning "on David's throne and over his kingdom" (Isaiah 9:6-7). The New Testament pictures this as a time when Christ rules on earth with His bride, the church, for 1000 years (Revelation 20:1-6). We will "reign on the earth" as kings and priests with Christ (Revelation 5:10). Those who survive the Tribulation will live on into the millennial kingdom as life continues on earth for 1000 years.

The Great White Throne Judgment

After the 1000-year reign, God will let Satan loose from the abyss, and Satan will attempt one last time to overthrow the kingdom of God (Revelation 20:7-10). God will permanently defeat him and cast him into the lake of fire. The millennial kingdom will be transferred into the eternal kingdom of God (1 Corinthians 15:24), and the Great White Throne judgment will settle the eternal condemnation of all the lost of all time, those whose names are "not found written in the book of life" (Revelation 20:11-15). At that time, even "death and hell" will be thrown into the lake of fire, the "second death."

Eternity

The Bible pictures the eternal state as one of perpetual bliss where paradise is regained. The "tree of life" is restored (Revelation 22:2), and the redeemed of all time live together in the "new heavens" and "new earth" with the "new Jerusalem" as their central dwelling place (Revelation 21:1-23). God will wipe away all tears, and His people will experience "no more death or mourning or crying or pain" (Revelation 21:4). Isaiah (65:19) predicted, "The sound of weeping and crying will be heard no more." God the Father and Christ the Lamb will be the light and the temple of the eternal city (Revelation 21:22-23). The 12 gates of the city are named for the 12 tribes of Israel, and the 12 foundations for the 12 apostles, emphasizing the eternal unity of the redeemed people of God (Revelation 21:11-14).

Jesus said, "I am the resurrection and the life. He who believes in me will live, even though he dies" (John 11:25). This is the great promise of Christ. He calls us to faith in Him and then promises to reward us with eternal life (John 3:16; 4:36; 5:24). The Bible pictures eternity as a place of great activity as we serve Christ forever.

A CONSTANT READINESS

Until the trumpet sounds or death comes to usher us into eternity, we are to keep our eyes on the Savior (Hebrews 12:2). He is the focus of Bible prophecy. The prophets predicted His first coming with incredible accuracy, and they have done the same for His second coming. Jesus said, "When these things begin to take place, stand up and lift up your heads, because your redemption is drawing near" (Luke 21:28). Whatever else is coming in the future, we can rest assured that Jesus is coming again!

—ED HINDSON

BIBLIOGRAPHY

Hindson, Ed. *Final Signs*. Eugene, OR: Harvest House Publishers, 1996.

LaHaye, Tim. *Understanding the Last Days*. Eugene, OR: Harvest House Publishers, 1998.

MacArthur, John F. *The Second Coming: Signs of Christ's Return and the End of the Age*. Wheaton, IL: Crossway Books, 1999.

Pentecost, J. Dwight. *Things to Come*. Grand Rapids: Zondervan, 1971.

SIX HUNDRED SIXTY-SIX

REVELATION 13:18 IDENTIFIES the Antichrist using the enigmatic number 666. This verse provides the means by which the intelligent reader can compute the number of the beast. The term "wisdom" (Greek, *sophia*) refers to the skill and understanding necessary to interpret the meaning of this number (see Daniel

9:22). The God-given ability to interpret this number will come from the special intelligence given to believers during the Tribulation period.

The calculation of the number is derived by "counting" (from the Greek word for "pebble," since the ancients used pebbles for counting). The precise translation of the command in this verse is, "Let [him] count the number." Giving this phrase a general meaning with no arithmetic complexities, reducing it to a simple call to discern the identity of the beast from broad symbolism, is contrary to the plain meaning of the text and ignores the command to "count." The view that 666 represents man in general overlooks the writer's obvious intention that the number be understood to identify a specific individual.

Revelation 13:18 may be referring to the calculation technique called *gematria*. In ancient times, letters of the alphabet served as numbers. The first nine letters stood for the numbers one through nine, and the next nine for the numbers ten through ninety. Certain obsolete letters and signs supplemented the system. Every name yielded a number, the deciphering of which proved to be a fascinating riddle. An example of this practice occurs in the Sibylline Oracles 1.324-329, where the number of the name *Iesous* ("Jesus") is 888.

Those who would apply gematria to Revelation 13:18 should heed a precaution that the early church father Irenaeus offered long ago: We should not speculate about the identity of the person represented by the number 666 until that person arrives on the scene. This precaution answers the objection based on the unreliable and imaginative speculations resulting from the use of gematria. The number 666 does have a secondary implication regarding human limitation, but its primary use will be to help believers of the future recognize the false Christ when he becomes a public figure.

The conjunction "for" (Greek, *gar*) offers the reason that the calculation should be made. It is because it is the number of a man. The inescapable conclusion is that the expression means this is a mysterious hint about a man whose name gives the number 666. It is the name of the beast as well as that of one of the beast's heads. He is a king or emperor who at times in the narrative is emblematic of the empire he rules.

If 666 is the number of a future Antichrist who will rise to power after the rapture, then all attempts to identify him with past or present entities are futile. Attempts to calculate his name as Nero Caesar or Caligula require the use of a Hebrew transliteration of the Greek or Latin forms of their names for a readership who knew little or no Hebrew. In the case of Nero, the identification involves a defective spelling that necessitates changing Nero to Neron in order to make the calculation work. Robertson (pp. 406–07) notes that some Greek manuscripts read 616 instead of 666, which may be based on the Latin form of Nero (without the final "n").

The number is actually 666 (Greek, *hexakosioi hexekonta hex*). Its significance is not just three sixes; it must add up to 666. The clear purpose of the number is to help Tribulation-era believers to identify the Antichrist during the time when he will be in power. If one takes the pretribulational and futurist view of Revelation in general, the Antichrist's identification is obviously a matter of future discernment.

Second Thessalonians 2:3-8 clearly states that the Antichrist's identity will not be revealed until after the removal of the Restrainer, presumably at the rapture. The better part of wisdom then is to be content that the Antichrist's identity is not yet known but will be revealed when he ascends to his evil throne. In the meantime, any human curiosity on our part will have to remain unsatisfied until the time of fulfillment arrives. Thus, church-age believers are told to keep watching (Matthew 24:42) for Jesus to come, not for the Antichrist's arrival. Only after the rapture of the church will Satan be free to move the "man of sin" onto the world scene. Until then, he must wait until God makes the next move on the prophetic calendar of future events.

—ROBERT THOMAS AND ED HINDSON

BIBLIOGRAPHY

Hindson, Ed. *The Book of Revelation*. Chattanooga: AMG Publishers, 2002.

Robertson, A.T. *Word Pictures in the New Testament*, vol. 6. Grand Rapids: Baker Books, 1980.

Tenney, Merrill. *Interpreting Revelation*. Grand Rapids: Eerdmans Publishing Company, 1957.

Thomas, Robert L. *Revelation 8–22: An Exegetical Commentary*. Chicago: Moody Press, 1995.

Walvoord, John F. *The Revelation of Jesus Christ*. Chicago: Moody Press, 1966.

SON OF GOD

THIS IS ONE OF THE MOST definitive names for the Lord Jesus Christ in all of Scripture and particularly in the New Testament. "Son of God" points to the deity of Christ; the expression "Son of Man" defines His work as Christ, the Messiah. These noun phrases could be translated "the Son who relates to God" and "the Son who relates to mankind."

PSALM 2

The Messiah is first called God's Son in the great messianic Psalm 2. This psalm is a prophecy of the coming of the Son of God to the earth and of His future kingly role over Zion. The psalm follows this outline:

Verse 1: Why are the nations so angry?

Verses 2-3: The rulers of earth stand against the Lord and His Anointed (the Messiah).

Verse 4: The Lord in heaven scoffs at the rebellion of the peoples of earth.

Verses 5-6: God will someday reply in anger and install His King on the throne in Zion.

Verse 7: The Messiah speaks, and God calls Him His Son.

Verses 8-9: The Son will someday possess the earth and will rule the nations with a rod of iron.

Verses 10-12: The rulers of earth must pay homage to God's Son or face His wrath.

The thrust of this psalm is that God will someday send His Son to reign in Zion over the whole earth. At that time the world must recognize Him as the Son of God, pay homage, and take refuge in Him.

JOHN'S PROLOGUE

The New Testament picks up on the importance of this psalm and of the title "Son of God." John 1:1-5 goes into great detail to show that Jesus is that Son. The apostle gives one of the most grammatically powerful presentations of His deity in all of the New Testament. The Greek text points out that He always existed in the past as the Word of God, that this Word was always with God, and that He always existed as God. The past tenses describe a past linear action: He was always existing in the past this way!

John reinforces the fact of the deity of the Son of God: "No one has seen God at any time; the only begotten God who is in the bosom of the Father, He has explained Him" (John 1:18 NASB). Though this verse contains a textual problem, it nonetheless demonstrates the deity of the Son. The *Textus Receptus* reads "the only begotten Son," while the older Greek manuscripts read "the only begotten God." After much thought and study, most evangelical scholars believe the older manuscript readings should stand. Without question this is pointing to the incarnation of the Son as expressed so clearly in Psalm 2:7. The point of John 1:18 is that the Son is qualified to reveal the Father by reason of the continual fellowship (*en*, "in" His bosom) He has with Him. Verse 18 has been called the "prologue in which the Logos is pictured in marvelous fashion as the Word of God in human flesh, the Son of God with the Glory of God in him, showing men who God is and what he is" (Robertson, 5:17).

When John speaks of "the only begotten God," he uses the Greek word *monogenous*. This word marks the unique relation of the Father to the Son, and it applies to no one else besides them. This also points out and distinguishes the eternal relationship between the Father and the Son.

John 1:35-51 prominently alludes to Psalm 2. Andrew tells his brother Peter, "We have found the Messiah (which translated means Christ)" (verse 41). This is a reference to Psalm 2:2, which refers to the Son of God as God's Anointed (Hebrew, *Meshiach;* Greek, *Christos*). Nathaniel recognizes Jesus to be the Son of God, the king (see Psalm 2:6). To this Jesus adds the messianic expression "the Son of Man."

OTHER NEW TESTAMENT REFERENCES

The New Testament often quotes Psalm 2. Both God the Father and John the Baptist attested that Christ is God's Son (Matthew 3:17; John 1:34). The demons also knew that He was the Christ, the Son of God (Luke 4:41). Yet while Christ was on earth, no one had a comprehensive understanding of His relationship with the Father. Jesus said, "All things have been handed over to Me by My Father, and no one knows who the Son is except the Father, and who the Father is except the Son, and anyone to whom the Son wills to reveal Him" (10:22). Before He was arrested and crucified, Christ explained more about this mysterious relationship between Himself and the Father in the Upper Room Discourse (John 13–17). He told His disciples that after His ascension He would come and indwell each believer, as would the Father and the Holy Spirit (14:23-26).

In the epistles we read that the saved are reconciled to God by the death of His Son (Romans 5:10), and God calls them into the fellowship of His Son (1 Corinthians 1:9). God has sent forth the Spirit from His Son (Galatians 4:6), and Christ sent forth the Holy Spirit from Himself also (Romans 8:9,11). God sent the Son as a propitiation and Savior, and whoever confesses that Jesus is the Son of God abides in God (1 John 4:9,14-15). Saving faith is the act of believing in God's testimony about His Son (5:9-10). The apostle John adds, "The testimony is this, that God has given us eternal life, and this life is in His Son. He who has the Son has the life; he who does not have the Son of God does not have the life. These things I have written to you who believe in the name of the Son of God, so that you may know that you have eternal life" (5:11-13).

Prophecy encourages the church to eagerly await the rapture—the catching away to be with Christ. Paul commended the Thessalonian congregation because they were continually serving the "living and true God" and were waiting "for His Son from heaven, whom He raised from the dead, that is Jesus, who rescues us from the wrath to come" (1 Thessalonians 1:9-10). The apostle later expands on this theme, saying, "The Lord Himself will descend from heaven with a shout, with the voice of the archangel and with the trumpet of God, and the dead in Christ will rise first. Then we who are alive and remain will be caught up together with them in the clouds to meet the Lord in the air, and so we shall always be with the Lord" (4:16-17). The Son of God is the Lord who here raises the dead church saints and transforms those who are alive and carries them up to His presence.

As the book of Revelation begins, John sees the Son of God in glory, standing with His hair like white wool, eyes like a flame of fire, and His feet like "burnished bronze" (Revelation 1:14-15). Jesus says to the church at Thyatira, "The Son of God, who has eyes like a flame of fire, and His feet are like burnished bronze, says this..." (2:18). This is a reminder that the Son of God even now relates to the churches, and He will return someday (2:25).

At the conclusion of the 1000-year kingdom reign, Christ delivers up the kingdom to God His Father, when He has abolished all earthly rule, authority, and power (1 Corinthians 15:24). When death is finally abolished (verse 26), and all is subjected to Him, "then the Son [of God] Himself also will be subjected to the One who subjected all things to Him, so that God may be all in all" (verse 28).

—MAL COUCH

BIBLIOGRAPHY

Couch, Mal. *The Hope of Christ's Return.* Chattanooga: AMG Publishers, 2001.

Dana, H.E., and Julius R. Mantey. *A Manual Grammar of the Greek New Testament.* New York: Macmillan, 1958.

Kroll, Woodrow. *The Book of Romans.* Chattanooga: AMG Publishers, 2002.

Ridderbos, Herman. *The Gospel of John.* Grand Rapids: Eerdmans Publishing Company, 1991.

Robertson, A.T. *Word Pictures in the New Testament.* 6 Vols. Nashville: Broadman Press, 1932.

Towns, Elmer. *The Gospel of John.* Chattanooga: AMG Publishers, 2002.

Unger, Merrill F. *Unger's Commentary on the Old Testament.* Chattanooga: AMG Publishers, 2002.

SON OF MAN

THE EXPRESSIONS "Son of God" and "Son of Man" are two of the most important descriptions of Christ in the Scriptures. "Son of God" shows that He is the *Son who is related to God.* "Son of Man" shows that He is the *Son who is related to mankind.* Both descriptions dominate the four Gospels.

The Jews considered "Son of Man" as one of the most important titles for the Messiah in the Old Testament. However, as a messianic designation it is only used once—in Daniel 7:13. The expression "son of man" is often used in the Old Testament simply to describe one who is part of humanity. God uses it many times in addressing the prophet Ezekiel. The angel Gabriel uses it once, speaking to Daniel in a vision (Daniel 8:17).

Matthew uses "Son of Man" 28 times, Mark uses it 11 times, Luke uses it 23 times, and John uses it 13 times. Half of the Gospel usages are in Matthew 19–26. However, the most significant usages are found in the Olivet Discourse (24–25) and the chapter that follows. In these chapters Christ tells His disciples about His impending death and His future return to reign as King over Israel. It would only be natural that He would use the messianic expression that was so familiar to the Jews—"the Son of Man."

Acts uses "Son of Man" only once. As Stephen, filled with the Holy Spirit, was about to be stoned, he said, "Behold, I see the heavens opened up and the Son of Man standing at the right hand of God" (Acts 7:56 NASB). The Jews clearly grasped that Stephen was seeing a vision of the Messiah described in Daniel 7:13 and Psalm 110:1-2. With blinding rage "they cried out with a loud voice, and covered their ears and rushed at him with one impulse" (Acts 7:57) and stoned him to death.

None of the New Testament epistles use the expression "Son of Man." The reason may be obvious: The messianic kingdom has been postponed and the church age has begun. About halfway through the book of Acts, the gospel message moves out of Israel and goes to the Gentiles. The age of grace, the church age, comes forward and moves throughout the world. The reign of the Son of Man will not take place until after the rapture of the church and the Tribulation.

Though some interpreters dispute that they are messianic references, the expression "son of man" occurs twice in the book of Revelation (1:13; 14:14). Many Bible versions do not capitalize "Son" and "Man" in these verses. The Greek text has no definite article preceding the phrase "son of man" in these verses, so many translations, such as the NIV and the NASB, simply say "a son of man." This follows the Aramaic reading of Daniel 7:13, which has no definite article before "son of man." However, since ancient times the rabbis have made it clear that the Messiah is in view here. In both Daniel 7:13 and Revelation 1:13; 14:14, to translate the passages "a son of man" is not quite accurate. Without a definite article, it could read "like Son of Man...."

The Old Testament Messiah is clearly in view in Revelation 1:13. The verse reads literally, "One like a son of man, clothed in a robe reaching to the feet..." The full context pictures Jesus "coming with the clouds" (verse 7)—another reference to Daniel 7:13. Revelation 14:14 reads literally, "Behold, a white cloud, and sitting on the cloud was one like a son of man...."

Jesus told His disciples the Son of Man did not come the first time "to be served, but to serve, and to give His life a ransom for many"

(Matthew 20:28). He added in the Olivet Discourse that at the second coming, the Son of Man would come suddenly like lightning that flashes across the sky (24:27). He would come in the clouds "with power and great glory," gather the elect of Israel, and come in an hour not expected (24:30-31,44). The Son of Man will come with His angels, and "He will sit on His glorious throne. All the nations will be gathered before Him" (25:31-32). As the Lord's King, the Son of Man will say, "Come, you who are blessed of My Father, inherit the kingdom prepared for you from the foundation of the world" (25:34). But before all this could happen, the Son of Man had to die. He told His disciples, hours before His arrest, "You know that after two days the Passover is coming, and the Son of Man is to be handed over for crucifixion" (26:2).

Matthew 26:57-68 tells us that following His arrest, Jesus stood silent before the Jewish council and the high priest, Caiaphas. Referring to Psalm 2, Caiaphas said, "Tell us whether You are the Christ, the Son of God." Jesus answered, "You have said it," or "You have spoken correctly." He added, "I tell you, hereafter you shall see the Son of Man sitting at the right hand of Power, and coming on the clouds of heaven." Caiaphas knew Old Testament theology and understood what Jesus was saying. He tore his robes and accused Jesus of blasphemy. This may indicate the Jews realized the Son of Man was somehow related to God.

Most of what is known of the Son of Man in the Old Testament comes from Daniel 7. God, the Ancient of Days, takes His seat upon His heavenly throne (verses 9-10). Daniel records that suddenly, "Behold, with the clouds of heaven One like a Son of Man was coming, and He came up to the Ancient of Days and was presented before Him. And to Him was given dominion, glory and a kingdom, that all the peoples, nations, and men of every language might serve Him. His dominion is an everlasting dominion which will not pass away; and His kingdom is one which will not be destroyed" (verses 13-14).

When does this Son who is related to mankind arrive in glory to be presented to the Ancient of Days? Perhaps this happened at Christ's ascension, when in His resurrected eternal body, He returned to His Father and was seated on His throne in heavenly glory (Psalm 110:1-2). He is in glory until the Lord *(Yahweh)* says, "I make Your enemies a footstool for Your feet." God will then stretch forth the scepter of the Son from the earthly Zion and say, "Rule in the midst of Your enemies."

Orthodox Jewish rabbis realize all of these verses are messianic. Of Daniel 7:13, the rabbis say, "If Israel is worthy, the Messiah will come riding the clouds; if not, he will come in the guise of a poor man riding an ass" (Sanhedrin 98a). Of the clause that reads, "One like a Son of Man," the rabbis say "it refers to the regenerated people of Israel. [Ancient] Rabbinical exegesis applied it to the Messiah" (Cohen, p. 60).

The Son of Man riding upon the clouds is a prominent theme in orthodox Jewish literature. The Babylonian Talmud, completed in A.D. 500, ascribes to the Messiah the name *Bar Nifle,* which means "Son of the Clouds." The Targum also says the Messiah is called *Anani,* meaning "He of the Clouds." And in a Midrash fragment the Messiah is said to come "riding on the cloud," which the Midrash says is first a reference to God who is "riding upon the heaven" (Deuteronomy 33:26) and "riding upon a swift cloud" (Isaiah 19:1). The rabbis took notice of this and realized they must "exercise great restraint in attributing the same divine feat to the Messiah as well" (Patai, p. 81). This may indicate that at a very early point, even in New Testament times, the Jews had some indication that somehow and in some way the Messiah would be related to deity. (See the article titled "Son of God.")

—MAL COUCH

BIBLIOGRAPHY

Avi-Yonah, Michael, and Zvi Baras. *Society and Religion in the Second Temple Period.* Jerusalem: Massada Publishing, 1977.

Cohen, A. *Daniel, Ezra, Nehemiah.* London: Soncino Press, 1968.

Fruchtenbaum, Arnold. *The Footsteps of the Messiah.* Tustin, CA: Ariel Ministries, 2003.

Hindson, Ed. *The Book of Revelation.* Chattanooga: AMG Publishers, 2002.

Patai, Raphael. *The Messiah Texts.* Detroit, MI: Wayne State University Press, 1979.

Pentecost, J. Dwight. *Things to Come.* Grand Rapids: Zondervan, 1964.

TEMPLE

THE TEMPLE IN JERUSALEM is the focal point of God's restoration of national Israel and the source of His blessing for the world (Isaiah 2:2-3; 4:4-6; 56:6-7; 60:7-14; 66:18-21; Jeremiah 3:17-18; 33:14-18; Ezekiel 37:25-28; 40–48; Joel 3:26-27; Micah 4:1-8; Zephaniah 3:11-13; Haggai 2:6-9; Zechariah 2:10-12; 6:12-15; 8:3). The most common Hebrew Old Testament terms for the Jerusalem Temple are *beit 'adonai* (the "house of the Lord") and *beit 'elohim* (the "house of God"). These expressions indicate the Temple is a place where God dwells, as was the *mishkan* ("Tabernacle"). Another Hebrew term for the Temple, found particularly in the prophets, is *mikdash* ("Holy [Place]" or "Sanctuary"). The New Testament continues the Septuagint's use of the Greek term *naos*, a noun derived from the verb *naio* ("to dwell" or "inhabit") that usually has reference to the inner part of the Temple (the Holy of Holies). The book of Revelation uses this term for both the earthly and heavenly Temples (Revelation 11:1,19; 15:8; 21:22).

THE FIRST TEMPLE

The history of the Temple unfolds progressively in the prophetic record. On Mount Moriah, God showed Abraham where the Temple would one day be built (Genesis 22:2,14). Moses received prophetic instructions for establishing the Temple service at this site (Exodus 15:17) and creating its sacred vessels (Exodus 25:8-9,40). King David received a prophetic revelation of the Temple (1 Chronicles 28:11,19) to communicate to his son Solomon, who would construct the Temple

according to the prophetic covenant established with his father (2 Samuel 7:12-13; 1 Kings 5:5; 6:12-13). David purchased the threshing floor on Mount Moriah and erected an altar there as the place for the First Temple (2 Samuel 24:18-25; 1 Chronicles 21:18–22:1) in confirmation of the Abrahamic covenant and God's promise to make spiritual provision there (Genesis 22:14). This placement was also in confirmation of the Davidic covenant and the promise of a son (Solomon) who would build God's house and whose house God would build until the messianic Son would establish His throne there forever (1 Chronicles 17:14; 22:10).

The Davidic covenant provided for a Temple in Jerusalem as the symbol of God's presence among and blessing of Israel, conditioned upon the nation's obedience. Therefore, depending upon Israel's spiritual fidelity, the Temple could be removed or restored. The prophets warned of the destruction of the First Temple as evidence of divine judgment and prophesied the rebuilding of a Second Temple after the nation repented and had completed a period of punishment in exile. The Second Temple (515 B.C.) pointed to the prophetic ideal of a Restoration Temple (see Haggai 2:1-9), and the prophet Ezekiel received the blueprint for this final Temple and its service (Ezekiel 40–48).

THE SECOND TEMPLE

The Second Temple did not fulfill the restoration ideal, which included the complete restoration of Israel and the Davidic dynasty (Ezekiel 37:21-25; Amos 9:11-15; Zechariah 8:7-13), the conversion of the nations, their homage to Israel's God, and tribute to His Temple (Isaiah 2:2-3; 66:18-20; Haggai 2:7-9; Zechariah 6:12-15; 8:21-23; 14:16-19; see Revelation 21:24-26). To the contrary, the Second Temple was built under foreign occupation with most of the Jewish nation continuing in exile outside the Land. Throughout most of its 586-year history, the Second Temple continued to be under foreign domination and subject to desolation. During its later phase it was refurbished completely by the non-Jewish Judean king Herod the Great and controlled by a non-Zadokite priesthood, whose high priests were politically appointed. These shortcomings revealed the Second Temple had not fulfilled the prophecies of the Restoration Temple (the final Temple). Israel's rejection of Jesus as Messiah doomed the Second Temple to judicial destruction.

Jesus' prophetic pronouncements of the Temple's destruction (Matthew 24:2; Mark 13:2; Luke 21:6,20-24) must be viewed in this light and not as a rejection or replacement of the Temple as a legitimate institution in the plan of God. Jesus also made positive statements concerning the Temple (Matthew 12:4; 17:24-27; 23:16-21; John 2:16-17). In His Olivet Discourse (Matthew 24:15; Mark 13:14) He indicated the Temple would be continued in the future, prior to the time of His second advent. Therefore, in continuity with the Old Testament program expected for Israel's restoration, Jesus and the New Testament writers looked ahead to a rebuilt Temple in Jerusalem as part of the eschatological program.

THE FUTURE TEMPLES

A final Temple in the millennial kingdom will be part of the greater restoration promised to national Israel. This promise was made at the close of the First Temple period (Isaiah 1:24–2:4; 4:2-6; 11:1–12:6; Jeremiah 30–33; Ezekiel 36–48; Joel 2:28–3:21; Amos 9:11-15; Micah 4–5; 7:11-20; Zephaniah 3:9-20), again by the prophets who prophesied after the return from captivity (see Daniel 9–12; Haggai 2:5-9; Zechariah 8–14; Malachi 3–4), and reaffirmed in the New Testament (see Acts 3:19-26; Romans 11:1-32). It contained inseparably linked elements of fulfillment:

- the return of Israel to the Land of Israel (in unbelief)
- the experience of the time of Jacob's trouble (Tribulation)
- the rebuilding of the Temple
- the return of Messiah
- the redemption of Israel
- the restoration of Israel's glory (the millennium)

Consequently, these texts reveal that the future Temple will have two phases, one within the Tribulation (Third Temple) and one within the millennium (final or Restoration Temple).

The Temple is the symbol of Israel's national and spiritual existence, and this future program involves both national desecration (in the Tribulation) and spiritual restoration (in the millennium). (For the desecration, see Ezra 5:11-12; Ezekiel 8:6-18; Zephaniah 1:9. For the restoration, see Haggai 1:7-9; 2:15-19; Zechariah 1:15-16; Malachi 3:7-12.) The Temple of the Tribulation will be built by unbelieving Jews and desecrated by the Antichrist (Isaiah 66:1-6; Daniel 9:27; 11:36-45; 2 Thessalonians 2:3-4; Revelation 11:1-2). The Millennial Temple will be built by the Messiah (Zechariah 6:12-13), redeemed Jews, and (as a particular sign of restoration) representatives from Gentile nations (Haggai 2:7; Zechariah 6:15; see Isaiah 60:10). It will be distinguished from the Temple of the Tribulation by a return of the shekinah glory of God (Ezekiel 43:1-7; see 10:4,18-19; 11:22-23) and by Gentile worship (Isaiah 60:6; Zephaniah 3:10; Zechariah 2:11; 8:22; 14:16-19).

The Tribulation Temple

The Temple of the Tribulation apparently continues until the beginning of the messianic kingdom (Zechariah 14:3-9), at which time the Messiah will rebuild the Temple to fulfill the restoration ideal (Zechariah 6:12-15). The covenant established in Daniel 9:27 may result in the rebuilding of the Third Temple because the breaking of the covenant occurs by the interruption of the renewed sacrificial system through "the abomination that makes desolate."

The apostle Paul predicted the Antichrist would perform this desecration (implied in Daniel's "prince that shall come," Daniel 9:26) by seating himself within the Temple and usurping the place of divine manifestation (2 Thessalonians 2:3-4; see Exodus 25:22; Psalm 132:7,13-14; Ezekiel 43:5-7). Paul indicated that this act of desecration would identify the Antichrist to Israel (2 Thessalonians 2:3,8-9; see Revelation 13:13-15). John, who likewise expected the Antichrist (1 John 2:18), placed him in the Temple courts as the Gentile forces invade Jerusalem (Revelation 11:1-2). And Jesus declared the Antichrist's presence would signal the seventieth week, separating the initial experience of wrath or birthpangs (see Matthew 24:4-14; Revelation 6:1-17) from the concluding period of wrath, the Great Tribulation, which climaxes with the second advent (Matthew 24:15-31; Mark 13:14-26).

The Millennial Temple

The Millennial Temple is distinct from any previous historical Temple. The First Temple lacked Gentile worshipers, and the Second Temple further lacked the shekinah, as will the Third Temple. The Millennial Temple, by contrast, will include all of these elements (Isaiah 2:2-4; 60:7,13; Jeremiah 33:18; Ezekiel 37:26-28; 43:1-7; Haggai 2:9; Zechariah 6:12-13; 14:20), a distinct architecture, and an expanded Temple Mount (Ezekiel 40–48). Isaiah 2:2-3 (NASB) explains that in the last days, the world will come to the Millennial Temple to learn God's law as the basis of millennial government: "The mountain of the house of the LORD [the Millennial Temple erected on the Temple Mount] will be established as the chief of the mountains…and all the nations will stream to it. And many peoples will come and say, 'Come, let us go up to the mountain of the LORD [the Temple mount], to the house of the God of Jacob [the Temple]; that He may teach us concerning His ways and that we may walk in His paths.' For the law will go forth from Zion and the word of the LORD from Jerusalem" (see also Micah 4:2-3). Therefore, in the millennium, the Temple will be the sign of the fulfillment of the New Covenant for Israel, which will be protected and will prosper under its terms (Isaiah 59:20-21; Jeremiah 31:27-40; 32:37-40; Ezekiel 16:60-63; 37:21-28). Israel will never violate the covenant because the people will all have "new hearts and new spirits" to obey the Lord (Ezekiel 36:26-27).

The prophets announced an eschatological rest in the peaceful conditions of the millennial kingdom (Isaiah 2:3-4; Micah 4:3-4). The exile had interrupted the promise of a permanent rest within the Land, and the destruction of the Temple had removed the symbol of that rest and the presence of the Lord, the giver of rest. Isaiah predicted a future rest for Israel after her last exile that would be evidenced by a renewal and transformation of nature (Isaiah 11:10-12; 14:3-4,7; 28:12; 32:17). This rest will be maintained, according to Ezekiel, through the restoration of the Temple and its priestly service (Ezekiel 44:30). As the destruction of the Temple caused a loss of rest, so its rebuilding under millennial conditions would restore that rest.

The Millennial Temple will also reunite world Jewry and all the nations of the earth under the sovereignty of the Messiah (Zechariah 14:9). Judaism had been divided and in opposition to the nations, causing frequent desecration and destruction of the Temple by the nations. In the millennium, the Temple will become the center that unites Jew and Gentile in the worship and service of God (Isaiah 2:2-3; 56:6-7; 66:18-21; Zechariah 14:16-21) as the nations yearly assemble in Jerusalem for the Feast of Booths (Zechariah 14:16).

In the millennial kingdom, the future blessings of restoration include the renewal of the Land as a result of the river flowing from under the altar of the Temple (Ezekiel 47:1-12; Zechariah 14:8) and because of agricultural blessings connected with rain (Zechariah 14:16-17). This rain, so vital to an agrarian society, will be provided based on Israelite and non-Israelite faithfulness to worship at the Temple at the appointed feasts. Thus, the national blessings secured by the future Temple will be extended internationally to all of the inhabitants of the kingdom, fulfilling the mandate of the Abrahamic covenant that through Israel all of the families of the earth would be blessed (Genesis 12:3). Such texts as Isaiah 2:2-4; 11:1-11; 60–66; Micah 4:1-5; and Zechariah 8:23; 14:16 predict the Millennial Temple as the center of world renewal and blessing, turning all the nations to Temple worship. Isaiah 56:6-7 predicts that the Temple will serve this universal purpose as a sacrificial center and a "house of prayer for all peoples." Jesus Himself employed this verse against the money changers in the Temple. Their vulgar practice demonstrated the present lack of fulfillment of this great prophetic purpose.

The Heavenly Temple

The book of Revelation depicts a heavenly Temple as well (Revelation 11:19; 15:5-8; see also Hebrews 9:11). The heavenly Temple served as the model for the earthly Tabernacle and Temple (Exodus 25:8,40; 1 Chronicles 28:11-19; Hebrews 9:23) and will exist throughout eternity as it has from eternity past (Psalm 11:4; Hebrews 1:8). The New Jerusalem will not contain a Temple, for the Lord God and the Lamb will be its Temple (Revelation 21:22). However, the dimensions of the New Jerusalem form a cube (Revelation 21:16) and in this sense are reminiscent of the earthly Temple's Holy of Holies (1 Kings 6:19-20). Therefore, the abode of the saints in the eternal state will be within a celestial Temple comprised of the heavenly city itself with the glory of God in its center, and the saints will serve as its priests day and night and forever (Revelation 7:15; 22:3).

—RANDALL PRICE

BIBLIOGRAPHY

Ice, Thomas, and Randall Price. *Ready to Rebuild.* Eugene, OR: Harvest House Publishers, 1992.

Ice, Thomas, and Timothy J. Demy. *The Truth About the Last Days' Temple.* Eugene, OR: Harvest House Publishers, 1995.

Price, Randall. *The Coming Last Days' Temple.* Eugene, OR: Harvest House Publishers, 1998.

———. *The Battle for the Last Days' Temple.* Eugene, OR: Harvest House Publishers, 2004.

Richman, Chaim. *The Odyssey of the Third Temple.* Jerusalem: The Temple Institute, 1994.

THESSALONIANS, ESCHATOLOGY OF

THE TWO EPISTLES OF PAUL to the Thessalonians together give more information on Bible prophecy than all of the other New Testament epistles combined. In 1 and 2 Thessalonians, Paul gives prophecies about the resurrection, the rapture, the Tribulation, the Antichrist, the second coming, the judgment of the lost at Christ's return, and the kingdom. It is possible that these two books, written several months apart (about A.D. 51), are the first epistles the apostle wrote (though some believe Galatians was his first book). Clearly great prophetic themes were on Paul's mind early in his writing ministry.

Paul describes future prophetic events against the backdrop of the suffering and persecution that the Thessalonian church was enduring. Their current afflictions would be vindicated by their future deliverance. The Lord from heaven would rescue the church, liberating them from their troubles and pains.

The predominant prophetic sections in these books include these subjects:

- the resurrection of the church (1 Thessalonians 4:13-18)
- the rapture (1 Thessalonians 1:9-10; 2:19; 3:13; 4:13-18; 5:9-10,23; 2 Thessalonians 2:1-3a)
- the Tribulation and day of the Lord (1 Thessalonians 1:10; 5:1-4)
- the Antichrist (2 Thessalonians 2:3b-12)
- the judgment after the Tribulation (2 Thessalonians 1:6-10; 2:8)
- the kingdom (1 Thessalonians 2:12; 2 Thessalonians 1:5)

The doctrine of the rapture is the most predominate prophetic theme in the Thessalonian epistles. Paul apparently mentioned the rapture in a previous letter or teaching session, but the Thessalonian Christians were still confused about the sequence of events because they thought they were possibly already in the Tribulation (the day of the Lord).

These two letters emphasize the importance of understanding dispensational distinctions in Bible study. It would be quite simple to mix up all of the prophetic sequences and become totally confused about the end times. The doctrine of the church deals with those who are "in Christ." The church is neither the kingdom of God nor the kingdom of heaven so prominently mentioned in the Gospels. It is neither a replacement for Israel nor a spiritual Israel. Paul in no way suggests such a correlation between the church and Israel. By studying the Thessalonian letters carefully, one can see that these are kept separate. The church is not Israel, the rapture is not the second coming of Christ, and the Antichrist does not arrive until the church is taken out of the way and the Tribulation begins.

The apostle Paul mentions the kingdom of God in each of these letters (1 Thessalonians 2:12; 2 Thessalonians 1:5), which some commentators interpret as an allusion to the church. The argument is that the church has replaced Israel and become that kingdom promised in the Old Testament. In both letters Paul refers to the kingdom of God, but he never says that kingdom is the church.

Paul also describes the Tribulation, which is depicted graphically as the "birth pangs" (1 Thessalonians 5:3). This alludes to Jeremiah 30:6-7, where the prophet describes "that great day" as the "woman in childbirth." He adds, "There is none like it; and it is the time of Jacob's distress [Hebrew, za-rah, 'tribulation']." The Lord Jesus quotes Jeremiah 30, describing the coming wrath as "a great tribulation" (Matthew 24:21). As did Jeremiah, Christ calls this period a day "as has not occurred since the beginning of the world until now, nor ever shall [be]." In the same context, the Lord calls it "the beginning of the birth pangs" (24:8 NASB). Paul later quotes Jeremiah and Jesus to describe the Tribulation in the same way—the sudden birth pangs (1 Thessalonians 5:3).

Paul quotes Christ again when he writes, "that you may not be quickly shaken from your composure or be disturbed, either by a spirit or a messenger or a letter as if from us, to the effect that the day of the Lord has come" (2 Thessalonians 2:2). The word "shaken" in the Greek text is *throeo* and means "to be terrified, traumatized." The apostle's point is that they are not now in the Tribulation. "Do not be so shocked!" The Lord Jesus said the same to the disciples. He said many things would come upon the world, but the

Tribulation would not have begun. "Then, do not be traumatized!" (see Matthew 24:6; Mark 13:7). Christ used the word *throeo* only once as recorded in Matthew and Mark. Paul picks the word up and uses it almost the same way grammatically, and he is clearly quoting Jesus and reminding the Thessalonian believers that the day of the Lord had not started even though they were living in a time of terrible persecution.

The letters to the church at Thessalonica give powerful messages about prophecy, and especially the doctrine of the rapture. Paul wanted to make sure the church understood the flow of future events.

—MAL COUCH

BIBLIOGRAPHY

Benware, Paul N. *Understanding End Times Prophecy*. Chicago: Moody Press, 1995.

Couch, Mal. *The Hope of Christ's Return*. Chattanooga: AMG Publishers, 2001.

Ice, Tommy, and Timothy Demy, gen. eds. *When the Trumpet Sounds*. Eugene, OR: Harvest House Publishers, 1995.

Milligan, George. *St. Paul's Epistles to the Thessalonians*. Minneapolis: Klock & Klock, 1980.

Pentecost, J. Dwight. *Things to Come*. Grand Rapids: Zondervan, 1964.

Strombeck, J.F. *First the Rapture*. Grand Rapids: Kregel, 1992.

Walvoord, John F. *The Rapture Question*. Grand Rapids: Zondervan, 1979.

THRONE OF DAVID

PROPHECIES ABOUT DAVID'S THRONE form a prevalent subject in Scripture. Hints of this set of promises exist in Jacob's prophecies about his sons in Genesis 49. The throne of David concerns the right to rule over the nation of Israel and the world in the millennial reign of David's Son, the Messiah, the Lord Jesus Christ.

JUDAH—THE TRIBE OF THE KING

The kings of Israel would come through Jacob's son Judah. His eleven brothers "shall praise" him and even "bow down" to him. And as a king subdues his opponents, the hands of Judah "shall be on the neck of [his] enemies" (Genesis 49:8 NASB). In other words, Judah's line will have royal and kingly authority, and even his own brothers and their descendants will honor him and his descendants.

Jacob also predicts that Judah will be like a young lion (a lion's whelp), strong and cunning for prey, with no one opposing him (49:9). The kingly royal scepter will not depart from the tribe of Judah, "nor the ruler's staff from between his feet" (49:10). The scepter was the ancient club used by the warrior king, and as the sovereign sat on his throne to make judgment, his royal staff would be resting between his feet. The kingly scepter would remain as a standing prophetic symbol until "Shiloh comes, and to him shall be the obedience of the peoples." This verse is indicating that the kingly hope would always be with the tribe of Judah until the ultimate and final king of the Jews arrives who is called *Shiloh,* meaning "the one who brings peace." This verse is patently messianic; both Christians and Jews agree that it applies to the promised Messiah who will someday rule the world (Unger, p. 97). This promise that the Messiah would be the peacemaker (the Prince of Peace) is repeated in the great messianic passage, Isaiah 9:6-9.

THE SCEPTER AND THE STAR

In Numbers 24:17, a pagan seer named Balaam gives a prophecy concerning this Son of Jacob. Intending to curse Israel, this man is moved by God to prophesy that "a star will come forth from Jacob" and "a scepter shall rise from Israel" who will someday in the far future crush Moab, the ongoing enemies of the Jewish people. The language here is similar to Genesis 49. However, the one coming who carries the scepter is called the star (Hebrew, *koh-chahv*) who "comes forth from Jacob."

> The "Star" represents the Lord appearing to be the consummation of all that is cherished in the hopes of the saints by

virtue of Christ's redemptive work. The "Scepter" envisions the Lord coming to rule the earth as absolute King and Lord (Rev. 19:16). The "Scepter" is owned first in Zion (Psalm 110:2) and extends to the ends of the earth when Shiloh comes (Gen. 49:10; Psalm 45:6-17; Isa. 11:9-10). Although the royal insignia "star" and "scepter" include David, they only find their fulfillment in the greater David at His second advent and Kingdom (Unger, p. 218).

THE THRONE OF DAVID

These verses in the writings of Genesis and Numbers lead to the Davidic covenant and the fact that David's future Son would rule on the throne of David. The Lord, speaking through the prophet Nathan, told David that He would establish his kingdom with his immediate descendant Solomon. And Solomon "shall build a house for My name, and I will establish the throne of his kingdom forever" (2 Samuel 7:13). David's house (lineage), kingdom (land and people), and throne (the right to rule) "shall be established forever" (7:16). This "covenant" is repeated in Psalm 89. God swore by His holiness that He would not lie to David: "His descendants shall endure forever and his throne as the sun before Me" (Psalm 89:36). David's throne "shall be established forever like the moon" (89:37).

Isaiah the prophet continues to reveal more about the promised Messiah and says that He will bring unending peace. He will be called Wonderful Counselor, Mighty God, Eternal Father, Prince of Peace (Isaiah 9:6) as He sits on the future throne of David and establishes and upholds David's kingdom with justice and righteousness forevermore (9:7). The Holy Spirit will rest upon Him (11:2), and from the throne of David He will judge earth with fairness (11:3-5).

This universal extent of the reign of the Messiah on David's throne is well understood by Jewish commentators. They write that the Messiah will conquer all the nations, and then His rule will be the kingdom of heaven established on earth as He sits on the throne of David in Jerusalem (Patai, chapter 26). The Jewish writing *The Testament of Levi* (18) refers to the messianic promise in Numbers 24:17 and says that the Messiah's "star shall arise in heaven as the star of a king....And there shall be peace in all the earth." *The Testament of Judah* (24) states that "a star shall rise for you from Jacob in peace, and a man shall arise from my seed (Judah's), like unto the sun of righteousness.... Then shall the scepter of My kingdom shine forth, and from your root shall arise a stem [the Messiah], and from it shall grow a rod of righteousness to the nations, to judge and save all that call upon the Lord."

The rabbis also knew that the Messiah comes from the house of David, that He will have dominion from sea to sea (Psalm 72:8), that all kings will prostrate themselves before Him (72:11), and that He is the Son of Man who will receive "dominion, glory, and a kingdom, that all the peoples, nations, and men of every language should serve Him" (Daniel 7:13-14) (Patai, chapter 26).

THE NEW TESTAMENT CONFIRMATION

The angel Gabriel repeats these great promises to Mary. He tells her of the impending birth of her Son Jesus (Luke 1:31). "He will be great and will be called the Son of the Most High; and the Lord God will give Him the throne of His father David; and He will reign over the house of Jacob forever, and His kingdom will have no end" (1:32-33 NASB).

When the Messiah, the Son of Man, comes, "He will sit on His glorious throne" (Matthew 25:31)—that is, the throne of His earthly father David. He will be the messianic King to whom the heavenly Father will summon the righteous in order that they might inherit the kingdom prepared for them "from the foundation of the world" (25:34). The Lord Jesus is that Messiah, and Jeremiah calls Him the "Branch of David" who will execute justice and righteousness on the earth (Jeremiah 33:15), and who will sit on the throne of the house of Israel (33:17). God will not break His covenant

He made with David; David will have a Son to reign on his throne (33:21).

David will be resurrected to co-reign with his Son the Messiah. During the Jewish kingdom reign, David will be God's servant (Ezekiel 34:23), the "prince among them" (34:24), and he will take the role of shepherd over the people of Israel (37:24-25). David's resurrection is prophesied in Jeremiah 30:9: The people of Israel "shall serve the LORD their God, and David their king, whom I will raise up for them." Some have taken these words to refer to the Messiah, but the Scriptures are clear that David will be co-reigning. The literal interpretation of these verses means that David will be in the kingdom co-reigning. David will be appointed a regent over the Holy Land in the millennium and will rule over the land as prince, ministering under the authority of his Son, Jesus Christ the King (Pentecost, pp. 498–500). William R. Newell adds:

> We must not confuse in our minds this situation. We must believe the plain words of God. David is not the Son of David. Christ, as Son of David, will be King; and David, His father after the flesh, will be *prince*, during the Millennium (p. 323).

Progressive dispensationalists say that Christ is now reigning on the throne of David in heaven (Psalm 110:1-2), but this is not true. The Lord entered the throne room of God in heaven to be seated at God's right hand until the Father makes His "enemies a footstool for [His] feet." Then God will make the Messiah's "strong scepter" stretch forth from Zion, not heaven, to rule in the midst of the Messiah's enemies. "Zion" here is not heaven but the earthly center of the King's reign from Jerusalem. If heaven were now the Davidic throne and kingdom, then the scepter would be wielded from glory and would be used to subdue the evilness of earth from a kind of spiritual Jerusalem. But that earthly authority will not be exercised until Jesus Christ returns to reign from the holy city. In time, the throne of David will be established in the Holy Land.

SPIRITUALIZING THE THRONE OF DAVID

Amillennialists say that the throne of David is not to be taken literally. Some believe this refers to Christ's present reign over the church. On Matthew 25:31, Barnes writes that His splendid throne "is not to be taken literally, as if there would be a material throne or seat for the King in Zion" (Barnes, p. 270). On "throne of David" and "house of Jacob" in Luke 1:32-33, Lenski says that this rule has to do with "the spiritual descendants" of all the righteous and "not merely the Jewish nation as such." He adds that Christ now simply has a "spiritual rule" (Lenski, p. 67). Lenski then writes, "We are, however, told that we should not let the Old Testament prophecies control our New Testament exegesis" (Lenski, p. 68). Hendriksen writes, "It should not be unnecessary to state that according to our Lord's own explanation it is not an earthly or political kingdom (and throne) that is in view here, but rather the kingdom or rule of grace and truth established in the hearts and lives of all those who have the God of Jacob as their refuge" (p. 87). On "the throne of His father David," *The Preacher's Homiletic Commentary* notes that "Jesus is head over all things to His Church. He establishes His gentle sway over the hearts of His people, subduing them to Himself, ruling and defending them, and restraining and conquering all His own and all their enemies" (p. 27).

It is easy to see how amillennial thinking makes null and void the messianic promises that center on the throne of David. This throne is allegorized and ripped from its literal moorings. Christ is dethroned from His place in history as the King who will reign over the righteous Jewish people and the world from the city of Jerusalem in the Holy Land.

A LITERAL REIGN

The fact that Christ will reign over the earth is of course imbedded in practically every prophecy concerning the millennial kingdom. The absolute character of His reign is found in Isaiah 11:3-5. The angel Gabriel mentions this great prophecy to Mary when he predicts the coming birth of Jesus: "He will be great and will be called the Son of the Most High; and the Lord God will give Him the throne of His father David" (Luke 1:32-33). Obviously, these prophecies are not now fulfilled in the church age, nor are they simply speaking of God's overall sovereignty in the heavens. Many other passages prove the reign of the Lord Jesus as King in the millennium (Isaiah 2:1-4; 9:6-7; 11:1-10; 16:5; 24:23; 32:1-2; 40:1-11; 42:3-4; 52:7-15; 55:4; Daniel 2:44; 7:27; Micah 4:1-8; 5:2-5; Zechariah 9:9; 14:16-17). Such statements, if interpreted in their ordinary, natural, and literal way, lead to the conclusion that the Lord Jesus will someday reign on the throne of David as King over the earth in the millennial period (Walvoord, pp. 299–300).

—MAL COUCH

BIBLIOGRAPHY

Barnes, Albert. *Barnes' Notes*. Vol. 9. Grand Rapids: Baker Books, 1983.

Hendriksen, William. *The Gospel of Luke*. Grand Rapids: Baker Books, 1981.

Lenski, R.C.H. *St. Luke's Gospel*. Minneapolis: Augsburg Publishing House, 1961.

Newell, William R. *Revelation*. Grand Rapids: Kregel, 1994.

Patai, Raphael. *The Messiah Texts*. Detroit, MI: Wayne State University Press, 1979.

Pentecost, J. Dwight. *Things to Come*. Grand Rapids: Kregel, 1964.

Peters, George N.H. *The Theocratic Kingdom*. 3 Vols. Grand Rapids: Kregel, 1957.

Unger, Merrill F. *Unger's Commentary on the Old Testament*. Chattanooga: AMG Publishers, 2002.

Walvoord, John F. *The Millennial Kingdom*. Findlay, OH: Dunham, 1959.

Willcock, J. *The Preacher's Homiletic Commentary, Luke*. Grand Rapids: Baker Books, n.d.

THRONE OF GOD

THE TERM *THRONE OF GOD* EMPHASIZES the fact that God is absolutely sovereign in all of the affairs of His universe. However, this expression has more than one context. Fully understanding the concept of the Lord's throne requires surveying Scripture references from 1 Kings through Revelation. The word *throne* is a metaphor of God's authority and sovereignty. Scripture employs it as a visual illustration of the Lord's majesty and kingship over all that belongs to Him.

The Hebrew Old Testament word for *throne* is *kis-seh*. Related words are *kehs* (Exodus 17:16, "to swear") and *keh-she* (Proverbs 7:20, "to appoint"). Thus the word *throne* represents the king's domain from which he sends forth orders, appointments, or edicts.

THE SOVEREIGN THRONE OF HEAVEN

From this throne God rules His universe and all the affairs of earth. His edicts and plans will be carried out despite the rebellion of the fallen angels and the evil intentions of humanity. The first mention of God's throne is by the prophet Micaiah, who said to rebellious Ahab, "Therefore, hear the word of the LORD. I saw the LORD sitting on His throne, and all the host of heaven standing by Him on His right and on His left" (1 Kings 22:19 NASB). With such heavenly revelations the prophet established his authority. He was given the vision of God enthroned with the vast angelic host arrayed about Him, ready to do His bidding.

Isaiah graphically describes the awesomeness of the throne of God. The prophet saw the Lord on His throne "lofty and exalted, with the train of His robe filling the [heavenly] temple" (Isaiah 6:1). Before Him was the angelic host crying out "Holy, Holy, Holy, is the Lord of hosts" (6:3). Unger assigns this to Christ and writes,

> Isaiah saw the glory of the preincarnate Christ (John 12:41) in about 740 B.C., in the year of King Uzziah's death. The prophet could only have "seen" the eternal Word who was with God and was God (1:1-3), divine essence. It was apparently a vision to strengthen him in a career already in progress (Isa. 1–5) and to bolster his faith in prospect of obstinacy and opposition from those

to whom he would minister (vv. 9-12). The vision itself was the sight of the Lord (Christ) high and lifted up (Rev. 4:2-3), sitting...upon His throne, denoting the place of authority and government of the universe (Unger, p. 1157).

David says of the eternal God that He has established His throne for judgment, and from it He will judge the world and all peoples in righteousness (Psalm 9:6-7). The Lord's throne in heaven is also His holy temple, from which His eyes test the sons of man (11:4-5). His heavenly throne is eternal and holy (47:8; 93:2), and from there He wields His scepter of righteousness, the scepter of His vast, sovereign kingdom (45:6). His "sovereignty rules over all" (103:19). Besides the fact that righteousness comes from His domain, both righteousness and justice form "the foundation of His throne" (97:2), the throne of His glory (Jeremiah 14:21). By the Lord's hand, He "made all these things, thus all these things [of the universe] came into being" (Isaiah 66:2). And with this He has the right to rule because as He says, "Heaven is My throne, and the earth is My footstool" (66:1).

THE HEAVENLY THRONE AND THE ASCENDED SON OF MAN

When the Lord Jesus left His disciples, He ascended back to His heavenly Father. The Father is called the "Ancient of Days" in Daniel 7:9. Daniel saw His throne in a vision with wheels burning with fire, indicating that from here His judgments would be pronounced. The Lord Jesus comes to God as the "Son of Man," meaning that with His ascension He returns to glory as the Son who is related to mankind (7:13-14). Christ was made as a man in flesh who then died for the sins of humanity. In His eternal body He now resides with the Father, waiting for His messianic return to earth as Israel's King. When He entered the heavenly presence, the Lord (Yahweh) said to Him (the Lord of David, Adonai), "Sit at My right hand, until I make Your enemies a footstool for Your feet" (Psalm 110:1). In this incredible passage David is given the vision of the ascended Messiah sitting at the right hand of God until the Lord stretches forth Christ's "strong scepter from Zion, saying, 'Rule in the midst of Your enemies'" (110:2). When He came before His Father, Christ was given everlasting dominion "which will not pass away; and His kingdom is one which will not be destroyed" (Daniel 7:14). The earthly 1000-year millennial reign of Christ will be this promised kingdom fulfilled on earth. Though all dominion and authority has been given Christ, His sovereignty has not been consummated. This will happen at His second coming as prophesied by the writer of Hebrews, who wrote, "In subjecting all things to him, [God] left nothing that is not subject to him. But we do not yet see all things subjected to him" (Hebrews 2:8). Presently then, Christ is seated on the throne of His Father, waiting for His time to come to the earth to reign and rule (Revelation 3:21).

THE THRONE OF GOD AND TRIBULATION EVENTS

God's heavenly throne is seen as full of spiritual activity during the period of the seven-year Tribulation. The throne of God is mentioned in the book of Revelation almost more than any other individual book of the Bible. The sevenfold manifestation of the Spirit is seen before the throne (Revelation 1:4; Isaiah 11:1-2). John sees God on His throne (4:2) with "a rainbow [iris] around the throne" (4:3). And around the throne of the Lord are 24 additional thrones with the 24 elders seated, whom some say represent the church (4:4). From this heavenly seat of authority John sees flashes of lightning and hears peals of thunder as God prepares to shower earth with His displeasure and wrath because of the sins of humanity (4:5). God on His throne holds the scroll that will begin the Tribulation events on earth (5:1). Only Christ, the Lion of Judah and the Root of David, is worthy to open the seals of the book (5:5). Angels' voices are heard around the throne (5:11) with the anthem of

blessing both to the Lord on His throne and to the Lamb (5:13).

Coming out of the Tribulation in martyrdom is a great company of people who come before the throne of God in heaven and before the Lamb, clothed in white robes (7:9). They have suffered in the great Tribulation and now attend God before His throne day and night (7:15). In the center of the throne is the Lamb of God (7:17). Before the throne is the heavenly altar, before which a censer is waved with the prayers of the saints who perished on earth (8:3). At the end of the kingdom period, God will judge the unbelieving dead of all generations at the Great White Throne. Some see the Judge as Christ, but others see Him as the Lord God Himself (20:11). This judgment is for the eternal destiny of the lost, those who have rejected God with their evil deeds and their denial of Christ (20:12-15).

THE THRONE OF THE DAVIDIC KINGDOM

The Davidic throne represents the earthly messianic authority by which the Lord Jesus will reign. This throne is also the possession of God. The Lord will give the Davidic throne to His Son as an everlasting throne that is as eternal "as the days of heaven" (Psalm 89:29). The Davidic kingdom also belongs to God the Father. Through David's son Solomon, the Lord said that he would "sit on the throne of the kingdom of the LORD over Israel" (1 Chronicles 28:5; 29:23). This earthly kingdom also belongs to the Lord God, yet His Son is the One who will occupy it. "But when the Son of Man comes in His glory, and all the angels with Him, then He will sit on His glorious throne" (Matthew 25:31).

THE FUTURE ETERNAL THRONE OF THE FATHER AND THE SON

Finally, with the beginning of eternity and the coming of the new heaven and the new earth, from the throne of God the announcement is heard, "Behold, the tabernacle of God is among men, and He shall dwell among them, and they shall be His people, and God Himself shall be among them" (Revelation 21:3). Again from the throne comes the blessed news, "Behold, I am making all things new" (21:5). When eternity begins with the new heavens and earth, the new city of Jerusalem will come down from heaven with a throne, "the throne of God and of the Lamb" (Revelation 22:1,3). Those looking into the face of Christ will know that they are seeing God also (22:4). The Lord God Almighty and the Lamb are the temple (21:22) and the light (21:23) of this new city.

Whenever Scripture references God's throne, it gives the distinct sense of His absolute sovereignty over the affairs of His universal kingdom.

—MAL COUCH

BIBLIOGRAPHY

Bultema, Harry. *Commentary on Daniel*. Grand Rapids: Kregel, 1988.

Couch, Mal, gen. ed. *Dictionary of Premillennial Theology*. Grand Rapids: Kregel, 1996.

Hindson, Ed. *The Book of Revelation*. Chattanooga: AMG Publishers, 2002.

Keil, C.F., and F. Delitzsch. *Commentary on the Old Testament: Ezekiel, Daniel*. Vol. 9. Peabody, MA: Hendrickson, 1989.

Pentecost, J. Dwight. *Things to Come*. Grand Rapids: Zondervan, 1964.

Peters, George N.H. *The Theocratic Kingdom*. 3 Vols. Grand Rapids: Kregel, 1957.

Unger, Merrill F. *Unger's Commentary on the Old Testament*. Chattanooga: AMG Publishers, 2002.

Walvoord, John F. *Daniel*. Chicago: Moody Press, 1971.

TIMES OF THE GENTILES

THE PHRASE "THE TIMES OF THE GENTILES" (Luke 21:24) refers to the extensive period of history when the Gentiles are the dominant world powers and the people of Israel are subject to those powers. The phrase occurs only once in the Bible—in Luke 21:24, during a discourse by Jesus (Luke 21:5-38) concerning the fall and destruction of Jerusalem and the Tribulation. Jesus declared, "They will fall by the edge of the sword, and all will be led captive into all the nations; and Jerusalem will be trampled underfoot by the Gentiles until the times of the Gentiles are fulfilled" (NASB). This verse comes in a section of Luke's Gospel that is parallel to the Olivet Discourse of Matthew 24. Although the phrase occurs only once, the prophetic period covered by its duration is enormous, and the concept is a major component of God's prophetic plan.

Luke likely uses the word for "times" (Greek, *kairoi*) as one of two technical terms for an eschatological period. *Kairoi* refers to the present age and part of the future, and the other term (Greek, *chronos*) refers to the latter part of the Tribulation (Bock, pp. 1681–82). Luke's technical use of this phrase describes the long period of time from the Babylonian capture of Jerusalem under Nebuchadnezzar (586 B.C.) and continues through to the yet future Tribulation (Revelation 11:2). It includes the destruction of Jerusalem in A.D. 70 and the entire current age.

The phrase does not rule out temporary Jewish control of Jerusalem as has occurred in the past during the Maccabean era (164–63 B.C.), the first Jewish revolt against Rome (A.D. 66–70), the second Jewish revolt (A.D. 132–135), and now since 1967 and the Six-Day War. However, this control is only temporary because Revelation 11:1-2 predicts at least another three-and-one-half years of Gentile domination during the last half of the Tribulation. "Any Jewish takeover of the City of Jerusalem before the Second Coming must therefore be viewed as a temporary one and does not mean that the Times of the Gentiles have ended. The Times of the Gentiles can only end when the Gentiles can no longer tread down the City of Jerusalem" (Fruchtenbaum, p. 21).

Four prophetic texts, each building and elaborating on the previous one, provide a panorama of the "times of the Gentiles": Daniel 2:31-45; 7:1-28; Revelation 13:1-10; 17:7-14. These texts give a prophetic perspective on history from the time of the Babylonian Empire (612–539 B.C.) through the Medo-Persian Empire (538–331 B.C.) and the Greek Empire (330–63 B.C.) to the Roman Empire (63 B.C.–A.D. 476) and include a revived Roman Empire during the Tribulation.

AN OVERVIEW OF THE TIMES OF THE GENTILES

Some of God's most significant revelation concerning the times of the Gentiles was given when Babylon was the dominant world power and Nebuchadnezzar was king of Babylon. Much of this revelation came in a dream Nebuchadnezzar had, which is recorded in Daniel 2.

The Setting of the Dream (Daniel 2:1-30)

In 603 B.C. King Nebuchadnezzar, the greatest of ancient Babylon's kings, had a dream that disturbed him so much that he could not continue to sleep. The king demanded that his wise men tell him both the content and interpretation of the dream. The wise men could not fulfill the king's demand (Daniel 2:1-13).

Daniel, a young Jew who was taken from Jerusalem as a hostage, asked God to reveal the content and interpretation of the king's dream to him. God granted Daniel's request. As a result, Daniel was able to tell the king what would happen in the future ("the latter days," 2:14-30).

The Content of the Dream (Daniel 2:31-35)

The dream consisted of two major objects: an image and a stone. The image was of a human and was terrifying to see because of its huge size and brilliance. It had a head of gold, arms and breast of silver, belly and two thighs of bronze, two legs of iron, and feet and toes that were a mixture of iron and clay.

The stone had been cut without hands out of the side of a mountain (2:45). This indicated that it was not human in origin. The stone struck the feet of the image with such force that the feet were crushed and the image disintegrated into chaff. The wind blew away every remnant of the image. Then the stone became a large mountain that filled the whole earth.

The Interpretation of the Dream (Daniel 2:36-45)

In the interpretation, Daniel progressed from the top to the bottom of the image. This downward movement represented the passage of time. Thus, the upper parts of the image portrayed earlier time, and the lower parts represented later time.

Daniel signified that the head of gold represented both the Babylonian kingdom and its great king (2:38-39). Orientals regarded kings and their kingdoms synonymously.

Babylon was to be succeeded by a second Gentile kingdom, represented by the image's two arms and breast of silver (2:39). That kingdom was Medo-Persia. Two arms coming together to form one breast pictured this kingdom well. Two distinct peoples, the Medes and the Persians, were united together in 550 B.C. under the same king to form one great power. This part of the prophetic dream was fulfilled when Medo-Persia conquered Babylon in 539 B.C.

Medo-Persia was to be succeeded by a third Gentile kingdom, represented by the image's belly and thighs of bronze (2:39). This was the kingdom of Greece under Alexander the Great and his successors. One belly subdivided into two thighs was an accurate portrayal of the Grecian kingdom. After Alexander had extended and unified his kingdom, he died at a young age. His kingdom was then divided among his four leading generals. But only two of those divisions played important roles in Jewish history. They headquartered in Syria and Egypt.

Daniel said that Greece would rule over all the earth, referring to the world then known to Daniel and his contemporaries. Alexander's kingdom ruled considerably more of the earth than did Babylon and Medo-Persia. This part of the prophetic dream was fulfilled when Greece conquered the Medo-Persian kingdom in 331 B.C.

Greece was to be succeeded by a fourth Gentile kingdom, represented by the image's two legs of iron and feet and toes of iron and clay (2:40-43). This proved to be the Roman Empire. Two legs were an apt portrayal of Rome, for the ancient Roman Empire ruled extensive areas of both the western and eastern divisions of the world. As a result of becoming huge in size, it was divided into two political divisions in A.D. 364—the Western Roman Empire with Rome as its capital, and the

Eastern Roman Empire with Constantinople as its capital.

When Daniel interpreted the last part of the image—the feet and toes—he was dealing with the final form of Gentile world dominion in time. The language of 2:41 indicates that the feet and toes were part of the portrayal of the Roman kingdom. Thus, they represented the Roman Empire in its final stage of existence in contrast with its earlier "leg" stage.

The legs of this fourth Gentile kingdom consisted of iron, but the feet and toes were a mixture of iron and clay. This distinction in substance indicated that the Roman Empire would experience at least two distinct stages of existence—an earlier and a later stage.

Just as iron is strong, so the final stage of the Roman Empire will be strong militarily. Just as clay is characterized by brittleness, so the final stage of the Roman Empire will be characterized by division. Different groups of people will combine with one another to form the final stage of the empire, but they will not adhere completely to one another, just as iron and clay cannot adhere completely with each other.

It would appear, then, that the final stage of the Roman Empire will consist of a federation of several divisions. These divisions will federate for the sake of military strength, but they will not integrate to the extent of losing their ethnic and cultural identities. Because the image of the dream was human in form, it would have had ten toes. This indicated that the final stage of the Roman Empire will consist of a ten-division federation. Indeed, Daniel 7:23-24 signifies that eventually the Roman kingdom will consist of a federation of ten divisions with ten equal rulers (see Revelation 17:12).

When will this "feet and toes" stage of the Roman Empire exist? Because the Roman Empire has never consisted of a ten-division federation with ten equal rulers, one is forced to conclude that this stage of Rome's existence will take place in the future.

So, sometime in the future, a revived form of the Roman Empire will be established. The empire that collapsed in Western Europe in A.D. 476 will be brought to life again in the form of a ten-division federation that will ultimately give its allegiance to the Antichrist (Revelation 17).

THE END OF THE TIMES OF THE GENTILES

The Description

Daniel indicated that the Roman Empire was to be succeeded by a fifth kingdom represented by the stone in the dream (2:44-45). This kingdom will be set up by the God of heaven, not by man. It will never be destroyed, no other kingdoms will ever succeed it, it will end and destroy all the Gentile kingdoms portrayed in the image of the dream, and it will endure forever. These characteristics of God's kingdom contrast sharply with those of the Gentile kingdoms.

In the dream, the stone struck the huge image at its feet, causing the entire image to disintegrate. This indicated several things. First, the coming of the kingdom of God will take place when the last stage of Rome—the revived Roman Empire—is in existence. Second, when the kingdom of God comes, it will destroy the revived Roman Empire. Third, when God's kingdom destroys the last stage of the Roman Empire, it thereby will destroy all of Gentile world dominion.

After every remnant of the image was removed from the earth, the stone became a great mountain and filled the whole earth (2:35). This shows that although the fifth kingdom will be set up by the God of heaven, it will be a kingdom on earth just as the four Gentile kingdoms have been. It will rule the earth of its day just as the Gentile kingdoms ruled the known earth of their days.

Because ancient Orientals regarded kings and kingdoms synonymously, the stone of the dream must represent not only the future kingdom of God but also its King. That King will be the Messiah (Psalm 2:2,6), the Son of God (Psalm 2:4-12), the Son of Man who comes with the clouds of heaven (Daniel 7:13-14). The Bible also indicates that Jesus Christ is that person (Matthew 16:16; 26:63-64). So the stone represented the future kingdom of God and Jesus Christ Himself. More than once the Bible refers to Jesus as "the stone" (Matthew 21:33-45; 1 Peter 2:4-8).

The Timing

Because the stone represented both the kingdom of God and Jesus Christ, its appearance in the dream portrayed the coming of Christ to establish that kingdom. The fact that the Bible presents two comings of Christ prompts an important question: Would Christ establish the future kingdom of God during His first or second coming? Some have concluded that the divine kingdom of Daniel 2 was established by Christ during His first coming and that the kingdom is totally spiritual in nature. According to this view, the kingdom consists either of the church or the spiritual rule of Christ in human hearts, and the Gentile kingdom that was crushed by the kingdom of God was the ancient Roman Empire, not a future revived Roman Empire.

Others assert that the future kingdom of God foretold in Daniel 2 has already been established by Christ in a spiritual sense during His first coming, but that it has not yet been established in its political sense. According to this view, Christ will not establish the kingdom in its political sense until His second coming.

Several things militate against both of these views. First, according to the imagery and Daniel's interpretation of the king's dream, the stone did not appear and destroy the image until the "feet and toes" stage (the ten-division federation stage) of the fourth kingdom (Rome). Earlier it was observed that this stage of the Roman Empire must yet be future because that empire never consisted of a ten-division federation in the past. This prompts the conclusions that the coming of Christ portrayed by the dream must be His future second coming and that the dream was indicating that the future kingdom of God would not be established until that coming.

Second, Daniel stated that the future kingdom of God would be set up "in the days of those kings" (2:44). Because this statement was part of Daniel's interpretation of the "feet and toes" stage of the Roman Empire, "those kings" must be a reference to the kings who will rule the future, federated, revived Roman Empire (see Daniel 7:23-24; Revelation 17:12-13). Thus, Daniel's statement signified that Christ will come to establish God's kingdom when the future revived Roman Empire dominates the world. He did not do it when the ancient Roman Empire was the dominant Gentile power.

Third, the imagery of the king's dream suggested that there would be no coexistence of the Roman Empire and the future kingdom of God. The appearing of the stone represented the coming of Christ to establish God's kingdom. After the stone crushed the image, every remnant of the image was blown away before the stone became a great mountain and filled the whole earth (Daniel 2:34-35). This indicated that every remnant of Gentile world dominion, including its last form (the Roman Empire), would be gone before the future kingdom of God would be established to rule the earth.

In contrast with this imagery, both views that assert that the future kingdom of God foretold in Nebuchadnezzar's dream was established (in at least some form) during Christ's first coming would require several centuries of coexistence between the Roman Empire and the future kingdom of God. It is a fact of history that the Western Roman Empire lasted more than 400 years after Christ's first coming, and the Eastern Roman Empire lasted more than 1400 years after that coming.

Fourth, the imagery of the dream corresponds with the apostle John's description of Christ's second coming and millennial rule. In Revelation 19–20, John indicates that Christ will crush Gentile world power at His second coming and will rule the earth for 1000 years.

Fifth, those views that assert that the future kingdom of God foretold in the king's dream was established (in at least some form) during Christ's first coming teach that the throne of God on which Christ presently sits with the Father in heaven is the throne on which He was to sit when He would rule over the kingdom of God (see Isaiah 9:6-7; Jeremiah 23:5; Luke 1:31-33). By contrast, several decades after Christ's first coming and ascension to heaven, He drew a distinction between the throne of God on which He presently sits with the Father in heaven and the throne on which He will sit in the future (Revelation 3:21). In addition, during His first coming Christ indicated that He would take His seat on His throne when He comes in His glorious second coming and when He gives people entrance into the kingdom of God (Matthew 25:31,34).

THE CLIMAX OF THE TIMES OF THE GENTILES

Through the prophetic dream that God gave to King Nebuchadnezzar, God revealed that "the times of the Gentiles," which began six centuries before Christ, would continue until the second coming of Jesus Christ to the earth. This means that the Gentiles would be the dominant world powers and the people of Israel would be subject to those powers for an extended period of time. That period has continued now for more than two-and-one-half millennia and will again be the dominant political condition of the Great Tribulation to come.

During that last three-and-one-half years of the Tribulation (Matthew 24:21; Revelation 7:14), the Jews will again be persecuted and driven out of Jerusalem. This period begins with the abomination of desolation (Daniel 9:27; Matthew 24:15) and will be the climax of the "times of the Gentiles" under the control and persecution of the Antichrist. Its duration will be 42 months (Revelation 11:2), 1260 days (Revelation 12:6), or "time, times, and half a time" (Daniel 7:25; Revelation 12:14). The times of the Gentiles will end with the second coming of Jesus Christ and the establishment of His millennial kingdom. From that time forward, Jerusalem will never again be subjected to Gentile domination. The nation of Israel will be the spiritual and political center of the world (Isaiah 2:2-4; 61:6; Micah 4:1-3; Zechariah 8:22-23; 14:16-19).

—TIMOTHY J. DEMY AND
JOHN F. WALVOORD

BIBLIOGRAPHY

Bock, Darrell L. *Luke 9:51–21:43. Baker Exegetical Commentary on the New Testament.* Grand Rapids: Baker Books, 1996.

Fruchtenbaum, Arnold G. *The Footsteps of the Messiah.* Rev. ed. Tustin, CA: Ariel Ministries, 2003.

Pentecost, J. Dwight. *Things to Come.* Grand Rapids: Dunham Publishing Company, 1958.

Showers, Renald E. *The Most High God.* Bellmawr, NJ: The Friends of Israel Gospel Ministry, 1982.

Walvoord, John F. *Major Bible Prophecies: 37 Crucial Prophecies that Affect You Today.* Grand Rapids: Zondervan, 1991.

———. *The Nations in Prophecy.* Grand Rapids: Zondervan, 1967.

TRIBULATION

THE TRIBULATION WILL COME AFTER the rapture of the church and will be the greatest period of suffering the world has ever known. The Bible has more to say about these seven years than any other prophetic time period. During this period, the Antichrist will emerge, persecution of new believers will ensue, and the great battle of Armageddon and the second coming of Christ will transpire.

The New Testament teaches that the current church age will also include trials and tribulation. Jesus said, "In the world you have tribulation, but take courage; I have overcome the world" (John 16:33 NASB). The apostle Paul warned, "Indeed, all who desire to live godly in Christ Jesus will be persecuted" (2 Timothy 3:12). However, the persecution of the church in this age is not the wrath of God. The future Tribulation will be a time of God's wrath upon a Christ-rejecting world. Our Lord has promised to exempt the church from it (Revelation 3:10).

OLD TESTAMENT TRIBULATION TERMS

The Bible includes many direct and indirect references to the Tribulation. One of the first Old Testament passages to prophesy of this period is Deuteronomy 4:27-31. These verses foretell both the scattering of the Jews and their restoration to the Land when they seek the Lord. Deuteronomy includes an outline of Israel's entire history, revealed by God before Israel had set foot in the Promised Land. Their destiny is to experience a time of "distress" or "tribulation" (KJV) "in the latter days" right before Israel "will return to the LORD [their] God and listen to His voice."

The Tribulation will be a period of divine judgment preceding Israel's redemption and the establishment of God's kingdom on earth. God's covenant with Israel included this provision. The doctrine of the Tribulation begins in the Old Testament, and the Olivet Discourse and the book of Revelation cite and allude to the Old Testament frequently. For this reason an understanding of the "day of the Lord" in the Old Testament is essential when interpreting the New Testament teaching concerning the Tribulation.

The Old Testament often refers to Israel's "last days" (see Deuteronomy 4:30-31; 32:35-43; Isaiah 26:9-21; Jeremiah 30:4-24) and to the "day of the Lord" (see Ezekiel 13:1-7; Joel 2:1-11; 3:1-21; Amos 5:18-20; Zephaniah 1:7-13). It also uses other terms to describe divine intervention through judgment:

- the great and terrible day of the Lord (Malachi 4:5)

- distress (Deuteronomy 4:30)

- the time (or day) of trouble (Daniel 12:1 KJV; Zephaniah 1:15)

- the day of Jacob's trouble (Jeremiah 30:7 KJV)

- birth pangs (Isaiah 21:3; 26:17-18; 66:7; Jeremiah 4:31; Micah 4:10)

- the day of vengeance (Isaiah 34:8; 35:4; 61:2; 63:4)

- the day of the Lord's wrath (Zephaniah 1:18)

These terms do not all refer to the end-times Tribulation. The contexts of these verses usually include phrases that point to a definite time or to the indefinite future. In some cases, such as "the day of the Lord," the idiomatic nature of prophetic speech points to events such as the Assyrian or Babylonian invasions or to a more remote future event (the Tribulation and millennium). The prophets often used the Hebrew phrase b^e ʾ ah^a rit hayyamim ("the latter days") for the Tribulation (see Isaiah 2:2; Jeremiah 23:20; 48:47; 49:39; Ezekiel 38:16; Daniel 2:28; 8:19,23; 10:14; Hosea 3:5; Micah 4:1).

One of the most important passages for the study of the future is Daniel 9:24-27, which includes the 70-weeks prophecy and tells us how long the Tribulation will last (seven years). Like Jeremiah, Daniel 12:1 calls this future period "a time of distress." Daniel emphasizes that Israel will also be rescued.

NEW TESTAMENT TRIBULATION TERMS

The New Testament builds upon the Old Testament foundation and expands our picture of the Tribulation. The first extended passage in the New Testament dealing with the Tribulation is the Olivet Discourse (Matthew 24:4-28; see Mark 13; Luke 17:22-37; 21:5-36 for parallel passages). In this discourse, Jesus describes the Tribulation period. In Matthew 24:4-14, He speaks about the first half of the Tribulation, and in 24:15-28, He describes the second half, leading up to His second coming. According to Jesus, the Tribulation will be intense and extensive and will include both human and natural disasters. Jesus told the disciples that the trauma and suffering will escalate to such a point that it would end only after the battle of Armageddon and the second coming of Christ.

Some commentators have called Paul's Thessalonian epistles "the Pauline Apocalypse" because they deal extensively with the last days. Twice Paul refers to the Tribulation when speaking of a future time of wrath (1 Thessalonians 1:10; 5:9; see also Romans 5:9). In 2 Thessalonians 2:1-2, Paul tells his readers that they should not be deceived into thinking that the Tribulation (the day of the Lord) had already started. Paul continues, "Let no one in any way deceive you, for it will not come unless the apostasy comes first, and the man of lawlessness is revealed, the son of destruction, who opposes and exalts himself above every so-called god or object of worship, so that he takes his seat in the temple of God, displaying himself as being God."

Revelation 6–19 includes the Bible's most extensive description of the Tribulation. These chapters are rich in both imagery and content and leave little doubt in the reader's mind regarding the extent of the crisis that is yet to come.

The Great Tribulation

We believe the Bible distinguishes between the Tribulation period (seven years) and the Great Tribulation (the final three-and-one-half years). In Matthew 24:9 the term "tribulation" most likely refers to the full seven-year period of the Tribulation. On the other hand, Matthew 24:21 speaks of the "great tribulation," beginning with the abomination of desolation, which takes place at the midpoint of the seven-year period (Matthew 24:15).

In Matthew 24:15-20, Jesus told His disciples that in the middle of the Tribulation the Antichrist will break his covenant with Israel and persecution will increase. "Then there will be a great tribulation, such as has not occurred since the beginning of the world until now, nor ever will" (Matthew 24:21). We believe that the "great tribulation" most likely refers to only the last three-and-a-half-year period of the Tribulation.

The Wrath of God

"The time of God's wrath" and "the tribulation" evidently encompass the same seven-year time period. We have seen that Deuteronomy 4:30 describes this latter-day time period as a time of tribulation. Zephaniah 1:15 calls this same "day of trouble and distress" (tribulation) "a day of wrath." New Testament writers use this Old Testament term in relation to the seven-year Tribulation because it is a time when God's wrath breaks loose within human history and moves to repay a Christ-rejecting world, which will be motivated by Satan to persecute Christians and Jews (Romans 2:5; 5:9; Colossians 3:6; Revelation 14:10,19; 15:1,7; 16:1,19; 19:15).

The Day of the Lord

The Old Testament uses the phrase "day of the Lord" to refer to the Tribulation (Zephaniah 1:14-15). Paul continues this usage (1 Thessalonians 5:2; 2 Thessalonians 2:2). From God's perspective, the Tribulation will be the day of the Lord. It will be a time dominated and directly under the control of God. No longer will the Lord control history indirectly through invisible means. He will visibly intervene in human history. From man's perspective, it will be a time of suffering. Divine intervention produces human tribulation.

Birth Pangs

In Matthew 24:4-7, Jesus describes some of the beginning signs of the Tribulation. He then states in verse 8, "But all these things are merely the beginning of birth pangs." He was clearly using the imagery of Jeremiah 30:5-7 to describe intense suffering and expectation.

THE PURPOSE OF THE TRIBULATION

God's purpose is for the Tribulation to be a time of judgment (though His grace will still be available in the gospel) that will precede Christ's glorious 1000-year reign in Jerusalem from David's throne. Arnold Fruchtenbaum (pp. 177–81) divides God's purpose into three elements:

1. *To make an end of wickedness (Isaiah 13:9; 24:19-20).* One reason for the Tribulation is to punish the whole world for its sins against God, much as He punished the world through the global flood in Noah's days (Matthew 24:37-39).

2. *To bring about a worldwide revival (Revelation 7:1-17).* During the first half of the Tribulation, God will evangelize the world by the means of the 144,000 Jews and thus fulfill Jesus' prophecy that the gospel will be preached to the whole world (Matthew 24:14).

3. *To break the power of the holy people Israel (Daniel 12:5-7)*. Finally, God will use the Tribulation to prepare Israel for its conversion. When the Jews acknowledge that Jesus is the Messiah and call upon Him, He will come again to deliver them. In Daniel 11 and 12, the prophet was given a vision of what conditions will be like for Israel during the Tribulation. Daniel 12:5-7 asks how long the suffering will continue, and Daniel is told the events would end when "they finish shattering the power of the holy people."

EVENTS IN THE FIRST HALF OF THE TRIBULATION

1. *The Seal Judgments*. Revelation 6 outlines six of the seven seal judgments (the seventh contains the trumpet judgments) that initiate the Tribulation. The first four seals are also known as the four horsemen of the Apocalypse. These judgments are the beginnings of God's wrath on the earth.

2. *The Rise of Antichrist and the Ten-Nation Confederacy*. The beginning of the Tribulation will be marked by the signing of a covenant between Israel and the Antichrist (Daniel 9:26-27). The Antichrist will come on the scene in the first half of the Tribulation, and he will be the head of a ten-nation confederacy (Daniel 2:42,44; 7:7,24; Revelation 12:3; 13:1; 17:12,16) that will rule the world during the Tribulation.

3. *The Ministry of Elijah*. The ministry of Elijah (Malachi 4:5-6), which may be fulfilled through the ministry of the two witnesses, will be one of restoration toward the nation of Israel. It will be "before the coming of the great and terrible day of the LORD," so it will occur during the first half of the Tribulation.

4. *The Revival Through the 144,000 Jewish Evangelists*. Revelation 7 details the call and ministry of 144,000 Jewish evangelists who preach the gospel during the first half of the Tribulation.

5. *The Trumpet Judgments*. Revelation 8–9 describes six of the seven trumpet judgments. As with the seal judgments, the last trumpet introduces the next series of judgments (in this case, the bowl judgments). These judgments focus on nature and include two of the three woe judgments.

6. *The Ministry of the Two Witnesses*. Just as the 144,000 are engaged in world evangelism, the two witnesses are sealed by God (Revelation 11:3-6) to be a special witness to Jerusalem and Israel.

7. *The False Church*. Also known as "ecclesiastical Babylon," the apostate church will have great power and influence during the first half of the Tribulation (Revelation 17:1-6). This will aid the Antichrist in his deception.

EVENTS IN THE MIDDLE OF THE TRIBULATION

1. *The Little Scroll*. In Revelation 10:9-11, the apostle John is commanded by the interpreting angel to eat a scroll. The content of the scroll is prophecy relating to the middle and second half of the Tribulation. Biblical prophecy is considered good (sweet) by many people, but the message of judgment is hard to take (bitter).

2. *The Antichrist Is Killed*. Revelation 13:3 notes that the seventh head (a reference to Antichrist) is killed. "I saw one of his heads as if it had been slain, and his fatal wound was healed. And the whole earth was amazed and followed after the beast."

3. *Satan Is Cast Down to the Earth from Heaven*. Revelation 12:7-9 reveals that Michael and his angels defeat Satan and cast him and his fallen angels to the

earth. As a result, the trials during the second half of the Tribulation intensify.

4. *The Resurrection of the Antichrist.* One of the first things Satan does on earth after being cast out of heaven is to resurrect the Antichrist. Revelation 13:3-4 records this event through which the Antichrist attempts to counterfeit Jesus, the Messiah.

5. *Three Kings Are Killed and Seven Submit.* After his death and resurrection, the Antichrist consolidates his worldwide rule by killing three of the ten kings, which leads to the other seven submitting to him voluntarily. This event provides the political basis from which the Antichrist will project his power during the last half of the Tribulation (Revelation 17:12-13).

6. *Destruction of the False Church.* As history has shown, when a tyrant reaches his goal of total political control, he destroys those who helped him reach that point. The Antichrist now destroys the harlot, "ecclesiastical Babylon," as noted in Revelation 17:16. "And the ten horns which you saw, and the beast, these will hate the harlot and will make her desolate and naked, and will eat her flesh and will burn her up with fire."

7. *The Death and Resurrection of the Two Witnesses.* During the first half of the Tribulation, the two witnesses were miraculously protected by God. Now, God allows the deception of the Antichrist to deepen as he murders the two witnesses in Jerusalem and the whole world rejoices. However, after three-and-one-half days, the two witnesses will be resurrected and taken to heaven in the sight of all. Fear then grips those who have followed after the beast.

8. *The Worship of the Antichrist.* Since the "earth dwellers" prefer the counterfeit over the genuine, they will be deceived into worshiping the Antichrist as God. In reality they will be worshiping Satan. "And all who dwell on the earth will worship him, everyone whose name has not been written from the foundation of the world in the book of life of the Lamb" (Revelation 13:8).

9. *The False Prophet.* This person is a counterfeit of the ministry of the Holy Spirit in that he is temporarily empowered to do false signs, wonders, and miracles that greatly aid the Antichrist's rise to power. False religion is the vehicle of deception for this second beast—the False Prophet.

10. *666—the Mark of the Beast.* Another "ministry" of the False Prophet will be the administration of the counterfeit seal of the Holy Spirit, the famous mark of the beast—666. Placement of this mark on the forehead or right hand will be required for anyone who wants to conduct economic transactions during the second half of the Tribulation. It should be noted that any person receiving this mark cannot be saved. This mark will not be distributed during the first half of the Tribulation.

11. *The Seven-Year Covenant Broken.* It is not at all surprising that the Antichrist should break his covenant with Israel. Such a move is in keeping with his character. This betrayal will involve the Antichrist's military invasion of Israel. "He will also enter the Beautiful Land, and many [countries] will fall; but these will be rescued out of his hand: Edom, Moab and the foremost of the sons of Ammon" (Daniel 11:41).

12. *The Abomination of Desolation.* When the Antichrist breaks his covenant with Israel at the midpoint of the Tribulation, he will set himself up as God to be worshiped in the rebuilt Jewish Temple. This defiling act is called "the

abomination of desolation." This will be a sign to the Jews to flee Jerusalem.

13. *The Persecution of the Jews.* The second half of the Tribulation will be characterized by an extreme attempt to wipe out the Jews. Likely, Satan thinks that if the Jews are exterminated, God's plan for history will be thwarted. Satan might think that this would somehow prevent the second coming. This persecution is pictured in Revelation 12:1-6.

EVENTS OF THE SECOND HALF OF THE TRIBULATION

1. *The Bowl Judgments.* The bowl judgments are the most severe judgments of the entire Tribulation. They occur in the second half of the Tribulation, devastate the Antichrist's kingdom, and prepare the way for the second coming of Christ. The bowl judgments are the result of the prayers of the saints for God to take revenge on their behalf (Revelation 15:1-8). Revelation 16 describes the bowl judgments.

2. *The Protection of the Jewish Remnant.* At the midpoint of the Tribulation when the Antichrist commits the abomination of desolation, the Jews will flee Jerusalem. Apparently these Jews will be protected in the Jordanian village of Bozrah, known also as Petra. A remnant will be preserved through this and other means.

3. *The Conversion of Israel.* Right before the second coming, the people of Israel will accept the messiahship of Jesus and become saved from their sins. This will prepare them for their role in the millennial kingdom after the second advent. "And I will pour out on the house of David and on the inhabitants of Jerusalem, the Spirit of grace and of supplication, so that they will look on Me whom they have pierced; and they will mourn for Him, as one mourns for

an only son, and they will weep bitterly over Him, like the bitter weeping over a firstborn" (Zechariah 12:10).

A SEVEN-YEAR TRIBULATION

The prophetic calendar of Daniel 9:24-27, specifically verse 27, shows that the Tribulation will last for seven years: "He [the Antichrist] will make a firm covenant with the many for one week [that is, seven years], but in the middle of the week he will put a stop to sacrifice and grain offering; and on the wing of abominations will come one who makes desolate, even until a complete destruction, one that is decreed, is poured out on the one who makes desolate." The "week" that Daniel writes of is understood by most prophecy scholars to be a week of years or seven years. These years follow the interval of the "seven weeks and sixty-two weeks" found in Daniel 9:25.

The book of Revelation gives a number of time indicators, including these:

- times, time, and half a time (Revelation 12:14)
- 1260 days (Revelation 11:3)
- 42 months (Revelation 11:2; 13:5)

These time indicators, each a different way of indicating three-and-a-half years, reflect the two halves of the seven-year Tribulation period—the seventieth week of Daniel 9:24-27.

TRAGEDY AND TRIUMPH

Human history has been filled with personal, national, and international tragedy and despair. Every century, every empire, and every era has seen multiple manifestations of original sin, the fall, and satanic activity. Passages of biblical prophecy (and other portions of Scripture) clearly teach that the future will bring a specific period of increased trauma and tragedy during which terror and tribulation will be both intense and global. This era will last for seven years, and following the battle of Armageddon, it will culminate in the second coming of the Lord

Jesus Christ to establish His millennial kingdom and reign on earth.

This Tribulation era of destruction and persecution will follow the rapture of the church. However, the fact we will not enter the Tribulation does not alleviate us of our daily responsibilities, evangelism, discipleship, or holy living. Tribulation is certain, but so is triumph. In the meantime, we are called to evangelize the lost and edify the saints.

—THOMAS ICE AND RANDALL PRICE

BIBLIOGRAPHY

Fruchtenbaum, Arnold. *Footsteps of the Messiah.* Tustin, CA: Ariel Press, 1995.

Ice, Thomas. "The Seventy Weeks of Daniel." In *End Times Controversy.* Eds. Tim LaHaye and Thomas Ice. Eugene, OR: Harvest House Publishers, 2003.

Price, Randall. "Old Testament Tribulation Terms" In *When the Trumpet Sounds.* Eugene, OR: Harvest House Publishers, 1995.

Showers, Renald. *Maranatha: Our Lord Come!* Bellmawr, NJ: Friends of Israel Ministry, 1995.

Walvoord, John F. *The Blessed Hope and the Tribulation.* Grand Rapids: Zondervan, 1971.

TRIBULATION SAINTS AND MARTYRS

THE TERM *TRIBULATION SAINTS* designates individuals who will become Christians during the seven-year Tribulation that follows the rapture. In Revelation 7:9-17, John describes them and declares that their numbers are so great he cannot count them. He also declares that they come from every nation, language, and tribe on earth. They are clothed in white robes because they have believed in Jesus Christ.

These verses confirm that even amidst the horrors, deception, and great difficulties of the Tribulation, many people will reject the Antichrist, accept Jesus Christ, and follow Him. The description of these saints in 7:9-17 follows immediately after John's discussion of the 144,000 Israelites who will be sealed

for protection and special ministry during the Tribulation, so it's likely these Gentile saints came to belief in the Messiah as a result of the preaching of the 144,000 (Fruchtenbaum, p. 224).

The presence of these Christians during the Tribulation is also an indication that the regenerating work of the Holy Spirit will continue on earth after the rapture. Although the Holy Spirit will no longer be restraining evil during the Tribulation, He will continue carrying out His other ministries, such as filling and sealing believers. These ministries will result in worldwide revival during the Tribulation even though many people will choose to follow the Antichrist instead.

Some of the Tribulation saints will be martyred for their faith. These Tribulation martyrs are mentioned in Revelation 6:9-11, which describes the fifth seal judgment. These persecuted saints are those who come to faith in Jesus Christ during the first part of the Tribulation.

Revelation 6:9 pictures the Tribulation martyrs "underneath the altar" because in the Old Testament the blood of sacrifices was poured out under the altar (Exodus 29:12; Leviticus 4:7). In Revelation 6:10 John hears them cry out, asking why God has not avenged their deaths and judged their persecutors. Their prayer is similar to prayers in the imprecatory psalms of the Old Testament, such as Psalm 74:10. The reply, in Revelation 6:11, is that they must wait a short time longer before divine retribution is exacted so that the plan of God can be completed. This short time is the remainder of the Tribulation. Their prayer of vengeance is fully realized in Revelation 16:4-7 during the third bowl judgment.

The martyred saints will be raised at the end of the Tribulation and will enter into the blessing of the millennium and reign with Jesus Christ (Revelation 20:4-6). It is at this time that they will receive their resurrection bodies.

—TIMOTHY J. DEMY

BIBLIOGRAPHY

Fruchtenbaum, Arnold G. *The Footsteps of the Messiah.* Rev. ed. Tustin, CA: Ariel Ministries, 2003.

LaHaye, Tim, and Thomas Ice. *Charting the End Times.* Eugene OR: Harvest House Publishers, 2001.

Thomas, Robert L. *Revelation 1–7: An Exegetical Commentary.* Chicago: Moody Press, 1992.

———. *Revelation 8–22: An Exegetical Commentary.* Chicago: Moody Press, 1995.

Walvoord, John F. *Major Bible Prophecies: 37 Crucial Prophecies That Affect You Today.* Grand Rapids: Zondervan, 1991.

———. *The Revelation of Jesus Christ: A Commentary.* Chicago: Moody Press, 1966.

TRUMPET JUDGMENTS

THE BIBLE TELLS OF PEOPLE USING trumpets in several ways:

1. Trumpets signal the end of something, such as the end of the harvest.
2. Trumpets alert a city of impending danger.
3. Trumpets call the people of God to worship and sound their praise.
4. Trumpets rally troops to combat.

In 1 Corinthians 15:52 Paul describes a trumpet at the rapture of the church as "the last trumpet." By "last" (Greek, *eschate*) he means the trumpet that closes the church age. He also calls this trumpet "the trumpet of God" that brings those "in Christ" from the dead and catches up "we who are alive and remain" (1 Thessalonians 4:16-17). The rapture trumpet is therefore a sort of harvest trumpet.

God also uses a trumpet to bring His elect to the kingdom when the Messiah, the Son of Man, comes down to earth to reign. Jesus told His disciples the Son of Man "will send forth His angels with a great trumpet and they will gather together His elect from the four winds, from one end of the sky to the other" (Matthew 24:31 NASB). This trumpet is another harvest trumpet that calls the believers to the kingdom at the end of the Tribulation. This trumpet should not be confused with the rapture trumpet that calls the church saints into glory.

The seven trumpets of the book of Revelation warn of attacks—that is, of the Lord's fury against the evil forces on earth during the seven-year Tribulation period. Revelation describes three series of judgments that fall consecutively upon the earth. They begin with the seven seals that are broken on the scroll that only Christ can open (Revelation 5:1-5). Jesus is the One who brings about God's judgment on sinful human beings and ultimately upon the Antichrist and the False Prophet. The seven seals (6:1–8:6) lead to the seven trumpets (8:7–11:19), which then lead to the seven bowls "of the wrath of God" (16:1-21). The seals, trumpets, and bowls bring on the earth an ever-increasing weight of judgment because those on earth continue in their sin and in their loyalty to the Antichrist and False Prophet. John writes toward the end of the bowl judgments, "The fifth angel poured out his bowl upon the throne of the beast, and his kingdom became darkened; and [men] gnawed their tongues because of pain, and they blasphemed the God of heaven because of their pains and their sores; and they did not repent of their deeds" (16:10-11).

The seventh seal brings "peals of thunder and sounds and flashes of lightning" (8:5), but it also brings "seven angels who had the seven trumpets prepared themselves to sound them" (8:6). This verse indicates that these three series of judgments were "prepared" by the Lord because He foreknew where the earth was headed—to the final revolt against and rejection of the Lord and of His Christ (Psalm 2).

THE FIRST TRUMPET

What comes upon the earth from these seven trumpets? The first trumpet (Revelation 8:7) brings hail and fire "mixed with blood." A third of the earth is burned up, a third of the trees are consumed, and "all the green grass…burned." "Blood" (Greek, *haima*) is often used in Scripture to describe pollution or even disease after it has been exposed for a long time on clothes or skin. Blood was not to be eaten (Leviticus 7:26), and because bathing was at a premium in a hot climate, women were unclean for a time after menstruation (12:4). The reason is that blood putrefies so quickly and rapidly becomes germ-ridden. Blood then becomes a metaphor in Revelation 8:7 of a terrible disaster of awful circumstances that come upon the earth.

What is the significance of "a third," mentioned in connection with six of the seven trumpets? More than likely this definite numerical reference is literal, though not meaning to be mathematically precise. In other words, the figure is rounded off but shows that approximately a third of the trees, sea creatures, and other living things perish in the devastation that comes upon the planet. Interestingly, *all* of the grass is burned up. John stresses the negative effect on the ecology and the climatology of the globe and shows that all of life is in jeopardy.

THE SECOND TRUMPET

With the sounding of the second trumpet (8:8-9) the horror on earth accelerates with "a great mountain burning with fire…thrown into the sea." A third of the sea becomes blood, a third of the living creatures of the sea die, and a third of the ships on the ocean are destroyed! Some have suggested the mountain falling into the ocean represents a mushroom cloud from an atomic explosion that pollutes the waters.

Other possibilities exist, however. Half of the island of Krakatoa in the Javanese Strait of Sunda exploded and disappeared in the year 1883. Ships at sea were thrown miles inland on other islands, and many more were sunk. Millions of fish died and polluted the waters. Many sea creatures were electrified and boiled by the heat and static voltage. The explosive rumblings of the island were heard a third of the way around the world! The explosion was so loud that the sound waves killed many people.

When the Mediterranean island of Thera, an island near Patmos, exploded in approximately 1440 B.C., the sea became red as blood.

The fact that such natural phenomena really can occur would indicate that the events described in relation to the second trumpet can come about in a similar literal way. "As under the first Egyptian plague (Exodus 7:21; cf. Zephaniah 1:3), the fish in the blood-filled environment perished" (Thomas, p. 19).

THE THIRD TRUMPET

When an angel sounds the third trumpet, a "great star" named Wormwood falls from heaven and pollutes the earth's rivers and springs (Revelation 8:10-11). Wormwood (Greek, *apsinthos*) is a bitter-tasting plant found in Palestine. The Old Testament refers to it to describe God's just and divine punishment (Jeremiah 9:15; 23:15; Lamentations 3:15,19). As a result of this "great star" that falls from heaven, the waters of earth become so polluted that "many men died from the waters, because they were made bitter" (Revelation 8:11). The "star" more than likely is an asteroid (Greek, *astēr*). Its impact upon the earth brings about terrible destruction and lethal pollution.

THE FOURTH TRUMPET

At the sounding of the fourth trumpet, the light from the moon, sun, and stars are "struck," and their light appears to be diminished (8:12). Some commentators suggest that these lights appear "struck" because of atmospheric pollution surrounding the earth. The text, however, says these heavenly objects themselves "were struck" so that their light rays are weakened. This event would be most frightening to those on earth.

Verse 13 records a painful, loud cry from a heavenly angel. It is the first of three "woes" (Greek, *ouai*) "to those who dwell on the earth, because of the remaining blasts of the trumpet of the three angels who are about to sound." This may indicate that those on earth are forewarned that more judgment is coming. Sadly, Revelation seems to indicate that most of the people on earth are not moved to repentance even though the judgments are so terrible.

THE FIFTH TRUMPET

With the sounding of the fifth trumpet, a star falls from heaven holding "the key to the bottomless pit" (9:1). The star is actually a "he" (9:2), indicating that this being is likely an angel. He may be an elect angel sent by God, he may be an evil angel doing Satan's work, or he may be Satan himself (Walvoord, p. 159). It seems quite possible that this being is an angel of God (Hindson, pp. 105–07). "In either view the angel will carry out an order from the Lord Himself" (Couch, p. 246).

Next, a plague of locusts appears from the pit (9:3). Almost all Bible scholars believe this represents a horde of demonic beings coming upon earth to torment people. They are instructed not to harm the greenery left on the globe, but they are allowed to harm humans. John vividly describes their march of terror. Ten times in twelve verses, John uses comparative expressions such as "like," "as it were," and "as." With this, the first woe is finished, but "behold, two woes are still coming after these things" (9:12).

THE SIXTH TRUMPET

The second woe introduces the sixth trumpet, sounded by the sixth angel (9:13-21). An angel from the heavenly golden altar commands the sixth angel to release the "four angels who are bound at the great river Euphrates" (9:14). These beings must also be fallen angels—demonic creatures who are chained or bound.

What is the significance of the Euphrates River? The Euphrates begins its journey in the Armenian mountains just south of Russia. The river flows until it joins the Tigris River in lower Iraq (ancient Babylon). These two rivers form an 1800-mile waterway through Iraq. Mankind's original corporate revolt against God began in this part of the world with the aggression of Nimrod (Genesis 10:8-10). It is also the general area of Shinar, where the Tower of Babel was built (11:1-9). From here polytheism and astrology began and spread throughout the entire world. It is only natural that from this region more demonic activity would proliferate in the last days.

At this time, 200 million "horsemen" come to torment humanity (9:16-17). They kill a third of the people of the earth (9:18) with their "plagues" that come upon humanity like "fire and…smoke and…brimstone, which proceeded out of their mouths." Those not killed "did not repent of the works of their hands, so as not to worship demons, and the idols of gold and silver…and they did not repent of their murders nor of their sorceries nor of their immorality nor of their thefts" (9:20). As the Tribulation progresses, resistance seems to grow against the Lord even though peoples' pain intensifies.

THE SEVENTH TRUMPET

The seventh trumpet (11:15-19) is partly a preview of what is to come. With a reference to the book of Daniel, John says the earthly kingdom of the Antichrist will become "the kingdom of our Lord and of His Christ; and He will reign forever and ever" (11:15; see Daniel 2:44; 7:18-27). It will be the "everlasting kingdom," where all the dominions of the world and of heaven serve Him. "It doesn't get any better than this! There is no greater statement of triumph in all the Revelation, with the possible exception of 19:11-16, where Christ actually returns to earth to reign and rule….What started as hell on earth has become heaven revealed" in these verses (Hindson, p. 128).

The world, of course, is enraged with this prophecy. And God's wrath continues until the end, when He judges the dead and rewards His servants (Revelation 11:18). With this last trumpet come more flashes of lightning, peals of thunder, an earthquake, and a great hailstorm (11:19). The seven angels with the trumpets lead into the seven plagues described in 15:1-8, which are actually the "last" plagues—the wrath of God, which will be finished in the bowl judgments (15:1). The bowl judgments bring forth the worst of the torments and close the main portion of the Tribulation itself. (See the articles titled "Seal Judgments" and "Bowl Judgments.")

—MAL COUCH

BIBLIOGRAPHY

Couch, Mal, gen. ed. *A Bible Handbook to Revelation.* Grand Rapids: Kregel, 2001.

Hindson, Ed. *The Book of Revelation.* Chattanooga: AMG Publishers, 2002.

Seiss, Joseph A. *The Apocalypse.* Grand Rapids: Kregel, 1987.

Swete, Henry Barclay. *Commentary on Revelation.* Grand Rapids: Kregel, 1977.

Thomas, Robert L. *Revelation 8–22: An Exegetical Commentary.* Chicago: Moody Press, 1995.

Walvoord, John F. *The Revelation of Jesus Christ.* Chicago: Moody Press, 1966.

Winchester, Simon. *Kratatoa.* New York: HarperCollins, 2003.

TRUMPET OF GOD

IN THE BIBLE, TRUMPETS WERE USED for various purposes, including the worship of God. Psalm 47:5 speaks of God ascending with a shout and with "the sound of a trumpet." The King of Israel and the King of all the earth reigns over the nations and "sits on His holy throne." The trumpet is clearly an instrument of praise to the Lord.

Zechariah 9:11-16 seems to be an awesome prediction about the coming Maccabean era (in the second century B.C.), when the sons of Zion would defeat the sons of Greece. This included the defeat of the cruel madman who was reigning over Jerusalem, Antiochus Epiphanes. Zechariah predicted that the Lord would fire His arrows at the Greeks like lightning, and "the LORD GOD will blow the trumpet" and defend His people (9:14-15 NASB). "And the LORD their God will save them in that day" (9:16).

When the Lord Jesus comes again as the Son of Man, the promised Messiah, He will sound "a great trumpet," and His angels will gather together the elect from one end of the earth to the other. When the King comes "in His glory, and all the angels with Him, then He will sit on His glorious throne" with the nations presented at His feet for judgment (Matthew 24:31; 25:31-32). The context shows that this coming to Jerusalem with the sound of "a great trumpet" has to do with the millennial reign, after the Tribulation. The King comes to earth "on the clouds of the sky with power and great glory" (24:30).

Jesus said these words to His disciples in His Olivet Discourse. The Jewish people were very familiar with what the Lord was speaking about; the trumpet would announce the Davidic reign on earth.

The apostle Paul also mentions an earlier event, that involves another trumpet. Before the Tribulation, "the trumpet of God" will call home the believers of this dispensation, those "who have fallen asleep in Jesus" (1 Thessalonians 4:14). These who are asleep are the "dead in Christ" (4:16). In addition to these, those who "are alive and remain until the coming of the Lord" (4:15) will be summoned upward with "a shout, with the voice of the archangel, and with the trumpet of God." This event is both the resurrection of the "sleeping" church saints (those who have died in Christ) and the rapture of those living "to meet the Lord in the air" (4:17).

The "shout" (Greek, *keleuo,* "summon") is a classical and military term meaning to "give a command" and is used for the purpose of gathering groups together. Christ is coming for His church with absolute and certain authority! "The archangel" is the highest angel, Michael (Jude 9). No article appears before the name in Greek, and it could be read "with [preposition *en*] the voice of an archangel," leaving some to speculate that there could be other archangels.

As with "archangel," there is no article before "trumpet." It could read "with [preposition *en*] a trumpet [belonging to] God." This trumpet belonging to God is also the "last" (Greek, *eschatos*) trumpet, which will close the church age (1 Corinthians 15:51-53). As in 1 Thessalonians 4, this "trumpet will sound, and the dead will be raised imperishable, and we will be changed" (1 Corinthians 15:52). In verses 51-52 the apostle Paul reveals that the rapture is something not previously revealed; it is a *mystery* in which "we will not all sleep, but we will all be changed, in a moment, in the twinkling of an eye."

Some interpreters attempt to tie the last trumpet (1 Corinthians 15:52) and the trumpet of God (1 Thessalonians 4:16) to the seventh trumpet of Revelation 11:15-19. But the key to biblical interpretation is not simply the comparison of like words, such as *trumpet*, but more importantly, the context of various passages of Scripture. The seventh trumpet of Revelation 11 announces the soon-to-come eternal earthly reign of the Lord's Christ (verse 15). The seventh trumpet sounds forth in the midst of the Tribulation and has nothing to do with the rapture of the church. It announces the Lord coming down to rule, not the catching away of the church and the resurrected saints with Him to glory.

With the announcement that Christ will soon reign, the nations are enraged (Revelation 11:18). The seventh trumpet heralds more wrath upon the earth, accompanied with peals of thunder, an earthquake, and a great hailstorm (11:19).

Therefore, the trumpet of God sounds before the Tribulation and calls the church up to meet the Lord in the clouds (1 Thessalonians 4:16-17)—a joyous "harvest" occasion when God calls His workers home. On the other hand, the seventh trumpet of Revelation 11:15 sounds during the Tribulation and is a war trumpet that announces a final military victory of Christ and more judgment on the rebellious earth. (See the article titled "Trumpet Judgments.")

—MAL COUCH

BIBLIOGRAPHY

Blackstone, William A. *Jesus Is Coming*. Grand Rapids: Kregel, 1989.

Couch, Mal. *The Hope of Christ's Return*. Chattanooga: AMG Publishers, 2001.

Hindson, Ed. *The Book of Revelation*. Chattanooga: AMG Publishers, 2002.

LaHaye, Tim. *The Rapture*. Eugene, OR: Harvest House Publishers, 2002.

Pache, Rene. *The Return of Jesus Christ*. Chicago: Moody Press, 1955.

TYPOLOGY

A TYPE IS A DIVINELY INTENDED Old Testament foreshadowing of some spiritual reality in the New Testament. It usually consists of a correspondence or resemblance between a person, event, or thing in the Old Testament and some aspect of the person or activity of Jesus Christ.

Types can be persons (such as Adam or Melchizedek), events (such as the flood), objects (such as lambs or incense), institutions (such as Passover or service in the Tabernacle), places (such as Jerusalem), and offices (such as prophet, priest, or king) (Sterrett, p. 107).

The term *type* originated from the Greek word *typos* (used 15 times in the New Testament), which referred to a "pattern" or "image" such as the die from which coins were struck. A type is the pattern found in the Old Testament (such as the Passover lamb). The antitype (Greek, *antitypos*) is the "representation" (see Hebrews 9:24) or fulfillment found in the New Testament (such as Jesus as the Lamb of God).

The legitimacy of typology is based not only on this New Testament vocabulary but also on two other factors. Typology is part of prophecy, and the prophetic relationship between the Old and New Testaments ties them together in this latent fashion. Also, Jesus taught and demonstrated that the entire Old Testament speaks of Him (Luke 24:25-44; John 5:39-44). God has designed the earlier portion of Scripture to reflect and portray His Son in many ways.

THE CHARACTERISTICS OF TYPES

To be genuine, a type must be purposed and ordained by God. The Bible must indicate that God intended the correspondence between the type and its fulfillment (antitype) and that it doesn't simply spring from the fertile mind of creative interpreters. When the New Testament teaches such correspondence, it leaves no room for doubt. Types do not include the many simple parallels between things in the two Testaments.

A type is a real entity with a real, literal existence in Old Testament passages (it has historical reality), but is nevertheless considered by New Testament authors to foreshadow a greater spiritual reality in its New Testament fulfillment (especially in Christ). For example, the mercy seat in the Tabernacle existed physically and literally, but it also pointed to the ultimate reality of Christ as the propitiation of God for our sins.

A type also usually involves a symbol in its own context. A symbol is something that carries a meaning in addition to its ordinary meaning—a sign that suggests another meaning rather than stating it. For example, a national flag is a symbol of the country it represents. In the Bible, the bronze serpent in Numbers 21:4-9 symbolized faith for healing, but it was a type of the crucifixion of Christ and redemption through Him (John 3:14-15).

A type is a form of prophecy. As Zuck says, "Prophecy is prediction by means of words, whereas typology is prediction by correspondence between two realities, the type and the antitype." But not every correspondence is a type. To be a genuine type, "the correspondence or resemblance must have a predictive element, a foreshadowing and anticipation of the antitype." That is, it has a "forward focus" (Zuck, p. 173).

THE INTERPRETATION OF TYPES

Interpreting typology is not as simple as interpreting prophecy because the type is not given as a direct prediction, and the fulfillment is normally not described in detail. These general principles of interpretation can help identify types:

1. Study first the context of each type. The typological meaning of the bronze serpent, for example, must be based on the context of Numbers 21.

2. Note the natural qualities of the type to avoid including them in the meaning of the type. Jesus referred to the bronze serpent being "lifted up" in the wilderness before applying that pattern to His own crucifixion. However, the fact that it was bronze has no significance whatever.

3. Be certain that the type and antitype are parallel and congruous. God told Moses that the people should "look" and "live" (Numbers 21:8). Though Jesus changes this to "believe" (John 3:15), spiritually the ideas are parallel (see John 3:16-18).

4. Remember that the fulfillment is greater than the type. For example, Jesus as the Lamb of God (John 1:29) is greater than any Old Testament animal.

5. The correspondence between the type and antitype generally has one or two principal points. According to 1 Corinthians 5:7-8, for instance, Christ is our Passover Lamb. He was sacrificed, and we must receive Him to experience any benefit. Melchizedek was both a king and a priest, and he was superior to Aaron, typifying Christ as King and Priest with a greater high priesthood than Aaron's (see Psalm 110:4). Points of contrast or dissimilarity should also be noted in order to avoid including those in the typology (Zuck, p. 182).

6. The fulfillment arises out of the normal meaning of the type. Interpretations should not be arbitrary (such as concluding that clean animals that chew the cud [Leviticus 11:4-6] are types of Christians who should talk well or meditate on Scripture).

7. Types should not be based on numbers, shapes, or colors. These may be symbols (if shown to be so by their contexts), but are not foreshadowings of spiritual realities.

8. Avoid speculation. Parallelism alone does not imply typology. For example, the statement of Paul to Philemon about putting Onesimus' wrongs on Paul's account (Philemon 17-18) is parallel to God's reckoning to Christ the sins of the world (2 Corinthians 5:19; 1 Peter 2:24), but this does not make Paul a type of Christ. Some interpreters seem to feel discouraged that others are seeing types and symbols where they cannot, and so they invent them and frequently err in doing so.

9. Do not develop doctrines based primarily on types.

Recognizing Types

Note the following suggested criteria for recognizing types:

The safest way to recognize types in the Old Testament is to watch for statements in the New Testament that they are types, or at least to find a clear implication of it. Some scholars suggest that this is the only way to avoid taking all parallels between Old and New Testament persons and events as types. For example, resemblances and parallels can be found between Christ on the one hand, and Joseph, Moses, Isaac, Samuel, Solomon, Elijah, Jeremiah, and Daniel on the other hand. Yet none of these men are said in the New Testament to be types or prefigurements of Christ. One way to draw the line between types and mere parallels is to say that a genuine type must be so designated in the New Testament. On that basis, Zuck defines a type as follows: "An Old Testament person, event, or thing having historical reality and designed by God to prefigure (foreshadow) in a preparatory way a real person, event, or thing so designated in the New Testament and that corresponds to and fulfills (heightens) the type" (Zuck, p. 176).

Another potential criterion is to note a symbolic significance either stated or implied by an Old Testament author. The various articles that were included in the Old Testament Tabernacle may be suggested as both symbolic in

their time and as potential types of Christ and New Testament salvation, given the fact that the Tabernacle itself is a type (see Ramm, p. 230).

Roy Zuck lists 17 persons, events, and things that he considers to be genuine types, based on New Testament evidence (Zuck, pp. 179-80). Most of these were fulfilled specifically in Christ:

1. Melchizedek (Hebrews 7:3,15-17)

2. Aaron (Hebrews 5:4-5)

3. Feast of Passover (1 Corinthians 5:7)

4. Feast of Unleavened Bread (1 Corinthians 5:7-8)

5. Feast of Firstfruits (1 Corinthians 15:20-23)

6. Feast of Pentecost (Joel 2:28; Acts 2:1-47)

7. Feast of Trumpets (Matthew 24:21-23)

8. Day of Atonement (Zechariah 12:10; Romans 11:26-27; Hebrews 9:19-28)

9. Feast of Tabernacles (John 7:2,37-39)

10. Sabbath (Colossians 2:17; Hebrews 4:3,9,11)

11. Tabernacle (Hebrews 8:5; 9:23-24)

12. Tabernacle curtain (Hebrews 10:20)

13. Burnt offering (Leviticus 1; Ephesians 5:2; Hebrews 10:5-7)

14. Grain offering (Leviticus 2; Hebrews 10:8)

15. Fellowship offering (Leviticus 3; Ephesians 2:14; Colossians 1:20)

16. Sin offering (Leviticus 4:1–5:13; Hebrews 13:11-12)

17. Guilt offering (Leviticus 5:14–6:7; Hebrews 10:12)

Although only the Passover (among Israel's feasts) is specifically called a type in the New Testament, the other feasts can be included on the basis of Paul's statement in Colossians 2:16-17 that the festivals were "a shadow of things to come." Other scholars would also include Adam (Romans 5:14), Jonah (Matthew 12:40), and the bronze serpent (John 3:14-15) in the list. Pressing the criteria even further, some also identify Israel (Matthew 2:15) and God's judgment on Israel (1 Corinthians 10:1-11) as types (Virkler, p. 188).

Types Relating to Future Events

It is easier to spot types that have already been fulfilled in the New Testament than types whose fulfillment is still future. If types must be divinely purposed and perhaps divinely identified, one cannot know for sure that a future fulfillment of a presumed type is intended by God unless the Bible actually calls it a type and states that its fulfillment is still future. This is rare.

But certainly the feasts of Israel whose prophetic significance are not yet finally fulfilled would qualify here: (1) the Feast of Trumpets—the regathering of Israel (Matthew 24:21-23); (2) the Day of Atonement—Israel's national conversion (Romans 11:26-27); and (3) the Feast of Tabernacles—Israel enjoying kingdom blessings (John 7:2,37-39). The Feast of Firstfruits not only pictures Christ's resurrection, but also the resurrection of all saints (1 Corinthians 15:20-23). And the Feast of Pentecost began to be fulfilled in Acts 2, but ultimately awaits a universal outpouring of the Spirit on "all flesh" (Joel 2:28) associated with the arrival of Christ's future kingdom.

In addition, the ministry of Christ as a High Priest after the order of Melchizedek has typological relevance not only throughout the church age, but on an even greater scale during the millennial kingdom (as Christ not only reigns as King but also continues to minister as Priest) and the eternal state (as described magnificently in the New Jerusalem—Revelation 21:22; see Hebrews 7:17).

—WAYNE A. BRINDLE

BIBLIOGRAPHY

Mickelsen, A. Berkeley. *Interpreting the Bible.* Grand Rapids: Eerdmans Publishing Company, 1963.

Ramm, Bernard. *Protestant Biblical Interpretation.* Third rev. ed. Grand Rapids: Baker Books, 1970.

Sterrett, T. Norton. *How to Understand Your Bible.* Rev. ed. Downers Grove: InterVarsity Press, 1974.

Virkler, Henry A. *Hermeneutics: Principles and Processes of Biblical Interpretation.* Grand Rapids: Baker Books, 1981.

Zuck, Roy B. *Basic Bible Interpretation.* Wheaton, IL: Victor Books, 1991.

VENGEANCE

CHRIST USES THE WORD "VENGEANCE" (Luke 21:22) to describe the destruction that would come upon Jerusalem in A.D. 70. Prophesying that Jerusalem would be surrounded and brought down to desolation (verses 21-24), the Lord made it clear to His disciples that Israel's rejection of their King would bring ruin, dispersion, distress, and wrath. He added that the Jewish people would "fall by the edge of the sword, and will be led captive into all the nations; and Jerusalem will be trampled under foot by the Gentiles until the times of the Gentiles are fulfilled" (NASB).

Luke uses the Greek word *ekdikasis* ("vengeance") in a technical sense for "vengeance or punishment." The root verb, *dikaioo,* is translated "to justify, do justice, vindicate." With the preposition *ek,* the thought is "justice going forth" as a response to some specific crime. The New Testament uses the word (in its noun and verb forms) 14 times for "vengeance" or "revenge." God will exact a price from the nation of the Jews for their stubborn rejection of their Messiah.

Before the A.D. 70 destruction of the temple and Jerusalem, the apostles and thousands of Jewish and Gentile Christians would suffer and die for their faith. The Jews of that generation were building a mountain of wrath that would soon fall on them. Israel was not simply at war with Christians and later with the Romans; they were also at war with the Lord.

In the Olivet Discourse (Luke 21:5-38), the Lord discusses the vengeance that would someday come upon Israel (verses 12-26). His larger context is the future Tribulation, which will include "terrors and great signs from heaven" (21:11). But He then shifts His thoughts to Jerusalem and says, "But before all these things…" (21:12). Here He is teaching about the prophesied A.D. 70 event. He continues, "When you see Jerusalem surrounded by armies, then recognize that her desolation is near" (21:20). Christ resumes His discussion of the Tribulation in verse 25, where He prophesies that "there will be signs in sun and moon and stars, and on the earth dismay among nations, in perplexity at the roaring of the sea and the waves." These terrible events will be concluded when the world "will see the Son of Man coming in a cloud with power and great glory" (21:27).

When the forces of General Titus broke into the city of Jerusalem in A.D. 70, the slaughter was terrible. Josephus writes, "There was no one left for the soldiers to kill or plunder, not a soul on which to vent their fury; for mercy would never have made them keep their hands off anyone as long as action was possible. So Caesar now ordered them to raze the whole City and Sanctuary to the ground."

The Lord adds that when the days of vengeance come upon Jerusalem, "all things which are written will be fulfilled" (21:22). Most interpreters believe He is referring to the fulfillment of Hosea 9, where several verses appear to be speaking about Israel's final rejection and final dispersion worldwide. Hosea writes: "The days of punishment [will] come, the days of retribution [will] come….because of the grossness of your iniquity, and because your hostility is so great" (9:7). He adds, "My God will cast [His people] away because they have not listened to Him; and they will be wanderers among the nations" (9:17).

In Hosea 9:7, the words "punishment" (Hebrew, *pequddah*) and "retribution" (Hebrew, *shalum*) carry the idea of vengeance. *Pequddah* is translated "punishment" in Isaiah 10:3. *Shalum* is often translated as "recompense" (Psalm 91:8). Therefore, Jesus may well have had Hosea 9 in mind when He mentioned the coming days of vengeance that would fall on Jerusalem. He also called the days of vengeance the days of "great distress" and "wrath" that would fall upon "this people"

(Luke 21:23). While the Lord speaks of the distant wrath of the seven-year Tribulation in most of the Olivet Discourse, in verse 23 He is referring to the destruction of the Temple and the city of Jerusalem.

The mention of the vengeance in Luke 21 seems to tie Luke's Gospel to the Jews' resistance to Christ as the Savior as seen in the book of Acts, also written by Luke. The Gospel of Luke and the book of Acts are like two volumes of the same story. Acts is but a continuation of the story of rebellion and denial of Jesus by the Jews. Acts closes with the words of Paul to the Jewish elders in Rome. After quoting the judgment prophesied by Isaiah the prophet (Isaiah 6:9-10), Paul said, "Let it be known to you, that this salvation of God has been sent to the Gentiles, they will also listen" (Acts 28:28).

About the vengeance, Barnes writes:

Judgment had been threatened by almost all the prophets against [Jerusalem]. They had spoken of its crimes and threatened its ruin. Once God had destroyed Jerusalem and carried the people to Babylon; but their crimes had been repeated when they returned, and God had again threatened their ruin (p. 142).

The vengeance of A.D. 70, then, is God's vindication or retribution for the sin of unbelief and for Jerusalem's crimes against the gospel and for her stubborn rejection of God and His Messiah.

—MAL COUCH

BIBLIOGRAPHY

Barnes, Albert. "Luke and John." In *Notes on the New Testament*. Grand Rapids: Baker Books, 1983.

Cohen, Abraham, ed. *The Twelve Prophets*. London: Soncino, 1970.

Couch, Mal, gen. ed. *A Bible Handbook to the Book of Acts*. Grand Rapids: Kregel, 1999.

———, gen. ed. *The Dictionary of Premillennial Theology*. Grand Rapids: Kregel, 1996.

Gilbert, Martin, ed. *The Illustrated Atlas of Jewish Civilization*. New York: Macmillan Publishing, 1990.

Holladay, William I. *A Concise Hebrew and Aramaic Lexicon of the Old Testament*. Grand Rapids: Eerdmans Publishing Company, 1974.

Josephus. *The Jewish War*. New York: Penguin Books, 1981.

Lenski, R.C.H. *St. Luke's Gospel*. Minneapolis: Augsburg, 1961.

Price, Randall. *When the Stones Cry Out*. Eugene, OR: Harvest House Publishers, 1997.

Wood, Leon J. "Hosea." In *The Expositor's Bible Commentary*. Frank E. Gaebelein, gen. ed. 12 Vols. Grand Rapids: Zondervan, 1981.

WAR IN HEAVEN

DURING THE FIRST HALF OF THE seven years following the rapture of the church, while God's judgment is being poured out upon the earth, the church will appear before the judgment seat of Christ. The purpose of this judgment is twofold: to determine eternal rewards to be given to the church-age believers, and to demonstrate that they possess the righteousness of Christ and therefore rightly belong in heaven. The prosecutor will apparently be Satan himself. He will futilely attempt to prove that each saint does not belong there and should be banished from God's presence. The judgment will last three-and-one-half years. Satan will fail to convict a single saint. When the judgment is all over, God the Father will declare, "Satan, I've put up with you in my heaven long enough! Michael, throw him out!"

At that time, according to Revelation 12:7, "war broke out in heaven." The contestants are Michael and his angels fighting against the dragon (Satan) and his angels (demons). The war is short and the outcome is not in doubt, for Satan and his angels "did not prevail, nor was a place found for them in heaven any longer" (Revelation 12:8 NKJV). Though this event is yet future, its occurrence and outcome are so certain that they are described in the past tense. As a result of this war in heaven, Satan and his angels will be cast down to the earth and will turn with a vengeance against the nation of Israel in a futile attempt to destroy it and frustrate God's promise to Abraham to make Israel a great nation (Daniel 12:1; Revelation 12:9-17).

—PAUL FINK

BIBLIOGRAPHY

Hindson, Ed. *The Book of Revelation*. Chattanooga: AMG Publishers, 2002.

Walvoord, John F. *The Prophecy Knowledge Handbook*. Wheaton, IL: Victor Books, 1990.

———. *The Revelation of Jesus Christ*. Chicago: Moody Press, 1966.

WITNESSES, TWO

REVELATION 11:3-13 DESCRIBES THE work of two unique individuals who will proclaim the gospel for 1260 days during the first part of the Tribulation. Referred to as the "two witnesses," the supernatural ministry of these two people is directed toward Jerusalem and the nation of Israel, to whom they provide a special witness of God's program of judgment. In spite of severe Gentile opposition and oppression of Israel during the last half of the Tribulation (Revelation 11:2), God will continue to provide opportunity for repentance, and His sovereignty over human history and nature will be displayed throughout the entire Tribulation.

In the Old Testament, two witnesses were required for competent legal testimony to secure conviction (Deuteronomy 17:6; 19:15; Numbers 35:30). However, the work of these two people is more prophetic than procedural. According to Revelation 11:3, the witnesses belong to God and are special prophetic messengers dressed in sackcloth. Their attire, indicating distress, humiliation, and sorrow, is reminiscent of that of Old Testament prophets and symbolic of the fact that the witnesses are prophets of doom calling the nation Israel to repentance (see Psalm 69:11; Isaiah 37:1-2; Daniel 9:3; Joel 1:13; Jonah 3:5-8).

THEIR IDENTIFICATION

Many prophecy teachers have identified the two witnesses as Moses and Elijah, although other options have also been offered. Among the other historical pairs suggested by interpreters through the centuries are Enoch and Elijah (since both were taken to heaven without dying), Jeremiah and Elijah, James and John, Peter and Paul, two Christians martyred by the Roman general Titus, and two future Jewish prophets who have not previously lived. Some interpreters, noting that the witnesses are called "lampstands" in Revelation 11:4 and that lampstands are symbols for churches in 1:20, argue that the witnesses are symbolic of the church. However, this interpretation assumes the entire passage (11:3-13) is symbolic. In addition, only individuals can wear sackcloth, and the description of the witnesses states that they have unique and specific powers and identities, as did prophets in the Old Testament. Such a symbolic view also requires that all believers of this time undergo martyrdom. Some have also argued that the two witnesses are a blending of historic and symbolic figures.

Perhaps the simplest solution is to understand the witnesses to be Moses and Elijah. Both men reappeared at the transfiguration of Jesus (Matthew 17:3; Mark 9:4; Luke 9:30), and the miraculous signs performed by the two witnesses (Revelation 11:5-6) match those performed by Moses and Elijah. Moses turned water into blood and brought forth plagues upon the Egyptians (Exodus 7:14–11:10). Similarly, Elijah called down fire from heaven (2 Kings 1:10) and kept the heavens from raining (1 Kings 17:1; see Luke 4:25; James 5:17). The duration of the drought in Elijah's time is also the same as in this period. Additional support for the identification of the two witnesses as Moses and Elijah comes from Malachi 4:5, which states that Elijah will be sent again by God to Israel "before the coming of the great and terrible day of the LORD" (NASB).

Some interpreters object to the identification of the witnesses as Moses and Elijah because John the Baptist fulfilled Malachi's prophecy and because Moses did die, and dying a second time (Revelation 11:7) is problematic. But even though John the Baptist was like Elijah, he did not restore all things as prophesied. Regarding Moses, two deaths for one individual are unique, but they are not unprecedented, for Lazarus had the same experience.

Another question is whether Elijah was glorified after he "went up to heaven" by a whirlwind (2 Kings 2:11). If he was, how can he come back to the earth in a physical, mortal body and die? An important factor in solving this problem may be found in a statement of Jesus: "No one has ascended into heaven, but...the Son of Man" (John 3:13). His statement seems to exclude the possibility that anyone, including Enoch and Elijah, could ever have ascended to the heaven of God's throne. Jesus was "the first fruits of those who are asleep" in the sense of receiving a glorified resurrection body. No one else will receive such a body until the rapture (1 Corinthians 15:20-23); indeed, no one could possibly have been glorified before Jesus Himself. Perhaps, then, neither Enoch nor Elijah received glorified bodies when God took them from the earth. Like Paul (2 Corinthians 12:2-4), they might have been caught up to God's heaven (or paradise) for a period of time. Then they both returned to the earth temporarily to appear with Jesus at His transfiguration (Matthew 17:3). And finally, both may once again enter mortal life at the beginning of the Tribulation and die again three-and-a-half years later.

The reason Moses is a better choice than Enoch is that Enoch would not be an appropriate fellow-witness with Elijah in a prophetic ministry directed exclusively to Israel. For a future apostate nation of Israel, following the rapture of the church, no two men in Israel's entire history would receive greater respect and appreciation than Moses and Elijah. Moses was God's great deliverer and lawgiver for Israel (see Deuteronomy 34:10-12). First-century Jews actually thought that Moses had given them the manna in the wilderness (John 6:32). And God raised up Elijah to confront Israel in a time of great national apostasy. God vindicated him by sending fire from heaven and "a chariot of fire and horses of fire" to escort him out of this world. So highly did the Jews of Jesus' day think of Elijah that when they saw Jesus' miracles, some people concluded that Elijah had returned (Matthew 16:14).

THEIR MINISTRY

The ministry of the two witnesses will include preaching, prophesying, and performing miracles. They will call people to repentance, foretell future events, and announce that the kingdom is at hand. Like Zerubbabel and Joshua, who sought to restore Israel to her land, the two witnesses will encourage faithfulness to God regardless of one's circumstances.

Revelation 11:4 describes the witnesses as "the two olive trees and the two lampstands that stand before the Lord of the earth." This verse is an allusion to Zechariah 4:3,11,14, in which Zerubbabel and Joshua the high priest, the leaders of Israel in Zechariah's time, are portrayed as a lampstand or light to Israel. They are fueled by olive oil, representing the power of the Holy Spirit. So too, in the last days will the two witnesses arise by the power of God and function in their prophetic office.

God will protect the two witnesses from those who try to harm them before their mission is complete. Revelation 11:5-6 records the miraculous powers given to these witnesses and states that any who seek to harm them will be destroyed by fire. This is parallel to the protection given to Elijah, who on two occasions called down fire from heaven when soldiers sought to arrest him (2 Kings 1). Similarly, idolaters and enemies of Moses were destroyed by fire (Numbers 16:35).

THEIR DEATH AND RESURRECTION

By divine decree, the ministry of the witnesses will last 1260 days. For three-and-a-half years they will minister in Jerusalem, "the great city...where also their Lord was crucified" (Revelation 11:8), without being harmed. At the end of this period, God will withdraw

His special protection and the two witnesses will be killed by the Beast. He will "make war with them" (11:7), a phrase reminiscent of Daniel 7:21 and foreshadowing Revelation 13:7. During this time, Jerusalem is likened spiritually to Sodom and Egypt. The figurative likeness suggests complete moral and spiritual degradation and antagonism toward God and His people.

According to Revelation 11:9, the bodies of the two witnesses will be left unburied on the streets of Jerusalem for three-and-a-half days as a spectacle for all people to view. This was one of the worst means of defiling a body in biblical times (Psalm 79:2-3). There will be worldwide rejoicing over the witnesses' deaths by "those who dwell on the earth" (11:10). This phrase is an apocalyptic formula for the unbelieving world (Revelation 3:10; 6:10). The prophets will die in the same city as did their Lord, and like Him, they too will be physically resurrected from the dead and be taken to heaven in a cloud (Revelation 11:11-12; cf. Acts 1:9), just as the church will have been raptured (1 Thessalonians 4:17).

The ascension of the two witnesses will be public and in sight of their enemies and mockers (Revelation 11:12). Following the rapture of the witnesses, an earthquake will destroy one-tenth of Jerusalem and kill 7000 people, after which the remainder will turn to God in repentance. The repentance comes toward the end of the bowl judgments, offering encouragement in the midst of the world's greatest horror.

—TIMOTHY J. DEMY AND
JOHN C. WHITCOMB

BIBLIOGRAPHY

Fruchtenbaum, Arnold G. *The Footsteps of the Messiah.* Rev. ed. Tustin, CA: Ariel Ministries, 2003.

LaHaye, Tim, and Thomas Ice. *Charting the End Times.* Eugene, OR: Harvest House Publishers, 2001.

Thomas, Robert L. *Revelation 1–7: An Exegetical Commentary.* Chicago: Moody Press, 1992.

———. *Revelation 8–22: An Exegetical Commentary.* Chicago: Moody Press, 1992.

Walvoord, John F. *The Revelation of Jesus Christ.* Chicago: Moody Press, 1966.

WORLD EMPIRE

THE FINAL WORLD EMPIRE WILL dominate the world during the Tribulation period and will be destroyed by the Lord Jesus Christ when He comes at the end of the Tribulation to establish the millennial kingdom.

THE TIMES OF THE GENTILES

In answer to the disciples' question about the end of the age and His return, Jesus said, "They [the Jewish people] will fall by the edge of the sword, and will be led captive into all the nations; and Jerusalem will be trampled under foot by the Gentiles until the times of the Gentiles are fulfilled" (Luke 21:24 NASB).

The times of the Gentiles began when the Babylonians, led by Nebuchadnezzar, captured Jerusalem in 586 B.C., and the times of the Gentiles will end with the second coming of Christ (Luke 21:25-28). This means that the world is currently in the times of the Gentiles and that this period will continue through the Tribulation. The fact that this period of Gentile domination over Israel will eventually be "fulfilled" implies that Israel will one day regain prominence in God's prophetic program. According to Zechariah, Gentiles will again conquer and devastate Jerusalem during the Tribulation (Zechariah 14:1-2). But at the end of the seven-year Tribulation, Jesus Christ will return as Lord of lords and King of kings. He will crush all opposition, rescue the Jewish people, and establish a kingdom of righteousness and peace.

In regard to the fulfillment of the "times of the Gentiles," there are some key questions prophecy students often ask: What will happen at the end of the current era? Who will lead the final world government? What is the nature of the final Gentile world power? The Bible does not answer these questions with the kind of specificity that we might like. But it does paint in broad strokes a fascinating and frightening portrait of the last world empire.

A REVIVED ROMAN EMPIRE AND A PSEUDOPEACEMAKER

Daniel 2 and 7 give a description of the final world empire using the imagery of a huge metallic image and a terrifying wild beast. Daniel 2 records Nebuchadnezzar's dream of a gigantic metal statue composed of gold, silver, bronze, and iron, with each of the four metals representing one of four kingdoms. The feet and toes, however, are comprised of iron mixed with clay. Since the iron (the fourth metal) represents the Roman Empire, the feet and toes (representing the fifth and final empire) symbolize some type of revived Roman Empire that will arise at the end of the church age and dominate the world during the Tribulation. In Daniel 7, Daniel describes a dream involving the same kingdoms represented by the statue in Daniel 2, but here, they are represented by four terrifying beasts. From man's perspective (Nebuchadnezzar's dream) the kingdoms of this world are valuable metals, but from God's perspective (Daniel's vision) the kingdoms of this world are vicious beasts. The fourth beast in Daniel's dream has ten horns, three of which are uprooted by a "little horn," the ruler who will dominate the world during the Tribulation (Daniel 7:7-8). He is a charismatic individual who will propel himself into prominence as a world leader by brokering peace with Israel at the beginning of the Tribulation (Daniel 9:27).

This ruler is commonly referred to as the Antichrist, but the Bible does not specifically use that title for this individual. He is called the Antichrist because of his intense hatred for Christ. The Scriptures give him numerous other titles that are indicative of his character and his program.

He is identified as a "little horn" in Daniel 7:8: "While I was thinking about the horns, there before me was another horn, a little one, which came up among them." Daniel says that the "little horn" had "eyes like the eyes of a man and a mouth that spoke boastfully." The Antichrist is a man of strength. Horns on an animal represent its strength for attack and defense. He is intelligent ("the eyes of a man") and arrogant ("a mouth uttering great boasts"). He defies God, persecutes the nation Israel, and brings Israel under his authority (Daniel 7:25).

He is simply called a "ruler" in Daniel 9:26, but what he accomplishes sets the stage for one of the most terrifying and destructive eras in the history of the world. According to Daniel 9:27, "the ruler" will make a covenant with Israel at the beginning of Daniel's seventieth week, the seven-year Tribulation. As the head of a powerful coalition of nations, he guarantees the security of God's people. The treaty is a ruse, but it convinces Israel that "the ruler" is their best hope for peace. Unfortunately, in the middle of the Tribulation, he betrays Israel and establishes himself as the political and religious ruler of the world (Daniel 9:27). Though he promised peace, he will set the Middle East ablaze with destruction and death. His crowning achievement will be his boldest and most despicable act. After eradicating Israel's religious system, he will erect an image of himself on the Temple mount in Jerusalem and compel the world to worship him as God. Christ referred to this blasphemous act as the "abomination that causes desolation" (Matthew 24:15).

Paul calls this ruler "the man of lawlessness" and "the man doomed for destruction" (2 Thessalonians 2:3,8). The title "man of lawlessness" implies that the Antichrist is a ruthless, hardened criminal who rejects all law, especially God's. But as Paul indicates, he is also "the man doomed for destruction," a reference to the fact that Christ will destroy him at His second coming. Paul gives perhaps the clearest reference to the Antichrist's blasphemous attempt to make himself God in the middle of the Tribulation. Seeking to replace the worship of the one and only God, he will proclaim that he is God and will set up a throne in the sanctuary of the Temple (2 Thessalonians 2:4).

John calls the Antichrist "the beast out of the sea" in Revelation 13:1. The sea symbolizes the demonic origin of the Antichrist.

According to Revelation 11:7, he came out of the "abyss" (see 17:8), the source of satanic opposition to God. The Antichrist is a henchman of Satan and the second person in an unholy trinity made up of the dragon (Satan) and "the beast out of the earth" (the False Prophet). Satan's goal from the beginning has been to overthrow God and rule the world. At the end of the age he will turn to two beasts, forming an unholy trinity that is a clever and sinister imitation of God the Father, God the Son, and God the Holy Spirit. In this unholy trinity, Satan assumes the place of God, the Antichrist the place of Christ, and the False Prophet the place of the Holy Spirit.

John adds that the beast has seven heads and ten horns with ten crowns on his ten horns (Revelation 13:1). The ten horns connect the Antichrist with the fourth beast in Daniel 7, which also has ten horns. According to Revelation 17:12, the ten horns are ten kings, who will become allies with the Antichrist to form an empire that is incredibly powerful and evil.

WORLD DOMINION

This empire ultimately covers the whole world (Revelation 13:7). Ezekiel 38–39 pictures an invasion of Israel by a northern kingdom (Gog and Magog) that results in that kingdom's total defeat. With the northern kingdom out of the way, no major political force will be left standing in the way of the Antichrist's empire. Perhaps world dominion will be achieved simply by proclamation and intimidation.

John's description becomes even more chilling when he reveals that the Antichrist is energized by Satan (Revelation 13:2). He gains world renown when he makes an amazing recovery from what is apparently a mortal wound (Revelation 13:3). He is either supernaturally healed or at least gives the appearance that he has recovered from a fatal wound. In either case, the deception works: "The whole earth was amazed and followed after the beast" (Revelation 13:3). The world will worship not only the beast but also Satan himself, and Satan will have seemingly achieved his ultimate goal: to usurp God and to receive the worship that God alone deserves. Once the Antichrist has consolidated his power, achieving total political and spiritual domination of the entire world, he will go on a rampage of terror against Tribulation saints.

Though he will control Israel, the Antichrist's thirst for power and glory will not be satisfied. Midway through the Tribulation, he will use his political and military might to claim absolute power in the religious realm. Like the infamous Antiochus Epiphanes, who ruthlessly persecuted Jews in the second century B.C., the Antichrist will blaspheme God, disregard all organized religion, repudiate all messianic hopes, and magnify himself as God (Daniel 11:36-37; see Revelation 13:4-8).

The final empire will support an evil and seductive counterfeit of the worship of God—a powerful and pervasive religious, political, and economic system (called a "great harlot" in Revelation 17:1). Initially, the Antichrist supports this apostate system. But in order to satisfy his lust for glory, at the midpoint of the Tribulation, he will destroy the ecumenical world religious system, proclaim himself God, and require that everyone worship him (Revelation 17:16).

THE FALSE PROPHET

The Antichrist is not the only beast in the final world empire. In addition to the "beast out of the sea," John sees a "beast out of the earth" (Revelation 13:11). The second beast, or the False Prophet as he is commonly called, will work in close association with the Antichrist. Just as the Antichrist serves on behalf of Satan, the False Prophet promotes the worship of the Antichrist. His activities are somewhat similar to those of the prophet Elijah. Like Elijah, he will perform spectacular signs and wonders. He will be extremely persuasive and deceive many into worshiping the first beast. One of his intriguing feats will be somehow infusing life into an image of the Antichrist, even making it speak (Revelation 13:15). He will have the authority to kill all those who refuse to worship the image. He will also control the world's economic system and require people to bear the mark of the beast. Without this on either their right hand or forehead to prove that they worship the beast, no one can buy or sell (Revelation 13:16-17). (See the article titled "Six Hundred Sixty-Six.")

THE PRINCE OF PEACE

In Jesus' final lament for the city of Jerusalem, He warned that God would abandon His people for rejecting His Son. But God is faithful to His covenant promises and will not abandon Israel forever. Jesus will come to Israel a second time, and at His second coming, Israel will accept Him as their Lord and King.

One of God's primary purposes for the Tribulation is to break the stubborn hearts of His covenant people. The horrors of the Tribulation and the testimony of a host of faithful witnesses will spark a spiritual awakening in Israel. Many will turn to Christ, and many of them will die for their faith. And when Jesus returns in power and glory, the nation will experience the deep anguish of someone who realizes that they have made a terrible mistake. Instead of mocking and condemning Jesus as they did at His first coming, they will mourn and weep because they will realize that Jesus was indeed Israel's true Messiah and King and that He is coming to judge them for rejecting Him (Zechariah 12:10–13:6). But their mourning will turn to rejoicing when they realize that the Lord has not come to punish but to cleanse their sins and destroy their enemies.

The Antichrist will consolidate his armies in the Middle East to either repel an attack from the south and the north or to crush a rebellion in Israel that he provoked by breaking the treaty with Israel and desecrating the Temple. Some of the combatants will have been lured to the battle arena by demons (Revelation 16:12-16). When the total annihilation of God's covenant people seems inevitable, Jesus Christ will suddenly appear along with the armies of heaven. He will tread on the armies of earth as one treads grapes in a winepress (Revelation 14:14-20). Nothing in the history of war will compare to the carnage of Armageddon. Millions will die in a satanically inspired but insane attempt to do battle with the King of kings and the Lord of lords. With apocalyptic imagery, John sees an angel calling for the birds of heaven to gorge themselves at "the great supper of God" (Revelation 19:17-18). With the defeat of this last Gentile world empire, the nation of Israel will at last enjoy rest in the Promised Land and peace in Jerusalem.

—W.H. MARTY

BIBLIOGRAPHY

Benware, Paul N. *Understanding End Times Prophecy.* Chicago: Moody Press, 1995.

Marty, William H. "The Nations in Transition: The Shape of the Final Superpower." In *Storm Clouds on the Horizon.* Ed. Charles H. Dyer. Chicago: Moody Press, 2001.

Pentecost, J. Dwight. *Things to Come.* Grand Rapids: Dunham Publishing Company, 1958.

Scofield, C.I. "The Last World Empire and Armageddon." *Bibliotheca Sacra* 108:431 (July 1951), pp. 356–58.

Walvoord, John F. *Prophecy in the New Millennium.* Grand Rapids: Kregel, 2001.

———. *The Nations in Prophecy.* Grand Rapids: Zondervan, 1967.

WRATH OF GOD

THE DOCTRINE OF DIVINE WRATH is a recurring theme throughout the Bible. The subject of the wrath of the Lord may not be popular, but the grace of God through the Lord Jesus Christ provides for repentant sinners an opportunity to know exemption from God's wrath.

THE WORDS FOR WRATH

Old Testament Words for "Wrath"

The Old Testament uses eleven words to describe wrathful anger, including these three:

(1) The Hebrew word *aph* can describe the face or nose but often pictures the anger in a person's face or the nose turning red in fury. Jeremiah speaks of the "fierce anger" of the Lord against the nations (Jeremiah 30:24), and by this same anger the Lord drove His people into other lands (32:37). (2) The Hebrew word *zah'gaph* describes the rage or anger that the Lord had against Egypt and Assyria. "The LORD will cause His voice of authority to be heard, and the descending of His arm to be seen in *fierce anger,* and in the flame of a consuming fire" (Isaiah 30:30 NASB). (3) The Hebrew word *kah'tzaph* carries the idea of being provoked or flying into a rage. The noun is used mostly of God. Jeremiah uses the word to describe the Lord's indignation against Babylon and adds that Babylon "will be completely desolate" (Jeremiah 50:13).

While not translated "wrath," the Hebrew word *tzah'rah* speaks of the distress that humans may inflict or that God may bring about in order to punish sinners and produce righteousness. The noun is related to the word *tzohr* ("a sharp stone or knife"). *Tzah'rah* is used to describe "Jacob's distress" (Jeremiah 30:7), referring to the distress that will come upon Israel in the last days (Daniel 12:1). It is also used in Zephaniah 1:15-17, where the prophet says the day of the Lord is coming. "A day of wrath is that day, a day of trouble and *distress,* a day of destruction and desolation, a day of darkness and gloom, a day of clouds and thick darkness, a day of trumpet and battle cry....I will bring *distress* on men...because they have sinned against the LORD" (emphasis added). This day is "the day of the LORD'S wrath; and all the earth will be devoured" (1:18).

New Testament Words for "Wrath"

The Greek word *thumos* refers to burning anger. It is used ten times in the book of Revelation and only eight times in the rest of the New Testament. Most of the references in Revelation refer to the wrath of God poured out upon the evil taking place during the Tribulation.

The Greek word *orgē* speaks of anger but also of righteous judgment and indignation against sin. The apostle Paul makes the sobering observation that "the wrath of God comes upon the sons of disobedience" (Ephesians 5:6).

THE FORMS OF WRATH

Judicial Wrath

God will certainly pour out His wrath on sin. He is a righteous God who cannot tolerate sin in His presence. Because of this, sin must be punished. God's wrath hangs over the heads of all sinners (Romans 1:18), and the lost are said to be the children of wrath by nature (Ephesians 2:3). The lost are also said to be the vessels of wrath who will experience the certainty of God's wrath (Romans 9:22). God's holy law points out sin and makes certain the wrath of God (4:15).

The Final Eternal Wrath

In most cases the final wrath is the same as judicial wrath. In other words, those who reject Christ are waiting for the final judgment and will be cast into outer darkness in an eternal separation from God. Those who have placed their faith in Christ are covered by His blood and thus will not experience this wrath. Those who have not accepted Him are judged, "every one of them according to their deeds" (Revelation 20:13), and face the eternal lake of fire (20:14-15). Jesus put it this way: "He who believes in the Son has eternal life; but he who does not obey the Son will not see life, but the wrath of God abides on him" (John 3:36). The Great White Throne judgment will take place at the end of the millennium and just before the beginning of the eternal state.

The Tribulation as Wrath

Seven times the book of Revelation describes the "wrath of God" using the Greek word *thumos*. God will be furious with those who take the mark of the beast and worship him. He who does this "will drink of the wine of the wrath of God, which is mixed in full strength in the cup of His anger; and he will be tormented with fire and brimstone in the presence of the holy angels and in the presence of the Lamb" (14:9-10). In the final months of the Tribulation, the nations of the earth will be thrown "into the great wine press of the wrath of God" (14:19), and the last great plagues will bring on more of the wrath of God (15:1). In seven terrible stages, bowls of God's wrath will be poured down upon the earth (15:7; 16:1) and bring about loathsome pain upon the populace. God's wrath during the Tribulation is "fierce." In fact, in 16:19, both words for wrath are used. The apostle John writes about the judgment of Babylon the harlot and says that God gave her "the cup of the wine of His fierce wrath" (Greek, *tou thumou tas orgas,* "the wrath the fierce"). This construction implies a double wrath or judgment on the harlot for all of her evil religious deceptions.

At the end of the Tribulation, the Lord Jesus will come in a flash of glory. He will come as the Faithful and True One (Revelation 19:11-16), the righteous Judge who has eyes of flaming fire. He will possess many crowns, and His robe will be dipped in blood, signifying His death for sinners. He is called "the Word of God," and He will smite the nations, rule with a scepter of iron, and tread "the wine press of the fierce wrath of God, the Almighty." This verse doubles the force of the terribleness of God's wrath, using a grammatical construction identical to the one in 16:19.

In the book of Revelation, *orgē* is also used alone to describe God's wrath. In 11:17, the apostle gives a preview of the fact that the Lord's power has arrived and He will begin to reign. The nations resist this, and because of their resistance, "Your wrath came," and the judgment of the dead will follow. God will destroy those who destroy the earth (11:18), and to show His wrath, He will send lightning, peals of thunder, an earthquake, and a great hailstorm (11:19).

The Wrath of the Lamb

Though all judgment is God's judgment, all adjudication has been given into the hands of the Lord Jesus (John 5:22) because He died for the sins of humanity. It is only reasonable that the Son of God also participates with His heavenly Father in passing out the sentence of wrathful punishment.

As the Tribulation begins on earth in Revelation 6:1-17, both the Father and the Son of God, the Lamb, preside over it from the throne in heaven. John tells us that the world will cry out to the rocks, "Fall on us and hide us from the presence of Him who sits on the throne, and from the wrath of the Lamb; for the great day of their wrath has come; and who is able to stand?" Verse 17 better reads, "Their wrath *came* [aorist tense], and who is able to stand?" This seems to say that the Tribulation wrath begins with chapter 6, and it is so terrible that few can survive under its onslaught.

The Son of God, the King of kings and Lord of lords, also pronounces judgment and wrath from His mouth, as if it were a sharp sword. He will smite the nations and tread the winepress of the fierce wrath of God the Almighty (19:15). The wrath of the Son will come down upon the kings of the earth who have joined the beast, the Antichrist, in an attempt to make war against Him (19:19). Christ will defeat the beast and the False Prophet and cast them into the lake of fire (19:20). The righteous then "will reign with Him for a thousand years" (20:6). The prophet Isaiah also predicted this coming judgment of the Lamb of God; he wrote that someday the Son of David would "strike the earth with the rod of His mouth, and with the breath of His lips He will slay the wicked" (Isaiah 11:4).

At the end of the millennium, judgment will go forth from the Great White Throne (20:11-15). The apostle Paul says that God "has fixed a day in which He will judge the world in righteousness through a Man whom He has appointed, having furnished proof to all men by raising Him from the dead" (Acts 17:31). On the judgmental wrath of the Lamb in Isaiah 11:4, Merrill F. Unger writes:

He will govern forcefully, smiting (striking) the earth (the wicked upon the earth at His second coming) with the rod of his mouth (19:15,21) to usher in His glorious millennial reign against the opposition of wicked rebels (Psalm 2:9-12; Rev. 8:1—20:3). With the breath of his lips (19:15) He will slay the wicked (19:20-21), notably that "wicked [lawless] one" (2 Thess. 2:8), the Antichrist. As "The Word of God" (Rev. 19:13), He will come to strike the blow that will decide His claim to the Kingdom usurped by the Antichrist, to whom Satan will delegate his power (Unger, p. 1174).

In summarizing the doctrine of the wrath of God, G. Harry Leafe writes:

There is...eschatological significance to God's wrath. The establishment of Messiah's kingdom and the events attendant to it are described by Zephaniah as a day of wrath (1:15), and a day of the Lord's wrath (1:18). These expressions correspond to the wrath of the Lamb (Rev. 6:16), Jesus Christ, that will come upon the ungodly in association with His Second Advent. This future expression of the wrath of God (cf. Rom. 2:5,8; 9:22; 1 Thess. 1:10) follows the removal of the church to heaven (cf. 1 Thess. 4:15-17), an event that delivers church-age believers from that wrath (1 Thess. 5:9; Rev. 3:10). The last great judgment of human history, taking place at the Great White Throne (Rev. 20:11), represents the final manifestation of God's wrath against the ungodly, even though the term *anger* or *wrath* are not used (Leafe, p. 425).

—MAL COUCH

BIBLIOGRAPHY

Balz, Horst, and Gerhard Schneider, eds. *Exegetical Dictionary of the New Testament,* 3 Vols. Grand Rapids: Eerdmans Publishing Company, 1994.

Couch, Mal, and Ed Hindson, gen. eds. *Revelation*. Chattanooga: AMG Publishers, 2002.

Leafe, G. Harry. "Wrath." In *Dictionary of Premillennial Theology*. Mal Couch, gen. ed. Grand Rapids: Kregel, 1996.

Ryrie, Charles C. *Basic Theology*. Chicago: Moody Press, 1999.

Unger, Merrill F. *Unger's Commentary on the Old Testament*. Chattanooga: AMG Publishers, 2002.

Walvoord, John F. *The Revelation of Jesus Christ*. Chicago: Moody Press, 1966.

WRATH OF THE LAMB

NEW TESTAMENT WRITERS used two Greek words to describe the wrath of God—*thumos* and *orgē*. *Thumos* was used to speak of God's burning indignation against evil and against sin. It appears more in the book of Revelation than in all of the rest of the New Testament. The noun *orgē* and the verb *orgizomai* refer to God's anger and His judicial wrath and vengeance against evil and injustice.

WRATH OF THE MESSIAH

The Bible first mentions the wrath of the Messiah, the Lamb of God, in Psalm 2. This psalm teaches that the Son will someday execute judgment on the earth. David writes that the Lord will bring forth His Son and give Him the earth for His inheritance (2:7-8). At the end of history, the Son will break the inhabitants of the earth "with a rod of iron," and He "shall shatter them like earthenware" (2:9 NASB). If the world does not pay homage to the Son, He will become angry, "For His wrath may soon be kindled" against them (2:12). Putting these words from Psalm 2 with the rest of prophetic scripture, especially the book of Revelation, we see that this wrath will first come at the beginning of the Tribulation and will be consummated at the end of that seven-year period.

The prophet Isaiah refers to the wrath of the Messiah when he reveals that the "stem of Jesse," the King, will receive power from the Spirit of the Lord (Isaiah 11:1-5). During the Tribulation, or at the end of that terrible time, the Messiah "will strike the earth with the rod of His mouth, and with the breath of His lips He will slay the wicked" (11:4). This did not happen at the first coming of Jesus the Messiah, but it will take place during the judgments of the Tribulation and certainly at the very end of that time, when the King comes to establish His kingdom.

When the Messiah comes at the end of the Tribulation and sits upon His glorious throne, "all the nations will be gathered before Him; and He will separate them from one another, as the shepherd separates the sheep from the goats" (Matthew 25:32). Here the nations will be judged for their mistreatment of Christ's brothers, the Jews (25:40). A harsh judgment follows, and sinners will "go away into eternal punishment, but the righteous into eternal life" (25:46). At that time, "by the appearance of His coming," He will "slay with the breath of His mouth and bring to an end" the reign of the lawless one, the Antichrist (2 Thessalonians 2:8). He will also judge all who do not believe the truth, "but took pleasure in wickedness" (2:12).

WRATH OF THE LAMB

In Revelation 6:16-17 we find the expression "the wrath of the Lamb." At the start of the Tribulation, the world will cry out to the rocks and the mountains, "Fall on us and hide us from the presence of Him who sits on the throne, and from the wrath of the Lamb; for the great day of their wrath has come; and who is able to stand?" The source of this wrath is God, who is seated on His throne, but also His Son, the Lamb of God. The imagery of the Lamb comes from the great Suffering Servant passage of Isaiah 53. Here the Lamb, the Messiah, is led to the slaughter (53:7) in order to die as a substitute for the sins of God's people. He is pierced through "for our transgressions" (53:5), and "the Lord has caused the iniquity of us all to fall on Him" (53:6).

John the Baptist realized that Jesus would fulfill Isaiah 53. Seeing his cousin Jesus near the Jordan River, he cried out, "Behold, the Lamb of God who takes away the sin of the world!" (John 1:29). Jesus is called the Lamb in many other places in the New Testament (John 1:36; Acts 8:32; 1 Peter 1:19, Revelation 5:6,8,12).

Because Christ died for the sins of humanity, God gave Him full authority to judge those who refuse Him. His wrath, along with the wrath of His Father, will be unleashed at the beginning of the Tribulation. However, His wrath comes to a head at the end of the Tribulation when He arrives from glory as the "Faithful and True" (Revelation 19:11), "The Word of God" (19:13), who with a sharp sword in His mouth will "strike down the nations" (19:15). He will then "rule them with a rod of iron; and He treads the winepress of the fierce wrath of God, the Almighty. And on His robe and on His thigh He has a name written, KING OF KINGS, AND LORD OF LORDS" (19:15-16).

FINAL JUDGMENT

The Lamb's wrath will not conclude with the judgments that take place at the end of the Tribulation. Following His millennial reign, Christ, probably along with His heavenly Father, will judge from the Great White Throne (20:11-15). "More than likely the Judge will be Jesus, because He stated that the Father 'has given all judgment to the Son, in order that all may honor the Son, even as they honor the Father....For just as the Father has life in Himself, even so He gave to the Son also to have life in Himself; and He gave Him authority to execute judgment, because He is the Son of Man [the Messiah]' (John 5:22-23,26-27)" (Couch, p. 296). The apostle Paul warned the Athenians that God "will judge the world in righteousness through a Man whom He has appointed, having furnished proof to all men by raising Him from the dead" (Acts 17:31).

It is not simply the Son who is judging. "The Son sits with [His Father] (Revelation 3:21; 22:1,3,12; cf. John 5:26-27; Hebrews 1:3) and works with Him (John 5:19-21; 10:30; see Matthew 25:31-46; Acts 10:42; 17:31). This passage [Revelation 20:11] has no reference to the Son, but John elsewhere indicates His involvement in judgment (22:12)" (Thomas, *Revelation 8–22*, p. 429). All the unbelieving dead, small and great, are judged before the Great White Throne from books that have recorded their deeds of unrighteousness (20:12). They have no expiation by His blood that was shed at the cross. They must be judged "every one of them according to their deeds" (20:13). This results in the second death, spiritual death, and eternal separation from God. "If anyone's name was not found in the book of life, he was thrown into the lake of fire" (20:15).

With this final act of judgment, the wrath of God and of the Lamb is abated and satisfied. Evil, along with all of its consequences to humanity and the universe, is purged forever. The Lord Jesus Christ will never exhibit wrath again!

"Consignment to the lake of fire will be forever. God has gone out of His way to give mankind every possible chance to repent, but this last act of rebellion after 1000 years of blessing [the millennium] will mark the end of His patience. And all who rejected Christ as Lord will be condemned to the lake of fire" (Hindson, p. 206).

—MAL COUCH

BIBLIOGRAPHY

Chafer, Lewis Sperry. *Major Bible Themes*. Grand Rapids: Zondervan, 1974.

Couch, Mal, gen. ed. *A Bible Handbook to Revelation*. Grand Rapids: Kregel, 2001.

Hindson, Ed. *The Book of Revelation*. Chattanooga: AMG Publishers, 2002.

Pentecost, J. Dwight. *Things to Come*. Grand Rapids: Zondervan, 1964.

Thomas, Robert L. *Revelation 1–7: An Exegetical Commentary*. Chicago: Moody Press, 1992.

———. *Revelation 8–22: An Exegetical Commentary*. Chicago: Moody Press, 1995.

ZECHARIAH, ESCHATOLOGY OF

A FAMILIARITY WITH THE BOOK of Zechariah is essential for developing a clear and more complete understanding of God's prophetic plan, but it is among the least studied of the Old Testament books. Yet the New Testament authors directly quote from or allude to Zechariah's content 40 times, making it one of the most quoted Old Testament works.

Zechariah reveals more about the coming Messiah than all the other minor prophets combined. He is truly the minor prophet with the major message. Within the pages of Zechariah we find many of messianic prophecy's "greatest hits" concerning the restoration of Jerusalem and the coming messianic King.

AUTHOR

The prophet Zechariah, whose name means "the one whom the Lord remembers," is mentioned among the 50,000 returning Jewish exiles listed in Ezra 5:1; 6:14. He was born during the Babylonian exile, of priestly descent, and thus is the third in the trinity of prophet–priests associated with the Babylonian exile: Jeremiah, whose ministry was preexilic; Ezekiel, whose ministry was exilic; and Zechariah, whose ministry was postexilic. Zechariah carefully dates his prophecies, which began in late 520 B.C.

STRUCTURE

The body of Zechariah's message is divided into three main portions. The first section, chapters 1–6, contains eight apocalyptic visions with accompanying angelic interpretations. The second section, chapters 7–8, is an example of ethical prophecy, or exhortation. The final section, chapters 9–14, is predictive future prophecy, the kind of foretelling that commonly comes to mind when one thinks of prophetic ministry.

CONTENT

The book has two specific emphases. The first is that of the powerful appearance of the Lord to destroy the enemies of His people Israel and, once all is subjugated under His control, to personally dwell among His people. The second is the specific election and glorification of His city, Jerusalem, the home of His Temple and the center of Israel's (and eventually the

world's) worship of God. Zechariah mentions Jerusalem (and its synonym, Zion) 50 times in his 14 chapters. The restoration and supernatural glorification of the city of the messianic King is clearly a central focus of this prophet.

PURPOSE

Zechariah relays God's word to encourage the returned Jewish exiles to take heart amid uncertain circumstances and to finish rebuilding the Temple. He explains the Lord's plans to establish the Temple as the center of His kingdom when He personally returns and glorifies His city, Jerusalem. This will result in the fulfillment of all covenant promises, the final deliverance of His people, Israel, and their facilitation of the universal worship of the Lord.

THEMES

The Restoration of Jerusalem and of the Jewish People to Their Land

The Lord promises to restore the Jewish people, regardless of their failings, because of His overwhelming protective passion for them. Zechariah relates four specific divine promises:

1. In the imminent future, the Lord will personally return to Jerusalem and permanently dwell among His people, providing protection, provision, prosperity, peace, and security (8:3-5).

2. His presence in Jerusalem will glorify and sanctify the city. His manifest glory will be visible to all (2:5-12).

3. Regardless of the condition of Israel's covenantal commitment toward Him, His covenantal obligation toward the nation as a whole will not falter (9:11-13).

4. Regardless of how distantly the Jewish people have been dispersed, the Lord guarantees He will personally return His people to Jerusalem and restore their covenantal relationship with Him by a sovereign act of gracious authority (8:7-8). Zechariah vividly describes the exiles'

return from this worldwide dispersion as a second exodus. The returning exiles will be so numerous that they will swamp the land, and Israel's borders will need to be expanded (10:8-11). The Lord will bless the renewed population of Israel, and they will worship Him (10:12).

God's Judgment on Israel

Prior to any future divine blessings and prosperity, God will judge and cleanse everyone within the covenant community who was guilty of breaking that covenant through the violation of God's law. In order for God to personally dwell in the midst of His people, they must be purged of covenantal impurity. The entire land of Israel will be devastated (11:1-3) because of Israel's rejection of the Lord's chosen Shepherd, the Messiah (11:4-17). The people are destined to experience dreadful suffering on account of their repudiation of God's chosen Leader (11:8-9). In the future, they will reenter their land, yet two thirds of the inhabitants will be slain (13:8). The survivors of this genocide will be purified through their suffering and will worship the Lord with a covenant lifestyle (12:10–13:1).

The Coming Messiah

Zechariah reveals the arrival of the Lord's representative agent, the Messiah (9:9-10), who is to rule for the Lord as the righteous and victorious King of Israel. He describes the Messiah as humble and conveying a kingdom of peace, entering Jerusalem not on a warhorse but on a donkey. The kingdom of Israel's borders will expand in all directions to their promised extent under their Messiah's righteous and peaceful reign, and this King of Israel will actually reign over the whole earth.

When the Messiah appears on the scene, He will complete the construction of the Temple and will powerfully rule Israel by the fusion of the offices of king and high priest, removing the Jewish people's sin, and inaugurating a period of tremendous blessing for the people and the Land (3:1-10).

Significant ambiguity clouds the relationship between the return of the Lord to His people and the coming of the Messiah. The Lord and His Messiah are so closely associated in Zechariah that at certain points, their identities appear to merge.

God's Judgment and Restoration of the Nations

The wrath of God is to be poured out upon all nations that have participated or will participate in the dispersion of the Jewish people. By persecuting the Jewish people, the guilty nations have personally and painfully abused the Lord, with whom the Jewish people are bound in covenantal relationship (2:8). Yet when the Lord takes up residence in Jerusalem and fills it with His protective glory, great numbers of Gentiles will join the Jewish people in their relationship to the Lord and worship together with them (2:12-13). Multitudes from surrounding nations will be attracted to the Lord and will eagerly pilgrimage to Jerusalem to worship Him in the Temple alongside the Jewish people.

By virtue of the Jews' covenant relationship with the Lord, they will serve as His mediators and will be granted a position of prominence among the Gentiles (8:9-23). Following the Messiah's final triumph, the whole earth will recognize the Lord, and His covenant community will expand accordingly (14:9). The nations' survivors will all worship the Lord with the Jewish people in Jerusalem at the Temple, the location of His manifest presence. Ambassadors from all nations will make annual pilgrimage to Jerusalem to celebrate the Feast of Tabernacles, the great holy day related to the appeal for rain, the public reading of the Torah, and covenant renewal (14:16-19).

Messiah's Final Victory at Jerusalem

Zechariah chronicles God's systematic deliverance of Judah from surrounding national enemies and the coming of the Messiah to establish His kingdom (9:1–11:17). He reveals the harrowing yet exhilarating circumstances immediately preceding the ultimate victory of the messianic King and the establishment of His kingdom (12–14).

Zechariah reveals that every nation will make war against the Jewish people, and their capital, Jerusalem, will be besieged on every side by an international coalition (14). However, the Lord will intervene on behalf of His people and incapacitate their enemies (12:2-3).

When the nations appear to be ready to completely overrun Jerusalem (with half the population of the city having been taken captive and deported and the remainder having seen their possessions despoiled and their women brutally raped [14:1-2]), and it seems that the nations will complete their victory with a "final solution," the Lord personally enters the battle and engages the nations on behalf of His people (14:3). He arrives just east of the city on the Mount of Olives, accompanied by angelic armies at His command.

The Messiah is powerfully revealed as the manifest Lord Himself. Upon His appearance, the Mount of Olives will divide in two (reminiscent of the parting of the Red Sea), creating a valley that serves as an escape route (14:5). The Lord's conclusive victory leads to ultimate blessing for His people, the establishment of His kingdom, and the final fulfillment of all covenant promises.

When the threat posed by Israel's national enemies is finally defused, the Lord will infuse the Jewish people with spiritual conviction and contrition. He will enable the Jewish people to perceive their need for divine forgiveness, and the entire nation of Israel will repent. The reason for their repentance will be their prior rejection of the Messiah, the representative agent of the Lord's loving leadership.

Zechariah integrates the Lord's identity with the Messiah's. He declares that when the Jewish people see the Lord, they will suddenly comprehend that in mortally wounding the Messiah, they had physically pierced the Lord Himself. Upon this realization, their grief will be enormous (12:10). Following this period of grief and repentance, the Lord will forgive His people for their rejection of His leadership and will direct their spiritual purification (13:1).

—STEVEN C. GER

BIBLIOGRAPHY

Baldwin, Joyce. *Haggai, Zechariah and Malachi: Tyndale Old Testament Commentary Series.* Downers Grove, IL: InterVarsity, 1972.

Chisholm, Robert B. *Interpreting the Minor Prophets.* Grand Rapids: Academie, 1990.

Feinberg, Charles L. *The Minor Prophets.* Chicago: Moody Press, 1990.

Lindsey, Duane. "Zechariah." In *The Bible Knowledge Commentary: Old Testament.* Wheaton, IL: Victor, 1986.

Merrill, Eugene. *An Exegetical Commentary: Haggai, Zechariah, Malachi.* Chicago: Moody Press, 1994.

Unger, Merrill F. *Zechariah.* Grand Rapids: Zondervan, 1963.

Cohen, Gary. *Understanding Revelation.* Chicago: Moody Press, 1968.

Couch, Mal. *A Bible Handbook to Revelation.* Grand Rapids: Kregel, 2001.

Couch, Mal, gen. ed. *Dictionary of Premillennial Theology.* Grand Rapids: Kregel, 1996.

Fruchtenbaum, Arnold. *The Footsteps of the Messiah: A Study of the Sequence of Prophetic Events.* San Antonio, TX: Ariel Press, 1982.

Grudem, Wayne. *Systematic Theology.* Downers Grove, IL: InterVarsity Press, 1994.

Hindson, Ed. *The Book of Revelation.* Chattanooga: AMG Publishers, 2002.

Hitchcock, Mark. *101 Answers to the Most Asked Questions about the End Times.* Sisters, OR: Multnomah Publishers, 2001.

Ice, Thomas, and Timothy J. Demy. *Fast Facts on Bible Prophecy from A to Z.* Eugene, OR: Harvest House Publishers, 2004.

LaHaye, Tim. *The Merciful God of Prophecy.* New York: Warner Books, 2002.

————. *Revelation Unveiled.* Grand Rapids: Zondervan, 1999.

————. *Tim LaHaye Prophecy Study Bible.* Chattanooga: AMG Publishers, 2001.

LaHaye, Tim and Jerry Jenkins. *Are We Living in the End Times?* Wheaton, IL: Tyndale House, 1999.

MacArthur, John, Jr. *Revelation 1-11.* Chicago: Moody Press, 1999.

————. *Revelation 12-22.* Chicago: Moody Press, 2000.

————. *The Second Coming.* Wheaton, IL: Crossway Books, 1999.

Pentecost, J. Dwight. *Things to Come.* Grand Rapids, Zondervan, 1958.

Price, Randall. *The Coming Last Days Temple.* Eugene, OR: Harvest House Publishers, 1999.

————. *Jerusalem in Prophecy.* Eugene, OR: Harvest House Publishers, 1998.

Ryrie, Charles C. *Dispensationalism.* Chicago: Moody Press, 1995.

Thomas, Robert. *Revelation 1-7: An Exegetical Commentary.* Chicago: Moody Press, 1992.

————. *Revelation 8-22: An Exegetical Commentary.* Chicago: Moody Press, 1995.

Walvoord, John F. *Daniel: The Key to Prophetic Revelation.* Chicago: Moody Press, 1971.

————. *Major Bible Prophecies.* Grand Rapids: Zondervan, 1991.

————. *The Prophecy Knowledge Handbook.* Wheaton, IL: Victor Books, 1990.

————. *The Revelation of Jesus Christ.* Chicago: Moody Press, 1966.

Walvoord, John F., and Roy B. Zuck. *The Bible Knowledge Commentary: An Exposition of the Scriptures by Dallas Seminary Faculty,* New Testament. Wheaton, IL: Victor Books, 1983.

Wiersbe, Warren W. *Be Victorious.* Colorado Springs: Chariot Victor, 1985.

ABOUT THE PRE-TRIB RESEARCH CENTER

IN 1991, DR. TIM LAHAYE BECAME CONCERNED ABOUT the growing number of Bible teachers and Christians who were attacking the pretribulational view of the rapture as well as the literal interpretation of Bible prophecy. In response, he wrote *No Fear of the Storm* (Multnomah Publishers, 1992; now titled *The Rapture*). In the process of writing this book, Tim was impressed by the Christian leaders who, in Great Britain during the 1820s and 1830s, set up conferences for the purpose of discussing Bible prophecy. In 1992, Tim contacted Thomas Ice about the possibility of setting up similar meetings, which led to the first gathering of what is now known as the Pre-Trib Study Group in December 1992.

In 1993, Dr. LaHaye and Dr. Ice founded the Pre-Trib Research Center (PTRC) for the purpose of encouraging the research, teaching, propagation, and defense of the pretribulational rapture and related Bible prophecy doctrines. It is the PTRC that has sponsored the annual study group meetings since that time, and there are now over 200 members comprised of top prophecy scholars, authors, Bible teachers, and prophecy students.

LaHaye and Ice, along with other members of the PTRC, have since produced an impressive array of literature in support of the pretribulational view of the rapture as well as the literal interpretation of Bible prophecy. Some of these members are among the contributors to this encyclopedia. Members of the PTRC are available to speak at prophecy conferences and churches. The organization has a monthly publication titled Pre-Trib Perspectives.

To find out more about the PTRC and its publications, write to:

Pre-Trib Research Center
1971 University Blvd.
Lynchburg, VA 24502

You can also get information through the Web site:
www.pre-trib.org